The Nature of Emotion

SERIES IN AFFECTIVE SCIENCE

THE NATURE OF EMOTION

Fundamental Questions

Edited by
Paul Ekman
Richard J. Davidson

New York Oxford
OXFORD UNIVERSITY PRESS
1994

Oxford University Press

Oxford New York Toronto
Delhi Bombay Calcutta Madras Karachi
Kuala Lumpur Singapore Hong Kong Tokyo
Nairobi Dar es Salaam Cape Town
Melbourne Auckland Madrid

and associated companies in
Berlin Ibadan

Published by Oxford University Press, Inc.
200 Madison Avenue, New York, New York 10016

Library of Congress Cataloging-in-Publication Data
The Nature of Emotion : fundamental questions /
edited by Paul Ekman, Richard J. Davidson.
p. cm.
Includes bibliographical references and index.
ISBN 0-19-508943-X (cloth). – ISBN 0-19-508944-8 (paper)
1. Emotions.
I. Ekman, Paul. II. Davidson, Richard J.
BF531.N38 1994 152.4–c20 94-18638

9 8 7 6 5 4 3 2 1

Printed in the United States of America
on acid-free paper

For Silvan S. Tomkins
who pioneered our understanding of
the nature of emotion

Acknowledgments

The idea for this book arose in the course of teaching the yearlong seminar on emotion in 1990 to graduate students and postdoctoral fellows in the NIMH supported Postdoctoral Training Program on Emotion Research (Number to come). We wish to thank the NIMH program officers who helped us in developing the plans for that training program: Mollie Oliveri, Lynn Huffman, and a special thanks to Stan Schneider who suggested the need for such a program to Paul Ekman.

Wanda Matsubayashi, who works at Paul Ekman's lab, and Michele Albert at Richie Davidson's lab, each provided invaluable help in the near herculean task of keeping track of the many parts and pieces that were assembled to form this book. Joan Bossert, our editor at Oxford University Press, has offered good advice and encouragement throughout.

Paul Ekman's work was supported by a Research Scientist Award from the National Institute of Mental Health (MH 06092), a grant from the National Heart, Lung and Blood Institute (HL46192), and a grant from the National Science Foundation (IRI19217831). Richard J. Davidson's work was supported by a Research Scientist Development Award from the National Institute of Mental Health (MH00875) and by NIMH grants MH40747 and MH43454, by the NIMH Center for Behavioral Sciences Research Grant (P50-MH52354) and by a grant from the Network on Mind-Body Interactions of the John D. and Catherine T. MacArthur Foundation.

P. E.
R. J. D.

Contents

Contributors

JAMES R. AVERILL
Department of Psychology
University of Massachusetts
Amherst, Massachusetts

GORDON H. BOWER
Department of Psychology
Stanford University
Stanford California

LINDA A. CAMRAS
Department of Psychology
DePaul University
Chicago, Illinois

LEE ANN CLARK
Department of Psychology
University of Iowa
Iowa City, Iowa

GERALD L. CLORE
Department of Psychology
University of Illinois
Champaign, IL

RICHARD J. DAVIDSON
Department of Psychology and Psychiatry
University of Wisconsin
Madison, Wisconsin

JUDY DUNN
Department of Human Development and Family Studies
Pennsylvania State University
University Park, PA

PAUL EKMAN
Department of Psychiatry
University of California
San Francisco, California

PHOEBE C. ELLSWORTH
Department of Psychology
University of Michigan
Ann Arbor, Michigan

NICO H. FRIJDA
Department of Psychology
University of Amsterdam
Amsterdam, Netherlands

H. HILL GOLDSMITH
Department of Psychology
University of Wisconsin
Madison, Wisconsin

JEFFREY A. GRAY
Institute of Psychiatry
Department of Psychology
University of London
London, United Kingdom

CARROLL E. IZARD
Department of Psychology
University of Delaware
Newark, Delaware

JEROME KAGAN
Department of Psychology
Harvard University
Cambridge, Massachusetts

RICHARD LAZARUS
Department of Psychology
University of California
Berkeley, California

JOSEPH E. LEDOUX
Center for Neural Science
New York University
New York, New York

ROBERT W. LEVENSON
Department of Psychology
University of California
Berkeley, California

JAAK PANKSEPP
Department of Psychology
Bowling Green State University
Bowling Green, Ohio

MARY K. ROTHBART
Department of Psychology
University of Oregon
Eugene, Oregon

KLAUS R. SCHERER
Section of Psychology
University of Geneva
Geneva, Switzerland

RICHARD A. SHWEDER
Committee on Human Development
Department of Psychology
University of Chicago
Chicago, Illinois

DAVID WATSON
Department of Psychology
University of Iowa
Iowa City, Iowa

ROBERT B. ZAJONC
Institute for Social Research
Department of Psychology
University of Michigan
Ann Arbor, Michigan

The Nature of Emotion

Introduction

A rapid growth in research and theory about emotion has occurred in the last decade. As should be expected, currently only a few widely replicated findings exist, and even those are subject to some controversy about how they can be explained. There are many promising findings, many more leads, a variety of theoretical stances, and even a few different, fairly complete theoretical accounts.

Our goal in this book is to move the field forward by focusing attention on some of the most important questions about the nature of emotion that confront research and theory alike. We consider the divergence of views and arguments in the psychology of emotion. There are no commonly accepted answers to the twelve questions that form this book—that is why they were chosen. Instead there are very different proposals and forecasts about what the answers may turn out to be.

We did not include all the questions that have been raised about the nature of emotion, nor all those who have become known by their research and theoretical work in this area. Certain topics within emotion research have attracted a considerable amount of activity, with multiple investigators working on similar questions. In such cases, we could not include all those active contributors, but rather had to select a representative exemplar.

We excluded some questions because little research or theory covers them. We excluded other questions because so much research exists that there is not much argument any longer about them, or the argument is limited to a single issue. We limited our questions to the psychology and biology of emotion, and our contributors to psychologists and neuroscientists. Our one exception is the lone anthropologist Richard A. Shweder, who contributed to the question about basic emotions. We omitted our colleagues in sociology, anthropology, linguistics, and psychiatry, not because of a lack of interest in their work but because including them would have made the book unwieldy. However, several scholars who have contributed to this volume have intellectual connections to and are informed by many of these border disciplines. However, those studying emotion in these other disciplines are, for the most part, raising other questions about emotion.

We hope to challenge both readers and contributors. Reading this book should motivate the current and next generation of scientists to do the research and the thinking that will, in turn, provide new findings and new conceptual accounts. If this book fulfills our hopes, in a few years some of these questions may be answered. For other questions, the range of feasible alternatives will be narrowed, or the questions will have to be reformulated. And a new set of questions about the nature of emotion will be generated.

Twenty-four contributors provided sixty-three separate replies. Each of the twelve chapters is a question about emotion, and within that chapter are the separate contributions of some of the most prominent scientists studying emotion. The book's organization is designed to reveal how different scientists approach each question, rather than explicate the entire position of any one contributor. At the end of each question we have written an Afterword, in which we highlight some of the areas of agreement and disagreement among contributors.

The twelve questions themselves are interesting in their own right, quite apart from what the contributors have written about them. They arose, in part, from an earlier list of questions about the nature of emotion that were developed years ago (Ekman & Scherer, 1984), forming the basis for a conference on emotion that was subsequently reported in a book (Scherer & Ekman, 1984). That book, however, was organized more traditionally by authors, not questions. The questions only served to index the author's contributions.

In this book the twelve questions include six of the seven questions from Ekman and Scherer's list: how to distinguish emotions (Question 2); what is the function of emotions (Question 3); how to explain evidence of universals in antecedents (Question 4); what are the minimal cognitive prerequisites for emotion (Question 5); is there emotion-specific physiology (Question 6); and, can we control our emotions (Question 7). The only question omitted from the 1984 list involved the expression of emotion. We chose not to include it because there are, regrettably, only a few scientists working on the many remaining questions about expression (see Ekman, 1993, for a recent discussion of unanswered questions about expression). As editors, we added other questions, and when we invited contributors to write about specific questions, we also asked them to modify or add to the questions. Despite the large number of contributors, there were few new questions added or other changes made over the initial year in which this book was planned.

In writing the Afterwords for each question, we were excited by the possibilities that the contributors raised. Oftentimes, consideration of the chapter question triggered other, related questions that the contributors posed. We believe that the research agenda for many different areas of emotion research are charted by these contributors. It is also clear that new methods are being infused into the emotion research area. For the first time in its history, the methodological sophistication of emotion research is on par with many other areas in the biobehavioral sciences. The combination of these new methods and novel conceptualizations bodes well for the future. Just as cognitive science took hold in the 1970s and 1980s, we expect that emotion research will witness a similar burgeoning of activity in the 1990s. No longer relegated to a subordinate position in the academy, a science of the emotions has arrived center stage. It is our hope that this volume will serve as a guide for students and researchers and help to define the research agenda for affective science into the next century. We have provided our own vision of that research agenda in the last chapter.

Question 1

Are There Basic Emotions?

In the Eyes of the Beholder

JAMES R. AVERILL

The idea that some emotions are more basic than others has had a subtle and yet profound influence on psychological research and theory. However, the issue of being "basic" is not limited to the emotions. It arises whenever phenomena require classification, and some objects or events are given priority over others "in the scheme of things." Folk classifications (of minerals, plants, animals, human behavior, or whatever) are universal; people could not live in a world where each object or event had to be treated as unique. Classification is also the starting point of all science. Many disciplines have subspecialities devoted specifically to classification—for example, taxonomy in zoology and nosology in medicine. Psychologists, however, have shown a surprising lack of interest in problems of classification. Most classification schemes in psychology hardly go beyond the folk level. That is certainly the case with respect to the emotions.

These considerations raise a potential source of ambiguity that should be addressed at the outset. Does being basic refer to a logical feature of a classification scheme, or does it also say something about the objects classified? I would argue in favor of the former, at least as far as emotions are concerned. That is, being basic is a property of our concepts, not of emotions per se. However, I must qualify this observation in a very important respect. Emotions are not like inanimate objects that remain unchanged regardless of how they are conceived. As a form of human behavior, emotions are constituted, at least in part, by the same "implicit theories" that lend emotional concepts their meaning. Logical and substantive issues are therefore inextricably intertwined. However, not all features of an emotional concept can be extrapolated without qualification to the corresponding emotional response. Specifically, simply because an emotional concept is basic within some classification scheme, it does not follow that the corresponding emotion is somehow more fundamental than other emotions.

For simplicity in the following discussion, I will not always draw a clear distinction between basic emotional concepts and basic emotions per se, but will rely on context to make my meaning clear. In the final analysis, I wish to make three main points. First, there are many different ways in which one emotion (or emotional concept) can be said to be more basic than others. Second, because of the many possible meanings of "basicness," all with some claim to legitimacy, the notion of basic emotions is a source of more confusion than clarity. Third, rather than limit the notion of basic emotions to any one of its potential meanings, we would be better off (from a strictly scientific point of view) to eliminate the notion entirely.

To substantiate these points, it is necessary to consider the logic of classification in general, as well as the more specific criteria typically used to identify basic emotions. A classification scheme can be horizontal (unilevel), vertical (multilevel), and, most often, a combination of both. I will consider first the notion of what is basic as it applies to horizontal classification schemes.

Prototypicality

Horizontal schemes are like democracies: all categories are created equal, at least in theory. In practice, however, some categories may be treated as more equal (basic) than others. To illustrate, consider a hypothetical classification scheme for birds (sparrows, vultures, robbins, penguins, ostriches, etc.). From a scientific or definitional point of view, all species of birds may be given equal status. But in a typical folk taxonomy, some species (robbins, say, as opposed to penguins) are considered more basic—representative of the class of all birds—than are others. In keeping with common practice, I will call the property of being basic in this sense "prototypicality."

Are some emotions more prototypic than others? Certainly. In our folk categorization of emotions, anger is more prototypic than chagrin, fear is more prototypic than anxiety, and so forth. In recent years, the concept of a prototype has been developed into a mini-theory to help explain the acquisition and meaning of concepts, including emotional concepts (e.g., Russell, 1991; Shaver, Schwartz, Kirson, & O'Connor, 1987). The basic idea is that objects are categorized, not on the basis of necessary and sufficient conditions (the "essence" of the category), but on the basis of their resemblance to some prototype (the "best exemplar" of the category). The exact nature of the prototype or best exemplar is subject to dispute (e.g., a representative member, ideal member, or average member of the class), and the nature of the prototype may in fact vary from one kind of object to another. That issue need not concern us here (see Russell, 1991; Clore & Ortony, 1991). I do, however, want to say a few words about some of the potential pitfalls inherent in a prototype approach to the classification of emotions.

Prototype theory was introduced, in part, in recognition of the fact that many concepts of ordinary language cannot be defined "classically"—that is, in terms of necessary and sufficient conditions. Classically defined concepts have an important role to play in science (Hull, 1976). However, they also have certain limitations when applied to objects and events that occur in the natural world (as opposed to theoretical entities). Stated briefly, most naturally occurring objects do not have essences—that is, the necessary and sufficient conditions stipulated by a classically defined concept. I will not belabor the problems associated with essentialism as it applies to emotions (Averill, 1980, 1984, 1991). One example will suffice. If physiological arousal, say, is an essential feature of emotion, then the temporal course of emotional episodes must necessarily follow the temporal course of physiological reactions. The emotion cannot outlive its essential feature. Prototype theories carry no such necessary implications. Nevertheless, an implicit assumption is often made that "real" emotions must somehow conform to the prototype. Thus, if prototypic emotions are characterized by physiological arousal, it may be assumed that other responses are emotional just to the extent that they, too, exhibit physiological arousal.

Another difficulty with prototypic conceptions of emotion stems from the fact that everyone wants to investigate what is basic, not what is secondary or derived (just as everyone wants to investigate what is essential and not what is accidental). However, a preoccupation with prototypic or basic emotions (anger, fear, grief, etc.) may not be the best strategy in the long run. We can sometimes learn more from unusual or odd cases than from the more commonplace. For example, a platypus is hardly a prototypic mammal, but it is precisely its unusualness that makes it so interesting and potentially informative. Similarly, more attention needs to be devoted to nonprototypic emotions if we are to develop a general theory of emotion. What would our theories of emotion be like if we devoted as much attention to such nonprototypic emotions as hope, pride, and guilt as we have devoted to anger, fear, and grief? (For a partial answer to this question, see Averill, Catlin, & Chon, 1990.)

In short, although prototype theory is often presented as an alternative to essentialism, it can lead to similar pitfalls. This is not to say that prototype theory is wrong or uninformative in all respects. Prototypes help us think about phenomena; we could not get along without them, especially in everyday affairs. But prototypes can also mislead. We even have a separate term for misleading prototypes—namely, stereotypes.

To the extent that prototypes serve as a basis for recognizing or identifying members of a category, they can be considered basic—but in no other sense should they be construed as more fundamental than other members of the category. In this respect, it might be well to recall Wittgenstein's (1953) notion of "family resemblances," which provided much of the philosophical rationale for prototype theory. One family member may be more representative of the group than others, but not therefore more important, fundamental, etc., in any other respect.

What is true of families is also true of entire species (e.g., the "family of man"). Sokal and Sneath (1963) have coined the term "polythetic" to refer to the fact that not all members of a species need share a common characteristic (essence). Emotions, too, are polythetic (Averill, 1980). Two main implications can be drawn from this fact: First, it makes no more sense to talk of basic emotions than of basic species; and, second, emotions can evolve and change depending on the circumstances. In contrast to species, however, emotional innovation and change are not limited to biological evolution, but can be seen in social history and individual development as well (Averill, 1984; Averill & Nunley, 1992; Averill & Thomas-Knowles, 1991). I will have more to say about such "emotional creativity" in response to Question 7: Can we control our emotions?

Level of Classification

I turn now from unilevel to multilevel classifications—that is, from comparisons within to between levels in a hierarchy. Consider the following simplified folk classification of household goods:

Level	*Example*
4. Inclusive Form	Household goods
3. Generic Class	Furniture, Appliances
2. Specific Type	Chair, Stove
1. Subtype or Variety	Kitchen chair, Gas range

According to criteria proposed by Mervis and Rosch (1981), Level 2, which comprises specific types of furniture such as chairs and stoves, is the most basic level of categorization. Specifically, these authors define as basic that level in a hierarchy "at which the information value of attribute clusters is maximized. This is the level at which categories maximize within-category similarity relative to between-category similarity" (p. 92). Emotions can also be organized in a hierarchical fashion (Storm & Storm, 1987; Shaver et al., 1987). As I will discuss shortly, however, not all emotion theorists accept Mervis and Rosch's criteria for basic-level categories. The result is that emotions located at either higher or lower levels in the hierarchy have been defined as basic. But before getting to that, I need to say something about hierarchical organizations in general.

Hierarchical orderings can be based on either class-inclusion or part-whole relations. The above simplified taxonomy of household goods illustrates class inclusion, as do zoological taxonomies on a more formal level. However, class inclusion is not the only basis for a hierarchical ordering of categories. Consider, for example, the classification of body parts: the hand is a part of, not a subclass of the arm. Sometimes both class-inclusion and part-whole relations are applied to the same phenomena. Thus, chemical elements at the atomic level can be grouped (by class inclusion) into higher-order categories (e.g., helium, neon, argon, krypton, xenon, and radon are subclasses within the group of noble gases). But chemical elements can also be grouped (by part-whole relations) according to the compounds they form (e.g., hydrogen compounds, carbon compounds). Both kinds of grouping are legitimate, but for different purposes.

In our folk taxonomy of emotion, it is not always clear whether the relation between levels is one of class inclusion or part-whole. For example, is indignation a species of anger (class inclusion) or an aspect of anger (part-whole)? As in the case of chemistry, both kinds of relation are possible—and common, depending on the context. I raise this issue because theorists who talk of basic-level emotions often take it for granted that emotions are organized hierarchically on the basis of class inclusion.

It makes little sense to speak of basicness in part-whole relations. (Is the hand more basic than the arm?) Therefore, let us assume for the sake of argument that emotions are organized solely on the basis of class inclusion. We are still faced with several difficulties. One of these difficulties is the problem of missing levels. Not every level in a hierarchy need be separately named. This is a common occurrence in folk taxonomies (Berlin, Breedlove, & Raven, 1968). For example, a particular culture may not have a separate name for birds and yet members of the culture may show by their behavior that they recognize birds as a separate life form. Similarly, as the work by Storm and Storm (1987) illustrates, not all categories in our folk taxonomy of emotion are distinctly named.

When a category is not named, a term from another category, typically one from a lower level in the hierarchy, may be used "to fill in the blank," so to speak. The term selected is usually one that is prototypic of the relevant subcategory. For example, if we had no name for birds in general, we might use "robin" to refer both to a specific type of bird and to birds as a generic class. When a less inclusive term is used for a more inclusive category, or vice versa, the term so used is known as a synecdoche. Synecdoches are common figures of speech in the area of emotion, where the same term may be used to refer to both a general class and to a specific member of that class. Consider "anger." Contrary to popular stereotype, anger as a specific emotion seldom eventuates in aggression (Averill, 1982). Nevertheless, "anger" has become a commonly used synecdoche for all kinds of aggressive syndromes. A failure to distinguish between the specific and generic uses of "anger" has led some theorists to assume that what is true of anger as a general category must also be true of anger as a specific emotion—for example, that because aggression is universal anger must also be universal.

Going further, let us assume not only that our taxonomy of emotion is based on class inclusion, but that it also has no missing categories, so that confusions of the above type are obviated. We are still faced with the problem of which level is the most basic. As noted previously, in Rosch's scheme the basic level is intermediate in the hierarchy, where the information value of a member category is maximized (Mervis & Rosch, 1981). This is the position adopted by Shaver et al. (1987) with respect to basic emotions. But that is not the only possibility. In chemistry, the atomic level (i.e., the level at which elements are no longer divisible into subvarieties of the same kind) has traditionally been taken as basic. (The discovery of a plethora of subatomic particles might seem to make this traditional conception obsolete; but note that the relation of subatomic to atomic particles is part-whole, not class-inclusion.) Plutchik (1980) and Oatley and Johnson-Laird (1987), among others, have argued that basic emotions should also be defined at the most elementary level—that is, as those emotions which are no longer divisible into more elementary emotions. Going in the opposite direction, still other theorists (e.g., de Rivera, 1977) seem to take the most inclusive or superordinate categories within a hierarchy as basic.

I am not concerned with whether one level of classification (elementary, intermediate, or superordinate) is *really* more basic than the others. Legitimate arguments can be made for each. The choice depends on broader theoretical issues and the subject under investigation. The main thing I wish to emphasize is the possibilities for confusion and needless debate that exist when the criteria for identifying a basic level are not clearly articulated or are used inconsistently.

Principles of Organization

Thus far I have been concerned with the logic of classification in general, and some of the ways that categories can be considered basic, both within and between levels of a hierarchy. All of my remarks could have been made without reference to emotions. I will now consider briefly some of the criteria that have been used to identify basic emotions in particular, independent of the broader issues of classification. For the sake of simplicity, I will limit consideration to a few observations on the principles by which emotions become organized into coherent syndromes or systems of behavior. These principles are of three general kinds: biological (information encoded in the genes), social (rules and other cultural artifacts), and psychological (schemas or knowledge structures). But before getting to that, I need to say a few words on the functions of emotions, for in the organization of behavior, form follows function. (In response to Question 3 – What is the function of emotions? – I will discuss in greater detail the possible functions of emotions.)

In everyday affairs, we consider something basic, fundamental, or primary if it fulfills an important function. Indeed, the prototype or presumed essence of an object may include functional criteria (e.g., the prototypic knife is a good cutting instrument, the prototypic automobile is a good transportation vehicle, and the prototypic bird is one that can fly). This everyday meaning of basic finds its counterpart in discussions of emotions. That is, basic emotions presumably are those that fulfill vital functions. Having taken this step, we may ask: vital for what or whom? Three general possibilities exist. An emotion may be vital to survival of the species (biological criteria), the society (social criteria), or the self (psychological criteria).

Of the three possibilities, which is the most fundamental? Currently, the most popular answer to this question is: biology. That is, basic emotions are those that fulfill vital biological functions. Having adopted this answer, a number of more precise criteria for basic emotions can easily be specified. For example, basic emotions should be universal among the human species, they should be observable in rudimentary form in nonhuman primates, and they should be heritable.

But why should we accept the notion that biological criteria are the most fundamental? In one sense, the answer is obvious. As a species, human beings are the product of millions of years of evolution, and in that sense biological principles of organization are prior to either social or psychological principles.

Biology, however, sets only loose constraints on human behavior. If we are talking about standard emotions (i.e., those recognized and named within a culture), social principles determine the form the emotions actually take. Thus, among the Japanese, attachment to another human being takes a special form called *amae* (a kind of "sweet dependency"), which is considered a basic emotion; in Western cultures, attachment is no less important from a biological perspective, but it takes different forms, fashioned by different social rules (Doi, 1973). To take another example, among the head-hunting Ilongot of the Philippines, the emotion of *liget* (a kind of exhilaration experienced when taking a head) is fundamental. There is no Western equivalent to *liget*, although Rosaldo (1980) has used "anger" as a partial and very inexact translation. Or consider the vicissitudes of hope within Western societies: During the Middle Ages, hope was classified as a basic emotion; today it is regarded as secondary or derived by most emotion theorists, if it is regarded at all (Averill et al., 1990). In short, emotional syndromes are not only constituted by social rules, but some are among the defining features of a culture and an age. The latter are basic emotions in a social sense.

Social and biological principles must ultimately be manifested through the behavior of individuals, and there is always some "slippage" in the process. In this sense, psychological principles might be considered the most basic. By psychological principles, I mean the personal rules, plans, and knowledge structures that determine a person's sense of self. When people are asked to recount emotional episodes that evoked their "true feelings," they typically describe incidents that reinforce, transform, or enhance their sense of self (Morgan & Averill, 1992). Emotional experiences of this type are psychologically basic. (Parenthetically, the sense of self need not be positive. The depressed person who feels dejected and guilty is preserving a sense of self, no matter how maladaptive such behavior might be in the long run.)

When a psychologically basic emotion comes to dominate a person's life, it may be called (in a somewhat antiquated terminology) a "ruling passion" or "master sentiment." Some people are ruled by fear, others by anger, love, pride, shame, or whatever. That is a maladaptive extreme that only points to a larger truth. "Reason is, and ought only to be, the slave of the passions, and can never pretend to any other office than to serve and obey them" (Hume, 1739/1967, II(iii)3, p. 415). This passage is often quoted, if only to be dismissed as either an empty tautology or a blatant falsehood. But let us not be too critical, or interpret Hume too literally. The fact remains: Each of us on occasion is, and ought to be, a slave to our passions; to be otherwise is to lack a firm sense of self and engagement in the world.

In short, the term "basic" can be applied to emotions from biological, social, or psychological perspectives. To pick one of these (the biological, say) as primary is an a priori assumption, not an empirical discovery. There is nothing wrong with a priori assumptions as long as they are clearly recognized as such. All inquiry must start somewhere. And whether one assumption is better than another ultimately depends on its fruitfulness in accounting for observed data and in raising interesting questions for further research. The assumption that basic emotions are organized according to biological principles has had undeniable heuristic value; however, for reasons presented elsewhere, I believe this assumption has outlived its usefulness and now inhibits rather than facilitates our understanding (Averill, 1980, 1984, 1990a). Would we be served any better if we adopted social or psychological criteria for the identification of basic emotions? I don't think so, for the problem lies not with the criteria but with the very notion of basic emotions.

Concluding Observations

To summarize briefly, there are many ways in which an emotion can be said to be basic (e.g., according to its prototypicality, level of classification, and principles of organization). These various ways are often conflated, as when a prototypic emotion at one level of classification is interpreted in terms relevant to another (either higher or lower, but presumably more basic) level of classification, or when an emotion that serves a vital function for the society or individual is interpreted as basic in a biological sense.

If confusion were the only difficulty, we might solve the problem by settling on one set of criteria for being basic and applying those criteria consistently. That strategy is not likely to succeed, however, for the criteria that one theorist might deem appropriate, another might reject on equally valid grounds. Fortunately, from a theoretical point of view, there appears to be no compelling reason to postulate basic emotions, regardless of the criteria used. If our goal is a general theory of emotion, we must transcend parochial allegiances. Basic emotions have no more place in psychology than basic animals in zoology or basic diseases in medicine.

All Emotions Are Basic

PAUL EKMAN

The phrase *basic emotions* has been used in a number of different ways by emotion theorists. My use of the term *basic* is to emphasize the role that evolution has played in shaping both the unique and the common features that emotions display, as well as their current function. Innate factors play a role in accounting for both the characteristics shared by emotions and for those that distinguish one emotion from another.

Emotions evolved for their adaptive value in dealing with fundamental life tasks. There are a number of ways to describe these fundamental life tasks. Johnson-Laird and Oatley (1992) say they are "universal human predicaments, such as achievements, losses, frustrations, etc. . . . [E]ach emotion thus prompts us in a direction which in the course of evolution has done better than other solutions in recurring circumstances that are relevant to goals." (See also Lazarus's discussion of core relational themes, 1991, p. 202, and also Stein & Trabasso, 1992).

Tooby and Cosmides emphasize the crucial role of evolution in understanding our emotions today, telling us that emotions impose "on the present world an interpretative landscape derived from the covariant structure of the past." Emotions they say deal with recurrent "adaptive situations[,] [f]ighting, falling in love, escaping predators, confronting sexual infidelity, and so on, each [of which] recurred innumerable times in evolutionary history" (1990, pp. 407–408). What distinguishes emotions from other psychological phenomena, I believe, is that our appraisal of a current event, and at least some of our responses to it, is influenced by what Tooby and Cosmides have called our ancestral past.

Some years ago I described the nature of that appraisal as follows.

> There must be an appraiser mechanism which selectively attends to those stimuli (external or internal) which are the occasion for . . . [one or another emotion]. Since the interval between stimulus and emotional response is sometimes extraordinarily short, the appraisal mechanism must be capable of operating with great speed. Often the appraisal is not only quick but it happens without awareness, so I must postulate that the appraisal mechanism is able to operate *automatically*. It must be constructed so that it quickly attends to some stimuli, determining not only that they

> pertain to emotion, but to which emotion . . . . Appraisal is not always automatic. Sometimes the evaluation of what is happening is slow, deliberate and conscious. With such a more extended appraisal there may be some automatic arousal, but perhaps not of a kind which is differentiated. The person could be said to be aroused or alerted, but no specific emotion is operative. Cognition plays the important role in determining what will transpire. During such extended appraisal the evaluation may match to the selective filters of the automatic appraiser . . . . It need not be, however; the experience may be diffuse rather than specific to one emotion (Ekman, 1977, pp. 58–59).

This view of appraisal is similar to positions subsequently developed by Zajonc (1985) and Ohman (1986).

Automatic appraisal does not simply and solely operate on what is given biologically, dealing only with stimulus events that exactly fit what is given. In all likelihood not enough is given for automatic appraisal to ever operate without considerable amplification and detailing through social learning. (See especially Ohman, 1986, on this point.) Individual differences in our experience allow for enormous variations in the specifics of what calls forth emotion that are attributable to personality, family, and culture. And yet what calls forth an emotion is not totally malleable—there are some commonalities.

> The ancestrally recurrent structured situation that the organism categorizes itself as being in is the "meaning" of the situation for that organism. It "sees," i.e., is organized to respond to, previous fitness contingencies, not present ones. . . . Emotions . . . lead organisms to act as if certain things were true about the present circumstances whether or not they are because they were true of past circumstances. . . . In this lies their strength and their weakness. . . . [The automatic appraisal] cannot detect when the invariances that held true ancestrally no longer obtain (Tooby & Cosmides, 1990, pp. 418–419).

Let me more briefly describe some other characteristics of emotion that directly follow from viewing emotions as having evolved to deal with fundamental life tasks in ways that have been adaptive phylogenetically. (1) There are some common elements in the contexts in which emotions are found to occur, despite differences due to individual and cultural differences in social learning. (2) Emotions are likely to be observable in other primates. It is possible that there might be some emotions unique to humans, but no convincing evidence exists that is so. (Of course, we should also note that the capacity to represent emotional experience in words changes many aspects of emotional experience in ways which I cannot describe here.) (3) Emotions can begin so quickly that they can happen before one is aware that they have begun. Quick onset is central to the adaptive value of emotions, mobilizing us quickly to respond to important events.

It is also adaptive for the response changes that can occur so quickly not to last very long unless the emotion is evoked again. Here is not the place to argue about just how long an emotion typically lasts, but certainly it is not hours or days, but more in the realm of minutes and seconds. I believe those who claim emotions endure for much longer time periods are summating what is actually a series of briefer emotion episodes.

Because emotions can occur with a very rapid onset, through automatic appraisal, with little awareness, and with involuntary changes in expression and physiology (which I will describe), we often experience emotions as happening to us, not as chosen by us. We do not simply decide when to have a particular emotion. "An automatic involuntary aspect is present in the experience of all emotion" (Stein & Trabasso, 1992).

I have so far characterized emotional responses in terms of their potential for quick onset, brief duration, and involuntary nature, such that they are experienced as happening to us rather than as chosen. Let me now describe two further aspects of emotion, their physiology and expression.

There is evidence (Ekman, Levenson, & Friesen, 1983; Levenson, Ekman, & Friesen, 1990) for distinctive patterns of autonomic nervous system (ANS) activity for anger, fear, and disgust, and it appears that there may also be a distinctive pattern for sadness (Levenson, Carstensen, Friesen, & Ekman, 1991). These findings have now been replicated in four separate experiments, in two different age groups. Although there are some inconsistencies between the ANS patterns found and the findings of other investigators, we should not ignore the many consistencies with the results of Schwartz, Weinberger, and Singer (1981), Ax (1953), Roberts and Weerts (1982), and Graham (1962).

The only recent challenge to our findings was Stemmler's (1989) report that ANS patterning was specific to how the emotion was elicited. However, this may be due to a number of methodological problems including measuring physiology a considerable period after the induction was over and studying very low emotional intensities, as well as including a substantial number of subjects who reported not experiencing the emotion. We have preliminary evidence in two different studies (Ekman & Davidson, 1993; Levenson, Carstensen et al. 1991) of the same emotion-specific pattern when emotion was elicited in very different ways.

We presume that these ANS patterns evolved because they subserve patterns of motor behavior that were adaptive for each of these emotions, preparing the organism for quite different actions. For example, fighting might well have been the adaptive action in anger, which is consistent with the finding that blood goes to the hands in anger. If no specific pattern of motor activity had survival value for an emotion, then there would be no reason to expect a specific pattern of ANS activity to have been established for that emotion. That is why I think we have not found an emotion-specific pattern, a pattern that differs from each of the other emotions, for either surprise or enjoyment.

I have no argument with Davidson's belief that approaching versus withdrawing is a fundamental issue in terms of the action plans associated with each basic emotion. But there is no definitive evidence to show that all positive emotions always involve just approach. And certainly anger, fear, and disgust can involve approach or withdrawal. Is Davidson arguing that for each emotion, evolution prepares us to *either* approach or avoid, and only social learning may add the other action pattern? If that was so, it might be possible to measure electromyographically the beginning of that tendency even when the action taken is different. For now, I propose we do not regard either an action readiness or emotion-specific ANS activity as the *sine qua non* for defining emotions.

However, it is necessary to posit emotion-specific central nervous system (CNS) activity in my account of basic emotions. The distinctive features of each emotion, including the changes not just in expression but in memories, imagery, expectations, and other cognitive activities, could not occur without central nervous system organization and direction. There must be *unique* physiological patterns for each emotion, and these CNS patterns should be specific to these emotions and not found in other mental activity. Here I am reaching far beyond the data, but not far beyond what the new techniques for measuring brain activity may allow us to discover in this decade of the brain.

I have so far described seven characteristics of emotion: automatic appraisal, commonalities in antecedent events, presence in other primates, quick onset, brief duration, unbidden occurrence, and distinctive physiology. I believe the evidence will show that these characteristics are found in amusement, anger, awe, contempt, contentment, disgust, embarrassment, excitement, fear, guilt, interest, pride in achievement, relief, sadness, satisfaction, sensory pleasure, and shame. Not all of these emotions are known to have a distinctive, universal signal, the last characteristic I will consider.

Emotions could have all the features I have described and not communicate any information to others, but in fact at least some emotions often do. A distinctive universal signal has been identified for anger, fear, disgust, and sadness (see Ekman, 1989, for a review of the evidence and arguments about universals). There is argument about contempt (Ekman & Friesen, 1986; Ekman, O'Sullivan, &Matsumoto, in press; Russell, in press), and some newly emerging evidence for embarrassment (Keltner, personal communication, October 1991).

There has been no study of a possible signal for awe, and it is not certain if there is a signal for either excitement or interest (which unlike Tomkins, 1963, or Izard, 1971, I consider to be separate states). I believe the evidence is also not definitive for a separate signal for guilt or shame, which differ from the sadness signal. While there is evidence of a universal signal for surprise, there are other reasons for doubting whether surprise is an emotion (see Ekman, 1992).

A universal signal should not *ipso facto* be considered evidence of an emotion. Nor should the lack of a universal signal be used to say a phenomenon is not an emotion. We should, however, expect to find that emotions that do not have distinctive signals differ in other ways, which I do not have space here to describe, from emotions that do have universal signals.

Most interesting is the likelihood that positive emotions such as amusement, contentment, excitement, pride in achievement, satisfaction, sensory pleasure and relief, all share a single signal—a particular type of smile (Ekman, Davidson, & Friesen, 1990). I am convinced from the research I and others have done on facial expression that no other facial signals will be found that differentiate among these positive emotions. Perhaps a distinctive vocal signal will be discovered.

There are other characteristics of emotion beyond the eight I have described, which deserve and are receiving study. Of particular importance is when emotions appear developmentally, how emotions regulate the way in which we think, and the subjective experience of emotion.

A caveat about thinking of emotions in terms of the characteristics they share. Emotions also differ from each other, as, for example, some may not have distinctive signals. There may be some characteristics that are very important for one emotion and of little significance for another. It may never be possible to have an adequate comprehensive theory of emotion. Instead we may need to have a separate theory for each emotion, to best capture its uniqueness.

Before closing, let me mention the concept of emotion families that may help to clear away some of the argument about how many emotions there are. Each emotion is not a single affective state but a family of related states. Each member of an emotion family shares the eight characteristics I have described. These shared characteristics within a family differ between emotion families, distinguishing one family from another. Put in other terms, each emotion family can be considered to constitute a theme and variations. The theme is composed of the characteristics unique to that family, the variations on that theme are the product of individual differences, and differences in the specific occasion in which an emotion occurs. The themes are the product of evolution, while the variations reflect learning.

By now it should be clear that I do not allow for nonbasic emotions. Every emotion has at least seven of the characteristics I have described. These characteristics allow us to begin to deal with fundamental life tasks quickly without much elaborated planning in ways that have been adaptive in our evolutionary past. Emotions do also typically include informing others which specific negative emotion is occurring or if a positive emotion of some kind is occurring. Much research needs to be done to delineate each of the characteristics I have described, to discover other characteristics shared by these emotions, and to determine whether there are indeed other emotions beyond those I have described.

Note

Much of this reply is drawn from a longer article on this topic, "An Argument for Basic Emotions," which appeared in *Cognition and Emotion*, Spring, 1992. I have, however, changed some of my views in this presentation. The preparation of that article was supported by a Research Scientist Award from the National Institute of Mental Health (MH 06092).

The Basics of Basic Emotion

JAAK PANKSEPP

Were one to ask "Is there *something* basic about emotions?," every sensible commentator would have to respond in the affirmative. The most important events in all our lives are filled with feelings, whether we show them or not. Few individuals need any formal training to know what it means to feel happy, sad, frustrated and angry, scared, full of lust or other innumerable desires, or to identify the environmental events that trigger these feelings. Also, is not the most obvious aspect of infantile behavior its high degree of emotionality? Only the most extreme skeptic would be tempted to argue that babies' passionate flailings do not reflect the ingrained inherited potentials of their nervous systems. The general function of emotions also seems obvious if one assumes they provide coherent and ingrained ways of coping with major challenges to the welfare of an organism.

However, were one to ask "What is basic about emotions?," one would surely get embroiled in controversy, both in terms of what is meant by "basic" and what it means to be an "emotion" (e.g., Ortony & Turner, 1990; Turner & Ortony, 1992; and commentaries by Ekman, 1992; Izard, 1992; and Panksepp, 1992). "Basic" is easier to define than "emotion," since it can be taken to reflect the unfolding of genetic potentials. Unfortunately, we can rarely specify where the influence of genetic unfolding ends and the role of ever-present environmental influences begins. Of course, they are intextricably intwined. In all but the most well-controlled circumstances, we cannot credibly distinguish the spontaneous unfolding of genetic potentials from the fertilization that the environment provides (see Plomin & Bergeman, 1991, for the ongoing debate).

With the enormous recent growth in our understanding of genetic mechanisms, it is becoming increasingly clear that many genetic potentials are expressed in specific environments, which further compounds the difficulty in clearly differentiating the influences of nature and nurture. In other words, genes are not just passive repositories of ancestral knowledge, but dynamically responsive information stores. More than ever before, we are beginning to appreciate the full complexity of the epigenetic blending of inherited and environmental potentials (for more details, see my response to Question 11: What develops in emotional development?). As a general principle, it appears that predilections for most of the common behavioral potentials are genetically provided (through generalized, nondetailed "blueprints" that guide the construction of the nervous system). Many of the behavioral potentials of the nervous system are ingrained, although all must be environmentally molded to achieve any level of coordinated sophistication. Still, it remains remarkable how widely the genesis of behavioral traits are attributed to the ever-present environmental guidance rather than the incredibly sophisticated genetically coded neural mechanisms which provide the fundamental operating systems that allow organisms to behave in the categorical ways they do. Of course, the delusion is understandable. It is much harder to see into the dark recesses of genes and the brain circuits they help construct than to describe the well-illuminated environmental events that bombard our every waking moment. These difficulties are compounded by the fact that our most analytical brain functions appear to have been designed, through evolutionary selection, to discern causal relationships in the external world. In short, as scientific observers, we, as all other humans, may be genetically prepared to believe that many developmental changes are largely due to environmental events, while in fact they are as much the result of the epigenetic unfolding of hereditary tendencies stored within DNA. The brain is full of special and general-purpose mechanisms that have been constructed through evolutionary reinforcement. At least in rough outline, the basic emotions are such entities. They provide organisms with relatively complex behavioral potentials (i.e., instinctual tendencies), and they also elaborate the intrinsic values that guide most of subsequent learning. In other words, these systems continue to regulate behavior throughout the lifespan of an organism—first in very impulsive ways and then in more measured ways.

Although the reinforcement histories of individual lives create vast tapestries of detailed differences among the members of each species, the general groundplans for these potentials are provided as hereditary gifts. It is amazing that this point needs to be emphasized, but all too many scholars are still willing to argue that the brain is something akin to a "blank slate" and that humans are a species with no instincts. Far from it. We are as laden with emotional instincts as lower animals, but because of our enlarged cortices (which resemble the random access memory [RAM] space of general-purpose computers [Panksepp, 1989]), we are not as constrained by the dictates of these instincts. We have more choices available to us than other species. We can leave our emotions internalized as feelings to guide unseen cognitive strategies. Still, if our emotional instincts reflect general solutions that have been well conserved across mammalian and other vertebrate species, the use of appropriate animal models will be essential for grasping the nature of the underlying brain mechanisms (Panksepp, 1991). Unfortunately, the neuroscientific approach remains poorly developed (partially because of the insidious influence of a simpleminded "behaviorism" that inhibited psychoneurological thought during the middle of this century; see Panksepp, 1990)

So, what is so basic about emotions? At present, one can assert with great confidence that most species possess some unique sensory-perceptual inputs that lead to emotionality: For instance, for a rat to exhibit "fearful" behaviors to the smell of a cat requires no life experiences with cats (Crepeau & Panksepp, 1988). But a mere analysis of the inputs will not take us to the heart of the matter. One can likewise defend that there is something basic about the motor outputs of emotions: For instance, emotional responses have been evoked by localized brain stimulation in even very young animals before they have had much chance to learn to express emotive behaviors (Moran, Schwartz, & Blass, 1983; Roberts & Berquist, 1968). But a mere analysis of the outputs also does not take us to the heart of the matter. One would be taking a more controversial stance if one were to claim that basic emotional circuits exist within that "great intermediate neural net" that intervenes between inputs and outputs, but how else could we explain the variety of emotive tendencies, accompanied by appropriate affective states, that can be reliably evoked by localized brain stimulation of essentially the same brain areas across a diversity of species (Panksepp, 1981, 1982, 1985)? To believe that such behaviors were acquired by individual learning by members of vastly different species is highly implausible. To believe that such brain systems, conserved throughout mammalian evolution, no longer move the human mind, is to plead a privileged metaphysical status for the human condition. I often fear that those who advocate such positions are playing deconstructive intellectual games (which is so readily promoted by the complexity of our cortical potentials) or perhaps some are committed to maintaining the hegemony of long-standing cultural biases (such as metaphysical/spiritual views of mental organization). Of course there are less sinister causes. Those who are not conversant with the neuroscientific evidence tend to avoid the conclusions such evidence supports. But this is a two-way problem. An equally small percentage of psychologists and neuroscientists appreciate each other's approaches. Without a familiarity and respect for various levels of analysis, fruitful interchange and cross-fertilization cannot occur (Bunge, 1990).

Which, then, are the basic emotions from a defensible interdisciplinary perspective? It should come as no surprise that they are the most common and well-accepted ones. At the folk-psychological level, it is reasonably easy to agree on some major items that should top any list, functions such as desire, anger, fear, sadness, sexual lust, joy and maternal acceptance/nurturance. And they are the ones most clearly supported by evidence from brain research. There is no credible evidence that these commonly accepted items are constructed through associative learning from more basic brain components through life experiences in either animal or human children. Indeed, there is abundant data, summarized elsewhere (LeDoux, 1987; MacLean, 1990; Panksepp, 1982, 1985, 1986, 1989, 1990b, 1991, 1992, 1993), that such emotions arise from the highly conserved subcortical brain mechanisms we still share with other species.

As most taxonomies acknowledge, there are many other affective states (Plutchik, 1980), but the cardinal neuroscientific issue, and an important psychological issue as well, is whether there are common principles among the underlying circuit functions of the brain that should encourage us to place only certain items in the same category. Should we have several taxa of affective processes, with only one set being considered to be bona-fide emotions? I believe we should, and I believe at least three general levels of complexity are present:

Category 1. There are the very low-level emotive responses that are almost reflexive, such as startle, disgust, and the various hungers, that are time locked with precipitating conditions (although they may come to have metaphoric representations in higher cognitive sentiments, as in surprise and social contempt).

Category 2. These I would call the the "blue-ribbon grade-A" emotions. They arise from extensive sensorimotor command circuits of the brain that can have sustained behavioral and affective consequence that outlast precipitating conditions. They generate flexible behavioral states and help coordinate a great deal of brain activity.

Category 3. Finally, there are the systems for various higher sentiments that remain largely internalized as subjective states, and hence are open to empirical analysis only in humans.

I would suggest that the taxonomy issues will never be resolved until we begin to include brain circuit criteria in our discussion of the underlying issues.

My personal research perspective is utilitarian, guided by the view that psychobiology needs to expend the greatest effort on the basic nature of the "trunk-line" issues for those big items in Category 2 that all emotional lists contain (Panksepp, 1991; 1992). Further, I suspect that the most useful type of analysis will be the characterization of the neurochemical codes that help mediate these "primes" (Buck, 1985; Panksepp, 1986, 1992). In short, my position is not to deny the reality of many affective states in the brain, but to accept, with considerable disappointment, that many subtle ones (Category 3) cannot be well explicated by our nascent brain sciences at present. Pursuit of others (such as those in Category 1) will have minimal impact on our understanding of emotional and psychiatric disorders.

A concerted effort devoted to understanding the neural underpinning of the big items in Category 2 will eventually provide powerful new levels of prediction and control in biological psychiatry. Indeed, through the application of such a strategy (Panksepp, 1979), we have achieved modest success in the treatment of an intractable psychiatric disorder, early childhood autism, with the opiate antagonist naltrexone (Leboyer et al.,1992; Panksepp & Lensing, 1991,). At the neural level, the analysis of basic emotions is unlikely to be a repetitive exercise in systematically revealing the obvious, but an ever-deepening journey into the true nature of human and animal existence—a journey where many mistakes must be made along the way.

Without neurobiological and neurobehavioral anchor points, the discussion of "basic emotions" can easily regress into a battle of empirically bolstered opinions (e.g., see the Turner and Ortony 1992 controversy). Thus I would reemphasize that a useful starting point for establishing the basic cross-species homologies in emotional operating systems is to define the basic emotions at least in part with respect to neural circuit characteristics (Panksepp, 1982, 1986, 1992). At the most global level, I think it is reasonable to view basic emotions as arising from coherent brain operating systems that have a considerable number of shared neural characteristics. One major attribute is that such brain systems can orchestrate and coordinate a large number of output systems in response to specific inputs. They coordinate diverse outputs so that relevant physiological/hormonal, behavioral, and psychological processes are well integrated with relatively stereotyped action tendencies. Emotional systems also generate characteristic internal feeling states (which may have been the most efficient neurosymbolic way to encode incoming information with values). Without internal biological values, I doubt if any credible model of behavior could ever be generated, and it is long overdue for disciplines concerned with the objective behavior of animals to take such issues seriously.

To some extent, the emotional operating systems of mammals resemble command-motor systems that have been elucidated in invertebrates. Indeed, recent work on invertebrate and simple vertebrate systems has highlighted how sophisticated and flexible these systems actually are (Berkinblit, Feldman, & Fukson, 1986; Larimer, 1988). For instance, a large array of interconnected neurons will participate in the coordination of a motor output (with no single neuron assuming an exclusive command mode). It is also clear that emotional command systems affect the intensity of emotions in "mass-action" ways": An individual emotional state intensifies as more neurons within the system are recruited, whether it be by the increased activity of specific neural circuits through electrical stimulation or by increasing synaptic potentials by administration of relevant transmitters into the brain (e.g., all neuropeptides that modulate emotions do so with increasing intensities as administered doses are increased, and they can sustain a specific emotional state for hours (Panksepp, 1990c, 1993)). Also, emotional systems have the intrinsic capacity to inhibit antagonistic emotional systems and arouse synergistic ones. There is no space here to go into the details of these systems, but they have been summarized before (see previous reviews cited above). Recent data related to the *rage* system has been well covered by Bandler (1988) and Siegel and Brutus (1990); a detailed analysis of *fear* has been provided by Gray (1987), Panksepp (1990b), and Panksepp, Sacks, Crepeau, and Abbott (1991); *expectancy/behavioral facilitation system* by Depue and Iacono (1989) and Panksepp (1981, 1986); and *separation-distress/panic* by Newman (1988), Panksepp, Siviy, and Normansell (1985), and Panksepp, Normansell, Herman, Bishop, and Crepeau (1988).

In short, the evidence strongly suggests that the neurodynamics of human emotional states arise from lawful principles that can be revealed through animal brain research (Panksepp, 1991). This is not to claim that the more recent evolutionary and culturally molded socio-affective processes of humans can also be revealed by such work. Clearly they cannot, but the primitive shared emotional substrates are so powerful that useful homologies will continue to emerge with remarkable clarity (Panksepp, 1985, 1993).

Toward a Concept of "Modal Emotions"

KLAUS R. SCHERER

The claim for basic or fundamental emotions is usually based on empirical evidence for the universality of verbal labels, facial expression patterns, and antecedent eliciting situations. On closer investigation, this evidence is less conclusive than is often claimed. I believe that any attempt to settle this issue must address the question whether there really is evidence for a limited number of universal and invariant response patterns (for a few "basic" emotions) or whether, instead, the evidence points toward the existence of a large number of universal "response elements," with some combinations tending to occur more frequently than others as part of an emotional reaction. This question has important implications for the definition of emotion.

Brief Review of the Evidence for Basic Emotions

Verbal Labels

Equivalents for most of the emotion terms commonly considered part of the "basic" category seem to exist in almost all major languages of the world. In an interculturally comparative study of emotion experiences in 37 countries (Scherer & Wallbott, 1994; Wallbott & Scherer, 1986), we were able to translate the English terms for the seven emotions studied (anger, fear, sadness, joy, disgust, shame, and guilt) into the various languages spoken in these countries to the satisfaction of our local collaborators. However, as we discovered in many informal discussions, major divergences in connotations also exist. Some careful studies of the respective semantic fields have shown important differences, even between closely related languages (such as German and Swiss German; Dünker, 1979). Quite a few anthropologists maintain that in many of the more exotic cultures one does not always find single terms comparable to the basic emotion terms used in Western languages. While this is not convincing evidence that the respective emotion does not exist, such differences and the economic use of short labels may well reflect meaningful cultural differences (see Mesquita & Frijda, 1992).

Facial Expression

There is good evidence that prototypical Western facial expressions are well recognized in non-Western countries (Ekman, 1972; Ekman et al., 1987; Izard, 1971; Matsumoto & Ekman, 1989). There is also some evidence that people in very different cultures produce very similar facial expressions in response to certain situations or when portraying their reactions to a standard imagined situation (Eibl-Eibesfeldt, 1972; Ekman, 1972). However, reports in the literature also suggest differences in the type of expressions used for the same emotion between cultures and even within a single culture (Ricci-Bitti, 1989). Most important, much of the evidence can be interpreted in terms of the universality of the innervation of some major elements of facial expression (particularly the corrugator and zygomatic muscles). To my knowledge, there is as yet no large-scale study on naturally occurring facial expressions to standard situations in a cross-culturally comparative fashion (or in any one single culture) that could establish the amount of prototypicality and variability of the respective facial expression. One might find that some major elements do in fact occur almost invariably but that the total pattern of expression is quite variable (see Gosselin, Kirouac, & Doré, submitted). If this were indeed the case, we need to ask whether the differences in overall pattern indicate differences in the underlying emotional state.

Antecedents

There is evidence that specific situations or events will evoke similar emotions in different cultures (Boucher, 1983; Scherer, Wallbott, & Summerfield, 1986). But there is also some evidence for cultural differences in this respect (Scherer, 1988; see also my comment on Question 4 in this volume). I believe that it is not the situations themselves that are universal but the pattern of appraisal reflecting the meaning of certain events for the individual. In this sense, structural, transactional features of situational meaning—such as loss, danger, gratification, injustice—are indeed universal and phylogenetically continuous (see Johnson-Laird & Oatley, 1989). Again, central elements of the appraisal process will be invariant but the complete pattern may be quite variable. We can then ask whether the differences in overall appraisal outcome reflect differences in the underlying emotional state. Even more striking than the cultural differences that have been observed is the important role of individual differences within a single culture. The same situation does not necessarily provoke the same emotional expression nor the use of the same label in two individuals (or even in the same individual on two different occasions). It is not a question of a common repertoire, which certainly exists, but one of the stereotypy or prototypicality of the patterns observed. Do we find relatively standardized, invariant overall patterns for a few basic or fundamental emotions, or do we find that—while central elements or components are invariant responses to situations with a universal meaning for an individual—the total reaction pattern may be quite variable? Given the lack of real-life observational data, we do not know how invariant or variable the appraisal, expression, and labeling patterns really are. My bet is that they are quite variable. Again, if this were the case, we need to ask whether such differences in overall pattern reflect differences in the underlying emotional state.

Defining Emotion as a Process

One can argue that variability of patterning does not exclude the existence of a "basic" category (especially if one assumes prototypicality and fuzzy sets). However, the issue then becomes one of defining emotion. If one claims that emotion is a theoretical construct that can be exemplified by rather variable patterns of elicitation and reaction as long as there is an underlying central core, one needs to clearly explain what constitutes this "core." Some attempts in this direction have been made: Tomkins (1984) and Ekman (1992) see this core in what they perceive as a limited number of typical facial expression patterns based on innate neuromotor programs, Panksepp (1982) claims innate neurophysiological pathways, Lazarus (1991c) argues for "themes," prototype theorists rely on the results of factor or cluster analyses (Russell, 1983; Shaver, Schwartz, Kirson, & O'Connor, 1987). I believe that all these attempts to define the core of basic emotions suffer from the post hoc nature of the explanation. They all reflect the fact that we generally experience emotion in a discrete fashion and that there seems to be a "bunching" of the different emotional states around a limited number of types. Certain patterns of expression (and possibly autonomic arousal) occur more frequently than others in response to certain types of structurally equivalent (in terms of underlying appraisal) situations and most languages provide convenient labels to refer to this "bunching." However, I have not yet seen a convincing a priori argument, let alone evidence, that establishes the existence of basic or fundamental emotions as independent and integral biological or psychological categories or mechanisms.

My own view is rather different, mostly due to a radical difference in my definition of emotion. I have defined emotion as a sequence of interrelated, synchronized changes in the states of all organismic subsystems (information processing/cognition, support/ANS, execution/motivation, action/SNS, monitoring/subjective feeling) in response to the evaluation of an external or internal stimulus event that is relevant to central concerns of the organism (see Scherer, 1993a). In this sense, *the pattern of all synchronized changes in the different components over time constitutes the emotion* and even small differences in this pattern are expected to reflect real differences in the nature of the emotional state.

It is important to note the cumulative aspect of the synchronization process. Emotion is not considered as a steady state triggered by a prototypical eliciting event with the immediate onset of a full-fledged, ready-made effector program (as seems to be the case in the tradition of discrete emotion theories; see Ekman, 1992; Izard, 1971, 1977; Tomkins, 1984). Instead, I see emotion as an episode, a time window, during which the different components get synchronized and desynchronized in a highly differentiated fashion, with cumulative changes depending, in addition to multiple feedback and feedforward effects, on changes in the constant evaluation of significant ongoing situational change for the organism. Consequently, contrary to the postulates of discrete emotion theories or prototype approaches, I expect that emotion episodes are as variable as these appraisal-determined cumulative patterns of component synchronizations.

In trying to predict which type of emotional state is likely to result from the cumulative evaluation of organism-relevant changes in internal or external stimulation, I have proposed a sequence of five stimulus evaluation checks (novelty, intrinsic pleasantness, goal conduciveness, coping potential, norm/self compatibility; see Scherer, 1984a, 1986b, 1993b and my contribution to Question 4 for greater detail) that I consider necessary and sufficient to account for the differentiation of most of the modal emotions.

During the 1980s a large number of very similar models, attempting to differentiate the emotions on the basis of specific patterns of event appraisal, were suggested in the literature (see Scherer, 1988a, for a comparative review). Few of these appraisal theorists, however, attempted to link the appraisal mechanism directly to other components of the emotion process (for an exception, see Smith, 1989; Smith & Ellsworth, 1985). This link constitutes the core proposal of the component process model (see Scherer, 1984). Taking a functional point of view, I argued that the result of each stimulus evaluation check should bring about an appropriate adaptive reaction in the other organismic components. I have ventured detailed predictions (see Scherer, 1984b, 1986) concerning the changes in ANS responding, facial and vocal expression, and other modalities of an emotional reaction that are theoretically expected for particular outcomes of stimulus evaluation checks. The figure illustrates the suggested sequential, cumulative process using the successive "overlay" of facial expression as produced by the stimulus evaluation checks "novel, unpleasant, discrepant, high power," resulting in what would commonly be called an "anger face" (reproduced from Scherer, 1992). In fact, componential patterning theory, as I have called it, suggests that many of these elements (e.g., an orienting response as a consequence of novelty appraisal) are innate, largely phylogenetically continuous, and thus universal.

The Concept of Modal Emotions

As previously mentioned, many different combinations of results from the stimulus evaluation checks are possible (especially since evaluation is thought to occur in a graduated fashion, determining not only the type but also the intensity of the emotional arousal). In consequence, the number of potential emotional states (as defined by the process of synchronized patterning of all components in the emotion episode time window) is virtually infinite. However, there are some major patterns of adaptation in the life of animate organisms that reflect frequently recurring patterns of environmental evaluation results (see also my comment on Question 4 concerning the universality of antecedents and minimal prerequisites). All organisms, at all stages of ontogenetic development, encounter blocks to need satisfaction or goal achievement at least some of the time. Thus, frustration in a very general sense is universal and ubiquitous. Equally universal are the two major

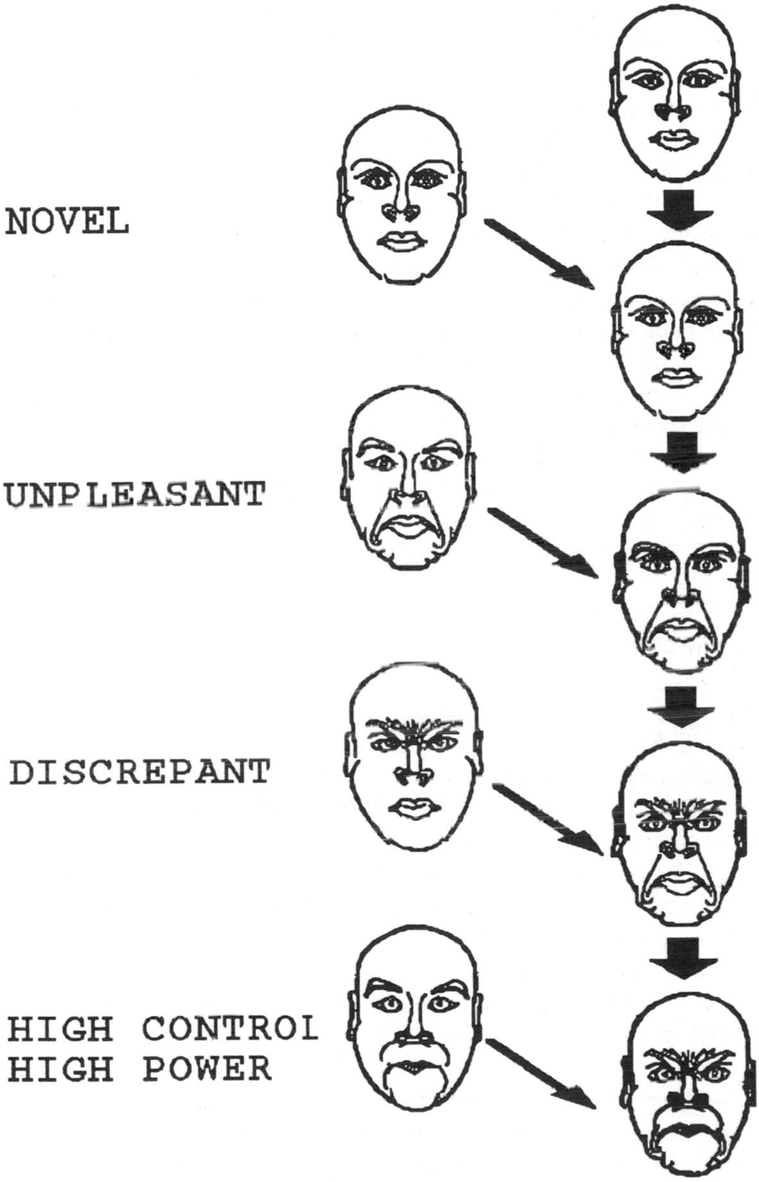

Sequential cumulative changes in facial expression as a result of specific SEC outcomes (as predicted by component process theory). Reproduced from Scherer (1992).

reaction patterns—fight and flight. Consequently, it is not surprising that the emotional states that often elicit these behaviors—anger and fear, respectively—seem universal and present in many species. In terms of the model proposed here, it is highly likely that, if one were to compile a frequency distribution of stimulus evaluation check patterns, some combinations of evaluation check results would be very frequently encountered by many types of organisms, giving rise to specific, recurring patterns of state changes.

I have suggested (Scherer, 1984b) the term *modal emotions* for the states resulting from these predominant stimulus evaluation checks. Just as certain stimulus evaluation checks in response to certain types of situations are more frequent, the patterning of elements in other emotion components would also occur more frequently. Modal emotions are therefore characterized by a prototypical pattern of appraisals and the corresponding patterning of expression, autonomic arousal, action tendencies, and feeling states. This would account, it seems, for the evidence for universal prototypical patterns mentioned at the outset. However, I find it important to highlight the central difference of the modal emotion concept to the postulate of basic or fundamental emotions: No effort is made to find or define a definite number of homogeneous, integral categories or mechanisms that justify an a priori definition of basic or fundamental. Instead, we need to empirically study the frequency with which certain patterns of sequential, synchronized changes in the different components of emotion episodes occur. I believe that the study of verbal labeling plays a special role in the empirical assessment of modality or "bunching."

The Role of Verbal Labeling

Given the prominence and frequency of occurrence of these episodes of highly similar emotional experiences, it is not surprising that they have been labeled with a short verbal expression, mostly a single word, in most languages. This would be predicted on the basis of a principle of economical verbal coding of objects of communication (see Clark & Clark, 1977, pp. 552–557; Whorf, 1956; Zipf, 1949). Thus, discreteness is—at least in part—bestowed by linguistic categorization and the cultural prototypes these categories reflect (see Shaver, et al., 1987). Linguistic categories conceptually order the world for us in many domains, and they do so for emotion. Among the many advantages of this categorical organization are cognitive economy and communicability of underlying referents. One can venture rather specific theoretical predictions as to the patterns of stimulus evaluation checks that are likely to produce such modal emotions as they are labeled in many different languages of the world (see Scherer, 1986, 1988). In fact, we can show that a simple expert system allows us to predict the use of verbal labels for emotional experiences on the basis of the subject's recalled appraisal processes (Scherer, 1993b).

Verbal emotion labels are only one type of representation of the emotion process. It can be argued that they represent the reflexive part of the monitor subsystem previously described. Whereas the monitor subsystem as a whole reflects the changes in the states of all other subsystems, there is, at least in humans, a conscious part. This is the component of the emotion process available for reflection and verbal description. The conscious part of the monitor system may reflect many aspects of the other emotion components—such as the evaluation of the situation, the neurophysiological changes, expression, and action tendencies—and so do many emotion words, particularly those considered to stand for "fundamental" emotions.

However, we must keep in mind that the activity of labeling is independent of the emotion process, and of emotional experience as a whole. To some degree, it is arbitrary which aspects of the emotion process are selected and labeled by a word in the language, depending on the communicators' intentions. Thus, some words appear to highlight the physiological reaction component, as in the case of "aroused" or "tired." Some are quite cognitive, like "bewildered" or "curious." Others focus on somewhat specific sociomotivational antecedents like the word "jealous." Still others emphasize the action tendency, as in "hostile." The special importance of the "basic emotion words" may reside in the fact that they refer to a more global set of changes in many of the subsystems of our emotion construct (see Scherer, 1984).

And yet the existence of a specific emotion label in one or even several languages does not establish the existence of a corresponding, frequently occurring pattern of stimulus evaluation checks with respective componential response patterning—that is, a modal emotion. This would seem to be a matter for empirical investigation. Consequently, a verbal emotion label cannot be used as an explanans (as it often is in the psychology of emotion). Instead, it is an explanandum. Emotion labels may in part be based on typical reactions of the social environment that may be quite similar for rather different emotions (cf. the constructionist view held by Averill, 1980; see also Mesquita & Frijda, 1992). Consequently, we really need empirical investigation to determine how patterns of event appraisal and the nature of the subsequent subsystem responses result in our use of a particular emotion word or expression.

"You're Not Sick, You're Just in Love": Emotion as an Interpretive System

RICHARD A. SHWEDER

"Are there basic emotions?" is such a deceptively simple question that it deserves to be deconstructed. So before answering "yes," "no," "maybe," or "don't trust anyone who says they really know," I want to puzzle a bit over the meaning of the two key terms in the question, for their meanings are deeply contested and by no means obvious.

When it comes to questions about "emotions"—for example, whether some of them are "basic"—there is a good deal of "cross-talk" in the relevant literatures in psychology, anthropology, and biology. This is largely because theorists from different schools of thought, guided by somewhat different assumptions about psyche, symbol, soma, and nature, have used those common everyday English words to construct somewhat different objects of investigation. Scholars have talked past each other because they have answered the question "Are there basic emotions" with different intellectual objects in mind.

The goals of this essay are twofold. To trace the broad outlines of a "symbolic," "interpretive," or "intentional" theory of the emotions[1] by setting it in contrast with other theories of somatic and affective experience. To address the question "Are there basic emotions?" (1) by asking whether people everywhere in the world give meaning and shape to their somatic and affective experiences as "emotions"; and (2) by asking whether those peoples around the world who do "emotionalize" their somatic and affective experiences tend to use the same emotions to give meaning and shape to their experiences. To both questions I give the answer "do not trust anyone who says they really know."

My general claim is that "emotion" terms are names for particular interpretive schemes (e.g., "remorse," "guilt," "anger," "shame") of a particular story-like, script-like, or narrative kind that any people in the world might (or might not) make use of to give meaning and shape to their somatic and affective "feelings." More specifically, "feelings" (both somatic and affective) have the shape and meaning of an "emotion" when they are experienced as a perception of some self-relevant condition of the world and as a plan of action for the protection of dignity, honor, and self-esteem. My claim is that we do not yet know whether all peoples of the world emotionalize their feelings to the same extent, or whether they emotionalize their feelings with the same "emotion" schemes when they do. I suggest that alternative interpretive schemes for the diagnosis of somatic and affective experience include schemes for "sickness," "bewitchment," and moral "suffering."

Part 1: Basics and Emotions

The phrase "essentially contested concept" was not coined with the "emotions" in mind, but it might have been. Everything from their substance to their distribution to their logical form is a subject of debate.

With regard to their *substance*, for every William James who claims that the emotions are reducible to feelings of bodily states there is an Errol Bedford (1962) who claims they have nothing to do with feelings or sensations or psychological facts at all, but are rather linguistic ploys for imputing responsibility and blame and for praising and criticizing conduct (as, for example, in "I hope you are ashamed of yourself, or "I sure envy your technique").

With regard to the *distribution* of the emotions, for every Johnson-Laird and Oatley (1989; pp. 90) who claim that there exists "a set of basic emotion modes" (viz., happiness, sadness, anger, fear, and disgust) that "should be universally accepted as discriminable categories of direct experience"[2] or for every Paul Ekman (1973; pp. 219–220) who claims that regardless of language, culture, and history "these facial expressions are labeled with the same emotion terms: happiness, sadness, anger, fear, disgust and surprise" there is an Anna Wierzbicka (n.d., also see 1990) who points out (with those assertions by Johnson-Laird & Oatley and Ekman explicitly in mind) that the whole world does not speak English; that English words such as happiness, sadness, anger, fear, and disgust encode concepts that are "different from those encoded in the emotion terms of different languages"; that "in fact, there are NO emotion terms which can be matched neatly across language and culture boundaries"; that "there are NO universal emotion concepts, lexicalized in all the languages of the world"; and that it is all too easy in the translation process to unwittingly assimilate other peoples' linguistic meanings to an ethnocentric set of analytic categories—the abstract "emotional" states favored by the English-speaking world.

Undoubtedly most anthropologists will appreciate Wierzbicka's sensitivity to the all too often glossed over problem of translation. In my own experience the mapping of lexical items across languages has always seemed especially hazardous when it comes to the characterization of psychological states, in part because of the way culture and psyche are interdependent and make each other up. Across languages, the range of implications, suggestions, and connotations of psychological state terms do not easily map, at least not *lexically*; and to adequately understand the meaning of the terms in either language is to understand a good deal about different local systems of values and particular ways of life. Under such circumstances of hazardous lexical mapping, any strong claim about the actual distribution around the world of the "emotions," as we define them, is bound to be controversial, and cannot be settled by innocently pointing out that according to some dictionary or bilingual informant there is in this or that language a term for this or that emotion.

Indeed, when it comes to the "emotions," even their *logical form* (as expressed in such commonplace English language terms as "sad," "happy," "angry," "envious," "remorseful," "homesick," or "ashamed") is a matter of dispute. Some argue that emotions are "concepts," that is to say, logicosemantic forms such as triangles or bachelors, which can, through conceptual analysis, be given strict definitions in terms of necessary and sufficient standards or logical essences. Which "standards" (physiological events, "feelings," verbal reports using terms for feelings, antecedent events, verbally expressed interpretations of antecedent events, facial expressions, etc.) should be included in the definition is itself quite unsettled.

"Concepts subsist" (so it is said) outside of time and space, which is why one does not have to travel anywhere in this world to discover whether a "bachelor" is a "marriageable unmarried male." The universal validity of a "concept" is guaranteed by its definition. The way one discovers the meaning of "bachelor" is through conceptual (logical) analysis. One asks competent speakers of the English language Would you call the Pope a "bachelor"? Is a married male with one wife in a polygamous society a "bachelor"? In this way one discovers, as in the case of the Pope, that there is more to being a "bachelor" than just being an unmarried male. "Marriageability" is also a necessary standard, although, as in the case of the legal polygamist, it is not sufficient. And so forth. Any anthropologists who came up with an exotic counterclaim (e.g., that among the Bongo-Bongo "bachelors" are monogamously married virginal females) would simply reveal that they misunderstood the meaning of the English term.

If there is a "concept" named "sadness" defined by a strict standard (e.g., for sake of argument, paralleling Smedslund, 1991, a concept with a stipulated logical essence meaning "the way human beings feel when the things they want are thought to be permanently unattainable"), then that is what it universally and eternally means (for if it meant anything else it would not be the concept named "sadness"). It would be foolhardy to go searching in the world for the concept, for it subsists in its definition, and *must* exist, by definition, everywhere in the world where there are human beings who have wants and feelings, and where the things they want are thought to have become permanently unattainable.

With regard to the logical form of the emotions, an alternative view is that "emotions" are more like natural objects such as plants and animals, whose essence can only be known by finding them in time and space, inspecting them, and intercorrelating their perceptible properties (e.g., body posture, facial movements, skin temperature, heart rate acceleration, causal antecedent events, etc.).

Yet still others (and I am one of them) argue that "sadness" and "guilt" and other "emotions" are not really natural objects at all. Unlike tigers and elm trees, which exist in the world as perceptible kinds that one can directly point at and inspect, the "emotions," it is claimed, are transcendent "narratives" or "scripts" and the biochemical states, social events, expressive signals, phenomenological reports, action tendencies, and judgments that we associate with "emotions" as symptoms or indexes are not unified in the same way as are such clusters of natural object attributes as stripes, fur, sharp nails, whiskers, and a capacity to deliver a dangerous bite. Precisely what that other way might be is a subject of this essay.

Not only are there disagreements about the substance, distribution, and logical form of the "emotions," but there are difficulties with the idea of "basic" as well. In the psychological, linguistic, and philosophical literatures on "basic objects," "basic terms," and "basic concepts" the idea of a basic object, term, or concept has been used quite variously to connote any or all of the following: the elementary, the inherent, the salient, the abstract, the widely distributed, the empirically universal, the logically necessary, the functionally indispensable, the important, the natural, the deeply seated, the unalterable, the perceivable, the minimal set, the ontogenetically original, the phylogenetically original, the generic in a taxonomic scheme of classification, the level at which perception, thought, memory, and communication take place. There may be other senses as well.

In the context of studies of basic "concepts," "basic" often refers to those concepts that are the elementary, primitive, nonreducible building blocks for all definitions. By that line of reasoning (e.g., Wierzbicka) there are no basic emotions because emotion concepts (e.g., angry, sad) are not conceptual simples; they are themselves complexes, which are reducible to more elementary or primitive concepts (e.g., feel, bad, want, think). Most cluster and scaling analyses of emotions classify the emotions by reducing them to nonemotional primitives such as arousal (+ / –) and feels good (+ / –).

In the context of studies of basic "terms," "basic" often refers to those linguistic expressions that are monolexemic, abstract, and general (e.g., "red" rather than "strawberry," "cherry," "crimson," or "blood-like"). If one adheres to that approach, basic emotions exist only in those languages that lexicalize their expressions into monolexemic, abstract, and general terms, although the psychological importance of the linguistic shift from a metaphorical nonbasic expression such as "a broken heart" to a basic abstraction such as "sad" or from a metonymic nonbasic expression such as "to bite your tongue" to a basic abstraction such as "shame" is entirely obscure. (For a discussion of biting the tongue as a facial sign and linguistic idiom of "shame" in Orissa, India, see Menon & Shweder, 1992.)

In the context of studies of basic "objects," intellectual anarchy is more the rule. "Basic" emotions are sometimes said to be that minimal set of simple emotions out of which all others can be generated through blends or through parameter setting, although it is by no means clear in what sense the postulated "basic" emotions ("sadness," "fear," etc.) are simpler than postulated nonbasic emotions such as love, homesickness, trepidation, regret, interest, or boredom. It is not even clear why some "objects" (surprise) are treated as emotions while others (curiosity, awe, optimism, piety, sympathy) are not.

"Basic" emotions are sometimes said to be that small set of "generic" emotions out of which all other emotions can be taxonomized as subordinates. Research on object taxonomies (see D'Andrade, 1991; Wierzbicka, 1985) has revealed that any folk hierarchical system of classification has no less than three and not more than six levels of classification. An example of a six-level taxonomic hierarchy is "plant-tree-evergreen-pine-white pine-Western white pine," although it might be argued (as

Anna Wierzbicka has argued to me in a personal communication) that this example mixes together folk and scientific lexical labels (in folk discourse, as Wierzbicka notes, one can point at a pine and say "look at that tree," but it seems quite unfolksy or somewhat technical to say while pointing at a pine "look at that evergreen" or "look at that plant").

It has proved impossible to determine the generic or basic or psychologically salient object from principles of taxonomy per se (D'Andrade, 1991). In "color" classification the generic or basic or salient level is the most inclusive level ("blue" rather than "turquoise") that exists just *one* level below the level of "color." In "plant" classification, depending on how one constructs the classification, the generic or basic or salient level might be the most inclusive level ("evergreen" instead of "pine") that exists just *two* levels below "plant." "Tree" exists one level below "plant" but it is not a basic or generic or salient object. It has yet to be demonstrated that the various properties of the "emotions" in fact form a taxonomy or can be arranged such that (e.g.) all the properties of "anger" (e.g., the desire to attack) are included among the properties of "scorn," all the properties of "sadness" (e.g., the inclination to withdraw from interpersonal contacts) included among the properties of "regret," or all the properties of "fear" (e.g., the desire to flee) included among the properties of "trepidation." Loose analogies to genuine taxonomic systems abound but they are not very convincing.

It is known from research on basic objects that those objects that are more salient (frequency of use, ease of recall) are not predictable from their formal or structural level in a taxonomy. Instead, the most salient "objects" are the ones that are concrete and visual (e.g., an apple, a chair, a knife, a cat). Salience seems to measure perceptibility. Nonperceptible abstractions (superordinates, collections, or functions such as fruit, furniture, weapon, pet) are not psychologically salient (D'Andrade, 1991; Wierzbicka, 1985). It might follow that psychological states (e.g., pain, happiness, embarrassment) for which there are perceptible facial icons (a grimace, a smile) or visible signs (e.g., blushing) might be more salient than other states. It does not seem coincidental that the "emotions" held out by Western theorists as "basic" emotions are those interpretive schemes associated with a memorable visual image, which, in extreme cases, is sometimes taken to be the very object of the emotion itself. Some of our most important emotion schemes (e.g., guilt, love, empathy, remorse), however, contain no facial icon or other visible sign.

Basic emotions are sometimes said to have universal antecedent events that serve as their cause. The notion of an "antecedent event" is doubly misleading here. It is a trivial exercise for any anthropologist to generate long lists of antecedent events (ingesting cow urine, eating chicken five days after your father dies, kissing the genitals of an infant boy, being complimented about your pregnancy, caning a child, touching some one's foot or shoulder, being addressed by your first name by your wife, ad infinitum) about which the emotional judgments of a Western observer would not correspond to the native's evaluative response.

One part of the muddle here is that the phrase "antecedent event" is not really meant to refer to an event at all but rather to a self-involving state of the world and one's relationship to it, to an (abstract) interpretation of an event as (e.g.) loss, injustice, abuse, frustration, danger, status degradation, etc. Another part of the muddle is that these kinds of abstract interpretations are not causally antecedent to the emotion; they are part and parcel of the narrative structure that gives shape and meaning to the emotion (see Shweder, 1993).

In other words, the identity of the "emotion" is not conceptually independent of the identity of the interpreted event as (e.g.) "loss" or "injustice" or "abuse" or "danger" or what have you. The experience of the Bongo-Bongo would not be "sadness" if the story to be told was about the somatic experiences (e.g., fatigue and loss of appetite), affects (e.g., emptiness and feelings of "soul loss"), and actions (withdrawal from social contacts) associated with the occurrence of "novelty" or of "fame," unless we were willing (as is so often gratuitously done in cross-cultural attributions of mental states) to interpret their "novelty" or "fame" as a disguised or hidden or unconscious form of "loss." If Bongo-Bongo mothers smiled and celebrated whenever their children died, we would either interpret the death as some kind of hidden gain or we would interpret their smile and celebration as some kind of defense against sadness. We would not say that "loss" has now been observed to be an antecedent to "happiness." The interpretive scheme labeled "happiness" has no place in its narrative structure for true "loss" as an antecedent event.

Indeed, who needs to invoke the Bongo-Bongo to make the point that "antecedent events" are neither events nor real causal antecedents but rather slots in our script-like or narrative interpretive schemes? Imagine people in our own culture who feel listless, deflated, disinclined to smile and who lose interest in the world when they get the things they want. Because our official theory of the emotions has no explicit scheme for making reflective sense of those feelings and action tendencies in that context, you may find yourself tempted to think of their "gain" as merely apparent, disguising some kind of unspoken or unacknowledged loss.

In other words, the universality of the connection between an "antecedent event" (more accurately an "interpretation of a condition of the world and of our relationship to it, for example, as "loss") and an "emotion" (e.g., "sadness") is guaranteed by our very conception of the emotion. What is not guaranteed is that our feelings (our somatic and affective experiences) must be given shape and meaning as "emotions," or that when our feelings are "emotionalized" the same script-like or narrative structures will link the same "antecedent events" to the same somatic and affective experiences and to the same action tendencies around the world or even across individuals within the same culture. Not only is *that* not guaranteed, it has never been shown.

Part 2: What Is a Theory of Basic Emotions About?

To summarize so far, "emotions" are neither "concepts" nor "things" nor "terms" in a language. They are complex narrative structures that give shape and meaning to somatic and affective experiences—feelings of the body (e.g., muscle tension) and of the soul (e.g., emptiness), whose unity is to be found neither in strict logical criteria nor in the perceptible features of objects, but rather in the types of self-involving stories they make it possible for us to tell about our feelings.

In each of those "emotion" stories (the story of "fear" or "shame" or "sadness"), somatic and affective experience (e.g., tiredness, arousal, emptiness, loss of appetite) is represented as a perception of some self-involving state of the world (e.g., of loss) leading to a plan (e.g., the desire to die). Each story combines within a single plot some concept of the conditions of the world and one's relationship to it (e.g., loss, frustration, transgression) that would make this or that somatic and/or affective experience (e.g., tension, tiredness, emptiness, headaches) accurate, valid, or justified, as well as some concept of the missions (e.g., to hide, to confess, to attack, to protect) motivated by a perceptive body.

These "stories" or "scripts" or "narratives" are not the kinds of things that are the exclusive property of those who have books or narrate tales to one another on special occasions. They are instead the script-like or story-like interpretive schemes that organize lived experience. Of course, they need to be explicitly formulated if one has a theoretical interest in emotional functioning, but one can give emotional shape and meaning to one's somatic and affective experiences without reflective knowledge of the script. The narratives or scripts are implicit in the feelings they give shape and meaning to, and it is for us, as students of the emotions, to spell them out.

Most important, for those whose feelings have the meaning and shape of an "emotion" story, the experience of "fear" or "shame" or "sadness" is not something independent of or separable from the conditions that justify it or from the actions it demands. The "emotion" is the whole story, the whole package deal—a kind of somatic event (fatigue, chest pain, goose flesh) and/or affective event (panic, expansiveness, emptiness) experienced as a kind of perception (of loss, gain, threat, possibility) linked to a kind of plan (attack, withdraw, confess, hide, explore).

As story-like interpretive schemes the "emotions" can, of course, be classified and reclassified in numerous ways, by attending to different slots in the script—the self-involving state of the world, the somatic experience, the affective experience, the mission or plan for action, perhaps even the expressive mode.

Thus, for example, focusing on the missions of the emotions, there are "affiliative" emotions such as love, happiness, interest, and guilt, which lead you to seek out others for some purpose (e.g., to express affection or to celebrate or to confess), and "avoidant" emotions such as sadness, contempt, disgust, and shame, which lead you to hide or distance yourself or withdraw or to engage in solitary melancholy contemplation.

There are some emotions, such as happiness or anger, that can be arranged along a somatic temperature scale from "warm" to "hot" and other emotions, such as sadness or fear, that can be arranged along a somatic temperature scale from "cool" to "cold."

And there are some emotions, such as happiness and love, that can be placed in an affect cluster associated with feeling puffed up, full, and open, and other emotions such as sadness and guilt, which can be placed in an affect cluster associated with feeling deflated, empty, and closed.[3]

There are emotions, such as grief, envy, and rage, that you are advised to manage by "standing up to them" or suppressing them, and other emotions, such as joy or love, that we manage by giving them encouragement or permission to "flood" our somatic and affective experiences.

There are some emotions, such as happiness, anger, and disgust that, like pain (a nonemotional feeling), are associated with perceptible facial icons (the grimace, the smile, the frown), some of which are universal, and other emotions (e.g., guilt, remorse, optimism, empathy) for which there is no facial expression.

There are humoral classifications of the emotions, which group the emotions by their presumed psychobiological or somatic causal links to a particular fluid of a particular internal organ. For example, even in our contemporary culture, which has long since officially abandoned humoral theories of human functioning, many people associate emotions such as anger, fear, love, sympathy, envy, and sadness with conditions of the blood, a humor of the heart. The blood boils (anger). It curdles (fear). It flows profusely because the heart pounds or breaks (love). It tires or ceases to flow because the heart is heavy or there is a stone resting on one's heart (sadness) or because one has a heart of stone (lacking in sympathy). Because of a lack of blood flow one can turn green (with envy), and so on.

Organs and fluids serve taxonomic functions in the ethnosciences and cultural psychologies of many peoples of the world and it is not hard to understand why. For example, normal versus abnormal conditions of the liver (a cool liver, a splitting liver) can be used as a way of talking about, explaining, and classifying positive (purified) versus negative (poisonous) feeling states. It can serve this taxonomic function because of various beliefs about the function of the liver—for example, that it removes toxins from the blood and harbors poisons. From a cross-cultural and historical perspective the psychobiological imagination has had a field day mapping liver malfunctions (and the envisioned release of toxins into one's "system") onto various kinds of negative feeling states, somatic and affective.

Nevertheless, however one chooses to sort or resort the "emotions" and however useful or pointless, defensible or indefensible the classification, a somatic or affective experience (a "feeling" of body or soul, e.g., muscle tension, emptiness, agitation, shakiness, a pain in the chest, nausea) becomes an "emotional" experience (e.g., anger, disgust) rather than just a somatic or affective experience (muscle tension, emptiness, agitation, shakiness, a pain in the chest, nausea) when physical, social, and moral events (loss of control, violations of expectations, success at goal attainment, insult, ethical failure, community censure, a challenge from an unworthy inferior, vulnerability to danger, transgressions of the natural order of things) psychosomatically reach in and touch one's feelings in ways that implicate the self.

It is primarily for that reason that the "emotions" should be viewed as the symbolic/intentional/interpretive side of somatic and affective experience. To emotionalize one's feelings (e.g.) as "guilt," "pity," "fury," "contempt," or "dread" is to give a "reading" to somatic and affective experience, to look through the tension, palpitations, nausea, and heat to what they are about. The "emotions" re-present somatic and affective experience not simply as a feeling (as tiredness or tension or a heartache) but as a perception (e.g., betrayal by trusted allies) and a plan (e.g., retaliation, realignment, withdrawal, and so forth). An "emotion" is a feeling that activates a self-esteem program or person schema. It is a somatic or affective experience with a mission and with more than (or other than) just a biochemical or somatic cause.

Every culture I know or have read about seems to have many different linguistic resources for representing somatic and affective experiences. Thus, I am going to assume (with due respect to radical skeptism and the androids of science fiction) that all peoples of the world have "feelings." In my conception, the capacity to feel is a "basic" feature of normal human functioning. Once that assumption is made, the variety of linguistic resources for representing somatic and affective experience deserves close examination, for there are subtle and not so subtle problems in translating these representations and it is all too easy to succumb to the illusion that other peoples are representing their feelings as "emotions" when they are not. These problems of translation should be apparent even from a moment of reflection on our own language use.

Within our own language and culture there are multiple ways to give expression to somatic experience, which may or may not involve a discourse of "emotions." To be "nauseous" is not the same as to be "disgusted"; nausea is a nonemotionalized feeling of the body that is neutral as to its cause, while "disgust" is "nausea" emotionalized by interpreting it as a perception (directing our attention to some agent which is its cause) with a mission (disappropriation, distancing, avoidance). Because the "emotions" (love, anger, sadness) are interpretive or symbolic forms integrating a somatic or affective experience into a single story as perception and plan, our names for the "emotions" make no direct reference to experience per se. Our actual "feelings" become transparent when emotionalized. By the time we have given shape and meaning to our experience as "being in love" or "being angry," we have seen through our feelings to the self-affirming and self-denying realities of our (physical, interpersonal, and moral) world.

Every culture, I believe, has a vast linguistic arsenal for giving expression to somatic and affective experiences in nonemotionalized terms. Thus, in our own culture we speak of feeling or being tired, hungry, relaxed, empty, shaky, weak, nauseous, clean, thirsty, dizzy, in pain, short of breath, itchy, tense, agitated, calm. To "walk on air" is to feel "lightheaded." To have "tired blood" is a way of talking about generalized fatigue. It may or may not be a body-part metaphor for the emotion of "sadness" or "depression."

This is true in other cultures as well. One must beware when translating the linguistic expressions of other people not to casually assimilate expressions for nonemotional feelings into our own reigning theory of the emotionalization of experience. The translation found in the dictionary or given to you by some bilingual informant may read "anger," but all the native may have said was "my liver is splitting," which, quite possibly, may be his or her way of giving expression to a nonemotional feeling (tension, heat) by means of a biochemical humoral theory of its genesis. It may not imply the same thing as "anger" at all, although it might.

In making translation decisions it is important to recognize that our contemporary theory of the "emotions" plays a rather special part in the history of human self-consciousness because it intrudes into an interpretative space that is occupied in many other cultures by theories of "bewitchment" (sorcery, evil eye, black magic, spirit attack) and "suffering" (sin, moral transgression, karma, spiritual debts that are acquired or inherited). In such cultures, theories of "bewitchment" and "suffering" typically compete, not only with each other, but also with local theories of "sickness" (biochemical imbalance, fluid and fiber dysfunction, organ pathology, disease) to explain and help people manage the pleasant or painful, arousing or enervating immediacies of somatic and affective experience, and this is no less true of our contemporary theory of the "emotions." The metaphysics of nature and of transcendent realities that supported theories of "bewitchment" and "suffering" may no longer be popular in our official mainstream scientific culture but the problem they addressed—how to make sense of those somatic and affective experiences that have more than (or other than) just a somatic cause—has not gone away.

On a worldwide or historical scale the most frequent folk theories of somatic and affective experience are of three general kinds: (1) theories of "sickness" (a biochemical theory); (2) theories of "bewitchment" (an interpersonal theory); and (3) theories of "suffering" (a moral theory). (See Shweder, Much, Mahapatra, & Park, in press.) In the official culture of the contemporary Western world, theories of "bewitchment" (e.g., ghost attack) and of "suffering" (nature itself punishing those who sin) have been displaced by a general theory of mental or psychosomatic causation, of which the theory of the "emotions" is a subclass.

Not only do all cultures have multiple linguistic resources for representing nonemotionalized feelings, but every culture I know or have read about also seems to understand that there are three big causes—biochemical, interpersonal, and moral—of somatic or affective experience. What we seem to have contributed to the discussion is the suggestion that (unlike the biochemical causes of feelings, which we view as direct somatic causes) the interpersonal and moral causes of somatic and affective experiences are mediated by mental entities that come in the form of a limited number of abstract interpretive or symbolic schemes (which in English have been designated with names such as "anger," "sadness," "envy," "happiness," and "guilt," etc.).

While it may be debatable whether our theory of the "emotions" and of psychosomatic causation are superior to those other schools of interpretation preceding it, or whether they represent a fall in human self-consciousness, the only choice today that makes cultural common sense in popular and scientific Western discourse about feelings is the choice between a somatic (biochemical) interpretation and a psychosomatic (mental or emotional) one. As the songwriter knew so well, when it comes to the contemporary world, either you are "sick" or "you're just in love." You're never truly bewitched or suffering from karma.

Within the halls of the academy, Irving Berlin is not recognized as an expert in cultural psychology, yet within the lyrics of one of his many famous melodies can be found an expression of this culturally constituted choice between a somatic and psychosomatic reading of our feelings. The following lyrics are by Berlin. The bracketed, nonlyrical comments are, of course, my own.

"I hear music and there's no one there. [Auditory hallucinations] I smell blossoms and the trees are bare. [Olafactory hallucinations] All day long I seem to walk on air. [Dizziness] I wonder why. I wonder why. [Somatic experience as an invitation to investigate, to wonder what those feelings reveal about the state of one's body as a biochemical system or about the state of one's self as a mental system] I keep tossing in my sleep at night. [Insomnia, restlessness] And what's more I've lost my appetite. [Loss of interest in food] Stars that used to twinkle in the sky are twinkling in my eyes. [Subject-object confusion] I wonder why. [Again, somatic experience as an invitation to investigate] You don't need analyzing. It is not so surprising. [These experiences are part of a manifest cultural script; depth (psycho) analysis is not required] That you feel very strange but nice. [Pleasant arousal] Your heart goes pitter patter. [Palpitations in the chest] I know just what's the matter. Cause I've been there once or twice." [These experiences are common in our culture]

And then, after a head on the shoulder of "someone who's older" and a "rub down with a velvet glove" (!) the lyrics conclude: "There is nothing you can take to relieve that pleasant ache. You're not sick, you're just in love." [The culturally constituted choice between a somatic versus psychosomatic explanation of our feelings]

What I am suggesting is that our contemporary theory of the emotions is our culture's contribution to a universal intellectual enterprise aimed at the interpretation of feelings. A somatic or affective experience is an invitation to wonder why, to ask what those feelings reveal, to investigate various orders of reality (biochemical, interpersonal, moral), to diagnose one's biochemical, interpersonal, and moral standing in the world, and to make plans accordingly. Indeed, that may be one of the significant functions of feelings, to serve as a feedback system at the level of individual consciousness so that one can be alert to one's standing in the world (see Levy, 1984b).

It then becomes relevant to ask: What does our contemporary theory of the "emotions" distinctively contribute to this universal intellectual enterprise? Are the "emotions" the only way to give shape and meaning to somatic and affective experience? To what degree are feelings emotionalized or not emotionalized in different cultures and by means of which particular "emotion" and "nonemotionalized" schemes?

Of course, none of this is to deny the possible existence of "basic" self-involving conditions of the world and of our relationship to it (e.g., loss and gain, protection and threat), "basic" somatic feelings (e.g., muscle tension, pain, dizziness, nausea, fatigue, breathlessness), "basic" affective feelings (e.g., agitation, emptiness, expansiveness), "basic" plans for self-management (e.g., to flee, to retaliate, to repair, to celebrate, to invest) or even the possible existence of "basic" emotions. Instead, the point of this deconstruction is to help focus the question "Are there basic emotions?" in the following way.

If there are "basic" emotions, then some subset of the script-like or narrative structures we name "sadness," "anger," "guilt," "love," "pity," "shame," "contempt," "pining," "sulky," etc., will give shape and lend meaning to the somatic and affective experiences (the "feelings") of people in all cultures. If there are basic emotions everyone in the world will, by means of their feelings, link the same self-involving conditions of the world (status loss and status gain, success and failure, protection and threat, blocking of a goal, novelty, etc.) to the same somatic and affective subsystems (fatigue, agitation, chest pain, emptiness, headaches, etc.) and to the same action tendencies or self-management strategies (to attack, to withdraw, to hide, to confess, to repair, etc.). At this point in the social sciences we know relatively little about the narrative structure of experience in different cultures, about the possibilities for coupling or decoupling "antecedent" conditions, somatic and affective feelings, and action tendencies in the way we live in the world. We do not even know if the subsystems controlling somatic feeling in different populations are the same. There is no a priori reason to assume they are. Before we can answer questions about "basic emotions" with any real confidence, far more comparative research is needed unencumbered of ethnocentric illusions, philosophical naiveté, and question-begging methodologies. As we stand on the threshold of what I believe to be a bright new age of collaborative research on "cultural psychology" (Shweder, 1991a; Shweder & Sullivan, 1993), my answer to the question "Are there basic emotions?" is "Do not trust anyone who says they really know."

Notes

My thoughts for this essay were developed while I was a Visiting Scholar at the Russell Sage Foundation. I am also grateful to Roy D'Andrade, Shinobu Kitayama and Anna Wierzbicka for their evaluations of an earlier draft, and to the MacArthur Foundation Research Network on Health Related Behavior and the MacArthur Foundation Research Network on Successful Mid-Life Development for their generous support.

1. Perhaps the most profound formulation of what today would be called a "symbolic" theory of the "emotions"—a theory of the "rasas" and their relationship to the "bhavas" and other psychological facts of various kinds—can be found in ancient and medieval Hindu Sanskrit writings and commentaries on drama and aesthetics—in particular, in the famous sixth chapter, the "Rasadhyaya," of the *Natyasastra*, a third-century text, as explicated by the tenth-century Kashmiri Brahman and philosopher Abhivanagupta (see Masson & Patwardhan, 1970; Shweder, 1992).

2. The meaning of the term "direct" is ambiguous here, for it is unclear whether it means something like "already on-line" or "free of interpretation or symbolic mediation." When it comes to questions about "directness," some scholars might argue that acts of interpretation or symbolic mediation are performed so rapidly and at such a deep level that they are not consciously distinguishable from experience itself, which creates the illusion that they are unmediated or direct. On top of this argument might be placed another: We come into the world already equipped with complex and differentiated interpretive schemes, some of which undergo transformation throughout the life course as a result of interaction with cultural institutions and practices (including linguistic practices), which is what one ought to mean by "learning." Nothing in a symbolic-interpretive-intentional theory requires that one adhere to the innocent naive view that children come into the world innocent, naive, or as tabula rasa.

3. Notice how affects, which are the feelings of the self or the soul, require metaphorical designations—empty, full, closed, deflated. It is crucial for a symbolic-interpretive-intentional theory of the emotions that a distinction is drawn between emotions and affects. Affects are but one part of or slot in the more complex narrative organization of an emotion.

Most cluster analyses of large sets of terms for the emotions (e.g., Shaver et al., 1987) discover roughly similar metaphorical groupings. My speculation about the implications of this evidence is that informants simplify the demands of the sorting task by attending to similarities in the affect slot (see Gerber, 1986, for a cluster analysis of Samoan emotion terms and a thoughtful discussion of the affects). The researcher then selects one emotion term from the cluster to represent or designate the entire cluster, but this seems to me arbitrary and a great mistake. I would argue that the clusters discovered in these studies should not be designated with any "emotion" label, such as fear or sadness or anger. They are more properly thought of as affect clusters not as emotion clusters, in which various complex narrative structures such as sadness or guilt have been grouped together on the basis of some one point of similarity in their script. For example, in the case of the cluster D labeled as "sadness" by Shaver et al. (1987, p. 1067), some of the co-elements in the cluster are the terms guilt, shame, and sadness. Why should this cluster be labeled "sadness"? It might just as well have been designated as a cluster unified by the affective experience of emptiness, deflation, and closure. I would relabel the clusters found by Shaver et al. with affect descriptors such as expansive, tight, deflated, aroused, puffed up, and panic. Descriptors from the slot of somatic experience (e.g., tired, trembling, erotically aroused) might be appropriate as well.

Looking at cluster analyses from around the world, one might speculate that there is an abstract affect space consisting of three or four contrastive dimensions–the self or the soul may feel empty versus full, expansive versus contracted, agitated versus still, pleased or displeased. Affect, not emotion, is in my view what the cluster analyses are about, despite the misleading emotion labels assigned to the clusters. The affective part of the narrative structure of anger consists of feelings of the self that are contracted, full, agitated, and unpleasant, but there is much more to anger or to any emotion than the specifications for its affect slot.

Afterword: Are There Basic Emotions?

PAUL EKMAN
RICHARD J. DAVIDSON

Three contributors—Averill, Scherer, Shweder—say the answer should be No. Scherer begins by challenging the evidence for basic emotions in studies of verbal labels and antecedents. While there is considerable evidence, he says it is not complete. His theoretical stance is that it is the elements found in emotions that are universal, not the gestalts or patterns. He seems, however, to modify this position somewhat in acknowledging that "bunching" of these elements is fairly common. His own theory of appraisal steps allows for a great deal of variability in emotional responses, but his recognition of the widespread occurrence of what he calls "modal" emotions does not appear to be very different from the view argued by Ekman.

Averill provides a number of arguments against the usefulness of proposing that there are basic emotions. He gives a useful explanation of the concept of prototypicality, and says that emotions do not have essential elements, such as physiological changes. Another problem for Averill is that a concern with basic emotions may lead us away from studying nonbasic emotions. (Note that for Ekman and Panksepp there are no nonbasic emotions; they use the term basic to refer to the biological contribution to a number of discrete emotions.)

It is useful to contrast Averill's metaphor of a rope with Ekman's metaphor of a family, with a theme and variations. Averill is concerned that focus on a theme will lead us to ignore the variations. Averill also explains how the concept of "basicness" can imply hierarchical levels, and argues against the applicability of such hierarchies to emotion (Ekman and Panksepp would agree with him about that). Averill recognizes what Ekman and Panksepp suggest is the reason for calling the emotions they describe as basic when he says "basic emotions should be universal among the human species, they should be observable in rudimentary form in nonhuman primates, and so forth." After saying this, Averill argues that the amount that biology contributes to our emotions is minimal.

Shweder takes the most radical position, questioning whether emotions exist in this sense in every society and culture. Even if all people were found to "emotionalize," to interpret their feelings of body and soul, Shweder argues the same emotions would not be found. Shweder acknowledges that all people have feelings, but not that all people interpret any of their feelings as emotions. He uses the title of a song for the title of his contribution, to underline that there are many ways to interpret feelings. Emotion is one contemporary way, but not the only, not the universal, not the necessary, and certainly not any natural way to account for feelings. Shweder says it is just the Western way.

In challenging Ekman and also Johnson-Laird and Oatley, Shweder cites Wierzbicka's arguments about language differences. Even Scherer would not accept Wierzbicka's position about the total variability in the lexicon of emotion. Shweder fails to note that the evidence for universality is not limited to words, but includes studies of expression that did not involve words as well as studies of physiology, antecedents, and so on.

Shweder makes clear his view that emotions are transcendent interpretive scripts or schemes, not natural objects. It is not clear whether Averill would go that far. Scherer would certainly appreciate Shweder's position that emotions such as anger or fear are reducible to elements that presumably can recombine into totally different states. For Shweder these combinations are endless, and not necessarily interpreted as emotions. With his notions of bunching and concept of "modal" emotions, Scherer recognizes that some combinations of elements co-occur much more often than others, which Shweder argues against.

For Panksepp the term basic refers to the unfolding of genetic potentials, emphasizing that genes are "dynamically responsive [To specific environmental influences] information stores." All our behavioral potentials, he says, are genetically provided. He appears to take the position that basic emotional circuits exist that intervene between inputs and outputs, and proposes that emotions such as anger, fear, sadness, and so forth, are not the result of associative learning. Panksepp distinguishes emotions such as fear and anger from more reflexive states, such as the startle, and more internalized sentiments. He argues for a research strategy that focuses on understanding the brain circuits for his "blue ribbon" emotions, such as fear and anger.

Ekman considers all emotions to be basic in the sense that evolution played a role in shaping both the features unique to each emotion, the features emotions share, and their functions. He distinguishes eight characteristics, at least seven of which are found in all emotions. The one characteristic that may not occur in all emotions is a distinctive signal. The characteristics Ekman says distinguish the emotions from other phenomena allow us to respond to fundamental life tasks quickly, without much elaborated planning, in ways that have been adaptive in our evolutionary past. He also introduces the concept of an emotion family, proposing that each emotion is not a single state but a family of related affective states. Each of these families has a theme and many variations on that theme. The themes, he says, are the products of evolution and their variations reflect learning.

Clearly there is great divergence on this question. For Shweder and Scherer emotions are not givens; there is no biological contribution to emotions such as anger, fear, or sadness. Shweder believes emotions are interpretative ideas we may or may not invent to account for our feelings; there is no reason to expect that we will all make such inventions, let alone the same ones. Scherer is less radical, proposing that biology contributes to a number of elements that often combine in certain ways to form what we call the emotions, but they presumably could be arranged to form totally different emotions. For Scherer it might be unlikely to have an emotion unique to a culture or to an individual within that culture, but it could happen. For Shweder it is likely that there are individuals who have no emotions and cultures that have no emotions. Averill takes a more moderate stance, acknowledging that biology contributes to some emotions. He just does not believe that those emotions that include an important biological contribution are necessarily the most important emotions, and he argues for emotions that may be totally socially constructed.

Ekman and Panksepp do not disagree with one another, although they emphasize different issues. For both there are a limited number of emotions, and each emotion is universal and the product of our evolution. They both emphasize the importance of specific environments in influencing the unfolding and development of emotions. Our emotions reflect our ancestral past and are not completely malleable.

Although everyone agrees that more data are needed, they disagree about how much reliable data are now available, and what kind of data will be most useful in furthering our understanding of the emotions.

Question 2

How Are Emotions Distinguished from Moods, Temperament, and Other Related Affective Constructs?

On Emotion, Mood, and Related Affective Constructs

RICHARD J. DAVIDSON

Mood and emotion are two words that are used by psychologists and laypeople alike to refer to certain aspects of affect. Some psychologists have used these terms interchangeably or have, at least, not been motivated to distinguish between them. For other psychologists, these terms imply different types of mental states (e.g., Ekman, 1984).

In the first part of this brief essay I propose a new functional definition of mood. The scheme I propose is admittedly quite speculative, but I will attempt to show how it is testable. In the second part, I examine the concepts of temperament and affective style and show how they are related to and different from emotions and moods.

For some students of affect, the primary difference between mood and emotion lies in the duration of each. Emotions are held to be brief, while moods last longer. Other common distinctions include the proposal that emotions are accompanied by distinctive facial expressions while moods are not. Some have also argued that emotions are preceded by recognizable antecedent events, while the antecedents of mood are not always identifiable.

Most of these distinctions, however, can be found wanting when carefully scrutinized. For example, Ekman (1992) has suggested that not all emotions are accompanied by distinctive facial expressions, so facial expression as a criterion to distinguish between moods and emotions is problematic. The idea that emotions are preceded by recognizable antecedents while moods are not also appears inconsistent with the experimental evidence. A number of investigators have demonstrated that brief emotional episodes can be produced in subjects by using procedures that bypass conscious awareness. For example, Öhman, Dimberg, and Esteves (1989) found that fear conditioning can be produced in response to stimuli that have been degraded to make subjects unaware of what was actually presented. Similarly, Kunst-Wilson and Zajonc (1980) have demonstrated that subjects can be induced to favor objects that they have been exposed to through subliminal presentation. These examples illustrate that emotions can be produced in the absence of recognizable antecedents, thus calling into question this criterion to distinguish between moods and emotions.

The criterion that remains from the initial list is duration. It is appealing to view moods as longer in duration than emotions and it may be that most instances of each do honor this difference. However, this criterion is merely descriptive and it is likely that instances of short-lived mood and longer-lived emotion can be found. But we need to better understand the essential differences between each before we can entertain this possibility.

Emotions and Moods: A Functional Account

I wish to propose that the essential difference between moods and emotions can be found through a functional analysis of each. A number of theorists have proposed that the primary function of emotion is to modulate or bias action (e.g., Frijda, Kuipers, & ter Schure, 1989). Emotions most often arise in situations where adaptive action is required. Autonomic activity typically accompanies emotion and supports the action that coincides with the emotion (e.g., Levenson, Ekman, & Friesen, 1990).

The primary function of moods, on the other hand, is to modulate or bias cognition. Mood serves as a primary mechanism for altering information-processing priorities and for shifting modes of information processing. Mood will accentuate the accessibility of some and attenuate the accessibility of other cognitive contents and semantic networks. For example, individuals in a depressed mood have increased accessibility to sad memories and decreased accessibility to happy memories (e.g., Teasdale & Fogarty, 1979; see review by Mineka & Sutton, 1992). Moods may also function to shift not just cognitive content, but processing mode as well. For example, Isen (1987) has found that positive moods facilitate cognitive flexibility. They result in more creative responses, more remote associations, and an increase in the perception of relatedness among cognitions.

In at least a weak sense, moods may always be present. Moods provide the affective background, the emotional color, to all that we do. Emotions can be viewed as phasic perturbations that are superimposed on this background activity. To the extent that moods are continually present, it can also be said that our cognitive processes are always biased or modulated.

How do we know when an affective state is a mood or an emotion? This is a very difficult question to answer given our present knowledge. If moods are continuously present, as suggested above, the question can be reframed in the following way. What evidence might we use to infer a difference between one mood versus another? Since emotions occur against a background of mood, they can be present or not, and so we must ask: What evidence supports the presence of an emotion compared with a period during which no emotion is present.

Mood is often reflected in subjective experience. In adult subjects, we can ask people to rate their moods and find that such self-reports correspond to other more objective indicators. However, there is no reason to believe that moods do not occur in preverbal infants, or in other species. How might we infer the presence of moods in such organisms? I believe that we might eventually be able to characterize the presence of a mood based upon systematic shifts within subjects in basic information-processing characteristics. For example, we can look at biases in the retrieval (both implicit and explicit) of particular types of information (e.g., Tobias, Kihlstrom, & Schacter, 1992), biases in preattentive mechanisms (e.g., Mathews et al., 1990), measures of cognitive flexibility (e.g., Isen, 1990), and indexes of perceptual function. An information-processing battery might be developed to characterize systematic patterns of cognitive function that appear to accompany different moods. Shifts in the pattern of information processing may reliably index shifts in mood in the absence of any requirement to provide reports of associated subjective experience. Unlike emotion, we would not expect shifts in autonomic function to reliably accompany shifts in mood. However, more enduring changes in the state of the central nervous system would be expected.

Another important difference between moods and emotions is the nature of the antecedent events that elicit each. Emotions appear to be precipitated by events that are perceived as occurring quickly and without warning, while moods may be more likely to follow events that are perceived as occurring over a slower time course. The initial physiological change in response to adaptively significant and sudden events is almost always the triggering of an emotion. Losing control of your car on an icy road will provoke fear, accompanied by pronounced autonomic changes and a rapid change in action to deal with the threat. Triggers of mood are usually quite different. Weather can often affect mood. A dreary, rainy day can produce a depressed mood, while a bright, warm sunny day can engender a positive mood (e.g., Schwartz & Clore, 1983). Moods can also be produced in a cumulative fashion over time. For example, a series of mild negative interactions (each of which might initially elicit a negative emotion) might cumulatively produce a negative mood over the course of a day. Similarly, a series of mild positive events can together result in a positive mood over time.

It also appears to be the case that moods and emotions dynamically interact in important ways. Emotions can lead to particular moods and moods can alter the probability that particular emotions will be triggered. Precisely what the eliciting events are in these situations is very complex. For example, when a mood follows an emotion, just what is the critical elicitor? Is it the emotion itself, or the event that initially triggered the emotion? If it is the emotion, is the trigger the ascending or descending limb of the emotion? To introduce further complication, different response systems have different time courses so that the ascending and descending slopes for facial expression are likely different from those of autonomic activity, and so on. Virtually no systematic data have been gathered on these questions to date.

On Temperament and Affective Style

I have used the term affective style to refer to the entire domain of individual differences that modulate a person's reactivity to emotional events (Davidson, 1992a). Such individual differences are conceptualized as trait-like constructs that are consistent over time. Thus, mood would not be included within the rubric of affective style. However, certain personality traits might be considered to reflect affective style to the extent that they are associated with systematic differences in affective reactivity (e.g., Larsen & Ketelaar, 1991). In addition, certain patterns of central nervous system function that vary across individuals and show consistency within individuals reflect affective style. For example, our own research has repeatedly shown that asymmetric activation in anterior cortical regions (prefrontal and anterior temporal) has been found to reflect consistent differences in emotional reactivity (e.g., Davidson & Fox, 1989; Tomarken, Davidson, & Henriques, 1990; Tomarken, Davidson, Wheeler, & Doss, 1992). And, according to this scheme, temperament would be considered a part of affective style.

Temperament refers to early consistent differences that are assumed to be at least in part under genetic control, as evidenced in responses to environmental challenges. Temperamental differences among children can lead to systematic biases in emotional reactivity (e.g., Goldsmith, 1993). Moreover, temperament in children and affective style in adults appear to be mediated through the same central circuitry, since similar patterns of anterior cortical activation are associated with each (see Davidson, 1992b, for review).

It is likely that temperament and affective style are associated with differences in the nervous system that can persist over longer durations, such as differences in the receptor densities for particular neurotransmitters or neuromodulators, and indeed a long research tradition has developed around rats that have been bred for different emotional characteristics. The Maudsley reactive strain has been bred for many generations to exhibit qualities of fearfulness, and a number of studies have revealed that the reactive rats (those who display heightened fearfulness) have fewer benzodiazepine receptors compared with those who are low in fearfulness (nonreactives) (e.g., Robertson, Martin, & Candy, 1978). It is also likely that these individual differences in affective style that are present early in development are impacted by learning in significant ways. Several authors have commented on the unique importance of early stressful events in the development of subsequent affective style, particularly of a pathological nature. Not only do behavioral and psychoanalytic perspectives place a premium on early life events, but biologically oriented theorists (e.g., Jacobs & Nadel, 1985; Jacobs, Nadel, & Hayden, 1992) also underscore the salient role of early stress in the production of enduring affective changes. According to the Jacobs and Nadel (1985) model, if aversive learning episodes occur prior to the anatomical and physiological maturation of the hippocampus, then a stress later in life can temporarily "disable" the hippocampus and lead to a restoration of the aversive learning that was acquired prior to hippocampal maturation. Although there is a paucity of data relevant to the evaluation of this model, it does provide a cogent scheme that accounts for many facts about simple phobias and panic attacks (see Jacobs et al., 1992, for review).

Summary and Conclusions

Emotion, mood, temperament, and affective style—all have been used to describe different features of affective phenomena. A number of these terms have been used interchangeably in the literature, while others have been used imprecisely. I have argued for a functional account of differences between emotion and mood. Emotions bias action, while moods bias cognition. Although this distinction might seem arbitrary, it is offered in the hope of providing a sharp contrast to stimulate research. It also underscores the need for new strategies in research that examine relations between affective phenomena and other domains in the biobehavioral sciences. Here affective style was defined as all individual differences that form consistent patterns of emotional reactivity. Such enduring differences among people would include temperament, but would also encompass other enduring traits that are significantly affected by early learning.

Moods, Emotions, and Traits

PAUL EKMAN

In response to Question 1 (Are there basic emotions?), I described a number of characteristics that distinguish emotions from other affective states (see also, Ekman, 1992). Here I will focus on how moods differ from emotions, describing a number of features that distinguish one from the other.

Moods can be distinguished from emotions in terms of their time course and therefore presumably also in terms of what should be found in the neural circuitry that directs and maintains each of these affective states. What we call moods last much longer than emotions. While there is no agreement about how long an emotion typically lasts, most of those who distinguish emotions from moods recognize that moods last longer. I have maintained (Ekman, 1984) that emotions can be very brief, typically lasting a matter of seconds or at most minutes. When we speak of an emotion lasting for hours, we probably are summating the recurrent emotion episodes within that time period. Moods last for hours, sometimes for days. If the state endures for weeks or months, however, it is not a mood but more properly identified as an affective disorder.

Those who rely solely on lexical distinctions to conceptualize the domain of emotion may be confused about this distinction (Ortony & Turner, 1990) since laypeople do not always use language precisely. While the term "irritable" may refer to a long-lasting mood as distinct from the related but briefer emotion of anger, it is not always used in that fashion. Irritable may also be used to refer to low-intensity anger or to the beginning of an anger episode. What people say, particularly what they say on questionnaires or interviews when they are not having the emotion they are describing, is interesting but should not be the only or the definitive data source for distinguishing among affective states. If we closely examine expression and physiology during emotion episodes, I believe we will find it possible to distinguish single emotion episodes and multiple emotion episodes from sustained moods. I think also that if we were to talk to a person when a person is experiencing a mood or in the midst of an emotion episode we would find that people can then make the distinctions I am proposing.

Although it is the most obvious difference, duration is not the sole criterion for distinguishing moods from emotions. Moods seem to lower the threshold for arousing the emotions, which occur most frequently during a particular mood. When a person is in an irritable mood, for example, that person becomes angry more readily than usual. Events that might ordinarily not be as likely to bring forth anger now do so easily. In an irritable mood people construe the world around them in a way that permits, if not calls for, an angry response. It is as if the person is seeking an opportunity to indulge the emotion relevant to the mood. The research has not been done to determine whether the person in an irritable mood is in a continuous low level of anger, which readily is provoked to more intense outbursts, or if instead it is a difference in threshold and related cognitive appraisals that characterizes the mood. Perhaps all of this occurs during a mood.

Another feature that distinguishes moods from emotions is the apparent difficulty in modulating an emotion if it occurs during a mood. Presumably, a person in an irritable mood will not be as able to modulate an episode of anger as that person would be if not in an irritable mood. Not only should the anger during an irritable mood be more intense and less controlled, it should decay more slowly.

Another feature distinguishing moods from emotions is that moods do not own their own unique facial expression while many of the emotions do. One infers an irritable mood by seeing many facial expressions of anger, but there is no distinctive facial expression of irritability itself, nor is there for any other mood, or for that matter for emotional traits, or affective disorders. Perhaps there is a distinctive unique vocal signal for each mood, but no one has yet identified one. More likely, there might be a particular pattern of facial tonus measurable with electromyography that could distinguish one mood from another, but this would not be an observable signal.

While it seems evident that a mood potentiates a particular emotion (anger for irritability, positive emotions when in a euphoric mood, sadness when in a blue mood, fear when in an apprehensive mood), I do not know of research that has actually examined this possibility using expressive or physiological measures. Nor has there been any exploration of whether a mood inhibits the likelihood of eliciting a nonrelevant emotion. Is the irritable person less able to experience disgust, contempt, sadness, or fear? Or just sadness and fear? Or just positive emotions that are harder to arouse?

Another feature differentiating moods from emotions is what calls them forth. Although I know of no direct evidence to support my claim, I propose that people usually can specify the event that called forth an emotion, and often cannot do so for a mood. The event that calls forth an emotion may be in the environment, a memory, or imagined. To say that a person can specify what called forth their emotional reaction is not to suggest that people typically are aware of the event provoking the emotion as it is called forth. Sometimes they are, particularly when the event unfolds slowly, but often the awareness of the source of the emotional reaction occurs afterward, or during the emotional episode. Moods are more opaque in this regard.

I suggest two different ways in which moods are brought forth. First, and most obviously, moods can be brought forth by changes in one's neurohormonal, biochemical state. It is beyond my expertise to specify just what those internal chemical changes are, beyond proposing that they involve phenomena that have a longer life than the internal changes that sustain emotions. Lack of sleep and lack of food are two obvious physiological changes that would in turn change one's internal chemistry, but this may occur also on a cyclical basis, more obviously for premenopausal women, but presumably for males as well, and at other ages for both sexes. It is common in children and adults for a lack of sleep to lead to an irritable mood. Parents call it crankiness when it is manifest in their children. I have seen instances, however, when a lack of sleep can instead cause hilarity, if a pleasing event occurs before irritability becomes manifest.

There may be a second, quite different route for arousing a mood. I propose that moods can be generated by a *dense* emotional experience. By "dense" I mean an occasion in which a specific emotion is called forth at very high intensity, again and again, with little time between each evocation. Suppose someone insults you and you become very, very angry, but before the anger completely subsides the person insults you again, and again, and then again. You experience intense anger repeatedly with only a few seconds in between bursts of anger. In such a dense emotional occasion, I presume a threshold is crossed that produces a biochemical change that then sustains a mood. In my example, the subsequent mood after a series of insults would be irritability that could last for hours. I suspect that if the expression of the emotion is inhibited, for one reason or another, then the likelihood of generating a mood is enhanced. Observation suggests that this is so for negative but not for positive emotions. Again in my example, if you were not able to express your anger, if the person insulting you had power over you so that you had to inhibit your angry expressions, that would increase the likelihood that you would be in an irritable mood afterwards.

Space does not allow me to do more than raise the question of how moods are related to emotional traits, such as hostility, euphoria, shyness, melancholia. While everyone has an irritable mood from time to time, not every one is a hostile character. We do not know how or when these emotional traits arise, or whether they endure over the entire life span. Nor do we know if people with a particular emotional trait can be characterized as having a very high incidence of the related mood.

Varieties of Affect: Emotions and Episodes, Moods, and Sentiments

NICO H. FRIJDA

Emotion words are used to refer to a large variety of psychological states or events. This variety is reflected in the distinctions made between emotions, feelings, moods, sentiments, and personalities, and in the different ways of speaking, such as "being frightened by an event," "feeling frightened because of an event," "envisaging a frightening event," "feeling frightened" or "feeling anxious," "being afraid of a given sort of event," and "having an anxious nature, or one that is easily frightened." The phenomena or constructs meant by these terms and expressions differ along several dimensions: duration, origins, reference to a particular object or to a more general or undefined class of objects, and so forth. But we must not think that it will be possible to "discover" the true nature of emotions, moods, sentiments, and so on, because these are natural-language words invented to distinguish now along this line, and then along that one. Neither can we expect that each of these words refers to a distinct class of events, neatly separated from the others. But the words do indicate that distinctions exist that are worth making, the bases of which are worth following up.

The major and most important bases for distinctions between affective phenomena, which are hidden in the uses of those words, are, I think, two. These bases are independent of, and orthogonal to, one another: whether or not a relation between the subject and a particular object or event is involved; and whether or not an acute process or state is referred to or, rather, reference is made to a more or less enduring disposition.

Intentional and Nonintentional States

It is a basic fact of psychological analysis that many psychological states or processes involve a relationship of a subject with an object. Such psychological states or processes are said to possess the feature of "intentionality" and include the emotions.

Emotions imply and involve relationships of the subject with a particular object: One is afraid of something, angry at someone, happy about something, and so on. The feature of intentionality not only applies to emotional experience, but also to emotional behavior. Angry behavior is directed at someone or something, fearful behavior is directed away from something. Even being frozen from anxiety involves such intentionality and direction: It concerns an object, one is paralyzed in front of it, one can neither flee from it nor approach it, and one's attention is focused on it. Since Hume, a distinction has been made between the object of an emotion and its cause. An emotion's cause and its object may be different entities. The cause of one's anger may be an insult; the object of that anger is the antagonist who insulted you. In principle, it would be possible for an affective state to have a cause and no object, or to have an object without the person being aware of its cause. Emotions have objects by definition, although one might, in a particular instance, be unaware of their cause. I might, in such an instance, not know where my irrational anger came from.

One can thus say that emotions involve relations to some object. A better, more precise way of saying this is of course to say that there exist object-related affective states of mind, along with object-related states of behavioral readiness (and, usually, combinations of these), and that these states coincide with what usually are called emotions. This statement is of interest because there also exist affective states of mind that are not intentional, or that are not intentional in the same way (definitions in the literature vary; see below). The domain of nonintentional affective state is different from that of the domain of intentional affective states just described. It roughly coincides with that of the phenomena usually called "moods." Of course, this corresponds to the fact that moods are often characterized as being "diffuse" or "global," as compared to emotions (e.g., Morris, 1989), and that emotion words felt by subjects to refer to more global states (like "cheerful"), as opposed to more focal ones (like "amused"), are also felt to be referring to moods (Frijda, 1987). It is natural that the domain of "nonintentional affective states" coincides with that of states called "moods" only roughly because natural-language words like "mood" never are used in fully consistent fashion and do not consistently correspond to a particular necessary feature.

Hume's distinction between objects and causes of affective states is highly relevant for the analysis of mood. Naturally, moods have causes, and the cause of a particular mood may be a particular emotionally charged event; still, that event or the person focal in that event does not constitute its object. One may know that one's bad mood has been precipitated by a slight one received during the day; this does not preclude one's feeling irritable or depressed "in general," and doubtful about one's merits in ways that have nothing to do with the received slight.

I said that what we call moods are nonintentional states. Analyses differ in this regard, though. Some authors (e.g., Brentano, 1874) argue that, indeed, they are nonintentional. Others (e.g., Stumpf, 1899; see Reisenzein & Schönpflug, 1992) hold that, being states of consciousness, they are intentional states by definition. However, under that view their object does not consist of a particular object but of the "world as a whole," the environment entirely and diffusely.

Analysis of Emotions and Moods

Differences between affective states consist of differences in affect, appraisal, action readiness, and physiological response. "Affect" here refers to pleasant or unpleasant feeling. "Appraisal" refers to the perception and evaluation of the emotional event, with regard to its valence and its relevant properties for dealing with it (e.g., goal conduciveness or obstructiveness, outcome certainty, others' agency, controllability, etc.). "Action readiness" refers to action tendencies or impulses to establish or disrupt relationships to the environment, and to states of activation in doing so. Affective states are composed of all the above: of a particular affect, a particular appraisal, a particular state of action readiness, with or without corresponding motor involvement, and a particular pattern of physiological response. They may also include a conscious awareness of the state of appraisal, a felt action readiness, and awareness of one's bodily response. A particular emotion can be described in those terms.

Moods, too, can be described in those terms. There is a difference, however: In the states that we call emotions, affect, appraisal and action readiness are object-focused, whereas in those that we call moods these elements lack such a focus. Depressed mood can be understood as diffuse negative affect, a generalized absence of goals for striving, and generalized low inclination (or even disinclination) to undertake action, or to relate to the environment.

Variations in our state of action readiness, as a feature of moods, are prominently manifest in variations in thresholds for corresponding emotional responses. Investigating correlations between moods and emotional response thresholds is, of course, an active domain of investigation (Morris, 1989). However, theoretically these threshold changes belong to the definitory aspects of moods. Anxious mood in part is defined by persistent, diffuse anxious feeling, and in part by the number and frequency with which even minor events evoke anxious responses; angry mood is defined in part by diffuse angry feeling, and in part by irritability and the enhanced tendency to view events as frustrations, obstructions, or manifestations of ill will in others. The research in fact aims at assessing the degree of correlation between the various defining aspects.

Emotion Episodes

One of the features often mentioned as distinguishing emotions from moods is duration: Emotions, it is said, tend to be of short duration; moods may persist for a day or even more. However, the use of the word "emotion" in daily language is not restricted to states lasting for only a few minutes or an hour or so. More important, the duration of an affective state is uncorrelated with whether the state is an intentional or a nonintentional state, that is, whether or not it relates to an object. When subjects were asked to report a recent emotional incident, 50 percent of these incidents was described as having lasted for longer than one hour, and 22 percent for longer than 24 hours (Frijda, Mesquita, Sonnemans, & Van Goozen, 1991). It was clear from the descriptions of these incidents that the affective states focused on the emotional object or event during those entire intervals, either continuously or intermittently. If intermittently, the successive phases were felt to belong together and not represent a succession of individual emotions. In the study in which these data were reported, subjects were also asked "to draw a diagram of the course of their emotion over time." The diagrams show a beginning and an end, separated by the time intervals indicated; between those beginnings and ends, emotional intensity fluctuated, showing peaks and valleys that reflect the intermittency meant.

In the reports of emotional incidents, more or less extended duration appears to be the rule rather than the exception. In other words, emotional events tend to lead to emotion episodes that, typically, last for an hour or more. "Emotion episode" is indeed the term that appears appropriate to designate these affective states since they clearly do not represent moods, as evidenced by the fact that there is an object of focus.

The extended durations of emotion episodes have various causes, to judge from the reports. They may be due to the duration of the emotion-arousing event or event sequence; an example is the incident of fear in which the subject was being threatened by a knife-toting vagrant for several hours. Extended durations can also arise from the magnitude of the aroused emotion the event elicited, exemplified by the female subject who, after having been the subject of vulgar remarks when walking down the street, felt upset, angry, and nauseated for the rest of the evening, the night, and part of the next morning (the examples come from Frijda et al., 1991).

There is good reason to distinguish such "emotion episodes" from "emotions," even though subjects in recollection experiments do not make that distinction. Overall intensity fluctuates over the episode, as the diagrams reflected. The emotional state does not remain the same during the episode. The nature of the emotion usually also varies. Although the incidents were reported as exemplars of a given emotion (say, anger, fear, or joy), they were described as sequences in which one emotion followed another: annoyance followed by anger, followed by disgust, followed by upset and indignation, for instance, or the various emotions may have been present at the same time. What this means is that the cognitive content of thought, and the concomitant appraisal of the event as viewed at the time of the event, changed, as well as the prevailing mode of action readiness. In the example of the woman walking down the street, action readiness changed from rejecting the event, and readiness to oppose, over actual antagonistic thoughts and impulses, to rejecting the event or its content, in thought or overt behavior, to restlessness and inability to focus thoughts on something else, and articulate thoughts about the inacceptability of the event.

At the same time, the successive phases are not felt as independent; nor is the actual state of readiness. Activation tends to persist or show a course over time; enhanced activation during an emotion episode may be manifest even during sleep, in sleep disturbance and restless dreaming, and attention tends to remain focused on the event continuously. Subjects report the episodes as wholes, as unbroken engagements with the emotion-arousing event. During the episodes, more acute phases and less acute phases succeed one another. During acute phases, motor readiness, physiological arousal, expressive activity, and interference with other activities are pronounced; during less acute phases, feelings and thoughts are present either as foreground or as background for other activities. During the less acute phases, the individual's state might be characterized as a "mood," except that an object may be the focus of attention or may be reinstalled as such at any moment.

Are Emotions, Emotion Episodes, and Moods Distinct Processes?

Are emotions, emotion episodes, and moods distinct categories of affective processes? I think they are, when the emphasis is on "processes" and not on "categories." Psychology often still is in the grips of Aristotelian or medieval science, in which the essences of classes of objects were sought (Lewin, 1935; Cassirer, 1908). In my distinctions I tried to describe different processes rather than categories or states: the processes of object-focused, intentional affective activity; non-object-focused or nonintentional affective activity; sequences of such processes (mostly of the first kind) that go on in continuous fashion over the course of a particular transaction with a particular object or event.

But at the same time, these processes do not necessarily represent different states. I think it can be safely said that every emotion tends to prolong itself into a mood or, more properly perhaps, that every emotion tends to entail consequences of diffuse, global responsiveness—that is, tends to entail a mood change. While angry at one child, a parent may snap at others as well; while happy and proud when an object of praise and celebration, one tends to be generous to others. It would, I think, be silly to say that in those instances emotions and moods alternate in lightning fashion. Rather, the corresponding processes alternate, or may even be active simultaneously. The same applies, incidentally, to individual emotions. It is inadequate to say that during an emotion episode one emotion succeeds another. This way of describing the event invites the unsolvable problem of determining when one emotion ends and the next one begins. Instead, the component processes of appraisals, of activation of action readiness mechanisms, of activation of specific behaviors and of physiological responses wax and wane, either successively or, in the event, at overlapping periods or simultaneously.

Consequences of Emotions and Moods

Distinguishing different sorts of affective phenomena, I argued, makes sense to the extent that the distinguished phenomena carry differential consequences or implications. The global feature implied by the definition of moods implies consequences that differ from those implied by the object-focused feature of emotions. Among those consequences are generalized threshold changes, which one would not expect in emotions, and nonspecific changes in judgments. Indeed, both expectations are borne out. A by now large amount of research has demonstrated that negative moods tend to bias judgments of life satisfaction, or the probability estimates of negative events, in a negative direction (Morris, 1989; Frijda, in press; Clore & Parrott, 1991; Schwarz, Bless, & Bohner, 1991). Belief changes, by contrast, only appear to follow emotions. The emotion of anger enhances the attribution of blame, while an angry mood appears not to do so (Schwarz, Bless, & Bohner, 1991).

The various cognitive consequences of moods have been discussed in the literature mainly under the heading of effects of memory structure and process; according to Bower's (1981) network theory, instances of mood, and particular moods generally, serve as memory nodes. However, the various effects can be better understood from an analysis of the nature and structure of moods as affective states; in particular, the differences between emotions and moods, and their cognitive consequences, can be better understood from that perspective. Moods as well as emotions are sources of information, to the subject, with regard to his or her current global state of action readiness and evaluation of the life situation, or with regard to affectively important events.

Sentiments

The acute or dispositional nature of an affective event is the second feature, next to intentionality, that I consider useful in distinguishing among psychological states and constructs.

Human beings possess dispositions to respond affectively to particular objects or kinds of event. More precisely, we attribute affective dispositions to individuals to account for their propensities to respond affectively, and to account for individual differences in this regard. Such dispositions are called sentiments or emotional attitudes. They are usually referred to as "likes" or "dislikes," or else by emotion words followed by an object name or generic expression ("I hate pitbull terriers"). Most sentiments are, it is generally assumed, acquired on the basis of previous experience or social learning; however, certain sentiments (e.g., dislike for seeing blood or of unstable surfaces) may have an innate basis and be fairly common among human beings.

Certain common emotion words tend to refer to sentiments rather than to emotions—"love" and "hate" are the most prominent. Both words usually refer to ways of seeing and treating a given object rather than to momentary responses. Verbal usage, however, is confusing in this regard, because the same words are being used for particular emotions, as in the expressions "I felt an upsurge of love" or "He was overwhelmed by a feeling of hatred"; the temporal implications make the distinction clear. Confusions are understandable, and both "love" and "hate" occur among the most frequently mentioned words when subjects are asked to name as many emotions as they can (Fehr & Russell, 1984; Van Goozen & Frijda, 1992). The confusion (or lack of distinction) is understandable if we consider the fact that sentiments are the bases for emotions when something happens in which the object is involved, that they form the source of emotions with the same name when just seeing or meeting or hearing about the object (the "upsurges" mentioned), and that the structures of sentiments are similar to those of the corresponding emotions, in involving appraisals, and (latent) motivations.

It is thus incorrect to say that love and hate "are" not emotions but sentiments. The labels can apply both to some acute state and to some disposition. Moreover, these dispositions can also be felt, that is, one can be aware of them; one generally knows that one hates or loves a particular individual or group of people. Emotions and sentiments stand in a close and reciprocal relationship, in that the sentiment of love can originate in emotions of love, precipitated by a particular event, and emotions of love can be precipitated by meeting or thinking of an individual toward whom a sentiment of love exists.

The structure of sentiments can be described in two ways. First, sentiments consist of cognitive dispositions to appraise an object in a particular way; the mode of appraisal is similar to that of the corresponding emotion. Sentiments can be understood as cognitive schemas (Fiske, 1982), whose informational content gives rise to the appraisal when meeting the object. Furthermore, the schema is actualized when the subject consciously reflects on a sentiment. On such occasions, an emotion with the same content is elicited, as when in thought or in conversation saying "I hate that man!" or "I just love Bach's partitas for solo violin."

Second, sentiments are dispositions to treat the object in a way corresponding to that of the action readiness during the emotions; they constitute latent motivations that become acute on actual or possible confrontation with the relevant object. Fearful sentiments lead to anticipatory avoidance of the object. Hate has similarities to anger: It forms the motivation for hurting or harming an object, or for acclaiming such hurting or harming when performed by others. Sentiments indeed often can be described as desires. Love, for instance, has been defined as the desire to increase the well-being of the object (Scheler, 1923).

Individuals can be aware of their sentiments through both aspects. One can be reflexively aware of one's cognitive schemas (expectations, etc.) and of one's desires and wishes. In addition, of course, one may be familiar with one's sentiments through anticipation or recollection of emotions about the objects concerned.

Characterizing sentiments as dispositions, and distinguishing them from emotions and moods by that aspect, is not without its problems. Emotions as well as moods may function as dispositions. Emotions involve states of action readiness that, by their nature, are dispositions for the matching variety of actions. They have indeed been characterized as "episodic dispositions" (Averill, in press). I have indicated the dispositional aspects of mood above. Nevertheless, the core of both emotions and moods consists of actual, occurrent aspects (Ryle, 1949); that is to say that feelings, perceptions, motor responses, all are elements with temporal specification. This is not the case with sentiments. Or, again to be precise, "emotions" and "moods" are constructs devised to refer to particular occurrent phenomena; "sentiment" refers to the individual's cognitions that such occurring phenomena may be evoked, or else it is a construct devised to account for the fact that such occurrent phenomena are in fact evoked by particular objects or events that do not, at that moment, appear to justify the appearance of those responses.

This is not the place to enlarge on the origins of sentiments (but see Shand, 1920; Frijda et al., 1991). Suffice it to say that they may stem either from earlier emotional encounters with the objects concerned (e.g., sentiments of fear originating in traumatic encounters) or from social learning (e.g., culturally determined food aversions, sentiments toward one's nation or one's religious symbols). In addition, some sentiments may have facilitating sources in innate propensities (see the "preparedness" notion to explain certain phobias; Seligman, 1971).

Personality Dispositions

The term "sentiment" was coined to refer to differential propensities to respond emotionally to specific types of events; but differences of less specific, more general kinds exist, too. Examples of such differential propensities are seen in differences in thresholds for fearful emotions, and in positive emotions (emotional instability or "neuroticism" or trait anxiety, and extraversion, or "positive affect"; Eysenck, 1967; Spielberger, 1975; Watson & Tellegen, 1985), in proneness to anger ("trait anger," Spielberger et al., 1985), and in the tendency to seek strong emotions ("sensation seeking," Zuckerman, 1979).

Emotional personality dispositions are often referred to by emotion words; language refers to an anxious or fearful person, a happy person, and the like. These dispositions can be understood as propensities to appraise events in terms corresponding to particular emotions. Anger propensity can be viewed as the tendency to appraise unpleasant events as being caused by someone else's agency; trait anxiety can be interpreted as a propensity to view novel or uncertain events as possible threats, or even to view familiar events as novel and with uncertain implications. Alternatively, emotional personality dispositions can be understood as low thresholds for the response patterns characterizing different emotions: anger trait as a low threshold for aggressive behavior; trait anxiety as a low threshold for autonomic arousal and response inhibition. Emotional personality traits are often referred to as traits of temperament.

The notion of personality trait carries the assumption of relative temporal stability. Empirical data, of course, are needed to decide whether a particular emotional propensity is more or less permanent, or subject to changes over the life cycle. Evidence exists that several emotional personality traits (notably emotional instability, extraversion, and sensation seeking) have some innate basis. However, life experience may be equally responsible, as it is usually adduced for explaining depressed personality. Biological (e.g., hormonal) changes, too, may account for personality changes in these respects. In fact, the difference between moods and emotional personality traits is one of degree of duration and, thus, of taste. One of the ways to define moods is by low threshold for a particular class of emotions; the notion of personality trait does not imply innateness or life-long persistence.

Conclusions

Verbal expressions containing emotion words refer to a variety of phenomena or constructs. Several useful and meaningful distinctions can be made among them, and that made in the language between emotions and moods is related to one of these distinctions—namely, object-relatedness. That between emotions and sentiments derives from another one—namely, acute or dispositional nature. The two distinctions are orthogonal. Emotions stand to sentiments as moods stand to emotional personality traits, or temperament. My further distinction of emotion episodes refers to the structural complexity in the manifestation of emotions.

My analyses make it intelligible, I think, why emotion terms are confusingly involved in all these different classes of events. They have features in common. They all refer to appraisal structures, either object focused or not, and either as actual structures of experience or as cognitive schemas that may underlie such experiences. Again, they all refer to modes of action readiness, either as actual states of readiness or as propensities or goals underlying willingness or inclination to intentional behavior. I have tried to place the various usages of emotion words in an intelligible relationship to one another, with respect to the phenomena the words refer to and the constructs used to account for them.

The phenomena under the different headings have intimate and obvious relationships, which adds to the reasons for the blurring of distinctions. Emotions may fade into moods; but moods may give rise to emotions, since they often imply a lowering of threshold for particular emotions. Sentiments may be the precipitate of emotions, and may underlie the emergence of emotions, because that is how they are defined. Traits of temperament or personality give rise to both emotions and moods, again because it is the occurrence of those emotions and moods that prompt us to attribute such traits to a particular individual.

Parsing the Emotional Domain from a Developmental Perspective

H. H. GOLDSMITH

Carving the human personality into smaller domains on the basis of our present knowledge to facilitate scientific analysis involves some stipulation, some intuition, and a willingness to accept the strong likelihood of eventually being judged as arbitrary, simplistic, or just ignorant. I suggest that the three concepts that can be most fruitfully distinguished are discrete emotional reactions, moods, and temperamental traits.[1] Here I attempt to defend a set of distinctions that might facilitate research.

I suspect that the editors posed this question because the term "emotion" is used to describe reactions, states, moods, sentiments, traits, and disorders (three of which I shall largely ignore). We tend to use one word and its variants for so many purposes—"he reacted with anger"; "she's in an angry mood"; "he tends to be an angry person." Consider a very rough analogy of these emotion-related concepts to the concepts involving the phenomenon of magnetism. When a paper clip seems to jump across my desk to attach itself to a magnet, I call the event "magnetic attraction." The structure called the "magnet" is not confused with the event of magnetic attraction. The magnet has the dispositional property, even in the absence of my paper clip, of being "magnetic." And this property will be manifest in other relevant contexts—for instance, when an unfortunate floppy disk lands nearby. Furthermore, my scissors made mostly of iron have a higher-order dispositional property of being "magnetizable." A temperamental disposition of, say, anger proneness, is analogous to my scissors: If certain ill-understood processes occur, the anger-prone disposition results in behavioral properties that make events of anger expression more likely. Thus, the facial, vocalic, and other indicators of an emotional reaction are analogous to the observable movement of the paper clip toward the magnet. There are other indicators of the emotional state besides the observable reaction, such as the elementary appraisals that are analogous to whatever it is that scrambles the data on my floppy disk. Just as physicists understand the processes that result in my floppy disk's data being scrambled by exposure to the magnet, we emotion researchers seek to understand componential processes of the emotional state that are not observable in overt behavior. Thus, the emotional state of the organism (or from a functionalist viewpoint, the state of the organism's relation to the environment—especially the social environment) is analogous to the processes occurring during the "interaction" of the magnet and the paper clip.

With this orientation, I now try to define and distinguish temperamental traits, moods, and emotional reactions, emphasizing temperament because it is my primary research area.

Temperament as Emotional Traits

We may think of temperamental traits as **characteristic individual differences in the way basic emotions are experienced and expressed** (Goldsmith & Campos, 1982, 1986). The reader will immediately ask what I mean by "emotion." Emotion, in functionalist perspective, refers to the organism's "sense" (perception, appraisal, evaluation) that a significant change has occurred in the relation of the self, either physical or symbolic, to social other(s), either actual or implied, or occasionally to the world of objects. Thus, emotions are generally interpersonal, and phenomena we call thirst, sleepiness, and startle are not emotional. Campos and his colleagues have elaborated this definition (Barrett & Campos, 1987; Campos, Campos, & Barrett, 1989; Campos, Barrett, Lamb, Goldsmith, & Stenberg, 1983), and some theorists have emphasized the social interactional nature of emotion even more strongly; for instance, Averill (1980) referred to emotions as "transitory social roles" several years ago. In structuralist perspective, emotion involves not only the feeling state mentioned above, but also an associated action tendency (e.g., Frijda, 1986). Emotions are structured as families (Shaver, Schwartz, Kirson, & O'Conner, 1987), with common eliciting and expressive features, the latter including vocalic, facial, gestural, postural, and instrumental components. Lists of which emotion families should be considered basic vary from one theorist to the next. A recent and fairly extensive list by Ekman (1992) includes anger, awe, contempt, disgust, embarrassment, excitement, fear, guilt, interest, sadness, shame, surprise, and enjoyment, with enjoyment having several variants. Of these, only anger, excitement, fear, interest, and enjoyment have been investigated extensively from a temperamental perspective, and this investigation has sometimes been conducted using different labels such as, respectively, anger proneness (an element of emotional—as opposed to instrumental—aggressiveness), sensation-seeking, anxiety, persistence, and positive emotionality.

The reader will also ask what I mean by "characteristic" in the definition at the beginning of the previous paragraph. There are two key expectations that personality theorists hold of a trait: cross-situational consistency and temporal stability. Cross-situational consistency is not expected across any set of situations. The property of cross-situational consistency is qualified in at least three ways. If consistency is to be expected, the situations must have common incentive properties, they must afford significant behavioral options, and they must be relevant to the individual's goals.

Likewise, temporal stability is only expected between periods of major behavioral reorganization, and the stability is not expected to override other sources of variation. Furthermore, temperamental continuity sometimes is apparent only under conditions of stress, novelty, or other extraordinary situations (Thomas & Chess, 1977). These two properties of personality traits transfer to temperamental traits, and sometimes a third expectation, that of constitutional (Rothbart, 1989a) or genetic (Buss & Plomin, 1984) origins is added. There is no necessary reason for stable and consistent traits to be rooted in the genetic code, however. Consistencies can inhere in cognitive structures, such as chronically accessible schemas, or from learning and generalization, as in the case of classically conditioned fears.

With these issues covered, let us return to the definition of temperament. It does not stretch the concept of temperamental traits too much to define them as tendencies to enter into an emotional state or perhaps to remain in an emotional mood. A similar perspective views temperamental traits as "emotional biases" (Malatesta, 1990). However, other temperament researchers broaden the domain of temperament beyond the strictly emotional, as reflected by views expressed in a roundtable exchange on the topic (Goldsmith et al., 1987). Logical and empirical reservations concerning the practice of *defining* temperamental traits as constitutional or heritable are on record (Goldsmith, 1986; McCall, 1986; Hinde, 1987). Despite the inadvisability of prematurely incorporating etiology as part of the definition of a concept that is otherwise understood at the behavioral level, I do search for etiologic factors within the biological realm (Goldsmith, 1989). Definitions of temperament at one or more biological levels may soon be possible, but there is little reason to expect that the biological concepts will be isomorphic with the behavioral concepts of temperament currently popular in research (Goldsmith, 1993).

Concepts of emotional individuality overlap broadly with current concepts of temperament. Goldsmith and Campos (1982) documented that most scale names on temperament questionnaires are easily reinterpreted in terms of a basic emotion family and parameters of response (e.g., intensity or latency). Most contemporary research on temperament in the United States centers on infancy and early childhood. As the child develops, it becomes increasingly arbitrary to distinguish temperament traits from personality traits. Thus, I view temperamental traits as being emotional in nature, and, as noted by Strelau (1987) in commenting on earlier versions of my approach, this may be an apt characterization for the infancy period. Of course, considering the entire lifespan, temperament is not the whole of personality and arguably not even the whole of emotional individuality. The personality characteristics that are distinguished from temperament include social attitudes, self-related characteristics, and other more complex personality structures. Are there also emotional traits that can usefully be distinguished from temperament? The answer harkens back to the first question posed by the editors: Are there basic emotions? I cannot rehash the debate of this difficult issue here. However, those who are convinced of the usefulness of Ekman's (1992) criteria for distinguishing basic emotions (e.g., anger) from other emotion-related phenomena (such as the attitude of hatred) will find analogous grounds for distinguishing temperamental traits from other emotional traits. A key distinction between temperament and other emotional traits will be developmental, with temperamental traits becoming organized earlier.

Recently, I have offered another, related definition of temperament (Goldsmith, 1993). This definition draws on a systems perspective to counterbalance reductionistic tendencies in the field of temperament. One property of some systems is sensitivity to initial conditions, and temperament is a prime candidate for an initial condition, where "initial" refers not to presence at birth, but to presence at any time a system becomes organized or undergoes transition. A similar idea is inherent in other developmental approaches to emotionality and temperament, most notably in the study of emotional regulation (Kopp, 1989; Rothbart, 1989b). The study of emotional regulation best links the concept of temperament to systems theory-like approaches. Regulatory processes include attention allocation, communication with others, self-mediated processes, coping styles, and other processes. Emotional regulatory processes can be considered either as internal (or specific) to emotional systems or as external (or more general) systems that interact with emotion developmentally. This definitional issue may not be critical at our present stage of knowledge. Another tenet of dynamic systems theory is that a process is most fruitfully analyzed at times of transition, when new components might enter the system and when rate-controlling processes of the system might change. Bearing these considerations in mind, it is desirable to define temperament as **variability in developing emotion systems**. The proper study of temperament, then, would involve analysis of how individuals negotiate significant transitions. Some significant transitions occur on a daily basis and involve new relations of the self, others, and the object world (e.g., meeting a stranger). Other significant transitions are more pervasive and constitute a new setting for the daily transitions (e.g., starting school). As the individual grows, some consistency likely develops in how these transitions are negotiated, and such consistency is termed temperamental. In fact, consistency is perhaps most apparent at times of transition, as suggested in the long-term follow-up of subjects by Thomas and Chess (1977).

Distinguishing Temperament, Mood, and Emotional Reactions

With this brief treatment of temperament as background, let us turn to the task posed by the editors. Table 1 depicts my conceptualization of emotional reactions, moods, and temperamental traits. Before proceeding, I should qualify my views by stating my research perspective. I primarily study infants, and I primarily use behavioral methods. Thus, some idealized distinctions I attempt to draw may be murky when applied to adults.

The depiction of emotional responses in Table 1 is not novel; it overlaps broadly with the views of Ekman (1992), Lazarus (1991a), and others. The depiction of mood in Table 1 borrows from Mayer and Salovey and their colleagues, who have contributed important conceptual analyses of mood (e.g., Mayer, Salovey, Gomberg-Kaufman, & Blainey, 1991). These researchers suggest that emotion-management processes are also key components of moods. Frijda (1986) captures a similar idea by stating that, "In emotional responding generally there is no succession of discrete events so much as the flow of varying attitudes, acceptances, rejections, abandonments, and reserves" (p. 479). Such a view of mood implies that many of our studies

TABLE 1. Features That Distinguish Temperament, Mood, and Emotional Reactions

	Emotion-Related Concept		
Distinguishing Features	*Emotional Reaction*	*Mood*	*Temperament*
Type entity	Coordinated event, with associated brief state	Longer-term state	Disposition, or trait
Temporal properties	Duration of seconds, unless stimulus persists	Duration of minutes to days; intensity varies; episodic quality	Stability over periods ranging from months to years; activated in relevant contexts
Cognitive components	Some appraisal required; can be elementary or automatic	Includes emotion-management processes, attributions, and other complex cognitions	Limited in early development, but central as temperament is transformed into personality traits
Antecedents	Species-general relational themes or perceptions of significant changes in the environment	Can be after-effect of emotional reaction, or result from other poorly understood processes	Differences in genotype and/or experience
Role of situations	Confined to features of emotion-eliciting stimulus	Help maintain or terminate state	Complementary to temperament as influence on behavior
Universality vs. individuality	Universal in occurrence, if not form	Features of both universality and individuality, with the latter primarily in emotion management	Conceptualized as an individual-difference variable; traits vary in salience from person to person
Developmental considerations	Distinctive reactions evident in first year of life for several emotions, and in second and third years for others	Seldom studied; moods expected to become longer-lasting as cognitive capacities develop	Traits become organized and stable on different schedules, beginning in first year; relative standing on traits can change during development

of emotion actually involve assessment of mood, and this is widely recognized in, for instance, the literature on mood and memory. Most social psychology experiments involve manipulation of mood rather than discrete emotional responses (Batson, Shaw, & Oleson, 1992), and responses to checklists of emotion words should also be assimilated to the framework of mood rather than emotional response (Watson & Tellegen, 1985). In part, this is because complex emotional schemas are invoked in mood states, and these emotional schemas can be distinguished from intellectual schemas (Averill, 1990). Of course, it is too simplistic to view moods as emotional states imbued with activation of cognitive representations. Even the most elemental emotional reactions in infants probably involve basic appraisal processes, even though the appraisal may be rapid, unconscious, and more "perceptual" than "cognitive." (This issue has, of course, been debated at length; see Lazarus, 1991b, and references therein.) Distinctions among classes of mood states are also reasonable. The mood following an acute emotional response and lasting, say, an hour can usefully be distinguished from the more chronic and episodic moods that extend for days.

Given the extensive treatment of temperament here, there is little need to elaborate the criteria that distinguish it from emotional responses and mood in Table 1. However, it is worth mentioning that trait concepts tend to be caricatured outside the field of personality. That is, traits are sometimes depicted as constantly operative and rigidly stable in ways that would seem foreign even to classical trait theorists, such as Allport (1937), Cattell (1946), and Stern (1938). It is also worth emphasizing that some trait names carry more meaning than the emotional state that lies at their core. For instance, "emotional aggressiveness" carries connotations well beyond the state of anger (Berkowitz, in press).

Understanding the intent of Table 1 requires that the reader incorporate developmental considerations. In particular, emotional reactions are apparent before mood states during development, and the behavioral indicators of temperament change gradually as the child ages. Although Table 1 helps us map the conceptual domains of emotion, mood, and temperament, it has limited utility for directing research. Much better would be frameworks for particular emotions, such as anger, and associated moods and traits.

The reader will note that Table 1 does not incorporate biological criteria, but it seems likely that emotional responses, emotional states, and temperamental states will be distinguished by biological criteria in the future. I am not confident in attempting this biological differentiation in a comprehensive way now, but I hope some other respondents to this question will take up the challenge (see Frijda, 1986).

A final point is that distinguishing among various affective phenomena is only an initial task. Explaining concurrent and developmental interactions is both more important and more difficult.

Note

1. A fourth construct of "affect" could possibly be differentiated from these three, along the lines suggested by Batson et al. (1992).

Distinctions Among Emotions, Moods, and Temperamental Qualities

JEROME KAGAN

The distinctions among the related concepts of acute emotion, chronic mood, and temperamental quality are theoretically useful, for each has a unique sense as well as referential meaning. An acute emotion is understood by most investigators to refer to a temporary change in psychological and biological processes to particular classes of incentives. There is, in addition, the assumption that some acute emotions are universal.

A chronic mood is generally understood to refer to a salient, enduring emotional quality displayed in a variety of situations and distinguishing one class of people from another. Unlike acute emotions, which are usually provoked by particular incentives, moods transcend contexts.

Finally, a temperamental quality usually refers to an inherited profile of behavior and biology that predisposes a person to experience a particular affective reaction, given a relevant incentive. Like a mood, a temperamental quality is an individual-difference construct. But, unlike mood, which does not imply a genetic pedigree, a temperamental quality does imply some genetic influence. Individuals who are chronically anxious because they inherited a temperamental vulnerability to this emotion are displaying both a mood and a temperament.

The state of fatigue provides an appropriate analogy. The fatigue produced by a poor night's sleep is an acute feeling state. A mood of chronic fatigue can be due to responsibility for caring for triplets for the first five years of their lives. Finally, the fatigue of a person who inherited a mild hypothyroidism is analogous to a temperamental quality.

Three Uses of Affect Concepts

A major difference between most biologists and most behavioral scientists is that biologists prefer to start with robust phenomena and invent construct names a posteriori after reliable functional relations have been established. Many psychologists, by contrast, prefer to begin their inquiry by assuming the reality of a priori, idealized concepts that they try to find in nature. Thus, it is profitable to ask: What are the reliable phenomena psychologists wish to explain with affect concepts?

First, there are the acute changes in physiology, cognition, and action that occur in response to novelty, challenge, loss, attack, or frustration. These changes are sudden, usually temporary, and resemble the meaning of the discrete emotions posited by Tomkins, Ekman, and Izard.

A second set of phenomena refers to the longer lasting affect states created by experiences over months or years. These chronic moods can result, for example, from membership in a particular social group, a decade of academic failure, or repeated social rejection. These chronic moods bias a person to react to incentives in particular ways. Folk theory, as well as research reports, make the distinction between acute states and chronic moods. When we say, "Paul is angry because he was pushed," we understand that Paul's state is different from the one implied by the sentence, "Paul is angry because of his chronic life of poverty," even though the word—"angry"—is used in both sentences. Because the physiological states and cognitions are probably different in the acute and chronic states, it seems reasonable to apply different names to them.

Finally, there is individual variation in the biologically based biases to react to certain events with particular profiles. These inherited biases are called temperaments. Neither folk belief nor contemporary theory makes a distinction between chronic emotional moods and temperamental biases, even though nineteenth-century writers did.

For the family of affects we call anxiety, I suggest there should be at least three different terms used for three states that are members of this affect family. A similar conclusion holds for all other affect families. Concrete examples of the three states follow.

1. A person given a challenging problem displays increases in heart rate and pupillary dilation, as well as a loss in the quality of recall memory. Most scientists would call this temporary change in sympathetic reactivity and memory impairment an instance of acute anxiety. They might write: "When adults are in a challenging situation and have no coping response, they become anxious."
2. A person who grew up in poverty and left school early because of failure does not persist when cognitive tasks are presented, shows self-effacing behavior and reluctance to persist with challenge, but does not show any change in physiological functioning in most test situations. Investigators are likely to regard this profile as indicative of chronic anxiety, implying that the stable profile is a result of a prolonged history of failure. These scientists would write: "Adults who have consistently failed to meet standards for intellectual mastery are anxious."
3. A person who had been a temperamentally irritable infant and fearful child shows a rise and stabilization of heart rate and an increase in cortisol level in unfamiliar test or social situations. Psychologists are apt to call this person "temperamentally anxious" and write: "Temperamentally inhibited adults are anxious in unfamiliar, challenging situations," implying that such persons began life with a distinct physiology and, as a result of experience, became vulnerable to uncertainty.

Because the sources of evidence for the term "anxious" are different in the three instances described, the theoretical meaning of anxiety is not the same. The use of anxiety in the first instance usually implies a quantitative dimension, somewhat like the fever of a patient with an infection or the degree of receptivity to mating in a female macaque. By contrast, the term "anxious" in the second instance implies a distinctive acquired quality, like the profile of a domesticated horse compared with that of the wild type. The term "anxious" in the third instance implies a qualitative category that is genetic in origin, analogous to related strains of dogs, monkeys, or birds.

The history of biology indicates the utility of distinguishing between a quantitative feature that is shared by many different members of a species, on the one hand, and the qualitatively distinct species categories, on the other. Basal metabolic rate (BMR) is a continuum on which all animal species can be placed. But the physiological bases for a low BMR are not the same in hibernating bears and crocodiles. That is one reason why these animals belong to very different categories. Similarly, the processes that occur when a temperamentally inhibited child faces temporary challenge are not identical to those in a timid child who does not belong to this temperamental category. We now consider the idea of temperament in more detail.

Temperamental Vulnerability to Fear States

We have recently discovered two distinct behavioral profiles that are displayed to visual, auditory, and olfactory stimuli in 16-week-old infants that predict inhibited or uninhibited behavior in the second year (Kagan & Snidman, 1991a, 1991b). One group is characterized by extreme degrees of motor activity combined with fretting or crying to the presentation of dynamic visual stimuli, speech, or butyl alcohol. The highly motoric infants arch their backs, pump and extend their arms and legs with vigor, and about two-thirds of them will, on 15 to 25 percent of the trials, fret or cry during a period of high motor activity. About two-thirds of the infants who display both the high motor activity and frequent crying (called high reactive) show above average levels of fear to unfamiliar events in laboratory settings at 14 and 21 months, while less than 10 percent show low levels of fear. Among the contrast group of infants who display low levels of motor activity combined with little or no fretting (called low reactive), two-thirds are minimally fearful and about 10 percent show high levels of fear. Display of high motor activity with minimal crying or low motor activity with high crying, rather than the combination, is predictive of intermediate levels of fear, as well as different autonomic and affective reactions in the second year.

The four-month-old high reactive, compared with low reactive, infants have higher heart rates in the weeks prior to birth and at two weeks of age (while sleeping in an erect posture), and showed larger magnitudes of cardiac acceleration to selected unfamiliar events at 14 and 21 months. For example, high reactive infants show larger heart rate accelerations to a sour taste at 14 months and to a rotating wheel that produces a moderately loud, unpleasant noise at 21 months of age (Snidman & Kagan, unpublished).

One interpretation of this corpus of evidence rests on the assumption that high reactive infants inherit a low threshold of excitability in the amygdala and its projections to the lateral hypothalamus and sympathetic nervous system, as well as to motor systems served by the ventral striatum and central grey. The complementary group of low reactive infants inherits a high threshold in the amygdala and these circuits. Further, we suspect that the neurochemical bases for these two categories are qualitatively different. Although future research will have to evaluate the fruitfulness of that suggestion, recent work by Adamec supports these ideas.

Adamec (1991) has found that about 15 percent of house cats (*Felis catus*) show a behavioral pattern resembling that of the inhibited child. These cats withdraw from novelty, are slow to explore unfamiliar events, and do not attack rats, although they will attack mice. By contrast, there is a larger group of cats who attack rats and do not show defensive or avoidant behavior to novelty.

The defensive cats display their salient trait as early as the second month of life—which is comparable to 12 to 14 months in humans—and they retain this behavior through adulthood. One class of experience that will decrease preservation of the defensiveness is exposure to subdued rats while hungry—an event mimicked in life when the adult cat brings injured prey to offspring when they are hungry. However, exposing defensive kittens to live prey early in life—or not exposing them to any prey at all—increases the likelihood that they will remain defensive throughout life.

Adamec has measured activity of sites in the amygdala and hypothalamus and found that neurons in and near the large basal area of the amygdala are more reactive to threatening stimuli in defensive, compared with nondefensive, cats. Further, the projections from the basal area of the amygdala to the ventromedial hypothalamus (VMH) are more excitable in defensive animals, for electrical stimulation of the amygdala produces greater output voltages in the VMH of defensive, compared with nondefensive, cats. The enhanced responsiveness of the basal amygdala in defensive cats occurs only to events that would be perceived as threatening (e.g., the howl of an adult cat), and not to the sounds of a cat purring or ordinary noise. The fact that reactivity in the circuit from the amygdala to the VMH is independent of the reactivity of the basal amygdala to threat suggests that inhibited children differ in both the threshold of responsiveness to unfamiliar events as well as in the excitability of projections from the amygdala to the hypothalamus.

Moreover, unpublished research by Fox suggests that high reactive infants, who are likely to become inhibited, have greater activation of the EEG (desynchronization of frequencies from 6 to 12 Hz) in the right frontal pole, while the low reactive infants, who become uninhibited, have greater activation in the left frontal pole. Both Fox (1991) and Davidson (1992), in collaborative and independent work, have found that greater activation in the right frontal area is predictive of fearfulness in infants and dysphoric affect in adults.

These findings are in accord with a right-left asymmetry in facial temperature. The arterioles under the surface of the skin are under sympathetic control; some are alpha adrenergic and some beta adrenergic. Constriction of arterioles mediated by alpha adrenergic receptors reduces blood flow to the skin and, as a consequence, produces surface cooling.

A surprising fact discovered during the last 20 years provides the theoretical basis for expecting lateral asymmetry in facial temperatures. It appears that discharge of the sympathetic nervous system is slightly greater on the right than on the left side of the body. For example, stimulation of the right stellate ganglion in dogs leads to a tachycardia that is absent following stimulation of the left stellate ganglion (Randall & Priola, 1965). Further, the anatomical connections between the amygdala and hypothalamus, on the one hand, and sympathetic ganglia, on the other, appear to be stronger on the ipsilateral than on the contralateral side (Saper, Loewy, Swanson, & Cowan, 1976). Finally, extensive reviews by Cutting (1990) and Silberman and Weingartner (1986) suggest a functional association between asymmetry of activity in those brain areas that influence the sympathetic nervous system and individual variation in behavior or physiology that is assumed to accompany states of anxiety or fear. We have found in a large group of 21-month-old children that those who smiled frequently in laboratory batteries at 14 and 21 months were significantly more likely to have a cooler left forehead while those who smiled infrequently were more likely to have a cooler right forehead (chi square $= 8.5$; $p < .01$). These two groups appear to differ in the ease and frequency with which they experience the families of states we call joy or happiness, on the one hand, and anxiety, fear, and uncertainty, on the other. Contemporary research implies that the positive affect states are mediated more completely by the left hemisphere, while the dysphoric states of anxiety and fear are mediated more completely by the right hemisphere (Cutting, 1990). As early as two months of age high reactive-inhibited children show significantly less smiling to laboratory episodes than do low reactive, uninhibited, children, and the former retain their dysphoric mood in laboratory assessments through 21 months of age.

Imagine 100 adults in a laboratory exposed to a cognitive stressor. The investigator measures desynchronization of 6 to 12 Hz activity in the EEG, heart rate acceleration, changes in blood pressure, salivary cortisol, and muscle tension. The individuals who show a modest change in three or more of these variables may be experiencing an acute emotion of anxiety. The smaller proportion of individuals who showed a similar profile on these dependent variables before the cognitive stressor was imposed can be characterized as possessing a chronic mood of uncertainty. The individuals who showed an exaggerated response on these measures probably have a temperamental vulnerability to becoming anxious to challenge.

Summary

Most biological phenomena are categorized with respect to their history, time course and degree of variation; hence, it is probably helpful to use these features to classify affective phenomena and to distinguish among acute emotions, chronic moods, and temperamental types. More rapid progress in understanding emotions is likely to follow accommodation to these distinctions in future empirical work.

Acknowledgments

This research was supported in part by grants from the John D. and Catherine T. MacArthur Foundation and the Leon Lowenstein Foundation.

The Stable and the Unstable in Emotion

RICHARD LAZARUS

Philosophers and psychologists have long been at pains to define the concept of emotion and to make distinctions among diverse but overlapping emotion concepts. The task here is to clarify what is meant by emotion as a state or trait, a temperamental quality, and an acute emotion or mood. Belaboring some distinctions, such as between emotion states and traits, is apt to be a dull enterprise because of well-established and oft-examined habits of thought, unless some of their more interesting implications are explored, which I will try to do. Others, such as the distinction between acute emotions and mood, are more challenging and require that we turn to emotion metatheory and theory to help in their resolution. When I consider these latter cases, I draw on my cognitive-motivational-relational theory of the emotions (Lazarus, 1991a, 1991c) to facilitate the argument.

Trait Versus State

The simplest, most basic, and least controversial of the several distinctions is between emotion state and trait. An emotion *state* usually refers to a transient reaction to specific kinds of adaptational encounters. We say that someone is displaying or experiencing anger at a particular time and place; the state comes and goes with the circumstances. An emotion *trait*, on the other hand, usually refers to a disposition or tendency to react in a particular emotional way to an adaptational encounter. To speak of trait implies frequent recurrence of the state in diverse but specifiable circumstances.

The simplest definition of an emotion trait is the tendency of an emotion state to recur in a person. We speak of angry (or prideful, affectionate, or guilt-ridden) persons, which implies that this person is not always angry but is made angry more often or more easily than most people or, when angry, displays or experiences it more intensely than other people.

A more inferential or interpretive version explains the recurrence by reference to some personality characteristic of the person or an environmental configuration. For example, we say that a person reacts emotionally because of some personality trait, say, a goal or belief system, or a disposition to appraise or cope with a social situation in a certain way, which presumably contributes to the generation of anger, anxiety, or whatever. Later, in place of either person *or* environment, I shall emphasize the *person-environment relationship* in the emotion process because I think this way of phrasing things is more complete and accurate.

I might note in passing that, because of these inferential interpretations based on goals, beliefs, and ways of coping, clinicians are especially interested in emotion traits; traits involving recurrent forms of chronic emotional distress such as anxiety, and depression, and anger, and the adaptational dysfunctions associated with them, constitute one of the main reasons why people seek professional help. Treatment often consists of trying to understand and change motivational, cognitive, and coping tendencies that are regarded as causal in the emotional distress and dysfunction.

The concept of trait overlaps substantially with *sentiment* and attitude, which are not emotions but dispositions to respond positively or negatively toward a given person or event. To eventuate in an emotion, a sentiment or attitude must be activated by an encounter with that person or event, whether actual or imagined. The anger lies in wait, as it were, for some provocation to make it salient; even a recollection may constitute the provocation. As Ortony, Clore, and their associates (Clore, Ortony, & Foss, 1987; Ortony, Clore, & Foss, 1987; Ortony, Clore, & Collins, 1988) have emphasized, to feel the emotion of pride (a state) is not the same as to be a proud person (a trait) because a proud person does not always feel the emotion of pride unless he or she is personally in a pride-inducing social situation.

So far so good. The distinction I have been making is basically simple and is easily understood. One implication of this distinction is that state and trait are merely two sides of the same coin, as it were, and we ask different but interdependent questions about each. For example, when emotion is viewed as a state, we want to know what it is about the *situation* that generates anger, say, as distinguished from pride or another emotion. When emotion is viewed as a trait, we want to know what it is about the *person* that accounts for the recurrent response of anger, pride, or another emotion.

Furthermore, whether we are interested in emotion states or traits influences what we pay attention to—for example, we may look at the stability or *consistency* of the emotion response over time or across circumstances, or at the instability or *inconsistency* of the response over time or across circumstances. When there is high consistency in the reaction—which means that a person responds with the same emotion recurrently—the focus is on the emotion as a trait, and we are concerned with stable, structural properties of the person-environment relationship that help account for this. When there is low consistency, the focus is on the emotion as a state, and we are concerned with how changes in the person-environment relationship help account for this.

Traditionally, we think of relatively consistent personality structures as traits. For example, a person with a strong belief that the world is dangerous, and that he or she lacks the resources to cope with it effectively, is more likely than others to react with anxiety. And although we usually don't use the term trait to refer to stable environmental structures, it is perfectly consistent and appropriate to think of these structures as environmental traits that dispose us to respond emotionally. For example, an environment whose demands tax or exceed a person's coping resources is likely to result in threat or thwarting and, therefore, depending on the particular conditions, it increases the probability of one or another of the so-called negative or stress emotions, such as anger, anxiety, guilt, or sadness.

Temperament

The distinction I have been making between emotion state and trait applies also to the concept of *temperament*. The definition given by Campos, Barrett, Lamb, Goldsmith, and Stenberg (1983), for example, which overlaps heavily with an earlier one by Allport (1937), emphasizes individual differences in the intensive and temporal parameters of behavioral regulation, expression of arousal, and emotionality, and the way these individual differences influence intrapersonal and interpersonal processes (see also Derryberry & Rothbart, 1984, for an overlapping but distinctive approach).

Although temperament has been defined in a number of different ways, it is usually treated as a trait or dispositional concept. I am familiar with no influential approach to temperament that does not treat it basically as a set of dispositional properties or *traits* that are either inherited, learned, or a product of both; all center on consistent individual differences largely, but not exclusively, in variables of emotionality. Emotions and emotionality are, presumably, influenced by temperament, which is what makes temperament a trait or disposition.

Although a viable theory of how temperament might actually influence emotional development is still lacking, temperament is an early-appearing disposition of neonates that makes a difference in how the emotional life, in general, is structured, and how a child responds in specific interactions with its environment.

However, herein lies a problem. Concern with how a temperamental trait, once established, influences emotional development obscures a question that should suggest itself prior to this one—namely, how temperament itself develops. To what extent is it inherited? A product of intrauterine and neonatal social experience? The interaction of both? Evidence on this complex question is still limited. Nevertheless, the question invites us to think of early manifestations of temperament as states with their own causal antecedents. Although ultimately they may become established as traits, high stability in these manifestations implies a marked and important trait; low stability implies a state whose manifestations depend on the presence or absence of evanescent causal antecedents.

Relational Meaning

Whether an emotion is recurrent (trait) or evanescent (state), it is the *relationship* between the person and the environment, rather than separate personality or environmental variables, that permits a full analysis of the emotion process. An emotion is the result not solely of a personality trait (e.g., a goal or a belief) or a property of the environment (e.g., an external demand, constraint, or resource), but depends on a functional *conjunction* between both.

The way this works is that personality traits, such as an individual goal hierarchy in which some goals are more important than others, make some environmental circumstances salient for that individual in the emotion-generating process. For that individual, too, other environmental circumstances are less salient and hence less likely to generate that emotion. Thus, a person with a strong desire to achieve does not react with one of the stress emotions, such as anger, anxiety, or sadness, unless also confronted with an environment that threatens or thwarts that desire. And an environment that makes achievement difficult or impossible will not generate stress emotions in a person for whom achievement is of no importance.

Furthermore, to some extent people select, or find themselves confronting again and again, an environmental context that is salient for their goals and beliefs, thereby recurrently making that environmental context an emotional one. Likewise, to some extent people confront diverse and changing conditions that are sometimes salient but at other times not, thereby leading to emotional states that vary from occasion to occasion. To understand and predict emotions programmatically, we always need to study the *conjunction* of personality traits *and* environmental traits.

Therefore, it is careless usage to speak of emotion traits as properties of persons—although they are to some extent—since emotions, whether recurrent or not, always depend on the conjunction of particular personality traits, such as goal patterns or beliefs, with particular environmental properties whose emotion-generating capacities are defined by and depend on these personality traits.

From the point of view of a cognitive-motivational-relational theory, I would add that what accounts for an emotion trait is a *relational meaning* that is based on an *appraisal* of recurrent, functional conjunctions between relevant variables of the person and environment. The relational meaning derived from these conjunctions does not arise from either a person or environmental variable alone, but depends on both. Thus, anger could be said to involve the relational meaning of an unwarranted offense against me and mine, anxiety an existential threat, guilt having acted against a moral standard, and sadness having experienced an irrevocable loss, to suggest some examples of the relational meanings (or core relational themes, as I have elsewhere referred to them; Lazarus, 1991a, 1991b, 1991c), which underlie different emotions.

Acute Emotions Versus Moods

Now to a more difficult problem, involving strong definitional traditions, but about which I believe a cognitive-motivational-relational theory of the emotions has something distinctive to offer. I use the term "acute emotions" to refer to usually brief emotional phenomena that arise in particular adaptational encounters with the environment. This differentiates these states from the other kind of emotional responses that we call moods which, as I shall elaborate shortly, operate as background states based on existential, lifespan issues rather than as figural adaptational encounters.

How are we to distinguish an acute emotion from a mood? Without a theory of the emotion process, we are left with an inadequate basis for making the distinction, one that depends on the peripheral response characteristics or "feel" of the emotion. Is happiness an acute emotion or a mood? How about sadness? One answer might be that sometimes they are one and sometimes the other.

The most common basis of the distinction between acute emotions and moods is to treat moods as traits or dispositions and acute emotions as states. Since a mood has consequences for subsequent thought and action, it is tempting to think of it in that sense as a trait. For example, being in an irritable mood disposes one to become angry or distraught more readily than being in some other mood; being in a sad mood disposes one more readily than otherwise to react to neutral or even positive events misanthropically; being in a happy mood disposes one more readily than otherwise to overlook negative events. Perhaps the same could be said about an acute emotion too—though this has not been the subject of much research in contrast with moods—but this voids the basis of the trait-state distinction.

Consistent with the idea of mood as a dispositional variable is the idea that a mood is experienced over longer time spans than acute emotions, which typically are extremely brief (cf. Ekman, 1984). Duration has become one of the traditional response criteria for distinguishing moods from acute emotions. It is often true that moods are more enduring than acute emotions; however, some moods seem to be relatively brief, which should make us wary of centering on duration as an essential defining attribute. Although it may be the predominant emotional outlook of a particular period, we are not always in a given mood; the mood state may seem to come and go, depending on what else we are doing and thinking. Similarly, we may react with acute anger, which doesn't last long as we turn our attention to other issues, yet because the issue that generated the anger has not been resolved, it remains latent and recurs shortly, perhaps again and again. Therefore, both acute emotions and moods may be better described as latent or recurrent rather than as chronic.

Thus, when a couple has an argument one morning, which is marked by intense and mutual verbal expressions of anger, the anger tends to disappear as the two go off to work and attend to the demands of their jobs. However, when they come home from work that evening it may return, though perhaps in different form, with verbal attack giving way to coldness and sulking. Although the emotional pattern seems to have an on-off quality, it remains a latent property of the relationship until the conflict and hurt are somehow resolved. The same could be said about moods.

So it seems to me that duration of a response state is not a good basis for making a distinction between acute emotions and moods. As an inconsistent and superficial feature of the response, it is not essential to distinguish between acute emotions and moods. We are also apt to be more aware of a mood when we are not, perforce, engaged in situationally focused adaptational struggles.

There is also an important logical danger in treating moods in trait or dispositional terms. Although some people are more disposed to be melancholy or cheerful than others, most of us can experience both kinds of mood. It is simplistic and possibly misleading to say that moods are like a personality trait, whereas acute emotions are situationally generated. To put this differently, when we speak of a person as in an irritable or hostile mood, this does not necessarily refer to a personality trait but rather to a disposition to react negatively to whatever happens, which applies only during the presence of this mood.

Therefore, we should distinguish between two kinds of dispositional concepts, a *personality* disposition and a *temporal* or *contextual* disposition. Both have causal significance for subsequent states of mind, but consist of different kinds of variables that work in different ways. A mood should always be regarded first as a response state, even though, as such, it also disposes the person to react in specifiable emotional ways to adaptational encounters. The primary question is always how the mood state is brought about—that is, what is it about the person and the environmental context (the person-environment relationship) that has generated it. How it influences subsequent emotional reactions is important but secondary, and treating moods as traits or dispositions obscures the emotion process unless we make the distinction between the two kinds of dispositions.

I think the *fundamental difference* between acute emotions and moods depends on the motivational and cognitive conditions that shape the appraisals bringing each about. Although acute emotions and moods are both brought about by the way one appraises ongoing relationships with the environment, what is being appraised in each case is quite different. Acute emotions refer to the immediate adaptational business in an encounter with the environment, the fate of a specific and narrow goal that confronts a beneficial or harmful (or threatening) environmental condition. Elsewhere (Lazarus, 1991a, 1991b, 1991c), I have referred to this as the motivational principle, which defines what is important or unimportant to the person and, therefore, provides the stakes on which harm or benefit is based and gives the encounter its emotional potential.

This is why acute emotions tend to be brief compared with moods, though I would not make this response feature a definitional criterion. When the specific adaptational encounter ends, especially when the goal-centered issue is resolved, so usually does the emotion. Acute emotions operate as *figural* adaptational events or transactions in our lives to which we must direct our attention. If we want to go to graduate school and be successful professionally, we need first to confront numerous specific encounters, such as exams or other public performances the results of which influence whether our long-range, more existential goal agendas can be realized.

Moods, on the other hand, are products of appraisals of the *existential background* of our lives. This background has to do with who we are, now and in the long run, and how we are doing in life overall. Although, if pressed, we might try to explain a mood by pointing to a specific event, when we are in a mood we rarely pin it down to anything specific, which is why moods are so vague and pervasive. However, the events we can legitimately point to in explaining a mood are apt to be profound in that they have major existential implications, such as the death of a loved one, loss of occupational roles, an assault on cherished lifelong beliefs, a life-threatening or disabling illness, and the like.

When our mood is negative, it is not because a particular encounter has gone wrong but because life overall seems sour, which could be a partial result of that encounter; we denigrate ourselves and others, the world, the meanings on which our sense of self depend, our loved ones, our future, and we live out the scenario of the "theater of the absurd," which treats human existence as meaningless and ridiculous, as in Becket's *Waiting for Godot*, or Ionesco's *Rhinoceros*. Figural positive events seem unable to affect us. On the other hand, when our mood is positive, it is because life seems good; our loved ones love and respect us, the world is just, the meanings on which we depend are reaffirmed, and our immediate and existential problems recede. Figural negative events seem unable to affect us.

A major assumption underlying what I have said here is that, in trying to define emotion, the task of discriminating among some emotion concepts is difficult, ambiguous, and sometimes daunting when it is addressed on the basis solely of descriptions of the peripheral response state. Making useful and internally consistent distinctions is facilitated by attention to the central emotion process of mind, especially the relational meaning that underlies each emotion which, in turn, depends on how the person construes and evaluates what is happening, with its implications for personal well-being.

Basic Emotions Ramify Widely in the Brain, Yielding Many Concepts That Cannot Be Distinguished Unambiguously . . . Yet

JAAK PANKSEPP

There is no well-anchored, nonstipulative way to distinguish among these concepts. But it is useful to consider various options, for conceptual exercises may eventually lead to objective analyses. One useful general way to distinguish emotions from moods is to suggest that emotions reflect the intense arousal of brain systems that strongly encourage organisms to act impulsively, while moods reflect milder and more sustained arousal of affective systems that tend to encourage organisms to remain more "reflective." But such distinctions do not lead to obvious empirical endpoints in the brain research laboratory. Accordingly, I prefer to view these concepts in terms of the different types of brain processes that may distinguish them. As outlined in my response to Question 1, emotions may consist of precipitous arousal of specific types of brain operating systems. These systems can interact with each other as well as with many other brain systems, and many concepts may be needed to describe these interactions. Emotional systems can presumably be tonically activated at low levels by a variety of comparatively weak perceptual inputs as well as internal stimuli, ranging from modes of thought to internal metabolic states. Thus, I would consider an optimal working definition of "mood" to be a low tonic level of arousal within emotional operating systems, while "emotions" reflect precipitous arousal in these same systems. High arousal of emotional systems will tend to inhibit other emotional systems (Panksepp, 1982, Figure 2, p. 412), while mild arousal may permit several systems to be concurrently active, leading to the possibility of a vast panoply of mood states compared to the limited number of basic emotional states. It has often been said that a few emotional systems could hardly explain the vast subtlety of human moods and feelings. I believe this is a misplaced argument. Had molecular biologists been fooled by comparable assertions, they may never have attempted to seek an explanation for the vast diversity of life in the permutations of the four nucleotides in DNA.

The synaptic subtleties and fluctuating neuroelectric patterns within the underlying basic command systems for emotions can surely yield more semantic distinctions (and perhaps distinct moods) than are useful in understanding the general organization of the primary emotional systems. As a simple mathematical exercise, if one had four innate emotional systems in the brain that could subsist in all on-off permutations (an unrealistic assumption for sure!), one could generate a minimum of 24 distinct concepts (4 factorial) to describe the possible combinatorial states of the systems. If one adds several additional attributes, such as overall intensity, time courses of activity, and level of interaction within the systems, one could generate thousands of permutations. If there are at least 8 basic systems as most theorists, including myself, believe (Panksepp, 1989, 1991, 1992, 1993), then the number of permutations increases to millions. If one adds the likelihood that multiple unconditional and multiple cognitive inputs can converge on each system, the possible permutations increase to billions, and if one adds the full range of presumable non-"emotional" affective feelings such as hunger, thirst, tiredness, and so forth, to the combinatorial brew, the permutations become incalculable. Faced with these mind-boggling numbers, it is wonderous that semantic regularities reflective of major types of emotional experience can be so readily abstracted from the jungle of possible permutations. However, I suspect that without neurological anchor-points for major concepts, the field may continue to be hampered by the splitting of semantic hairs. Objective measures of moods will be difficult to formulate until we know much more about the neural nature of the emotional primes (Panksepp, 1993). Also, if moods are reflected largely by internal feeling states instead of explicit behaviors, then animal models will not be very useful until credible electrophysiological and neurochemical indices of such states are developed. Such indices could be validated by measuring bodily changes during sustained low-level activation of specific emotional circuits in animals. Until such understanding is achieved, human subjective reports, and correlated autonomic, postural, and facial expressions, will remain the main indices of moods for a long time to come.

The concept of "temperament" must obviously be related to long-term emotional traits of an individual, and mechanistically it may be related to specific types of neurobiological interactions that can occur between emotional systems and other neural systems with which they communicate. Temperaments may also be usefully viewed as the types of habitual interactions between cognitive and emotional systems that an individual is prone to exhibit. Not only do emotional systems interact unconditionally with brain mechanisms that elaborate thoughts (Beagley & Holley, 1977; Roberts, 1980), thoughts can evoke and sustain emotions and mood states (presumably via unknown emotion-specific reinforcement processes that help solidify specific thinking patterns). Thus, the concept of temperament may subsume both the unconditional cognitive inputs (evolutionarily prepared perceptions, such as facial and bodily action patterns) and the conditional ones that come to have strong interactions with the basic emotional systems through learning. In short, the concept of temperament is presumably closely related to emotional personality traits of an individual, whether they be learned or unlearned. Of course, these will remain difficult concepts for neuroscientifically oriented investigators for a long time.

However, even in animal research, pursuit of such concepts may not be hopeless. Different species do exhibit different emotional strengths and weaknesses. Predators exhibit curiosity and predatory and aggressive emotions more than herbivores. Herbivores, on the other hand, are more likely to exhibit fear, timidity, and panic. These are probably genetically imposed temperamental traits, which can vary as a function of the life cycle of an animal. For instance, Shapiro and Insel (1990) have found marked brain oxytocin receptor differences between highly social prairie voles and seclusive montane voles. However, during the time of life when they temporarily become more social (i.e., during motherhood), the oxytocin receptor patterns of the montane vole begin to resemble the pattern of the highly social prairie vole (see Insel, 1992).

Many chronic emotional tendencies clearly have strong heritability components, and this has been repeatedly affirmed by genetic selection experiments. For instance, selective breeding for fearful reactivity is successful within three generations (Broadhurst, 1975), as is selection for aggression (Hyde & Sawyer, 1979; Maxson, Shrenker, & Vigue, 1983) and many other behavioral traits (Fuller & Thompson, 1978), including selections for specific circuit functions such as those that sustain self-stimulation in the brain (Moreau, Cohen, & Lieblich, 1984). These studies may well have selected for differential activities of certain brain neurochemical systems, but we typically do not know what brain systems were intensified or weakened. However, selection for specific brain chemical parameters, such as high acetylcholine levels, can yield animals with different temperaments and cognitive abilities (Will, 1977). Although the bleak violent history of the twentieth century makes us reluctant to generalize such concepts to the human level, we have to face the fact that neurochemical strengths and weaknesses do dictate human temperamental tendencies (Depue & Spoont, 1987; Zuckerman, 1984). What we do with such a fact is a separate matter. Even culturologists have recently toyed with the idea that different national groups have defining temperamental traits (Gachev, 1987), and, if they do, we should not be loathe to believe that these could be caused as readily by distinct neurochemical attributes as by acquired attitudes.

Emotions, Moods, Traits, and Temperaments: Conceptual Distinctions and Empirical Findings

DAVID WATSON
LEE ANNA CLARK

Emotion Versus Mood

To many people, an *emotion* is a strong, highly valenced feeling state. For instance, if asked to characterize the emotion of anger, many individuals would simply describe feelings of rage and resentment. Such feelings are an important aspect of emotions, but they cannot be equated with emotions themselves, which we can define as distinct, integrated psychophysiological response systems. Even this more complete definition does not do full justice to the complex phenomena of emotions, for, in essence, an emotion represents an organized, highly structured reaction to an event that is relevant to the needs, goals, or survival of the organism.

An emotion contains three differentiable components: (1) a prototypic form of expression (typically facial), (2) a pattern of consistent autonomic changes, and (3) a distinct subjective feeling state (Izard, 1977). For instance, the emotion of fear is characterized by a distinctive facial expression in which the eyebrows are raised and drawn together, the eyes are opened widely, the lower lip is tensed, and the lips are stretched back (Ekman & Friesen, 1975). At the same time, fear is also associated with marked autonomic changes, including rapid increases in heart rate and skin conductance (Ekman, Levenson, & Friesen, 1983). Finally, consistent with the commonsensical view noted earlier, fear involves a characteristic experiential state in which the individual feels scared, frightened, nervous, and apprehensive (Izard, 1977; Watson & Clark, 1992a).

In addition to these three components, other characteristics also help to define an emotion. Most notably, each emotion represents a response to specific types of events, and each gives rise to characteristic forms of adaptive behavior. For instance, fear is a reaction to situations of perceived risk or danger and motivates various behaviors (e.g., flight) that are designed to eliminate that danger. Moreover, because emotions are reactions to specific circumstances, they are typically quite shortlived in their full form, lasting only a few seconds or perhaps minutes.

In contrast, the concept of *mood* is much closer to the commonsensical view of emotion described earlier. That is, we can broadly define a mood as a transient episode of feeling or affect. As such, moods are highly similar to the subjective component of emotions. One important difference, however, is that moods typically are much longer in duration. For instance, whereas the full emotion of anger may last for only a few seconds or minutes, an annoyed or irritable mood may last for several hours or even for a few days.

More fundamentally, it would be a mistake to equate moods simply with the feeling component of emotions because the concept of mood is much broader; that is, mood states are not restricted to those feelings that accompany specific emotions. In fact, distinct emotions account for a relatively small percentage of the mood states that an individual experiences. The average person has approximately 1000 waking minutes each day. On a typical day, how many of these minutes are spent in states that clearly correspond to classic emotions such as fear, anger, or joy? Available data offer no definitive answer to this question, but our own extensive analyses of momentary and daily mood (e.g., Clark, Watson, & Leeka, 1989; Watson, 1988a) suggest that the bulk of waking life is spent in nonemotional states.

However, this does not mean that most of daily life is devoid of important or meaningful feelings. On the contrary, waking consciousness is experienced as a continuous *stream of affect*, such that people are always experiencing some type of mood. Much of the time they may be experiencing milder, attenuated versions of the classic emotions: For instance, they may be feeling annoyed or irritated, rather than the full-blown emotion of anger; or they may be in a pleasant, cheerful state that does not fully conform to the emotion of joy. On many occasions, people experience mixed states that represent complex combinations of basic emotions. For example, when beginning a new relationship, a person may experience mixed feelings of joy, excitement, and fear. At other times, a person may be feeling nostalgic, a mixed state that combines elements of joy and sadness. Finally, people frequently experience low-activation states that generally signal the absence of any strong emotion. For instance, they may report feeling tired or sluggish (an unpleasant state that we call fatigue; see Watson & Clark, 1991), or calm and relaxed (the pleasant mood state of serenity; see Watson & Clark, 1992a).

The basic emotions are enormously important in a number of areas, and no complete psychological treatment can ignore them or their implications. Nevertheless, we believe that an approach that emphasizes distinct emotions fails to capture the essential nature of everyday, ongoing affective experience. As we have argued, individuals are always feeling something, but are only infrequently experiencing a full, distinct emotion. How, then, can we capture this stream of affect more accurately? Building on the seminal studies of Tellegen (1985), our own research has demonstrated the value of an alternative structural approach that focuses on two very broad mood factors—Negative Affect and Positive Affect—rather than distinct types of emotions (Watson, 1988b; Watson, Clark, & Tellegen, 1988; Watson & Tellegen,

1985). In brief, Negative Affect represents the extent to which an individual is currently upset or distressed. Persons experiencing high Negative Affect typically would report various negative mood states, including feelings of nervousness, dissatisfaction, discouragement, and irritability; conversely, individuals experiencing low levels of Negative Affect would describe themselves as calm and relaxed. Incidentally, the fact that individuals simultaneously report a broad array of negative mood states—including those related to different basic affects, such as fear, anger, and sadness—is further evidence that specific emotions are not well distinguished in everyday life (see Watson & Clark, 1992a).

In contrast, Positive Affect reflects one's current level of pleasure and enthusiasm. Individuals in a state of high Positive Affect typically experience a broad range of positive mood states, including feelings of cheerfulness, excitement, energy, alertness, self-confidence, and so on. Conversely, persons experiencing low levels of Positive Affect typically report feeling sluggish, unenergetic, and disinterested in their environment. Again, the fact that individuals concomitantly report various types of positive feelings indicates that these feelings are not clearly distinguished from one another in normal, ongoing daily life.

This initial description might suggest that these two mood factors are polar opposites and that they are, therefore, mutually exclusive. That is, it might seem that someone who is experiencing high levels of Negative Affect must necessarily be experiencing low levels of Positive Affect, and vice versa. This is true in a limited sense, confined to extremely high levels of affect. Individuals experiencing very high levels of Negative Affect usually report low levels of Positive Affect; conversely, states of very high Positive Affect are largely incompatible with substantially elevated Negative Affect (Diener & Iran-Nejad, 1986; Watson, 1988b). A notable exception to this rule is when the negative affective state (usually fear) is sought out and anticipated, as when one rides a roller coaster or watches a horror movie with enthusiasm and excitement.

At more moderate levels of affect—which constitute the bulk of normal everyday experience—these two mood factors are largely independent of one another (Diener & Iran-Nejad, 1986; Watson, 1988b). For instance, individuals who are currently experiencing low Negative Affect (i.e., they are feeling calm and relaxed) are not necessarily feeling happy or enthusiastic; in fact, they may fall anywhere on the continuum ranging from low to high Positive Affect. Conversely, persons experiencing relatively low levels of Positive Affect (i.e., they are feeling sluggish and disinterested) are not necessarily upset, fearful, or angry. Thus, at any given point in time, we can characterize mood in terms of both Negative and Positive Affect. Accordingly, a complete consideration of mood requires that we examine both these general factors.

Trait Affect and Temperament

Thus far, we have discussed only transient affective episodes, what traditionally has been called "state affect" (e.g., Cattell & Scheier, 1961). However, it is also necessary to consider consistent, long-term individual differences in affective experience—that is, what has often been termed "trait affect," or what we will here call *emotional traits*. Emotional traits can be defined simply as stable individual differences in the tendency to experience a corresponding mood state. For instance, an individual who is high in the trait of fearfulness is prone to more frequent or more intense episodes of fear. Conversely, an individual who is low in the trait of fearfulness will experience less frequent or less intense states of fear.

Consistent with our earlier discussion, we believe that the two most important emotional traits are the dispositional counterparts of Negative and Positive Affect. Extensive evidence indicates that both these mood factors have a strong dispositional component, such that individuals exhibit broad and consistent differences in their tendency to experience them. This evidence is of two basic types. First, scores on both Negative and Positive Affect are strongly stable over time (e.g., Diener & Larsen, 1984; Ormel & Schaufeli, 1991; Watson & Slack, 1993). For example, Watson and Slack (1993) retested an adult sample over an average time span of 27 months. Trait scores on Positive Affect (r = .74) and Negative Affect (r = .63) were both strongly stable over this retest interval. Even more striking are the results of Ormel and Schaufeli (1991) who retested Negative Affect levels across time intervals of 7 and 8 years; both analyses revealed impressive stability (*rs* = .57 and .52, respectively). Thus, individuals differ widely in their characteristic tendency to experience both Negative and Positive Affect, and these differences persist over time.

Second, individual differences in affect are consistent across various life situations (e.g., Diener & Larsen, 1984; Watson & Clark, 1984). For instance, Diener and Larsen (1984) reported strong correlations between mean affect scores assessed during socializing and corresponding values obtained when the subjects were alone (*rs* = .70 for Negative Affect, .58 for Positive Affect). Similarly, they found that mean affect scores were strongly correlated across work versus recreational settings (*rs* = .74 for Negative Affect, .70 for Positive Affect). Clearly, these marked dispositional differences are crucially important in understanding the affective experiences of individuals.

What, then, is the difference between these emotional traits and *temperament*? In our view, these constructs differ in two basic ways. First, positing the existence of an emotional trait simply acknowledges that stable individual differences in emotional experience exist, but makes no assumption regarding *why* they exist—that is, what is the nature and origins of these traits? Accordingly, these broad and stable differences may arise from hereditary influences, environmental factors, or some combination of the two. In contrast, the concept of temperament clearly implies that these observed individual differences are at least partly heritable, and that they are—to some extent—already present at birth (e.g., Buss & Plomin, 1984).

Second, we believe that temperaments emerge as broader, more general dispositional constructs that subsume various emotional traits, along with other associated cognitive and behavioral characteristics. Thus, trait differences in Negative and Positive Affect each represent central, core components of still more general dimensions of temperament. Specifically, trait Negative Affect is a centrally defining feature of a personality dimension that is usually called "Neuroticism" or "Negative Affectivity" (see McCrae & Costa, 1987; Watson & Clark, 1984, 1992b). Individuals who are high in Neuroticism are prone to experience a diverse array of negative mood states, including frequent episodes of anxiety, depression, and hostility. In addition to this marked affective distress, however, high levels of Neuroticism are also associated with various other cognitive and perceptual characteristics. For instance, high scorers on this dimension tend to be somewhat introspective and ruminative; perhaps as a result, they are prone to various types of psychosomatic complaints. They also have a negativistic cognitive/explanatory style, and focus differentially on negative aspects of themselves, other people, and the world in general. Consequently, they have a less favorable self-view and tend to be highly dissatisfied. Finally, they report relatively high levels of both chronic and transient stress, and appear to cope poorly with this stress. In contrast, individuals who are low in Neuroticism tend to be content, secure, and self-satisfied, and to report relatively low levels of both physical and psychological problems (McCrae & Costa, 1987; Watson & Clark, 1984; Watson & Pennebaker, 1989).

Trait differences in Positive Affect are, in turn, a core component of the broad personality dimension of Extraversion or Positive Affectivity (McCrae & Costa, 1987; Watson & Clark, 1992b). Thus, extraverts tend to experience strong levels of positive mood; they characterize themselves as cheerful, optimistic, and enthusiastic, and report that their lives are full and interesting. Introverts, in contrast, experience relatively low levels of Positive Affect. Beyond this positive affective core, however, Extraversion also has broad social/interpersonal implications. That is, extraverts are gregarious, friendly, assertive, and socially facile, whereas introverts tend to be reserved, retiring, and somewhat aloof. Finally, extraversion may be related to various other characteristics, such as the tendency to seek intense, highly stimulating experiences (McCrae & Costa, 1987).

Consistent with our definition of temperament, Neuroticism/Negative Affectivity and Extraversion/Positive Affectivity are both strongly heritable. For instance, Tellegen and his associates (1988) investigated over 400 pairs of identical and fraternal twins, reared either together or apart. Approximately 55 percent of the variance on Neuroticism/Negative Affectivity could be attributed to genetic factors, compared to only 2 percent for the shared familial environment. Similarly, 40 percent of the variance on Extraversion/Positive Affectivity was estimated to be heritable, compared with 22 percent attributable to shared family experiences. Other studies have reported very similar findings (e.g., Fulker, 1981).

What factors are responsible for these broad and heritable differences in temperament? Tellegen (1985) has proposed that Neuroticism/Negative Affectivity and Extraversion/Positive Affectivity reflect differential sensitivities to signals of punishment and reward, respectively. In Tellegen's view, the core affective traits do not simply reflect differing life experiences; that is, individuals high in Neuroticism do not experience greater Negative Affect simply because they are subjected to higher levels of life stress, and extraverts do not report greater Positive Affect solely because of their increased frequency of socializing. Rather, these two dimensions of temperament, at least in part, reflect systematic differences in how individuals respond to the same life circumstances. Thus, those who are high in Neuroticism are unusually sensitive to stimuli that generate Negative Affect; conversely, extraverts have an increased readiness to respond with pleasure to the events and experiences of their lives. Tellegen's formulation offers a good working model for understanding these two temperaments, and it is noteworthy that corroborating evidence has recently been reported by Larsen and Ketelaar (1991).

Afterword:
How Are Emotions Distinguished from Moods, Temperament, and Other Related Affective Constructs?

RICHARD J. DAVIDSON
PAUL EKMAN

All the contributors to this question make a distinction between emotion and mood. Although these terms are often used interchangeably by laypeople, most researchers interested in affect insist on distinguishing between them. The criteria that are highlighted as most important in this distinction differ across investigators, however.

Some contributors have underscored the importance of duration as a criterion. For both Ekman and Kagan, duration is an important feature that distinguishes between these two related constructs. Lazarus questions whether moods are always much longer than emotions, and proposes that both are recurrent. Both Ekman and Kagan draw other distinctions as well between moods and emotions; Ekman focuses on differences in antecedent events and Kagan on the different biological processes involved.

A number of theorists have commented on the relation between mood and emotion as a way of differentiating between them. Thus, for Ekman and Panksepp, moods alter the threshold for the elicitation of particular emotions. Emotions, in turn, may facilitate the development of particular moods. Panksepp suggests the interesting possibility that high arousal of an emotion system will inhibit other emotions occurring at the same time, but moods that involve lower levels of arousal may allow a panoply of moods to be experienced simultaneously.

Frijda takes quite a different stance, suggesting that every emotion tends to prolong itself in a mood, while Watson and Clark propose that we are always in a mood state, albeit not necessarily a very strong one, and therefore emotions always occur in the context of a mood. Watson and Clark argue against considering moods in terms of the more specific states such as apprehensiveness or irritability and, instead, put all negative moods into one category and all positive states into another independent mood.

Ekman also uses facial expression to distinguish between emotion and mood. According to Ekman, emotion is often associated with a unique facial expression, while mood itself has no visible facial expression. Ekman offers the interesting speculation that nonvisible patterns of facial muscle tonus (assessed with electromyography) may reflect differences in mood.

A number of theorists have commented on the differences in antecedents of emotions and moods. Ekman has noted that antecedents of emotion are typically more accessible to consciousness, and he proposes that moods may be brought about either by highly dense emotional episodes or autonomous changes in neurochemistry. Frijda introduces the distinction between intentional and nonintentional affective states. Emotions are intentional—they always have an object. Moods are nonintentional in the sense of not being object related. Thus, one is angry at someone or something, but one is nonspecifically irritable. Lazarus endorses a similar distinction when he suggests that emotions refer to the immediate adaptational business in an encounter with the environment, while moods are products of appraisals of the "existential background of our lives." Lazarus explains that when our mood is negative "it is not because a particular encounter has gone wrong but because life overall seems sour."

Some commentators have underscored the importance of the differential consequences of emotions and moods. Davidson argues that emotions bias action, while moods bias cognition. Consistent with this formulation is Frijda's idea that moods produce generalized cognitive consequences—for example, nonspecific changes in judgments (e.g., of life satisfaction)—while emotions alter action readiness.

Different authors have also introduced a number of other affect-related constructs including affective style, temperament, sentiments, emotional traits, and personality dispositions. Davidson has proposed that the term affective style be used as a supraordinate term to include all other constructs that refer to dispositional or traitlike constructs. Included among them would be temperament, sentiment, emotional trait, and certain personality traits that have an affective core, such as extroversion.

Temperament was considered by many of the contributors, and all agree that it refers to early dispositional differences that are associated with emotional reactivity. Most explicit with such a definition is Goldsmith who proposes that temperamental traits are "characteristic individual differences in the way basic emotions are experienced and expressed." Most contributors also agree that temperament is, at least in part, under genetic control, although Goldsmith cautions that we should not incorporate etiology as part of the definition of a concept that is otherwise understood at the behavioral level. Kagan reminds us that the meaning of a construct is a function of the procedures that we use to measure it, and that the term "anxiety," for example, may mean very different things depending on the context and how it is measured. "Temperamental anxiety" is a form of anxiety that implies origins in early development and suggests a distinctive physiology, according to Kagan. Whatever the distal cause, the existence of a temperamental quality invites analysis of the underlying biological mechanisms that give rise to such individual differences. Kagan speculates that in the case of "temperamental anxiety" or behavioral inhibition, the underlying biological predisposition is a difference in the threshold of excitability for an amygdala-based circuit. Watson and Clark explain that temperament is a broader concept than emotional trait, since temperament includes nonaffective components.

In particular, they suggest that in addition to referring to differences in affective reactivity, temperament also includes associated cognitive and behavioral characteristics.

Both Frijda and Lazarus introduce the term sentiment and both explain the construct in the same way. Sentiments are affective dispositions to particular objects or kinds of events. For example, "I hate pit bull terriers" or "I love to ski" are examples of affective dispositions. Sentiments differ from both moods and emotions in referring to phenomena that are nonoccurrent. They refer to emotional changes that may be evoked with exposure to the critical object or event.

Emotional trait is a term introduced by Watson and Clark. It refers to broad mood qualities, such as positive affect (PA) and negative affect (NA) that are stable over time. These theorists note that PA and NA overlap with temperament since they are heritable. These broad emotional traits are represented in subjective experience and account for much more of the variance in self-reported affect than basic emotions.

Personality dispositions are related to affective traits. Many personality traits, such as extroversion and neuroticism, include a significant affective core. Frijda notes that personality traits are the dispositional equivalent of moods in that they are nonobject related or nonintentional, unlike emotions and sentiments, which are focused on specific objects.

Question 3

What Is the Function of Emotions?

Emotions Are Many Splendored Things

JAMES R. AVERILL

Questions about function are among the most important we can ask. Emotions do not simply occur; they occur for reasons. Nevertheless, functional explanations have a bad reputation. They smack of "final causes"—those seemingly ghostly entities from the future that somehow haunt the past. But that back from the future scenario represents a misconception. Final causes are not causes in the ordinary (Humean) sense. Stated most simply, a functional explanation specifies the consequences a response is "designed" to achieve within a relevant environment. Such consequences are empirically verifiable, although often obscure to casual observation.

To take an everyday example, I go to the dentist to get a tooth extracted. Having my tooth extracted is the consequence that my behavior was designed (or intended) to achieve, and in respect to which my behavior could be considered functional. (When speaking of human purposeful behavior, we can substitute "intended" for "designed.") The design of a response need not be conscious or voluntary, as in this example, but can be a result of biological evolution, social custom, or well-ingrained habits unique to the individual.

In theory, then, functional explanations are innocent enough; in practice, unfortunately, their bad reputation is often deserved. With sufficient ingenuity, it is possible to invent a rationale for almost any consequence. Functional explanations, therefore, often say more about the inventiveness of the investigator than about the nature of the behavior under investigation.

From the One to the Many

One impediment to functional explanations of emotion is the assumption, more often implicit than acknowledged, that all emotions may have the same function. (Note that the question we are presently addressing—What is the function of emotions?—carries this implication.) I have stated that a functional explanation specifies the consequences that a response is "designed" to achieve within a relevant environment. The consequences of a response, however, can be many and varied. At the minimum, distinctions must be made between (1) intended and unintended consequences; (2) short-term and long-term consequences; (3) singular and average or predictable consequences; and (4) individual and group (biological and social) consequences.

Intended Versus Unintended Consequences

Not all consequences are functional. Returning to the example of visiting the dentist, one consequence of having a tooth extracted is the experience of pain. That, however, is not what the behavior was designed (intended) to achieve. The distinction between intended and unintended consequences is not always as easy to make as this example might suggest. It has been postulated, for example, that "emotions function to rearrange the priorities of goals" (Oatley & Jenkins, 1992, p. 60). Most emotional episodes do, in fact, involve a change in priorities, but is that their function or simply an unintended consequence? To make the question more specific, is the function of fear to shift goals or to escape danger?

Short-term Versus Long-term Consequences

Behavior that is functional in the short term may be nonfunctional or even dysfunctional in the long term, and vice versa. Thus, an outburst of anger may get me what I want now, but at the cost of my long-term relationship with the target. Conversely, an immediate result of anger may be negative (resistance and confrontation on the part of the target); nevertheless, the long-term consequences may—and often do—prove beneficial, for example, by preventing a recurrence of the instigating circumstances (Averill, 1982).

Singular Versus Average or Predictable Consequences

Much speculation about the functions of emotions has focused on singular or dramatic episodes. For example, when anger is manifested in physical aggression, the results are often dramatic—and dysfunctional. However, the typical episode of anger is not particularly aggressive, and it is the typical not the extreme episodes that determine whatever function anger might have (Averill, 1982).

Individual Versus Group Consequences

As discussed earlier in response to Question 1, an emotion may be functional for the individual (psychological consequences), the species (biological consequences), and the society (social consequences). While these three types of consequences may be mutually reinforcing, that is not always the case. What is good for the individual is not necessarily good for the group (species or society); and on the group level, biological and social ends are frequently in conflict. An emotion may thus be both functional and dysfunctional at the same time, depending on whether one takes the perspective of the individual, the species, or the society (Averill, 1990b).

Typically, when theorists speak of the function of emotions they have in mind the consequences that emotions might have for the survival of the species. However, there is no reason to give biological criteria priority in this regard (cf. my response to Question 1). Psychological and social factors can be just as important (and in many cases may be more important) than biology in the determining the "design" of emotional syndromes.

Consequences Are Only the Beginning

Having considered some of the ways that emotional consequences might be functional, let us put those issues aside for the moment. Even if we were to limit consideration to one type of outcome (e.g., short-term, average, biological consequences), our problems are just beginning. Emotions represent a heterogenous category. To ask whether all emotions serve the same function is like asking whether all thoughts serve the same function. The question is simply too broad to allow a meaningful answer. Each emotion must be analyzed in its own right. Only by completely ignoring context can we speak of love, say, as serving the same function as fear or anger.

And what is true of emotion as a general category is also true *mutatis mutandis* of specific emotions. Emotions are not unitary phenomena. They comprise diverse reactions ("part-emotions," if you will), and functions may vary depending on the aspect of the emotion under consideration. Grief provides an extreme but instructive example (Averill, 1979; Averill & Nunley, 1988). Grief typically proceeds in stages over many months. The initial grief reactions—the agitated searching and yearning for the lost object—represent biologically based responses to separation. Quite similar reactions have been observed in a variety of species in which social living is a basic adaptation. Since most separations are temporary, these initial responses are typically effective in promoting reunion. However, if reunion is impossible because of the death of the other, certain other responses may ensue (e.g., withdrawal, lethargy, etc.). These latter responses may, as Kaufman and Rosenblum (1967) suggest, function to prevent a needless expenditure of energy in a "lost cause." Still other common reactions during grief, such as anorexia, sleep disturbance, and self-mutilation, may be of no functional significance in their own right; like the common backache, they may simply be unintended and unfortunate consequences of another biological adaptation (upright posture in the case of backaches and group living in the case of grief).

This description refers only to some of the possible biological functions of grief. Death has important implications for a society as well as for the species. Not surprisingly, therefore, most societies add elements (ritualized mourning practices) that serve to reinforce social cohesion following bereavement. Grief thus becomes a social duty and not just a biological imperative. This duty is sometimes imposed on individuals regardless of their personal welfare, as when a wife throws herself on her husband's funeral pyre (cf. the custom of suttee).

Turning to the psychological level of analysis, not all social and biological reactions during grief are detrimental to the individual. For example, the bereaved may be afforded certain rights during mourning (e.g., release from obligations) that people in more favorable circumstances do not enjoy. Such secondary gain may keep a person in the grieving role longer than biology or society might dictate. In the extreme, some people experience "hysterical" grief reactions in the absence of bereavement.

In short, my answer to the question, What is the function of emotions? is that any given emotion can have a multiplicity of functions depending on the aspect of the emotion under consideration, the nature of the consequences being considered (e.g., short term vs long term), and whether the point of reference is the individual, species, or society.

Inhibition Versus Exhibition

If the expression of an emotion is functional within a given context, then the inhibition of the emotion *in that same context* will be dysfunctional, or at least nonfunctional. This truism would hardly seem to require elaboration. However, the mechanisms by which emotional inhibition can have deleterious effects are poorly understood; and, in the absence of understanding, the pendulum has tended to swing to the opposite extreme, that is, toward emotional exhibitionism.

Most speculation on the dysfunctional effects of unexpressed emotions has focused on the possible consequences of sustained physiological arousal, including hindrance of the immune system. I think that emphasis is misplaced. Situations that arouse emotions typically are those that demand some form of action or resolution. If the emotion remains unexpressed, the situation is liable to continue unchanged, to the detriment of the individual or the group. Sustained physiological arousal may also be a problem, but it probably is not as important as is commonly assumed (Averill, 1989).

The inhibition of emotion is simply one aspect of a larger issue, namely, the control of emotion. Since I will address the issue of control in detail in response to Question 7 – Can we control our emotions? – the present remarks will be limited to a single point. As I have noted, many people interpret the opposite of inhibition to be exhibition, a "let-it-all-hang-out" attitude, although few would phrase it so bluntly. ("Catharsis" might be a preferred way of expressing the idea.) Sometimes, however, inhibition is precisely what the situation calls for, and exhibition then becomes the problem. Physical and mental health come from neither emotional inhibition nor exhibition per se, but from flexibility (Averill & Nunley, 1992). That is easy enough to say, but difficult to put into practice; it does not help that most of our current theories tend to emphasize the intractable qualities of emotions.

Concluding Observations

Functional questions are among the most difficult to answer with confidence. This is because emotions are complex syndromes that have multiple consequences, and because no behavior is ever functional in and of itself, but only within a particular context. These difficulties are well recognized but easily ignored. It is particularly tempting to treat all emotions as though they had a common function, ignoring differences between (and even within) emotions, as well as differences in context. It is tempting, but it is a temptation we should resist, for it almost always leads to false conclusions.

Why Emotions Are Felt

GERALD C. CLORE

> One afternoon in 1989 a gunman fired a semi-automatic assault rifle into a Stockton California schoolyard killing five children. A year later the parents of one of the slain girls was interviewed on PBS radio. In the year since the tragedy the lives of this southeast Asian couple had come to a halt. The father spent most of his time simply lying in bed looking at a picture of his daughter, and each day the couple watched a videotape of their child at play.

In contrast to the complete immersion of this couple in their grief, consider the behavior of victims of physical or sexual abuse who often grow up thinking as little as possible about their unfortunate experiences and telling no one. Pennebaker (1991), for example, has studied a number of individuals who experienced distressing events about which they had never expressed themselves. Typical of these is an account of a young man physically abused by his stepfather (p. 29):

> . . . his stepfather had physically abused him starting when he was fourteen and continuing about three years. . . . he refused to tell his mother for fear of tearing the family apart. During the abusive periods, Jimmy experienced intense migraine headaches. At age seventeen, Jimmy attempted suicide and was hospitalized.

I shall argue that a primary function of emotion is to provide information (Schwarz & Clore, 1983). Emotions supply information to others through distinctive facial and vocal expressions and to oneself through distinctive thoughts and feelings. From this perspective, whether the expression of emotion is functional or dysfunctional depends on what it does to the information value of the accompanying affective experience. The previous examples suggest that both the expression and inhibition of emotion can be dysfunctional. The continual expression of grief by the parents of the murdered girl and the complete silence of abused individuals may lead to equally poor coping. Whether one thinks about a traumatic event constantly or tries to avoid it, the accompanying emotional reactions can cease to belong to a specific time, place, and circumstance. When the experience is cognitively unconstrained, that is, when it is no longer clearly tied to a specific object, it may color the judgment of any situation to which it might appear relevant.

The affective experience of the parents of the murdered girl became unconstrained because they maintained an overt state of grief and mourning over a long period of time. But the private affective experience of the victims of abuse may also become unconstrained. Refusing to talk to others about emotional events does not keep one from thinking about them. And, indeed, refusing to think explicitly about the event does not keep representations of it from being activated in memory and having affective consequences (Wegner, 1989). By not thinking about the event, the resulting affective cues may be diffuse and ill defined, so that the range of things to which they can be attributed is potentially broad. The abuse victim, for example, may carry feelings of resignation, conflict, and anxiety everywhere; as a result, instead of being a reaction to a specific past event, these feelings become part of everyday experience, judgments, and decisions.

I am proposing, then, that whether the feedback from emotional experience provides information or misinformation depends on how one parses one's experience. For emotions to be functional requires not only that one feel them but that the feelings convey discriminative information. This same idea is suggested by a simple experiment reported by Martin (1986). Subjects initially engaged in a task in which emotional thoughts and feelings were activated. Later, they read an evaluatively ambiguous description of a person and rated how much they liked him. The results showed that subjects' perceptions of the ambiguous person were biased by their prior affective experience. Subjects whose happy thoughts and feelings had been activated saw him more positively than did subjects entertaining sad thoughts.

Such affective phenomena are frequently reported, but Martin's experiment is especially interesting because he was also able to control them. A simple instructional manipulation governed whether or not a prior affective experience contaminated their later judgments. After the initial affective task, Martin told one group that they were completely finished with that task (Completed Condition), while he told another group that they would return to that task in a minute (Interrupted Condition). The effect of this instruction was to cause the interrupted group to keep their affective experience on-line, so that it contaminated their subsequent judgment. By contrast, the completed task group was able to mentally punctuate their affective experience so that the prior and subsequent experiences were kept distinct, and the usual contamination of judgment did not occur. The experiment nicely shows that whether an affective experience contaminates subsequent judgments depends critically on how one mentally parses one's experience.

Pennebaker (1991) reports in his studies of people who kept their traumatic experiences secret that when they related their experience to someone else, dramatic changes in their anxiety and arousal sometimes resulted. When one expresses the circumstances of one's distress to another, the act of framing that distress into a communication may make the associated affective reactions more likely to be seen as part of a particular time, place, and circumstance. Conversely, not talking about the event may keep the person from separating the emotional experience from subsequent experiences. The resulting affective cues then seem potentially relevant to anything and everything, resulting in contaminated judgments.

These proposals about the effects of expressing and inhibiting emotion rest on a particular view about the function of emotion. According to the affect-as-information view (Schwarz and Clore, 1983; 1988), a primary function of emotion is to provide information about how a situation has been appraised. This information is conveyed internally by emotional experience. It serves as data for judgment and decision-making processes (Carver & Scheier, 1990; Clore, 1992) and also for reordering processing priorities (Clore, Schwarz, & Conway, in press; Schwarz, 1990; Simon, 1967). I will now discuss these two emotional consequences.

Emotion and Judgment

Like rose-colored glasses, emotional states color one's perception of the world. Just about anything is judged more positively when one is happy and more negatively when one is sad. These are among the most reliable affective phenomena. They are readily observable in everyday life as well as in the laboratory (e.g., Isen, Shalker, Clark, & Karp, 1978; Forgas & Bower, 1988). In a typical experiment, subjects watch an emotionally involving film or are induced by some other means to experience a mild emotional state. Afterward they engage in tasks that involve judgments of some kind. For example, Gallagher and Clore (1985, May) found that frightened subjects overestimate the risks of various accidents, crimes, and diseases, while angry subjects make exaggerated judgments of blame.

Irrationality. One's response to an angry or frightening situation depends in part on judgments about how blameworthy someone's actions seem or how threatening a situation appears. But a primary source of information for such judgments (especially in unfamiliar situations) is the intensity of one's own feelings of anger or fear. The affective system allows one to respond rapidly and seems generally adaptive, but it is also subject to certain errors. The problem is that one cannot generally discriminate between reactions to the situation in question and similar feelings of irritation or anxiety that are left over from prior situations or are induced by being reminded of similar events. As a result, emotional situations sometimes escalate. Already irritated individuals who are frustrated can become furious, and already anxious individuals who are frightened can become panicked. Emotions are believed to make people irrational. In hindsight, intense reactions may seem unjustified because, by then, the background cues of irritation or anxiety that fueled the reaction may no longer be present. Because people's judgments depend in part on how they feel in the moment, affective cues from extraneous sources can provide misinformation.

This is perhaps a good place to note another source of irrationality associated with emotion, one that is due to the other major function of emotion—the reordering of processing priorities. Emotions guide one's attention to things that are relevant to goals and concerns that are implicated in the emotional situation (Simon, 1967). Such processes ensure that what appears most important is attended to first. However, giving exclusive priority to emotionally relevant concerns means that one can quite literally lose perspective. Acting as though one's momentarily active goals are the only concerns of importance can lead to excess. Later, in the context of other concerns, one may feel that one has been shortsighted. In the course of an argument, for example, winning may seem of overriding importance, but, afterward, one may judge that winning was too expensive in terms of sacrificing other goals, such as maintaining good social relations. Again, a highly functional aspect of the emotional processing system can be seen to have problematic side effects.

Misattributions. Although the processes I have described can lead to excesses, the use of momentary affective feedback would seem to be utterly essential in a self-guided system with its own motivations. Such feedback is especially important in human judgment. The incorporation of affect into judgment is such a smooth and seamless process that it is generally difficult to isolate the processes involved. One way we can study these processes is in experiments that focus on people's attributions for their feelings.

In one attribution study, students responded to a life-satisfaction interview on either cold and rainy or warm and sunny spring days (Schwarz & Clore, 1983). Respondents were happier on warm, sunny days than when it was cold and rainy, and they judged themselves to be more satisfied with their lives. In some cases, however, the interviewer mentioned the weather in order to make this true cause of respondents' feelings salient. When the external cause of their feelings was made apparent in this way, subjects' life-satisfaction ratings were immune to mood effects. Those who attributed their feelings to the weather did not see them as an indication of life satisfaction. The act of making the weather salient did not change subjects' moods, but only how they diagnosed the associated feelings. The moods of the rainy day respondents were still negative, but those feelings were not used in making judgments of life satisfaction.

Moods Versus Emotions. Many studies on the effect of emotion on judgment, including the one just described, employ general moods rather than specific emotions. The reason is that the processes are easier to study with moods than with emotions. Both are affective states, but emotions generally have a specific object and are usually briefer in duration, while moods usually have less salient causes and last longer. The importance of this fact is that studies of affect and judgment generally depend on implicit misattributions, and such misattributions and judgment biases are more common when the true cause of one's state is vague and remote than when it is clear and immediate. But our primary interest in judgment bias is simply that it offers a chance to observe the inner workings of the usual, unbiased process of affective judgment. The interface between feeling and judgment is the same, whether based on correct or incorrect implicit attributions.

Applications of Affect-as-information Principles. The principles we learn from the study of emotion and judgment represent only a formalization of what is already well known among those engaged in persuasion, seduction, or sales, and perhaps also by those skilled at resisting persuasion, seduction, and sales. Romance, for example, often depends on the inability (or the disinclination) of partners to separate their experience of alcohol, soft lights, or music from their experience of the exciting attributes of a partner. Outcomes ranging from buying encyclopedias to religious conversions can depend heavily on whether or not one confuses reactions to the mellifluous voice of a persuader with reactions to the content of a message. And one of the oldest advertising strategies is to encourage male consumers to confuse their interest in an alluring female model with their interest in the product she is associated with.

A moment's reflection makes these familiar strategies transparent. But they are so universal and so effective because people routinely turn to their feelings for information when making judgments and decisions. If this were not the case, advertisers, politicians, and suitors would probably not go to such lengths to elicit feelings in others and encourage their misattribution. Analogous processes are also apparent in other social practices. Judges in courtrooms, for example, are elevated on a high platform so that the experience of physically looking up to the judge merges with the experience of psychologically looking up to this person as an authority. In a related vein, banks were traditionally housed in large stone buildings with massive classical columns, presumably so that one's experience of the bank's physical solidity could be easily confused with assumptions about its financial solidity. I am not suggesting that the sense of solidity and the experience of looking up to someone are emotions; indeed they are not. The point is that the experience of emotion shares with these other experiences informational properties that we routinely integrate into judgments and decisions, and that producing such information and conveying it via affective experience is the central business of emotion.

Direct Versus Indirect Effects. The explanation of emotional effects on judgment—that emotions affect judgment because people routinely use even minimal affective cues in their ongoing judgments and decisions—is quite different from the explanations traditionally offered for how we change attitudes and judgments. Social psychologists have long assumed that influences on judgment are mediated by changes in beliefs about the object of judgment, or in the weights attached to those beliefs (e.g., Anderson, 1971; Fishbein & Ajzen, 1975). This same assumption has also been made more recently by social cognition researchers. During the last decade or so, social cognition research has been preoccupied with problems of how information about people is represented, stored, and retrieved (Wyer & Srull, 1984). As attention turned toward the effects of mood and emotion on judgment, a natural tendency was to appeal to this same framework and assume that mood effects on judgment are also indirect. Thus, it has been generally assumed that the influence of mood is on how something is represented or on what part of the representation is retrieved (e.g., Bower, 1981; Isen, 1984). The affect-as-information hypothesis, by contrast, hypothesizes that mood and emotion have *direct effects* instead of, or in addition to, such *indirect effects* (Clore, 1992).

We can view the difference between these approaches by considering how one might make the kinds of judgments for which experiential information is clearly relevant. How, for example, does one answer such questions as "How do you like your lunch?" Traditional models of judgment imply that one would proceed by identifying the ingredients, looking up the stored liking values for each ingredient, and then integrating these values into a judgment of how much one likes the dish. A more modern social cognition view would have us categorize the dish as, say, lasagna, look up the stored value for lasagna, and then answer accordingly—"I must like my lunch because it is lasagna, and I know I like lasagna." Such an account seems to be missing something. Surely liking also reflects information from the direct experience of tasting the lasagna as well as indirect influences from the retrieval of previously stored knowledge about lasagna.

A similar process also presumably underlies other on-line affective appraisals. If asked, for example, how much we like a person we have only recently met, we are likely to formulate an answer by bringing the person to mind and noting any resulting affective reactions. Often we may not be able to say why we like or dislike the individual because we may have made the judgment without accessing reasons—we may have simply read the affective cues in our momentary experience and used that information directly. We can test various predictions from this view. For example, the direct, or informational, hypothesis (Schwarz & Clore, 1983) predicts that emotion enters the equation at the judgment stage instead of solely at the encoding stage (Clore, Parrott, Schwarz, & Wilkin, 1990). This hypothesis also predicts that mood affects subjects' evaluations independently of their representation of the object of judgment (Schwarz, Robbins, & Clore, 1985, May).

The evidence discussed so far suggests that positive and negative affective states tend to influence evaluative judgments. The ease with which these affective biases can be shown implies that people may frequently base their judgments and decisions directly on how they feel at the moment, and that one of the important functions of emotion involves the information provided by feelings for making judgments and decisions. But this assertion also has important implications for other influences on judgment, including the role of emotional experiences other than feelings (e.g., emotional thoughts), and the role of other feelings that are not emotional (e.g., feeling certain, feeling confused).

Nonfeeling Components of Emotion

Emotions involve not only distinctive feelings but also distinctive thoughts. The jealous lover not only feels longing, fear, and anger but also finds himself conjuring up images of the loved person in the arms of another, entertaining depressing thoughts about himself, and considering extreme plans of action (Parrott, 1988). Like his feelings, the experience of these thoughts provides information to the lover about the nature and seriousness of his situation. These products of unconscious mental computation often appear as if from nowhere. If they occur in the right place and at the right time, they may affect judgments very much as feelings do.

Recent studies confirm that the attributional processes responsible for mood effects on judgment also operate when primed thoughts affect judgment. Whether primed thoughts influence judgments or not depends on whether one experiences them as a reaction to the object of judgment (Clore & Parrott, 1991). Merely activating a concept is not sufficient for ensuring that judgment and recall will be influenced in the direction of a primed concept. Priming requires subtlety because it depends on misattribution.

Several recent studies have tested this hypothesis explicitly. They show that when priming manipulations are subtle (Strack, Schwarz, Bless, Kubler, and Wanke, 1990) or when subjects experiencing blatant priming are distracted (Martin, Seta, and Crelia, 1990), the presence of a primed thought in consciousness is likely to be misattributed as a reaction to the object of judgment. But if reminded of a subtle priming manipulation, or if not distracted after a blatant priming manipulation, subjects are likely to discount the relevance of any primed thoughts they encounter so that they have no effect on judgment.

Nonemotional Feelings and Judgment

I have discussed the informational value of affective feelings and affective thoughts, but the same can be said for nonaffective feelings. The term "feeling" is often assumed to refer to affective feelings, but this need not be the case. Many of the most common feelings are not affective. For example, when we say we feel "hungry," "tired," or "dizzy," we are not referring to emotions but to bodily feelings or feedback about our bodily state. Similarly, when we say we feel "certain," "confused," or "surprised," these are not emotional feelings but what might be called "cognitive feelings" or feedback about our state of knowledge. The same feedback processes that govern the role of affective feeling in evaluative judgments also turn out to govern the role of these nonaffective feelings in nonevaluative judgments (see Clore, 1992). Thus, when asked if we want to eat lunch, we might consult our feelings of hunger for decision-relevant information. Similarly, in an argument, we may consult our feelings of certainty as a source of information about whether to continue to press our point. As in the case of affective thoughts and feelings, whether one's judgment is influenced by nonaffective feelings that are present depends on what they are implicitly attributed to. For example, subjects were more likely to believe that they understood a poem when the feelings of uncertainty they experienced were attributed to a prior experimental manipulation than when they saw them as part of their reaction to the poem (Clore & Parrott, 1994). Thus, the informational or feedback function characteristic of emotional feelings and thoughts is also a central function of other nonemotional experiences.

Emotion and Processing Implications

I have focused on the implications of emotions for judgments (cognitive content), but they also have implications for how problems are solved (cognitive style). In recent years much as been written about the cognitive eliciting conditions of emotions (e.g., Ortony, Clore, & Collins, 1988; Roseman, 1984; Smith & Ellsworth, 1985). But attention is just beginning to be devoted to the cognitive output of emotion. It appears, however, that positive and negative affective experiences cue different processing styles. These have been studied primarily by inducing positive and negative moods (Clore, Schwarz, & Conway, 1994; Schwarz, 1990). The usual finding is that positive affect leads subjects to engage in more heuristic processing. Individuals in positive affective states are more likely to use stereotypes, scripts, schemas, and other

other organizing information and less prone to focus on the details of the information available. Subjects experiencing sad affect are more likely to engage in systematic processing, to be analytical, and to focus more on the presented details.

Recent results show, for example, that: happy subjects are more likely to (1) recall information consistent with applicable stereotypes and schemas (Forgas & Moylan, 1991; Bodenhausen, 1993), (2) cluster information more in recall (Bless, Hamilton, & Mackie, 1990), (3) make decisions faster and more efficiently (Isen & Means, 1983), (4) engage in more creative problem-solving (Isen, 1984), and (5) form more inclusive categories from lists of items (Isen, 1987). Sad subjects, on the other hand, are more likely to: (1) discriminate between strong and weak arguments in a persuasive message (Bless, Bohner, Schwarz, & Strack, 1990), (2) estimate correlations more accurately (Sinclair & Marks, 1992), and (3) solve syllogisms better than happy subjects (Melton, in press).

Such findings suggest that emotion influences cognitive processing, perhaps in very fundamental ways. Positive affect appears to encourage unconstrained, heuristic processing, sometimes with creative results, while sad affect seems to foster a focus on more controlled, systematic processing.

The best explanation for these processing differences is not yet clear. Schwarz (1990) suggests that the information provided by positive and negative affect activates different kinds of procedural knowledge. Another possibility, also based on the affect-as-information hypothesis, is that the processing effects of emotion are really judgment effects in disguise (Martin, Ward, Achee, & Wyer, 1993). That is, when we experience positive affective cues, we may interpret them as an affirmative answer to implicit questions about the viability of whatever responses we activated. As a result, any incipient responses, including unusual or novel ones, are more likely to be retained and less likely to be rejected, so that happy individuals appear more creative. Similarly, negative affect may provide a negative answer to questions about the viability of incipient responses, so that sad subjects reject more potential answers and therefore appear more analytical and discriminating.

Emotion and Behavior

Before leaving this question, we might make some comment about the relationship between emotion and behavior, since the function of emotion presumably has something to do with action. Emotional states may involve a number of processes that facilitate action in a general way without priming any particular behavior. It is easy to imagine that emotion involves changes in arousal, in blood distribution, in muscle tension, and so on. To the extent that these or related changes occur, the organism might be prepared to engage in action more quickly or forcefully. It seems less plausible, however, that emotions in humans involve activation of motor programs for particular actions.

Nevertheless, it is common to assume that fear involves behavioral tendencies to escape, that anger involves activation of aggressive responses, that shame involves tendencies to hide, and so on. But these links are probably more indirect than is generally assumed. Such words as "behavior," "response," and "action," even when qualified by such words as "tendencies," "readinesses," or "inclinations," imply that specific muscle groups and motor circuits are activated when one is angry, fearful, or ashamed. Such claims suggest, rather implausibly, that one's legs are programmed to run when afraid, one's arm is programmed to hit when one is angry, or one's hands programmed to cover one's face when ashamed. Of course emotions such as fear do involve a redistribution of blood from the viscera to the large muscles, and such effects would presumably enable one to engage in rapid action or extreme exertion. But such general activation is not at all the same thing as a specific action tendency or a motor program.

Fewer conceptual problems arise if one assumes that the direct effects of emotions are motivational rather than behavioral. One can achieve more agreement about the likely goals of angry, fearful, or ashamed persons than about their likely behaviors. It seems clear enough, for example, that fear involves a desire to avoid harm or loss, but not at all clear whether achievement of this goal would necessitate selling one's stocks, listening to the weather report, or running away. Thus, the immediate effects of emotion may be more mental than behavioral.

Summary

Emotional organisms are information-processing organisms. Emotions emerge from information processing and feed information back into the same system. Sources of emotions are the continual appraisals that take place as the organism moves through its world. The output of emotions is information conveyed by distinctive thoughts, feelings, and expressions. This experiential output serves as input to moment-to-moment judgment and decision making (Clore, 1992; Schwarz, 1990). It informs the individual about the results of unconscious computations concerning the significance of events for one's concerns. Thus informed, the individual can then allocate resources appropriately (Simon, 1967).

Emotions Are Functional, Most of the Time

NICO H. FRIJDA

That emotions fulfill some sort of function is a basic Darwinian presupposition that psychologists probably all share. It may be useful to remember, though, that this is not the only possible view. One can see emotions as disruptions of behavior and cognitive functioning caused by information overload, for instance, or to the absence of meaningful response options in the given situation (Hebb, 1949). Alternatively, emotions might be regarded as mere hereditary remnants of past adaptive responses, or as primitive adaptive responses whose purpose is much better served by more recent and advanced mental capacities. More fundamentally, emotions can be argued as expressing the individual's awareness of his or her position in the world, rather than serving as adaptations to that world.

I adhere to the Darwinian, functionalist position, in that I think that, indeed, emotions serve an adaptive purpose, and that they do so now, even in present-day human adults. At the same time, I think that not all occurrences of emotions, nor all their manifestations, serve a useful purpose. It is, I believe, necessary to distinguish sharply between the overall usefulness of a particular psychological function and the usefulness of each of its individual manifestations. Take language. The primary purpose of language is communication. However, not every sentence spoken serves that purpose, nor do all aspects of speech, as, for example, the faltering of someone out of breath after running.

In any case, and whatever our overall view, when we think that emotions do have a function, the problem remains of specifying that function. We must also validate the corresponding functional use for each emotional occurrence and each aspect of emotion manifestation or else account for the fact that emotions are sometimes useful and sometimes not.

Emotions possess two major aspects: that events are appraised as relevant, as pleasant or unpleasant, and that some experiential, behavioral, and physiological response is elicited. These two aspects require separate functional explanations.

The Function of Emotional Responsivity

The occurrence of emotions, whatever the emotion aroused, presupposes sensitivities for particular types of events. Emotions give evidence of dispositions in the individual that allow those events to be appraised as pleasant or unpleasant—that is, to elicit positive or negative affect. Emotional sensitivity represents a very fundamental and general process of evaluation, and emotions can be understood to represent a process of relevance signaling: of signaling events that are relevant to the individual's well-being or concerns to the cognitive and action systems. Emotions, from this angle, appear to serve that function. They can be considered the mechanism whereby the organism signals to its cognitive and action systems that events are favorable or harmful to its ends. It is the relevance signaling mechanism.

Indeed, how else could such relevance be detected, transmitted, and taken care of? It is true that Nature shows other options. One of those is by means of localized stimulus-response connections. With such stimulus-response connections, the "ends" of the system are not represented in a way that is accessible to the entire organism, but only to the localized provisions. This is how plants change their sap flow under shortages in available liquid and our wounds heal. Another similar provision is the reflex that, again, couples local sensitivities (e.g., irritation of the nasal cavity) to fairly specific prewired action programs (e.g., sneezing).

However, some more centralized signaling provision, producing more general shifts in action control and commanding action plans rather than specific actions, appears to be vastly more flexible and, indeed, indispensable for ensuring the safeguarding of its ends in systems that can respond to complex information in a variable environment. In such a provision, "ends" and "means" are separated. "Ends" are given independent representation (as desirable states of affairs, and as states of satisfaction or dissatisfaction), actions are flexibly guided by action plans or programs, and harmony and disharmony between "end" and "current state" are centrally signaled to the action system. Affects are just those signals. In the formulation by Oatley and Johnson-Laird (1987; Oatley, 1992), they represent "nonpropositional signals," which are elicited by the detection of "goal junctures."

In this interpretation of emotion (or at least of affect), the "ends" are what give the emotional event its emotional valence. Personal loss produces sadness because it conflicts with one's attachment to the lost person, frustrations madden because we desire to complete progress toward our goals, and so on. In the emotion literature the ends are referred to as motives, major goals, or well-being; I prefer to use the word *concerns*. Emotions signal the relevance of events to concerns. This interpretation implies that in each emotion-eliciting event some concern can be identified, and it can be argued that detecting concern-relevant events is useful for ensuring satisfaction or protection of these concerns.

This interpretation can be easily substantiated for a large number of emotions, given the events that elicit them. To a large extent, positive emotions are elicited by events that satisfy some motive, that enhance one's power of survival, or demonstrate the successful exercise of one's capabilities. Positive emotions tend to result from achieving such conditions of satisfaction, in which case they signal that activity toward the goal can terminate, consummatory behavior can be initiated, or resources freed for other exploits. "Enjoyment" quite often is the name given to the emotion that follows achievement. Other positive emotions result from increased likelihood of satisfaction: a desired object presents itself, or appears obtainable. Emotions signal that continuing on one's track is appropriate; they have reinforcement value.

Similarly, many negative emotions result from painful sensations and from threat or harm to some concern. These negative emotions alert the action system that some action should be undertaken to set things right or prevent unpleasant things from actually occurring. Different negative emotions result from different contingencies within this general frame. All this is plausible, and currently fairly widely accepted theory.

There is a class of emotion-eliciting events in which emotions clearly have an action-guiding, monitoring function: the vicissitudes of progress toward a valued goal. Goal-achievement represents a concern by itself; almost any goal, once we are committed to it, gives rise to emotions when relevant events are met on the road: when it is thwarted, when it is achieved if there has been some uncertainly about achieving it, and so on. Hope and fear, disappointment, anger (including self-directed anger), and dejection are emotions that signal the relationship between progress and expectations regarding one's rate of progress (Carver & Scheier, 1990), and that have implications for energy investments and ultimately for action termination or goal abandonment.

The Functions of Emotional Response

The second aspect of emotions consists of the emergence of emotional response: experiential, behavioral, and physiological reaction. Part of the experiential reaction has already been dealt with: affect, the experience of pleasure or pain, or the experience of the eliciting event as pleasant or unpleasant. Other aspects of experience reflect either awareness of the eliciting event and its meaning, or the impulses toward the behavioral response, and thus share in their meaning.

Emotions can roughly be regarded as motivators for the behavior meant to deal with the emotional events. Many emotions have a function in directly dealing with these events. Fear, presumably, motivates actions to protect oneself from the event that caused it, or to prevent the event from actually materializing, or to suppress activity until the threat has passed (as in anxious freezing). Anger serves to discourage the offender from doing what causes one's anger, or to mend one's ways. These emotions, in other words, have a function within the actual individual-environment interaction, or one's immediate goal achievement. The best characterization of what they aim at is the production of relational behavior; that is, they motivate behavior meant to maintain or modify a particular kind of relationship with the environment. They aim to change (or maintain) the relationship, not the environment itself. In addition, emotions adjust the energy resources brought into play in the interaction, or in interaction with the environment as a whole—the changes in level of activation.

Such a functional interpretation quite clearly does not easily apply to all emotions or their occurrences. It is hard to discern such a function in sadness and in joy, and, in particular, to discern a function that accounts for the behavioral manifestations tied to these emotions. True enough, sadness has been interpreted as the emotion that motivates calling for help; crying can be seen as a distress call. However, crying is only one of the manifestations of sadness, and calling for help does not impress as the most meaningful responses to the primary elicitor of sorrow, loss of an attachment figure.

Why should loss produce an emotion? One possible answer is that there is no real answer; sorrow might just happen to be there, as the painful outcome of thwarted desire and broken attachment. This, of course, is a nonfunctional interpretation and I will come back to it. It may be the appropriate one. However, functional interpretations are in fact possible and have indeed been advanced. One interpretation suggests a direct-dealing function. Klinger (1975) took his cue not from crying but from the apathy of grief. Apathy might serve the goals of emotional processing, which in this case would mean facilitating one's disengagement from the broken attachment. Passivity saves energy during recuperation and allows meaning change to take place; it is a mode of what has been called "secondary coping" (Rothbaum, Weisz, & Snyder, 1982). The hypothesis is plausible in part because grief is often filled with painful recollections that may serve as extinction stimuli, and in part because a similar hypothesis has been advanced to explain deep body pain—such pain motivates immobility that helps recuperation from illness (Bolles & Fanselow, 1980).

Quite a different hypothesis has been proposed by Averill (1968). The function of grief might not be situated in the direct dealings with the emotional event, the loss. It might instead be of an anticipatory and preventive nature. Not loss, but absence or probable loss could be the major elicitor of grief; grief might serve to motivate search for the lost object. More important, the anticipated possibility of grief might anticipatorily motivate effort not to lose the object of attachment; incipient grief might motivate efforts to prevent it from occurring. It might be, figuratively speaking, a rising sorrow that lets the stray lamb run back to the herd of sheep. Sorrow as the motivator of recuperation efforts is, of course, known from attachment theory (e.g., Bowlby, 1980).

Joy is not difficult to understand as the signal that is contingent on the various contingencies mentioned: goal achievement, increased trust in obtaining satisfaction, actual satisfaction. The problem lies more in explaining the increase in activation, that is, the manifestations of exuberance, the more upright stance, and the like—and, of course, laughter. Yet, the explanation may not be so difficult once we realize that the contingencies leading to joy, or other positive emotions, include more than just achievement of satisfaction. The other contingencies, indeed, make activation increase highly appropriate. The emotions of enjoyment sustain eating, obtaining sexual gratification, absorbing aesthetic impressions, or whatever is involved. They provide the motivations for consummatory behavior. In addition, the exuberance of joy to a large extent manifests activation that has become freely available after a problematic or strenuous interaction has ended successfully. The high activation can be understood either as a leftover from the activation mobilized by the preceding interaction (the arousal-safety sequence in the theories of laughter by Rothbart, 1973, and Sroufe & Waters, 1976) or, alternatively, as mobilized by the appraisal of increased competence and accessibility of the environment, caused by the success.

In the examples given of the functions of emotional behavior, those functions involved directly dealing with that environment: establishing or breaking relationships, and the like. Much of that relational activity is social in nature–emotions motivate proximity seeking, social avoidance, chasing-off offenders. The functions in dealing with the emotion-arousing event may also be more purely social. Shyness, for instance, can be seen as the emotion aroused by social situations that require status- and role-conforming behavior. It can be understood as the emotion that signals such requirements and motivates corresponding submissive, respectful, or role-respecting behaviors, that is, recognition-of-social-distinctions displays. This hypothesis has been plausibly argued by Gomperts (1992) from the positive evaluation that shyness receives in cultures that value social status and sex-role distinctions [e.g., Oriental cultures, see Shweder, this volume; European culture before World War II (Gomperts, (1992)], and the emergence of negative evaluation (including the new diagnostic category "social phobia") in parallel with the abolishment of social distinctions and distinctiveness. The behaviors in shyness are in line with their interpretation as recognition-of-social-distinctions displays. Shyness is characterized by anxiety behavior, that is, by response inhibition (Gray, 1982). Movements are awkward, speech halts, thought stops. As with anxiety displays generally, these manifestations can be understood as "inconspicuousness behaviors." They fit with the more specifically social inconspicuousness behaviors like gaze avoidance and the posture with eyes slanted downward, head drooping.

A number of other emotions can be understood in a similar way. Shame and guilt, for instance, serve as social regulators by motivating certain pro-social behaviors that prevent their occurrence. Recognizing events that *might* evoke shame leads to group-conforming or self-conforming behavior; recognizing situations that might evoke guilt if certain precautions or actions were neglected leads to taking these precautions or executing these actions. The actions and precautions are those geared to being careful with respect to other people, or to not losing *their* love, in the case of guilt, and to conform with group- or self-standards, and not losing their love, in the case of shame. The functions of shame and guilt are, it seems, first anticipatory and preventive; they are corrective only when one has not heeded their signals. Their functions appear to promote group coherence and interpersonal prudence (or to avoid punishments after transgressions), respectively.

Afunctional and Dysfunctional Emotions

The functional interpretations in these last sections are theoretically interesting. They suggest that emotions might not merely be functional because they watch the individual's interests, but also because they may serve as social regulators. Emotions belong to the fabric that keeps social interaction in shape, and they do so not merely through the joys of affection that are part of them or through the fear of uncontrolled emotion display. These interpretations also show that emotions which at first sight are merely dysfunctional disturbances may not on second thought appear to be so. Stage fright, for instance, may not so much be (or not merely be) fear of social ridicule, but a mode of control of social presumption; guilt emotion (or its precursor, being aggrieved by having harmed someone else) is not merely an internal pain but a prime mover for constructive social behavior.

These interpretations decrease the domain of dysfunctional and afunctional emotion manifestations but they do not make that domain disappear. Some emotions resist functional interpretation and, more important, many emotion occurrences appear to have no function within the context in which they arise.

Concerning afunctional emotions, I mentioned that grief and sorrow may be given functional interpretations; but these interpretations are not too convincing, at least not for everything included under the emotion labels. To the extent that apathetic sorrow is comparable to "learned helplessness," there is little that is functional about it. Conserving energy resources would be better served by calmly sitting it out. The deep activation decreases in many states of sorrow and depression would just seem to reflect the mode of operation of the organism under unmodifiable aversive circumstances.

Concerning clearly dysfunctional emotions, there are phobic fears and panics, guilt emotions without clear causes in social transgression or neglect, panics and states of desperation in clinical depressions, and unfounded jealousies. Much simpler examples come from a normal emotion like nostalgia. Nostalgia has a double meaning, and in other languages these meanings are separated (*Heimweh* and *Wehmut* in German, *homesickness* and *nostalgia* perhaps in English). The first meaning refers to a painful longing for home; the second to a bittersweet craving for things that have gone by—it is evoked by memories of childhood or other pleasurable past events (Bellelli, 1991). I can find no possible use in that emotion. Of course, it signals that the longing is alive, but that statement is a confused one since the longing has no existence or consequence beyond the nostalgic longing: It signals to what? It is true that this emotion enriches life, but that can hardly be considered its function. Like sorrow, it just is there, useless as it is.

Phobic fears have a somewhat similar nature. They are fears for objects or situations that the individual knows are harmless. Certainly, some unconscious or automatic appraisal process does make the object appear dangerous, but again this does no more than repeat that there is an unfounded, nonfunctional emotion; unfounded not in a historical sense, but having no contemporary meaning in dealing with problems and opportunities in the environment. Nothing would be lost by not having it.

The examples of sorrow, nostalgia, and panic indicate where the theoretical solution lies. If emotion manifests the operation of useful relevance-detection system, this need not imply that every manifestation of that system is useful. A burglar alarm is a useful contraption even if on occasion it goes off because a broken branch hits the windows, or if it sounds even when the police are too far away to hear. The first comparison applies to nostalgia, the second to grief with irretrievable loss. In other words, emotion, as a phenomenon and a provision, is useful; not every individual emotion necessarily is. Grief is not useful; the capacity that enables grief is. The same applies to the other emotions. How often emotion is useless and nonfunctional, one may say, is determined by how finely the system has been tuned. In the end, the usefulness of a provision depends on the proportion of hits to misses and to false alarms, and on the costs of the alarms.

Emotions as the Servants of Concerns

We have argued that the function of emotion is very general, even if the utility of individual emotions may be doubtful. Emotion—actual emotion, affective response, anticipation of future emotion—can be regarded as the primary source of decisions and, thus, of control of behavior. Preferences can be viewed as latent dispositions that determine whether behavior will go one way or another, but they actually affect behavior only by way of emotions or of anticipation of those emotions. What does "survival" mean to the individual besides the distress of pain or the horror at the idea of death?

Some remarks are needed to round off the perspective given here. First, in this view of emotions, emotional mechanisms are unspecific with regard to concerns. Anger occurs after frustration (among other things), whatever the goal that is frustrated, and sadness results from loss, whatever the kind of loss involved (an attachment person, a possession, an ideal, self-esteem). This is not true for all emotions, because some emotions (i.e., some emotion categories or labels) are defined by particular concerns; "lust" is an example. Furthermore, the social functions of some emotions suggest that these emotions are of a fairly special-purpose nature; for instance, the corrective function of anger, or the self-corrective function of guilt. That of others appears much more general—to discourage interfering agents, as a goal for so much anger, and self-protection against threats, for fear. It is unclear whether this difference is more apparent than real, or whether it can be fitted into the general analysis presented, which views emotions as the general-purpose servants of concerns.

A theoretically tricky issue regards the definition of "concerns" (or of motives or self-generated goals). The statement that emotions serve satisfaction or protection of one's concerns is meaningful only to the extent that concerns (or, again, motives or goals) can be defined or ascertained independently from emotions. This is not always without problems. Does evidence exist for attachment that is independent from the pleasure of being with a given person, or from the sadness on losing him or her? Some concerns can be defined in terms of underlying mechanisms (e.g., the need for heroin in heroin addiction, the need for food in ordinary hunger), or in terms of adaptive advantages (e.g., curiosity). For many concerns, however, this does not seem possible. It would seem particularly difficult for "hedonic concerns" (Frijda, 1986)—those that have getting pleasure as their primary motive, such as gluttony, sensation-seeking, and even sex. It would be odd to say that the joys of drinking champagne serve the concern of desiring champagne; it would be tautological. I think the following arguments meet this issue and I repeat them from Frijda (1986). The most important is that many concerns consist of representations of states of affairs that evoke pleasant or unpleasant affect. These concerns include hedonic concerns, but also what I call "surface concerns," those defined in terms of a particular object, such as the attachment to a particular person, the fear for a particular type of object, or the value attached to a particular abstract notion (e.g., the self ideal). The origin of surface concerns may be conditioning to other situations that had affective valence, or it may be specification of more basic concerns (like particular attachments being rooted in a general need for proximity). *Affect* elicited by objects or events defining such concerns cannot be said to "serve" these concerns; it merely expresses them. *Emotions* (affects plus some mode of action-readiness change) elicited by such objects do serve these concerns, by involving signals to the action system, and subsequent changes in action readiness.

"Set-points," or reference values that are to be attained, must logically be supposed to explain the emergence of both affect and emotion. Several of these set-points have been more or less clearly identified in a way that is independent of emotion arousal; optimal stimulation of opoid receptors, in the case of need for heroin, is an example. Beyond that, positing a concern means issuing the promissory note that some such set-point will one day be identified, or else something that is functionally equivalent. One can specify what such functionally equivalent entities might consist of. It can be argued that what we call concerns (that which underlies emotions as well as striving) are rooted in capabilities that the individual possesses. Affects can be viewed, not as contingent on particular stimulus events, but resulting from the optimal or non-optimal functioning of these capabilities. We like, and strive for, what we are capable of doing when that capability is not self-evident. Sex can be said to be pleasant because we can do it (we have the provisions for it), but to use these functions we have to be set for it. This also applies to cognitive assimilation (which is what curiosity achieves): We are capable of cognitive assimilation, and assimilating something gives pleasure when we did not already know it, or when assimilation is trivially simple. Affect monitors optimal functioning; emotion (affect plus a command to the action system with control precedence) goads or regulates action.

Emotional Behavior Patterns

I have discussed the function of emotions in general, not the functionality of their particular behavioral, psychological, physiological, and experiential manifestations. I will now briefly turn to this issue. Certain aspects of emotions appear extrinsic to the emotion process itself, and perhaps as nonfunctional or a hereditary remnant. Facial expressions and psychophysiological response, in particular, are sometimes so regarded: They may have been useful in our evolutionary or historical past, but at present they are nonfunctional and may even be dysfunctional. The issue is also relevant for dysfunctional emotion manifestations such as blind panic, self-destructive depression, violent anger, paralyzing stage fright, and destructive or oppressive jealousy. All these emotions can be considered functional when they are of moderate intensity, but disruptive in certain contexts and at high intensities.

The functional nature of most emotional response components is, in principle, fairly obvious. Some facial expressions, for instance, are elements in affective overall action patterns aiming at self-protection, retreat, aggressive approach, and the like. The fear expression, as analyzed by Darwin, combines backward withdrawal with attention to the fearful object; the surprised face results from inhibitory behavioral interruption (which makes the mouth fall open) and unfocused visual orientation (these arguments come from Darwin, 1872; Dumas, 1948; and Piderit, 1867). Other expressive movements can be functionally understood in perhaps a somewhat less obvious fashion. Anxious paralysis can be viewed as cautionary response inhibition, an automatic passive avoidance response, in line with Gray's (1982) interpretation of anxiety. Frowning, the response in any endeavor to overcome an obstacle, appears to be actually instrumental in concentrated effort, in some unclear fashion (Darwin, 1872). Other features, such as movement characteristics, manifest current activation levels.

Many expressive activities, especially facial and vocal ones, are interpersonally effective—as requests, commands, or threats. The angry glance (eyes widened with eyebrows drawn downward) is best understood as a menace, as intimidating behavior, together with foot-stamping, shouting, and slamming doors; the smile is an appeasement signal; other facial expressions and voice intonation patterns can be understood along similar lines. The communication value of these expressions tends to be instrumental within the emotional action tendency; just as aggressive behavior in anger tends to remove an obstacle, so does intimidating behavior.

The adaptive nature of physiological responses—again, in principle—is hardly a point of discussion, since Cannon's (1929) introduction of the emergency response concept. However, several important response components are functionally opaque. The purpose of skin conductance response, for instance, is unclear, because it is most noticeable in skin areas that contribute little to thermoregulation. Diarrhea, although an epinephrine response, seems to have little adaptive value. In fact I suspect that our energy mobilization interpretation of physiological response in emotion is a gross simplification, and may in part even be erroneous. We do not know to what extent physiological changes are responses to actual or anticipated physical energy expenditure when coping with the external event, to suppression of emotional impulses in order to continue following task demands, to keep concentration, or to assist in the process of attention and information registration. It has been argued that physiological responses in emotions are atavistic responses, useful only in creatures that had to fight bears, and not in humans, who only have to invent insults. Whether or not this is true vitally depends on the kinds of interpretation given to the various phenomena. In fact, the signal value of autonomic response in emotion has been emphasized by Mandler (1984) and by Wynne and Solomon (1955), and its role in event registration and subsequent habituation by Pribram and McGuinness (1975). It should be taken up in actual research.

To evaluate the functionality of emotions one must, I think, distinguish between their occurrence as such and their intensity. Intensity reflects two processes: those of emotion arousal and those of emotion control or inhibition. Any normal emotion is the result of their joint influence; inhibitory control processes are part and parcel of emotion mechanisms. Inhibitory control is the means whereby emotions get attuned to the seriousness of their cause. The attuning and moderating function of inhibitory control makes it likely that such control uses other and more information than what is used for emotional arousal. In fact, inhibition is primarily regulated by anticipation of the aversive consequences of the response to be controlled (Frijda, 1986; Gray, 1982). It may thus be inferred that inhibitory control occurs only when time for the additional processing of information is available, and that it is vulnerable to disturbance. Immoderately, dysfunctionally intense emotions may well reflect disturbance in the control mechanisms; the location may be in the cognitive apparatus triggering moderation, or in the effectiveness of the inhibition control resources.

What this amounts to, in the present discussion, is that functionally appropriate processes (restriction of attention allocation can be counted among them) may have dysfunctional consequences when the system is taxed beyond the limits of its capability.

This would seem to apply to many afunctional or dysfunctional aspects of emotions. The apathy of desperation and depression and the often severe disturbances of function in anxiety are probably best viewed as failures to meet unanswerable situations as well as disrupting consequences of coping mechanisms operating beyond their resources. States of exhaustion are examples. Exhaustion of energy resources leads to the irritability and anxiety bursts of the exhaustion syndrome; exhaustion of available coping modes results in the dysfunctional helplessness pattern. Another example where coping mechanisms work in vain involves conditions of conflict between action tendencies. The organism's means of operating under conflict are evidently limited. Inhibitory anxiety response in stage fright is incompatible with the responses needed for answering whatever goals underlie the stage performance. It is awkward to call the emotion itself dysfunctional, but its manifestations at that moment certainly are—not because of their very nature, but because of the state of conflict.

There is another category of nonfunctional responses, which we have already referred to when discussing nostalgia: responses that are useless under the given conditions, though meaningful under others. Their uselessness, in fact, appears under close scrutiny or, rather, could have appeared on close scrutiny by the subject him- or herself. Longing for something definitely lost is meaningless; so is vomiting after hearing morally disgusting information; so is freezing in anxiety when there is nobody to watch you or take advantage of your actions. However, if emotional response is to serve its purpose, it should be fast and work with minimal information. Whether that is functional or dysfunctional depends on the pay-off matrix: If risks are high, shoot before you ask questions. This is in fact the reason behind what I said earlier regarding inhibition: Inhibition is useful as a secondary provision, to be put in operation when time suffices and, of course, when the efforts of discrimination serve a purpose. Emotions like nostalgia indeed are, in a sense, luxuries that one indulges in for the sweetness of their bittersweetness, *if* one indulges in them—which one does only infrequently.

Conclusion

Emotion is a functional provision, even if not all its occurrences are. I think that there is ample ground for this judgment. The function of emotions is to signal events that are relevant to the individual's concerns, and to motivate behavior to deal with those events. Detailed analysis of emotional phenomena, such as the morphological analysis of expressive behavior, tends to corroborate that function.

As far as I can see, no emotional phenomena can properly be regarded as atavisms that have no current use, in the circumstances that human beings today have to meet. That is, emotions and their various manifestations do not appear to be atavisms, nonfunctional, or mere phenomena of disturbance. What may well be nonfunctional, and perhaps even atavistic, are the concerns that give events their emotional significance. It is difficult to find an advantage for many attachments or likings. Nevertheless, many nonfunctional or even dysfunctional emotions and emotional phenomena occur. They can largely be understood as consequences of a functional provision when operating under taxing circumstances and at the limits of its resources, and on occasion manifesting a functionally appropriate lack of selectivity in its operation. Part of the dysfunctional aspects probably are consequences of breakdowns or malfunctions in emotion-controlling processes.

Human Emotion: A Functional View

ROBERT W. LEVENSON

Emotions are short-lived psychological-physiological phenomena that represent efficient modes of adaptation to changing environmental demands. Psychologically, emotions alter attention, shift certain behaviors upward in response hierarchies, and activate relevant associative networks in memory. Physiologically, emotions rapidly organize the responses of different biological systems including facial expression, muscular tonus, voice, autonomic nervous system activity, and endocrine activity to produce a bodily milieu that is optimal for effective response. Emotions serve to establish our position vis-à-vis our environment, pulling us toward certain people, objects, actions, and ideas, and pushing us away from others. Emotions also function as a repository for innate and learned influences, possessing certain invariant features along with others that show considerable variation across individuals, groups, and cultures.

In my response to this question, I will briefly discuss these functions, with an implicit emphasis on emotions that occur when a person's physical and psychological well-being are at stake.

Intrapersonal Functions

Coordination of Response Systems

The essential function of emotion is organization. It has been widely observed that an emotional response includes manifestations in subjective experience, behavior, and physiology. The subjective aspect includes the phenomenological experience of the emotion, perceived physical sensations, and associated memories. The behavioral aspect includes facial expressions, posture, and voice tone. The physiological aspect includes the autonomic, somatic, central nervous systems as well as endocrine responses. Often an emotional episode occurs without warning and lasts for less than a minute. Given this lack of opportunity for preparation and this brevity, the amount of coordination and organization that is required to mount a unified and effective response is considerable. The complexity of this task of coordination is especially imposing because each of the component subjective, behavioral, and physiological systems has its own control mechanisms, and is capable of quite independent action.

Shifting Behavioral Hierarchies

Emotions have the capacity to activate certain behaviors, which might normally exist at the bottom of behavioral hierarchies. Thus, under the proper conditions, anger can drive the pacifist to fight; sadness can make the strong weep; and fear can cause the brave to cower. In this regard, emotion has the unique capacity to set aside, in a moment, a lifetime of individualized learning, refinement, culture, and style, revealing the common denominator of human response.

Recruitment of Physiological Support

Behaviors such as withdrawal, expulsion, fighting, fleeing, and nurturing each make different physiological demands. A most important function of emotion is to create the optimal physiological milieu to support the particular behavior that is called forth. Given that this milieu includes the central, somatic, and autonomic nervous systems, each with a number of important subsystems, and the importance of rapidity of response, the ability of emotion to choreograph the activity of these diverse systems has profound implications for our capacity to adapt and survive.

Short-circuiting Cognitive Processing

Evolution has endowed humans with exquisite cognitive powers, which provide myriad possibilities of action and inaction for responding to environmental challenges. Emotion is the antidote to the problems caused by this embarrassment of riches. Hearkening back to an earlier stage of phylogenetic development, emotions provide us with access to a limited number of simpler time-tested modes of efficient, effective adaptation.

Although rational thought and emotion are often depicted as locked in an eternal battle, there is typically more cooperation than strife. Nonetheless, any functional view of emotion must allow for the possibility that emotion and rational thought can sometimes work at cross-purposes. In those instances, and especially when the challenge to personal well-being and integrity is strongest, the more primitive emotion system often gains the upper hand. Clearly there are times when action is more appropriate than deliberation, when responding is more appropriate than considering, when doing is more appropriate than planning. In situations where hesitation could have the most dire of consequences, emotion functions to set aside cognitive processing that is too cumbersome, too obsessive, too self-indulgent, and, ultimately, too likely to be inconclusive.

Interpersonal Functions

Communication and Control

The expressive characteristics of emotion in voice, face, gesture, and posture serve an important function in communicating our emotional state to others. The value of these signals is twofold: first, by allowing others to know how we feel, and second, by influencing their behavior. The power of simple emotional signals to mobilize others can be seen quite vividly when fear expressed by one person causes a crowd to panic. At a more intimate level, the crying of an adult or a child powerfully calls forth nurturing behaviors on the part of others; a shared smile can defuse the most dangerous situation and can create an instant bonding among strangers.

Establishing Our Position in Relation to Other People, Ideas, and Objects

Emotion also functions to establish the spacing between us and the entities that populate our personal worlds. Acting via ubiquitous processes of approach and avoidance, emotions draw us toward some things and push us away from others. In this way emotion functions to establish and structure those things that define us as individuals. These include our social networks of friends and enemies (and all the gradients in between), our likes and dislikes (forming the basis for our aesthetic sensibilities), and our moral sense of what is right and what is wrong.

Repository for Influences of Evolution, Learning, and Culture

I embrace a biocultural model of emotion, which reflects a confluence between innate and learned influences. My elaboration of this model is depicted in the following figure[1]. As suggested by the figure, emotions arise from a transaction between the organism and its internal and external environment. Antecedent conditions, which may be *inter*personal or *intra*personal, are perceived and processed by an appraisal system that imbues them with meaning in terms of the organism's well-being, plans, and goals. Certain outcomes of this appraisal process evoke an emotion prototype, which recruits response tendencies in multiple systems encompassing subjective experience, behavior, and physiology. The configuration of these response tendencies represents a generalized solution for coping with the demands of the original antecedent condition. However, these response tendencies do not directly lead to measurable and observable emotional responses. Rather, they are acted on and often transformed by cultural learning, resulting in the emotional responses that can be observed by conspecifics and measured in the laboratory.

In this model, innate hard-wired influences are found in the connections between the emotion prototype and the recruited response tendencies (indicated by solid connecting lines in the figure). The primary loci of cultural influences are seen in the two shaded panels labeled "appraisal" and "cultural learning." In the realm of *appraisal*, culture greatly influences the sense we make of and the meaning we

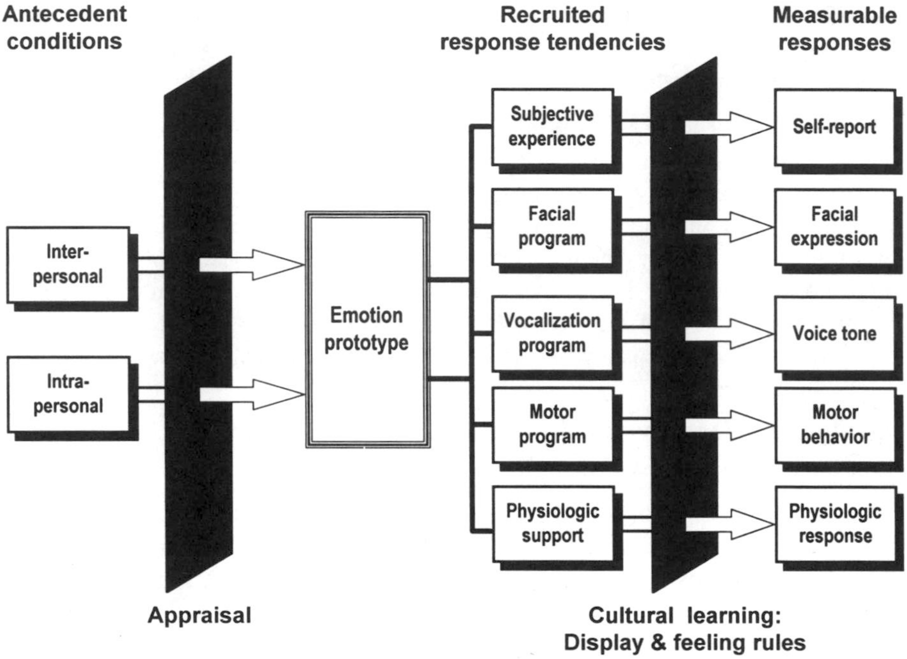

ascribe to our experiences. In the realm of *cultural learning*, display rules (e.g., Ekman & Friesen, 1969) influence the ways we visibly express our emotions, and *feeling rules* (e.g., Hochschild, 1979) influence how we experience and label our emotions.

Conclusion

As this brief overview should make clear, emotions serve an impressively large number of highly critical functions for individuals, groups, and cultures. A defining feature of the human condition, emotions serve as one of the major pathways along which both innate and learned influences are expressed.

Note

1. A number of theorists have offered models that include both hard-wired and learned influences, including those attributable to culture (e.g., Ekman, 1972, 1984; Heider, 1991b; Lazarus, 1991; Levy, 1973; Mesquita & Frijda, 1992).

Emotion Serves to Decouple Stimulus and Response

KLAUS R. SCHERER

One of the most exciting leads for answering this question is Donald Hebb's early but rarely cited assertion that man is the most emotional of all animals (Hebb, 1949). He based this claim on his observation of the frequency and complexity of emotional behavior in many different species of animals, and reached the conclusion that the degree of emotionality seems to be correlated with the phylogenetic development of sophisticated central nervous systems. Hebb explained the paradox that the most rational primate, man, is also considered the most emotional by pointing to the effect of sociocultural control mechanisms that mask the high level of human emotionality (see Elias, 1977).

If one accepts Hebb's claim (i.e., increasing potential for complex emotional behavior as one moves from fairly simple to more advanced species), one can attempt to identify which of the more sophisticated behaviors in the advanced species seem to benefit from an emotion mechanism. This may shed some light on the evolution of emotion. As one moves up the evolutionary scale, the following features appear to become more prominent: the ability to process more complex stimulus patterns in the environment, the simultaneous existence of a multitude of motivational tendencies, a highly flexible behavioral repertoire, and social interaction as the basis of social organization. Emotion seems to be centrally involved in determining the behavioral reaction to environmental, often social, events of major significance for the needs and goals of the organism.

I have used the analogy of emotion as an *interface* to refer to this mediation between environmental input and behavioral output. Since there are nonemotional reactions to environmental stimulation, other interfaces must also exist (e.g., reflexes or rational problem-solving). However, the special role of emotion seems to be that of an intelligent interface that mediates between input and output on the basis of what is most important to the organism at a particular time. It evaluates incoming information on the basis of a situationally weighted assessment of an event's relevance to central needs or goals and prepares appropriate adaptive action. Because of this strong tie to motivation, Tomkins (1984) has considered emotions as amplifiers of motives. Similarly, Frijda (1988) calls emotion a concern-realization system. Two other theories, proposed by Panksepp (1982) and Buck (1985), are also based on the motivational force behind emotions.

It may help to understand this function of emotion by considering how important adaptive reactions are controlled in organisms that appear not to have emotions. In very primitive organisms, such as the amoeba, adaptive reactions to relevant environmental events are assured by hard-wired detection and motor-response mechanisms, through reflexes. Similarly, in many other animals somewhat more elaborate fixed action patterns are quasi-automatically triggered when relevant environmental stimuli are registered by specialized feature detectors (Hinde, 1974). Even when such mechanisms are not innate but depend on learning, there is a fairly rigid link between a specific releaser stimulus and a particular behavioral response. In all these cases the relevance detection is largely preprogrammed and encoded in the feature detector or the conditioning pattern. While some of these mechanisms can be modified by learning and show some situational specificity, they are not flexible enough to control adaptive behavior in more advanced, socially living species with a highly variable behavioral repertoire such as many mammals and particularly primates.

I have proposed that emotion has evolved as a relevance detection and response preparation system in species in which organisms can perceive and evaluate a wide range of environmental stimuli and events (even those that are irrelevant for survival) and have an extensive repertoire of behavioral response alternatives at their disposal. More specifically, one can argue that emotion *decouples* stimulus and response (Scherer, 1984b). The two major advantages of this decoupling, which I believe to be one of the central characteristics of emotion, are (1) that a latency period intervenes between stimulus evaluation and reaction, and (2) that a response appropriate to the stimulus event is prepared and can be executed very quickly. The first advantage represents important progress over the more primitive reflexes and fixed action patterns: the second preserves the advantage of speed associated with the more automatic, phylogenetically older mechanisms in the service of emergency responding.

These features may become clearer if we look at them with an engineer's eye. The task is to design a mechanism with great flexibility in the evaluation of environmental events and in the choice of optimal behavioral responses without entirely losing the advantages of the older system that dealt with important situations for the organism's survival and well-being by providing reliable, quick, and appropriate responses. Emotion would seem to correspond very well to these demands, representing a major engineering feat: An appropriate action tendency as well as the energy to carry it out are prepared as soon as the stimulus is analyzed, but the motor action pattern is not immediately released. The latency time can be used to analyze and evaluate the stimulus event as well as one's repertoire of reaction or coping alternatives more thoroughly. On the basis of this additional information, the response can be modified appropriately (see also Crook, 1980, p. 147).

Before exploring further how the latency period is used for these purposes, we might find it useful to discuss the apparent paradox that, judging from everyday experience, the shorter the latency period, the stronger the emotion (Hörmann, personal communication). Since events vary in their significance for the organism—both in terms of the centrality of the needs or goals they affect and the urgency of the required response—emotion as a relevance detector can be expected to reflect the degree of importance of an event, and the corresponding degree of ego-involvement, on a continuous scale of intensity. It follows that the organism cannot take the risk of delaying a reponse in the case of very intense emotions. The solution is to fall back on the "wisdom of the body," in this case the phylogenetically preprogrammed action tendencies. In emergency situations the organism cannot afford the luxury of repeated evaluations and of careful consideration of response alternatives. There is a priority on speed of response and even though the outcome may be less than perfect or, in some cases, even disastrous, the probabibilty is high that the preprogrammed action tendencies are adaptive in the long run. Presumably, this is what they have been selected for in the course of evolution (unless there has been a major shift in the environment or in the social organization to which selective adaptation has not yet responded).

Thus, the paradox is only apparent. The inverse relationship between the intensity of an emotion and the length of the latency time is actually one of the most powerful design features of the emotion mechanism. It is interesting to note that the impulsivity of action under extreme emotion that follows from the short latency time has been the reason that "emotional behavior" is often considered "irrational" (because it lacks the careful sifting of alternatives and systematic and orderly thinking). Yet, in the sense of practical rationality (Max Weber's "Zweckrationalität"—i.e., optimal means-ends relationships; Weber, 1947), impulsive emotional behavior would have to be considered "rational" in emergency situations (Scherer, 1985).

In the normal course of events, situations in which the original stimulus evaluation will trigger a prepared action tendency immediately, without any latency period (the extreme case being the "innate releasing mechanism"), are likely to be rare. Generally, the emotion mechanism can be expected to work in such a way that the original stimulus evaluation immediately produces neurophysiological changes and a readiness for a particular type of action that prepare the organism for responding. Thus, the latency period needed for further information processing is used optimally for a generalized mode of response preparation.

We can now turn to a more detailed discussion of the uses made of the latency period created by the decoupling of stimulus and response. As we have already noted, the first major function is the ongoing analysis of the stimulus event, which allows the organism to arrive at more detailed or more realistic conclusions and may lead to a reevaluation and consequently a revision of the original appraisal. Lazarus (1966) has emphasized this important aspect of emotion, which he called "re-appraisal," as distinct from the initial evaluation. Instead of adopting his categorical distinction between initial appraisal and re-appraisal, which seems to imply that there is a clear demarcation between the two, I propose that the evaluation or appraisal process be viewed as essentially continuous with a constant potential for change in its outcome. While the latency period allows this evaluation process to operate before action is taken, it does not stop with its execution. The evaluation of the stimulus event continues, but the action and its consequences are now added to the total situation under evaluation. I have used the analogy to a constantly revolving radar antenna to describe this continuous evaluation process.

The second major function of the latency period in emotional responding is that it allows the organism to communicate signals of evaluative reactions and behavioral intent to others. Clearly, it is highly adaptive if the choice of a response takes into consideration the likely effects or consequences of this response. In social interaction, the outcome of a particular act usually depends partly on the reactions of the significant others in the encounter. Thus, the projection of how the other(s) will react to the different courses of action open to the organism largely determines its behavioral choice. The signaling of the emotion communicates the emoting organism's evaluative reaction to a stimulus event or act and thus narrows the possible range of behavioral intentions that are likely to be inferred by observers. In addition, because of the action tendency component of the emotion, the momentary behavioral intention will be expressed even more clearly.

Let us take an example from human interaction. The facial reaction to an ironic statement will reveal immediately whether the utterance was perceived as a joke or an insult. This information reduces the number of behavioral consequences to be expected. In addition, a raised fist may further specify the behavioral intentions of the emoting organism. In most cases there will be a latency time before the fist hits. The fact that the raised fist announces a behavioral intention will lead in turn to a noticeable emotional reaction and communication of intention in the other, allowing the prediction of the likely outcome of various response alternatives, such as hitting. It was Darwin (1872/1965) who stressed the major significance of emotional expressions as signals of behavioral intention and their role in social interaction. It can be shown that the signaling functions of the emotion displays are of such major importance that they are selected for communicative efficacy in the course of evolution (see Leyhausen, 1967).

Both the availability of a comprehensive stimulus evaluation process and the predictability of outcomes (one's own and those of others) based on the communication of intention signals allow the internal simulation and evaluation of several response alternatives before an appropriate choice of action is made. The latency period also gives the organism time to internally monitor (or even reflect on, in the case of man) these various processes—that is, stimulus and response outcome evaluation, organismic changes in support of various action tendencies, and expressive signaling. This monitoring process is likely to have a dual function. First, it serves to focus attention on an unresolved situation requiring an adaptive response, which keeps other events from intervening during the latency period and distracting the organism while it deals with the original event. Second, it integrates information about external and internal events and thus allows representation in memory, thereby facilitating learning.

Distinguishing Functional from Dysfunctional Affective Responses

LEE ANNA CLARK
DAVID WATSON

One approach to understanding the function of emotions is to study dysfunctional emotions, which is the focus of our response. We primarily address how and why emotional responses—which have developed and persisted because of their functional, adaptive qualities—may become maladaptive and dysfunctional. We begin with a brief consideration of certain normal, functional qualities of emotions. Broadly speaking, the functions of emotions can be divided into those that have basic evolutionary significance versus those of more contemporary origin. That is, certain aspects of emotions appear to be not only humanly universal but also identifiable across a wide range of animal species, and so may have originated in a common ancestry. For example, the emotion of fear in response to danger has served to enhance survival for eons through its associated behaviors of freezing or fleeing. On the other hand, more complex emotions such as nostalgia, love, or guilt seem uniquely human and have intrapsychic, interpersonal, and social functions that transcend (although they may encompass) their ancient origins. Given space limitations, we consider only the more basic emotional responses due to their more immediate relevance to dysfunctional emotions.

Universal Functions of Emotions

The most important emotional functions fall into three broad types: signal systems, resource mobilization, and resource conservation. First, triggered by environmental events, emotions act as salient internal stimuli that alert the organism to the need for further information gathering and action, with specific types of environmental events linked to different emotions. For example, fear signals the organism to escape an impending disaster, whereas disgust is the response to a bitter taste or noxious odor and warns the organism of a potentially lethal poison. In contrast, the emotion of joy—in response to the acquisition of a desired object or the completion of an important task—highlights the value of the object or task; likewise, the interest that is felt in a novel situation encourages further exploration, thereby increasing the likelihood of obtaining valuable information or objects (cf. Fowles, 1980).

From our point of view, it is not important whether these different situations directly trigger the emotional responses through an innate, precognitive, limbic mechanism or whether the emotion arises in response to a more central, higher order cognitive processing of the survival-relevant information in each of these contexts. Instead, we await the development of comprehensive models that integrate both cortical and limbic inputs, and endorse integrative models that view emotions and cognitions as interdependent processes with causal reciprocity (e.g., Greenberg & Safran, 1984). What is significant is that the triggering of an emotion renders a situation more strongly salient to an organism, so that an emotional response to an event has the survival-enhancing function of signaling an organism to focus needed attention on the event.

Why would such a dual cognitive-emotional system have developed? Why was the more primitive, emotional evaluation system not superseded by a purely cognitive one as higher order functions developed? First, a dual system takes advantage of both the immediacy of limbic responding and the flexibility added by higher order cognitions. Second, a dual system permits judicious use of higher order cognitive processes. Affectively neutral situations do not compel attention to the degree that emotionally laden ones do, so in the absence of emotional responses all situations have equal attention-getting value. Without an "automatic" judgment system, all situations would have to be evaluated cognitively for their survival value, which would severely tax cortical resources.

Consider the analogous case of children who lack the ability to experience pain. Although these children develop a cognitive appreciation of the danger value of objects and activities, this process takes far more time and effort than the pain-based system used by normal children. Only continual vigilance ensures their safety, whereas normal children quickly learn to avoid common dangers owing to the immediate feedback of their pain system. Analogously, without emotions, one would have to learn the positive and negative stimulus value of situations through strictly cognitive means.

A second function of emotions is resource mobilization. In addition to increasing the salience of a situation, emotions are accompanied by physiological responses that can be viewed as action potentials. For example, the autonomic nervous system prepares the body to respond physically to perceived danger with the flight or fight response. Similarly, the positive emotions are energizing and motivate a broad range of social and prosocial behavior (Watson & Clark, in press). Moreover, emotions affect not only internal resources, but also are associated with behavioral responses that mobilize external resources. For example, distress cries alert community members to the need for help, whereas shouts of excitement or joy invite others to join in the hunt or feast. As with the signal function of emotions, we surmise that these integrated emotion-behavior systems developed as highly efficient means of utilizing organismic resources.

Finally, at least one emotion—sadness or despair—appears to serve the function of resource conservation (Beck, 1987). When prolonged activity does not result in success, then reduction of effort or withdrawal from further action represents an adaptive strategy. Depue, Krauss, and Spoont (1987) have described a integrative biobehavioral system that ranges from high energy/activity levels, increased interest and alertness, heightened excitement- and pleasure-seeking, and euphoric mood to low energy/activity levels, withdrawal, decreased cognitive capacity, anhedonia, and sadness/depression. The characteristics of the low end of this continuum all suggest a mechanism "designed to conserve energy by slowing down the entire psychobiological apparatus" (Beck, 1987, p. 29). In essence, sadness results when sufficient energy has been expended without the gratification normally associated with the activity. In a coordinated fashion, the motivating biobehavioral system then shuts down, which discourages further action.

Are There Dysfunctional Emotions?

At first glance, the answer to this question seems obvious given the emotional suffering that clearly accompanies mental disorder. However, it may be argued that it is not emotions per se that are dysfunctional, but the fact that negative emotions often have the dysfunctional qualities of high intensity and frequency, long duration, and situational inappropriateness, whereas positive emotional responses may be weak, rare, short-lived, and difficult to elicit. We examine how these qualities combine to yield dysfunctional responses and discuss factors associated with the development of anxiety and depressive disorders. Anger is also an important clinical problem, but it is more strongly linked to the social/interpersonal functions that we do not discuss due to space limitations.

Anxiety Disorders

Consistent with our analysis of the normal function of emotions, traumas such as physical or sexual assault or abuse, combat, natural disasters, serious accidents, or death of a close relative elicit extreme emotional responses. These responses are normal and adaptive as long as there is a recovery of emotional equilibrium within a reasonable time limit. Under certain conditions, however, recovery is impeded and the response becomes dysfunctional because it does not serve any of the adaptive functions described (e.g., Posttraumatic Stress Disorder or Adjustment Disorder).

Severe, multiple, or prolonged trauma may increase the likelihood of disorder, especially if the trauma occurs at a young age, in which case the normal functioning of certain neurotransmitters may be impaired (Van der Kolk, 1987). In some cases, traumatic experience may have a priming effect, and there is a stronger, more prolonged emotional reaction to a subsequent event (Brown, Harris, & Copeland, 1977). Also, there are large individual differences in response to stressors (McFarlane, 1986) and those who react maladaptively are more likely to have preexisting personality characteristics such as a high level of Neuroticism/Negative

Affectivity (N/NA; see our response to Question 2: How do you distinguish emotions?) that predispose them to disorder (Merbaum & Hefez, 1976).

Most emotional disorders, however, occur in the absence of obvious situational stressors or when the emotional response clearly is disproportional to the situation. Simple phobias, for example, are extreme reactions to situations in which most people either would not feel fear (e.g., open places) or would be only mildly afraid (e.g., spiders, snakes). The latter type of phobia may be acquired more easily and extinguished less readily (Cook, Hodes, & Lang, 1986), which is consistent with Seligman's (1971) "preparedness" hypothesis that phobias are based in innate tendencies to respond fearfully to specific stimuli. These phobic reactions thus represent fear responses that phylogenetically were reasonably adaptive, but are not functional in modern society.

Even assuming a phylogenetic basis, however, we must explain the way in which these abnormal fear responses develop because not all people acquire phobias. Behavior theorists have hypothesized that phobias develop through a combination of classical and operant conditioning (Mowrer, 1947), but this has not been well supported by experimental evidence, nor can conditioning account for all cases of phobia (Davison & Neale, 1990). An alternative theory that focuses on information-processing biases has been proposed (Tomarken, Mineka, & Cook, 1989), but is not well established empirically. Temperamental differences also may play a role (Gray, 1985).

Some individuals experience panic attacks—strong anxiety accompanied by heightened autonomic arousal in the absence of any immediate stressor. Whereas an isolated panic attack is rarely dysfunctional, frequent attacks (i.e., Panic Disorder) can be extremely disabling. There is increasing evidence that Panic Disorder results from an interaction between biological and psychological characteristics; specifically implicated are abnormal norepinephrine activity (Gorman, Liebowitz, Fyer, & Stein, 1989) and hypersensitivity to physical sensations (Barlow, 1988). Moreover, this hypersensitivity has two aspects: (1) a propensity to notice and attend to (vs. ignore) physical sensations; and (2) a tendency to misinterpret normal somatic feelings as abnormal and thus react to physical sensations with worry and concern. Accordingly, the experience of physical sensation itself becomes a threatening situation, with resultant escalation into heightened anxiety.

These two aspects of somatic hypersensitivity—heightened perception and overconcern—are modestly correlated and both are components of the broad temperament of N/NA (see our response to Question 2; Watson & Pennebaker, 1989). This temperament is characterized by a general apprehensive hypervigilance to threat and has been linked with noradrenergic (and serotonergic) activity (Gray, 1985). Thus, it is plausible that the dual physiological and psychological propensities to panic attacks are part of a single, integrated reaction system. Individuals high in N/NA are predisposed both psychologically and physiologically to respond too readily to situations as if they were threatening. This view is consistent with the fact that individuals often experience their first panic attack during a stressful period in their lives (Pollard, Pollard, & Corn, 1989), when this system already is overburdened. In essence, therefore, Panic Disorder is an anxiety reaction that has become dysfunctional because it occurs in nonthreatening situations due to impairment in the psychophysiological system that signals danger.

Finally, some individuals develop Generalized Anxiety Disorder (GAD)—prolonged, moderately intense anxiety in the absence of an overt stressor. Similar to panickers, individuals with GAD have an abnormal anxiety response; however, they report more chronic, moderate psychophysiological symptoms rather than the extreme emotional peaks experienced by panickers. Thus, rather than possessing a "hair-trigger" emotional-reaction system, GAD sufferers have high tonic levels of autonomic arousal and cognitive worry that persist across time (e.g., durations of over two years are common; Breslau & Davis, 1985). Again, the general temperament of N/NA—which itself is relatively stable, due in part to its substantial heritability (Clark, 1989)—has been implicated in GAD (Clark & Watson, 1991b). GAD may also be more responsive than other mood and anxiety disorders to cumulative environmental events (Breslau, 1985), which suggests a parallel to the prolonged reactions of Posttraumatic Stress Syndrome.

Depressive Disorders

In contrast to anxiety disorders, which—because of progress in understanding their biological substrates—can be viewed as perturbations of normal fear reactions, there have been few plausible or compelling theories regarding the function or adaptive significance of depression. However, as mentioned earlier, Beck (1987) has proposed that depression is part of a mechanism for psychobiological slowdown in response to a lack of expected positive reinforcement and Depue et al. (1987) have described a biobehavioral system that regulates levels of positive emotions, energy, and social, behavioral, and cognitive activity. Fluctuations in this system (which we call Positive Affectivity [PA]; see our response to Question 2) have been linked to both diurnal and seasonal rhythms (Clark, Watson, & Leeka, 1989; Smith, 1979), including seasonal affective disorder (Kasper & Rosenthal, 1989). Moreover, changes in sleep architecture are diagnostic of depression (Giles, Rush, & Roffwarg, 1986), and some forms of depression may involve a dysregulation of endogenous circadian rhythms (Clark et al., 1989; Healy & Williams, 1988). Finally, Fox and Davidson (1984) have proposed a cortical model of emotional activity in which positive affective states are conceptualized as representing approach tendencies; in contrast, negative affective states are thought to involve active avoidance.

These various models describe mutually compatible aspects of a more comprehensive approach to understanding depression. For instance, if positive affect accompanies approach and exploration, then its absence is consistent with depressive withdrawal. Moreover, variation in energy level is a primary component of each model, and both diurnal and seasonal variation in activity/approach may be mechanisms for energy conservation: Reduction of exploration and other activity during the nonwaking hours of the day and the winter season clearly represents a more efficient use of resources than does a constant state of high activation. Thus, these models also are consistent with the fact that depression is a naturally cyclic disorder that tends to remit and recur over time.

Therefore, it is reasonable for us to view depression as a dysfunctionally prolonged slowdown in a normally cyclic PA or approach system. The etiological role of biological malfunction seems particularly clear for bipolar disorder, in which dysfunctional overactivation is also observed. Several lines of evidence support this contention: Bipolar disorder can be regulated using lithium, which has been shown to affect circadian bodily rhythms (Mellerup & Rafaelsen, 1979); depressive episodes respond, at least temporarily, to sleep-deprivation therapy, perhaps as a result of resynchronization of dysregulated circadian rhythms; and seasonal affective disorder is treated with phototherapy that mimics the lengthening of the solar day (Wehr et al., 1986).

It is less clear, however, what processes might trigger unipolar depression, whose biological underpinnings are less well understood. Potential clues lie in the observations that (1) anxiety and depressive disorders are highly comorbid (Clark, 1989; Clark & Watson, 1991b); (2) there is a typical sequence of emotional reactions to stressors such that fear/anxiety responses predominate initially and, if not ameliorated, are superseded or combined with sadness/depression (Akiskal, 1990); and (3) anxiety is linked primarily to N/NA, whereas depression is associated with both high N/NA and also with low levels of PA (Clark & Watson, 1991b). These observations are all consistent with the hypothesis that depression has its origins in a normally functional response to the failure to master an environmental threat. If initial anxiety and its concomitant avoidant behavioral response pattern are unsuccessful in resolving a crisis, it is not adaptive to continue in that mode, so stopping the response is both appropriate and functional. Accordingly, the organism gives up and passively withdraws from the situation. The further adaptive response is then to pursue other tasks after the crisis has passed. However, if the deactivation is intense or prolonged, depression ensues. A prototypic example of this phenomenon is the well-documented, two-stage primate response to loss/separation in which active protest is followed by passive despair (Bowlby, 1980).

It is important to note that the negative affective (i.e., anxiety-relevant) avoidance and the positive affective (i.e., depression-relevant) approach systems are relatively independent of each other and relate to distinctive sets of variables (Clark et al., 1989; Watson & Pennebaker, 1989). Thus, shutdown of the positive system can have deactivating behavioral effects without directly influencing the negative emotional system, which may remain aroused. However, anxiety and agitation are rare in severely retarded depression; thus, when the positive-activation system is at its passive nadir, it may dampen the negative-activation system.

This integrated view accounts for the cooccurrence of anxiety and depression and for their temporal sequencing; it is consistent with the view of depression as both an energy conservation strategy and as a component in a larger biobehavioral system of positive activation that has significant endogenous variation; and it provides an initial basis for understanding the interaction of Positive and Negative Affectivity in psychological disorder. There are clearly many other factors—particularly cognitive variables—that are relevant to mood and anxiety disorders and require incorporation into this highly general model. It is encouraging that researchers from various perspectives are striving actively toward developing comprehensive theories of anxiety and depression that both link these disorders to the normal functions of emotions and also consider the ways in which normally adaptive mechanisms become dysfunctional (e.g., Akiskal, 1990; Healy & Williams, 1988).

Afterword: What Is the Function of Emotions?

PAUL EKMAN
RICHARD J. DAVIDSON

Recruiting Physiological Changes Levenson and also Clark and Watson describe how physiological changes are recruited to support behavior that has been adaptive over the course of the evolution of the species. Frijda agrees in part, but he questions whether there is an evolutionary basis for some of the changes that occur in autonomic nervous system activity.

Action Readiness Clore challenges the idea that emotions involve action tendencies. Instead he proposes that emotions change our motivations, and what goals we seek rather the behaviors in which we might be impelled to engage. Fear thus involves, for Clore, an attempt to avoid harm, but he suggests that how one avoids harm would vary with the threat and is not best captured by the idea of an action readiness to flee. Frijda allows for more than one fear response, but proposes a limited, distinctive set of action readiness changes for each emotion. Scherer also endorses the notion of "phylogenetically preprogrammed action tendencies" for each emotion. Levenson's account that emotions prepare us to engage in actions that have had survival value implies also that there are distinctive, innate action tendencies for each (or most) emotions.

Changing Cognitive Activity The contributors differ in their account of how emotion influences cognition. According to Levenson, emotion short-circuits cognitive processing. Clark and Watson propose a dual cognitive-emotional system, with both the automatic phylogenetically adaptive responses that Levenson is concerned with, and a more elaborated information gathering and evaluating process in which emotions increase our need to gather more information and focus our attention. Their position is very similar to Scherer's view.

Clore says that our feelings provide us with information. We use our awareness of our feelings to make evaluative judgments and decisions, based on how we feel. Frijda takes a similar position. Clore additionally proposes that for feelings to be functional in providing information we must be aware of those feelings. This seems to contradict Levenson's position and to some extent Clark and Watson's description of how emotions function to prepare the organism to respond without needing to cognitively evaluate every situation. Insofar as the antecedents of mood are more diffuse and less object focused than emotions, Clore suggests that they may have different functional consequences for cognition.

Facilitating Phylogenetically Adaptive Responses Levenson proposes that emotions can "set aside in a moment a lifetime of individualized learning, refinement, culture . . . revealing the common denominator of human response." By this reasoning the only source of individual differences in emotional response would be biology, not social learning. Levenson's view is in stark contrast to those who consider emotion to be nearly totally socially constructed, such as Schweder (in Question 1) and Averill (on this and other questions).

Scherer and also Clark and Watson take a more intermediate position. Scherer allows for more flexibility in emotional response, and for the influence of current learning, in proposing that emotions decouple stimulus and response, which allows the organism to detect the relevance of an event and the time to perceive and evaluate a wide variety of environmental stimuli. Yet Scherer also agrees with Levenson in saying that when intense emotions occur, phylogenetically preprogrammed action tendencies are brought into operation. Clark and Watson similarly see emotion as subject to dual influences.

Emotion Organizes/Disorganizes Levenson's stance that "the essential function of emotion is organization" contradicts the view that emotions disorganize behavior (see Frijda's opening discussion of Hebb). Those who have emphasized the disorganizing impact of emotion may have in mind extremely intense emotional moments (Frijda) and sustained affective states, such as anxiety, which may be better considered as moods than emotions (see Question 2 on distinguishing emotions from moods, temperament, and emotional traits). For Clore and also for Clark and Watson it is not a passing mood of anxiety or dysphoria that they describe as dysfunctional, but when those moods are sustained sufficiently long to be considered a manifestation of a particular temperament or emotional disorder.

Emotion-specific Functions Clark and Watson describe the function of sadness to be resource conservation. Frijda also recognizes that sadness is quite a different emotion from the other emotions he considers. Clark and Watson's discussion of sadness raises the possibility that there may be functions that are unique to only one emotion, in addition to functions that are shared across all emotions, such as those Levenson described. Averill takes this possibility further, suggesting that each emotion must be analyzed in its own right to determine its functions, and those functions will depend on the aspect of the emotion being considered. Averill argues that the functions of an emotion depend on short- or long-term consequences, and whether the reference point is the individual, the species, or society.

Dysfunctions Clark and Watson focused primarily on when emotions are dysfunctional, which they believe involves the intensity and frequency of negative as compared to positive emotions. The key distinction is that these negative emotional reactions are not situationally appropriate. Averill also says this is the issue. Clark and Watson's views on individual difference in emotional response are further explained in their consideration of temperament under Question 2.

Averill's discussion of short-term versus long-term consequences of an emotion can be integrated with Clark and Watson's discussion. An emotional reaction could in the short term be functional, but repeated again and again over the longer term would be dysfunctional.

Clore's' description of how a depressed person's continuing negative feelings impair judgment is quite consistent with Clark and Watson. Averill deals with a different type of dysfunction—not an overreaction but an inhibition of emotional response.

Interpersonal Functions Levenson briefly describes the interpersonal functions of emotion, as does Frijda, Scherer, and Clark and Watson. All note that emotional expressions serve to inform others about the expressers' intentions and motives, and function to motivate various actions on the part of the perceiver. Levenson also mentions that emotions influence tendencies to approach and avoid various persons.

While interpersonal functions have generally been given short shrift in comparison to intrapersonal functions, we must note that the intrapersonal functions considered mostly dealt with interpersonal events. All the contributors believe that emotions are brought into play most often by the actions of others, and, once aroused, emotions influence the course of interpersonal transactions.

Question 4

How Is Evidence of Universals in Antecedents of Emotion Explained?

It's a Small World, But a Large Stage

JAMES R. AVERILL

How do you explain evidence for universals in the antecedents of emotion? The way this question is posed, it assumes not only universal antecedents, but also universal emotions. It is, in fact, three questions in one: (1) Are there universal emotions (defined primarily in terms of response characteristics)? (2) If there are universal emotions, do they have universal antecedents (eliciting conditions); and (3) if there are universal antecedents, how do we explain them? For the vast majority of emotions, I would answer No to the first question, which leaves speculation regarding the second question meaningless and nothing to explain with reference to the third question.

The above "answer" is far too glib, for it trivializes an important set of observations. Evidence suggests that some aspects of behavior and situations commonly associated with emotions in one culture are also associated with emotions (not necessarily the same emotions) in other cultures. For example, certain facial expressions are universally recognized as connoting aggressive intent; moreover, certain situations (e.g., pain and betrayal) are liable to elicit aggressive responses among people in all cultures. It is reasonable to assume that any emotion that commonly involves an aggressive intent (e.g., anger, envy, and jealousy in our own culture) may also incorporate these facial displays. This does not mean, however, that anger *as a specific emotion* is universal across all cultures; or that aggressive emotional syndromes found in other cultures (e.g., *liget* among the Ilongot–Rosaldo, 1980) are simply variants of anger (cf. my response to Question 1).

The above example indicates an important conceptual issue that must be clarified before the question of universality of emotions can be addressed: *The more general a concept, the more universal its application*. Consider the familiar adage, "Bread is the staff of life." In this expression, "bread" is used as a synecdoche, that is, a figure of speech in which a subordinate category ("bread") is used to refer to a superordinate category ("food"). Is bread necessary for life? No, not if it is interpreted in its usual sense as one category of food; but Yes, if it is interpreted in the broader sense of food in general.

In folk taxonomies, not all categories need be named in ordinary language. As explained in response to Question 1, a common way of alluding to a covert (unnamed) category is by reference to one of its prototypic members or subcategories. For example, if there were no name for food in the English language, then "bread" might be used to refer both to a specific kind of food and to food in general.

Synecdoches are common in the case of emotion. For example, in its strictest sense "anger" may refer to a emotional syndrome, comparable to envy, jealousy, fear, hope, sadness, and the like (Averill, 1982). Storm and Storm (1987) also use "anger" to refer to a more comprehensive category that includes not only anger as a specific emotion, but also mad, fury, choler, rage, and wrath. Shaver, Schwartz, Kirson, and O'Connor (1987) use "anger" in an even more inclusive sense, to refer to an unnamed family of emotions that comprises "anger" in Storm and Storm's sense, and two other generic categories named by Storm and Storm, "hostility" and "disgust."

Is anger universal? Only if we interpret it in the very broad sense of Shaver et al., which includes not only anger as a specific emotion, but also annoyance, frustration, vengefulness, contempt, envy, to name but a few additional members of the category.

But even at the level of broad generalities, we must account for universality. There are three possibilities: (1) biological universals, (2) social universals, and (3) ecological universals. In practice, these three possibilities are often related. For example, social universals may reflect our biological heritage, and our biological heritage (being a result of natural selection) may reflect certain ecological conditions. However, the three possibilities need not be related, and sometimes may even be in opposition. Societies may impose conditions that are counter to biologically based tendencies (e.g., by restricting sexual practices). And the ecology of much of the world today is far different from the ecology in which the human species—and even most human societies—evolved; hence, current ecological conditions (e.g., in over-populated urban areas) may call for different emotional responses than either biology or society has prepared us for.

Again let me take anger to illustrate the point. At a very broad level of generality anger might be defined as (1) an impulse toward aggression, (2) an attempt to enforce social norms, and (3) a response to frustration. The first definition implies a biological universal; the second, a social universal; and the third, an ecological universal. With regard to biological universals, only the ideologically committed can overlook the substantial evidence that human beings are an aggressive species, and that there are a variety of eliciting conditions for aggression that are also universal, a painful stimulus being among the most common (Berkowitz, 1990). With regard to social universals, all societies entail norms that help regulate interactions among members of the group, and which help distinguish one group from another. These norms, if they are to function, must be enforced in some manner. On the interpersonal level, anger might be considered one such "enforcement mechanism," and in this sense a "violation of social norms" would be a universal antecedent of anger. With regard to ecological universals, no environment is so benign that all of an individual's desires or actions can be immediately fulfilled; hence, if frustration is inevitable, so, too, must be attempts to overcome frustration. These attempts need not be "hard-wired"; they could be learned, or they could be inculcated by society. Probably, biology, society, and individual learning all play a role. The point is simply that *if* anger is defined as a response to frustration, then anger is also likely to be universal.

Similar considerations apply to other emotions. For example, if love is defined very broadly as a strong sexual attraction (or, in the case of Freud, as "aim-inhibited sex"), then it is universal. However, romantic love, as a specific emotional syndrome, is peculiar to western cultures (Averill, 1985). Or take hope, which, presumably, "springs eternal in the human breast." People everywhere face an uncertain future in which they would like some events to occur, and others not. In that sense, hope is undoubtedly universal. But as a specific emotional syndrome, hope as we know it in Western cultures is not universal (Averill, Catlin, & Chon, 1990).

In short, the universality of a response leads us to look for universalities of eliciting conditions, and vice versa. Universality per se, however, does not tell us whether the origins of the response are to be found in biological evolution, social conditions, or individual experience with the environment (or some combination of all three). Also—and this point cannot be overemphasized—these considerations presume that the emotion is being interpreted in the most generic sense: The broader our concepts, the smaller (less differentiated) the world seems to be. On the other hand, the more specific we get, the less meaningful it is to speak of either universal antecedents or responses: All the world is a stage, and when we are dealing from the perspective of specific emotions, it is a very large stage, with many differentiated roles to be played.

What level of specificity is most appropriate when analyzing emotions? That depends on one's purpose. Some people maintain that emotions are so individually unique, they are incommensurate across persons. "You can never experience love the way I do, for you are not me." That is an extreme position, but one sometimes voiced by humanistically oriented psychologists. It precludes any scientific analysis of the emotions, which become the domain of poets and artists.

At the other end of the continuum are theorists who lump all emotions into a few very broad categories that apply not only across individuals but across cultures. This strategy has the advantage of at least appearing scientific, since it presumably deals with universal rather than specific aspects of emotion. Unfortunately, the resulting formulations typically have little direct relation to the actual experiences of people.

My own preference is to approach emotions at an intermediate level of generality, namely, at that level where abstract concepts such as "anger," "love," "grief," and so on, and their counterparts in other cultures, have meaning in everyday discourse. At this level, there is generality across individuals within a culture (otherwise, the common term would have no meaning); there is, however, little evidence for cross-cultural equivalency at this level.

I do not wish to leave the impression that an intermediate level of analysis is superior to the others in every respect or for all purposes. The important point is that we should not make what Ryle (1949) called a category mistake, that is, assuming that what is true of categories at one level of generality (e.g., of anger as a generic category) is also true of categories at other levels (e.g., of anger as a specific emotion). Questions about the universality of emotions are particularly conducive to category mistakes.

Antecedent Events and Emotion Metaphors

PAUL EKMAN

When I first wrote about emotion and its expression (Ekman & Friesen, 1969; Ekman, 1972), I believed that antecedent events for each emotion were socially learned and therefore likely to be culture-specific, although expressions of emotion were universal. A few years later my former student Jerry Boucher (Boucher & Brandt, 1981) showed that I was wrong about the antecedent events. He and his colleague asked subjects which events typically precede an emotion, and they found commonalities across very different non-Western cultures. These commonalities were evident on an abstract or conceptual level, not in terms of the very specific details that were described. This work has been further advanced by Klaus Scherer and his colleagues (Scherer, Wallbott, & Summerfield, 1986) in their research on the antecedents of emotion in a number of literate cultures.

I should have known that I was wrong in proposing total cultural variability in emotion antecedents because of my own experience working in a preliterate culture in New Guinea in 1967. In my initial trip I showed subjects photographs of facial expressions and asked them to tell me what had occurred to bring about each expression. The most common story for the fear expressions was being attacked by a wild pig. Substitute a rabid dog and the story would work in America for fear—different in detail, but similar in general theme: the threat of physical harm, in this instance by an animal. And so it was for each of the six emotions I studied. (The following year I reversed the procedure and told the subjects one of the emotion stories and asked them to pick which expression fit the picture [Ekman, 1972; Ekman & Friesen, 1971]).

Informed by Boucher's work I subsequently proposed "[t]here are variations in the particulars of what elicits a particular emotion, yet there are also common features in what are identified as the elicitors for an emotion . . . [across cultures]" (Ekman, 1977, p. 58). Based on Boucher's findings and our own observations, we (Ekman & Friesen, 1975) described what those common features were likely to be. An actual or threat of harm for fear. The loss of an object to which one was attached for sadness. An event that is either unexpected or contrary to expectation for surprise.

Something that is repulsive, to the senses or to one's beliefs, for disgust. Disapproving and feeling morally superior to someone for contempt. For anger we suggested five antecedents: frustration resulting from interference with one's activity; a physical threat; an insult; seeing someone do something that violates one's values; another person's anger directed at oneself. For happiness we suggested four antecedents: sensory pleasure; excitement; praise; relief when something unpleasant has ceased.

My descriptions are similar to what Lazarus (1991) later posited as the "core relational themes" for each emotion; they are nearly identical for sadness, fear, and disgust, and differ in some regards in the other emotions. We must note that such proposed commonalities in emotion antecedents are abstract rather than detailed. For example, there are many different ways in which someone's activity can be interfered with, many different ways in which to obtain sensory pleasure, and so on. It is hard at this time to judge the merit of these proposals, other than how well they fit folk beliefs about what brings forth emotions.

Hereafter, I will capitalize Antecedents whenever I am referring to these commonalities across cultures in the events that reportedly often call forth specific emotions. I say "often" because I believe individual experience probably can counteract an Antecedent. Perhaps it is also possible for an entire social group or culture to counteract an Antecedent, but no definitive evidence exists to prove that. The closest case is Levy's (1984) report that the Tahitians do not have a word for sadness, and do not recognize the constellation of sad behaviors as caused by the loss of a loved person. But this is not sufficient to assert that the relationship between the sadness Antecedent and sadness responses is absent in that culture. It would be necessary to find that the Tahitians do not show the constellation of sad behaviors when experiencing loss. That was not what Levy observed. The Tahitians did show sad behaviors in response to loss even though they did not label it as sadness, and attributed those responses to illness rather than to the loss.

I presume that the commonalities in the antecedent events that call forth each emotion are the product of our evolution and reflect the most important or frequent events our ancestors encountered. (See Panksepp's discussion of archetypal ancestral memories in Question 9: What is the relation between emotion and memory?). Our emotional responses are the product of that evolution, and begin to mobilize us to respond in ways that were adaptive for our ancestors. It is not a fixed or closed system, solely the product of phylogeny. Ontogeny also plays a large role. Our experience not only fills in the details of each Antecedent, and adds new events unrelated to the Antecedents, but also offers individualized responses that become part of an emotional episode as it unfolds.

The question is how to account for the commonalities in antecedent events and also allow for variability in the specifics of the events that call forth each emotion. There may be completely idiosyncratic events that elicit emotions unique to a single person, and these may be quite unrelated to the Antecedent for that emotion. There also could be an idiosyncratic event that calls forth an emotion that is related to an Antecedent. And there should be a variety of specific events that are shared by members of a social group or culture, which differ from other groups in detail but on a more abstract level show commonalities, and thus are derivative or at least conforming to an Antecedent.

Before addressing the question of how these commonalities in emotion antecedents are transmitted from one generation to another, I need to digress for a moment to describe two types of emotional appraisal. I distinguished *automatic* appraisal from *extended* appraisal (Ekman, 1977). In the automatic appraisal, the organism responds in milliseconds to an event, with the cascade of emotional response changes occurring immediately, and often coincident but not necessarily prior to awareness of what has occurred. The issue I will address shortly is: How does our evolutionary history influence automatic appraisal to respond to the commonalities in the antecedent events for each emotion? Extended appraisal involves an activity that resembles problem-solving rather than reflexive or habitual behavior. An event is evaluated, considered, and then after some time the cascade of emotional responses may occur.

Scherer and Ellsworth have each offered models of how emotional appraisal occurs, and presumably their models apply to both automatic and extended appraisal. (See also Roseman, 1991, and Stein and Trabasso, 1992, for still other such models.) I find no reason to argue with any of these models, but I do not view them as convincing descriptions of how the mind actually operates during an emotion. They are instead attempts to account for how people explain what brings about their emotions. This is important information; it may tell us much about how people represent their emotional experience, and this may be very relevant to how they cope, how they justify, how they remember, and how they discuss their emotions with others. These appraisal models perhaps also may have provided a veridical account of what transpires during extended appraisal, or at least for one's memory of or attempt to explain one's extended appraisals. But they cannot tell us what happens during automatic appraisal.

If we were to ask people about their emotions the moment we notice that they occur, we would not be much better off. I presume that most automatic appraisal takes place in milliseconds, prior to awareness. Furthermore, I expect that people do not have the ability to identify during the emotional episode, or afterwards, the initial processes that occurred in those milliseconds. Thus, I believe we should not rely on what people tell us for evidence about how automatic appraisal operates. This is not to deny the importance of what people say about their emotions in understanding many other aspects of emotion—it is just not likely to be useful for understanding automatic appraisals.

In trying to answer the question of how automatic appraisal can allow for both variability and commonalities in what calls forth each emotion, I have borne in mind the need to devise a proposal that has some hope of being subject to empirical test. As explained earlier, I posit a limited number of abstract, antecedent events for each emotion. Is information about these abstract events genetically transmitted—pretuning, alerting, or sensitizing in some fashion automatic appraisal to occurrences that conform to them? Possibly, but let me suggest a more limited view of what is transmitted genetically, using fear as my example. There may be only one or two fear-relevant events that are genetically transmitted, and all others may be acquired, more or less readily depending on how closely they resemble these fear events. Let me suggest four candidates, based on conjecture about what events might have been most frightening during our evolutionary history. (1) Anticipating physical pain. (2) An object moving very quickly toward you, which would injure you if you did not duck. (3) A sudden loss of physical support, so that you are falling through space.

(4) Being touched from behind when you do not believe anyone else is present.[1] Conceivably, there might be just one such event or a limited number that are *the* fear events.

Any antecedent event that resembles one of these four would be easily acquired; and the greater the resemblance, the more easily it would be acquired. These events stand as metaphors for most of the specific antecedents that become part of our repertoire for calling forth fear. I believe it should be possible to learn other specific antecedent events for fear–or any other emotion–that are not related to one of these three events, but it should take longer to acquire those unrelated fear antecedents.

Measuring the latency of emotional reactions when presented with an emotional event could be a way to test this formulation. I am presuming that when automatic appraisal operates, there might still be some variation in the speed of operation as a function of how closely any particular event resembles the given fear event(s). The greater the resemblance, the shorter the response. The responses to be examined in such research should not be peripheral, such as expression or autonomic nervous system activity, but measures of central nervous system activity. The place to begin is with one of the themes that I or anyone else has proposed, and to compare stimulus events that more or less resemble it.

No one knows how automatic appraisal operates to call forth emotion, in ways that both show commonalities and differences across people and cultures. The challenge is to figure out a way of beginning empirically to find some reasonable approximations.

Note

1. This was suggested by Alexandra Kostic (personal communication, May 1993).

Some Reasons to Expect Universal Antecedents of Emotion

PHOEBE C. ELLSWORTH

First, human beings are all of the same species. Their bodies, their autonomic nervous systems, their hormones, and their sense organs resemble each other in structure and in use, and there is no doubt that these brains, autonomic nervous systems, hormones, and sense organs are essential to emotion.

Second, in order to survive in the world, human beings must be able to appreciate changes in the environment that have important consequences for their well-being, and they must be able to respond to these changes effectively. They must cope with immediate perils and take advantage of immediate opportunities, and they must be concerned with the various threats and opportunities that are not so immediate. There are commonalities in the kinds of external events that make life better or worse for human beings, just as there are commonalities in our internal equipment. Like all species, humans are built to respond to the things that matter, and the way humans do it is by emotion. Enormous loud objects rapidly bearing down on us must be escaped, and fear provides the motivating force. Encouraging behavior from an attractive member of the opposite sex comes to evoke desire in most people at about the time they reach sexual maturity. If our species is to survive, our babies must grow up, and so their mothers must love them. When we need something, and see an opportunity to get it, we feel hopeful, perhaps challenged if we also perceive an obstacle, and are moved to go after it. When we get it, we feel relief or joy. Although physical and social environments around the world are all different from each other, they all include novelty, hazard, opportunity, attack, gratification, and loss. These are changes that people must deal with, and these are the kinds of events that generate emotion. To ignore them would make learning impossible, and would jeopardize life itself.

To respond appropriately to these consequential events, we must perceive them fairly accurately and recognize their importance. If our brains are similar, and our perceptions are accurate, it follows that this kind of important environmental event will be a universal antecedent of emotion across societies, although not necessarily among all individuals within any particular society. There are universal antecedents to emotion insofar as there are universal human needs and goals. (By "universal" I mean, as most psychologists do, "very general." There may be societies that deviate from these very abstract propositions in some respects, but "almost universal" is the best most social psychologists dare to aspire to.)

There is some evidence for quite specific emotion elicitors that are very common, if not universal, but there is not very much evidence. Loss of support or sense of direction, separation from a mother, sudden intense noises, abrupt movements, caresses, and secondary sexual characteristics have all been suggested as universal elicitors of specific emotional responses, but the actual research record is quite thin. Most studies compare only a handful of cultures, or only two, or show a similarity between humans and some other primate species (Suomi & Harlow, 1976). Aside from a few reflexive responses such as the startle response and responses to certain tastes, however, the specificity of the elicitors that have been proposed is questionable, if by "specificity" we mean that a particular, well-defined stimulus (e.g., separation from the mother) elicits a particular, well-defined emotional response (e.g., anxiety). Most of the specific universal elicitors described reliably lead to negative or positive emotions, but further specification is problematical (Frijda, 1986). Separation from the mother is arousing and unpleasant, but the specific response is by no means universal even within a culture, sometimes appearing as grief, sometimes as fear, sometimes with signs of anger. In humans, the potential for complexity is as universal as anything, and in order to find underlying consistency, appraisal theorists suggest that we consider stimuli at a more abstract level. Several more abstract elicitors have been proposed (cf. Arnold, 1960; Frijda, 1986; Ortony, Lazarus, 1991; Clore, & Collins, 1988; Roseman, 1984; Scherer, 1984; Smith & Ellsworth, 1985; Stein & Levine, 1989; Wiener, 1985).

Novelty or Strangeness

A change in one's environment merits attention and, I would argue, gets attention, universally. Such a change is a major entry point, arguably *the* major entry point, to the world of emotions. Novelty is not positive or negative in itself. It may result in interest, fear, relief, or any emotion, but, without it, emotions are unlikely. Novel events trigger an identifiable neural circuit, creating something like a predisposition or state of readiness for emotion (LeDoux, 1989; Posner & Rothbart, 1992). Of course, the novel stimulus need not be an external event; it can be a thought or a memory. If a person remembers the long-ago death of a child after many weeks of not thinking about it, the memory is novel in context, and the grief is elicited anew.

Valence

A rapid, seemingly automatic response to stimuli as positive or negative is also common to many emotional experiences and is very likely universal across cultures

(Zajonc, 1980). Many of the "specific" emotion elicitors that have been proposed are stimuli that trigger this sort of immediate positive or negative response, rather than further differentiated varieties of positive or negative response. The idea that pleasantness–unpleasantness is a fundamental characteristic of emotional experience is common to almost every theory of emotion, and valence accounts for the largest proportion of the variance in most studies of emotion.

A sense of valence is frequently assumed to be an immediate, inevitable response, but it is not *necessarily* so; sometimes people can feel that a stimulus is potentially significant, but not yet know enough to feel positive or negative (Ellsworth, 1991; Kagan, 1991). A stranger approaching one's door or an odd noise somewhere in the house may elicit alertness and a sense of intensity that will only turn into a valenced response as more information becomes available. Sometimes people can feel ambivalent over quite long periods of time. But even in these situations valence lurks as a universal, because it is the knowledge of the likelihood of a valenced response that makes the stimulus emotionally significant in the first place. The *possibility* of a valenced response—"this event may be good or bad for me"—is enough to elicit emotion.

Certainty and Uncertainty.

Besides responding immediately to novelty, a person may continue to experience some level of uncertainty about an event over a period of time. One may be uncertain about the valence of an event, as described above. When the valence is known, a person may still be uncertain about the probability of the event's occurring, his or her ability to deal with it appropriately, or just *how* good or bad it is. Uncertainty about probably positive events leads to interest and curiosity, or to hope. Uncertainty about probably negative events leads to anxiety and fear.

A sense of certainty may also color the emotional experience, and changes from a state of uncertainty to certainty or vice versa generally have emotional consequences. When certainty replaces uncertainty, fear turns to relief or despair, and hope may evolve into trust (Frijda, 1986, p. 209).

Obstacles and Control

Since emotions are motivating responses to consequential events in the environment, the perception of obstacles and the assessment of one's ability to cope with the situation are fundamental to emotional experiences. Lazarus and Folkman (1984) term these coping appraisals "secondary appraisals," as opposed to the "primary appraisals" of the event itself. If we assume that all people have implicit and explicit goals, and that obstacles exist in all cultures, then the perception of a goal obstacle is a highly likely universal elicitor of emotion. The particular emotion will depend on the size of the obstacle and the degree of confidence one feels about overcoming it (control). A fairly high sense of control may lead to a sense of challenge; as one's sense of control decreases, challenge may change to frustration or fear. Prolonged lack of control can lead to desperation, hopelessness, and resignation. In our research (Smith & Ellsworth, 1985), we have found that a sense of control is itself positively valenced; people are happier about events they think they've brought about themselves than they are about equally pleasant events brought about by others or by chance. There is no evidence that this correlation is universal.

Also, the perception of an obstacle and the sense of control, along with a third, related concept, the need to expend effort, are conceptually distinct. I've included them under the same heading here because the conceptual distinction has only sometimes been borne out in our empirical work.

Agency

If we know the cause of an event, we are often considerably better equipped to deal with it than if we don't know the cause. This is especially true of negative events, which typically demand more immediate and appropriate action than positive events (Rozin & Fallon, 1987). Missing opportunities is bad for survival, but ignoring significant threats is worse. We have consistently found that the attribution of agency is important in differentiating among the negative emotions of anger, sorrow, and guilt. Negative events seen as caused by other people evoke anger; negative events seen as caused by oneself evoke shame, guilt (or regret); negative events "caused" by fate or chance or uncontrollable circumstances result in sorrow.

I would tentatively suggest agency as a universal appraisal affecting the nature of people's emotional response. This still leaves a lot of room for cultural variation, however. First, cultural belief systems regarding the causes of events will affect emotional responses to those events; fate, for example, may play a much larger role in some cultures than in others. Second, there is some evidence that perceptions of agency are not as consistent in their relationship to specific emotions across cultures as are the other appraisals we have discussed. Mauro, Sato, and Tucker (1992), for example, found that attribution of agency was important in differentiating among emotions for Chinese and American subjects, but the Chinese were more likely to be saddened when negative events were caused by other people, whereas for Americans sadness is associated with the perception that the event was caused by circumstances beyond anyone's control.

Norm/Self-concept Compatibility

Scherer (1984) proposes a final ("final" in both the ontogenetic and phylogenetic sense) component of emotion that he calls "norm/self-concept compatibility," that is, the extent to which one sees some aspect of oneself as meeting or violating one's personal standards or the standard of one's reference group. Ostracism from one's group or rejection by one's parents (in childhood) or one's mate (in adulthood) are plausible candidates for universal sources of distress in a social species such as humans (Gray, 1971), and the perceived threat of such ostracism may make the awareness that one has violated important standards a highly general, perhaps universal, elicitor of emotion as well.

It should be obvious that I tend toward a view of emotion as process, rather than as a set of entities, and the "antecedents" I have suggested are perceptions that initiate or elaborate emotional processes or change their course, not stimuli that trigger a fully articulated experience corresponding to a categorically distinct "basic" emotion.

It should also be obvious that the antecedents I talk about are not generally the environmental events themselves, but the events-as-perceived by the person. It is in these "perceptions" or "appraisals" or "interpretations" that we may find evidence of universals, rarely in the external event.

The antecedents I've suggested show a rough progression from relatively simple, automatic, and less "cognitive" to relatively complex, potentially modifiable, and more "cognitive." I've considered the hypothesis that there is more room for individual and cultural variation in the more complex appraisals, such as agency and norm/self-concept compatibility, and thus that these will be less likely to be universal. There's a plausibility to the idea. On the other hand, even at the least "cognitive" levels—the perception of novelty or discrepancy and the primitive valence response—there is enormous room for individual and cultural variation in the events themselves. Culture and environment create familiarity and therefore define unfamiliarity. A car is unlikely to be "noticed" in an American city; a camel attracts attention. In a North African village, it is the other way around. At the most complex level, as I mentioned above, there is fairly good evidence that social ostracism may be a universal source of misery. The empirical record is still embarrassingly thin.

Universal Antecedents Exist, and Are Interesting

NICO H. FRIJDA

There is little systematic research on the universality of emotion antecedents except for the work by Scherer and his collaborators (Scherer, Walbott, & Summerfield, 1986; Scherer & Walbott, 1986). Apart from that, the evidence has to be pieced together from scattered mentions in the literature, and a satisfactory, well-founded evaluation of how much generality in emotion antecedents exists cannot be obtained without considerable effort. Most comparative studies of emotion antecedents have focused on specificity. Also, cultural differences strike the eye more readily than similarities, let alone universality. Specificity can be established on the basis of two cultures; universality only on the basis of all of them. Nevertheless, in trying to give an answer to the question of explaining evidence of universals, I have to form an opinion about that evidence. What evidence I know of indeed suggests a considerable degree of generality, if not universality, in emotion antecedents.

Evidence for Universal Antecedents

Degree of universality depends on the level of specificity chosen to categorize the antecedents: whether that of specific emotion events, of emotion-arousing themes as distinguished and labeled within given culture, or of themes defined at a psychologically and interpersonally relevant level of abstractness (Mesquita & Frijda, 1992). At that abstract level, a considerable degree of generality of emotion antecedents appears to exist (Scherer, Walbott, & Summerfield, 1986; Scherer & Walbott, 1986). Lazarus (1991) calls this level that of "core relation themes": antecedent themes such as harm, threat, loss, or success in achieving one's aims or goals. Which events are considered as harmful, as threats, or as losses may differ from one culture to another; whether they are so considered depends on how the events are coded, and which concerns or values they are considered to favor or threaten. It also depends on the way the events are appraised regarding their fit with the individual's capacities for dealing with them, since core relational themes correspond to patterns of appraisals

(Lazarus & Smith, 1988; Lazarus, 1991). A given event can be considered to spell future evil by one person or group, and not by another. But once a given event is conceived as representing some such theme—success, harm, loss, and the like—emotion appears to be aroused everywhere, and a similar emotion at that. "Similar emotion" is of course a somewhat tricky concept, since emotion labels are often not straightforwardly translated or translatable; in the present context it means emotional arousal, and readiness for similar actions and activation changes like mourning and dejection in response to loss, readiness for avoidance or self-protection in response to threat, repair efforts and help-seeking in response to harm, and negative social behavior upon offense.

There also is a close correspondence between certain universally occuring event types and the core relational theme that they represent and, consequently, the emotions they tend to evoke. These event types include physical danger, risk for material and social deprivation (for harm or threat or distress and fear), illness and death of close relatives (for loss or sorrow), achievement of material and social goals (for success or joy), and evil treatment by others of equal rank (for frustration or anger).

In addition, there probably are several event types that are not so easily grasped in terms of the core relational themes discussed by Lazarus, and that also appear to elicit emotions universally or near universally. Among these are: threats to exclusive sexual access, unless such access is explicitly granted (eliciting an emotion like jealousy; Buunk & Hupka, 1987); inequality of access to valued goods by social equals (envy); experiencing willfully inflicted harm to one's kin, possessions, or social status (anger, hatred, desire for vengeance), behavior or properties entailing risk of social rejection (shame), having unintentionally harmed someone within one's group (guilt), meeting others superior in social status (shyness, embarrassment; Shweder, this volume). I have added the typical English emotion categories, to clarify the kinds of event that are meant. Equivalent emotion categories may not exist in all cultures, nor will the event types necessarily evoke similar emotions in all cultures. I propose, however, that the event types indicated evoke some emotion (and for most of these types, some negative emotion) near universally.

I expect that almost none of these emotion antecedents is absolutely universal; neither will such event types invariably elicit some emotion, or a given emotion, in all individuals within a given group, or in a given individual at all times. That, by itself, does not conflict with the hypothesis that those event types represent universal elicitors of emotion. Propensities to respond emotionally to particular events are readily overridden by incompatible emotions (such as anger being easily overridden by fear of retaliation or of loss of love), or by cultural taboos. This does not render the propensity any less universal. Support for the notion that universality is involved, exceptions notwithstanding, comes from the high degree of generality with which the emotions are cross-culturally encountered. To conclude from generality-with-exceptions that some biologically universal disposition may be involved is familiar from other domains. The study of gender differences provides an example. Male dominance in society is the rule, though not universal; female dominance can be observed in a few cultures (Maccoby & Jacklin, 1974) and in chimpanzees in exceptional circumstances (De Waal, 1982). The very large difference in frequency of occurrence suggests that dominance is more easily established in males than in females. Similarly, although infringement on unique sexual access after bonding is not always or everywhere a cause for anger or upset (i.e., for jealousy), the generality of such upset suggests a universal sensitivity. Such a sensitivity can be neutralized, for instance, by extended cultural definitions of the self (Markus & Kitayama, 1991), or by norms of hospitality; there still is reason to assume its existence.

What Is to be Explained?

In examining explanations of generally occurring antecedents, we must distinguish two levels of generality. The first concerns the generality of emotional valence of particular events or environmental contingencies. For generality in this sense, particular event types should generally elicit *some* positive or negative emotion. The second concerns the generality with which particular event types elicit a particular emotion. The second level, of course, assumes that universal emotions exist, as defined by criteria other than the particular type of eliciting event. I will not go deeply into the arguments for the existence of universal emotions in this sense. I think that a small set of emotional response patterns does exist, each defined by a set of behaviors that share a common aim or relational intent (i.e., by a particular "mode of action readiness," such as self-protective, agonistic, proximity-seeking, exuberant, apathic; Frijda, 1986), and that can be observed with high cross-cultural generality. Note that this definition of universal emotions differs from the one given previously, which took universal emotions elicitors as its point of departure. I think there is sufficient evidence to assume the existence of a number of universal emotions, *in this sense*, examples of which are joy (defined as contact-enhancing exuberance), fear (self-protection), anger (provoked agonistic behavior), arrogance or dominance (unprovoked aggressive or menacing behavior), sadness (apathy and help-solliciting), anxiety (movement inhibition), shame (blushing and hiding behavior), aversion (a variety of physical-rejection behaviors). In addition, certain universal response modes exist that consist of unfocalized action tendencies, such as restless behavior (often labeled *excitement*), or apathetic or tense tendency to shut off stimulation (often labeled *distress*).

Universally Pleasant and Unpleasant Events

How do we explain the universalities? Several different mechanisms can plausibly be evoked, and I think they all apply and interact. The first and major one is that there are, I believe, a number of stimuli to which humans are innately affectively sensitive; these stimuli are in themselves capable of evoking affect. They tend innately to be liked or disliked, sought or avoided.

Affect arousal, liking and disliking, do not, by themselves, constitute emotions, if emotions are defined by changes in action readiness with control precedence. There is no emotion when someone likes the smell he or she smells. Additional factors are involved for an emotion to occur. Yet, affect is a decisive prerequisite for an emotion, and affect is often elicited by stimuli that act without learning, that is, without association to something else. The human organism just seems to be made that way. This would seem to apply to certain tastes and smells (sweet taste of moderate intensity is an example; Pfaffman, 1960) and, I would guess, also certain visual, olfactory, tactual, and perhaps auditory sexual stimuli (the literature on sexual stimuli in humans is curiously scant). It also applies, however, to more complex events. The number of innately pleasant or unpleasant events probably is fairly large. I enumerate a few, selected at random: unrestrained execution of self-initiated movement; cognitive assimilation; acceptance by the group or by valued group members; sense of self-efficacy (whatever the definition of the self and, thus, the precise content; see Markus & Kitayama, 1990). Of all these, I hold that they innately tend to evoke positive affect. Pain, sustained effort, physical conditions deviating appreciably from norm conditions—all innately evoke negative affect. Note, incidentally, that most of these inherently pleasant or unpleasant events are not in any real sense "stimuli." What elicits pleasure or what is felt as unpleasant is in many cases the execution or failure of execution of particular actions. Being accepted by one's group, too, can probably best be seen as the net outcome of group-approaching and group-inserting behaviors.

Certain affective values appear to originate on the basis of curious mixtures of learned and unlearned elements, as, for example, those that occur in imprinting and other forms of liking for stimuli that have become familiar (Bowlby, 1969; Hebb, 1949; Zajonc, 1968). These latter instances are highly instructive. That infants attach to a particular individual is a matter of learning; that they *attach* to that individual is not. That they encounter individuals to attach to is ubiquitous, or nearly so. That being close to such individuals, or meeting familiar objects becomes an affective stimulus, is a consequence of the way the organism is made, even if as such it is not innate.

I said that these stimuli or events innately, or through some general and unspecific form of learning, "tend" to elicit positive or negative affect. My hedging comes from two qualifications. First, the stimuli may be of subthreshold affective intensity, or have become so through habituation. Second, affective valence may be overruled by other simultaneous affective influence. The most interesting of these influences consists of affect evoked by the stimulus-evoked affect. Pain may cause enjoyment when that pain has an additional moral (as in martyrs) or sexual (as in masochists) meaning; sexual pleasure may incite feelings of guilt. Both qualifications modify the regularity of which affects are evoked by particular events without damaging the thesis of universality through innateness of affect arousal. Of course, these qualifications merely extend the qualifications that justify taking generality of emotion antecedents as sufficient evidence for their "universality."

Arousal of affect, as I just said, is not emotion. In fact, the affectively valenced stimuli or events constitute "concerns," that is, motives or reasons for striving to maintain or obtain the states of events involved, or to escape from them or prevent them from occurring in the case of negative affective valence. They evoke emotions when—and only when—achieving desirable states or avoiding undesirable ones is rendered uncertain, or when such uncertainty has been overcome. Together with several other theories, I hold that emotions are elicited when events challenge or did challenge one's ability to cope with affectively valenced events. Emotions are aroused when difficulties have arisen in dealing with events that are relevant to one's concerns or, in a related formulation, when achieving one's valued goals proceeds faster or slower than expected (Carver & Scheier, 1990; "faster than expected" is taken to be equivalent to "uncertainty overcome"). To the extent that affect-evoking events are universal, the concerns are universal; and to the extent that concerns are universal, events that challenge one's ability to deal with threats and opportunities with regard to them are universal emotion antecedents. If the presence of one or a few particular individuals is universally liked, then bonding to attachment figures is universal; if bonding to attachment figures is universal, than sickness or death of such a figure is a universal elicitor for emotion, and so is rejoining him or her after prolonged absence.

Just for completeness sake, let me add that emotions do not arise merely when there are difficulties in the achievement of one's concerns. They also arise when opportunities for satisfaction present themselves, and in the process of satisfying. "Love" is the name of one such emotion. Yet I think that the notion of uncertainty (or "faster than expected") is applicable here. When "love" is taken as referring to an emotion, to an acute inner movement, and not to a sentiment stretched out in time, it can be argued that love is felt only when the presence of the object is not taken for granted, is not self-evident.

Human concerns do not revolve solely around innate pleasant or unpleasant events. I suspect that certain issues are of general or universal concern as a consequence of the rewards and punishments provided by social interaction and group belongingness. Self-esteem and the integrity and status of one's social group or groups are examples. Self-esteem probably is a concern of high generality, even if the specific attributes on which self-esteem is based differ considerably from culture to culture. The same holds for the status of one's group; it forms a ready ground for intergroup violence and lesser forms of antagonism (Tajfel, 1982). Universal emotion antecedents derive from such concerns, too: Emotions arise when these concerns are hurt or when they receive satisfaction.

Universal Conditions for Emotion

Wherever you go in the world, emotions are aroused when affectively valenced events occur that are or were so constituted as to challenge one's ability to deal with them. That in itself is a general innate antecedent of emotions, independent of whether or not the event is universally felt as pleasant or unpleasant. It is a universal emotion antecedent at a higher level of analysis than when we talk about specific types of events; it also embodies the factor that turns universally affective events into emotion elicitors.

What gives events the character of challenges or difficulties in dealing with them would appear to include a solid core of universal, or at least relatively culture-independent, aspects. The notions of "challenge" and "difficulty" refer to obstacles and interferences on the way to reaching desired outcome or preventing undesired ones. These notions also point to the imminence of such outcomes, inasmuch as the shorter the time to grasp opportunity is, or to ward off harm, the greater the risk of not succeeding. Obstacles and interferences are partly of a physical, partly of a social nature, but they are at least to some considerable degree independent of the particular history of the individual or group concerned. What constitutes an obstacle or interference in large measure depends on the actual powers and coping propensities of the individual, in relation to those of the obstructing or interfering agent, and thus has as much to do with the laws of physics and basic social interaction as with cultural learning, or norms and values.

Universal Antecedents of Specific Emotions

This whole line of argument points to an explanation of whatever universality there is in the antecedents of particular emotions. In my view, different emotions, as defined by modes of action readiness, are elicited by different patterns of event features often referred to as "appraisal patterns." Appraisal patterns consist of patterns of context features that are relevant for designing coping actions, as perceived by the subject on the basis of actual cues or expectations. These context features include interruption, unexpectedness, uncertainty, others' agency, anticipation regarding future benefit or harm, (un)controllability, (ir)remediability, and focality (Frijda, Kuipers, & Terschure, 1989; Lazarus, 1991; Roseman, 1991; Scherer, 1984; Smith & Ellsworth, 1985). Different emotions are elicited by different appraisal patterns; these patterns represent the proximal eliciting stimuli for the various emotional responses as well as the internal structure of Lazarus' core relational themes. Personal loss, for instance, is manifest most directly to the individual as decrease or absence of a pleasant or satisfying conditions, when that decrease or absence is sensed to be irremediable. Evidence is accumulating that most or all of these features are universal in defining different emotion structures (Mauro, Sato, & Tucker, 1992), which is not too surprising. They reflect appraisals of what one can do to or with events. The feature "irremediable" may simply mean that recuperative efforts have failed and the repertoire of recuperative efforts is exhausted.

It is clear what this means for the explanation of universal elicitors for particular emotions. Personal loss leads universally to grief (sorrow, sadness, *fago*, or whatever nameless state of mourning and apathy) because personal loss corresponds to the eliciting pattern of the grief response, namely, irremediable absence. Frustration and insults lead to anger (readiness for intimidation, threat, and harming) when and because frustrations and insults are aversive events with the features of behavior obstruction and agency by others, and so on. The link between appraisal pattern and form of action readiness is itself a universal or near-universal. It forms the spine of our emotional makeup, the core of the emotion mechanisms. Emotional response patterns like self-protection, agonistic readiness, behavior interruption, and activation increase, and activation decrease are not operants. They therefore must have wired-in eliciting conditions. These conditions are to be found in the particular stimulus structures, or cognitive structures, that I termed appraisal patterns.

I do not think, incidentally, that emotional responses are always triggered by the appraisal patterns in the ways indicated. If sufficiently primed, fragments of such patterns might be sufficient for elicitation of a particular emotion. The priming may be due to the individual's makeup, predisposing the person to a particular type of emotional response. Any aversive stimulus may elicit anger in some people, or in someone whose angry response readiness has been aroused by previous frustrations. Any unclarity about how to deal with the event that presents itself may evoke apprehension and defensive withdrawal in an individual high on the trait of Negative Affect (Watson & Clark, 1984) or Neuroticism (Eysenck, 1967). Other forms of priming may come from the socially conditioned expectation that a specific emotion will be shown in a specific context.

Conclusions: The Explanations of Universal Emotion Antecedents

I have sketched several mechanisms that, in my view, account for universal emotion elicitors: innate affective stimulus sensitivities, the general (innate or other) conditions for emotions as such, universal concerns, general occurrence of emotion-keying appraisal cues in events with more or less universal affective appeal.

This does not exhaust the possible explanations of universal emotion elicitors. As Hebb (1970) has argued, particular reactions may be universal because particular events happen to occur universally. It could, for instance, be that jealousy springs from an innate sensitivity to the appearance of sexual rivals (animal behavior would suggest this; De Waal, 1982). It could also be, however, that the only thing that is innate is the negative affective valence of threat of loss, and that rivals happen to be around and active wherever you turn.

In fact, many of the general or universal emotion antecedents may well have much more complex origins. One should not too easily reach for simple and straightforward explanations in terms of innateness, and devise evolutionary explanations for them. For instance, one of the very general classes of emotion elicitors consists of offenses to the integrity or status of one's social group. Current events in the Balkans or countries of the former Soviet Union illustrate how readily anger can be evoked, and shared by large groups of individuals, in this domain. Audience reactions in football also illustrates how easily violent emotions, again including anger, are evoked by what happens to a team one identifies with. Why should this be so? One possible explanation is an ingrained tendency to identify with one's group, created by evolution because of the obvious advantages that this produces. The rewards of group loyalty may well be considerable. But it is equally possible that such identification arises because others take you as a member of your group. The emotions might originate in the, possibly universal, fact that others, members of another group as much as of your own, treat you as one of that group, and more or less force your loyalty on you.

I think it is clear that plausible explanations for universal emotion elicitors are easy to come by. Compelling evidence is more difficult to obtain. Such evidence is not absent but, as I said in the beginning, should be amplified by systematic search. First, there is the evidence for innate emotional response patterns, in the human and animal species-specific response patterns (Bolles, 1970), that include facial expressions but are not exhausted by these. These patterns logically must have prewired, and thus universal, eliciting conditions. Whether those conditions consist of more or less general feature patterns (like appraisal patterns) or particular types of events (like group expulsion) remains to be analyzed. Second, evidence is accumulating on the widespread occurrence of certain event types as emotion elicitors, as well as the affective valence of the general emotion-eliciting conditions such as interruption, thwarting of expectations or goal achievement, and challenge to coping. Third, the growing evidence for the universality of appraisal dimensions and patterns suggests that emotion elicitors in fact are universal, at least on that plane of abstraction. Massive data have, in fact, been assembled by various investigators, in the data bank of emotion antecedents being established by the CERE-group in Western Europe, under Scherer's initiative, that might make valid assessments possible.

Universal Antecedents of the Emotions

RICHARD LAZARUS

The wording of this question is particularly interesting for several reasons, each worthy of note: First, the question assumes that universals exist rather than soliciting evidence for or against; second, instead of centering attention on the peripheral features of the emotional response, such as expressive or physiological patterns—which is what most research on universals addresses—the question is directed at the antecedents of emotion; third, the question is not about universals, per se, but asks how we might explain them, which points us toward theory.

Of the many difficult issues that must be resolved by a theory of emotion, I consider among the most important to be reconciling biological universals with cultural sources of variability. I present my own attempt to do this with five basic propositions, beginning with three about biological universals, one that draws on both biology and culture, and a fifth that centers on cultural sources of variability.

Biological Universals in the Antecedents of Emotion

Proposition I is central to all cognitive approaches in presuming that all complex creatures capable of learning—especially mammals—are characterized by the fundamental biological property of constantly evaluating what is happening with respect to their well-being. The more biologically advanced and intelligent a creature, the more complex, subtle, and symbolic these evaluations can be, though they may also be simple, hasty, and concrete.

It is by means of this evaluation process, which I call *appraisal*, that we know how to respond selectively to conditions signifying harm, threat, and benefit and, thereby, to cope adaptively. These conditions often require long-range coping strategies based on a sophistocated anticipation of the future. Emotions constitute the main evolutionary-adaptational system in intelligent creatures, and they depend on motivational, cognitive, and coping activities that orient these creatures selectively to relevant features of their environments.

Proposition II takes as its premise that the appraised significance of what is happening involves a particular kind of *relational meaning*. As I indicated in my response to Question 2, the significance for well-being, whether of harm, threat, or benefit, depends on the conjunction of the conditions present in the environment with personal goals, beliefs, and adaptational resources. Relational meaning, therefore, has to do with the adaptational match or mismatch between an individual and the environmental conditions being faced. Harms and threats lead to negative emotions; benefits to positive ones. And anger implies a particular kind of harm or threat, anxiety another, and so on; similarly, happiness implies a particular kind of benefit, pride another, and so on.

Anger, anxiety, pride, and so on, consist of separate and distinct emotion families, though each occurrence of a given emotion is apt to be somewhat different from the prototypical ideal (see Lazarus, 1991b, Chapter 2). I have already proposed distinctive core relational themes (CRT) for each emotion (Lazarus, 1991a, 1991b, 1991c). Although the details are open to argument and further evidence, and one could suggest additional emotions or deletions from the list, the core relational themes and the emotions they serve are presented in Table 1.

A core relational theme is the molar, cognitive-motivational-relational essence of a prototypical emotion, a configuration that defines the key harm or benefit implied in the person-environment relationship. Knowing the CRT should enable us to explain and predict the emotion that is aroused. In addition, to fully understand the emotion process requires knowledge of the molecular appraisals by means of which the individual arrives at the core relational theme that underlies each emotion. I have dealt with this in detail in Lazarus (1991a, 1991b, 1991c), and need not repeat that analysis here.

Proposition III is that the connection between relational meaning and each emotion is innate, a characteristic of the species. Specifically, and stated as an "if-then" form of reasoning, if a person appraises his or her relationship to the environ-

TABLE 1 Core Relational Themes for Each Emotion

Anger	A demeaning offense against me and mine.
Anxiety	Facing uncertain, existential threat.
Fright	An immediate, concrete, and overwhelming physical danger.
Guilt	Having transgressed a moral imperative.
Shame	Failing to live up to an ego-ideal.
Sadness	Having experienced an irrevocable loss.
Envy	Wanting what someone else has.
Jealousy	Resenting a third party for loss or threat to another's affection or favor.
Disgust	Taking in or being too close to an indigestiable object or idea (metaphorically speaking).
Happiness	Making reasonable progress toward the realization of a goal.
Pride	Enhancement of one's ego-identity by taking credit for a valued object or achievement, either one's own or that of someone or a group with whom we identify.
Relief	A distressing goal-incongruent condition that has changed for the better or gone away.
Hope	Fearing the worst but wanting better.
Love	Desiring or participating in affection, usually but not necessarily reciprocated.
Compassion	Being moved by another's suffering and wanting to help.

ment in a particular way, then a specific emotion—which is tied to the appraisal pattern—always follows. All persons will react with the emotion that is defined by its core relational theme and the appraisal pattern, which express the essential relational meaning. The "if-then" formula is, in effect, a *psychobiological principle*, which helps us understand universals in the antecedents of emotions.

From this standpoint, the task of normative analysis and research is to examine the core relational theme and appraisal pattern for each emotion. With an individual's adaptational transaction, however, the task is to decipher the relational meaning that inheres in an individual's particular adaptational encounter. Some details of the proposed normative relational meanings are clearly controversial, for example, whether adult anger requires the sense of being demeaned or belittled or, alternatively as Berkowitz (1989) has argued, that personal insult merely enhances or moderates the capacity of frustration to generate anger. Insofar as possible, we should attempt to resolve such controversies through programmatic research that could sharpen our understanding of the process for each emotion.

To put Proposition III a bit differently, we could say that—regardless of the actual environmental conditions—if two individuals appraise the relational meaning of an encounter in the same way, they will inevitably react with the same emotion; if they confront different environmental conditions but make the same appraisal, they will also react with the same emotion; and if they confront the same conditions but appraise them differently—perhaps as a result of different goals or belief systems—they will react with different emotions. In this brief essay, unfortunately, it is necessary to beg a number of important questions that arise from this analysis, such as whether the emotional reaction is evident to the observer or to the individual who reacts, and whether and how the emotion experienced or displayed can be modified in consciousness or in expression. These issues are extremely complicated and require careful examination (see Lazarus, 1991c).

Universals imply some kind of innate process. Eibel-Eibesfeldt (1989, Ch. 2) has examined evidence for innateness from an ethological point of view (However, see Lehrman, 1953, for a critique.) The gist of his argument may be found in a statement that opens his most recent book (1989, p. 19):

> A blue whale swims with fully coordinated movements immediately after birth. A newborn gnu trots or gallops after its mother when danger threatens, and a freshly hatched duckling waddles into the water, swims with no prior practice, sifts through the mud for food, drinks, and oils its feathers without requiring any model or instructions for these behavior patterns. Hatching the duckling's eggs among those of a hen's brood would not alter any of these typical duck behavior patterns. A duckling that hatched with a brood of chicks would, quite contrary to its foster mother's behavior, go straight into the water.

Somewhat later in his account, Eibel-Eibesfeldt applies this position about innate mechanisms provocatively, albeit all too briefly and incompletely, to human emotion. Much to my surprise, what he says (1989, p. 72) has some similarity in its essential thrust to my own position on relational meaning which, I claim, underlies each of the emotions (Lazarus, 1991a, 1991b, 1991c):

> We find, for example, that all cultures identify the same kinds of emotions: anger, hatred, love, jealousy, envy, fear, a bad conscience, to name but a few. This is noteworthy, because we could not have taught each other all these emotions. We cannot learn the subjective correlates to specific behavior or perceptions; what we learn is the *object* of the hatred or love and not the emotion itself. We can talk to others about our emotions, and the fact that we can communicate about emotions presupposes a shared biological basis. (Emphasis mine)

There are three main difficulties with this statement: (1) It fails to specify the innate mechanisms that are involved in the generation of an emotion. A more detailed and useful approach has been offered by Lehrman (1964)—interpreting his classic research on the reproductive cycle of the ring dove—in which a number of separate mechanisms are strung together in a stereotypical pattern whose timing and control are partly environmental, and which I shall examine later; (2) with respect to the contents of the innate mechanism, the statement does not specify how one emotion process differs from another—that is, in the conditions generating anger, say, compared with those generating anxiety, guilt, shame, sadness, and so on; and (3) although Eibel-Eibesfeldt suggests an organism-environment interaction in his comment about learning the object of hatred or love from the culture rather than learning the emotions, per se, he does not help us understand how culture influences the development of the emotion process in interaction with biology.

Elaborating a bit more on point 3, we must recognize that innate mechanisms do not completely preempt what happens in the complex emotional response configuration because the emotion process can be regulated by coping, which may influence the emotional display or transform it by changing the appraisal, thereby producing a truncated or even different emotion by virtue of the altered relational meaning.

I have long argued that coping can alter emotions in three fundamental ways (Folkman & Lazarus, 1990): first by actions on the environment or person, which change the troubled relationship, hence the relational meaning, and the resulting emotion; second, by affecting attention deployment, as in psychological avoidance, which takes one's mind off the trouble—even if only temporarily—without changing the relational meaning; third, by changing the way the relationship is appraised, hence the relational meaning, and the resulting emotion. Denial and distancing are good examples of how this kind of process works, since to deny successfully is to alter the subjective basis of threat and to distance is to pay attention only to the threat's nonemotional aspects.

So to deal with the flexible and fluid nature of emotions, especially in humans, we must have Proposition IV, which states that *coping* changes emotions by changing the appraisals on which emotions rest. Since coping is a universal capacity of all species, and human coping draws on acquired knowledge and values, this proposition draws on both biology and culture and has qualities that result in both universality and variability.

As his second quotation suggests, Eibel-Eibesfelt considers it unlikely that the connection between relational themes and emotions could be taught to each generation. Others (e.g., Levy, 1973, 1978, 1984) have suggested that emotions are innately given but may be regulated or modified in their expression—which emphasizes the innateness of the emotion process, but the malleability of its expression. About this malleability I would certainly have to agree, even extending it to emotion generation itself (see also Hochschild, 1979, concerning the concept of emotion work). Some anthropologists (e.g., Briggs, 1970, 1978) have even suggested that in some cultures anger is unknown—which emphasizes that emotions are learned in a culture. My doubts about Brigg's claim stem from uncertainty about the thoroughness and depth of her cross-cultural observations and, in fact, about most such observations, which are not usually suitable for identifying layers of meaning at the conscious, preconscious, and unconscious levels of mind.

Throughout history, in literature, and in most if not all cultures, the same emotions—with limited exceptions that, for methodological reasons, cannot be firmly documented—appear again and again, though certain emotions are emphasized or deemphasized in certain cultures (Heider, 1991; Levy, 1973). Although a strong statement cannot be made, in part because it is so difficult to distinguish between emotional experience and emotional display, and in part because we cannot go back historically to make fresh observations, a plausible and reasonable case for universality in the relational meanings that underly each emotion can, I believe, be made fruitfully. However, the innate connection I have proposed between a core relational theme and the emotion that is generated by it is difficult to prove. A fierce debate is also taking place about whether it is possible to make any universal statements about human development from a biological standpoint without considering the cultural context (e.g., Cushman, 1991, who makes a constructivist critique of Stern's 1985 analysis of the development of the self).

Nevertheless, if we allow the matter to rest here, we will have failed to acknowledge and deal with the obvious variability of the emotion process among peoples of diverse cultures and individuals with different personalities. It is necessary, therefore, to suggest the ways culture influences the emotion process, a task to which I now turn.

Cultural Sources of Variability

Proposition V, which is an *ontogenetic principle*, is that variability in the emotion process arises from the divergent ways in which person-environment relationships are appraised. Since individual appraisals are made at the confluence of an environmental display and the goals and beliefs of that individual, culture can have a strong influence on the emotions, those both experienced and displayed, through its influence on the values and meanings on which appraisal itself rests. The social structure (i.e., interpersonal roles and behavior patterns) also affects appraisal, but its mode of operation is somewhat different from that of culture (see Lazarus, 1991c), so I will limit my discussion here to culture.

Variations in the emotion process arise because personality, whether viewed individually or as a shared product of the same culture, and the ways it affects coping, influence the "if" in the "if-then" formula. This creates a functional intersection between the psychobiological and ontogenetic principles; biological universals link the if with the then, and cultural sources of variability affect the if by influencing—sometimes via coping—the appraisal of the personal significance of what is happening.

Imagine, if you will, two individuals who have experienced a failure, say, in school or interpersonally. Imagine too that one of them has internalized the cultural value that it is personally damaging to have the failure blamed on lack of effort; a second individual, however, has internalized the cultural value that it is damaging to have the failure blamed on lack of ability. In the first case, to suggest that the failure is due to lack of effort is a source of shame or anger, while in the second case, there is little or no negative emotional spinoff from such an attribution; lack of effort in this case might even provide a socially acceptable excuse for the failure. In the second case, to suggest that lack of ability is a source of shame or anger, while lack of effort as an attribution for the failure carries no sting.

This mirrors a cultural difference in the way failure is viewed by Japanese and Americans. Japanese appear to regard lack of effort rather than lack of ability as ego-alien, while Americans regard lack of ability rather than lack of effort as ego-alien. In this hypothetical example, we see a way in which cultural values—defining what is offensive or threatening—could influence the "if" of the "if-then" formula by shaping the appraisal on which consequent emotions depend, thereby resulting in different emotions or at least different degrees of the same emotion.

Consider a second, quite different illustration. Among middle-class persons in the United States, physical attack when one is insulted is anathema while verbal attack is more acceptable. In contrast, among working-class persons (especially males), and some ethnic groups, not to respond to an insult with physical attack is to allow oneself to be demeaned. Presumably, when offended middle-class individuals become angry, they inhibit its expression or limit it to verbal retaliation, whereas working class persons become angry but feel obliged to retaliate with physical aggression.

Notice that the first illustration deals with the actual process whereby an emotion is generated. The second illustration, however, deals with the shaping of the expression or display of an emotion, rather than its generation. Some cultural anthropologists distinguish between these two ways that culture influences the emotion process. Levy (1973) uses the term *constitutive rules* to refer to cultural definitions of social situations that influence the emotion that is experienced, and *regulative rules* to refer to how an emotion, once aroused, should be expressed. Heider (1991) uses *cultural definitions* as the term for the former, and *display rules* for the latter. Regulative or display rules surely affect how people cope with common sources of emotion. In any case, these distinctions, whatever language is used, clearly identify two different points at which cultures influence the emotion process, one (constitutive rules) occurring between the provoking event and the experienced emotional reaction, the other (regulative rules) occurring between the emotional state that is being experienced and the observable outcome in expression.

Levy (1973, p. 287) illustrates regulative rules about anger in his description of the Tahitian outlook about anger. Notice his use of the word coping:

> Doctrines about anger and violence . . . lead to [the following] strategies for coping with anger; try not to get into situations which will make you mad. Don't take things

> seriously or withdraw if possible. If someone else is mad at you, try not to let it build up. If you do get angry, however, express it by talking out your anger, so that things can be corrected and you will not be holding it in. Express your anger, if possible, by verbal rather than physical means. If you use physical means try to use symbolic actions, not touching the person. If you touch him, be careful not to hurt him.

As to constitutive rules, as offered by anthropologists such as Lutz and White (1986), for example, culture provides the basis for knowing when we have been demeaned (for anger), what constitutes an enhancement of one's ego-identity (for pride), the conditions of existential threat (for anxiety), when we have failed to live up to an ego-ideal (for shame), when we have violated a moral proscription (for guilt), what is a loss (for sadness), what is an altruistic gift (for gratitude), and so on (see Lazarus, 1991c, for a more detailed account).

The Psychobiology of the Emotion Process

The final task of this essay is to return to the innate mechanism of the emotion process, in effect, to what some (e.g., Ekman, 1977) have called *affect programs*. The question I want to raise concerns how the innate mechanism implied in the psychobiological principle of universal, species-linked connections between core relational themes and the emotions might work. Is it consistent with what we know about innate mechanisms, for example, to suggest that, once triggered by the appropriate appraisal, the mechanism unfolds, perforce, as preprogrammed until turned off by a change in the person-environment relationship?

I think not, and my analysis has been much influenced by Lehrman's (1964) classic research on reproduction in the ring dove. The old and discredited instinct concept assumed that the entire, complex, but seemingly stereotyped and universal action pattern unfolds over time (many weeks in the case of the reproduction cycle of the ring dove). Lehrman demonstrated that a number of specific mechanisms were strung together over time, each highly responsive to environmental triggers that stimulate hormonal activity, leading to the observed and universal sequence of building a nest, laying eggs, sitting on them till hatched, feeding the young, and so on.

Lehrman observed, for example, that if the male and female are placed in a cage in which there are nesting materials with two eggs already laid, they do not sit but act as if the eggs were not there. They proceed to court, build their own nest, lay their own eggs, and then sit on them. A lone female does not lay eggs; she must respond to the sight of a receptive male. A lone male shows no interest in the materials to make a nest, in eggs, or in young; he needs to be stimulated by the female.

There is, in effect, a complex interplay between environmental and hormonal influences in the reproductive cycle, with each major event depending on specific environmental and hormonal triggers occurring at the right time, before the process can proceed to the next step. The stereotypical cycle that we observe is made up of a number of separate innate and interactive mechanisms that are joined if the right conditions are met.

If we follow this model, it is not appropriate to think of apparently universal and complex action sequences taking place over time as a built-in affect program, which when triggered by appropriate conditions, then unfolds in toto. Rather, a finite number of innate, independent mechanisms are capable of being turned on interdependently and regulated by factors within the organism whose role in the total sequence is heavily influenced by what is happening environmentally each step of the way.

We should then think of the emotion-generating process as triggered by an innate mechanism that links a particular relational theme with each emotion. When the appropriate core relational theme has been appraised, anger, anxiety, pride, or whatever is generated, along with the innate action tendency that goes with it and provides part of the basis for the physiological changes associated with that emotion. However, the process can be turned off easily by learned coping processes, including defensive reappraisals, that alter the relational meaning. And, as noted earlier, the emotional display may be inhibited or transformed as a result of cultural or individual values. Although some of this is innate, much of it is also a product of acquired psychological processes that are capable of regulating every aspect of the emotion process except what flows from the innate linkage between a particular appraisal pattern and the specific emotion that goes with it.

In addition to the innate linkage between the core relational themes and the particular emotional reaction, what gives the emotion-generating process an instinctive, universal appearance are the common adaptational requirements inherent in the relationship as appraised at each stage in the process. The overall pattern for each emotion then should appear similar within a species, and sometimes perhaps even across species, because each engenders a more or less similar pattern of perceptions, appraisals, and coping processes which, in turn, produce common motor requirements, homeostatic processes, and physiological changes. What is called for in thought and action when we are made angry is shared, more or less, just as it is when we are made anxious or feel guilt or shame. The shared plight leads to overlapping patterns of reaction within a person across occasions and among persons.

Thus, although there are differences, all instances, say, of anger share a common core relational theme and appraisal pattern, with variations around a central theme. Appraisals, once generated (the "if" of the "if-then" formula), generate common intents and action impulses depending on what is at stake adaptationally—for example, restoring a wounded self-esteem in anger, hiding one's failure to live up to an ego-ideal in shame, and so on. The motor patterns required by such appraisals and intents result in distinctive physiological requirements for each emotion that have their own metabolic sequelae to sustain action or inhibit it.

On the other hand, I don't want to overstate the peremptory nature of the innate connection between core relational themes and the emotion response configuration by underestimating the extent to which coping and feedback from its effects can override what is set in motion, change the appraisal in the wink of an eye, and produce a diminution or cessation of one emotion—though the physiological effects might persist a bit longer—and the emergence of another. The capacity of coping to conceal what is going on and to create rapid changes is what provides such adaptional flexibility in the emotion process in humans, but it also obscures the theoretically ideal psychobiological response pattern when we try to study it. And the fact that each response system serves other masters, for example, homeostatic regulation when the environmental conditions are physiologically hostile, adds to the noise that makes it difficult to identify the distinctive psychophysiological characteristics of each emotion.

And so, in my view, some aspects of the emotion process are innate, and others are influenced by cultural values and individual differences in personality and the resulting coping process. To advance our understanding of what is universal and variable, we must concern ourselves with the details of how innate mechanisms interact with each other to produce a pattern that looks more or less universal in each of the emotions, and in turn how these innate mechanisms interact with sociocultural influences, developmental (individual, personality-centered) variations, and adventitious—that is, responsive to the situation—as well as stable patterns of coping, in shaping the fluid emotion process.

Evidence for Both Universality and Cultural Specificity of Emotion Elicitation

KLAUS R. SCHERER

While some rationalist philosophers have treated emotion as a regrettable flaw in an otherwise perfect cognitive machine (cf. Scherer, 1985), most psychologists do not question the adaptive function of emotion or its phylogenetic origin. Assuming that this view is correct, it is rather likely that the antecedents of emotion are comparable across phylae to the extent that organisms find themselves confronted with similar types of situations, particularly emergencies such as frustration of needs, danger to survival, or loss of relatives or mates. If such structural equivalence of antecedent situations requiring emotional adaptation was to be found across species, it seems a foregone conclusion that we ought to find a high degree of universality across cultures, at least at the level of the "deep structure," for emotion-eliciting situations.

While the phylogenetic continuity of motivation-situation-emotion linkages can be argued theoretically and on the basis of limited comparative evidence for some animal species (see Plutchik, 1980), there is little hard data on the equivalence of the eliciting situation and the type of emotional reaction across animal and human species. Fortunately we do have some hard data on the universality of emotion-antecedent situations across different human culture groups. While there has been indirect evidence from a number of emotion researchers (including Darwin's pioneering cross-cultural inquiries, Darwin, 1872/1964; see also Ekman, 1973), more systematic attempts to determine to what degree similar situations elicit similar emotions are more recent. One of the earliest studies was conducted by Boucher and Brandt (1981) who found that American and Malay stories representing emotion-antecedent situations had very similar theme structures and that both were easily recognized by American judges. They concluded that emotion-antecedents seemed pancultural (but see Heider, 1991, for a critique).

In collaboration with a large number of scholars in different countries, I have conducted a series of questionnaire studies in over 40 countries on five continents to determine the way in which universal, psychobiological factors and culture-specific, socio-normative factors interact with respect to the emotion elicitation and reaction patterns. These studies are based on verbal report of recalled emotion situations and have limited generality since student respondents were studied exclusively. It should be noted, however, that this choice of respondents allows us to compare the data to the vast majority of empirical studies in the psychology of emotion, which have also used students. The results, briefly reviewed here, have encouraged us to develop more specific hypotheses for further work in this area.

In our first study (see Scherer, Wallbott, & Summerfield, 1986, for details) we compared eight European countries (including Israel) with respect to emotional experiences concerning anger, fear, joy, and sadness. Respondents were asked to report the eliciting situation and give details on various reaction modalities (subjective feeling, physiological symptoms, verbal and nonverbal expression, as well as control efforts) on a structured but open-response questionnaire. To study the nature and universality or cultural relativity of the antecedent situations, our research group developed and used a detailed coding system to determine types and important structural elements of the antecedent situations (see Scherer et al., 1986). While the richness and complexity of the results required a full book, our main findings can be summarized as indicating relatively few and rather weak differences between the European cultures studied. The major national differences found were a predominance of "basic pleasures" as joy elicitors for the British subjects, the importance of closed, interior settings as a physical context for the Belgian subjects, and an unexpectedly lively emotionality of the Swiss German subjects (see Scherer et al., 1986, for details)

Using the same open-ended questionnaire, we then extended the comparison to the United States and Japan (Scherer, Wallbott, Matsumoto, & Kudoh, 1988). As one might have expected, the addition of non-European cultures yielded many more culture effects. This was particularly true for the comparison between Japanese culture on the one hand and American and European cultures on the other. For example, Japanese respondents reported less body-related joy, fewer death- and separation-induced sadness episodes, less stranger-induced fear but much more stranger-induced anger, and fewer anger episodes produced by perceived injustice (see Scherer et al., 1988, for details). We speculated that the sources of these cultural differences implicate cultural values, norms, and interactional practices but also demographic and socioeconomic factors, as well as the frequency of certain types of events, such as crime.

This encouraged us to broaden the scope of the emotions studied (adding disgust, shame, and guilt) and to include as many countries around the globe as we could practically manage. We ended up with over 3000 student respondents in 37 countries (Scherer & Wallbott, 1994; Wallbott & Scherer, 1986). Given the difficulties to be expected for coding free-response items for such a large number of different subjects in such a massive study, we resorted to pre-coded response questionnaires (using the data from the earlier studies as guidelines for the creation of categories). The eliciting situation is fully reported in the form of a descriptive paragraph. Unfortunately, our energy has not been sufficient so far to code the over 21,000 situations thus collected with the antecedent coding scheme we developed earlier.

However, we had added an element to the questionnaire that allows us to approach the question of the universality of emotion antecedents from a different angle, namely the dimension of *appraisal*. The questions used for this purpose were directly based on the set of stimulus evaluation checks (SECs) that I have suggested as necessary and sufficient to explain the elicitation of emotion (Scherer, 1984b, 1986). These appraisal criteria correspond closely to similar dimensions postulated by other appraisal theorists (see Lazarus & Smith, 1988; Scherer, 1988a). Specifically, I propose five major checks or appraisal dimensions, including several subchecks:

1. *Novelty check* Determines whether there is a change in the pattern of external or internal stimulation, particularly whether a novel event occurred or is to be expected.
2. *Intrinsic pleasantness check* Determines whether a stimulus event is pleasant, inducing approach tendencies, or unpleasant, inducing avoidance tendencies; based on innate feature detectors or on learned associations.
3. *Goal/need significance* Check determines whether a stimulus event is relevant to important goals or needs of the organism (relevance subcheck), whether the outcome is consistent with or discrepant from the state expected for this point in the goal/plan sequence (expectation subcheck), and whether it is conducive or obstructive to reaching the respective goals or satisfying the relevant needs (conduciveness subcheck).
4. *Coping potential check* Determines the causation of a stimulus event (causation subcheck) and the coping potential available to the organism, particularly the degree of control over the event or its consequences (control subcheck), the relative power of the organism to change or avoid the outcome through fight or flight (power subcheck), and the potential for adjustment to the final outcome via internal restructuring (adjustment subcheck).
5. *Norm/self compatibility check* Determines whether the event, particularly an action, conforms to social norms, cultural conventions, or expectations of significant others (external standards subcheck), and whether it is consistent with internalized norms or standards as part of the self-concept or ideal self (internal standards subcheck).

In our large-scale cross-cultural study we attempted to obtain information on the recalled outcomes of the appraisal processes that had presumably preceded the emotion episode. Unfortunately, given the mass of information to be collected on all aspects of the emotional experience, we had to greatly restrict the number and complexity of the questions relating to recalled appraisal processes. Relatively simple questions were used to obtain information on the novelty, pleasantness, goal conduciveness, fairness, agency, coping ability, and morality of the emotion-antecedent events (see the reproduction of the complete questionnaire in Scherer, 1988b, pp. 201–203).

Based on the results for this grid of appraisal dimensions, characterizing the antecedent situations with respect to the respondent's evaluation of the situation, we can estimate the relative importance of universality versus cultural relativity. The data show that the relative effect sizes for country differences are consistently below those for emotion differences, often amounting to only about one-third of the emotion effect sizes. Emotion by country-interaction effect sizes exist but are relatively low (see Scherer, submitted). The only appraisal variables for which this pattern is somewhat different are the perceived morality of the situation, the expectation of the eliciting event, and the perceived causes or agency.

In trying to understand the possible sources of the country differences, we used Hofstede's (1984) cultural value dimensions. Interesting patterns emerge: for example, the more individualistic a country and the lower the power distance and the uncertainty avoidance, the more the emotion-eliciting event has been expected. Similarly, the higher the individualism, and the lower uncertainty avoidance and power distance, the more the event is seen as immoral.

A case that is of particular interest concerns the self-reflexive or moral emotions—shame and guilt. We found rather interesting differences for these emotions across cultures, particularly with respect to the perceived immorality of the eliciting event. In individualistic cultures both shame and guilt seem to have rather similar antecedents, strongly characterized by immorality of the eliciting behavior. The reported reactions are also quite similar for both emotions. For collectivistic cultures, however, we find more clear-cut differences between shame and guilt: Guilt antecedents are perceived as more immoral than shame antecedents. Similarly, the expressive and physiological responses seem to be quite different for shame and guilt in collective cultures, shame being a shorter, "hotter" affect burst than guilt (see Wallbott & Scherer, in press).

Based on these data sets I reach a conclusion that is very similar to Heider's (1991): Emotion antecedent situations are *both* universal—with respect to many structural characteristics—*and* culturally specific—due to differences in values, practices, history, interaction patterns, demography, climate, economy, and social structure. One could assume that some basic eliciting themes are very similar, especially for simple emotions like disgust, anger, sadness, and fear. As soon as norms, values, and cultural practices become important, especially for complex emotions such as shame and guilt, the eliciting situations and their meaning become vastly more complicated and culture will obviously play a much bigger role with respect to the nature of the eliciting situations.

Afterword: How Is Evidence of Universals in Antecedents of Emotion Explained?

PAUL EKMAN
RICHARD J. DAVIDSON

Averill tells us that the more general a concept is, the more universal it is. That principle applies to the amount of consensus among the contributors in this chapter. On a general level there is a great deal of agreement, but when we consider the specifics of what they say there is divergence.

All agree that there is evidence of universality for emotions, that there is less evidence but some, for universals in the antecedents of emotion, and that biology and culture both play a role in accounting for these universals. They all believe that it is the appraisal, not the stimulus event, that is crucial to understanding which emotion occurs when. Beyond this summary there is divergence.

Scherer has provided the best evidence about universals in antecedent events, and he acknowledges its limitations. His evidence shows more commonality across countries for what he calls the simple emotions—disgust, sadness, anger and fear—than for what he terms the more complex emotions—shame and guilt. Shame and guilt are emotions in which moral judgments are at issue, and might therefore be ones in which differences in cultural values might have more relevance. His research does show the importance of further studying how and why emotions may differ in the extent of commonality in antecedent events and appraisals across countries. Lazarus, Frijda, and Ellsworth all emphasize that whatever biological base there may be for an event's being appraised in a common way across persons within a culture or across cultures is very limited, fragile, and easily overwhelmed by social/cultural/personality influences. Implied is the idea that there may be a hierarchy of events in terms of the likelihood of the events being appraised in a common fashion, but there is no empirical work on this. Ellsworth suggests that what is most likely to be universal is whether an event elicits positive or negative emotion, not the specifics of which emotion. This is another interesting idea that merits investigation. Frijda agrees with Ellsworth that valence is likely to be innately based, but he calls that valenced state affect, not emotion.

Lazarus, Scherer, and Ellsworth emphasize appraisal and each provides a different theoretical account of how that appraisal operates. Lazarus's core relational themes seem to fit at least Western experience, and resemble similar accounts of the antecedent events for each emotion made by Ekman and Friesen (Ekman & Friesen 1975; Ekman 1977). Lazarus tells us that it is the connection between the core relational theme and emotion that is set by biology (though easily overwhelmed by coping). His focus is on the output of the appraisal, how the event has been appraised. He argues that the process of appraisal must involve a process not a "program," but he does not describe what that process might be. Ellsworth and Scherer each provide theoretical accounts of that process, but they differ from each other. It is not clear from their accounts what kind of research might test the difference between their proposals.

Ekman challenges Lazarus, Scherer, and Ellsworth, proposing that the appraisals that occur automatically with emotions happen so quickly that it is unlikely that people can report on what occurred. Ekman views the proposals of Lazarus, Scherer, and Ellsworth as accounts not of appraisal as it actually occurs, but how people subsequently explain and account for the emotions they have. Ekman focuses on the issue of what might be transmitted genetically, which allows for both commonalities and variability across cultures.

Averill usefully argues that evidence for universality in expression or antecedents requires that we consider not specific emotions but emotion families (See Ekman, Question 1). He elaborates three sources of universals: biological, social, and ecological; presumably Lazarus' discussion of personality would be subsumed within the social, although it might be useful within social to deal with sources common to a social grouping, and those likely to be variable within any social group. At the conclusion of his discussion Averill provides a useful caution to end this discussion: Evidence of universality does not tell us the source of the universality.

Question 5

What Are the Minimal Cognitive Prerequisites for Emotion?

Why Emotions Require Cognition

GERALD L. CLORE

The phrasing of this question betrays a view in which cognition and emotion are separate and distinct, rather than thoroughly intertwined, and a view in which it would be possible for the role of cognition to be minimal. My own view is that emotions are mental states, so that cognitive involvement is substantial, by definition. Asserting that emotions are mental states in no way implies that emotions are not also bodily states and legacies of our evolutionary past. It does not mean that emotional persons know why they are emotional, or that they cannot be surprised by their emotions. It requires only that emotion be seen as part of a larger information-processing system. A variety of valid answers might be given to this question, but the adequacy of each would seem to depend on certain assumptions. These include assumptions about *the situation* in which the emotion is to occur, the *definition of emotion*, the implicit *model of emotion elicitation*, and *the particular emotion* in question. I will discuss each of these considerations briefly.

The Situation

Processing and Knowledge Prerequisites

A prerequisite for emotion is that a situation be perceived as positive or negative for one's concerns. This is true of all emotions; and if a reaction is not positive or negative, then it cannot be a genuine emotion (Clore & Ortony, 1988; Ortony, Clore, & Collins, 1988). If one accepts a view in which valence is a necessary feature of emotion, then it would follow that the conditions for generating such positive or negative evaluations might also be prerequisites. But the conditions required to arrive at such evaluations turn out to depend on the kind of situation one is confronted with.

In some situations, the minimum processing required to generate an affective reaction may be extensive, conscious, and deliberative. For business executives to determine how they feel about revisions in the tax code surely requires extended cognitive processing. At the other extreme, however, reacting to a highly charged symbol, like a swastika, would presumably involve much less processing. But even in that situation, one's reaction might be contingent on inferences about who was displaying the swastika and why. Also, one would need to make some mental connection between the symbol and what one knows about the horror that it represents.

In many situations, some of the usual processing steps may be omitted, as when one adopts the evaluations of others or when one retrieves prior evaluations of one's own. But such shortcuts merely allow one to take advantage of the cognitive processing done by others or by oneself at a previous time; they do not alter the assertion that emotions require cognitive appraisals of situations as positive or negative. Similarly, the fact that emotions may occur quickly or that one can be surprised by one's emotional reaction also does not diminish the cognitive contribution, since the requisite computations generally occur outside of awareness.

Less obvious than the processing requirements for emotion are the knowledge requirements. When appraisals are made quickly without much bottom-up processing, they often require correspondingly more top-down processing. In a game of chess, for example, generating an affective reaction to a move by one's opponent requires a lot of knowledge. For that matter, vast stores of knowledge are needed to cope with even the simplest of everyday situations, unless one encounters only one situation over and over again. One of the great contributions of cognitive psychology during the last 25 years has been to discover the importance of stored knowledge in the appropriate execution of even the most mundane behavior. Designers of robotic systems, for example, have succeeded only when their robots are dedicated to repetitive tasks in impoverished environments. One problem is that there is no way to give robots the world knowledge that even small children have at their disposal. This obstacle is crucial, because even if the robots had all the physiological and expressive machinery of the most emotional person, they would remain stonyfaced and impassive to everything that happened to them. This is true because a minimal cognitive prerequisite for emotion is the world knowledge required for things to have meaning. Only then can things take on positive or negative value.

Quasi-Emotions Without Cognitive Mediation

Situations characterized by little or no cognitive processing often include only components of emotion rather than emotions as such. In search of a situation involving emotion but not requiring access to world knowledge, one might consider examples involving sudden fright. Suppose someone were to leap out and say "Boo!" unexpectedly or clap their hands near someone's ear when the person was lost in thought. Would the unsuspecting victim react with fear before accessing any world knowledge? I am inclined to say no. It is true that motorically, physiologically, and in terms of facial expressive behavior the person might look emotional, but such reactions might be better classified as part of a startle reflex than as the emotion of fear. And startle, although it includes some emotion-like reactions, is not generally seen as an emotion. These reactions might well lower one's threshold for fear, but they would not by themselves constitute fear.

The same problem may arise in cases of stimuli believed to have innate emotional potential. Chickens, for example, are said to have an innate fear of chicken hawks. The sight of the short-necked silhouette of a hawk has been reported to release innate avoidance responses. This kind of example requires, however, that one assume that the avoidance behavior is mediated by an emotional state rather than being a reflex or fixed action pattern (cf., Mandler, 1984). To the extent that the avoidance appears to be a reflex or fixed action pattern, then emotion is not required. Scherer (1984), for example, has an excellent discussion of how the evolutionary emergence of emotion brought with it behavioral flexibility, a great advantage over the limitations of reflexes and fixed action patterns (see also Toates, 1988).

What about stimuli that are innately pleasing, like sweet tastes, or displeasing, like physical pain? Surely, little cognitive processing is required to approach pleasure and avoid pain. True enough, but none of these—pleasure, pain, approach, or avoidance—are emotions. From a cognitive view, the term "emotion" would refer in this instance to the reaction of being *pleased* or *displeased* at the experience of physical pleasure or pain, not to the raw experience of physical pleasure or pain itself.

Other examples of minimal cognitive involvement could include instances in which the weather makes someone depressed. Some of our own research shows that people tend to be less happy on cold and rainy spring days than on warm and sunny ones (Schwarz & Clore, 1983). However, this example also does not establish emotion without cognition. The weather presumably elicits certain physiological reactions that are experienced as sad feelings, but since they have no object, what is elicited by the weather is a mood rather than a specific emotion. There is general consensus that emotions are intentional, which in the philosophical use of the term means that they must be about something (Harré, 1986).

Still other examples of minimal cognitive involvement might include instances in which the characteristic feelings and physiological responses of emotions are triggered simply by making emotional facial expressions (e.g., Strack, Martin, & Stepper, 1988), listening to emotional music (Kenealy, 1988), or watching someone else react emotionally. These are all intriguing phenomena that are potentially informative about the emotional cycle, but they too do not demonstrate emotion without cognitive mediation. Whatever feelings and physiological responses are produced directly by these noncognitive means may be just that—feelings and physiological responses. Even though these are constituents of emotion and may trigger or amplify emotions, they are not emotions by themselves.

Some of the examples mentioned above—being startled, deprived of sunlight, experiencing distinctive facial and physiological feedback—do appear to lower the threshold for the elicitation of emotions. That is, they may activate related mental content or make one vigilant for stimuli that become objects of emotions. But the elicitation of part of an emotion is not itself an emotion, even if it causes an emotion to follow. The fact that emotion-relevant physiology, feeling, or expression can be made to occur by manipulating aspects of the well-integrated emotion system ought not to distract us from the cognitive nature of emotion.

It may seem like semantic gerrymandering to make such fine distinctions about when a reaction does and does not constitute an emotion, but it is not. The task for emotion theory is to arrive at a coherent view of emotion that allows us to use emotion terms in a consistent and meaningful way. The goal is to be able to account for relevant phenomena without changing definitions to accommodate unusual cases. I believe that the current view has the advantage that it is coherent, and that its terms can be used consistently.

Implicit Definitions of Emotion

A question of enduring importance in the study of emotion concerns how to characterize emotion in a way that is both precise and captures what is meant in everyday uses of the term. In an effort to do this, Andrew Ortony and I conducted an analysis of 600 putative emotion terms (Clore & Ortony, 1988). The goal was to arrive at a principled basis on which to determine the words in English that do and do not refer to emotions. The general characterization we arrived at is that emotion terms refer to *internal mental states that are primarily focused on affect* (where "affect" simply refers to the perceived goodness or badness of something). Poor examples of emotion terms generally fail to satisfy one or more of these critical conditions. Some of the rejected terms refer to external conditions (e.g., abandoned) rather than to internal conditions, some refer to bodily states (e.g., tired) rather than to mental states, and some do not refer to states at all (e.g., faithful). Some words did not qualify because the states on which they focused are behavioral states (e.g., cowering) or cognitive states (e.g., confused) rather than affective states (e.g., happy). As a result of this research, a subset of about 200 affective terms was isolated (Clore, Ortony, & Foss, 1987). This study made it clear that good examples of emotion terms do not refer directly to events, bodily reactions, feelings, or behavior, but to mental events with relevance to all these things.

Conceptions of Emotion Based on Physiology and Feelings

Although I argue for the necessity of cognition in emotion, different assumptions can follow from analyses that define emotions on the basis of physiology or distinctive feeling states rather than on the basis of appraisal. Gray (1971), for example, has outlined the kinds of mechanisms in the nervous system that might be responsible for some emotions, including the positive emotions, the active negative emotions, such as anger, and the passive negative emotions, such as fear. If localization of specific emotions could be made, and emotions were to be specified solely at the physiological level, then it would follow that activation of the physiology underlying specific emotions could give rise to emotional feelings and emotional behavior without any cognitive appraisals whatsoever.

The same conclusion might also be reached from a different starting point. Oatley and Johnson-Laird (1987) argue that basic emotions are defined by the occurrence of distinctive feeling states. Theirs is a cognitive account of emotion, but by reducing basic emotions to particular feeling states, their position would seem to allow emotions to occur whenever these feelings are experienced, regardless of how they are triggered. Like a position based solely on physiological criteria, this position too would include as emotions feelings generated artificially by electrical stimulation, hormone injection, or some other noncognitive means whereby the feelings lack their appropriate signal value.

Conceptions of Emotion Based on Appraisal

From my own perspective, neither physiology nor feeling states provide an optimal starting place for a characterization of emotion. To be an emotion, feelings must signify the results of an appraisal of some kind (Ortony & Clore, 1989). Sadness is not simply a particular kind of feeling, but a particular kind of feeling for a particular kind of reason. Diseases also typically involve particular physical and experiential symptoms, but the concept of disease is appropriate only if those symptoms are assumed to have particular causes. In the case of emotions, the valid use of the concept depends on the feelings having emotional causes. A patient complaining of a tight feeling in the chest, for example, is experiencing a panic reaction only if the feeling is caused by fearful preoccupations, not if it is caused by a heart attack.

An example provided by Ortony and Clore (1989) illustrates this point. Imagine an experiment in which electrical stimulation of some region of the brain gives rise to feelings of anger. A subject in such an experiment might conclude that the reason he was having feelings associated with anger was because of the stimulation from the electrodes. The subject might say, "This is just the *feeling* of anger. I presume I have this feeling because of the electrical stimulation. I'm not really angry."

An experiment could only produce such results, however, for psychological states in which the experience is dissociable from other components, especially the cause. Thus, it could not be done for the feeling of a headache. Someone either does or does not have a headache and no verification is required. One cannot have the feeling of a headache while not really having a headache. Some terms refer simply to feelings, and some refer to feelings as symptoms of psychological states. The existence of these two kinds of feeling terms suggests that a definition of emotion solely in terms of feelings (or any other symptom) is inadequate. Emotion terms appear to refer to something beyond feelings, to psychological states of which feelings are perhaps a necessary but not a sufficient condition.[1]

Cognitive Requirements for Appraisals

If the prerequisites for emotion include cognitive processes sufficient to make or retrieve an appraisal of a situation, how exactly are such appraisals made? A preliminary account has been proposed by Ortony, Clore, and Collins (Ortony et al., 1988), which I shall refer to as the **OCC** account. The OCC account is congenial to, but different from, that of a number of other cognitively oriented emotion theories (e.g., Abelson, 1983; Mandler, 1984; Roseman, 1984; Scherer, 1984; Smith &

Ellsworth, 1985; Weiner, 1985). It specifies the cognitivc bases of emotion in general as well as the cognitive requirements for specific emotions.

Cognitive Structure

The theory proposes three broad classes of emotions distinguished in terms of the cognitive focus involved. One can focus on events, actions, or objects. Specifically, one can focus on the outcomes of events, the agency of actions, the attributes of objects, or on combinations. All emotions involve positive or negative (affective) reactions to one of these. If one focuses on events, the basic affective reaction is referred to as being *pleased or displeased about the outcomes of events*. Hope, fear, relief, disappointment, happiness, sadness, and related emotions appear in the left branch of the following figure.

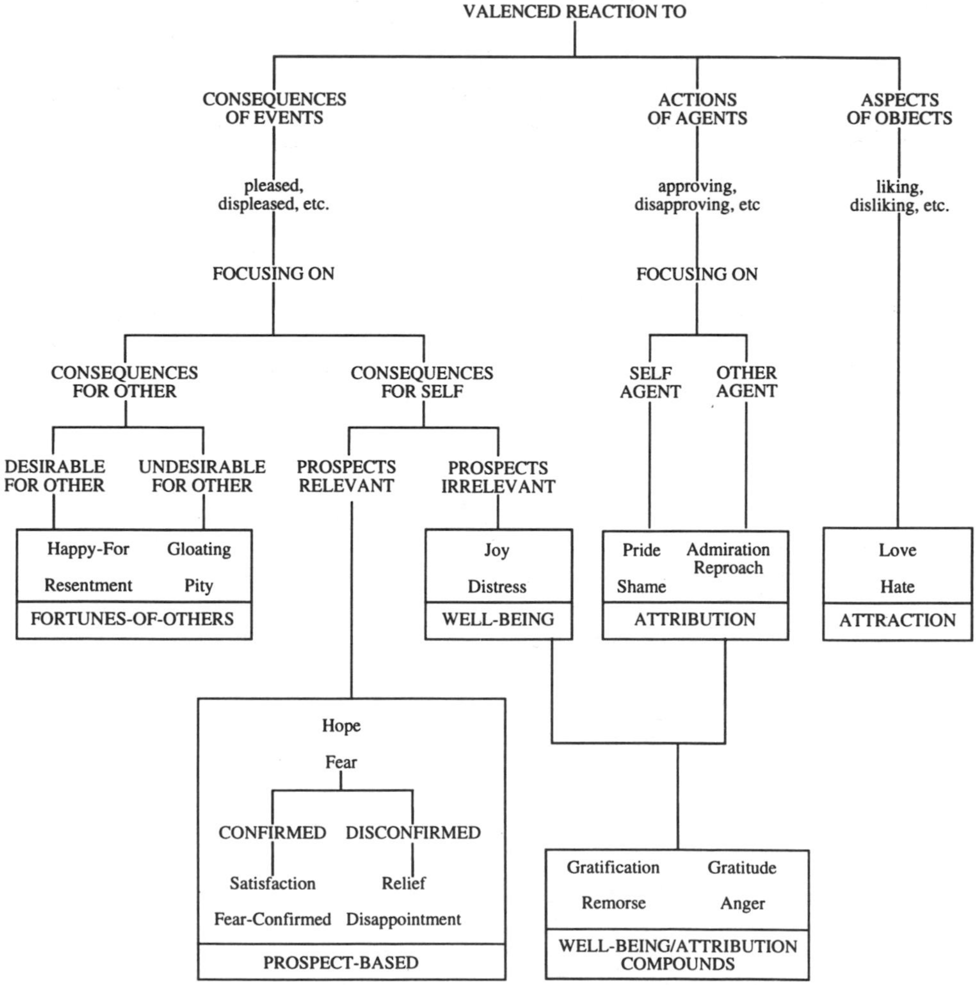

The cognitive eliciting conditions for 22 emotion types according to Ortony, Clore, and Collins (1988).

They are some of the ways of being pleased or displeased at the outcomes or possible outcomes of events. If one focuses not on events but on someone's actions, the relevant affective reaction is referred to as *approving or disapproving of the actions of an agent*. Pride, shame, admiration, and reproach appear in the middle branch of the figure. They are some of the ways of approving or disapproving of the actions of agents. Finally, when focusing on objects, the relevant affective reaction is to *like or dislike the attributes of an object*. Love, hate, and disgust appear in the rightmost branch of the figure. They are forms of liking or disliking the attributes of objects. Thus, according to the OCC account, there are three possible aspects of a situation on which one can focus, and the resulting emotion depends on which of these is taken. In addition, one can also simultaneously focus on two aspects of a situation. For example, gratitude and anger are ways both of being pleased or displeased about the outcome of an event and of approving or disapproving of relevant actions at the same time.

Whether one's affective reactions are positive or negative depends on perceptions of the goodness or badness of what one is focusing on. In the case of events, one has the affective reaction of being pleased only if one sees the outcome of events as *desirable*. In the case of actions, one has the affective reaction of approval only if one sees someone's action as *praiseworthy*. And in the case of objects, one has the affective reaction of liking only if one finds the attributes of an object *appealing*. These perceptions arise from a process of appraising the implications of a situation for one's personal concerns. And the kind of possible concern also varies with the focus. The outcome of events is appraised relative to one's *goals*, the actions of agents relative to one's *standards*, and the attributes of objects relative to one's *attitudes or tastes*.

According to the OCC account, three affective reactions (e.g., *pleased, approving, liking*) are based on three kinds of appraisals (e.g., *desirability, praiseworthiness*, and *appealingness*) of three kinds of things (*events, actions, objects*). And these three kinds of appraisals are made with respect to three kinds of cognitive structures (*goals, standards, attitudes*). All emotions can be seen as differentiated forms of these three general affective reactions—(1) *being pleased or displeased at the outcome of events that are appraised as desirable or undesirable for one's goals*, (2) *approving or disapproving of the actions of agents appraised as praiseworthy or blameworthy with respect to one's standards*, and (3) *liking or disliking the attributes of objects appraised as appealing or unappealing with respect to one's tastes or attitudes*.

A major aim of the theory is to use a consistent set of terms in a clear and precise way. To do this, some terms such as "pleased/displeased" or "desirable and undesirable event" take on specialized meanings. It should be noted that since emotions are states, the terms "liking" and "disliking" are used in the momentary sense of experiencing a feeling of liking or disliking rather than in the dispositional sense of having an attitude toward something. The emotion of love or hate, therefore, involves loving or hating something in the moment.

Virtual Cognitive Structure

The assumption that appraisals are made with respect to some sort of cognitive structures such as goals is standard for cognitive accounts of emotion. But a close inspection of that assumption raises some questions. Is it reasonable, for example, to assume that a representation of everything to which a person aspires or in which a person believes is permanently stored, no matter how trivial? It may not be sensible to assume that we maintain in our heads an endless archive of all our possible goals, standards, and concerns. An alternative possibility is that we construct them as we need them. Of such a cognitive structure, the OCC account (Ortony, et al, 1988, p. 35) maintains that

> . . . it seems more sensible to view it as an implicit or "virtual" structure. People behave *as if* there were such a representation. In fact, we suspect that many of the goals people have are constructed as and when needed, presumably as a result of inferential processes based upon relatively high-level, abstract aspirations, and relatively specific, local considerations.

The idea is that one has a variety of general goals, standards, and attitudes. These are cognitive prerequisites for emotion because without these structures nothing matters to the person. But these prerequisites, although we have referred to them as "cognitive structures," probably do not exist before the appraisal is made.

> Presumably most of what we have stored are high-level, relatively nonspecific goals, standards, and attitudes, all of which have powerful generative capabilities. For example, if one has as a standard that people ought not to inflict needless pain, one presumably has implicitly (or sometimes explicitly) a host of instantiations of this standard such as that one ought not to harm animals, and so on (Ortony et al., 1988, p. 47).

People continually propagate inferences about the implications of specific situations in which they find themselves. If these inferences make contact with elements in the appraisal structure, then goals, standards, or attitudes are activated. When this happens, the situation is seen by the person as relevant to his or her concerns and the possibility of emotional reactions arise. If an emotional reaction does occur, then the nature and urgency of the perceived relevance of the situation to one's concerns will be reflected in the experience of the emotion. (This part of the process is discussed further in response to Questions 3 and 12.)

Thus, in the typical situation, the minimal cognitive prerequisites for emotion include a variety of processes, including the retrieval of stored knowledge relevant to interpreting the situation, the propagation of inferences about the implications of the situation, and the appraisal of the relevance of the situation for one's virtual structure of goals, standards, and attitudes.

Cognitive Prerequisites of Specific Emotions

General affective reactions require an appraisal that implicates one's goals, standards, or attitudes. Specific differentiated emotions, such as anger, fear, pity, or shame require that certain other cognitive distinctions also be made. These include such distinctions as whether the implications for one's goals have already been realized or are only possibilities, whether the person responsible is oneself or another person, and so on. For example, *fear* is a differentiated form of "being displeased." The formal specification of fear in this system is "being displeased at the prospect of an undesirable event." To see what this means in the context of the figure on p. 186, follow the event-based branch. Assume one is focusing on the consequences for self (rather than for another), on the prospect of an event happening (rather than on an event that has definitely occurred), and on possible outcomes that are undesirable (rather than desirable). When these cognitive conditions exist, then the resulting affective reaction, if any, is a kind of fear emotion. In terms of the question posed, these eliciting conditions constitute the minimal cognitive prerequisites for the occurrence of fear. It is important to note that Figure 1 represents a logical and not a temporal structure. One does not first have a reaction of being pleased, for example, and then determine that the outcome about which one is pleased is one's own outcome rather than someone else's. Instead, the cognitive distinctions involved in particular emotions often occur simultaneously as features of a single perception.

The figure on page 186 gives the eliciting conditions for 22 emotion types. The emotions that share common eliciting conditions form groups (Fortunes-of-others emotions, Well-being emotions, Prospect emotions, Attribution emotions, Attraction emotions, Well-being-Attribution Compounds). It is not assumed that there are only 22 emotions. Presumably, the number of emotions that can be distinguished on some basis is large. Indeed, even these 22 emotion types encompass many emotion tokens—terms denoting specific states within the same type. The states denoted by these tokens may differ in several ways from others in the same type, but they all share the same general eliciting conditions.

Consider the Well-being emotions. This is a particularly large category, because it includes all states in which one focuses on events and is pleased or displeased at the desirable or undesirable outcomes for oneself. One might well find meaningful subtypes within this category, but many of them differ from each other mainly in the specific goal that is involved. For example, in the case of being distressed, one can grieve (be distressed at the loss of a loved one), be lonesome (distressed at being alone), be homesick (distressed at not being home), be lovesick (distressed at not being with a lover), and so on. Some well-being emotions may involve irrevocable losses, as in sadness, some may involve the interruption of subgoals on the way toward a larger goal, as in frustration. These various emotions may each have different implications but all share the same kind of eliciting conditions and hence are all considered for the present purposes as examples of the same emotion type, labeled for short "frustration" or "distress." The English terms given here as examples illustrate the kinds of emotions one might feel given a particular cognitive focus. The theory is not designed to sort words, however, but to systematize the emotion states referred to by such words.

The emotions in the figure are cognitively differentiated forms of one or more of the three affective reactions. They achieve their distinctiveness as they are cognitively constrained. The least cognitively differentiated are some of the object-based (Attraction) emotions. Disgust at the prospect of eating a cockroach (Rozin & Fallon, 1987), for example, would seem to require a minimum of cognitive involvement. Reactions of liking and disliking also seem to be experienced often as relatively undifferentiated reactions. People are frequently at a loss to explain why they like or dislike something, giving as a reason simply that they do like or dislike it. Critics who write about art, literature, film, or restaurants may give lengthy descriptions of what they like or dislike, but their descriptions rarely illuminate aesthetic appreciation as such. Of course, the fact that it is difficult to articulate the cognitive bases of taste does not imply that there are none. Appreciating the harmony and grace of beautiful forms may involve a different set of criteria and a different mode of processing than other emotional reactions without being any less cognitive. There is an extensive literature on the cognitive structure of attitude. However, comparable work on taste is lacking, although complementing the original pioneering work of Berlyne (1971), are more recent cognitive analyses by Mandler (1982) and Ortony (1991).

Summary

Answers to questions about the minimal cognitive prerequisites for emotion depend on various assumptions. These might include assumptions about the situation, about the necessary conditions for emotion, about how emotions are elicited, and about which specific emotion is involved. It was argued that the minimal conditions in some situations might involve extensive cognitive processing and stored knowledge. In some situations the processes involved in making a bottom-up appraisal may be circumvented by retrieving the results of prior processing or learning the results of another's processing. Still other situations may require very little processing, although the resulting physiological, experiential, or behavioral reactions often do not constitute emotions as such.

It was argued that characterizations of emotion solely in terms of physiology or in terms of feeling states are inadequate. Like symptoms indicating a disease, these point to an emotion only when they have an appropriate cause. In the case of emotion, the symptoms need to be caused by a perception of a situation as personally significant in some way. Analyses of the language of emotion suggest that the best examples of emotion terms refer to mental events rather than to feeling and behavior per se.

Proposals about the cognitive structure of emotion (Ortony et al., 1988) were reviewed. The account specifies 22 emotion types in terms of their cognitive eliciting conditions. These emotion types are differentiated forms of three basic affective reactions. The nature of the affective reaction (pleased, approving, liking) depends on whether one focuses on events, actions, or objects. Emotions such as hope, fear, happiness, sadness, relief, and disappointment all reflect appraisals of the outcome of events as desirable or undesirable with respect to one's goals. Pride, shame, admiration, and reproach reflect appraisals of the actions of agents as praiseworthy or blameworthy with respect to one's standards. And such emotions as love, hate, and disgust reflect appraisals of the attributes of objects as appealing or unappealing with respect to one's attitudes or tastes. It was argued that the goals, standards, and attitudes on the basis of which appraisals are made are probably best thought of as virtual cognitive structures constructed as needed from quite general aspirations in combination with specific local considerations.

Finally, some of the cognitive distinctions that characterize specific emotions were described. It was suggested that object-focused (Attraction) emotions such as love and disgust appear to be the least elaborated by such cognitive distinctions. Much work remains to be done to illustrate the processes involved in emotions that depend on taste.

Note

1. To the extent that they conflict, the current argument that feeling is not a sufficient condition for emotion should take precedence over an earlier statement that "Feeling is not just a component of emotion, it *is* the emotion" (Clore & Ortony, 1984).

Levels of Thought and Levels of Emotion

PHOEBE C. ELLSWORTH

I am not talking about unconscious emotions. If we have emotions that never ripple the surface of consciousness, they are beyond the scope of this discussion. I am talking about times when we are aware of emotional feelings, whether or not we can give these feelings a name.

Even for conscious emotional states, I think it is impossible to specify a set of minimal cognitive prerequisites. In some ways it is analogous to the attempt to specify the defining features of mental illness. Some people are delusional but not unhappy, some experience debilitating panic attacks even though they "know" there is nothing to be afraid of, some are racked with physical pain that has no identifiable physical cause. The history of attempts to define insanity in a way that bears some relation to reality is testimony to the futility of seeking necessary and sufficient causes.

Emotional experiences differ enormously in their degree of cognitive involvement. The emotional responses described by Clark Hull and those described by William Shakespeare seem almost incomparable. An ambiguous noise many create a sense of alert wariness, a smile or the sun breaking through the clouds may trigger happiness without analysis, without signification, without thought (Zajonc, 1980). At the opposite end of the spectrum we have Alexei Karamazov, Dorothea Brooke, and Stephen Dedalus navigating in mental worlds of infinite cognitive and emotional complexity, where any simple cognitive components have been transformed almost beyond recognition.

If one defines emotion as beginning at the point of entry into the emotional system, the contributing role of cognition will be less than if emotion is defined as the full-fledged manifestation of an identifiable emotion such as anger or sorrow or pride. Much of the debate about the role of cognition in emotion has been the result of different definitions of the key terms.

My own view, similar to that of several other appraisal theorists, is that usually the process of emotion (and I think of emotion as process) is initiated when one's attention is captured by some discrepancy or change. When this happens, one's state is different, physiologically and psychologically, from what it was before. This might be called a "state of preparedness" for an emotion, "alert attention," or the beginning of emotion (cf. Ellsworth, 1991; Kagan, 1991, LeDoux, 1989). Whether one considers it the beginning of emotion or some pre-emotional state is largely a matter of semantic preference. Viewing emotion as a process, I have no problem in defining emotion from the moment the process begins. If others prefer to define it as the moment the process results in the crystallization of the emotional (or pre-emotional) experience into a relatively stable emotion that has a name, that's fine with me, although not particularly interesting. It is the process that interests me. The process almost always begins before the name and almost always continues after it. The realization of the name undoubtedly changes the feeling, simplifying and clarifying. Eventually, most human emotion involves cognition most of the time.

If the novel stimulus is easily defined as inconsequential, the physiological response wanes, and the person typically moves out of the emotional system. If not, further appraisals occur.

Appraisal theories (Arnold, 1960; Frijda, 1986; Lazarus, 1991c; Roseman, 1984; Scherer, 1984; Smith & Ellsworth, 1985) typically begin with very simple appraisals as entry points into the realm of emotions: attention or novelty; a primitive sense of pleasure or aversion; a sense of uncertainty or certainty. Further appraisals are progressively more complex: the perception of an obstacle; a sense of control or lack of it; attribution of agency—was the event caused by oneself, someone else, or impersonal circumstances; legitimacy (Roseman, 1984); evaluation of the match between an event and prevailing social norms or one's own personal standards (Scherer, 1984).

One's answer to the question of minimal cognitive prerequisites depends on one's definition of cognition and on one's definition of emotion (as abundantly illustrated by the debate between Zajonc and Lazarus; see Scherer & Ekman, 1984). If sensory information processing is considered cognitive, then most if not all emotions will show some "cognitive" contribution. If one defines cognition as involving conscious propositional analysis, then a larger proportion of emotional experiences will be defined as noncognitive, at least at their onset.

We have found that attention, pleasantness, certainty, anticipated effort or obstacle, and attributions of agency reliably discriminate 13 different emotions, and that appraisals along some of these dimensions are especially important or central for some emotions—uncertainty for hope and fear, and agency for sadness, anger, and guilt, for example (Smith & Ellsworth, 1985; Ellsworth & Smith, 1988). We hypothesize that these appraisals are extremely common in the process of emotion, both within and across cultures. There may be other appraisals that are equally common; we do not claim that our initial efforts have produced an exhaustive list. At least some of these appraisals are associated with characteristic facial movements (Smith, 1989); perhaps all of them have recognizable physical manifestations. There are undoubtedly additional less common appraisals that affect emotion, some that occur in some cultures or classes of individuals but not others (Lutz & White, 1986; Ellsworth, in press), perhaps some that are culturally or individually idiosyncratic.

I think emotion is usually provoked by appraisals (including remembered appraisals) of the environment, and one's self in relation to the environment, and I believe the cognitive dimensions of appraisal we have found are likely candidates for very general, if not absolutely "necessary" cognitive components. There are, however, some situations that have been proposed as evidence against the proposition that there are any cognitive prerequisites to emotion. I will briefly consider four of these, two red herrings and two that raise real questions about the necessity of cognition for emotion. This list is not exhaustive either.

Two Red Herrings

1. Emotions at the Movies

People scream and gasp at horror movies, cheer when the underdog clobbers the evil power, cry when the lady dies bravely. If you ask people whether what is happening on the screen is really happening, most of them will look at you askance and say, "Of course not!" (The intellectuals will ask what you mean by "real.") Cognitively, they "know" that no one was hurt, that the monster was just a special effect, yet their emotions *seem* real. Their own well-being was never at stake; they do not need to cope with the perils before them; they are sitting in chairs in a comfortable environment surrounded by other people sitting in chairs. How can they be experiencing emotion if they lack the essential cognitive appraisals?

I do not think the emotions evoked by obviously fictional presentations contradict the logic of appraisal theories. One of the essential functions of emotion is to motivate the organism to respond quickly and effectively to environmental threats as they arise. Generally the costs of failing to respond soon enough are far greater than the costs of responding when it is not really necessary. Running away from an imaginary danger or taking needless extra precautions may waste one's time or make one look foolish, but standing there trying to decide whether or not the danger is real can cost one's life. It is far safer for an organism to be calibrated to feel emotion when it is not warranted—to have a hypersensitive system—than it is to have a system that postpones the initiation of emotional processes until there is no question that they are justified. Thus the emotions we feel in the movies are real. The events on the screen trigger processes that are initially identical, or at least highly similar, to those triggered by real events. The "higher cognition" that we are not in danger, that the events are not real, comes into play only after the process has been set in motion, modifying the experience and inhibiting the associated action tendency.

In young children the imbalance between the force of the immediate emotional response and the knowledge that the events on the screen are fictional is even greater. Young children often shout advice to the characters ("Not the *West Wing*! That's where the *Beast* is!"), and sometimes *do* try to run out of the theater when the monster appears. The emotions produced by an emotionally significant stimulus take precedence over the recognition that the stimulus is make-believe.

2. The Zajonc "Feelings Are First" Hypothesis

Likewise, I see no fundamental incompatibility between Zajonc's claim that "preferences need no inferences" and the claims of appraisal theories. The kinds of preference Zajonc discusses are immediate, automatic approach or avoidance tendencies that can occur even before the object is recognized and named. These preferences seem to correspond quite closely to the very simple appraisal of valence that characterizes several versions of appraisal theory. Nothing in appraisal theory says that an object must be recognized before a sense of pleasure or aversion can be felt.

From my point of view, Zajonc has engaged in extensive study of one of the basic and most important steps in the process, usually (though not necessarily) a very early step. Further appraisals—of obstacles, of control or coping potential, of agency—create emotions that are more differented than the simple sense of valence. Zajonc himself is quite clear on this point: "Of course, more complex emotions [more complex than "simple affective polarities"], such as pride, disappointment, jealousy, or contempt obviously require extensive participation of cognitive processes" (Zajonc, Murphy, & Inglehart, 1989).

Two Real Problems

1. Music

Explaining emotional responses to instrumental music is a real problem for appraisal theories, and may be a real threat to the generality of appraisals as elicitors of emotion. Appraisal theories can account for *some* emotional responses to music, as attention and valence certainly occur in listening to music just as they do in responding to other stimuli. The other appraisals that have been proposed—appraisals such as certainty, control, and agency—seem less relevant to music than they are to other kinds of events. Nonetheless, many people report responses to music that are far more elaborate than a simple sense of pleasure or displeasure. Casual research in our laboratory indicates that people can categorize their responses to musical selections as "sad," "fearful," "triumphant," and "happy" with fairly high levels of reliability, and as "angry" with somewhat lower levels. Some subjects, along with many writers (cf. Forster, 1939) struggle to communicate extraordinarily complex emotional "meanings" of musical selections.

I do not think that these responses can be accounted for by appraisals *of the music*; therefore, in this context, stimulus appraisals do not *cause* the emotion. But the same patterns of appraisals may still be *experienced* as part of the emotion, even if their causal role is delayed, muted, or nonexistent. Although I believe that emotions are usually the result of a sequence of appraisals, they are not simply a combination of cognitions. Instead, the appraisals have physiological and experiential correlates (Smith, 1989), which together with the appraisals themselves, *are* the emotional experience. Some of these physiological and experiential sensations may correspond to features of music such as crescendo and decrescendo (as suggested by Tomkins, 1963), staccato and legato, tempo and rhythm, ascending and descending scales. Musical phrases or longer excerpts that mimic the nonverbal, noncognitive aspects of an emotional feeling state may elicit aspects of the emotion itself, then at last the full emotion, including the characteristic appraisals (but not the action tendencies). The order of events is not the standard order described in the model, and the appraisals are not appraisals of one's own immediate circumstances, of course. Instead they are more generalized appraisals—without specific objects—appraisals of loss and uncontrollability, of uncertainty, or of power and self-agency.

This hypothesis suggests the possibility of cross-cultural commonalities in the ability of certain kinds of music to elicit certain emotionally relevant physiological responses. Alternatively, the emotional response to music and the associated appraisals may be learned within particular cultures. I know of no cross-cultural research on perceptions of the emotional tone of music.

2. Opponent Processes

Richard Solomon (1980) proposed an Opponent Process theory of emotion, in which the termination of one emotion (e.g., joy) automatically brings about the onset of the opposite emotion (e.g., sadness). Solomon's own research was largely concerned with heart-rate acceleration in frightened dogs, followed by pronounced deceleration below baseline when the fear stimulus was removed; the initial arousal was attenuated over many episodes, while the rebound effect was exaggerated. Speculating about the applicability of the theory to humans, he cited studies of novice parachute jumpers who experience a nightmare of panic and near incontinence before their first few jumps, followed by relief, compared to experienced jumpers, who are barely aroused before jumping, but experience an exhilarating "high" after they land.

Research on humans is sparse and usually flawed. Mauro (1988), however, in an elegant series of studies, has provided evidence that opponent "rebound" effects do occur in humans, at least for some emotions, and cannot easily be accounted for by changes in the person's appraisal of the situation. If such rebound effects prove to be reliable, they constitute a second challenge to the generality of appraisal theories, since the second, "rebound" emotion is caused only be the termination of the first and not by any new appraisals.

Let me close with a gentle reminder. Music and opponent processes are problematical for appraisal theories of emotion, but no other theories have done much better. The usual tactic is simply to omit any reference to these embarrassing mysteries, to rule out domains where our theories falter as irrelevant or "beyond the scope of the present paper." Nonetheless, the mysteries *are* the theoretical challenges, and sooner or later must be acknowledged.

Emotions Require Cognitions, Even If Simple Ones

NICO H. FRIJDA

"Cognition" has two different, separate meanings in the emotion literature: conscious awareness and complex information processing. Under both meanings, the role of cognition as an emotion antecedent is an issue for discussion and research. The two domains of cognition overlap but do not coincide. With conscious awareness, the question can be asked whether emotional behavior, or physiological response to emotionally meaningful stimuli, can occur without a conscious emotional experience. One can also ask whether occurrence of emotion depends on conscious awareness of the meaning of the eliciting event or on the stimulus properties that cause the emotion. This was the question Zajonc examined when showing that the affective effects of stimulus frequency do not depend on awareness of that frequency (Zajonc, 1980). With complex information processing, the question is whether or not full-blown emotions are being elicited, or can be, by simple stimuli that do not suppose the cooperation of elaborate knowledge structures in the individual, or elaborate processes of inference. Can emotions be elicited by simple sounds, shapes, or smells, and, if they can, how much actual or prior information processing is involved?

The issues are complex. There seems little doubt that the meaning of events (their implications for well-being and the achievement of goals and values), rather than their objective nature as stimuli, is the primary determinant of most emotions. There also seems little doubt that one often is aware of that meaning, at least dimly and partially. This awareness shapes both the emotional experience and its development over time. It provides the experience with articulation and is the basis for giving it a name; it is both the starting point and the product of pondering the events and their implications, elaborating them and ruminating about them. But determining the role of such awareness in the causation of emotion is another, problematic matter. Awareness of the meaning of emotional events is not only, not necessarily, and not always the cause of the emotion but it also is part of the emotional experience itself. It is a result of the processing that leads to emotion, as much as or more than being its prior condition. This can be illustrated by the example of the guilt feeling of a driver who accidentally hit a child who ran across the street: The guilt feeling includes one's sense of being responsible for what happened, which can only emerge after the distress caused by the accident; it may actually conflict with one's knowledge that one was not to blame (Kroon, 1988; see Frijda, 1993a). The theoretical question thus concerns the extent to which deliberation about the implications of an event precede and cause emotions, and there is little doubt that such prior deliberation is the exception rather than the rule. Many emotions arise with a certain immediacy and we should not exaggerate that degree of immediacy. I think that most emotions only arise after the meaning of the event "has dawned on" the subject, or that he or she has realized the implications. Also, many apparently immediate emotions are prepared by prior expectations. Expectations, including nonconscious expectancies and being set for certain things, usually have laid a groundwork, and the emotion only follows immediately on the final confirmation or contradiction. Still, I think one can say that prior deliberating awareness is the exception and, in any case, not a prerequisite.

We must briefly mention an issue that touches on the present questions and complicates them. There is much conscious deliberation that leaves emotions untouched. Awareness that one was in no way to blame hardly lessens the guilt feeling when having hit a child; in any case, it does not at a stroke abolish it. Whatever the role of cognitive deliberation in the emergence of emotions, there are ill-understood restrictions on it.

A deeper and more fundamental question concerns the role of awareness of the eliciting event as such. The question is a difficult one, because awareness of the eliciting event prior to the emotion and of that event as filled with emotional meaning are hard to separate. My assumption would be that, in many cases, the eliciting event is perceived as filled with emotional meaning at the very instant that it is perceived at all. Also, anecdotal evidence suggests it is possible that an event is perceived as emotionally neutral, and yet it appears to have elicited an emotional feeling, or a behavioral emotional change.

At a still deeper level, one may question whether or not there may be elicitation of emotion without any awareness of a stimulus at all. Here again, one must be careful. There is evidence of unconscious priming of emotions, but that is not at issue here; in cases of priming, the emotion still may follow conscious perception of the target stimulus.

Cognitive Processes in Emotion Elicitation

The second question is the more important one: What's the role of cognitive processes in the elicitation of emotion? The question of course is vague and does not admit a meaningful answer, since the notion of "cognitive" is vague and its paraphrase "complex information processing" hardly less so: How complex is complex to be complex? The proper question, I think, is: What is the minimal cognitive complexity that allows full-blown emotion to arise? Presumably, "cognitive" stands in opposition to simple stimuli or simple associations. More precisely, stimulus events that might elicit emotions can be arranged, not according to a dichotomy, but along a continuum from simple to complex. I think we may distinguish:

1. Internal stimuli (e.g., direct influences on biochemical or neural processes).
2. Simple sensory stimuli that directly act on the affective system (e.g., tastes, smells).
3. Complex stimuli that activate affect by template matching or association (e.g., the hawk silhouette for a duckling; the visual cliff for an infant; a visual or other stimulus previously paired with an affective stimulus like pain or suffocation).
4. Conditions that affect the ease or effort with which mental or physical actions can be executed.
5. Stimuli that more or less directly act through their assimilation to stored schemata or expectations (attachment figures, familiar stimuli), or through their failure to be assimilated to such schemata (novel and unexpected stimuli).
6. Stimuli that act through the inferential and meaning schemas to which they are assimilated.

How far up on this list are stimuli capable of eliciting emotion? We can only answer that question when we agree on a criterion for "emotions." Some distinctions are necessary for making any answer meaningful and I think the following distinctions will work. First, there exist pleasant and unpleasant feelings—I call these "affects." Second, there exist diffuse states of affect or of action readiness (or both), that is, states of feeling or action readiness that do not bear on some particular object; they are usually designated by the word "moods" (Frijda, 1986; Frijda, 1993b) this volume, Question 2. Third, there exist states of affective appraisal of some emotional object (external object or object of thought), linked to a change in action readiness bearing on that object. In accordance with habits of speech, these are what I call "emotions." Emotions, in other words, involve a change in action readiness and they are about something. They are intentional states, which moods are not, and affects not necessarily. The states of action readiness are felt by the subject, or inferred from behavior, or both.

The answers to the questions about the role of cognitive determinants are different for affects, moods, and emotions.

Elicitation of Affect and Mood

I think that there is no disagreement whatever on the possibility of noncognitive elicitation of affect and mood. I believe that nobody contests the essentially noncognitive determination of the likes and dislikes for particular smells, tastes, and bodily sensations, at least for certain ones. Nothing other than direct prewired determination appears to be involved in the practically universal liking for moderately sweet substances, caresses, and sexual climaxing. Most smells derive their affective value either from prewired preferences or direct associations to other primary affective stimuli. With caresses, the quieting effect of stroking is observed in animals and has been observed in an idiot (Gellhorn & Loofburrow, 1963). A non-empirical, logical side exists in all this. There is no way by which affective evaluation can be reduced to bodily sensations or cognitive judgments. Reduction to bodily sensations has been tried in introspective experimentation, but when these have affective valence they have that valence in addition to being felt as sensations (Frijda, 1986). Moreover, the affective valence of pain can disappear while nonaffective "pain sensation" remains (e.g., after frontal lobotomy). With cognitive judgments, there is no reason, other than an affective one, to prefer any goal whatever over some other. Cognitive reasoning may argue that a particular event could lead to loss of money or health or life, but so what? What is wrong with death, other than that it is disliked? What I am trying to say is that tracing the affective effect of a stimulus to its cognitive conditions, allows one, in the end, to find a stimulus that evokes affect without cognitive mediation.

A number of physiological agents evoke mood change. These stimuli thus are noncognitive in the second sense, and several of them do so without the intervention of awareness regarding their affective valence, or even their presence. Among these agents are subliminal olfactory stimuli, conditioning procedures that counteract conscious identification of the affectively operative procedures (Baeyens, Eelen, & Van den Bergh, 1990), the temperature of inhaled air (Zajonc, Murphy, & Inglehart, 1989), and drugs such as morphine. It is true that a word of caution is in order when considering drug data as arguments for the noncognitive (in the second sense) determination of affect. Subtle cognitive influences are often present and difficult to exclude from affective drug effects. Particular drugs do influence vitality or general activation (e.g., testosterone, ACTH; Schnurr, 1989) and thus may well influence sensed coping ability, self-confidence, and positive mood. That might also be the road whereby physical state—good health at one side, exhaustion at the other—influences mood.

It is worth noticing that, in cases like this, an essentially noncognitive factor such as physical state influences mood in a cognitive way, in which "cognitive" obviously has very little of the representational character that the word "cognitive" is usually associated with. It concerns stimuli at category 3 in the previous list.

The chemical influences on mood, incidentally, are theoretically somewhat outside the scope of our present discussion. It is obvious that under natural conditions the process of emotion traverses a path through the brain, in which neurochemical processes are implicated. In all likelihood, that path can be activated along the way in the same manner that the visual pathway can be activated by thumping the eyeball or electrically stimulating the optic tract. That says little about nonsensory factors in vision under normal conditions.

Elicitation of Emotions

Emotions involve change in action readiness, by definition. Changes in action readiness and its cues—involuntary expressive movements and sounds, activation changes, signs of control precedence such as task interruption and distraction—are the criterion. Which are the simplest stimuli that can evoke them?

The simplest stimuli eliciting emotions are, I think, simple as stimuli, but somewhat complex as eliciting constellations. I believe that the simplest stimuli that can elicit emotions in humans consist of unexpected intense stimuli, unexpected stimuli in unfamiliar surroundings, unfamiliar stimuli close by; body restraint and other interference in self-initiated movement, pain that persists after one's first reactions to remove it have failed, and loss of balance. If these indeed are the simplest conditions for emotion, even these all involve some measure of cognition, albeit quite elementary forms. They all include more than a single localized stimulus. They all involve comparing a stimulus against schemata or expectations, or failing execute some activity that was or would be initiated; they all fall into categories 4 and 5 of the previous list. These categories are theoretically interesting. Emotions may arise because desired actions cannot be executed or are interfered with. Frustration of course is the prime example of the latter, but "despair"—that is, helplessness—is as well since it results from the exhaustion of the repertoire of actions for coping with an aversive event. Both notions encompass primitive cognitions, elementary forms of information processing. Frustrations of the sort meant involve prior goal-setting. Other forms—"frustrative nonreward"—presuppose prior expectations of forthcoming reward. Separation distress requires expectancies of yet other kinds. It presupposes prior bonding and, hence, prior recognition of a particular person as the attachment figure. The emotions triggered by the unexpected and the unfamiliar—confusion, surprise, and fright—also presuppose being set to things other than those that arose, or the explicit absence or weakness of schemas with which to match the input. Of course, in all those cases "goal-setting" and "expectation" do not refer to articulate representations the subject has taken cognizance of. They are more akin to "neuronal models" (Sokolov, 1963), "phase sequences" (Hebb, 1949), or neural networks (McClelland & Rumelhart, 1986) than to propositional thoughts. They are cognitive in the second sense nevertheless.

Hardly less simple, perhaps, are the emotions elicited by confrontations with elementary aversive and appetitive stimuli, like unpleasant body sensations, tastes, smells, sweet tastes, caresses, and the like. But more than these stimuli per se is needed to have them trigger emotions. Additional conditions must have been fulfilled, because not every unpleasant or pleasant sensation is an emotion, in the sense of the definition given. Theory hypothesizes that these conditions consist of uncertainty about how to deal with the stimulus—that is, how to get rid of aversive ones, or how to bear them, and how to avail oneself of pleasant ones; expectancy issues seem to be essential here, too (Carver & Scheier, 1990; Frijda, 1986).

Different emotions are, presumably, elicited by different stimuli. So far, no convincing evidence exists that particular emotions are elicited by particular more or less simple stimuli. To the extent that anger, for instance, is elicited by frustration, it is evoked by a complex pattern, as indicated previously. Different emotions appear to be elicited by different patterns of cues in which the aversive or appetitive stimulus event is embedded.

Current cognitive emotion theory makes much of the appraisal process, in which events are judged based on a number of appraisal dimensions. Among these dimensions are agency, controllability, and uncertainty. All involve cognition, but all include cognition of elementary kinds. "Agency," for instance, means attribution of intent or personal causation, and it is plausible that most anger is elicited by the intervention of such attribution of agency. However, attribution of agency is not necessarily a high-level cognitive feat. Animals are capable of it, in the sense that they react differently to an animal (or a mechanical toy; Suomi & Harlow, 1976) introduced into their cages than to an inanimate object; also, a hypothalamically stimulated dog aggresses on the experimenter's hand, not on the apparatus. The toy example shows that, of course, no true "attribution" is involved, nor a recognition of "alive" as opposed to "moving without apparent cause" or something like that. The point is that "perceived intentionally" (like perceived causality) is a fairly elementary perceptual/cognitive category (Michotte, 1950; see Thines, Costall, & Butterworth, 1991).

The (admittedly modest) complex information processing just sketched may not be necessary, however, for the elicitation of true emotional reaction. Diffuse reactions exist that nevertheless are marked by activation change and control precedence, and go under the names of "excitement" or "upset." Even a more articulate emotion like anger (defined as defensive aggressive behavior with autonomic upset) is on occasion elicited by still more restricted stimulus conditions than those described. The old decortication experiments by Bard (1934) suggest that any unexpected stimulation is sufficient to provoke "sham rage" in the decorticate animal. Cognitive variables like agency and controllability may, in fact, serve to limit the occurrence of anger to controllable events caused by another individual, rather than their being part of its elicitation. This is a conclusion we can draw from these lesion experiments: cognition has perhaps more of a function in emotion control than in emotion arousal; this indeed is a conclusion that Bard and Mountcastle (1948) drew. That this might occur is supported by the observation that animals may aggress when occasion for cognitive preparation is absent, when startled, for instance (Lagerspetz, 1961); cats and dogs may indeed respond angrily when woken up with stroking by their master, which they do not do when cognitive preparation had been sufficient.

If this analysis is correct, it would suggest a very low level of cognitive involvement as the minimal prerequisite for emotional arousal: unexpectedness, and perhaps absence of adequate preparation or resources for coping. Similar suggestions can be made with regard to other emotions, such as fear, anxiety, disgust, or sexual excitement. Sexual excitement (which I consider an emotion) provides another pretty example of a very elementary emotional response that nevertheless strongly depends on all sorts of context variables, even in animals, at least among females. To repeat: It is completely needless to argue whether the processing of these context variables is or is not called "cognitive." The processes extend through categories 3 to 5. Most of them have to do with matching with previous experiences.

Summary

Many emotions—instances as well as types—vitally depend on cognitions, in the sense of conscious awareness of meanings, but full-grown emotions appear to be possible with fairly minimal cognitive involvement, and certainly without reflective awareness of meanings. However, some elementary cognitive involvement always appears to be present. This applies to that which makes an affectively valent event elicit an emotion and not merely an affect. When an emotion occurs, something like "unexpectedness" or "mismatch with one's cognitive schemas" or "uncertainty about the sufficiency of one's coping repertoire" is implicated, and most of the time with the utilization of additional cognitive elements such as the presence of intentional agency in the eliciting event.

Cognition Is One of Four Types of Emotion-Activating Systems

CARROLL E. IZARD

What are the minimal cognitive requirements for emotion activation? None.

This simple, unqualified answer requires explication. First, it assumes that cognition is not equivalent to information processing, which *is* required for emotion activation and virtually every other biological and psychological process. Second, the notion that cognition is not a *necessary* cause of emotion implies that there are *noncognitive* activators of emotions. Third, the idea that there are both noncognitive and cognitive activators of emotion calls for distinctions among noncognitive emotion-activating processes, cognition, and emotion. Instead of undertaking the impossible task of providing a universally acceptable definition for each of these concepts, I begin with an attempt to draw some working boundaries for them.

On Distinguishing Emotion and Cognition

In my answer to Question 11 and elsewhere (Izard, 1993; Izard & Malatesta, 1987), I discussed emotion in terms of three components: neural-evaluative, expressive, experiential. I defined emotion experience for a specific emotion as a particular feeling or motivational state, a state that is a direct product of the activity of the neurochemical substrates of that emotion. As such, the subjective state of an emotion, or emotion experience, can occur without cognitive mediation.

With regard to the experiential component of emotion, the distinction between emotion and cognition is often blurred. This happens because some theories hold that emotion experience includes imagery or thought (e.g., Ortony, Clore, & Collins, 1988), and others maintain that emotion-activating appraisal processes are part of the emotion experience (e.g., Lazarus, 1991). I have argued that defining emotion to include cognition makes it difficult to sort cognition as cause from cognition as consequence.

The cause-effect problem and the larger problem of studying emotion-cognition relations are alleviated if the neurochemically induced motivational state is considered as a boundary for emotion. It is, of course, a permeable boundary, or, perhaps more precisely, an interface. The experiential/motivational state in emotion connects and interacts with perceptual, cognitive, and motor processes.

The task of drawing boundaries around the concept of cognition is equally as difficult as that for emotion. I begin with an important contrast between emotion and cognition: Emotion is about motivation, cognition about knowledge. More specifically, I propose that cognition is dependent on some form of learning- or experience-based memory. Described in this way, cognition can be viewed as the "upper" end of a continuum of information processing, an idea that will be elaborated in the following section.

On Distinguishing Cognitive and Noncognitive Emotion-Activating Processes

The viability of the notion of noncognitive emotion activating processes depends on the acceptance of some working boundaries for the concept of cognition. Cognition is indeed a broad concept, and there are several contrasting types or levels of cognitive process—automatic versus deliberate, conscious versus unconscious, explicit versus implicit. However, all these types of cognition are based on experience and some form of learning and memory, and if cognition is limited to processes based on memory, then it cannot be equated with information processing.

Information processing occurs at all levels of organismic activity—from protean molecules, the simplest unit of living matter, to neural networks in the human brain, the most complex organ in the animal kingdom. I have proposed that the many levels of information processing can be conceived as segments on a continuum or as links or sets of links on a chain, with the encoding and decoding of genetic information at one end and cognition at the other (Izard, 1992).

Perhaps the idea of a continuum of information processing or the metaphor of a chain of information processes can be elucidated by considering an analogy from embryology. Genetic codes determine the differentiation of a single cell into the many types of cells that constitute the nervous system, the cardiovascular system, the sense organs, and all the other systems and organs of the developing animal. This is one of the great marvels of nature, all of it a function of the encoding and decoding of information essential to development and adaptation.

The formation of the very first nerve cells in the embryo marks the beginning of its neural activity, and the advent of neural activity raises a very interesting question. To paraphrase a leading geneticist (Sinnott, 1966), who can say when the information processing that controls a chick's embryological development ends and the information processing that mediates its behavior and mental life begins? When the chick first moves or starts to peck its way out of the shell? When it perceives the mother hen and imprinting results in following behavior? When it flees from the shadow of a hawk? All these behaviors are, at least in part, a function of the decoding of genetic information, and some of the same behaviors are, in part, a function of sensory input from the environment.

A similar analogy can be drawn for human fetal development. Fetal behavior begins a relatively short time after conception, and evidence suggests that well before birth the fetus responds to sense data from both the uterine and external environment. Immediately after birth infants can discriminate and respond differentially to odors and tastes (Fox & Davidson, 1986; Steiner, 1979), distinguish a human infant's cry from a computer-simulated cry (Sagi & Hoffman, 1976), and by age three weeks can produce a social smile in response to perception of the contours of a human face (Izard, 1991). The task of distinguishing the genetic and cognitive determinants of these behaviors, or even deciding whether cognition is involved, is equally as difficult as deciding when the chick's embryological development gives way to experience-based behavior. These dilemmas raise the question as to whether there is a fixed boundary between genetically and cognitively mediated behavior.

Yet there seems to be a need for some conceptual distinctions between such seemingly different processes as those that occur in genes and those that require complex neural networks in the brain. Between these two highly contrasting sets of processes, there is information processing that guides reflexes, instincts, and more complex genetically prepared behavior.

A Continuum of Information Processing

I have proposed that we order the various sorts of information processing from simplest to most complex and consider them as segments of a continuum or as interconnected links or "types" (Izard, 1993). For convenience, I refer to them simply as types and designate them as: cellular, organismic, biopsychological, and cognitive.

All four types of information processing activate emotions. The first two are strictly noncognitive, and the third has an important noncognitive component. The fourth type stretches across the several subtypes or levels of cognitive information processing.

Cellular information processing is exemplified by the encoding and decoding of information that occur in the simplest units of living matter and, most important, in genes. At this level, the encoding takes place primarily through natural selection and biological development. These processes generate emotion directly and influence other systems or types of emotion activation. I have hypothesized that cellular/genetic information processing is responsible for the emotion that constitutes a person's characteristic mood (Izard, 1992). Genetic processes effect trait emotionality (Diener & Emmons, 1984; Tellegen, 1985) through two mechanisms. First, it influences emotion thresholds and proneness to certain emotion experiences (cf. Kagan, Reznick, & Snidman, 1988; Rothbart & Derryberry, 1981). Second, it generates emotions through directed neural activity, activity that is spontaneous in that it requires no special external stimulation.

Organismic information processing also involves genetically coded data. Such biologically based data can lead to emotion, or at least emotion expression, with little or no input from exteroceptors and independently of cognition (see Izard & Malatesta, 1987). However, organismic information processing often involves sense data from the interoceptors that transmit signals from physiological drive states. Examples of emotion responses activated in this manner are taste-elicited disgust expressions (Steiner, 1979) and pain-activated anger (Berkowitz, 1990; Izard, Hembree, & Huebner, 1987).

Biopsychological information processing is based on interactions between genetic codes and acquired knowledge. Essentially, this is an interaction between biological and psychological (cognitive) processes. An example of an emotion activated by this type of information processing is fear in response to biologically/genetically prepared stimuli (Lanzetta & Orr, 1986; Mineka, Davidson, Cook, & Keir, 1984; Seligman, 1970). Biopsychological information processing may also explain how feces becomes a universal object of disgust (Rozin & Fallon, 1987). A biologically based and adaptive proneness to avoid feces is potentiated by cognitive development and social learning (toilet training). Rozin and Fallon's theory (1987) explains how dangerously contaminated primary disgust objects, like feces, can give rise to many secondary disgust responses through conditioning, generalization, and other forms of learning. This way of establishing learned disgust responses can be viewed as biopsychological information processing, the interaction of biological and individually acquired information.

Cognitive information processing consists of the mental processes that produce some form of memory and the processes that depend on such learning- or experience-based memory. This definition covers all the types of information processing and memory currently being studied by cognitive psychologists—automatic and deliberate processing, various types of unconscious and conscious processing, and various types of memory, such as episodic, semantic, explicit, and implicit. It does not include certain sensory and perceptual processes, such as those involved in unanticipated pain, the discrimination of certain tastes and odors, and the detection of genetically prepared stimulus features (e.g., facial contours), all of which can lead to emotion.

Cognition as defined here also covers the two most widely studied antecedents of emotion—appraisal and attribution. No one would argue with the notion that memory is a minimum requirement of the processes involved in causal attribution. A causal attribution, by definition, must be based on knowledge and memory (see Weiner, 1985). Lazarus (1984, 1991) has defined appraisal as the evaluation of the significance of knowledge: "Only the recognition that we have something to gain or lose, that is, that the outcome of a transaction is relevant to goals and well-being, generates emotion" (Lazarus, 1991, p. 354). Defined in this way, appraisal clearly depends on discriminations and comparisons made possible by learning- or experienced-based memory.

The foregoing depictions of cognition, appraisal, and attribution distinguish them from cellular and organismic information processing. Thus in the present framework, there are multiple well-used routes to emotion.

What Are the Minimum Cognitive Requirements for Emotion Activation?

I can answer the question of minimum cognitive requirements by placing it in a perspective that includes both noncognitive and cognitive emotion-activating processes. In this perspective, the question needs to be qualified: When cognition activates emotion, what are the minimum cognitive processes? The answer is almost as simple as my initial answer to the unqualified question. The minimal requirements are learning- or experienced-based memory and the discriminative and comparison processes necessary for appraisal and some form of judgment. I believe this is consistent with Lazarus's (1991) description of appraisal as "the recognition that we have something to gain or lose, that is, that the outcome of a transaction is relevant to goals and well-being" (p. 354). Certainly these processes require memory, discrimination, comparison of stored knowledge with incoming information, and judgment.

Summary

I have argued that there are both noncognitive and cognitive processes that activate emotion. The argument is based on the notion that a minimum requirement for cognition is learning- or experience-based memory. There must be some form of knowledge that can be indexed by some form of memory. This argument is also dependent on a definition of an emotion experience as a particular motivational state that can exist independent of cognition.

I have maintained that the minimum requirement for cognitively activated emotion is appraisal, defined as requiring at least rudimentary discrimination, comparison, and judgment. In the present framework, none of these phenomena is necessary for emotion activation through cellular and organismic information processing, and they are not necessarily the dominant determinant of emotion activated by biopsychological information processing.

Appraisal: The Long and the Short of It

RICHARD LAZARUS

I have written extensively about cognitive mediation as a necessary as well as sufficient condition of emotion (Lazarus, 1991a, 1991b, 1991c), and it will come as no surprise to anyone that I choose this question. The only surprise may be that to an extent I have reservations about its wording.

There are two problems with the wording. First, notice that the way the question has been asked prejudices the answer by speaking of emotion, any emotion, rather than a *particular* emotion. If we inquire about the minimal cognitive prerequisites for a particular emotion, for example, relief compared with anger or sadness, we discover that some emotions are cognitively more complex than others. Relief is probably the simplest of the emotions, cognitively speaking, whereas anger, pride, and sadness are cognitively much more complex. Relief begins with a distressing goal-incongruent condition, which changes subsequently for the better. Therefore, if we ask what is the cognitive minimum for emotion in general, and we consider relief as an example, our treatment of minimal cognitive prerequisites will hardly be representative of the cognitively more complex emotions.

The second problem is the sole emphasis on *minimal* cognitive prerequisites. To me this connotes an effort to reduce mind to its basic elements, as we do when we try to reduce complex psychological and social systems to DNA molecules in a futile effort at understanding from the bottom up. When I entered psychology after World War II, psychologists wanted to find the least common denominator of S-R reinforcement learning in the Norway white rat, a creature cognitively far simpler than humans. This creature became a primary object of study by thousands of experimental psychologists, mostly using mazes for the study of learning. As for me, I could never even solve the stylus maze when I was a human subject, but rats somehow did with comparable mazes. The presumption was that the fundamentals of learning could be established with simple creatures and applied to the most complex.

It is hard to resist a quotation here from Bolles (1990), who has been among the most articulate psychologists to criticize the assumption of S-R reinforcement psychology that all stimuli, all responses, and all organisms, are functionally alike in the learning process. He wrote (1990, pp. 112–113):

> Reinforcement people say things like "pick an arbitrary operant such as bar pressing" or "choose a representative animal, such as a rat." So we did a lot of paradigmatic experiments, but then when we varied things a little we did not find generalities, we found a lot of specificities. It seems it does make a difference what the animal is, what the cue is, what the reinforcer is, and what response is being required. Learning has a vastly richer texture than the old-timers ever dreamed of.

Although I think we are past the worst of this reductionism, the penchant to follow a reductive epistemology is still widespread, especially in fields with a strong evolutionary biology flavor, such as the emotions. If we trace the evolved tendencies back to their origin, presumably we will understand them better. I note that humans possess the richest, most abstract and symbolic capacity for thought of any creature on earth—and are the most emotional of animals—suggesting that in its highest species manifestations, its mind does not—to put it too strongly, of course—greatly resemble that of any other creature on earth.

I should not push this criticism too far, however, because, although the way the question is asked prejudices the answer, I can readily see the point of trying to speak about minimal cognitive prerequisites, as long as one also contrasts this with the process of emotion generation that draws on more symbolic processes. Although there are undoubtedly versions of emotion that are cognitively very simple, as in ontogenetically immature infants and relatively dumb mammals, I believe anger in a human adult commonly arises from complex and symbolic cognitive activity in which a person's self has been demeaned. Infant and adult human anger may well be quite different in their causation as well as in quality and consequences. But more of this later.

There are at least two ways of thinking of minimal cognitive prerequisites. The first concerns the cognitive *content* for the occurrence of any emotion, and I deal with this by considering the relational meaning and the appraisal components crucial to emotion, especially anger. The second way of thinking concerns the cognitive *process* whereby the relational meaning of the emotion is constructed in an adaptational encounter. I contrast evaluations that are automatic and unconscious with deliberate evaluations, which involve effortful, complex symbolic and conscious cognitive activity. These two ways lead to very different kinds of answers about minimal cognitive prerequisites.

The Cognitive Contents of Relational Meaning

To speak of minimal cognitive prerequisites directs our search to the question of how much information—and what kinds—is required about the person-environment relationship for an emotion to occur. An emotion is always about certain substantive features of the relationship between a person and an environment. Although this relationship can occur with the physical world, most emotions involve two people who are experiencing either a transient or stable interpersonal relationship of significance.

What makes the relationship personally significant, and hence worthy of an emotion, is that what happens is relevant to the well-being of one or both parties; in effect, each has personal goals at stake. The relationship involves either harm (i.e., thwarting of or threat to goal attainment) or benefit. The particular harms or benefits provide the details of the relational meaning, which must be sensed by one or both of the parties for an emotion to occur.

Notice that harm and benefit are fairly simple ideas predicated on what is important to one or both of the two persons—that is, a goal commitment. However, relational meaning refers to the juxtaposition of two conditions, the goal that is at stake in the encounter and the action or inaction of the other person that bears on the fate of that goal. Both events must be united in terms of a meaning, which must be appraised by the person as either a relational harm, potential or actual, or a benefit to produce an emotion. This is what relational meaning is all about.

A distinction must also be made by the person reacting with an emotion between an environmental condition that is harmful and one that is beneficial. If the relationship is appraised as harmful, the basis of a negative emotion is present, say, anger, anxiety, guilt, shame, sadness, envy, jealousy, or disgust. If the relationship is appraised as beneficial, the basis of a positive emotion is present, say, happiness, pride, relief, or love. The harm is different for each negative emotion and the benefit is different for each positive emotion. Both sets of information, the condition of the environment and the person's goals, are juggled—appraisal negotiates between them—in appraisal at the same time providing the cognitive basis of an emotion, that is, the relational meaning.

In my response to Question 4, I proposed that each emotion involved a special, and different relational meaning, which I referred to as *core relational themes*. For example, anger is the result of a demeaning offense against me and mine, anxiety is facing uncertain, existential threat, sadness is having experienced an irrevocable loss, pride is enhancement of one's ego-identity by taking credit for a valued object or achievement, and relief is a change of a negative condition for the better. (See Table 1, p. 164) If a core relational theme is sensed by a person as applicable in an encounter, the experience of the emotion associated with that theme is inevitable.

The Cognitive Contents of Appraisal

I believe the previous discussion expresses the minimal cognitive content for each emotion at a *molar* level of analysis. This content is arrived at through a set of separate appraisal decisions on a more *molecular* level, which, when combined, provides the cognitive pattern for each core relational theme. I (Lazarus, 1991c) specify six appraisal components, three primary and three secondary, that produce the cognitive patterns for each of the emotions. The primary appraisal components are all about *motivational* variables, the secondary appraisal questions all about *available coping options*. The core relational themes synthesize the separate appraisal components into a relational meaning.

If we think of the appraisal process as a decision tree, we proceed from the most general to the particular emotion; for example, whether or not there will be an emotion, which is defined by the presence of a goal at stake, or whether it will be a negative or positive emotion, which is defined by the presence of either goal *incongruence or congruence*. Ultimately, by adding further appraisal components, we get to a particular negative or positive emotion. I note, parenthetically, that I don't believe appraisal follows a sequential pattern, as Scherer (1984) argues. I speak of a decision tree for didactic reasons, not to describe how people actually review and synthesize each appraisal component into a pattern.

Thus, the bottom cognitive line that must prevail for an emotion to occur is that a goal is judged at stake in the encounter, which is called goal relevance. If there is no goal at stake, and none emerges from the encounter, there is no possibility of an emotion taking place. At some level, whether conscious or not, the person must sense goal relevance for an emotion to be aroused. Use of the language of goals rather than drives implies a concern with the means of goal attainment and defines this primary appraisal component as a cognitive one.

If a person terminates the appraisal inquiry short of the full deployment of the components necessary for a particular emotion, the reason why we must specify the particular emotion involved becomes apparent. The emotion could be a negative one, for example, anger, anxiety, or guilt, or a positive one, for example, happiness, relief, or pride. Which one it will be cannot be stated without taking into account more than goal relevance, namely, whether the encounter is goal incongruent or congruent. If it is goal incongruent, implying thwarting or conflict, the emotion will be negative, reflecting an unfavorable condition for goal attainment. If it is goal congruent, implying a favorable condition for goal attainment, the emotion will be positive. To narrow the choice of the emotion further requires additional appraisal components in the decision tree to distinguish the particular emotion that will be experienced.

So, the answer to the basic question posed here—at the level of separate appraisal components of cognitive content—is that the minimal cognitive prerequisite for an emotion, any emotion, is that one senses a goal-related stake in the encounter. However, if we are to predict whether the emotion will be positive or negative rather than just any emotion, we need to know whether conditions are appraised as favorable or unfavorable. And finally, to narrow down to one or another particular emotion requires additional cognitive prerequisites, for example, the type of ego-involvement, whether and where blame or credit is assigned, coping potentials, and future expectations. In other words, depending on the particular emotion predicted, the minimal requirements grow progressively more complex as one goes from an emotion, that is, any emotion, to a particular emotion.

I don't have the space here to present a complete appraisal-related account for each emotion as I did in Lazarus (1991c). I will, however, relate the case for anger in more detail to illustrate some of the nuances involved in cognitively more complex emotions.

The Appraisal Contents for Anger

I said previously that the appraisal pattern for some emotions is more complicated than for others, depending perhaps on whether we are dealing with an infant or an adult. Since this point is crucial for the argument about minimal and maximal cognitive prerequisites, allow me to present the key appraisals for prototypical anger in an adult, which I believe is cognitively quite complex, after which I will speculate about the same emotion in infants.

As with all other emotions, anger depends at the outset on there being goal relevance and goal incongruence, the latter implying that a relevant goal in the encounter has been thwarted or threatened. I think that a special type of *ego-involvement* is also crucial to adult anger, namely, the protection or enhancement of self-esteem. Remember that the core relational theme for anger is said to be "a demeaning offense against me and mine." What makes us angry is that we have been taken for less than we want to be by someone who is being either inconsiderate or malevolent.

To make such an appraisal requires that we *blame* someone other than ourselves for the personal slight, blame being the most important secondary appraisal component of anger. Blame depends on two attributes, namely, external accountability and the imputation that the person accountable could have controlled the demeaning actions if he or she wished. If the accountability is internal, the emotion will be either anger at oneself, guilt, or shame. If the accountable person could not have acted differently, the reasons for appraising blame are undermined. Anger is also facilitated if an attack on whomever we blame is viable and there are grounds for expecting the retaliation to repair one's wounded self-esteem (see Lazarus, 1991c, for a more complete account).

Imagine that you have gone to a department store to buy something, but you are made to wait for a long time by a clerk who seems intent on a personal telephone conversation. You become increasingly irate and ultimately make a caustic remark, only to discover that the clerk has been talking to the school nurse because the clerk's child has had an accident and was taken to a hospital emergency room. The anger suddenly dissipates and in its place may be guilt or shame. You have discovered that the clerk could not reasonably have acted differently, and so is not blameworthy for what seemed like a social slight.

There is, in effect, no slight at all, though the frustration remains. This frustration of having to wait must still be dealt with, for example, by seeking some other agent who is blameworthy. One can, for example, assign blame to oneself for leaving shopping for an inconvenient time, to the store management for having too few personnel available, or to the system, which assigns blame almost abstractly but in a way that may protect or repair many a person's shakey self-esteem. The psychosocial processes whereby one senses a slight, assigns someone to blame, and chooses to express it overtly or regulate it are extremely complex in human social encounters, despite the fact that anger can also be phylogenetically and ontogenetically simple and elemental.

Aside from the controversial role of imputed control or intent in the generation of anger (cf. Berkowitz, 1989), the most serious problem to be dealt with in this account of anger is developmental. If we are to argue that roughly four appraisal components are crucial to anger, then for anger to be generated in an infant requires that these appraisal components are within an infant's cognitive capacity and are, indeed, active components of their appraisals.

Stenberg and Campos (1990) have generated what seems like anger in babies at 3 to 7 months old by restraining the baby's arm. At 3 months the baby seems to show distress, but at 4 months the baby displays unmistakable anger. It struggles to free itself, suggesting that it is capable of grasping that its goal of free movement is being *thwarted*. At 4 months it also looks at the wrist that is restraining it, suggesting that it is capable of grasping that the *offending agent is external*. At 7 months, it looks at the face of the person who is restraining it, and even at the mother if she is present, suggesting that it recognizes that the *offending agent is a particular person* and that it wants or expects help from the mother.

Does a baby in this situation sense that its self-esteem has been slighted? What of the equally important components of accountability and imputed control, which I said was crucial for adult blaming? With respect to *self-esteem*, when a self or ego-identity emerges in an infant is an unsettled question. Stern (1985) argues that this is a gradual process that begins almost right away; Lewis and Michalson (1983) suggest that a sense of self comes much later; Bahrick and Watson's research implies that a baby at 5 months is aware of the contingency between its movements and what is shown of these movements on a TV monitor, so it must have an emerging sense of a self that is distinguishable from another (see also Papousek & Papousek, 1974, for discussions of this). Although a primitive sense of self does not necessarily imply anything as sophisticated as a self-esteem that is used in social comparison, it may not be totally fanciful to suggest that a 4-month-old baby might somehow sense that it is being treated badly when restrained. I have difficulty conceiving, however, that arbitrariness and intent are understood at this stage of life.

And what about accountability and imputed control? If adult blaming depends on the attribution of *accountability*, the 4-month-old baby shows the capacity to make this judgment (it looks at the restraining wrist), and at 7 months looks at the face of the person restraining it. I doubt very much, somehow, that the baby at this age is capable of an inference about the intent of that person, or about the control that person might have over actions.

What does all this mean concerning anger in the 4-month-old baby compared with adult anger? We probably should conclude that, in the absence of clear evidence of its ability to sense damage to self-esteem or to assign blame (as a result of an inference of imputed control) rather than merely accountability, the anger shown by these babies is probably not the same as it is in the adult version. Certain key processes of appraisal-related inference seem still to be missing.

Should we call the baby's reaction anger? Probably, as long as one also recognizes that there are many forms of anger, some more cognitively complex and prototypic than others. I believe that it is important to recognize more than one kind of anger, the variations having to do with the activity of certain appraisal components. Elsewhere (Lazarus, 1991c) I gave considerable attention to two particular forms, which I believe depend on secondary appraisal components related to coping. These forms are pouting and gloating, and they serve nicely to illustrate the subtle nuances of meaning, which different forms of anger may reflect.

A person who *pouts* feels that someone on whom he or she depends for succorance has not been paying sufficient attention. Pouting is a mild reproach, which expresses disappointment with the other from whom more was expected or needed. A needy person cannot afford an outright attack on the other but must blunt it in order to preserve succor.

A person who *gloats*, on the other hand, seems to be savoring another person's comeuppance, enjoying his or her bad fate. Such a person obtains a well-deserved vindication, which serves to repair self-esteem damage at the hands of the other. Gloaters mock the other person with malignant scorn and smiling satisfaction. They can afford an overt attack because of their sense of being in a one-up position with respect to the other.

On the surface, the difference between a pouter and a gloater would seem to depend on being either powerful or needy, expressed in the secondary appraisal component, *coping potential*. The pouter feels weak and needy; the gloater feels superior. I say on the surface because Whitman and Alexander (1968) have characterized gloaters as "sore winners" from a psychoanalytic perspective. They consider gloating to arise from a childhood history of envy of more successful siblings. Thus, gloating preserves the illusion that one is superior, but—in the psychoanalytic tradition that everything expresses its unconscious opposite—it is really a defensive maneuver against the opposite construal, namely, that one is inadequate or in a one-down position. Although pouters and gloaters may have more in common than may appear on the surface, the pouter seems, nevertheless, to accept his or her dependency while the gloater covers it up with a defense. We should be able to find personality correlates and personal history variables that explain these diverse anger-related traits.

Notice that in this example, involving multiple goals, perceptions, and unconscious defenses, I have moved from a perspective of minimal cognitive content prerequisites to that of near maximal. The examples are rich and full of subtle distinctions, both about the other person, one's own resources, the ongoing relationship between the two people involved, and the contradictory tendencies (including defenses) within the person experiencing the emotion. Solely to seek the minimal cognitive prerequisites of emotion would be to also overlook all this rich cognitive activity, filled with complex relational meanings and personal histories.

It is also important to recognize that the processes involved are apt to be overlearned and repeat prior struggles involving appraisal. The overlearning serves to simplify and automatize the appraisal process and makes it respond to minimal cues. Thus, when major adaptational problems recur, as they are apt to over our lifetime, we need not engage in an elaborate set of cognitive decisions to reach the appropriate core relational theme. Since we have made the same decisions in the past, we now need a very limited cue about the meaning of what is happening. This is tantamount to saying that we constantly simplify and automatize recurrent appraisals, which makes them simpler in process though rich and symbolic in content.

The Cognitive Process of Constructing Relational Meaning

There has come to be a widespread conviction in social cognition that animals as well as people are capable of automatic and unconscious appraisals, in contrast with deliberate and conscious ways of constructing relational meaning. Le Doux (1986, 1989) speaks of these as *subcortical* (reaching only as far as the amygdala).

Others use quite different imageries and metaphors for related though not identical processes, for example, *affordances* (Baron & Boudreau, 1987), *resonances* (Shepard, 1984), *intersubjectivities* (Trevarthen, 1979), *embodied intelligence*, (Merleau-Ponty, 1962), and *tacit knowledge* (Polanyi, 1966). Heidegger's (see Guignon, 1984) distinction between *being-in-a-situation* and observing oneself as an outsider is also relevant here. (See also Kihlstrom, 1987, and Brewin, 1989) for other variations on this distinction.)

In a recent effort to contrast cognitive science with human experience, Varela, Thompson, and Rosch (1991) regret the absence of experience in the approaches of cognitivists, which is relevant to the study of how people think and evaluate issues. I should also note that the distinction between automatic and deliberate modes of meaning generation has also been delineated by others who have been long concerned with emotion theory itself (such as Buck, 1985, Ekman, 1977, Leventhal, 1984, and Scherer, 1984).

The key theme of all this is that somehow, without elaborate and deliberate cognitive processing or even being conscious of doing so, we intuitively sense fundamental evaluative features of the significance of our person-environment relationships for our well-being.

We should be wary, however, of drawing the conclusion that automatic implies simple or primitive, because to sense relational meaning requires that we take into account two often complex sets of variables, personal goals and the environmental forces, such as demands, constraints, and opportunities, that bear on these sets of variables. What we also sense may be symbolic, abstract, and complex rather than simple and concrete. Cognitive prerequisites for an emotion draw on a process in which—however automatic and primitive—we must juggle these two considerations simultaneously. The 4-month-old baby senses not only its curtailment of freedom of action but also that there is an external agent responsible for it.

For people to react with an emotion, the relevance of what is happening to their well-being must be sensed, as well as whether this has negative or positive implications. We do not stop with a hasty and incomplete cognitive evaluation—this constitutes an incompleted task, which the person or animal is compelled to pursue further—until what is happening can be understood in a way that is relevant to efforts at coping. Although the initial appraisal may be hasty and limited, if the opportunity for further investigation of what is happening presents itself, it would be a strange creature that let things drop at that point before a full functional understanding has been achieved.

An emotion can be generated hastily, but to the extent that it differentiates into anger, anxiety, guilt, shame, sadness, envy, jealousy, or disgust on the negative side, or happiness, pride, relief, and love on the positive side, substantial additional meanings are surely required. So, when all is said and done, I am not very sanguine about the utility of the search for minimal cognitive prerequisites for the occurrence of emotion. At the very least, we should be concerned with both content and process, and with maximal as well as minimal prerequisites. Far more important, however, I believe, would be a search for the fundamental cognitions that differentiate among the many emotions of which humans are capable.

Cognitive-Emotional Interactions in the Brain

JOSEPH E. LEDOUX

The relation between "cognition" and "emotion" has been debated at length for the past several decades. In this essay, I will attempt to address the issue of cognitive-emotional interactions, specifically emotional dependence on cognition, from the perspective of one who works on the brain mechanisms of emotion and cognition. I believe that information about the neural organization of emotional and cognitive processes suggests insights into the functional organization of these processes and sets constraints for theories of cognitive-emotional interactions.

Cognition and Emotion: Brain Functions or Labels?

Just what do the terms cognition and emotion refer to? Do they refer to real functions that are represented in the brain or only to labels that we use as shorthand descriptions of real brain functions? It seems to me that labels is the answer. Before defending why, let me state why it matters.

To understand how cognition and emotion interact, we need to be clear about what the nature of such an interaction might be. Unless we are willing to embrace spiritualism, where the interaction might take place ephemerally, the interaction must take place in the brain. It is therefore important that we talk about cognition and emotion at levels that approximate the levels at which these processes are represented in the brain.

First, consider cognition. Just as trees produce specific fruits (apples, oranges, pears, etc.), brains mediate specific cognitive processes (attention, perception, memory, etc.). "Fruit" and "cognition" are categories, not real things. Cognition itself has no specific representation in the brain because it is nothing more than a word that we use to describe a group of related but diverse information-processing functions, including sensory processing, perception, imagery, attention, memory, reasoning, and problem-solving. But even this characterization is too simplistic.

Each specific cognitive process listed can be broken down into more specific categories. For example, there are many perceptual processes, each with its own distinct neural representations. A trivial example is the fact that the system that mediates visual perception is different from the system that mediates auditory perception. Less trivial is that within the visual system, object, color, motion, and spatial perception are mediated by somewhat different circuitries. This could be pushed even further. However, the important point is that the description of cognition in terms of specific processes gets us closer to the way the brain is organized than the term "cognition" does. This explains why we have very successful theories of specific perceptual, attentive, or imagery processes, but not much in the way of a successful general theory of cognition.

Similarly, "emotion" is best viewed not as a function of the brain but as a label that refers to a closely related set of brain functions. The brain has systems that mediate fear, anger, and pleasure, but not a system that mediates "emotion." At one time, it seemed that the limbic system might fill the role of a general-purpose emotion system (MacLean, 1952), but we now know that this is not the case (Brodal, 1982; Swanson, 1983; LeDoux, 1987, 1992c). The limbic system points us in the direction of some relevant parts of the brain for emotion but tells us very little about the brain mechanisms of any given emotional process. I believe that psychological and neural theories of "emotion" have failed because they have to do too much on the basis of too little. We need some solid anchors on which to hang emotional concepts. One way to get these anchors would be to focus on specific emotions, such as fear or anger or pleasure, and construct mini-theories of these. Possibly, a global theory of emotion would result from a synthesis across the various specific emotion theories. However, even if the global theory failed, we would at least have developed a more detailed understanding of specific emotions.

In summary, interactions between cognition and emotion must take place at the neural level. The global concepts (labels) "cognition" and "emotion" are far too removed from the actual functions that are represented in the brain to be useful as reference points for examining functional interactions. It is necessary to focus on specific cognitive and emotional psychological processes that closely approximate brain functions if we want to understand actual interactions. However, because the global terms each refer to such diverse phenomena, it is possible, if the representatives of each category are carefully selected, to successfully argue that emotion depends on cognition or is independent of cognition. We must state exactly what we mean when we use the terms cognition and emotion and must choose meaningful examples on each side when we examine interactions between them.

I will therefore focus on specific cognitive and emotional processes in an effort to show how these interact in the brain. By dwelling on specific cognitive and emotional processes, I run the risk of generating a limited picture of cognitive-emotional interactions. However, the picture that emerges will at least have some basis in fact.

Neural Bases of Cognitive and Emotional Processing

Much is known about the neural basis of certain cognitive processes. This is especially true in the areas of perception and memory. I will therefore use perception and memory as examples of cognitive processes to examine how cognitive and emotional processes interact. More specifically, I will focus on the systems underlying stimulus perception and the formation of explicit (declarative) memories about such stimuli. On the emotional side, I will focus on the mechanisms underlying the evaluation (appraisal) of emotional significance of sensory stimuli and the production of stereotyped, species-typical emotional responses in reaction to these stimuli, especially by the fear system of the brain.

Studies beginning around mid-century began to elucidate the neural basis of stimulus perception terms of anatomical pathways extending outward from neocortical sensory receiving areas. Neocortical sensory systems are classically viewed in terms of sequentially organized networks involving a primary receiving area, which receives the major topographically organized inputs from thalamic regions, and parallel streams of association areas, each of which can also be organized in terms of sequential processing stations (Whitlock & Nauta, 1956; Jones & Powell, 1970; Mesulam et al., 1977; Turner, Mishkin, & Knapp, 1980). These sensory-specific or "unimodal" association areas are believed to be involved in the representation of stimulus information as perceptual entities (Farah, 1990; Gross, 1973, 1992; Mishkin, 1966; Ungerleider & Mishkin, 1982). Unimodal association areas then give rise to projections to "polymodal" association areas, which integrate information across sensory modalities. A third tier of association areas includes "supramodal" regions, which receive inputs from two or more polymodal areas (Mesulam et al., 1977). As information is transmitted through these networks, the level of representation of the stimulus becomes more and more divorced from the original input and grows more and more abstract.

Thus, the perception of the form of a visual stimulus, say, an apple, is believed to be mediated by the flow of sensory information through the visual processing system to primary visual cortex and then, by way of corticocortical pathways, to the latest stages of unimodal visual processing in area TE of the temporal lobe; in contrast, the perception of where the apple is located in space involves a different visual stream flowing from primary visual areas into parietal rather than temporal cortex (e.g., Gross, 1973; Farah, 1990; Mishkin, 1965; Ungerleider & Mishkin, 1982; van Essen, 1985). The integration of visual object representations with stored knowledge (memories) involves more extensive networks, especially networks extending from unimodal visual association areas into polymodal (i.e., perirhinal cortex) and supramodal (i.e., entorhinal cortex and hippocampal formation) association areas and then back to polymodal and unimodal association areas (e.g., Squire, 1987). These networks underlie the ability to categorize a stimulus on the basis of the semantic organization and relationships of the stimulus (that apples are a kind of fruit) and practical facts about it (that certain types of apples are better for making pies than others) and the ability to place the stimulus in a personal-past context (to remember where we were and who we were with and what happened before and after the last time we ate an apple). While these mechanisms are best understood in the visual system, other sensory systems have similar connections that may subserve similar functions (e.g., Turner et al., 1980).

Many emotional-processing functions are critically dependent on the amygdala. It has been known for some time that the amygdala, a small structure buried deep in the temporal lobe, plays an important role in the coding of the emotional significance of sensory stimuli (Kluver & Bucy, 1937; Weiskrantz, 1956; Gloor, 1960; Downer, 1961; Goddard, 1964). Animals with amygdala lesions respond normally to the immediately available or remembered perceptual features of objects but are insensitive to the emotional significance of the same objects (for reviews, see Aggleton & Mishkin, 1986; LeDoux, 1987). Further, neurons in the amygdala are driven particularly strongly by stimuli with emotional significance (see Rolls, 1992; Ono & Nishijo, 1992; Brothers, Ring, & Kling, 1990). The amygdala has been implicated in many experimental tasks used to study the brain mechanisms of emotion and it appears to be a focal point in the brain system that determines (appraises) the emotional significance of many kinds of emotional stimuli (LeDoux, 1992a, 1992b). Nevertheless, the amygdala does not work as a unified whole in the mediation of these emotional functions. While it is tempting to describe the amygdala as a universal emotional computer, it is best not to think of it in this way. Different emotional functions require different inputs and outputs of different amygdaloid nuclei. The networks through which the amygdala is involved in fear processing are best understood and are the basis of most of the following discussion of emotional mechanisms (LeDoux, 1987, 1990, 1992; Davis, Hitchcock, & Rosen, 1987; Davis, 1992; Kapp et al., 1990, 1992).

Threatening stimuli often elicit immediate, stereotyped behavioral and visceral responses, so-called defense responses (the difference between these automatically elicited responses and later-occurring, emitted, instrumental responses is described in Question 7). The propensity of fear-related stimuli to lead to behavioral and visceral reactions is easily explained by the intimate connectivity of the amygdala with brainstem systems involved in the control of preprogrammed, species-typical behaviors and associated autonomic and endocrine reactions (see LeDoux et al., 1988; LeDoux, 1987, 1990; Davis et al., 1987; Kapp et al., 1984, 1990). Facial expressions are an important example of a species-typical behavioral response class that is expressed during fear and some other emotions in humans (Ekman, 1984; Tomkins, 1962; Izard, 1977) and the amygdala has access to the brainstem nuclei that control the face musculature (Holstege, Kuypers, & Dekker, 1977; Post & Mai, 1980). In contrast, most high-level association areas of the cortex lack this connectivity with brainstem motoric areas involved in stereotyped response control but do have connections with the motor control systems in the neocortex and basal ganglia (Jones & Powell, 1970; Alheid & Heimer, 1988), which are believed to be involved in voluntary motor control. This distinction in connectivity most certainly underlies the stereotyped, inflexible, involuntary nature of fear and some other primal emotional reactions and the variable, flexible, voluntary nature of behavioral responses controlled by cognitive events. Interestingly, the amygdala is also connected with the basal ganglia (deOlmos, Alheid, & Beltramino, 1985) and these connections may allow the amygdala to contribute, along with cortical cognitive systems, to instrumental (voluntary) emotional behavior responses emitted in an effort to cope with the involuntary emotional reactions that are elicited by emotional stimuli (see Question 7).

The propensity for fear-provoking and other emotional stimuli to elicit "arousal" may also be related to the connectivity of the amygdala. Arousal is a vague concept that has nevertheless played an important role in emotion theory for some time (see

Frijda, 1986). One of the mysteries about arousal is how it is initiated. The older notion was that the so-called reticular activating system was activated by collateral fibers from ascending sensory systems. However, these fibers arise very early in the sensory processing channel and are unlikely to "know" the difference between fear-arousing and insignificant sensory events. It would seem necessary for the arousal systems to receive inputs from forebrain areas (such as the amygdala) that are involved in the coding of stimulus significance. This turns out to be the case. For example, the brainstem cholinergic system has, in recent years, emerged as an important component of the activating system, especially in the regulation of ascending sensory information processed in thalamo-cortical relay systems during waking states and rapid eye movement (dream) sleep (Hobson & Steriade, 1986). It is thus significant that the amygdala projects to this system (Hopkins & Holstege, 1978; Takeuchi, McLean, & Hopkins, 1982; Krettek & Price, 1978). Such pathways may allow the detection of emotional significance by the amygdala to contribute to the triggering of brainstem arousal functions.

In summary, the amygdala seems to be particularly involved in emotional functions and to have considerably less direct involvement in cognitive ones. More is known about the contribution of the amygdala to fear than to other emotions, but it seems to be involved in other aversive and appetitive emotions as well. In contrast, cortical association areas (including the archicortex of the hippocampal formation as well as the neocortical association areas) are particularly involved in cognitive functions. An important approach for understanding the relation between cognition and fear and other amygdala-based emotions would be to understand the neural interactions between cortical association systems and the amygdala. Fortunately, this is well understood.

Cognitive-Emotional Interactions in the Brain: Clues to the Cognitive Prerequisites of Emotional Processes

The amygdala receives inputs from unimodal sensory processing areas in the thalamus, from unimodal association cortex, and from various levels of polymodal and supramodal association cortex (for review, see LeDoux, 1987; Amaral et al., 1992). These connections are illustrated in the following figure. Animal studies have implicated each of these inputs to the amygdala in different aspects of fear processing (see LeDoux, 1987, 1992b). Thalamo-amygdala projections are involved in processing the emotional significance of simple sensory events (sensory features as opposed to complete objects) (LeDoux, 1986), unimodal cortico-amygdala projections in processing the emotional significance of discriminated stimulus patterns or recognized objects (Jarrel et al., 1987), and polymodal/supramodal cortico-amygdala projections in processing the emotional significance of complex, multimodal representations, such as the memory of a context in which an emotional stimulus appeared (LeDoux, 1987; 1990; Phillips & LeDoux, 1992; Kim & Fanselow, 1992; Penick & Solomon, 1991). Presumably, hippocampal projections to amygdala would also be involved the elicitation of fear/anxiety on the basis of explicit or declarative memories, which depend on the hippocampal formation, but this has not been examined directly. Thus, the amygdala is an important site of fear processing; it can attach significance to any of several levels of stimulus representation, from the simplest to the most complex (see the accompanying figure).

From this neuroanatomical perspective, the cognitive prerequisites of fear processing can be minimal or extensive or both. Thalamic sensory processing areas are the gateway to the neocortex, where object representations and elaborations are constructed from incoming sensory signals. Thalamic areas are also a gateway to the amygdala, where emotional significance is attached to sensory signals. The amygdala can thus be activated from the thalamus at about the same time that the cortex can be activated from the thalamus. Object representation and emotional representation can thus proceed in parallel. We can, in other words, begin to respond to the emotional significance of a stimulus before we fully represent that stimulus. However, this means that the representations that activate the emotional system can be based on incomplete and fragmented information rather than on veridical perceptions. This may account for why we are not always aware of why we respond emotionally the way we do. This kind of organization is particularly useful as a first line of defense against threatening stimuli, but may sometimes lead to emotional errors of commission. However, the system is built to allow for error correction. Emotional responses that are inappropriately initiated by subcortical (thalamic) sensory inputs to the amygdala can be modified by cortical inputs, which provide multiple levels of representation to activate the amygdala. An important challenge facing neuroscientists studying emotional processing is to determine just how thalamic and cortical inputs to the amygdala interact in the initiation and control of emotional responses.

The importance of the distinction between the neural representation of affective and cognitive systems is strongly highlighted within the area of memory research. Studies of the anatomy of memory in humans and nonhuman primates have long pointed to the temporal lobe, and particularly to the hippocampal formation, in the establishment of explicit or declarative (consciously accessible) memories (Squire, 1992). For some time, the amygdala was included in this temporal lobe memory system (e.g., Mishkin, 1982), but it is now known that the amygdala does not

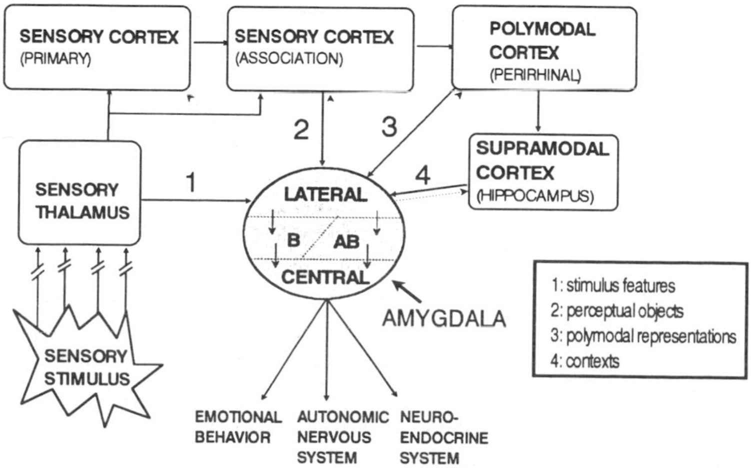

participate in declarative memory to any significant degree (Zola-Morgan et al., 1991; Murray, 1992). In contrast, the amygdala is an essential structure in the brain system involved in the formation of memories about the emotional significance of stimuli, especially but not exclusively aversive stimuli that elicit fear (e.g., LeDoux, 1992a, 1992b; Kapp et al., 1990; Davis, 1992). Lesions of the hippocampus leave the capacity for this kind of emotional memory formation intact, whereas lesions of the amygdala leave declarative memory undisturbed. In general, amygdala lesions do not affect the broad range of phenomena we tend to think of as falling in the domain of cognition. While the hippocampus plays a key role in Gray's (1982) model of emotion (anxiety), it may do so more as a cognitive than as an emotional processing system (LeDoux, 1992c). The hippocampus may be particularly involved in the "cognitive coping" (Lazarus, 1991) with the consequences of stress reactions that are initially activated by the amygdala (Henke, 1990, 1992). The hippocampus is also involved in contextual fear conditioning (Phillips & LeDoux, 1992; Kim & Fanselow, 1992), but appears to act more as a high-level sensory structure that provides inputs to the amgydala rather than as a key site of emotional learning.

Finally, it should be noted that the amygdala projects widely to neocortical systems (see dotted lines in the figure and Amaral et al., 1992). In fact, the projection field of the amygdala in the neocortex is wider than the field of neocortical areas that project to the amygdala. Processing in the amygdala can thus influence many cognitive processes organized at the cortical level, including the archicortex (i.e., hippocampus). Projections to the cortex from the amygdala may serve as channels through which emotional processing can influence cognitive processing (Rolls, 1990). Since these projections span all the way from primary sensory cortex through the highest (most complex) association fields, the possibilities for emotional modulation of cognition are enormous. These possibilities are further amplified by the fact that the amygdala also projects to brainstem (Hopkins & Holstedge, 1978; Takeuchi et al., 1982; Krettek & Price, 1978) and forebrain (Price & Amaral, 1981; Russchen, Amaral, & Price, 1985) cholinergic systems, each of which plays a role in cortical arousal and vigilance (Hobson & Steriade, 1986; Kapp et al., 1992). As described, the so-called nonspecific arousal that accompanies emotional activation must be due to the activation of nonspecific systems by processes that have first detected the significance of the stimulus. The amygdala can thus influence cognitive processing directly by way of back-projections to cortex and indirectly by way of nonspecific brainstem systems.

Conclusion

I believe that the neuroanatomy of cognitive processes (such as object perception and declarative memory) and emotional processes (especially the evaluation of fear-eliciting stimuli) helps us to see the interrelation of these processes in a clearer light. Emotional processing requires stimulus input and is therefore dependent to some extent on cognitive systems for stimulus transmission. However, emotional processing involves separate systems that are strongly connected with prewired response control networks and with arousal networks. These connections account for important differences between cognitive and emotional processing. Knowing these differences sets the stage for examining the links between the systems. These links, in turn, suggest insights into the nature of cognitive-emotional interactions.

The cognitive-emotional interactions that have been identified are specific and selective. Specificity allows us to have confidence in the conclusions since they are closely tied to brain organization, but selectivity limits the extent to which we can generalize beyond the specific processes to global notions of cognition and emotion. However, this seems to be a small price to pay for a clear, neuroanatomically based foundation, which should provide a base on which to build a more general understanding of cognitive-emotional interactions by adding, one at a time, additional pieces of emotion and cognition.

A Proper Distinction Between Affective and Cognitive Process Is Essential for Neuroscientific Progress

JAAK PANKSEPP

The answer to this question critically depends on one's definition of a cognitive process. If it is defined by thought or other forms of cortical information processing, then the clear answer is that there are no necessary cognitive preconditions (which is not to imply that such cognitive and emotional processes do not strongly interact under normal circumstances). If one liberalizes the definition of a cognitive process to include any incoming exteroceptive sensory input, then the answer is bound to be "quite a bit." After all, emotions are typically triggered by environmental events rather than local tissue irritations within the brain. However, the fact that sensory inputs typically trigger emotions is not the same as saying that these inputs are essential for the creation of emotions. The central integrative systems presumably continue to exist even if disconnected from the world. I think the emergence of patterned motor output generators has some primacy in brain evolution, and the fact that these systems eventually came to be under the obligatory guidance of various sensory/perceptual inputs does not negate that the central command systems probably still have an integrity that does not rely on the guidance mechanisms.

Let's us consider one minimalist example—the genetically ingrained tendency of a rat to exhibit fear in response to the smell of a cat. The information comes in via the vomeronasal nerve, which, after passing through the accessory olfactory bulb, synapses largely in the preoptic area and medial amygdala. From the medial amygdala, the information travels largely via the stria terminalis to the anterior hypothalamus, where the information travels largely via the stria terminalis to the anterior hypothalamus, where the information appears to be further integrated with fear command circuitry, which then descends to the periventricular gray (Panksepp, 1990a). At no point in this flow did the fearful smell have to be processed by thalamocortical systems, and even if the sensory input is removed, the animal can still exhibit fear responses. In a similar way, sounds can provoke fear with no cortical processing. Auditory information merely needs to get to the medial geniculate nucleus of the thalamus, from where it can directly activate the rostral extensions of fear circuitry in the amygdala (LeDoux, Ruggiero, & Reis, 1985; LeDoux, Sakaguchi & Reis, 1984). However, again, overall fear responsivity is preserved if these auditory inputs are disconnected. Although one could consider these "low" level forms of sensory processing to be in the cognitive domain, that tends to stretch the meaning of the concept excessively. To prevent the concept from covering everything and hence nothing, I believe the cognitive argument should be reserved largely for neocortical and hippocampal processing of exteroceptive information (and perhaps thalamic memory retrieval circuits). If one abides by such a restriction, the resounding answer to the posed question is that emotions require no cognitive inputs (although they may often be triggered by them).

This assertion is further verified by neodecortication experiments in young animals. This type of intervention leaves basic emotive tendencies intact, indeed intensified. For instance, rats that have been decorticated within the first week of birth are noteworthy for their outward normality—if anything, these animals exhibit more *species-typical* (and *class-characteristic*) "emotive energy" than neurologically intact animals. In studying such animals in my undergraduate laboratory classes, neophyte psychologists have been unable to correctly identify the decorticates, and routinely tend to guess that the decorticates rather than the intact animals are the normal ones in mixed pairs (and I doubt that fully trained psychologists, at least those who restrict their work to humans, could do much better). This mistake results from the fact that the decorticates exhibit unfettered emotional energies (i.e., they are generally disinhibited, and instinctually engaged with their sensory world). Such experiments affirm that cortico-cognitive processes are not essential for the expression of basic emotional tendencies.

Obviously, emotional and cognitive processes interact in untold ways. Emotions appear able to both guide and disrupt modes of thought, and provide mood- and emotion-congruent coding and retrieval of information. Thus, it is tempting to blend these concepts beyond distinction (Gray, 1990), but I believe the neurological evidence should advise us against such maneuvers (Panksepp, 1990b). The basic impulses for each appear to arise largely from distinct geographic areas of the brain (hypothalamo-limbic vs. thalamo-cortical). By sustaining reasonably well-demarcated distinctions between cognitive and emotional processes in the brain, we are more likely to make headway in substantive understanding of the many powerful, and often obligatory, interactions between them.

From the neuroscience perspective, several intriguing forms of interaction exist between cortico-cognitive processes and subcortical emotional systems that have specific neuropeptides within their core structures (Panksepp, 1993). Although most neuronal systems that express neuropeptides are heavily concentrated in viscero-limbic areas of the brain, the cortex often contains many receptors for these peptides (often with no corresponding axonal connections from subcortical areas). For some of these systems, peptidergic neurons and receptors are homogeneously, albeit sparsely, scattered throughout specific layers of the cortex. This scenario is present for CRF (Swanson, Sawachenko, Rivier, & Vale, 1983; Wynn, Hauger, Holmes, Millan, Catt, & Aguilera, 1984), CCK (Vanderhaeghen & Crawley, 1985), somatostatin (Brownstein, Arimura, Sato, Schally, & Kizer, 1975), VIP (Said & Mutt,

1988) and others. These interactions provide many neuronal as well as non-neuronal (e.g., paracrine) routes of interactions between emotional and cognitive processes.

Unfortunately, most of these brain systems are next to impossible to study in humans except via measurment of cerebrospinal fluid levels of peptides. Peripherally administered peptides typically do not cross the various barriers that exist between blood and brain. Once we develop better pharmacological means to modify these neurochemical systems, we may be in a position to study the subtleties of thought and mood that arise in the human brain from neuropeptidergic interactions. However, it is noteworthy that for some systems, entry into brain can be promoted by intranasal administration of neuropeptides (e.g., oxytocin and vasopressin) and the available work suggests some intriguing effects on selective attention which may be due to modification of specific types of emotional-arousal processes (Fehm-Wolfsdorf & Born, 1991; Naumann, Bartussek, Kaiser, & Gehm-Wolfsdorf (1991)).

An Emotion's Occurrence Depends on the Relevance of an Event to the Organism's Goal/Need Hierarchy

KLAUS R. SCHERER

The question concerning the minimal cognitive prerequisites for the occurrence of an emotion must be addressed regarding two issues: *level of processing* and *type of processing*.

The classic debate between Lazarus and Zajonc concerning the role of cognition in emotion (Zajonc, 1980, 1984; Lazarus, 1984)—which had a major impact on the psychology of emotion in the 1980s—mostly concerned *level of processing*. While Lazarus argued that there needed to be some type of "meaning analysis" for a stimulus to elicit an emotion, Zajonc pointed out, citing experimental evidence, that affective reactions could be elicted through very subtle, subcortical processes. Leventhal and Scherer (1987) have argued that the Lazarus/Zajonc debate was mostly about semantic issues, namely the definition of cognition. We suggested that, since both Lazarus and Zajonc assumed some type of stimulus processing or coding, be it at a very rudimentary level, the real issue concerned the level of processing. We further proposed that it would be more fruitful to determine the nature of the information processes antecedent to emotion, including the level on which emotion occurred and the type of cognitive and neurological equipment required. Marrying Leventhal's perceptual-motor theory of emotion (Leventhal, 1984) and my stimulus evaluation check model (Scherer, 1984), we proposed the classification of emotion-antecedent processing shown in Table 1 (reproduced from Leventhal & Scherer, 1987).

In terms of this model, any stimulus or event that is processed on the lowest level of sensory motor capacity, independent of links to stored schemata or conceptual-associative structures, would theoretically be capable of eliciting an emotion. LeDoux (1989) has suggested a very similar argument, mostly with respect to the requirement that the central nervous system of the organism has to perform some type of coding, independent of the level of sophistication of the structures that are involved. LeDoux's own work on direct projections to the amygdala from the sensory projection areas nicely demonstrates the feasibility of these assumptions.

TABLE 1. Processing Levels for Stimulus Evaluation Checks

Level	*Novelty*	*Pleasantness*	*Goal/Need Conduciveness*	*Coping Potential*	*Norm/Self-Compatibility*
Conceptual	Expectations: cause/effect, probability estimates	Recalled, anticipated, or derived positive-negative evaluations	Conscious goals, plans	Problem solving ability	Self-ideal, moral evaluation
Schematic	Familiarity: schemata matching	Learned preferences/aversions	Acquired needs, motives	Body schemata	Self/social schemata
Sensorimotor	Sudden, intense stimulation	Innate preferences/aversions	Basic needs	Available energy	(Empathic adaptation?)

Source: Reproduced from Leventhal & Scherer (1987).

The issue of minimal prerequesites is more difficult to answer regarding the *type of processing*. Clearly, not every stimulation that is processed by the organism on either a very low, rudimentary sensory motor level or on a more sophisticated higher level, involving association areas, will elicit an emotion. All organisms continuously process information on all levels without necessarily experiencing an emotion continuously. Actually, the notion advanced by some theorists in the area, namely that we are "affective" all the time and that it is just the intensity of the affect that is varying, does not seem to be very helpful in our attempt to understand emotional episodes. While one could conceive of a steady ebb and flow of affectivity superimposed on information processing, this would have to be dealt with in terms of a different phenomenon (possibly "affective tone") rather than as emotion in the sense of an emotional episode in which all response modalities of the organism are synchronized to deal with a significant event (see the definition of emotion I proposed in my response to Question 1).

What then could be the minimal prerequisite in terms of type of processing that is required to produce an emotional state in the sense outlined above? In one of the booming areas of the psychology of emotion, appraisal theory, a large number of different scholars have made predictions as to which types of appraisal dimensions are necessary to elicit a specific kind of emotion (Frijda, 1986, 1988; Lazarus, 1966, 1991c; Roseman, 1991; Smith & Ellsworth, 1985; and many others—see Scherer, 1988a, 1993b, for a review). As far as I can see (not having reexamined the literature for this question), there is not much discussion of what is *minimally* necessary to evoke an emotion.

In my own theory of appraisal, the Stimulus Evaluation Check (SEC) Model, I postulate five major stimulus evaluation checks and a series of subchecks in an effort to explain the elicitation and differentiation of the emotions (see my answer to Question 4 for a detailed list of these SECs). Although different appraisal theories have been developed in a largely independent fashion, there is a surprising degree of convergence regarding the nature of the appraisal dimensions (or criteria or evaluation checks) that are being suggested and the predictions concerning the patterns of such criteria expected to produce specific emotions (see Scherer, 1988a, 1993b, for a review). It should be noted in parentheses that the empirical work that has been done in this area (Smith & Ellsworth, 1985; Folkman & Lazarus, 1985; Frijda, Kuipers, & ter Schure, 1989; Gehm & Scherer, 1988; Reisenzein & Hofmann, 1990; Roseman, Spindel, & Jose, 1990) has clearly established the viability of this approach in terms of predicting the occurrence of specific emotions. I have been able to show that one can even use a relatively primitive expert system (GENESE—Geneva Expert System on Emotion) to rather successfully postdict emotion labels used by subjects to describe earlier experiences on the basis of questioning them about the stimulus evaluation checks that presumably took place prior to their experience (Scherer, 1993b).

In most empirical studies, subjects are questioned concerning their emotion-antecedent appraisal using recall procedures for experienced emotional episodes. Alternatively, a scenario method is used wherein subjects are expected to put themselves into a particular situation and judge the kind of emotion they are likely to experience. In both cases, the question is not what is minimally required to experience an emotion, but rather what combination or configuration of appraisal dimensions is likely to produce a specific differentiated emotion.

How could appraisal theory help to advance the issue of minimal prerequisites? In my own model, contrary to my appraisal colleagues, I postulate that the stimulus evaluation checks always occur in a fixed sequence (based on logical, phylogenetic, and ontogenetic arguments). While this postulate often evokes massive criticism from parallelists, the assumption of sequential processing is quite defensible and not at all at variance with the assumption of underlying massively parallel processing (see Scherer, 1993a). One could assume that this idea of sequential processing might help to settle the issue of minimal prerequisites, at least in terms of my system. One possibility would be, for example, that the result of the very first check—novelty—would constitute the minimal prerequisite for a particular emotion. However, this is not the case. For example, if there is a sudden onset of a very innocuous stimulus, this is likely to produce a novel response of the novelty check, but it is unlikely to lead to any emotion. In that sense, I would agree with Ekman and his collaborators that startle is not necessarily an emotion (see Ekman, Friesen, & Simons, 1985). The sequentiality argument does not imply that the result of the first or even the first two or three checks will automatically produce an emotion. For example, even a positive outcome of the intrinsic pleasantness check (e.g., the smell of a rose) may produce a particular affective state (e.g., an agreeable feeling), but may not necessarily elicit an emotion in the sense defined previously (see also my answer to Question 1).

What then is the minimal cognitive requirement for the type of check involved? I believe that this is an empirical question. While difficult and time consuming, one could imagine research that systematically varies events so that they have predictable effects on appraisal checks and to determine in this fashion which individual check or combination of checks is likely to produce the synchronization in the change of different response channels that I would require as evidence for the existence of an emotional episode strictu sensu. I will, however, venture a prediction as to which checks I have proposed will be minimally involved. One of the subchecks I postulate for the goal-conduciveness check is the relevance or pertinence of a stimulus or event for the organism's goals or needs. In fact, this is the first check in the sequence following the novelty and intrinsic pleasantness checks, which I believe are largely automatic and innate. Since sequential checking occurs not only once but in a highly repetitive fashion (like a radar antenna scanning the environment), one could assume that the intensity of scanning is directly related to the outcome of the pertinence of relevance checks. If an event is considered highly relevant to the organism's goals and needs, it is likely that processing will take on a rather different significance than if that is not the case.

Also, given the functional idea that emotions serve as emergency mechanisms to cope with significant events (see the comments to Question 3 concerning the function of emotion), and given the costs of emotional arousal to the organism in terms of energy depletion, one could imagine that the *evaluation of a stimulus or event as relevant to one's goals and needs* is in fact the minimal requirement for the elicitation of an emotion. This assumption would seem to fit well with the notion that is often found in writings about emotion, namely the idea that ego-involvement is required to produce strong emotional states and that the very same event will produce much a more emotional reaction in someone who is strongly ego-involved compared to someone who is not. We must note that the goals and plans that serve as the comparison standards for relevance are not limited to immediate desires or even long-term goals–they also include values. Thus, someone may react in a very violent, emotional manner on seeing injustice done to a total stranger. Ego-involvement does not require that one is directly and personally concerned by an event. It is quite sufficient that one holds particular values sufficiently strongly to find violation of these values directly pertinent regarding one's values system and requiring ego-involvement and even action. To avoid circularity of argumentation, it will be required, of course, to define ego-involvement or relevance to goal-need value structures independent of observed emotional reactions. This, I believe, is one of the major challenges of emotion psychology in the 1990s.

Afterword: What Are the Minimal Cognitive Prerequisites for Emotion?

RICHARD J. DAVIDSON
PAUL EKMAN

Most of the commentators on this question agree that the nature of their response hinges on their definition of cognition. Several authors distinguish among different classes of cognition. Virtually all of them agree that if "cognitive" is taken to include basic sensory information processing, then most, if not all, emotions will have some cognitive contribution. However, not all the commentators prefer to parse the domain in this way. The two biological theorists, LeDoux and Panksepp, both suggest that the brain circuitry subserving emotion and cognition is different. LeDoux implies and Panksepp explicitly notes that cognition depends on the neocortex and hippocampus. If one restricts the definition of cognition to those processes that are neocortical or hippocampal based, then emotion can occur in the virtual absence of such prerequisites since emotions arise in organisms with extensive neocortical and hippocampal lesions. As Panksepp has succinctly put it, "cortico-cognitive processes" are not essential for emotion. LeDoux's discussion of the connections between the thalamus and both the amygdala and the cortex allows him to provide a neuroanatomical explanation of why "representations that activate the emotional system can be based on incomplete and fragmented information rather than veridical perceptions . . . [and why] . . . we are not always aware of why we respond emotionally the way we do."

From a more psychological perspective, Izard strongly endorses this position and emphatically argues that emotions can be elicited via noncognitive routes. Here Izard takes a rather narrow view of cognition (the psychological equivalent to neocortical processing) and a broad view of emotion. He includes within the latter category temperament and mood, and suggests that genetic factors can directly set the values of these characteristics.

Many commentators note that while emotion might occasionally be elicited with minimal cognitive prerequisites, such occurrences may be rare and beg the more important question about emotion-cognition interaction. Lazarus, for example, believes it would be more profitable to study the fundamental cognition that differentiates among different emotions than to identify the minimal cognitive prerequisites for any particular emotion. This position is endorsed by those favoring appraisal models of emotion elicitation and include the commentaries of Clore, Ellsworth, Frijda, and Scherer, in addition to Lazarus. All these investigators argue that some cognitive processing is required for any emotion to be elicited. Most agree that such processes can be quite automatic and thus the sense of "immediacy" that Frijda describes as characteristic of emotion is not inconsistent with the cognitive appraisal that is putatively necessary for its elicitation. However, such models are not without their problems, as Ellsworth notes. She cites two important empirical challenges to traditional appraisal views of emotion generation. One is the elicition of emotion by music and the other is opponent process theory, which states that affective states of the opposite valence occur following termination of an initial affective state. These examples underscore the difficulty of any general account of emotion generation based on appraisal processes.

Clore and Frijda both acknowledge that certain affective states can occur with very minimal cognitive mediation (here the precise definition of cognition is not given). These feeling states, according to both authors, are not emotions, but rather can be moods. In contrast to emotions, moods do not have an object (see Question 2 for extensive commentary on this issue). Clore cites evidence to show that the weather can trigger a change in mood with minimal cognitive prerequisites. Certain stimuli are held to be intrinsically pleasing or displeasing, for example, certain tastes and smells and the feeling states that follow from exposure to such stimuli do not require extensive cognitive processing. Clore states very explicitly that for a state to be an emotion, it must signify the results of an appraisal of some kind.

Lazarus interestingly brings in a developmental perspective, contrasting the anger of a 7-month-old infant with the anger of an adult. While not all would agree with how he resolves the problem, he acknowledges in confronting the dilemma that the infant is not likely to be capable of the type of appraisals he claims are necessary for anger to occur; he does show the value of considering the issue of cognitive prerequisites developmentally. Parenthetically, it should be noted that the problem he raises of how to explain how a 4-month-old infant who exhibits anger could be capable of the type of appraisals he says are necessary for anger may be more apparent than real. There is serious argument about whether or not the expressions that Stenberg and Campos interpreted (on the basis of Izard's scoring system) as anger were indeed anger, or instead more undifferentiated expressions of distress (see Camras, 1993).

An important theme that was touched on by several commentators from very different perspectives is the two-way interaction between emotion and cognition. LeDoux summarizes the anatomy that makes such two-way interaction possible. He notes that bidirectional connections exist between neocortex and the amygdala that permit upstream emotion-related input from the amygdala to modulate cortical activity and downstream cognitive input from the cortex to modulate the amygdala's emotional information processing. Panksepp makes a similar point regarding the distribution of neuropeptides in brain circuits that subserve both emotion and cognition. Frijda highlights the importance of cognition in emotional control and suggests that its role in this type of process is more important than the role of cognition in the initial generation of emotion.

The older debate between Lazarus and Zajonc (see chapters in Scherer & Ekman, 1984) on whether emotion can be elicited in the absence of cognition has now advanced considerably. Most authors agree that the answer to this question fundamentally depends on how one defines cognition. Most students of emotion would acknowledge that emotion can be elicited in the absence of conscious cognition mediation. If a broad view of cognition is adopted, most would also agree that some cognitive processing is required for most emotion. The challenge that confronts modern emotion research is to specify with increasing precision the types of cognitive operations that may be critical to the emotion-generation process and to identify the neural circuitry that differentially subserves emotion and cognition. We also need to study the two-way interactions between these systems.

Question 6

Is There Emotion-Specific Physiology?

Complexities in the Search for Emotion-Specific Physiology

RICHARD J. DAVIDSON

Introduction

The question of whether different categories of emotion are associated with unique patterns of central and autonomic physiology is an old one with a checkered history. Since the beginning of the century with William James (1890), psychologists interested in emotion have taken a stand on this question. James implied that different emotions were associated with unique patterns of skeletal muscle and physiological changes since our experience of the emotion was a direct function of feedback from the periphery. The notion that different emotions might be distinguished on the basis of patterns of peripheral physiological activity fell out of favor following the publication by Schacter and Singer (1962) of their influential two-factor emotion theory. This theory held that different emotions was associated with the same basic state of undifferentiated arousal and what distinguished among emotions were cognitions. A generation of mostly social psychologists were heavily influenced by the Schacter and Singer model and performed numerous experiments that were predicated on the idea that different emotions were associated with the same state of arousal. In the past decade, the tide has turned once again, with the notion of psychophysiological differentiation among discrete emotions more popular, mostly due to the influential series of studies by Ekman, Levenson, and their colleagues (e.g., Ekman, Levenson, & Friesen, 1983; Levenson, Ekman, & Friesen, 1990; Levenson, Carstensen, Friesen, & Ekman, 1991; see review in Levenson, 1992).

In this essay, I will first analyze just what this question means and then propose a number of possible models of psychophysiological differentiation. The data on emotion-specific patterning in peripheral and central physiology will then be briefly and selectively reviewed. I will conclude by underscoring the challenge of characterizing what it is that is invariant across different instantiations of the same emotion and, in so doing, outline an agenda for future research on this topic.

Unpacking the Question

The first issue that confronts the scientist interested in the question of emotion-specific patterns of physiological activity is a methodological one. To demonstrate that physiological changes are emotion-specific, it is necessary to show that the same emotion elicited via very different procedures is associated with an invariant pattern of physiological change. Moreover, it is essential to compare among at least two emotions and also include a nonemotional condition that activates the same sensory and motor pathways as would be activated in emotion. Only in this way can the changes that are found during the emotion elicitation be linked to changes in actual emotion, rather than changes in other associated processes that accompany the emotional change. For example, if the experimenter used film clips to elicit emotion, it would be important to include a neutral film clip with equivalent visual and auditory components to compare against changes produced by the emotional clip. Only such a methodological strategy could uncover changes that are associated with emotion per se. Relatively few studies in the literature have included adequate controls of the sort described (see Davidson et al., 1990; Cacioppo et al., in press, for reviews).

A second issue is just what constitutes emotion-specific physiological activity. What is the nature of the mapping that is assumed between the underlying physiological activity and the emotion in question? What is the presumed causal status of the physiological changes? Is the putative physiological pattern sufficient for the occurrence of the emotion? Is it necessary? The data available for both peripheral and central measures are not clear on these questions. However, it is essential that future research on this topic be designed in a way to permit more focused analysis on the causal mechanisms involved.

A third issue hinges on one's model of emotion and whether a categorical or dimensional perspective is adopted. Although evidence of physiological differentiation among broad dimensions of emotion still presents a serious challenge to undifferentiated arousal theory, it represents a very different theoretical stance than that adopted by discrete emotions theorists who hold that unique patterns of peripheral and central physiology will be found for the so-called basic (see Question 1) emotions.

Peripheral Physiology

The autonomic nervous system has evolved primarily to provide the necessary metabolic supports for action. To the extent that emotions are reliably associated with different action tendencies, they should also differ in their autonomic patterns. Indeed, Levenson, Ekman, and Friesen (1990) note that autonomic changes associated with different discrete emotions "produce patterns of activity that will support the behavioral adaptations and associated motor programs that are most likely for that emotion" (p. 379). However, to the extent that the same emotion might be associated with different patterns of action, autonomic nervous system activity would be apt to show considerable variation. In fact, it is likely that the action tendencies associated with a number of common emotions are quite variable. In several previous publications, I have distinguished between different forms of positive affect based on the extent to which the emotion was associated with approach behavior. Different patterns of brain function were associated with each (see Davidson, 1993, for review). We do not know if different autonomic patterns would be observed as well. Fear can be associated with both fleeing and freezing, while anger is sometimes associated with approach movements (i.e., attack) and other times with withdrawal tendencies. The autonomic supports for these different forms of each emotion should differ considerably. For example, cardiovascular mobilization should be greater during fleeing than during freezing. Other research has demonstrated different central neurochemical substrates for different components of fear behavior in rhesus monkeys (e.g., Kalin & Shelton, 1989) and it is likely that the autonomic concomitants would also differ. It seems probable that, at least for the emotions of happiness, anger, and fear, different patterns of approach and withdrawal action tendencies may occur. Insofar as the same emotion is associated with different action tendencies, we would expect quite different patterns of autonomic activity for these different instantiations of the same emotion. Having said this, it is also important to underscore a proposal that I have previously made regarding the pairing of emotion and action (Davidson, 1993). I do not believe that such pairing is random and suggest that there are biological constraints on such pairing in the same sense in which we are biologically prepared to associate certain classes of stimuli with particular unconditioned responses (see Seligman & Hager, 1972). For example, it would be difficult to generate approach tendencies toward an object that elicits disgust. Similarly, it would be difficult to develop withdrawal tendencies toward stimuli that are strongly appetitive. For the emotions where the pairing may be very constrained, consistency within the autonomic nervous system may be more common. For those emotions where the constraints are less apparent (e.g., happiness, anger, and fear) less consistency in autonomic activity should be found.

It may be that the typical emotion induction procedures used in the laboratory with adult subjects themselves place constraints on the type of action that is possible for people to display and thus tend to accentuate the consistency of the autonomic patterns associated with different emotions. Using carefully constructed personalized imagery scripts and sophisticated measures of cardiovascular function derived from the impedance cardiogram, Sinha, Lovallo, and Parsons (1992) found systematic differences among several negative emotions, with the primary distinction between fear and anger. Anger was associated with greater diastolic blood pressure and greater peripheral resistance compared with fear. Levenson et al. (1990) also discovered systematic differences in finger temperature between anger and fear, with anger associated with increases and fear associated with decreases in temperature. Despite these encouraging reports, there is still a lack of consistency across studies and the evidence does not support the idea that different discrete emotions have unique and invariant autonomic signatures. Cacioppo and his colleagues (Cacioppo et al., 1993) have reviewed all studies that compared among two or more emotions elicited by any procedure and assessed two or more autonomic responses. These investigators conclude that little consistency is present in the literature. Moreover, they make the important point that whatever autonomic changes might occur, they are clearly not necessary for the appearance of discrete emotional states since there are abundant examples of differentiated emotion occurring in the absence of such autonomic differentiation.

A number of scientists examining the physiology of emotion have approached its study from a dimensional perspective. For the most part, they have sought to identify unique biological indices that reflect the valence and arousal dimensions of emotion, since these are the dimensions that consistently account for the most variance in factor analytic studies of the emotion space (see Russell & Mehrabian, 1977; Osgood, Suci, & Tannenbaum, 1957, for reviews). It is interesting to note that while consistent differences have been found in patterns of facial muscle tension, modulation of the reflex blink response, and measures of brain function, few reliable differences have been uncovered in autonomic measures between emotional states that differ in valence (but see Lang, Greenwald, Bradley, & Hamm, 1993, for a recent study where peak heart acceleration was related to reported pleasure). For example, Cacioppo and his colleagues (Cacioppo, Petty, Losch, & Kim, 1986) have reported on differences in facial electromyography, with positive affect associated with more zygomatic activity and less corrugator activity than negative affect. Lang and his colleagues (Lang, Bradley, & Cuthbert, 1992) have found greater potentiation of the eye-blink response to an acoustic startle stimulus when presented during negative compared with positive and neutral stimuli. And Davidson and his colleagues (Davidson, 1992b) have reported consistent differences in electrophysiological measures of anterior activation asymmetry with approach-related positive emotional states associated with left-sided anterior activation and withdrawal-related negative affective states associated with right-sided anterior activation.

Central Physiology

Historically, the study of the biological substrates of emotion has focused on subcortical limbic sites in animals. The notion that different emotional states are associated with unique patterns of central nervous system activity must, in a trivial sense, be true if we subscribe to the belief that no mental modification occurs without a corresponding change in brain activity. The challenge for us is to specify what the natural categories are and to identify what is invariant across different instantiations of the same emotion type. The mode by which an emotion is elicited will surely affect an individual's central state, so that visual elicitors will activate visual brain regions, while emotions that are produced by self-generated thought will begin with activation in association cortex, not primary sensory cortex. Presumably, if there is a quality within an emotion family (see Ekman, 1992, for a discussion of the concept of emotion families) that is invariant, it will be instantiated within an invariant pattern of neural activity that forms the "distillate" after the neural changes induced by the variable contextual and stimulus-related factors are partialled out. As yet, there are no convincing data on central nervous patterning specific to discrete emotions. However, it must be noted that no study has yet been undertaken with modern state-of-the-art neuroimaging procedures that would permit such an analysis. An interesting possibility that I have previously suggested (Davidson, 1992a) is that emotion-specific patterning at the discrete emotion level may be found in those brain circuits that are not exclusively devoted to emotional processing, but are also involved in higher-order cognitive processes, if the essential differences among emotions are to be found in the higher-order goals each is associated with (see Stein & Trabasso, 1992; Johnson-Laird & Oatley, 1992, for similar statements of this position).

Another approach that may bear fruit in future research is based on ethological/anatomical considerations. From the ethological study of mammalian behavior, MacLean (1990) identified six main forms of behavior that are identified with six well-recognized general affects. The six forms of behavior and their associated affects (in parentheses) include: (1) searching (desire); (2) aggressive (anger); (3) protective (fear); (4) dejected (sorrow); (5) gratulant (joy); and (6) caressive (affection). MacLean (1990) proposes specific brain systems that underlie each of these six different emotion systems that are preserved across phylogeny.

In contrast to the attempt to specify different neural systems that implement different emotion programs, other investigators have attempted to map out the generalized emotion circuitry in the brain and have argued that all emotion uses this circuitry. Presumably, different emotions are implemented by different patterns of activation within this circuitry. These different patterns of activation lead to distinct outputs. LeDoux (1987) has carefully documented an emotion network in the mammalian nervous system. The critical structure in this network is the amygdala and LeDoux argues that it is equally involved in both negative and positive emotion (see LeDoux, 1992). In part because of its size (relatively small) and location (in the medial portion of the temporal lobe), the amygdala has not been extensively studied in humans. It is essential that such studies be undertaken since some question has arisen about the precise role of the amygdala in human emotion. Tranel and Hyman (1990) have recently reported on a patient with Urbach-Wiethe disease. This is a rare autosomal recessive disease characterized by the deposition of calcifications in the region of anteromesial temporal lobes. The case they presented was of a 23-year-old woman with selective, bilateral damage to the amygdala. In this patient, they found intact skin conductance responses to emotional stimuli.

I (Davidson, 1984; 1992a, 1992b) have developed a model of the role of the left and right anterior (prefrontal and anterior temporal) regions in approach and withdrawal-related emotion. I have suggested that the left anterior region is implicated in approach-related positive affect and the right anterior region in withdrawal-related negative affect. Positive affect that is associated with approach should be accompanied by activation in the left anterior region. Certain types of negative affect may be associated primarily with a decrease in the approach system (e.g., sadness and its pathological manifestation, depression) and so should be associated with decreases in left anterior activation. Negative affect that is withdrawal-related (e.g., fear and disgust) is associated with activation in the right anterior region. I have also proposed that individuals differ in their tonic activation in these brain regions and that such individual differences serve as diatheses that affect an individual's vulnerability to particular affective states (see Davidson, 1992b, for review).

Future Challenges

The human brain is a product of millions of years of evolution; consequently, it has developed highly conserved and efficient modes of information processing. The same basic structures participate in a myriad of information-processing types. It is therefore unlikely that the neural implementation of emotion will be entirely distinct from other types of processing, such as cognition. Indeed, the frontal lobes have been identified as a region critically important to both emotion and cognition. This fact underscores the extensive interconnections between emotion and cognition and implies that the separation between these forms of processing may be artificial. It also suggests that different emotions will be characterized by different patterns of neural activity within the same structures. A major challenge that confronts us is how to define a pattern. Investigators examining both peripheral and central physiological substrates of emotion have often used the term "pattern" to describe emotion-specific configurations of physiological change. Yet it is difficult to formally describe the nature of pattern or to know if the predicted one actually occurred in a specific situation. New statistical techniques may be required to capture the invariant properties assumed to underlie such emotion-specific patterns.

It will also be critical in future research to dissect emotion into its underlying elementary processes. This strategy has been highly successful in cognitive neuroscience where processes that were assumed to be basic, such as imagery and attention, have yielded in the face of rigorous componential analysis (see Kosslyn et al., 1993). The same type of analysis will be required for emotion, where it is likely that appraisal, feeling state, and action will each be associated with different patterns of physiological change.

Three Fundamental Emotion Systems

JEFFREY A. GRAY

There is an old story, set for some reason in a street in Amsterdam, where one night a policeman sees a man looking for his watch under a lamp-post. The following dialogue ensues. "Where did you lose the watch?" "Over there," replies the man, pointing to a spot fifty yards away. "Then why are you looking over here?" "Because the light is brighter." That, in a nutshell, is why so much effort was expended in the earlier part of this century by physiological-minded psychologists seeking specific correlates of particular emotions in outputs of the autonomic nervous system (ANS) and endocrine system (ES). There was, at that time, very little light shining on the place where they really should have been conducting their search, namely, in the brain; so they looked where they *could* look—in the ANS and ES. All that has changed: experimental investigation of the psychological functions of the brain in animals now benefits from a wide variety of powerful tools; and *in vivo* neuroimaging techniques are promising to do the same for the investigation of these functions in the human brain.

The lamp-post analogy suggests that the ANS and ES, although easier to study, were the *wrong* places to look. There is reason to think that this is so. These systems are concerned essentially with housekeeping functions, energy metabolism, tissue repair, and the like. It would be surprising if these functions bore any specific relation to particular emotional states, since energy requirements, for example, are likely to be the same whenever an animal undertakes vigorous action, whatever the emotional significance of the action. As an example, consider an animal faced with danger from a predator who has three possible types of solution to its problem: fighting the predator; running to a burrow along familiar paths that have often led before to safety; or freezing and remaining silent. As we will see later, these three types of behavior (fight, active avoidance, and behavioral inhibition) are mediated by three different brain systems, each of which appears to be related to a different emotional state. But all require energy mobilization (even in the case of behavioral inhibition, the animal enters a state of high readiness for vigorous action), and the ANS and ES outputs necessary for such mobilization are therefore triggered in much the same way in every case. The rather meager results of the many studies of ANS and ES correlates of different emotional states (reviewed *in extenso* in Gray, 1987) conform to this pessimistic expectation. At best, they reveal somewhat different patterns of response to aversive stimuli depending on the degree to which active and passive motoric solutions are available to the subject of the experiment—coupled perhaps with a difference between response patterns related to emotional states elicited by aversive and appetitive stimuli respectively (Gray, 1987, pp. 68–69).

Interestingly, however, this harvest, poor though it may be, is consistent with studies of the involvement of the brain in emotional behavior. For these indicate the existence in the mammalian brain of three fundamental emotion-systems: one concerned with responses to appetitive stimuli; a second with the execution of active fight or flight behavior in response to aversive stimuli; and the third with the execution of behavioral inhibition in response to aversive stimuli. The parallel with the results of studies of the ANS and ES is fuzzy, but nonetheless suggestive. Pursuit of this parallel may throw some light on the organization of the ANS and ES. However, if one's primary interest lies in the organization of emotional behavior and the emotional states that underlie it, then it is clearly more profitable to concentrate on the brain; as we now shall.

There has been a substantial and growing investment in studies of brain mechanisms mediating emotional behavior in experimental animals. Workers in this field are by no means in agreement as to what these mechanisms are, how many of them can usefully be separately identified, or how they relate to the emotions that human beings are able to name. But there is considerable agreement on certain points—more so, I suspect, than among students of emotion in general. First (although not everyone would use the language, based in animal learning theory, in which I make this point), it is generally agreed that emotion is concerned with reactions to *reinforcers*, positive or negative, conditioned or unconditioned. This understanding of emotion has a long and fruitful history within animal learning (e.g., Amsel, 1958; Miller, 1951; Mowrer, 1960). It has its equivalent within philosophical and cognitive approaches to emotion, where, however, terms such as "appraisal" and "evaluation" are used to mean, roughly, "that process by which the subject determines the reinforcing value of a stimulus" (e.g., Lyons, 1980; Frijda, 1986). Second, it is generally agreed that there *are* specific emotion systems, and therefore specific emotions (e.g., Gray, 1994; LeDoux, 1987; Panksepp, 1986; Rolls, 1990); and that their number is rather few (most theorists are content with just three or four). Noone who studies the brain, so far as I am aware, postulates a single, nonspecific construct of "emotion-in-general." (Such nonspecific constructs are certainly used—"arousal" or "activation" are the typical terms—but they are seen as orthogonal to, or components of, specific emotion systems.)

At this point the disagreements begin. Some of them are more apparent than real, turning on nomenclature. For example, Graeff (1987) writes of the "behavioural aversive system." This can be abbreviated as "BAS," an acronym I use for the "behavioral approach system" and Fowles (1980) uses for the "behavioral activation system." Graeff's behavioral aversive system is essentially the same as my concept of the "fight/flight system"; and Fowles' behavioral activation system, the same as my behavioral approach system. And so on—examples can be multiplied (Gray, 1991). But there are also real disagreements: as to the best parceling of the brain into separate systems; as to the brain systems that mediate particular types of behavior; and as to the human emotions that correspond to particular combinations of brain system and types of behavior.

Fortunately, these are the kinds of disagreement on which science thrives: they are amenable to resolution by empirical data, and they act as a spur to the collection of such data. In what follows, I present my own model, leaving it to others to present theirs.

The model postulates the existence in the mammalian brain of three fundamental emotion systems: a behavioral approach system (BAS), a fight/flight system (FFS), and a behavioral inhibition system (BIS). A complete specification of the model would require a description of each of these systems at three levels: a behavioral level, indicating the (reinforcement-related) inputs and outputs that define a given emotion system functionally; a neural level, defining the brain structures and activity patterns that mediate the input-output relationships specified at the first level; and a cognitive or computational level, describing the information-processing functions discharged by the brain system specified at the neural level.

The input-output relationships that define the BAS, FFS, and BIS at the behavioral level are illustrated in the following figures.

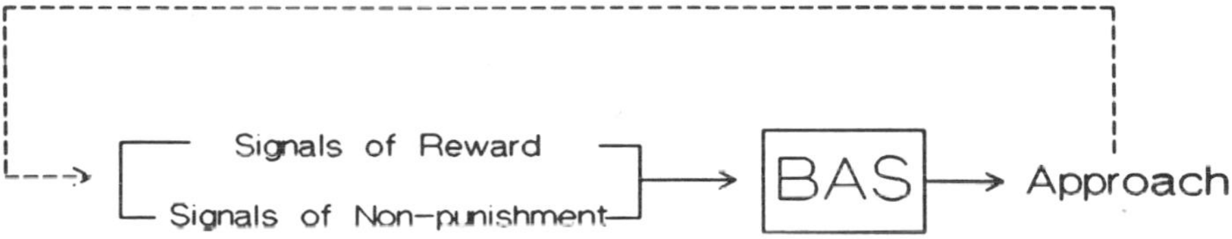

The Behavioral Approach System (BAS) as defined by its inputs and outputs.

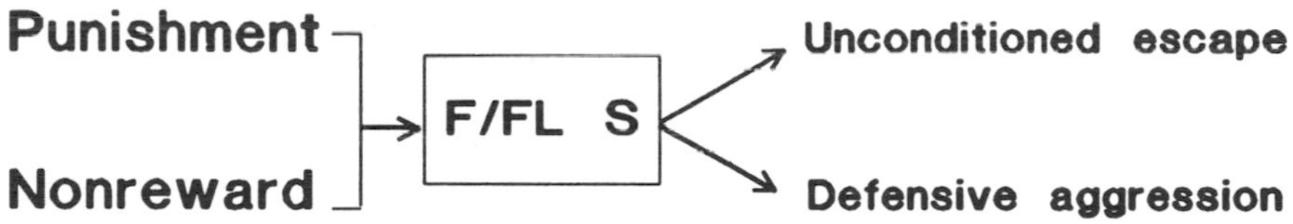

The Fight/Flight System (F/FLS) as defined by its inputs and outputs.

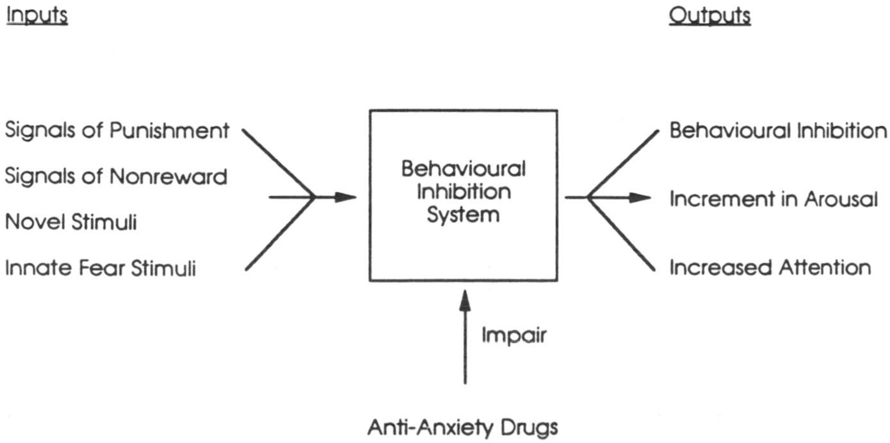

The Behavioral Inhibition System (BIS) as defined by its inputs and outputs.

These relationships are derived, in part, from considerations of a large body of data on animal learning, reviewed by Gray (1975, 1987). The brain structures (located mainly in the limbic system and basal ganglia; Gray, in press) that mediate these relationships have been described in detail by Gray et al. (1991) for the BAS and by Gray (1982a, b, 1987) for the BIS. Descriptions of the FFS, but not necessarily under this appellation, can be found in Adams (1979), Graeff (1987), and Panksepp (1982). These sources also document the considerable and varied evidential basis on which each of these systems is founded. Analysis of the third, cognitive, level has proceeded furthest for the BIS (Gray, 1982a, b), focused on the concept of a comparator that continuously monitors whether the current state of the world (as processed by neocortical sensory analyzers) matches the expected state of the world. The main informational components required for such a comparator process are illustrated in the following figure. A complementary cognitive analysis has also been offered for the BAS, focussing on its motor-programming function (Gray, 1994; Gray et al., 1991; Swerdlow & Koob, 1987). Recently, we have begun to convert these verbal descriptions of the cognitive processes mediated by these systems into a computational model, concentrating on certain features of the interactions between the BAS and BIS (Schmajuk, Lam, & Gray, in preparation).

This model provides the framework for an answer to the question posed here: Is there emotion-specific physiological activity? That answer is: Yes, in the brain; more specifically, activity in each of the fundamental emotion systems briefly outlined corresponds to a separate fundamental emotional state. But it is important to clarify the sense in which this assertion is made.

Clarification is perhaps best achieved by means of an analogy between activity in each of the fundamental emotion systems, on the one hand, and in each of the three retinal visual pigments on the other (Gray, 1985). Activity in only one visual pigment does not occur outside the laboratory; each color experience is the result of a blend of activity in retinal cones containing all three types of pigment, followed of course by massive further processing in the visual pathways and beyond. Similarly, any real emotional experience reflects a blend of activity in all three fundamental emotion systems. (Further complexities arise when emotional states are given names, but

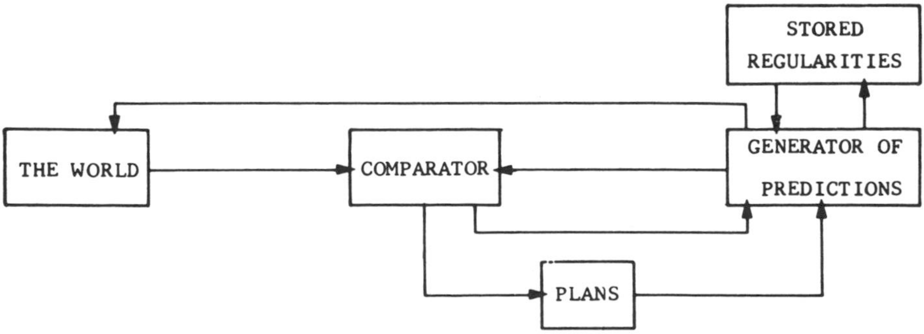

Information processing required for the comparator function of the Behavioral Inhibition System (BIS).

these are not considered here; see Gray, 1985a, for a brief discussion.) Thus, we must distinguish between what I have called fundamental emotional states, each corresponding to a given degree of activity in one of the fundamental emotion system, and experienced emotional states, each corresponding to a given blend of activity in all three systems. Viewed either way, however, there still is specific physiological activity corresponding to a specific emotion. (If this were not the case, what else could be meant by the notion of a "specific emotion" anyway?)

Pursuing the analogy with the visual pigments, one can go on to ask, "What are the 'purest' emotional states?" in the sense that some color experiences approximate more closely to activity in only one pigment than do others. For high activity in the BIS, the answer to this question is anxiety (given that the concept of the BIS is to a great extent based on empirical data concerning the actions of anxiolytic drugs, this is almost a necessary inference). The answers for the other two systems are less clear. For high activity in the FFS, panic or rage are possibilities (Graeff, 1987; Gray, 1994), for high activity in the BAS, hope or elation (Mowrer, 1960), happiness, or perhaps the "high" caused by addictive euphoriant drugs (Stewart, de Wit, & Eikelboom, 1984).

If we now return to the ANS and ES, we can ask: How is emotion-specific activity in the three brain systems outlined related to these peripheral systems? The connection is only loose. As already indicated, the ANS and ES are switched on in essentially the same way whenever vigorous action is required, whether this is as yet only preparing for action, as in anxiety (see the increased arousal output of Figure 3), or fight/flight behavior (panic/terror or rage), or active instrumental responding to obtain reward or avoid punishment (hope or elation). There are slight differences in the detailed patterns of ANS activation that accompany behavioral inhibition and fight/flight behavior, respectively; absence of ANS activity weakens the intensity of all emotional experience; and activity in the ANS for which the subject has no explanation biases experience toward negative rather than positive affect (Marshall & Zimbardo, 1979; Maslach, 1979); but there appears to be no more specific role for the ANS and ES than these (Gray, 1987).

Emotion-Specific Physiological Activity: Don't Forget About CNS Physiology

JOSEPH E. LEDOUX

One of the most pesty problems in emotion research has been that of determining whether different emotional states are accompanied by unique patterns of physiological activity. This research tradition is the legacy of the William James' feedback hypothesis, which suggested that feedback to the brain from the bodily changes that accompany emotional arousal determine the subjective emotional state that is experienced (James, 1884).

Much of the work that has been conducted in this area has involved measurements of peripheral autonomic nervous system activity. In general, investigators have failed to find clear and robust evidence for autonomic differentiation of emotion (e.g., Frijda, 1986). However, recent studies suggest that some emotions in some conditions are differentiated by autonomic activity (Levenson, 1992).

The emphasis of research in the area of emotional physiology on autonomic physiology is due in large part to Cannon's (1927) critique of the James' feedback hypothesis. Cannon's critique focused on autonomic feedback, but James had argued that feedback from the entire emotional act, which includes behavioral reactions as well, determines the subjective emotional experience. Inconclusive results on autonomic differentiation during emotion is thus not necessarily damaging to the feedback hypothesis, a point that facial feedback theorists have long argued (Izard, 1977).

To the extent that different emotions are expressed through unique behavioral patterns, the brain potentially receives different patterns of peripheral feedback. The problem then is explaining: (1) how emotion is experienced in the absence of overt behavior; (2) how different emotions might be experienced when their behavioral expression is similar; and (3) how emotional and nonemotional states involving the same behavior (i.e., running for exercise vs. running in fear) are experienced differently. Feedback may be important in emotion but it does not appear to be sufficient to explain emotion.

Failure to find emotion-specific autonomic activity is not evidence for its absence. Traditionally, relatively few autonomic variables have been measured. However, even when multiple measures are taken, they tend to be indirect indices of autonomic activity. The autonomic nervous system responds by altering neural activity at peripheral end organs. Measurements of organ responses (i.e., changes in blood pressure or circulating hormones) are measurements of the functional consequences of autonomic arousal, not direct measures of the neural response itself. Organ responses are potential sources of feedback to the brain but in the absence of a clear theoretical concept of what feedback is it is hard to define what an above-threshold feedback stimulus might be. There are unlimited responses that we could measure.

Even if appropriate measures could be made, other factors are at work against an accurate assessment of autonomic feedback during emotion. For practical reasons, experimental studies of human emotion are conducted in artificial laboratory situations using contrived conditions to arouse emotion. For ethical reasons, only relatively mild emotions can be aroused. Efforts are made to restrict overt behavioral reactions since any autonomic response observed might otherwise be secondary to the behavior rather than primary to the emotional state. However, in natural settings, where behavior is unrestricted by the instrumentation and the experimental design, the full range of feedback to the brain may involve interactions between primary and secondary changes in any and all response systems.

Regardless of how specific autonomic feedback turns out to be, even relatively nonspecific autonomic feedback should play an important role in emotion theory. Emotional states are characteristically more intense and longer lasting than other mental states. There are obvious reasons why this may be so. For example, if the intensity of a fear reaction is too weak or its duration too short, survival could be threatened. Nonspecific feedback provides a practical mechanism for sustaining the duration and intensity of emotional states.

One account that seems plausible to me is that in any condition involving strong emotional arousal there is probably a backdrop of undifferentiated autonomic activity, reflecting a generalized state of nonspecific arousal, against which more specific changes are expressed. Because the signal-to-noise ratio of the undifferentiated responses is so great compared to that for the specific responses, it leads to the conclusion that the specific responses are either absent or minor. The important point to keep in mind is that the magnitude of the undifferentiated, nonspecific arousal response should not be the gold-standard against which the other changes are measured. The resolution of our measuring instruments should not be mistaken for the resolving power of our minds and bodies. Differentiation, regardless of how small and difficult to measure, may be psychologically and/or physiologically significant. On the other hand, it may not be significant at all. The jury is still out on the extent to which autonomic responses are differentiated and on the significance of such differentiation, if it exists.

Although findings from the autonomic nervous system remain somewhat controversial, one need not look very far for extensive evidence for emotion-specific physiological activity in the central nervous system. Investigators using the technique of extracellular single- or multiple-unit recording techniques, which allow the measurement of potentials from individual neurons or small neuronal clusters, have identified many instances of emotion-specific activity. For example, experiments on awake primates have shown that neurons in the amygdala are differentially sensitive to rewarded versus unrewarded visual or auditory events (Ono & Nishijo, 1990; Rolls, 1992). Some amygdaloid neurons distinguish between stimuli associated with rewards from those associated with punishment. It is also possible to find neurons in the amygdala that modify their responsiveness as the significance of the stimulus is changed. However, amygdala neurons appear to be much more resistent to significance shifts than neurons in the orbito-frontal cortex, where neurons easily and rapidly adjust to changing environmental contingencies (Rolls, 1992). Amygdala neurons also respond in a specific and selective way to the presentation of the faces of conspecifics and to social encounters (Brothers et al., 1990).

Studies of unit activity changes during aversive classical conditioning have also shown the sensitivity of central neurons to emotional stimuli. Responses of neurons in many brain regions (e.g., amygdala, hippocampus, sensory thalamus, sensory cortex) change to an auditory conditioned stimulus after pairing with some aversive event (Kapp et al., 1992; Berger & Thompson, 1978; Gabriel et al., 1976; Ryugo & Weinberger, 1978; Weinberger et al., 1990). The level of discharge of the cell thus increases or decreases relative to baseline conditions and appropriate controls show that the changes are specific to the conditioning situation (i.e., are due to a learned association). In some studies the control procedure is such that one stimulus (CS+) is paired with the unconditioned stimulus (US) and a second stimulus (CS−) is not. This condition is particularly relevant since behavioral studies have shown that the CS+ elicits fear whereas the CS− inhibits or relieves fear (Rescorla, 1988; Mackintosh, 1983; Thomas, 1988). In this situation, cells in the same brain areas previously described show differential conditioning, that is they respond differently to the stimulus that predicts an aversive event from one that predicts safety from the aversive event.

The evidence for the differential representation of emotion in the brain can also be made from studies of the neural pathways underlying different emotional states. For example, the amygdala has been implicated in many emotional process that have been studied in animals (LeDoux, 1992a). One might therefore be inclined to view this as evidence against the specificity of emotional representation. However, the amygdala is an exceedingly complex brain region with many subareas, each with its own unique input and output connections. For example, the lateral nucleus of the amygdala receives the vast majority of the connections from sensory processing areas (LeDoux et al., 1990a; Amaral et al., 1992). (see the figure in Question 5) And while lesions of the lateral nucleus of the amygdala interfere with both appetitively and aversively conditioned emotions, presumably as a result of a disruption of the flow of sensory information, different output connections of the lateral nucleus appear to be involved in the different situations. Thus, projections (direct or indirect) from the lateral to the central nucleus of the amygdala appear to be important for controlling aversively conditioned fear responses (LeDoux, 1992) and projections to the nucleus accumbens for appetitively conditioned place preference response control (Hiori & White, 1991; Cador, Robbins, & Everitt, 1989; Everitt et al., 1991). As more and more emotional processes are studied with the idea of identifying the underlying microcircuitry, more and more anatomical distinctions between different emotional processes will surely emerge.

Theorists of emotion must be cognizant of the fact that different affective states are differentially represented in the brain. This does not mean that we should ignore the contribution of the periphery. Ultimately, we need a theory of emotion that accounts for the full range of physiological reactivity, specific and nonspecific, central and peripheral, that occurs during emotional states.

The Search for Autonomic Specificity

ROBERT W. LEVENSON

Ask a group of people to define "emotion" and most will include some form of physiological activity in their definition. Test the phenomenological limits, remove one feature at a time, query as to whether what is left is still "emotion," and, for many, physiological activity will be revealed as *a* necessary (or perhaps *the* necessary) condition for emotion. Then ask this group whether the same physiological changes occur when they are angry as when they are happy, when they are sad as when they are disgusted, and almost all will say no. There is a belief in the general population in emotion-specific physiological activity, and small wonder. Specificity in the physiology of emotion is manifest in many observable ways. Crying (an activity mediated by the parasympathetic branch of the autonomic nervous system) is often seen when people are sad, sometimes when they are happy, but almost never when they are angry or disgusted. We have sensations of warmth (which are mediated primarily by the sympathetic branch of the autonomic nervous system) when we are angry, sometimes when we are happy, but almost never when we are afraid. Our very language bespeaks a belief in emotion-specific physiological activity, especially in the metaphors we use to describe our feelings. We use metaphors of pressure (e.g., blowing your top) and heat (e.g., blood boiling) when we talk about our anger (Lakoff, 1987; Kovecses, 1989), but rarely, if ever, when we talk about other emotions such as sadness, disgust, or happiness. Of course, all this folk wisdom and linguistic convention do not establish the existence of emotion-specific physiology, but it is suggestive.

The Autonomic Nervous System and Emotion

In examining the current state of our knowledge in this area, I will be limiting my comments to the question of emotion-specific activity in the autonomic nervous system, a physiological system intimately tied to emotion.

The autonomic nervous system is a complex and highly differentiated constituent of human physiology. Among its many functions, two stand out. First, there is its regulatory function, operating to maintain a stable and consistent internal bodily milieu. This role as the "guardian" of homeostasis is the function most often emphasized in textbook accounts. The second important function of the autonomic nervous system is to provide support for behavioral demands; this role as the "disrupter" of homeostasis is arguably the function that is most relevant to emotion and most readily accommodates the notion of emotion-specific physiology.

Viewed in light of this second function, the argument for emotion-specific autonomic activity is a simple one. If the primary purpose of emotion is to organize efficiently and rapidly the organismic response to changing environmental demands, and if part of that response is the mobilization of appropriate adaptive behavior, then one would expect that some activation of the autonomic nervous system would be necessary to support that behavior. Whether or not this autonomic response is reliably different for different emotions depends on the answer to two different questions: first, whether or not the different emotions reliably call forth different patterns of behavior, and, second, whether or not these different behaviors require different configurations of autonomic support.

The first question can be exemplified by asking whether patterns of behaviors such as "fighting" and "shutting out" are equally likely to be called forth by all emotions or more likely to be called forth by some emotions than others. The equiprobability notion seems inconceivable to me; "fighting" is much more likely to be called forth in anger, while "shutting out" is much more likely to be called forth in disgust. Neither behavior pattern seems very likely to be called forth in happiness or sadness. The second question can be exemplified by asking whether a behavior such as "fighting" requires the same kind of autonomic support as does a behavior such as "shutting out." Again the notion of autonomic sameness seems farfetched.

Completing the logic of this functional analysis, if certain emotions are most closely allied with certain behavior patterns, and if different behaviors require different kinds of autonomic support, then there is a basis for some amount of emotion-specific autonomic activity. Assuming that the need for rapid mobilization is such that assemblage of the physiological support must be initiated before the behavior is fully manifest, it should be possible to find evidence of emotion-specific autonomic activity in the laboratory even under conditions in which the prototypical behavior never actually occurs. Thus, autonomic changes conducive to fighting should be seen during anger even if the subject never actually engages in fighting.[1]

Difficulties in Studying Emotion-Specific Autonomic Nervous System Activity

Studying emotion-specific autonomic nervous system in the laboratory is rife with problems—some soluble, others almost intractable (Levenson, 1988). Difficulties begin when we attempt to produce emotion. Ethical considerations place limits on the kinds of elicitors that can be used and, as a result, most emotional stimuli used in the laboratory do not produce very intense emotions. Further, many laboratory stimuli produce multiple emotions (either in blends or in sequences); this greatly complicates the task of studying the physiology of single emotions.

Other problems are inherent in the very nature of emotion and the autonomic nervous system. Most emotions are brief, and thus it is easy to miss them. While retrospection may have some cachet in the realm of self-report, it has little validity in the realm of physiology; if the autonomic activity associated with a brief emotional episode is not recorded when it occurs, it is forever lost. Temporal matching between emotion and the associated autonomic nervous system activity is crucial. The autonomic nervous system is not the exclusive servant to emotion, it is constantly responding to other metabolic demands, homeostatic needs, and certain cognitive and perceptual processes. One must extract from this flux those moments when the autonomic nervous system is acting primarily in the service of emotion. In the study of emotion-specific autonomic activity, those moments are the signal; all else is noise. Furthermore, within the autonomic nervous system, different functions (e.g., vascular constriction, sweat gland activity) have different latencies of onset, different durations of action, and different courses of offset, thus further complicating the temporal matching with emotion.

Individual variation presents challenges as well. A stimulus that produces disgust in 99 subjects might amuse the hundredth. Thus, care must be taken to determine which emotion or emotions, if any, were produced in each subject. Subjects may also have individual response stereotypies, which are idiosyncratic patterns of autonomic nervous system response (e.g., some may have highly reactive cardiovascular systems, others might have highly reactive sweat glands). Subjects come to the laboratory with very different attitudes and underlying moods. A subject's skepticism and irritation at having to be in an experiment could have a profound influence on his or her autonomic responses to an experimental stimulus designed to produce a positive emotional state.

And finally there are thorny methodological problems inherent in establishing baselines (subjects rarely, if ever, aren't feeling anything) and analyzing data (e.g., Do group averages have any meaning? How does one strike a balance between Type I and Type II error when measuring a large number of physiological functions during a large number of emotions?).

Autonomic Distinctions Among Emotions

Many dubious propositions are bandied about regarding autonomic distinctions among emotions. Perhaps most improbable is the notion that *every* emotion is autonomically different. It seems far more likely that reliable autonomic differences will only be found between emotions for which the associated prototypical behaviors are quite different. And even among that smaller set of emotions so defined, it is quite unlikely that each of them will be autonomically *unique*, sharing no features in common. Autonomic uniqueness is doubtful because quite different behaviors can make quite similar demands on certain elements of the autonomic nervous system. For example, both fighting and fleeing are likely to require increases in the blood supply to the muscles. Thus, we would expect that anger and fear—which are arguably associated respectively with these two behaviors—would both be characterized by autonomic activity that increases the availability of oxygenated blood (e.g., increases in heart rate, or in stroke volume). Of course, the muscles that are involved in fighting and those involved in fleeing are somewhat different; thus we would expect that anger and fear would be autonomically different in terms of the patterns of vasodilation and vasoconstriction that regulate the flow of blood to different muscle groups.

For the past 10 years, I have been involved in a series of studies of autonomic differences among emotions. In most of this work we have studied four negative emotions (anger, disgust, fear, sadness), one positive emotion (happiness), and the emotion of surprise. We think we have identified a small number of fairly reliable autonomic differences among the four negative emotions. We have also found some differences between the negative emotions as a group and the positive emotion of happiness.

In this research we have elicited emotions in several different ways. Most of our published work has utilized two eliciting tasks (Ekman, Levenson, & Friesen, 1983): (a) *directed facial action task*—subjects are instructed and coached to contract certain facial muscles to produce facial configurations that are morphologically identical to prototypical emotional facial expressions; and (b) *relived emotions task*—subjects recall and relive emotional memories. Most recently, we have begun studying autonomic differences among emotions that have been elicited by films or that occur spontaneously during the interactions of couples in intimate relationships.

Autonomic Differences Among Negative Emotions

We believe we have identified four reliable differences among the negative emotions of anger, disgust, fear, and sadness and have preliminary evidence for a possible fifth.

These are: (a) anger produces a larger increase in heart rate than disgust; (b) fear produces a larger increase in heart rate than disgust; (c) sadness produces a larger increase in heart rate than disgust; and (d) anger produces a larger increase in finger temperature than fear (Levenson, Ekman, & Friesen, 1990). The possible fifth difference is that sadness produces greater peripheral vascular dilation and greater speeding of blood to the periphery than the other negative emotions (Levenson, Ekman, Heider, & Friesen, 1992).

We have been able to demonstrate that these differences show consistency across subject populations differing in *profession* (actors and students: Levenson, Ekman, & Friesen, 1990); *age* (young subjects and subjects aged 71 to 90: Levenson, Carstensen, Friesen, & Ekman, 1991); *culture* (Americans and Minangkabau males living in West Sumatra, Indonesia: Levenson, Ekman, Heider, & Friesen, 1992); and *gender* (Levenson et al., 1990, 1991). We have also found that these differences show consistency across two *modes of emotion elicitation* (directed facial actions and relived emotions: Levenson et al., 1991), and that they are consistent with findings reported by a number of other investigators using the same and other methods (Levenson, 1992).

Interestingly, these found differences are fairly consistent with hypothetical functional models of autonomic change in emotion insofar as emotions such as fear and anger, which are thought to be associated with high activity/high metabolic demand behaviors such as fleeing and fighting, are more productive of autonomic changes that would be supportive of these behaviors (e.g., increased heart rate) than an emotion such as disgust, which is associated with low activity/low metabolic demand behaviors. Associations of heat with anger and coolness with fear, which are often found in the metaphorical language used to describe our feelings, are also supported by found differences in peripheral temperature between these two emotions.

Autonomic Differences Between Negative and Positive Emotions

We spent most of our early efforts focusing on differences among negative emotions because we considered them to be most interesting theoretically and to pose the strongest test for emotion-specific autonomic nervous system activity. Thus, our work with positive emotions advanced more slowly. Currently, our best evidence is for four autonomic differences between negative and positive emotions: (a) anger produces larger heart rate accelerations than happiness: (b) fear produces larger heart rate accelerations than happiness; (c) fear produces larger skin conductance increases than happiness; and (d) disgust produces larger skin conductance increases than happiness.

Our earlier work may have been hampered by using a very broad category of happiness. We are currently studying two varieties of happiness—amusement and contentment—and hope to determine whether the differences between the negative and positive emotions are the same for both.

Positive Emotions as Autonomic "Undoers"

One other reason we have not expended as much effort studying autonomic differences involving positive emotions is that there is reason to suspect that such differences might not exist. In an earlier paper (Levenson, 1988), I speculated that positive emotions might not be associated with specific patterns of autonomic activation because they were not associated with behavioral adaptations that required much in the way of autonomic support. Thus, emotions such as contentment might not be associated with any particular pattern of behavior, or if they are, it would be behavior characterized by low activity, which would make little metabolic demand on the autonomic nervous system. Instead of having distinctive autonomic signatures, I proposed that positive emotions might be associated with a state of physiological quiescence, and that their primary function might be to "*undo*" the autonomic activation produced by negative emotions. In this model, the function of certain positive emotions would be to restore the organism to its pre-arousal state in a more efficient and rapid manner than would be the case if the negative emotions were allowed to run their natural course.

Recently, we reported our first experimental test of this model (Fredrickson & Levenson, 1992). In this study, we induced fear in our subjects using a film stimulus and then determined whether the autonomic arousal associated with that fear would dissipate more quickly if they watched a film known to induce contentment than if they viewed films known to induce sadness or neutral affect. Results indicated that the cardiovascular arousal associated with fear did in fact dissipate more quickly when it was followed by the contentment film than by the sad or neutral films. Thus, the notion of positive affect as an efficient autonomic "*undoer*" received some preliminary support. This matter is far from settled, however, and we are continuing to work on this phenomenon.

Conclusion

I believe there is now sufficient empirical evidence to reject the notion that all emotions are autonomically the same. The available evidence lends some support to notions prevalent in folk beliefs about emotion, to hypothetical functional models of autonomic changes in emotion, and to physiological metaphors found in the language we use to describe our feelings. Whether the autonomic differences among emotions are limited to those found so far or whether others will also be revealed; whether the differences found so far will generalize to additional modes of emotion elicitation; and the viability of the notion that the positive emotions function as autonomic "undoers" all await further research. Although I think it extremely unlikely that we will find that *most* emotions are autonomically distinguishable, I believe we will continue to find support for the notion that *some* emotions can be reliably distinguished on the basis of their autonomic characteristics.

Note

1. Asserting emotion-specific autonomic activity on the basis of physiological support for behavioral prototypes is just one of several possible functional arguments. A similar case for autonomic specificity could be built on the basis of communicative signals in emotion such as crying, sweating, piloerection, flushing of the face, blushing, pupil dilation, and blanching. Given that each of these signals is produced by action of the autonomic nervous system, emotion-specific autonomic activity is implicated to the extent that these signals are associated with different emotions (e.g., crying associated primarily with sadness, blanching associated primarily with fear).

The Clearest Physiological Distinctions Between Emotions Will Be Found Among the Circuits of the Brain

JAAK PANKSEPP

If one conceives of primal emotions as being constructed from specific brain circuits in the way I have described, then there is no question that a considerable amount of emotional specificity exists in the brain substrates, and to some extent this specificity has to be expressed in both autonomic and enteric nervous systems as well as endocrine manifestations of emotions. Indeed, it is hard to construct a reasonable evolutionary scenario for the brain without positing a great deal of specificity, but it is a difficult matter to empirically untangle these specificites. In human research one will have to work largely on the input and output sides (anchored either by the presence of subjective reports of affect or external indicators such a facial expressions and bodily postures); in animal research one can also aspire to detail the properties of the intervening operating systems, and, once that is done, one may be able to precisely specify how various output controls are orchestrated by the emotional systems (Mancia & Zanchetti, 1981; Smith & DeVito, (1984). At present we only have vague hints of the possibilities, and I would share a few considerations that should be kept in mind while pursuing such issues.

Although several patterns of ANS-emotion specificity have been described in human investigations, (Levenson, Ekman, & Friesen, 1990), the details of the underlying mechanisms will have to be elucidated through well-controlled animal brain research. One of the persistent problems is that there is considerable overlap in the autonomic and endocrine outputs of the various basic emotional systems, which is to be expected. The main function of the autonomic and endocrine changes is to bring various bodily reactions in line with behavioral/psychological demands of each emotional system. For instance, brain anger circuits mobilize bodily energy resources (via catecholamine, glucocorticoid, and other catabolic hormone secretions), which are distributed around the body by the invigorated cardiac output. Similar changes may be needed during phases of fear, exploratory curiosity, playful arousal, as well as separation distress. Thus, it is not surprising that there is massive convergence of various emotional systems onto specific brainstem areas that direct autonomic processes—for instance, the parabrachial area and motornucleus of the vagus, as well as catecholaminergic cell groups such as the locus coeruleus that control overall brain arousal (for an overview, see Panksepp, 1986). Likewise, the endocrine patterns that accompany emotional states can be extremely diverse (Henry, 1986; Mason, 1975), but, despite many redundancies, there may be some specificities. For instance, the thermoregulatory changes of fear and separation distress (feeling cold) may be opposite to those of anger. Others may be so nonspecific as to resemble general emotion markers. For instance, practically every emotional state is capable of activating the pituitary adrenal axis (Puglisi-Allegra & Oliverio, 1990). In general, there are good reasons to anticipate much greater behavioral and affective specificity in emotional circuits of the brain than in the autonomic and hormonal responses they control, and I do not forsee a time when the precise type of emotionality that has been aroused within the brain can be credibly gauged simply via the analysis of peripheral physiological changes. Various forms of brain imaging have a better chance of succeeding at this (Davidson, Ekman, Saron, Senulis, & Friesen, 1990; Zappulla, LeFever, Jaeger, & Bilder, 1991).

In the context of the present question, one must also note that there will probably be some quite powerful feedbacks from autonomic changes onto the subcortical emotional command circuits. For instance, a massive symphony of neuropeptides has been described in the gastrointestinal system (i.e., the enteric nervous system) as well as in other visceral organs, especially the kidney, immune system, and heart (Furness, Bornstein, Murphy, & Pompolo, 1992). Although the CNS is generally protected from the influence of such peptides by blood-brain barriers, a remarkable number, including giants such as prolactin and insulin (Drago, 1990; Woods & Porte, 1983), do have feedback access to the ventricular system. The smaller and highly lipophilic sex steroids have been known for decades to possess the ability to cross readily into the brain (Joels & de Kloet, 1992). There are many reasons to believe that these hormonal inputs can modulate the tone of emotional and other brain circuits (and thereby help establish moods—see Question 2). Although the elucidation of these controls will eventually be an exciting chapter of emotional research, it would be counterproductive to take their existence as strong evidence for the resurrection of James-Langian theories of emotionality. The complexity of the systems merely goes to indicate that no part of the body can be ignored when one deals with emotions.

I believe the most important specificities will be found in neurochemical coding of the basic emotions. There are many reasons to believe that the neurochemical character of many emotional command systems will prove to be neuropeptidergic (Panksepp, 1993). At this point a great number of neuropeptides placed into the brain have been found to modify emotive behaviors and affective states in animals. For instance, CRF is strongly implicated in the genesis of anxiety and stress (Baldwin, Britton, & Koob, 1990; Dunn & Beridge, 1990), oxytocin and prolactin in maternal intent (Bridges et al., 1990; Pedersen, Caldwell, Jirikowski, & Insel, 1992), vasopressin in aggressive male dominance urges (DeVries et al., 1985; Koolhaas et al., 1990), TRH in some type of brain arousal, perhaps playfulness (Whybrow & Bauer, 1988), opioids and anti-opioids in the control of social processes (Panksepp, 1981; Panksepp, Siviy, & Normansell, 1985), MSH and ACTH in fearfulness (Panksepp &

Abbott, 1990), and a host of neuropeptides in the inhibitory and excitatory control of appetite (Baile, McLaughlin, & Della-Ferra, 1986; Morley & Blundell, 1988). All these peptides have typically strong and diverse effects on autonomic and hormonal outputs (Gardiner & Bennett, 1989; Fisher & Brown, 1990). Many other neuopeptides remain without clear functions, not because of negative evidence but largely because relevant psychobiological research remains to be done. That individual neuopeptide systems code specific classes of emotive behavior and regulatory processes seems all but certain, and this remains an open area for novel and important discoveries. When we have decoded the neuropeptide specificites of the subcortical emotive circuits, we may have some ideal strategies for experimentally disentangling how specific emotional processes modify specific physiological and hormonal output processes, and vice versa.

Afterword: Is There Emotion-Specific Physiology?

RICHARD J. DAVIDSON
PAUL EKMAN

All the contributors who have commented on this question agree that specific biological changes accompany and provide the substrate for different emotions. With the exception of Levenson, the remaining authors also believe that it is unlikely that the autonomic nervous system (ANS) will show much evidence of emotion-specific patterning. In noting that the ANS has evolved for the purpose of providing the necessary metabolic and energy requirements for different action, Gray questions whether different emotions are associated with sufficiently different energy and metabolic needs to be reflected in different patterns of autonomic activity, although he does not consider any of the evidence Levenson reports. Levenson agrees with Gray concerning the fundamental role of autonomic activity, but finds more specificity in the identification of the metabolic demands of different emotions. He proposes that differentiation in autonomic activity occurs to support different patterns of behavior that are associated with different emotions. Levenson does not specify whether the basis for this association is ontogenetic or phylogenetic, although presumably he thinks it is the phylogenetic.

The two primary autonomic differences that Levenson and his colleagues have identified are: (1) disgust is associated with lower heart rate than anger, fear, and sadness; and (2) anger is associated with greater skin temperature than fear. These differences have been found to be consistent across profession, age, gender, and culture. The most robust evidence for this patterning was obtained from the Directed Facial Action task where subjects are provided with muscle-by-muscle instructions to compose particular facial configurations that represent prototypic expressions.

Davidson, Gray, LeDoux, and Panksepp all agree that the location in which to search for emotion-specific patterning is in the central nervous system. Davidson and Gray both suggest that broad dimensions of emotion or emotional systems are implemented in different neural circuits. Davidson argues for the importance of approach and withdrawal-related processes, presuming that these tendencies are established phylogenetically. He suggests that the same emotion associated with different patterns of anterior brain function. While Gray includes both approach and withdrawal dimensions, he adds a third dimension—behavioral inhibition. Davidson suggests that the left and right prefrontal and anterior temporal cortical regions are differentially engaged in approach and withdrawal-related processes respectively.

LeDoux offers interesting ideas about why it may be difficult to find evidence of emotion-specific autonomic activity, and suggests that there also may always be a backdrop of undifferentiated autonomic nervous system activity for emotion. LeDoux's own research underscores the important role of the amygdala in emotion processing. He indicates that studies of the microcircuitry of the amygdala will provide important clues on emotion-specific physiological differentiation. For example, the outputs of the central nucleus of the amygdala are important for controlling aversively conditioned fear responses while projections to nucleus accumbens are critical for appetitively conditioned place preferences. Davidson cautions us about the role of the amygdala in human emotion, since several case studies have appeared that suggest apparently intact emotional responses in patients with bilateral destruction of the amygdala. It is clear that additional research on this issue is required using modern neuroimaging procedures in humans.

Panksepp highlights the importance of neurochemical specificity to emotion. In particular, he draws our attention to the neuropeptides that serve as important neuromodulators. For example, corticotropin releasing factor (CRF) appears to play an important role in anxiety and stress; oxytocin and prolactin are implicated in certain types of maternal, nurturing behaviors; vasopressin plays a role in male aggression; and the opioids have been implicated in a variety of social processes. Many of these substances are capable of acting with very short time courses and offer a potentially very promising window on physiological specificity associated with emotion.

Several contributions made the point that we are now on the cusp of a new era in physiological research with emotion since new neuroimaging procedures have recently become available and, for the first time, we can study complex neural networks that underlie emotion in the human brain.

Question 7

Can We Control Our Emotions?

Emotions Unbecoming and Becoming

JAMES R. AVERILL

When an emotion is unbecoming (inappropriate or improper), we attempt to control it, usually with considerable success. Although it is part of our conception of emotion that we are "gripped," "seized," and "overcome," episodes in which a person is literally "out of control" are rare. The answer to the question Can we control our emotions? is thus an obvious, Yes. We do so all the time. The more interesting question is: How does such control change the emotion? Or, to put it differently, what becomes of the unbecoming emotion?

Colloquially, when a person is "out of control" emotionally, his or her behavior is described as "unruly." These colloquialisms reflect the fact that emotional control implies the existence of rules by which emotions are governed. I will explain what I mean by rules of emotion shortly; but first we need to get on common ground regarding the meaning of "emotion."

Three Meanings of Emotion

The concept of emotion is used in psychological theory in three quite different ways, namely, to refer to (1) emotional syndromes, (2) emotional states, and (3) emotional reactions (Averill, 1991). An emotional *syndrome* is what we mean when we speak of anger, grief, fear, love, and so on in the abstract. These are folk-theoretical concepts that have both a descriptive and prescriptive aspect. For example, the syndrome of anger both describes and prescribes what a person may (or should) do when angry. An emotional *state* is a relatively short-term, reversible (episodic) disposition to respond in a manner representative of the corresponding emotional syndrome. For example, when in an angry state, a person is disposed to act in a manner that corresponds to the syndrome of anger. Finally, an emotional *reaction* is the actual (and highly variable) set of responses manifested by an individual when in an emotional state; these responses might include, for example, facial expressions, physiological changes, overt behavior, and subjective experience.

It is important to distinguish these three meanings of emotion, for they belong to different logical categories. To conflate them is to commit a "category mistake." Ryle (1949) illustrates the nature of category mistakes by reference to a hypothetical visitor to Oxford University. After viewing all the buildings, libraries, classrooms, and so on, and visiting with students, professors, and administrators, the visitor asks, "But where is the University?" Implicit in the visitor's question is the notion that Oxford University is some thing or activity on a logical par with other things and activities (e.g., buildings, teaching) that characterize the University.

Similarly, an emotional syndrome should not be confused with an emotional state (which, pursuing Ryle's example, might correspond to the University term currently in session) or to emotional reactions (the specific activities occurring during the term). How do emotions change as a function of control? That depends on whether we are talking about emotional syndromes, emotional states (episodes), or emotional reactions—and on the type of rule involved.

Rules of Emotion

As noted at the outset, emotional control implies the existence of rules by which emotions are governed. Three types of rules may be distinguished: constitutive, regulative, and procedural. (Strictly speaking, the distinction between these three types of rules does not represent a true trichotomy. Any given rule may have constitutive, regulative, and procedural implications, albeit to varying degrees. Also, the term "rule" must be interpreted somewhat metaphorically, roughly equivalent to "improvisational guideline.")

To illustrate these three types of rules with a nonemotional example, consider a game such as chess. Some rules (e.g., with regard to the way the various pieces may be moved) help *constitute* the game as a game of chess, as opposed, say, to a game of checkers. Other rules (e.g., limiting the time between moves) help to *regulate* how the game is played on any given occasion. Still other rules help determine the strategy of a game, that is, how well or poorly a game is played. I call this last class of rules *procedural*.

To take a more naturalistic example, consider the case of language. The rules of English grammar help *constitute* the language as English, as opposed, say, to Chinese or Russian. Other rules (e.g., "speak softly in a library") help *regulate* how we speak on a given occasion. Finally, *procedural* rules help determine the quality of speech; courses in rhetoric and elocution, for example, are concerned primarily with procedural rules for effective speech.

Like games and languages, emotions are both constituted and regulated by rules, and they require appropriate procedures for skilled performance. For example, if a constitutive rule of anger is broken, the emotion will not be counted as an instance of "true" anger, but of some other emotion or condition (cruelty, say, or sadism). If a regulative rule of anger is violated, the response will be recognized as a manifestation of anger, but it will be regarded as inappropriate or improper. Finally, if a procedural rule of anger is broken, the response may be considered appropriate in kind (e.g., a manifestation of anger), but amateurish in execution (Averill, 1982, 1991).

Regulative and procedural rules apply primarily to emotional reactions. We typically monitor our emotional behavior to conform to socially accepted standards (regulative rules) and to be effective (procedural rules). This is true not only with respect to overt behavior (cf. Ekman & Friesen's, 1969, notion of "display rules"), but to thoughts and feelings as well (Hochschild, 1979). And once one component reaction is altered, other responses may be brought into line, thus changing the entire course of an emotional episode (state). For example, taking a deep breadth to dampen physiological arousal can lessen the intensity and shorten the duration of an emotional episode.

These observations are relatively commonplace and noncontroversial. Most theorists recognize the importance of regulative and procedural rules for the control of emotional reactions and states. However, it is perhaps worth mentioning at this point that the concept of control does not imply direction. The person who cannot express emotion in an open and effective manner when appropriate is as much out of control as is the person who habitually "lets it all hang out." Control implies the ability to respond in the way one wants, whether that entails the inhibition or expression of a response.

Regulative and procedural rules do not necessarily alter the underlying nature of the emotion (i.e., the emotional syndrome), only the way the emotion is experienced and expressed. The situation is quite different concerning constitutive rules. As noted earlier, emotional syndromes are—like games and languages—constituted by rules. If the constitutive rules of an emotion are changed, the nature of the emotion itself is changed—fundamentally, not just in its manifestations. Thus, where constitutive rules are concerned, the notion of emotional control takes on additional meaning, namely, the construction of new and different emotional syndromes.

As long as we remain within our own cultural context, it is difficult to appreciate the role that constitutive rules play in the construction of emotional syndromes. Therefore, let us consider briefly an emotional syndrome from another culture. Rosaldo (1980) describes an emotion *liget* among the Ilongot, a headhunting people of Northern Luzon, the Philippines. Rosaldo glosses *liget* as "anger," but sometimes also as "vital energy," and "passion," depending on the context. None of these translations is completely appropriate. *Liget* is a highly rewarding experience occasioned by cutting off the head of another person. The identity of the victim is of no great importance—a man, woman, or child, anyone will do. The point of taking a head is not revenge or retribution; rather, taking a head is a way of establishing one's position as an equal member of society. Taking a head is thus an occasion for celebration, not only for the successful headhunter, but for other members of his group as well.

Liget has other occasions than the taking of heads. For example, concentrated in the sperm, it helps make babies. The important point I want to make is that *liget* is not simply a variety of anger. *Liget* and anger are constituted according to very different rules, and each can be understood—and experienced—only within its own cultural context.

Just as the constitutive rules of emotion can vary across cultures, so, too, can they vary across individuals within a culture. Socialization is never complete, but always allows for some individual variation and innovation. Along with variations in biological predispositions, this accounts for the fact that no two people experience and express exactly the same emotion. Your anger is, in a sense, a different emotion from my anger. For the most part, however, such individual differences in emotional syndromes are sufficiently minor that we have no difficulty in applying the same concept ("anger") to most variations within a culture.

But not all individual variations are so minor. As a result of (or in compensation for) physiological dysfunction, inadequate socialization, motivational distortion, and cognitive biases, a person may develop rules that depart significantly from the constitutive rules prescribed by society. Such personal (as opposed to social or shared) rules of emotion allow the expression of needs and desires, but in a highly idiosyncratic and often "disordered" fashion. One result can be a neurotic syndrome, such as an hysterical conversion reaction (Averill, 1988).

To illustrate, take the case of a person who, instead of becoming angry when unjustly treated, "punishes" the other by becoming physically incapacitated. This is not simply a case of normal anger being "repressed," only to surface in disguised form. Rather, the conversion reaction represents an emotional syndrome in its own right, one that shares some of the features of normal anger but also contains features idiosyncratic to the individual.

By definition, constitutive rules make an emotion the kind of emotion it is (anger, fear, love, or whatever). Thus, if the constitutive rules of an emotion are misconstrued too egregiously, the resulting syndrome will be unclassifiable. In such a case, we are tempted to say that something *more* is involved than meets the eye (e.g., repressed anger, fear, or whatever). But that "something more" is simply conformity to idiosyncratically developed, personal rules of emotion, as opposed to widely shared, culturally prescribed rules.

Not all changes in constitutive rules are maladaptive, as in neurotic syndromes. If a change in rules proves effective, we may speak of emotional creativity; that is, the development of a novel but adaptive emotional syndrome, one not generally recognized by the culture as a whole (Averill & Thomas-Knowles, 1991; Averill & Nunley, 1992). On occasion, the new emotion may actually prove beneficial to others and become widely adopted. What begins as a personal eccentricity thus becomes a new standard for society. The history of romantic love within Western societies provides a good example of this process (see, e.g., Hunt, 1959).

Concluding Observations

Too often, emotional control is viewed primarily as a matter of inhibition, and rules of emotion are regarded primarily as regulative. But control implies flexibility, not simply inhibition, and rules enable as well as regulate. For example, if the rules of English grammar were suddenly eliminated, people would not be able to speak English more freely, they would not be able to speak it at all. Similarly, remove the constitutive rules of emotion and people would not be emotionally more free, they would be emotionally inarticulate. It might be objected that, unlike language, emotions—at least "basic" emotions—have biological origins that provide them meaning independent of social norms and rules. It would, of course, be fatuous to deny that biological predispositions influence the development of emotional syndromes. However, the same is true of language. The capacity for language is a biological adaptation; but any specific language (English, say, or Chinese) is the product of social, not biological evolution. Similarly, emotions presume biological capacities, but any specific emotion (anger, say, or *liget*) is the product of social, not biological evolution (cf. my responses to Question 1 on basic emotions and Question 4 on the universality of emotions).

Emotional syndromes, to the extent they are constituted and not simply regulated by rules, are subject to change. Like genetic mutations, most such changes ultimately prove harmful or maladaptive ("unbecoming"), either for the individual or the group. Psychotherapy is basically a set of procedures designed to repair emotional maladaptations on the individual level. Some innovations, however, prove advantageous and deserve encouragement ("becoming"). Modern technology presents many challenges (e.g., weapons of mass destruction, urbanization, changing patters of intimate relationships, and a greatly expanded life expectancy) that require emotional as well as intellectual creativity if we are to continue to prevail and prosper as individuals and as a society (Averill & Nunley, 1992).

The Degree of Emotional Control Depends on the Kind of Response System Involved

JOSEPH E. LEDOUX

The question of emotional control, like most other questions about emotion, cannot be answered with a simple yes or no. The answer depends on which aspect of emotion we are seeking to control. I will focus on the question of whether we can control the expression of emotion responses and will limit my discussion to responses of the somatic musculature. The longstanding question of whether autonomic responses can be controlled will not be addressed.

In the presence of an emotional stimulus, the brain evaluates the significance of that stimulus and on the basis of that evaluation produces responses appropriate to the meaning of the stimulus. At the neural level, stimulus evaluation and response control are well understood for the brain's fear system. A key structure in both the evaluation of threatening events and the production of defensive responses is the amygdala (e.g., LeDoux, 1987). The contribution of the amygdala to stimulus evaluation has already been described (see Question 5). Here I concentrate on the production of emotional responses and will distinguish types of responses.

Type I responses are immediate. They are elicited when an affectively charged stimulus is evaluated by the amygdala (see Question 5). Type I responses reflect patterns of reaction that have been perfected through evolutionary experience of the species. The evolutionarily perfected responses are expressed largely the same from individual to individual within a species. These are automatic consequences of the initial evaluation of stimulus significance and are involuntary. Type I responses are somewhat akin to the fixed action patterns described by ethologists. In the presence of key stimuli or stimulus elements, the response patterns are automatically expressed or released. While it may be possible to willfully abort their full execution, their initiation is not under volitional control. Examples of Type I responses include freezing behavior and fearful facial expressions in the presence of a threatening event. Many autonomic and endocrine responses are also automatically elicited, evolutionarily determined responses and might be considered, along with somatic musculature responses, within the Type 1 category.

Type II responses are emitted rather than elicited emotional responses. These responses are specific to the individual and are not necessarily characteristic of the species. They reflect past experiences in similar or related situations as well as judgments and predictions about the immediate situation and the applicability of past experiences to the situation. Type II responses often follow Type I responses and, in these situations, represent the organism's strategy for coping with the consequences of emotional arousal. However, Type II responses may also appear in situations that are only mildly arousing and thus that do not first elicit Type I responses. Type II responses are largely expressed through the somatic musculature. Although autonomic and humoral responses may occur during Type II responses, they are secondary to the behavioral response rather than a primary response. Instrumental avoidance and approach responses are prototypical Type II responses. Type II responses are under volitional control.

Considerable progress has been made in identifying the neural system mediating Type I responses, at least within the domain of fear (see the figure in Question 5). As noted previously, a key link in this circuitry is the amygdala. The lateral nucleus of the amygdala receives inputs from sensory processing areas in the thalamus and cortex, as well as from cortical association areas, including the hippocampal formation (see Question 5). The lateral nucleus projects to the central nucleus, both directly and through intraamygdala connections with the basal and accessory basal nuclei (Pitkänen & Amaral, 1991; Stefanacci et al., 1992). The central nucleus has massive connections with brainstem areas involved in the control of species-typical behavior, stereotyped autonomic reactions, and endocrine responses. Lesions of the central nucleus eliminate an animal's ability to express these kinds of responses (Kapp et al., 1990; Davis, 1992; LeDoux, 1990), whereas lesions of individual projection targets eliminate specific response components, such as only the autonomic or behavioral response (e.g., Smith et al., 1980; LeDoux et al., 1988). Work in this area has focused mostly on defense responses elicited by threatening stimuli. Recent studies have also ventured into the role of the central amygdala in the regulation of stereotyped responses elicited by appetitive stimuli (Gallagher & Holland, 1992), but much more work is needed on this topic.

The amygdala also appears to participate in Type II responses. Lesions of the amgydala interfere with performance in avoidance conditioning (see LeDoux, 1992b, 1992c), which requires that a response be emitted to avoid the threatening stimlus. Recent studies have also begun to identify circuits through which voluntary (Type II) responses are controlled by the amygdala in appetitive conditioning tasks. Although much less is known about the contribution of the amygdala to these tasks, projections from the lateral and basal nucleus of the amygdala to the ventral striatum appear to be involved (Hiroi & White, 1991; Cador, Robbins, & Everitt, 1989; Everitt et al., 1991). It is not known whether aversive instrumental responses (avoidance) are also controlled by these connections between the amygdala and ventral striatum.

An important question concerns the mechanisms through which the immediate involuntary and the delayed voluntary responses are interrelated. On this point there is little evidence. However, a plausible neuroscenario involves the amygdala, particularly the lateral/basolateral nuclei. As described, the lateral nucleus is the sensory and cognitive port of entry to the amygdala. The lateral nucleus then projects to the basal nucleus. The basal nucleus has several projections of interest: central amygdala; striatum, including nucleus accumbens; neocortical association areas; hippocampal formation. The projection to the central amygdala appears to be involved in the expression of Type I responses and the other projections may contribute to Type II responses. The direct projection to the nucleus accumbens, as described, appears to be involved in some instrumental responses. Inputs to the neocortex and hippocampus may also enter into this. The outcome of emotional evaluation may be routed to the neocortex and hippocampus and from these areas back to the striatum, allowing very complex processing functions and circuits to participate in instrumental behavior that is emitted as a result of the evaluation of stimulus meaning by the amygdala and expressed through the striatum.

In this scheme, the emotional reaction may have both voluntary and involuntary components. To the extent that the emotional stimulus is one that the species has developed specific response strategies to cope with, the initial reaction will be automatic and involuntary and the secondary reaction will be voluntary. In contrast, in novel situations, where species-typical reactions are not available or appropriate, voluntary control may be required; involuntary responses may also occur in the form of displacement activities. To be effective, voluntary responses must be based on information about the stimulus, the situation, and possible outcomes of actions. By necessity, this kind of processing will utilize much of the cognitive capacities of the organism and involve the polymodal and supramodal association areas of the cortex. Involuntary, hard-wired responses eliminate the need for decision. They provide tried and true patterns that tend to work effectively in certain situations and can be executed with much less circuitry. Far too little is known about the interrelationship between Type I and Type II circuitry at this point and we can only speculate as to how the brain generates the integrated emotional response in a given situation.

Emotional Control: Variation and Consequences

ROBERT W. LEVENSON

Emotional control is quite ubiquitous. It is intertwined with the widest range of human activities spanning normal and abnormal development: maintenance of the social order; cultural convention; interpersonal bonding, power, and influence; optimization of performance, and processes of health and illness. A great deal has been written on the psychological and physiological consequences of inhibiting the free flow of emotion—many of which are depicted as dire and unhealthy.

Varieties of Emotional Control

Emotional control can take many forms, which differ in terms of *direction* of control (amplifying, inhibiting); *number* of emotions controlled (single emotions, multiple emotions in blends or sequences); nature of the *transformation* (altering intensity levels of emotions, substituting emotions for other emotions, masking emotions with other emotions); *locus* of attempted control (antecedent conditions, subjective experience, expressive behavior, physiology); *volition* (voluntary or involuntary); *awareness* (conscious or unconscious); *onset* of control (prior to emotion, following emotion); and *target* of control (our own emotions, those of others). Expanding this matrix produces myriad possible forms, delineating a large research agenda if emotional control is to be fully understood.

To study emotional control successfully in the laboratory, we must identify simple, ecologically valid models. For present purposes, I will focus on a very common form of emotional control: suppression—the conscious voluntary inhibition of expressive behavior beginning prior to the event that produces the emotion and continuing throughout that event. Life is replete with occasions for this kind of emotional control—situations in which we are motivated to inhibit the signs that would reveal how we are feeling. We try not to cry when we are hurt by bullies. We try not to laugh at pompous speeches, funerals, and the discomfort of others. We try not to let others see our fear when doing so would risk engendering their disapproval or inviting them to harm us. We try to hide our anger when it is directed at people we love. We dampen our contempt so as not to hurt or enrage others. We hold back our disgust when confronted with the ravages of illness and injury, or when a friend proudly serves us a special dish that revolts us.

I will also focus on one particular consequence of this kind of suppression—its effect on the autonomic nervous system. The question, simply stated, is: When one is emotionally aroused, does voluntary inhibition of expressive behavior *increase*, *decrease*, or have *no effect* on the level of autonomic activation? This question goes to the core of the relation between expression and physiology in emotion.

What Do We Know About Expression and Physiology in Emotion, and How Much Is Relevant to Emotional Suppression?

As it turns out, we know a great deal about the relation between expression and physiology in emotion; however, almost none of what we know is directly relevant to emotional suppression as I have defined it.

Empirical studies of the relation between expression and physiology can be divided into two paradigms: (1) *studies of dispositional expressivity* and (2) *studies of manipulated expressivity*.

Dispositional Expressivity

In studies of dispositional expressivity, aspects of the emotion response are examined in individuals who differ in how emotionally expressive they typically are. Research in both the "internalizer-externalizer" tradition (Buck, 1979; Field & Walden, 1982; Funkenstein, King, & Drolette, 1954; Jones, 1935, 1950, 1960; Notarius & Levenson, 1979) and in the "repressive coping style" literature (e.g., Levenson & Mades, 1980; Weinberger, Schwartz, & Davidson, 1979) support the conclusion that people who are characteristically unexpressive are *more* physiologically reactive than those who are characteristically expressive.

Does this mean that the effect of emotional suppression is to increase levels of physiological arousal? This is the precisely the conclusion that is often drawn, evoking metaphors of "hydraulic," or "cathartic" models. Unfortunately, such a conclusion is simply not justified. Dispositional studies of this sort do not establish whether emotional expression is actually being *suppressed*. To assert that a person who does not show a great deal of facial expression is actually inhibiting that expression is a wholly unjustified leap of logic.[2]

Manipulated Expressivity

In studies of manipulated expressivity, subjects are led to control their emotional expression and the effects of this control on other aspects of emotion are examined. A number of different experimental paradigms have been used in this sizable literature, with the two major variants involving either having subjects voluntarily construct emotional facial expressions or having them exaggerate or diminish naturally occurring facial expressions. In a recent review of 21 studies in this literature, we (Gross & Levenson, 1993) concluded that with only four exceptions, these studies all failed to provide a direct test of the physiological effects of emotional suppression because they: (1) did not arouse emotion in some way independent of the facial manipulation; (2) did not have subjects inhibit expression at all; or (3) did not measure physiology. Among the four exceptions,[3] the general finding was that inhibiting expressive behavior led to *lower* levels of physiological response.

New Studies of Emotional Suppression

We recently initiated a series of studies using a methodology that we believe will yield more definitive data regarding the effects of suppression. In designing these experiments, we rejected three assumptions that have been tacit in much of the existing work. *First*, we did not assume that the effects of suppression would be the same for all emotions; *second*, we did not assume that the effects of suppression would be the same for all aspects of emotion; and *third*, we did not assume that the physiological effects of suppression would await the start of the emotion-eliciting event. Thus, we planned to examine the effects of suppressing several different emotions; we measured the effects of suppression on subjective experience, expressive behavior, and physiology; and we measured physiology before and during the emotion-eliciting event.

Our experimental paradigm was simple. In the "no-suppression" condition, subjects were told that they would be seeing a short film; in the "suppression" condition, they were told that they would be seeing a short film and they should behave so that a person watching them would not know that they were feeling anything.

Studies of the Suppression of Disgust

Our first two studies were identical expect for the gender of subjects—the first conducted with males, and the second, a year later, conducted with females (Gross & Levenson, 1993). The stimulus film used in these studies portrayed a surgical amputation of a limb, which we had established as a reliable elicitor of both the subjective experience and facial expressions of disgust.[4]

Expressive Behavior. Subjects were clearly able to reduce the visible signs of the emotions they were feeling, as indicated by less overall facial movement and less disgust expressive behavior in the suppression condition than in the no-suppression condition. However, subjects could not *totally eliminate* all expressive signs of disgust. Furthermore, there was some "leakage" to another part of the face; suppression was accompanied by an increase in the rate of blinking.

Subjective Experience. Inhibiting the facial signs of emotion had *no effect* on the intensity of the subjective experience of disgust.

Autonomic and Somatic Physiology. When subjects inhibited the visible signs of emotion, they also reduced their overall level of body movement (both as coded by observers and measured by a motion sensor). Along with this reduction in bodily movement was a slowing of heart rate. This is consistent with the oft-observed coupling between somatic and cardiac activity, which is primarily mediated by the parasympathetic branch of the autonomic nervous system (Obrist, 1981). Thus far, the effects of suppression could be characterized as a *lowering* of the level of physiological activation, a finding comparable to the conclusions drawn from the four previous studies that we considered as adequate tests of the physiological effects of suppression.

However, elsewhere in the body, the effects of suppression involved a *heightening* of the level of activation. This was manifest in greater constriction of the peripheral vasculature, more pronounced shortening in the time it took the pulse pressure wave to travel from the heart to the finger (a sign that arterial blood pressure had risen), and greater electrodermal activity (i.e., increased skin conductance).[5] All these changes are consistent with the notion that suppression produces *heightened* activation of the sympathetic branch of the autonomic nervous system.

Sex Differences. There were no sex differences in the effects of suppression. Men are often said to control their emotions more than women, but, based on these findings, the effects of suppression, when it does occurs, appear to be the same regardless of the sex of the suppressor.

Temporal Course of Suppression. Most studies of emotional inhibition have only examined the responses that occur during the emotional stimulus. We were also interested in the *preparation* for suppression. Examining the period after subjects were told that they would be asked to inhibit visible signs of emotion, but before the film actually started, revealed that two signs of sympathetic nervous system activation—increased constriction of the peripheral vasculature and increased sweat gland activity—actually began appearing *prior* to the start of the film.

"Stonewalling": A Possible Naturalistic Analog of Suppression?

John Gottman and I have long been interested in the tendency of husbands to withdraw emotionally from conflictive marital interactions (Levenson & Gottman, 1985; Gottman & Levenson, 1988; see also Christensen & Heavey, 1990). Recently, we conducted an investigation of a particular variant of this behavior, which we termed "stonewalling" (Gottman & Levenson, 1993), that occurs when a spouse is subjectively experiencing negative emotion, but provides none of the behavioral signs that usually accompany those feelings. Examining the laboratory interactions of 79 married couples who were trying to resolve a marital conflict, we identified incidents on the basis of observational coding of the following behaviors: (1) no vocal or nonvocal backchannels—these are behaviors such as saying "uh huh" and head-nodding, which, when present, convey to the speaker that the listener is attending; (2) no facial movement; and (3) not looking at the speaker. We found that these behaviors were associated with: (1) highly negative subjective emotional experience; (2) low levels of bodily movement; and (3) high levels of electrodermal activity. Although husbands were more likely to stonewall than wives, the physiological effects of stonewalling were the same for husbands and wives.

I would argue that stonewalling is an interpersonal variant of emotional suppression. When spouses feel emotionally negative, inhibit facial movements, and reduce overall bodily movement, they are spontaneously producing a state much like the state we produced experimentally in our suppression studies. And, as with subjects in those studies who were asked to inhibit their expressive behavior, stonewalling spouses showed increased levels of sweat gland activity, an autonomic function thought to indicate behavioral inhibition (Fowles, 1980).

Emotional Control: Implications and Consequences

Our studies of suppression and stonewalling (and related research by others) indicate that people are quite adept at inhibiting the behavioral signs of emotion. Although they might not be able to do so completely (especially when the emotion is strong), and although there might be some "leakage" into other behavioral signs (e.g., blinking), the reduction in visible manifestations of emotion can be quite dramatic.

Our studies suggest that reducing the visible signs of emotion is *not* an effective way to reduce the subjective experience of emotion. In our suppression studies, the feelings elicited by the emotion-eliciting films were undiminished in the suppression condition; in our study of marital interaction, stonewallers continued to report feeling quite negative.

In our studies of suppression of emotional response to a disgust-eliciting film, we have found the physiological sequelae of suppression to consist of two quite different kinds of autonomic effects. First, there is a *reduction* in somatic activity and an attendant *reduction* in heart rate, which we believe is parasympathetically mediated. Second, there is an *increase* in vasoconstriction, an *increase* in the rate of blood flow to the periphery, and an *increase* in sweat gland activity, all indicating heightened sympathetic nervous system arousal. These findings point to the limitations of models of emotional inhibition that focus exclusively on increased sympathetic nervous activity (e.g., the model proposed by Cacioppo et al., 1992).

Why Is There Both Parasympathetic and Sympathetic Nervous System Activation During Suppression?

I have already indicated that we believe that the slowing of heart rate associated with emotional suppression is a parasympathetically mediated consequence of the reduction in somatic activity manifest by subjects in the suppression condition. But why, in the face of reduced somatic activity and its attendant decrease in metabolic demand, are there such clear signs of sympathetic nervous system arousal in other cardiac, vascular, and electrodermal systems?

One possible explanation is that the emotion that is being suppressed continues to recruit the same kinds of sympathetic nervous system support that it would if it were fully manifest. I do not believe this the case.[6]

Instead, I believe a more viable explanation for this sympathetic nervous system activation is that inhibiting the visible signs of emotion involves real work, and that this work makes significant metabolic demands. As I indicated in my answer to Question 4, emotions call forth powerful motor programs that mobilize activity in the muscles of the face, the trunk, the limbs, and other parts of the body. These motor programs enable the organism to adapt rapidly to the environmental demands that provoked the emotion. To eliminate the visible signs of emotion, emotional suppression likely mobilizes "bracing" and "braking" actions that attempt to hold these emerging somatic aspects of emotion in check. Thus, the observed heightened sympathetic activation (in sweat gland activity, pulse velocity, and vasoconstriction) is an indicator that such inhibitory work is being done. That some of these sympathetic nervous system changes occur *prior* to the commencement of the emotional stimulus, lends further credence to this "bracing" explanation.

Implications for Health

There is nothing inherently unhealthy about activating the autonomic nervous system. Physical exercise produces high levels of autonomic nervous system activity, and these are thought to be health-promoting. This begs the question of why emotion, which can also produce high levels of autonomic nervous system activity, would not also be health-promoting?

I would argue that there is little reason to suspect that the autonomic activity associated with emotion has any untoward health outcomes *except* when one or both of the following two conditions are met: (1) autonomic arousal is sustained and chronic; and (2) autonomic arousal exceeds metabolic demand.

Chronic autonomic reactivity has historically assumed a prominent role in etiological models that link psychosocial and emotional factors with early disease processes and with disease onset (e.g., Holroyd & Gorkin, 1983; Jemmott & Locke, 1984; Krantz & Manuck, 1984; MacDougall, Dembroski, & Krantz, 1981; Miller, 1978; Obrist, 1981; Steptoe, 1981). Recent studies of the effects of social stress on the development of atherosclerosis in monkeys (Kaplan, Pettersson, Manuck, & Olsson, 1991) provide strong experimental support for these notions.

As for the second condition, the notion of "physiological arousal in excess of metabolic demand" is a powerful explanatory construct. When people are running or engaged in other forms of aerobic exercise, a metabolic demand is created that is appropriate for the level of increased cardiovascular activity engendered by these activities. If this same level of cardiovascular arousal were produced when the person was relaxed and sitting still, then the arousal would be in excess of the metabolic demand. Similarly, when we *act* in the service of our emotions, the "motor programs" (Frijda, 1986) that are associated with different emotions create a level of metabolic demand that is appropriate for the level of arousal. If our emotions are aroused along with their attendant autonomic activation, and we do *not* act—because of some voluntary inhibition (as in suppression or stonewalling), some external restraining circumstance, or some involuntary, characterological or pathological inhibition—then there will *not* be a level of metabolic demand that is sufficient to accommodate the heightened physiological arousal.

The damaging effects of physiological arousal in excess of metabolic demands can be illustrated by simple analogy. Assume an old garden hose has several places where the rubber has become thin and brittle. No matter how high the water pressure, the hose will continue to function without damage as long as water is removed as powerfully from the distal end as it is pumped into the proximal end. If, however, the pumping force becomes greater than the extracting force, reflecting that less water is needed than is being pumped or that the hose has become blocked, the chances for the hose rupturing at one of its weak spots increases. And the likelihood of damage under these conditions is greatly increased the longer and the more often the water is turned on.

This crude hydraulic analogy notwithstanding, is there any evidence that chronic emotional inhibition is actually associated with negative health outcomes? One line of inquiry that is relevant to these issues suggests that behavioral inhibition (operationalized as not disclosing traumatic events) can have unfavorable effects on immune system functioning and on physical health (Pennebaker & Beall, 1986; Pennebaker, Hughes, & O'Heeron, 1987; Pennebaker, Kiecolt-Glaser, & Glaser, 1988a, 1988b). Although in no way settling this issue, these findings are certainly provocative, suggesting that certain kinds of emotional inhibition may well have adverse health consequences.

Notes

1. My response to this question draws on the work of James J. Gross, a doctoral student in my laboratory with whom I have been working collaboratively in the area of emotional control.

2. Cacioppo, Uchino, Crites, Snydersmith, Smith, Berntson, and Lang (1992) offer similar criticisms of the failure of such studies to actually test the "hydraulic" model. They then offer an alternative model based on dispositional differences in the "gain" of physiological and expressive channels. Unfortunately, they have not yet provided an empirical test of their model, or of the alternatives they criticize.

3. The exceptions involved suppression of expressive responses to electric shock (Colby, Lanzetta, & Kleck, 1977; Lanzetta, Cartwright-Smith, & Kleck, 1976); amusing films (Bush, Barr, McHugo, & Lanzetta, 1989); and pleasant and unpleasant films (Zuckerman, Klorman, Larrance, & Spiegel, 1981).

4. For his dissertation, Gross has recently completed another study using the same paradigm to examine inhibition of the visible signs of emotion with film stimuli known to elicit two other emotions: amusement and sadness, and a film known to elicit a neutral affective state. The results of this study should help answer the very important question of whether the effects of emotional suppression are consistent across emotions.

5. In Fowles' (1980) adaptation of Gray's two-factor learning theory, increased electrodermal activity is viewed as indicating activation of the "behavioral inhibition system." We consider emotional suppression as operationalized in this study to involve a form of behavioral inhibition.

6. A critical test of this explanation will be provided by our studies of the suppression of emotions other than disgust. Assuming some degree of emotion-specific autonomic nervous system activity (as I have posited in answer to Question 6), then if the suppressed emotion continues to recruit its characteristic pattern of autonomic nervous system activity, we would expect the physiological effects of suppression to be different for such emotions as disgust and sadness.

Afterword: Can We Control Our Emotions?

PAUL EKMAN
RICHARD J. DAVIDSON

Levenson provides the most complete description of what we refer to when we focus on the control of emotion, although he considers just one type of control, inhibition of expression. LeDoux also considers just the control of expression, in discussing the neural mechanisms that are involved. While Averill includes the inhibition of expression, which he terms "regulative rules" (see also the concept of display rules, Ekman, 1972; Ekman & Friesen, 1975), Averill is more interested in a quite different type of modification of emotion, the reconstituting of what an emotion is. Averill posits that it is not just the manifestations of an emotion that can be controlled. Through social experience, just what is an emotion and how it is constituted may differ radically. Although he grants a role for biology, it appears to be primarily in giving us the capacity to have emotions. He uses the analogy with language, where biology provides us with the necessary substrate to learn language, yet culture determines which language we learn. Which emotions we have, what those emotions constitute, are the product of "social not biological evolution." It can vary not only between societies but among individuals within a society, similar to the way dialects differ within a society. (For a similar view, see Shweder's answer to Question 1).

LeDoux takes nearly an opposite stance, although he allows for social as well as biological contributions. He posits two types of emotional responses. One is the product of evolution, involuntary, common to all members of the species. It is possible to abort but not to inhibit the initiation of these responses. Averill rejects this possibility. LeDoux's second type reflects social experience, representing what has been learned about how to cope, and it is here that LeDoux would put what Averill considers. LeDoux makes the interesting point that Type 1 responses occur only in regard to stimuli for which the species has developed response strategies. There are some antecedent events, for LeDoux, for which the organism is biologically prepared to respond with a certain emotion. The literature on human learned preparedness would be one example of such antecedent events (e.g., Seligman & Hager, 1972). Most of those who study the antecedents of emotion do not believe there are such events—it is the appraisal not the event that they believe sets off an emotion. (See the discussion of these issues in Question 4).

Levenson does not directly enter this argument, although he presumably would be in LeDoux's camp, certainly not in Averill's. Levenson summarizes a line of research that has begun to find out the effects of voluntary, deliberate inhibition on subjective experience and facial and autonomic responses. It is not clear from his contribution whether he would expect the same findings if the changes were brought about by well-established habit instead of choice of the moment. His section closes with provocative ideas about how and when emotions and their suppression may be unhealthy.

None of the contributors responded to one of the subquestions we provided: Is the capacity to control emotion relevant to whether people are responsible for their emotions or emotion behavior? This is perhaps too philosophical a question, but its answer does depend on whether we believe that emotion produces involuntary behavior, which cannot be controlled. Ekman (1977; 1992) proposed that the feeling that an emotion happens to us rather than being chosen is one of the essential defining characteristics of emotions. We are not capable of easily initiating any emotion we want to feel, nor are we capable of terminating an emotion completely by simple choice, he maintains. Levenson's and LeDoux's contributions might imply that we should be held responsible for what we do after the first moment or two, but not for the initial motor response, nor for the physiological and subjective changes that occur internally. On the other hand, Levenson's research indicates that the physiological manifestations of emotional control begin before the onset of the emotionally eliciting event. To the extent that such regulatory strategies become automated over time, there might never be a point where emotion is completely uncontrolled. Rather, it might be more appropriate to consider the degree of regulation that is in effect, not whether such regulation is present.

Question 8

Can Emotions Be Nonconscious?

Why Emotions Are Never Unconscious

GERALD L. CLORE

Defining Emotions as Conscious

Cognitive appraisals need not be conscious. Hence, it is quite possible to be surprised by one's own emotions. The emotions that result from such appraisals, however, must be conscious. In agreement with Freud, I would argue that it is not possible to have an unconscious emotion because emotion involves an experience, and one cannot have an experience that is not experienced. Freud (1915) indicated that he would still speak of unconscious emotion, but made it clear that this was a shorthand for unconscious beliefs with emotional implications. I am inclined to think that if Freud, who relied so much on unconscious processes, did not require a concept of unconscious emotion, then modern emotion theorists may not either. On the other hand, Freud did assume that the processes underlying emotions were unconscious, and he also had a concept of unconscious libidinal or psychic energy that he called "affect." This instinctual energy was unconscious, although it could leak out as unbound energy, which was then experienced as anxiety. Affect was believed to be the quantitative aspect of ideas and was responsible for driving them into consciousness (Freud, 1894).

From my point of view, emotion is mainly concerned with internal communication and motivation. The momentary experience of emotion informs the individual of the nature and importance of events, and the urgency of feeling motivates one to give priority in cognitive processing to emotion-relevant considerations. While the cognitive processing that causes emotion is unconscious, the informational and motivational effects of emotion depend on conscious experience in order to capture the attention of the experiencer.

According to this argument, emotions that are felt cannot be unconscious by definition. Does it then make sense to talk about emotions that are not felt? I am inclined toward a negative answer. If there are necessary features of emotions, feeling is a good candidate. Of all the features that emotions have in common, feeling seems the least dispensable. It is perfectly reasonable to say about one's anger, for example, "I was angry but I didn't do anything," but it would be odd to say, "I was angry but I didn't feel anything." As indicated in response to Question 5, feeling is not a sufficient condition for emotion, but, I would argue, it may be a necessary condition.

The feelings-as-information model (Clore, 1992; Schwarz & Clore, 1983; 1988) is based on the assumption that experience is an important mediator of the effects of mood and emotion on judgment and decision-making (see Question 3). The general idea is that people routinely use affective feedback in moment-to-moment judgments and decisions. For these processes to be as powerful and pervasive as we think they are would require a consistent mapping between emotional processing and the experiential readout of that processing. Otherwise the person could not be expected to use this feedback effectively.

Unconscious Fear

One counterargument to the idea that emotions must be felt (and hence must be conscious) can be found in the considerations raised by Lang (e.g., Lang, 1988) in his three systems view. He argues that emotion can be manifest in behavior, verbal report, or physiology, and that the level of the emotional response apparent in these systems is often not consistent. It should be noted that Lang is concerned with verbal report, while I am concerned with experience itself. Nevertheless, he provides evidence implying that emotion can be apparent in behavior or physiology without its having an experiential component.

To make this argument more concrete, consider the case of a particular assistant professor who was worried about getting tenure. The person had a good record, was generally assumed to be on safe ground, and did not report being worried. Nevertheless, she repeatedly awoke during the night with heart-attack-like symptoms. Extensive medical tests pursuing even the most exotic possibilities produced consistent evidence of good health. In addition, changes in diet and consumption of alcohol and caffeine had no effect. The problem was eventually solved by a positive outcome of the tenure review process.

From one perspective, this example is problematic for our assumption that conscious experience of emotion is essential. This assistant professor reported no fears and no rumination about tenure or other conscious mental content indicating such fear. She also engaged in no behavior that suggested fear, unless one interprets the absence of thought itself as avoidance. But despite the lack of relevant experience and behavior, the accompanying physiological activity suggests that unconsciously she was afraid. Stated more properly, fear-producing beliefs were unconsciously activated, or she unconsciously appraised her situation as one involving threat.

What seems to be missing at first glance is the experiential component, the thoughts and feelings of fear. (In my view, the absence of behavior and behavior tendencies is not a problem, since behavior is neither a necessary nor a sufficient condition for emotion). Of course, in one sense the experiential component is not missing. She did have explicit fearful thoughts and feelings, but they were about having a heart attack. But how did fear of failure become fear of a heart attack? As it happened, she experienced the symptoms only at night. During the day, she was well defended against her fears and thought little about the upcoming threat of tenure review. But when asleep and unable to maintain the same vigilance, these concerns were activated and produced the emotional symptoms that awoke her. But since the mental preoccupations occurred only in her sleep, she remained unaware of them. As a result, the racing heart became itself the focus of attention, and the feelings of fear became a fear that she was having a heart attack rather than fear of professional failure. Thus, the emotion did involve both physiology and verbal report of feelings, and since the emotion was experienced, it was also conscious. The curious nature of the example lies in the fact that she was unaware of what we presume to have been the real cause of her experience and hence the meaning of her emotion.

Whether one decides that one can or cannot have unconscious emotion depends on what one decides about the necessary conditions for emotion. One can take this case as an example of unconscious emotion, or one can define emotion as necessarily involving experience and then classify the unconscious threatening beliefs and the accompanying physiology as "fear potential" (Ortony, Clore, & Collins, 1988). Whether one chooses to refer to the unexperienced phenomena as "unconscious fear" or as "fear potential" is less important than being clear and consistent about how one uses the terms. Taking the position that emotions must be felt, and hence conscious, does not imply that people necessarily know what they are emotional about.

This example illustrates the functional nature of the usual sequence of emotion coping. Ordinarily, emotional experience directs one's attention both internally and externally to emotion-relevant considerations. But since the fear-eliciting thoughts remained unconscious, the feedback cycle was broken, and it was therefore unclear what concerns should be attended to. Deprived of the mental content that would have helped her perceive her emotion accurately, the assistant professor did none of the cognitive coping that might have stemmed the rising tide of anxiety (e.g., making favorable comparisons with those previously promoted). As a consequence she was seized by the symptoms of runaway fear unchecked by the reality testing that awareness of the presumed source of her fear would otherwise have triggered.

Being Unconscious of the Cause of Emotion

Some of the most important effects of emotion are mediated by the information conveyed by conscious experience (Clore, Schwarz, & Conway, 1994). The experience of emotion can include thoughts, feelings, and the feedback from emotional expressions and behavior. Whether these effects are narrow and specific or broad and general, however, depends on one's consciousness of the source of the emotions. If the source of an emotion remains unconscious, the emotion may be experienced as part of one's reaction to almost anything, and hence may color one's judgment of almost anything. If the source of an emotion is conscious, then its meaning will be constrained, and the range of judgments it colors will be limited. Hence, not only is the conscious experience of emotion important, but also consciousness of its cause and hence its meaning. Indeed, the convergence of a great deal of evidence from many different domains involving feelings (see Clore, 1992) shows this to be a very general principle.

In this regard, one of the primary differences between moods and emotions is the greater likelihood that one will be conscious of the cause and hence the significance or relevance of emotions as opposed to moods. Emotions tend to have a faster rise time and shorter durations than moods. Since moods last longer, their causes are likely to be more remote in time and hence less salient. As indicated in Question 3, moods are also typically less intense than emotions and therefore less likely to stand out as discrete events that are situated in time and place. The significance of these facts is simply that emotions per se are less likely to be problematic with respect to biasing irrelevant judgments and decisions. Again, a key to the effects of affective states on judgment lies in the degree to which the cause is salient in consciousness.

Freud. The problem addressed by research on mood and judgment is similar to the problem about which Freud was preoccupied. Freud was also concerned with the potential of emotion to have inappropriate effects on judgment. He was concerned with effects of intense emotion or trauma. Through his talking cure, he got people to remember the circumstances surrounding their original emotional experience, and this process of becoming aware of the cause often dramatically limited subsequent unwanted emotional effects on judgment. As a consequence, Freud developed a theory of unconscious mental processes and focused on the curative effects of making conscious what was unconscious.

Jacoby. Currently, psychologists are rediscovering some of these principles in a more mundane context. For example, Jacoby and his colleagues (Jacoby, Kelley, Brown, & Jasechko, 1989) report a series of experiments in which subjects are asked to pronounce a list of names. At a later time they participate in an ostensibly different experiment in which their task is to identify which names in a list are famous and which are not. There is a slight but reliable tendency for subjects to perceive the nonfamous names they had pronounced in the first study as famous. When they see them later in the second study, the sense of familiarity that these previously seen names engender is misinterpreted as a indication that the names are famous. The effect is obtained, however, only if subjects forget that these are some of the names they had seen earlier in the experiment. Jacoby concludes that he has demonstrated effects of unconscious experience on later judgment, and he shows that if he makes the experience conscious (i.e., if subjects remember seeing the names), the effect goes away.

This story seems adequate as far as it goes, but the implied model of unconscious processes is probably false. Freud's original model, for example, went something like this. Affect was seen as the energy in the mental system, and its aim was to be expressed. Being expressed generally required being attached to an idea, which it could then propel into consciousness. In the process of repression, an unacceptable idea would be kept from consciousness by having its energy stripped away. The aim of the energy to be expressed could then be achieved by attaching itself to an associated but harmless idea. Having been originally associated with an important idea, however, the repressed energy would sometimes be large in quantity, so that it would drive the harmless idea into consciousness with inappropriate force. This can be seen, said Freud, in obsessive-compulsive disorders, when a person becomes intensely preoccupied with a seemingly meaningless idea or action. Through such techniques as hypnosis or free association, the goal of therapy was to trace the symbolic link to the unconscious idea so that it could be expressed and the patient could be relieved of his or her symptoms.

Schwarz and Clore. Contemporary research on mood-biased judgment also seeks to explain how an initially modest idea can become inappropriately extreme by inheriting objectless affect. In this case too, the problem stems from the fact that one can be unaware of the true source of one's affective state, so that the affective value of an object becomes inflated by affective experience from a different source. As in the Freudian case, the cure for such distortion is to re-establish awareness of the true cause of the affective experience. Note that this affect-as-information explanation (Schwarz & Clore, 1983) is different from the analysis offered by Freud or Jacoby. In this view, the unconscious mental content does not influence judgment directly but only indirectly by reducing the informativeness of affective feedback. What is unconscious are the circumstances from which the affect arises; the reason this is important is that without such episodic constraints of time, place, and circumstance, the affective experience is unconstrained, without meaning, and hence potentially relevant to anything. In the previously cited research by Jacoby, and probably also in the cases cited by Freud, it is what is conscious, not what is unconscious that contaminates judgment. What is conscious is the experience of feeling happy, angry, fearful, or guilty. When this experience is one of free-floating affect (e.g., moods and diffuse states of irritability or anxiety) the experience can have wide-ranging influence. But when the experience is of "bound affect" (affect attached to a specific object), such influences are less likely to occur.

Displacement. The contrast between explanations of mood effects that focus on conscious versus unconscious processes can further be seen in cases of what Freud would have called "displaced aggression." If one were to kick one's dog instead of one's boss, a Freudian analysis would focus on the role of unconscious affect. It would maintain that the unconscious energy from repressed anger had accomplished its aim of being expressed by attaching itself to a safer, substitute object (the idea of the dog) somewhere in the unconscious. Our own view focuses not on the misdirection of unconscious affect, but on the misdirection of conscious affect. Without the constraints imposed by awareness of the source, the consciously experienced affect of anger is free to be attributed to (or experienced as a reaction to) some other event with anger potential.

This "displacement" process is a very common occurrence. Consider a tired parent whose child knocks his milk over, for example. In the experience of the parent, the background feelings of irritation left from a long day at work and the focal irritation of the split milk may become one irritation. The felt intensity of irritation informs the parent (inappropriately) that the spilt milk is a serious offense. This implicit judgment of extreme blameworthiness in turn elicits an outburst of anger and punitiveness. Later, when the parent is no longer in the same state, he or she may feel guilty for the outburst. Considered without the same baseline of irritation from work, the spilt milk is no longer experienced as so blameworthy. Then a punitive reaction no longer seems justifiable and indeed seems itself blameworthy. These things can then be cyclical, in that the irritation at one's own action raises the baserate of irritation, increasing the likelihood of a new outburst at some new infraction. This example thus illustrates the principle that what is lost when the source of an emotion is unconscious are the limits on the potential relevance of the associated cues. Without such limits, the information that the cues usually provide can easily become misinformation.

If a psychotherapist were to enter the situation just described, a prime goal would be to try to reduce the level of expressed anger. This could best be done by reducing the person's orientation of self-blame. This should help to the extent that it reduces the total background experience of irritation available for misattribution, so that the child's misdeeds would be less likely to be experienced as serious and hence less likely to elicit inappropriate outbursts.

Summary

In agreement with Freud (1915), the position was taken that emotions cannot be unconscious because they must be felt, and feelings are by definition conscious. The possibility of emotions that are not felt, and hence are not conscious, was entertained and rejected. Feeling was considered a necessary (although not a sufficient) condition for emotion. From the perspective of the affect-as-information hypothesis (Schwarz & Clore, 1983), a primary function of emotion is to provide feedback in the form of emotional experience. The realization of such an informational function requires that people be conscious of their emotions, otherwise the feedback loop would be broken.

Even though emotions themselves are conscious, the appraisals that elicit them often are not. Thus, people can be puzzled or surprised by their own emotions. When the cause is insufficiently salient in consciousness, emotions can bias judgments and decisions by being misattributed. This is more common for moods than for emotions, because the causes of emotions are generally more salient than the causes of moods. The affect-as-information model was contrasted to the model implicit in Freud's account and to a similar model implied in recent research by Jacoby and his colleagues. In each of these models a therapeutic effect is achieved by making conscious the cause of feelings that might otherwise become attached to an irrelevant idea.

Emotional Processing, But Not Emotions, Can Occur Unconsciously

JOSEPH E. LEDOUX

Nonconscious emotions need to be distinguished from nonconscious emotional processes. In my view, "emotions" are affectively charged, subjectively experienced states of awareness. Emotions, in other words, are conscious states. While nonconscious emotions do not exist, conscious emotional states are produced by unconscious processes. This is simply a statement about emotional consciousness that is often made about consciousness in general—that the content of consciousness is determined by processes that are themselves not accessible to consciousness (Jackendoff, 1987; Kihlstrom, 1987; Johnson-Laird, 1988; Lashley, 1956). Emotions, though conscious, emerge from nonconscious processes.

Previously, I have suggested that the evaluation of stimulus significance lies at the heart of emotional processing and is the basis of both the expression of emotion (behaviorally as well as viscerally) and the experience of emotion (LeDoux, 1984, 1986, 1987, 1989). To the extent that conscious emotional experience is a consequence of emotional evaluation, emotional evaluation occurs nonconsciously. Emotional evaluation is similar to the concept of cognitive appraisal (Arnold, 1960; Lazarus, 1982, 1991). However, in emotional evaluation the emphasis is on the emotional nature of the function, whereas in cognitive appraisal the emphasis is on the cognitive nature of the function. One advantage of my view is that I can localize emotional evaluation functions to the amygdala, at least for the processing of threatening events (see Question 5). The amygdala plays little role in the kinds of processes that most cognitive scientists think of as cognitive processes (see Question 5). In the absence of a clearer notion of what appraisal is and how it might relate to other cogntive processes with specific neural representations, the concept of an amygdala-based evaluation system seems more useful. However, in addition to this fundamental difference in how we view the evaluative process, I also differ with appraial theorists in another way. Appraisal theorists allow appraisal to be willful and conscious. I do not reject the possibility of conscious evaluations, but feel that it is useful to see how much of emotion can be explained without resorting to conscious intervention in the causation of emotion.

Interestingly, and not often recognized, most ideas about the origin of emotional experience implicitly assume an unconscious evaluative (appraisal) mechanism. For example, in bodily feedback (James, 1884; Lange, 1887), facial feedback (Izard, 1977; Tomkins, 1962), arousal (Duffy, 1941, 1962; Lindsley, 1951), and cognitive/arousal (Mandler, 1975; Schachter & Singer, 1962; Schachter, 1975) theories, the consequences of emotional arousal give rise to the conscious experiences we call emotions. These theories are mostly concerned with the proximal causes of conscious experience and tend to start with the assumption that the organism is emotionally aroused without asking what gives rise to the arousal in the first place. The brain must first evaluate the stimulus and determine that it is emotionally significant before producing the various manifestations of emotional arousal that then lead to conscious emotional experience of the stimulus. Since emotional evaluation leads to conscious emotional experience, evaluation, it would seem, must itself be a preconscious or unconscious process. The content of emotional consciousness, in other words, is determined by processes that occur unconsciously. As such, emotional experiences (i.e., feelings of fear or anger or love) reflect the representation in conscious awareness of the information processing occurring in brain systems specialized to mediate the various stimulus evaluation processes and the various behavioral and visceral responses characteristic of each emotion. This view is largely compatible with cognitive theories that emphasize unconscious processing as the entry point to emotional conscious emotional experience (e.g., Frijda, 1986; Johnson-Laird, 1988; Kihlstrom, 1990). However, I disagree with strong versions of cognitive theories of emotion that treat emotion as simply a subset of cognition. As I have argued in Question 5, the neural system that computes emotional significance is sufficiently different from the neural systems that perform cognitive computations so that these should be kept separate rather than simply folding emotion into cognition.

Finally, I would like to comment on the possibility of judging the extent to which an emotional process is conscious or not on the basis of its neural organization. My laboratory has for the past decade been studying the neural mechanisms of fear learning and the contribution of pathways that relay sensory information to the amygdala directly from the thalamus, without being first relayed through cortical systems (see the figure in Question 5). This work has often been cited as evidence for precognitive and preconscious emotional processing. As described in Question 5, whether thalamo-amygdala processing is precognitive or not depends on whether cognition starts in the thalamus or cortex. This is a question for cognitive, not for emotion, theory. Regardless of whehter thalamo-amygdala processing is precognitive or not, it is certainly preconscious. At the same time, this should not be taken to mean that information relayed to the amygdala from cortical systems involves conscious awareness. It is probably best to assume that information processing in the brain is carried out unconsciously unless it can be proven that it is actually conscious. To me, unconscious processing is the rule and conscious processing is what needs to be proven. If this view does nothing else, it shows how it is possible to study emotion similarly in organisms that have defensible consciousness (humans) and those for which consciousness cannot be proven (human infants and nonhuman animals).

Evidence for Nonconscious Emotions

ROBERT B. ZAJONC

Emotions are extremely complex phenomena. They involve the immediate sensory reaction to the eliciting stimulus, patterns of autonomic nervous system activations, activity in the central nervous system, muscular efference in the face and other parts of the body, the participation of cognitive processes for appraisal, meaning, or justification, subjective feeling states, and instrumental responses motivated by the emotional state. For emotion to be nonconscious, which of these correlates must also be nonconscious?

Asked in another way, what are the minimal observable indications neccessary for verifying that a nonconscious emotion is in fact being experienced? The most common phenomenon that presumes unconscious components of emotion is free-floating anxiety (Beck, 1976), a state that afflicts millions. Its milder forms are experienced by nearly everyone on a daily basis. We find ourselves somewhat depressed or disgruntled without knowing what brought it about and are ignorant about the object in the environment to which these states are directed or attached. Equally, we often find ourselves cheerful for reasons that escape us entirely. In these cases we are only aware of our feeling states, our moods. Now, if we were also not aware of the fact that we feel anxious or cheerful, would there be any *other* grounds to believe that we are experiencing a nonconscious emotion? I can see no way at present to answer this question with any confidence. Had there been neurochemical or neurophysiological signatures for all the emotions distinguishing each one from the others and all of them from all other psychological states, we could appeal to the corresponding physiological measures. But we are not yet in the position of the radiologist who can ascertain from a MRI test with very good reliability that the patient has a brain tumor even if the patient is not at all aware of having such a condition. So, for the time being, we need at the minimum some subjective affirmation by the person that something like an emotion is being experienced. These need not be direct depositions, such as "Yes, I am very sad," for there now exist indirect measures that some form of affective activation has taken place.

One cannot deal with the question of nonconscious emotions and ignore what Freud had to say about the matter. Curiously, Freud (1915) contradicted himself. At one point he asserts unambiguously

> It is surely the essence of emotion that we should be aware of it, i.e., that it should become known to consciousness. Thus the possibility of the attribute of unconsciousness would be completely excluded as far as emotions, feelings, and affects are concerned (p. 177).

Yet, having said that, he immediately notes

> But in psychoanalytic practice we are accustomed to speak of unconscious love, hate, anger, etc., and find it impossible to avoid the strange conjunction, "unconscious consciousness of guilt," or paradoxical "unconscious anxiety" (pp. 177–178).

The presence of nonconscious affect has been the subject of active research already from four decades ago and it is returning to the field prompted by new methods, techniques, and theories. The earlier interests focused on the phenomenon of perceptual defense (Erdelyi, 1974) and vigilance (Blum, 1954). The scope of nonconscious affective influences, however, soon broadened to include discrimination without awareness (Corteen & Wood, 1972; Lazarus & McCleary, 1951), affective influence of repeated degraded exposures (Bonnano & Stilling, 1986; Bornstein, 1987; Bornstein, Leone, & Galley, 1987; Kunst-Wilson & Zajonc, 1980; Mandler, Nakamura, & VanZandt, 1987; Seamon, Brody, & Kauff, 1983a, 1983b), and nonconscious affective priming (Edwards, 1990; Kitayama, 1991; Murphy & Zajonc, 1987, 1988, 1993; Niedenthal, 1987, 1990).

The clearest instance of nonconscious affective influence is to be found in exposure effects induced with degraded presentations of stimuli. The repeated exposure effect consists of a direct increase in the subject's attitude for an object as a consequence of mere repeated exposures of that object (see Bornstein, 1989, and Harrison, 1977, for reviews). The effect can also be obtained when the exposures are so degraded that the person is not aware that anything at all had been presented (Kunst-Wilson & Zajonc, 1980). There is a clear change in the preference for objects presented under these degraded conditions even when the subjects are unable to discriminate these objects from others that had not been presented, and even when they are unable to attribute the differences in their liking for some stimuli to their previous experience. This latter is also true when the exposures are given at optimal viewing conditions. That familiarity is not involved in these effects is shown by the fact that the liking scores depend almost entirely on the objective history of the persons' experiences with the object rather than their perceptions of familiarity of these objects (Matlin, 1971; Moreland & Zajonc, 1977, 1979). It is of some interest that Bornstein (1987) reports stronger exposure effects with suboptimal presentations.

The second technique for observing effects of nonconscious affect is in the nonconscious affective priming. When a photograph of a smiling face is presented at very short intervals, say 4 msec, just before another neutral and unrelated stimulus (say a Chinese ideograph) is shown for 1 second, the Chinese ideograph receives a higher affective rating than when nothing is shown previously or when a face with an angry expression is shown (Kitayama, 1991; Murphy & Zajonc, 1987, 1988, 1993; Niedenthal, 1987, 1990). Curiously, the same procedure involving the optimal presentation of the same affective primes produces no results. The ratings of Chinese ideographs remain uninfluenced. The explanation of these seemingly paradoxical results involves assuming the participation of nonconscious affect and its distinction from cases when affect is based on prior cognitive appraisal.

I have argued elsewhere (Zajonc, 1980) that affective influences can occur without the participation of cognitive processes and when such influences do take place, affect will be gross, diffuse, and possibly nonconscious. In arguing for the independence of affect from cognition, Kunst-Wilson and I tried to show that affective reactions can occur sooner than their cognitive counterparts, a hypothesis later empirically confirmed (Kunst-Wilson & Zajonc, 1980). Murphy and Zajonc (1993) explored this general proposition in a recent paper. In the case of nonconscious affective priming, we assume that the slide of a facial expression, present for a small fraction of a second, is sufficient to evoke an affective reaction. But this reaction is gross, diffuse, and nonspecific. Affective priming can elicit these affective states rapidly and it can do so when the exposures are well below the subject's awareness. However, under these conditions only affective polarity can be discriminated. No finer distinctions among affective influences are made. A smiling expression produces positive nonspecific affect and a frowning face produces negative nonspecific affect. The following figure shows these effects in curves A^+ and A^-.

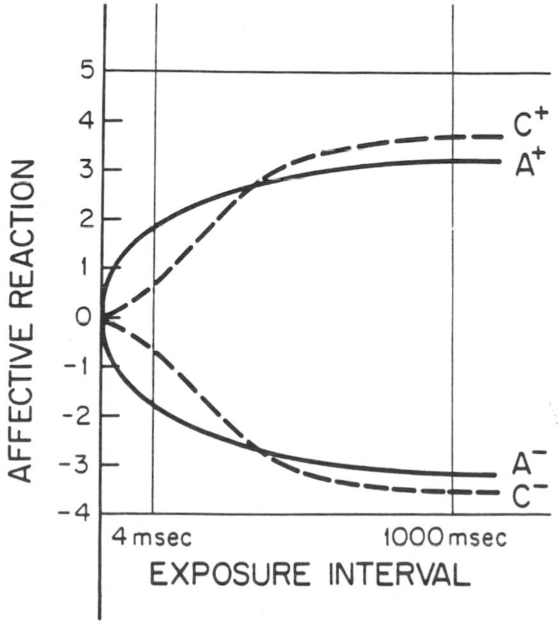

Theoretical values of affective reactions based on early affective (A^+ and A^-) and slower cognitive access (C^+ and C^-). From Murphy and Zajonc (1993).

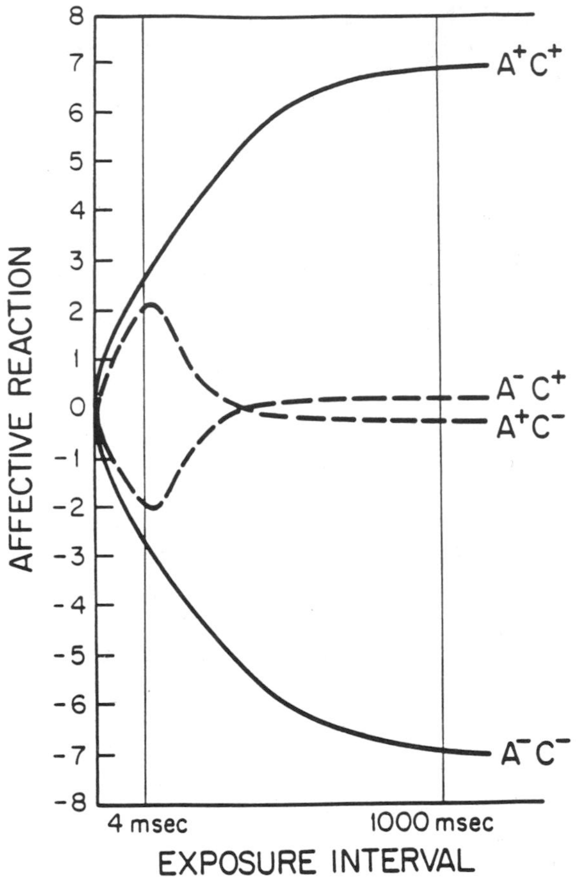

Theoretical values of affective reactions accumulating from early affective access and subsequent cognitive appraisal. Continuous curves represent accumulation when the two sources are consistent; broken curves represent inconsistent sources. From Murphy and Zajonc (1993).

Also shown in the figure are curves of growth of affect deriving from cognitive sources. Thus, we might find that the person in the slide is a highly decorated hero, a movie star, or a dreaded rapist. These affective influences based on cognitive sources are represented by the curves C^+ and C^- for positive and negative cognition-based affect. Note that affect formed from cognitive sources is slower to accumulate and rise. The important differences between nonconscious affect and nonconscious cognition lie in the specificity of these two processes. While nonconscious affect is gross and diffuse and its specificity is limited only to an approach-avoidance distinction, nonconscious cognition is content-specific. One can see this best in priming effects. Probably any stimulus can be subject to nonconscious affective priming. Thus, for instance, Murphy and Zajonc (1993) were able to use a slide of a facial expression to prime Chinese ideographs. However, nonconscious cognition is constrained by its content. Thus, semantic priming is referent-specific. One can prime the word CHAIR by the word TABLE, but not by the word GALAXY.

Now, if exposures are prolonged so that more stimulus information becomes available to the person, the affective reactions gain in specificity because cognitive appraisals are recruited. Under these enriched conditions finer distinctions can be made and the affect evoked gains in specificity. If the affective reaction that is brought about by a cognitive appraisal is congruent with the early nonconscious affective influence, the two effects will summate and there will be a stronger reaction. If, however, they are incongruent—if under longer exposures, the smiling face reveals some monstrous features, for example—the polarity of the affective reaction will be cancelled or even reversed. These patterns are shown in the following figure in which the A^+C^+ and A^-C^- are the cases where the polarities deriving from direct affect (say, that based on priming) and cognitive-based affect are congruent, and A^+C^- and A^-C^+ are incongruent. It is thus possible for nonconscious affective priming to have a stronger influence than priming induced at optimal levels of viewing, if A and C influences do not agree. These results were experimentally confirmed in a number of studies (Murphy & Zajonc, 1993). More recently, Murphy, Monahan, and Zajonc (under review), have shown that affect deriving from degraded repeated exposures and affect deriving from nonconscious priming are both diffuse and nonspecific for their joint effects manifest an additive pattern.

It is, of course, much more difficult to know much about emotions that are repressed, although Shevrin (1990) has been able to show indirect effects of repressed conflicts by using a combination of EEG and subliminal presentations. Here again, of course, some aspect of the emotion is at least partly accessible to awareness. Otherwise, the patient would not have come for help. The complete answer to the question of affect and awareness must wait until we know more about both affect and awareness, for we are still far from reaching a level of adequate scientific understanding in either of these problem areas.

Afterword: Can Emotions Be Nonconscious?

RICHARD J. DAVIDSON
PAUL EKMAN

Each of the commentators on this question agrees that components of emotional processing can occur in the absence of consciousness. Each also emphasizes different aspects of this problem, although there is considerable consensus.

Both Clore and LeDoux are explicit on the point that emotions per se are conscious states. Clore proposes that feelings are a necessary (but not sufficient) component of emotion and feelings are, by definition, conscious. LeDoux also concurs in the view that nonconscious emotions do not exist. However, LeDoux notes that conscious emotional states are products of unconscious processes. He further suggests that this appears to be a general principle of consciousness—that contents of consciousness are determined by processes that are themselves not accessible to consciousness. On this view emotions, though conscious, emerge from nonconscious processes.

Both Clore and Zajonc argue that if the source or eliciting context of an emotion is unconscious, the emotion will be diffuse. It may be experienced as part of one's reaction to almost anything and hence may color one's judgment of almost anything. Zajonc likens emotion elicited in this way to moisture, which can nonspecifically affect anything with which it comes into contact. Zajonc distinguishes nonconscious cognition from nonconscious affect (i.e., emotion elicited by a nonconscious source) by suggesting that the former is dedicated, while the latter is not. Nonconscious cognition must always have a referent; it is always about something. In contrast, nonconscious emotion can be free-floating and "spill over" from one stimulus to another.

LeDoux does not reject the possibility that emotional stimulus evaluations can be made consciously, but finds it useful to determine how much of emotion can be explained without resorting to conscious intervention. He believes that this view also underscores the utility of studying emotion in species in whom consciousness cannot be definitively established.

The complexity of the interaction between consciousness and emotion is no different than for the interaction between consciousness and other psychological processes such as cognition or attention. However, growing evidence does suggest that when emotion is elicited by stimuli outside conscious awareness, the emotion that is generated has different consequences compared with contexts in which the eliciting stimuli are conscious. Consciousness of the eliciting context appears to place constraints on the degree to which the affect is referent-free. While the present analyses illustrate one important way in which a component of emotion–its eliciting circumstances–can be nonconscious, they do not address the possibility that components of the emotional response itself may be nonconscious. For example, a person may be conscious of some of the changes in autonomic nervous system activity that are occurring but unaware of the changes in posture or expression. The reverse would seem less likely, but there is no evidence on that point. Also possible is the situation in which both the eliciting stimulus and the emotional response are conscious, but the person is unaware of the relation between them. People could also be aware of the eliciting stimulus, and their responses, but identify the emotion they are experiencing differently, presumably because of defenses against acknowledging that emotion.

We have reason to be optimistic about future contributions to this thorny issue since all the contributors illustrate new experimental paradigms in which these elusive questions will be treated empirically.

Question 9

What Is the Relation Between Emotion and Memory?

Some Relations Between Emotions and Memory

GORDON H. BOWER

Emotion and memory are related by several different causal strands. To begin with background, emotions are known to arise from many causes. Some are like "startle" reactions to sudden loud noises, slipping, or falling. Most other emotions arise as we translate our motives and concerns into goal-directed actions in a largely unpredictable environment. When our actions lead to outcomes appraised as achieving our concerns, or aiding plans to achieve them, we experience a positive emotion of pleasure, pride, delight, relief, or enjoyment. But events interpreted as thwarting our plans, as causing injury or loss of a goal-state, lead us to experience a negative emotion of sadness, fear, or anger. Which specific emotion is aroused depends on the circumstances and cognitions surrounding the event, including especially one's ability to cope with negative events.

A first major influence of emotion on memory is mediated through its influence on *attention*; attention in turn enhances later memory for the attended event. Attention is largely controlled by the "interestingness" of the event; that is partly determined by the unexpected character of the event (an "anomaly") and its affective significance (e.g., sex and violence).

A central idea in learning theory is that learning is driven by expectation failure; when events don't happen as expected, we have to learn more, to adjust our expectations to a changed reality. Such expectation failures are also likely to be causes of emotional reactions, as Mandler (1984) hypothesized in his "interruption" theory. When an action plan is blocked or thwarted due to some unsatisfied precondition (e.g., your car stalls, making you late for a job interview), that interruption causes frustration or upset which mobilizes attention and new learning that has two aims: (1) to search for some way to modify the ongoing plan to deal with the immediate blockage, and (2) to identify the unsatisfied precondition and devise means to prevent its recurrence on future occasions. Optimally, the emotional reaction to the interruption or unexpected outcome focuses attention on the relevant feature of the situation that might explain (or have caused) the failure, so that the person learns how to refine expectations adaptively.

Besides controlling attention to selected aspects of the external situation, a strong affective reaction after an event also causes the recycling, rehearsal, or "mulling over" in working memory of the trace of that event. This reactivation may reflect the persisting influence of hormones released during the emotional episode; but, even days later, the person may repeatedly resurrect the memory of the emotional event and relive it, thereby strengthening its memory. This tendency underlies the uncontrollable, traumatic flashbacks seen in extreme form in victims of post-traumatic stress disorder.

To summarize, emotions play three separate roles in directing learning. First, emotions frequently accompany failed expectations (or interruptions), and thus direct attention to accompanying events as important items to be learned. Second, emotions mobilize attention to those features of an external situation that learners judge to be sigificant or predictive of the cause of the failed expectation, and, in so doing, cause greater learning of them. Third, the inertial persistence of the emotional arousal, and its slow decay, leads to continued recycling or rehearsal of those encoded events viewed as causally belonging to the emotional reaction. All these factors promote better learning of relevant emotional material.

Abundant evidence indicates that people better remember events that evoke greater emotional reactions, whether positive or negative. The advantage appears not only in laboratory experiments that manipulate the emotional quality of material but even more strongly in studies of autobiographical memory. When people record and rate the emotional intensity of events in a daily diary, their later recall of an event is greater the more emotionally intense it had been rated originally.

Other influences arise because the mind accords a privileged status to emotional stimuli in its information processing. For example, in laboratory experiments, stimuli that arouse a strong emotional reaction (say, an erotic picture among a series of dull photographs) will be better remembered than the dull items around it. Moreover, because the emotional item captures priority of processing in working memory, it causes attentional resources to be withdrawn from neutral items that just preceded or just followed the emotional stimulus, so they are learned less well.

Similar mixed effects of emotional focussing can also be shown for a multiobject visual scene or film, say, of a bank robber accidentally shooting a bystander. Observers will remember the gist of the shooting very well but do worse than appropriate controls at remembering peripheral details, such as the wall clock, the color of the clothes on other bystanders, and so on. Thus, emotion does not enhance memory for all details of the arousing scene; instead, it focuses attention on the central part of the scene (the gun, the blood, etc.) so that that part is better remembered. But this enhanced memory occurs at the expense of peripheral details not perceived as relevant to the central event.

A corollary of this view—that emotions soak up processing resources—is that reactions to some emotionally significant feature of a scene can detract from processing information about some concurrent, independent event. This can have the consequence that the person stores in memory very little information about the concurrent event. Such "distraction" appears to be operative whenever emotions create decrements in learning and performance of some target behavior. For example, very anxious or depressed people are notoriously poor learners because their working memory is so preoccupied or "filled" with upsetting ruminations that few attentional resources are devoted to the learning or recall tasks being measured.

The idea that emotional arousal directs attention has also arisen in another set of studies concerned with mood-congruity effects in cognition and learning (see Bower, 1990, 1992). The hypothesis is that people in a given emotional or mood state attend more to stimulus events, objects, or situations that are affectively congruent with their emotional state. Thus, happy people find pleasant stimuli—words, descriptions, pictures, people, music—more attractive, salient, attention-provoking; as a result, such stimuli receive deeper processing and are better learned. Oddly, sad people seem to prefer the opposite types of stimuli—serious, somber, nostalgic music, movies, or stories—and such stimuli receive deeper processing when people are in a somber mood. Even when the processing time allotted to congruent and incongruent stimuli is equated, people still learn more about emotionally congruent stimuli. One explanation of this advantage is that emotionally congruent material evokes more plentiful associations that can be used to elaborate the material at the time it is being studied, thus linking it more firmly into memory.

A final relation of emotion to memory arises with emotion-state dependent memory (Bower, 1992). A memory learned in a given emotional state may be more retrievable later if the person returns to an emotional state similar to what prevailed during the original learning. Mood-dependent memory has proven to be a small, elusive effect, but it has been observed so frequently and reliably in circumscribed conditions that it must be considered a genuine phenomenon (Eich, 1992).

One explanation of the pattern of successful and unsuccessful demonstrations of mood-dependent memory uses a "causal belonging" hypothesis. This hypothesis states that subjects will most readily associate an emotion with a stimulus or a situation if they causally relate their emotional reaction to the occurrence of that stimulus. If they perceive the situation and the emotional reaction as causally belonging together, then according to this hypothesis they will forge a strong associative bond between the stimulus event and the emotion it evokes. As a result, later retrieval of the memory for that event should be aided by recurrence of that same emotional state. Emotional state-dependent memory has numerous implications for social and clinical phenomena that have been elaborated in several papers (Bower, 1990, 1992).

In summary, motivation and emotion serve multiple functions in the cognitive system. While motivation mobilizes resources for actions, directs attention, and guides execution of plans, emotions serve largely as "commentators" reacting to the present situation, evaluating the execution of plans and their outcomes. Emotions often signal to the cognitive system the important discrepancies (between actual and expected outcomes) that are to be reduced by further learning. The emotion directs attention to the causally significant aspects of the discrepant situation, serves to encode and index the unusual event in memory, and promotes persisting rehearsal of the corrective actions. In this way, new learning articulates a more accurate model of the current situation to guide future expectations about similar situations. Also, later arousal of an emotion retrieves associated thoughts, plans, and memories. This selective retrieval underlies such phenomena as mood-congruent biases in thinking, preferences, judgment, learning, and mood-state dependent memory.

The Past and the Present in Emotion

RICHARD LAZARUS

Two major themes may be found in current concerns with emotion or mood and memory. The first is that of *state-dependent recall*, which means that what one remembers depends on whether one's mood is positive or negative (e.g., Bower, 1981; Clark & Isen, 1982; Forgas, Bower, & Krantz, 1984). Although this has been challenged by Parrott and Sabini (1990), positive emotional experiences are often found to be recalled more when one's mood is positive, and negative emotional experiences are recalled more when one's mood is negative.

Second, the mood one is in, or the emotion being experienced, affects performance and prosocial behaviors, such as being helpful to others (see Forgas & Bower, 1987; Isen, 1970, 1984, who has used the expression "the warm glow of success" for this effect; Moore, Underwood, & Rosenhan, 1984).

Here I want to address why and how emotional memories are elicited and discuss the connection between the current encounter and the past emotional memory. I will use the terms mood and emotion interchangeably because they have never been distinguished in the research performed on this problem. My approach also differs from that of many who are connected with this research arena in important ways. My concept of relational meaning in particular shapes the way I view emotional memory.

The Molar Concept of Relational Meaning

The traditional approach to emotional memory is associationistic, that is, it deals with molecular elements, such as fleeting images and fragments of ideas, that ultimately become connected psychologically by association. When such connections are established through learning, the presence of one then calls forth the other—hence associative priming.

Emotions are always about some special harm or benefit that inheres in the relationship between the person and the environment. My concept of *core relational themes*, which I have already discussed in Questions 2 and 5, and elsewhere (Lazarus, 1991c) makes the point. Guilt carries the relational meaning that one has transgressed a moral imperative, shame that one has failed to live up to an ego-ideal, sadness that one has experienced an irrevocable loss, hope that one fears the worst but yearns for better, and so forth.

In my view, these relational meanings are not separate fragments connected by association, but express complex relationships whose bottom line is always, as J. A. Singer (1990) notes, the relevance of what is happening to the attainment or nonattainment of a person's goal commitments. Emotions really have to do with scenarios of meaning, stories or plots, as it were. They are present in the mind as core relational themes.

Although I suppose a fragment can be a cue to the whole scenario, it cannot express the relational meaning without invoking the theme, which in its detailed form is a complex story of the fate of one's goals in an encounter with the external world. This theme or basic plot—not the fragment—is what contains the emotional meaning. With additional detail, this is what we remember of an emotional experience. Each fragment or component of the story seems to connote the entire scenario of harm, threat, or benefit.

Though a researcher might center attention only on one element, it is always part of a larger configuration, which is what provides the personal meaning and expresses recurrent basic human struggles and outcomes, including interpersonal themes of being demeaned, failing, escaping harm, succeeding, losing, overcoming, gaining, giving, loving, and being admired as wonderful or rejected as inadequate or unworthy. Within this list of basic human struggles and outcomes are all the emotions, which result from one or another of these elemental plots or themes. Humans in all cultures and times have struggled with these themes, albeit in different ways and perhaps expressing them with different languages (see Russell, 1991).

Even though their approach is associationistic, Rholes, Riskind, and Lane (1987, p. 92) interpret their research findings on the effects of cognitive priming and mood on memory in a way that is quite compatible with what I have just said because its bottom line is cognitive, or what I refer to as relational meaning. They write:

> The effect of mood on memory retrieval may be at least partially accounted for in the following way. An emotion-producing event, such as a failure, occurs and produces both an affective state and a set of relevant cognitions (e.g., self-devaluation). The cognitions produced by the event then directly prime, or semantically cue, other items in long-term memory (e.g., life experiences) that are associated with them, thus increasing their recall accessibility. In other words, it may be mood-related cognitions, rather than affect per se, that at least in part influence memory retrieval. This cognitive process, of course, is not necessarily incompatible with state dependent learning. It is conceivable that both can operate at the same time.

Laird (1989) has pointed out the irony that the way researchers deal with effects of mood on memory is no different from the effects of any cognitive variable, suggesting that there is nothing special about emotion that isn't also cognitive. Moods and emotions are complex interpersonal events, and the term mood should be used to stand for the truly important components of the whole—that is, goals and their fate, thoughts, and meanings—not merely arousal. Laird lists six easily identified components of emotion (leaving out coping, however, which I would add as a seventh): the eliciting event, the appraisal of that event, patterns of autonomic reponse, expressive behavior, instrumental action, and the subjective feeling.

I would add that these components are always interdependent if we think of emotion, as I do, as a system. I suppose that any or all of the components can produce emotional effects on memory or lead to memory retrieval. However, what is most important, I believe, is the core relational theme, which carries the relational meaning on which the emotion depends. It is not the associational details that are crucial, but the relational meaning that links them all together in an emotional experience.

What Connects the Past with the Present?

It is usually said that one of the provocations to an emotion is the memory of a prior emotional encounter. This traditional approach to emotional memory turns inward to what is in memory rather than being relational, which should have to do with the functional connection between what a person wants and believes and what is happening in the environment.

What I think is missing from this tradition is that the memory does not occur in a vacuum, but is generated in an adaptational encounter or setting in which it is functionally connected with what is now happening. Most commonly, I suppose, one is struggling with one of the classic human problems such as I described earlier, which are apt to be recurrent. Most such problems in adults are not totally new, except in certain details, but reinstate struggles of the past that have not been resolved.

This sort of reasoning can be found in the Freudian notion of repetition compulsion in which unresolved difficulties of the past keep recurring in the present, presumably in the struggle to undo them. Although I do not find the mechanical feature of this idea useful, the principle that a functional connection exists between a memory or a dream about the past and what is happening now seems quite useful (see Breger, Hunter, & Lane, 1971; Horowitz, 1976, 1988). Most encounters are thought by the person experiencing them to be new. However, in most adults who have already struggled with many life issues, there must be general schemata in the mind for deciding whether similar or different appraisals and coping processes are called for. We can consider neurosis as a manifestation of rigidity about the past and present, and healthy coping as calling for flexibility, so that how we react and manage these classic struggles can be changed as advantageous or necessary.

The reason for the connection between the past emotional memory and the present adaptational encounter is easy to imagine from a superficial standpoint. Though it might not be obvious to the person involved, both encounters are functionally similar. Nevertheless, psychologists have long been confused about how formally (i.e., as a rule) to identify what makes the two events similar. The details may differ greatly even though the core relational theme is the same.

Freud's observations about the clinical case of Little Hans implied, reasonably, that the horse Hans feared symbolized his father, which helped explain why it was a phobic object. Indeed, our intuition invokes a similarity between a powerful male stallion and the father. The idea of this similarity seems right. However, similarity is typically a subjective product of individual history and subjective judgment rather than a matter of objective—rule-based—measurement of the qualities that seem to connect the two events or objects. The same problem applies to what might be said about private and universal symbols, which are part of dream interpretation and free association (see also Jung, 1960).

Furthermore, not only are no two adaptational encounters ever the same, but as we grow older, we form new schemata, and the reconstruction of past encounters tends to change. I believe that the notion of a core relational theme, which brings the details together in a gestalt of relational meaning, could serve as a useful criterion of functional similarity, for example, about being loved or rejected, experiencing gain or loss, being demeaned, or having one's ego-identity enhanced, and so forth.

It has also occurred to me that the core relational theme, because it is a meaningful plot or scenario, should help us remember better than any meaningless jumble of images and event fragments. When my wife and I watch old television movies, it often takes us quite a while into the movie to remember whether we have seen it before. Then suddenly we will recognize that we had. For a long time I did not understand why. I think what happens is that the early scenes—especially in some movies—often fail to reveal the plot or story line. The events operate in our minds like nonsense syllables, which, we know, are more difficult to learn than meaningful materials, such as a story line. The instant the plot, with its core relational theme, is revealed, we remember. I propose that emotional memory is always triggered by a core relational theme in the present that is functionally related to the one in memory; perhaps only a fragment can do this—I am not really sure—but the relational meaning always does because it is the most interpretable and salient feature of the emotional encounter (see also Lewis & Williams, 1989).

How Do Positive Moods Facilitate Performance and Pro-Social Acts?

Much research, some of which I cited at the outset, has shown that positive moods—without regard for the mood particulars—improve the quality of performance and generate prosocial behaviors, such as being helpful to others. Why should this be? Most interpretations draw on the concept of *associative priming* in which positive thoughts are primed by positive moods. People are said to store material in memory on the basis of its affective tone. The good mood is a cue that increases the probability of positive thoughts, so the person feeling good will evaluates others more favorably and is more ready to offer assistance. This explanation is molecular, that is, it has recourse to associative connections among fragments of core relational themes or relational meaning.

I prefer a more holistic and molar account of what is happening here, one that draws on the idea that we are constantly appraising our relationships with the environment from the standpoint of their bearing on our well-being, and reacting accordingly. When people have positive experiences, they tend to feel safe, self-confident, and expansive. Elsewhere (Lazarus, 1981; Lazarus & Folkman, 1984; Lazarus & Launier, 1978), and in the context of a performance, I have referred to this state as *challenged* in contrast with threat.

Whereas being threatened means we are in danger and need self-protection, threat leads us to be wary, constrained, inhibited, and defensive, which leads us to hold back so as not to increase the danger or make a fool of ourselves. Such a state of mind interferes with risk taking, trust, and smooth cognitive functioning. When we are challenged, on the other hand, thoughts flow easily (cf. Csikszentmihalyi, 1975). We are at one with the world, and view what is happening as benign or benefical. We think of others favorably and want to do good to them.

It should not surprise us that positive moods produce states like challenge, with their favorable consequences in human functioning, but that being threatened, hence anxious, has negative consequences. This is an old idea about which much research was conducted during the 1950s and 1960s (see reviews by Holzman & Bitterman, 1956, Horvath, 1959, Lazarus, 1966, Lazarus, Deese, & Osler, 1952, and Sarason, 1960, and a recent reexamination of the effects of stress or anxiety by Glanzmann, 1985). There continues to be interest in the problem in the form of the concept of test anxiety.

The failure of those whose work has focused on moods or emotions and social functioning to cite much older work (30 to 40 years ago) on stress and anxiety illustrates the parochial and unfortunate isolation that exists between the two literatures (Lazarus, 1993).

Memory Versus Emotional Memory in the Brain

JOSEPH E. LEDOUX

Emotion and memory are often discussed together, usually for the purpose of showing how emotion influences memory. The psychoanalytic theory of repression, the flashbulb-memory hypothesis, the Yerkes-Dodson law, the mood congruity hypothesis of memory, and hedonic theories of reinforcement are examples (see LeDoux, 1992d). However, besides being a factor that can influence memory, emotional information can also be stored as a memory. The important question is not whether emotional memory exists but instead whether it is a unique form of memory. The best evidence for its uniqueness comes from the neural organization of memory.

"Memory" usually refers to our ability to consciously reflect on past experiences. This kind of memory has come to be called explicit or declarative memory (e.g., Eichenbaum, 1992; Schacter, 1987; Squire, 1987; Tobias, Kihlstrom, & Schacter, 1992). The neural system underlying declarative memory has been identified through studies of humans and experimental animals over the past 30 to 40 years. This work has shown that the hippocampal formation is an essential component of the declarative memory system. Following damage to the hippocampus, the ability to store information so that it can be consciously recalled on later occasions is severely compromised. While the amygdala has long been thought to play an important role (Mishkin, 1982), recent studies suggest that the amygdala itself contributes little to declarative memory (Murray, 1992; Zola-Morgan et al., 1991).

The effects of hippocampal damage are relatively specific for declarative memory, leaving many other forms of memory intact. Examples of spared memory functions include certain aspects of motor skill learning, reflex conditioning, and priming (see Squire, 1987). Most significant for the present discussion is the fact that hippocampal lesions have no effect on the conditioning of emotional memories, which instead critically depend on the amygdala (see LeDoux, 1990, 1992a, 1992b).

When the amygdala is damaged, the emotional significance of a stimulus previously established by association with rewards or punishments is lost, along with the ability to form new associations of this kind (see Aggleton, 1992). Amygdala damage interferes with involuntary emotional responses "released" by conditioned or unconditioned stimuli, as well as with some (but certainly not all) voluntary, instrumental responses (see Question 7 for more details).

The hippocampal formation and amygdala thus form the hubs of two central memory networks. The hippocampus, but not the amygdala, is involved in explicit or declarative memory and the amygdala, but not the hippocampus, is involved in emotional memory. These systems operate in parallel and simultaneously lay down traces of a given experience.

It is important to distinguish emotional memory from memory of emotion. The latter is a declarative, conscious memory of an emotional experience. It is stored as a fact about an emotional episode. Emotional memory (mediated by the amygdala) and memory of emotion (mediated by the hippocampus) can be reactivated in parallel on later occasions, thereby giving new declarative memories an emotional flavor.

Because emotional memory and memory for emotion are stored through different brain systems, it is possible that the information stored will not always coincide. This may be due to the fact that the systems have different inputs (the amygdala but not the hippocampus receives inputs sensory processing areas in the thalamus and cortex; see the figure in Question 5), but may also be related to the fact that declarative memory can be operated on and modified by other kinds of declarative information in ways that nondeclarative emotional memory cannot. The opportunity for conflicts between declarative and emotional memory is thus there.

In summary, emotional and declarative memory about emotion are mediated by different brain systems. These systems operate simultaneously and in parallel during experiences. As a result, we can have conscious insight into our emotions and emotional memories. However, at the same time, because the systems are separate, this creates the possibility that they will not always coincide, possibly accounting for situations in which our conscious memory of a situation does not match our emotional reaction to the reoccurrence of the stimuli associated with that situation.

Subjectivity May Have Evolved in the Brain as a Simple Value-Coding Process That Promotes the Learning of New Behaviors

JAAK PANKSEPP

In the brain, as in everyday subjective experience, the relationships between emotional and memory mechanisms are bound to be intimate. If the basic emotional circuits encoded primal survival demands that confronted animals early in evolution, then it is reasonable to believe that the emergence of many higher brain mechanisms was premised on the utility of having higher spheres of influence devoted to providing increasing degrees of flexibility for the strategic concerns of the primal emotional systems. The everyday fact of human experience that highlights the tight relationship between emotions and memories is the ease of information retrieval that has been encoded during the powerful emotional experiences (the so-called "flashbulb" memories). In short, the easiest way to light up higher mental processes—of thought, strategies, and conniving—is to activate basic emotional systems (Gray, 1990). When these basic systems have been aroused, then cognitive activity flows spontaneously. Presumably, the basic emotional systems provide the underlying mechanisms for emotion-specific encoding and mood-congruent retrieval processes from long-term memory/knowledge structures. Humans exhibit no difficulty in relating the most frightening, anger provoking, sad, and happy situations that have affected them recently—such memories spill forth as if from artesian springs. It is not a large leap to envision that many memory mechanisms of the brain are intimately governed by those that elaborate emotions. For this reason, it is routine to establish strong conditions of motivation or emotion in animal experiments that are designed to analyze the nature of memory and learning.

Emotional command circuits presumably evolved to provide a rapid and coherent way of recruiting organismic resources (physiological, hormonal, behavioral, and psychological) in response to primal survival needs. In other words, emotional systems allowed organisms to respond adaptively with little need for cognitive activity. Still, there are many reasons to believe (on the basis of anatomical, behavioral, and psychological evidence) that these basic systems that establish primitive response priorities and basic organismic values (affects) eventually became guiding or chaneling forces for the evolution of specific modes of cognitive activity. One recent view along these lines is that "reinforcing events" reflect the fluctuation of activity in emotional systems of the brain (Panksepp, 1986, 1990d) although others believe that emotions reflect the operation of "reinforcing events" (Gray, 1990). However the matter goes much deeper.

The existence of emotional systems reflects the presence of powerful genetic memories in the brain. Indeed, the emotional operating systems are a *prima facia* piece of evidence for the existence of archetypal ancestral memories. Although these "memories" may have little cognitive resolution (and may be largely expressed as affective states), it is not farfetched to suppose that many human myths and legends, passed down through early oral traditions, reflected the existence of these archetypal affective memories in our brains. Traditions of folklore may reflect the ease with which the basic emotional feelings are capable of being linked to world events (to specific scripts) to provide powerful symbolic representations of our evolutionary heritage. Animals may achieve similar ends by the ability of their emotional systems to imbue affectively neutral environmental events with conditional affective values. In short, emotion-specific affective processes may be reflected in many long-standing cultural traditions, and emotion-specific "reinforcement processes" may be important ingredients in the genesis of the most compelling real-life memories that we possess. Although we know very little about the neurobiological details of such processes, a great number of neuropeptides that have been implicated in affective processes are also capable of modulating associative processes *(vide infra)*, and, as I noted in my response to Question 6, the cortex contains peptidergic interneurons and receptor systems for many of the elaborate subcortical peptide systems that appear to have executive roles in coordinating specific types of emotions (for review, see Panksepp, 1993).

In the context of the present question, we should highlight some interesting relationships between emotional memories and dreaming (or rapid-eye-movement (REM) sleep). It is quite remarkable that the dreaming stage of our basic daily rest-activity cycle is so full of emotionality, but that it is also characterized by poor long-term consolidation into our conscious waking memories (i.e., it is difficult to remember one's dreams). Perhaps this is because the REM mechanisms help interweave our unconditional emotional tendencies into conditional habit structures. In other words, the REM process may help solidify the subliminal relations between emotions and memories and thereby help establish the unconscious emotional temperaments of individuals.

In focusing on this emotion-cognition blending process of dreaming, I would also consider a possible way that REM-sleep emerged in evolution. I suspect that it occurred when part of the primal arousal mechanism for basic affective experiences was "forced underground" during brain evolution to assume a new role in routine brain dynamics—perhaps to provide a mechanism whereby the associative conjunction of complex life events and emotion-specific reinforcement processes are solidified. This may sound a bit arcane, but consider the perplexing fact that the REM-sleep generators are deeper in the brainstem than the classical waking circuits of the ascending reticular activating system (ARAS). Although it may seem perplexing to suggest that the dream came before waking in brain evolution, it certainly is the case that the executive mechanisms for REM are deeper (and hence presumably more ancient) in the brainstem than the executive ARAS mechanisms for waking arousal. A reasonable solution to this paradox is that what is now known as the REM mechanism was actually an ancient waking mechanism, one that was devoted exclusively to the arousal of relatively ingrained emotional processes. Indeed, this relationship is highlighted by the behavioral potentials that seem to be enacted during REM: In cats whose REM atonia has been blocked by brainstem lesions, spontaneous cascades of simple emotional scripts are displayed by the sleepwalking animals (Sastre & Jouvet, 1979). These cats exhibits fear, rage, and exploratory behaviors as well as hallucinatory grooming. I infer that the REM state reflects the existence of an ancient emotion-specific arousal mechanism, whose job was to activate emotional behaviors. As the cerebral cortex evolved in response to the evolutionary pressures of interanimal competition, such simple behavior patterns became less useful and were subjected to greater degrees of tonic inhibition. Concurrently, the thalamo-cortical axis came to have its own ARAS-based waking governor (Steriade et al., 1990; Steriade & Llinas, 1988), and the more ancient limbic arousal mechanism may have been relegated to the subsidiary role of reprocessing and amplifying emotional information during the internalized arousal of REM sleep. Perhaps in this way the brain was better able to consolidate complex patterns of exteroceptive and interoreceptive information that the animal had been exposed to in waking. In other words, REM may now provide a neurostatistical mechanism for collating and sifting apparent cause-and-effect relationships (especially the conjunctions of important external and internal events) from the many other coincidences that transpire during waking.

In short, the relationship between emotions and memory mechanisms is bound to be an intimate one, and I suspect that a proper conceptualization of the basic emotional processes of the brain and their respective neurochemistries will provide a powerful avenue for decoding the nature of memories, especially the state-specific retrieval processes that appear to be so abundant in the brain. In the past several years many peptides have been implicated in the control of memory processes, including somatostatin (DeNoble, Hepler, & Barto, 1989; Rubinow, 1986), galanin (Crawley & Wenk, 1989), bombesin (Flood & Morley, 1988), vasoactive intestinal peptide (Flood, Garland, & Morley, 1990) and vasopressin (Dantzer et al., 1987; DeWied & van Ree, 1989; Weingartner et al., 1981). Although emotion-cognition linkages are not well understood yet in terms of underlying mechanisms, we have finally reached a point when these issues can be broached with powerful new neurobiological tools instead of mere words. But to take advantage of these neuroscience riches, we now need to reconceptualize brain functions in animals in more realistic, psychological ways. It is unfortunate that doctrinaire behaviorism is still so influential in modern behavioral neuroscience. Its prejudices continue to retard the development of more realistic conceptions of how the nervous system is functionally organized.

Afterword: What Is the Relation Between Emotion and Memory?

RICHARD J. DAVIDSON
PAUL EKMAN

That a relation between emotion and memory exists has been apparent from the beginnings of research on emotion and is a salient feature of human experience. Individuals tend to remember emotionally charged events particularly well, though some events that have been associated with severe negative emotion may be especially inaccessible to consciousness (e.g., repressed).

Two commentators approach this question from a psychological perspective and two from a biological perspective. It is clear that both perspectives lead to the important realization of a special relation between emotion and memory. Yet neither the contributors from the psychological nor those from the biological perspectives take any account of the other.

Bower describes several different influences of emotion on memory. One influence is mediated through the effects of emotion on attention. We attend more to emotionally salient stimuli and this increased attention in turn enhances our later memory for the event that was attended to.

When emotion is elicited by a discrepancy between our expectations and an event, Bower proposes that our emotions mobilize attention to those features of the stimulus that learners judge to be significant or predictive of the cause of the failed expectation so that they can take the appropriate action to rectify the situation. Bower suggests that one function of emotion is to signal the cognitive system about important discrepancies that are to be reduced by further learning. Another way in which emotion influences memory is through the process of recycling and rehearsal. A strong affective reaction to an event will produce a "mulling over" of a trace of the event in working memory. This will enhance subsequent memory for the event. Bower is careful to note that emotion will not enhance memory for all details of an arousing scene but may act quite selectively. He cites evidence to suggest that strong emotion will enhance memory for the central or focal components of an event, but that such enhancement may occur at the expense of memory for peripheral details.

Bower also comments on two other influences of emotion or mood on memory. One is the mood congruity effect wherein people in a given emotional state attend more to stimuli that are congruent with their emotional state. This phenomenon is a powerful one that can be seen in normal behavior and in psychopathology. In abnormal behavior, the mood congruity effect can often serve to accentuate the psychopathology since the individual reinforces a maladaptive emotional state by overfocusing on stimuli congruent with this state. The second influence described by Bower is emotion-state dependent memory—when information that is learned in a particular emotional state may be more retrievable later if the person returns to an emotional state similar to what prevailed during the original learning. Although the empirical status of this effect has been somewhat shakey, under certain conditions it appears to be a reliable phenomenon.

According to Lazarus, the key component to understanding emotional memory is his notion of a core relational theme (see Questions 2 and 5). Lazarus proposes that the core relational theme is the most salient aspect of emotional experience and, consequently, what is encoded most importantly in memory. He suggests that the similarity in the core relational themes between our current encounters and past encounters is the thread connecting the past to the present. Lazarus argues that emotional memory is always triggered by a core relational theme in the present that is functionally related to one in memory.

While LeDoux and Panksepp both approach the issue of the relation between emotion and memory from a neural systems view, they focus on very different aspects of this relation. LeDoux notes that memory usually refers to our ability to consciously reflect on past experience. This is known in the memory literature as explicit or declarative memory. LeDoux cites evidence that underscores the role of the hippocampus in this form of memory. Emotional memories, LeDoux argues, are implemented in a different part of the brain, the amygdala. He notes that hippocampal lesions have no effect on the conditioned emotional associations while amygdala lesions do. LeDoux proposes that these two memory systems operate in parallel and simultaneously lay down memory traces. While information in each may coincide with one another, circumstances arise wherein they do not. This can result in interesting dissociations between explicit cognitive memory and implicit emotional memory.

Panksepp proposes the existence of powerful genetic memories in the brain, archetypal ancestral memories. (Is it possible that these might be related to Lazarus' core relational themes?) Panksepp views emotion and memory as emerging from the same basic neural substrates. He underscores the role of neuropeptides in both memory and emotion. Early in evolution prior to the development of the cerebral cortex, emotional systems allowed organisms to respond adaptively with little need for cognitive activity. As the cerebral cortex evolved with a concomitant shift in the importance of cognitive function for successful adaptation, Panksepp proposes that the emotional systems became guiding forces for the evolution of specific modes of cognitive activity. One domain in which this interaction can be observed is in REM sleep. Panksepp reflects on the fact that REM is so full of emotion, yet there appears to be poor long-term consolidation into waking conscious memory. Panksepp suggests that REM may solidify relations between emotions and memory unconsciously. In this sense, both LeDoux and Panksepp agree that emotions play an important role in implicit, rather than explicit memory. They each clearly underscore the importance of emotion for enhancing the subsequent retention of information, but suggest that this process may be largely isolated from consciousness. One implication of this view is that to study the relation between emotion and memory demands the use of procedures that are sensitive to implicit memory effects and it therefore precludes the use of traditional self-report measures.

Question 10

How Do Individuals Differ in Emotion-Related Activity?

Honoring Biology in the Study of Affective Style

RICHARD J. DAVIDSON

Introduction

Individual differences in emotion-related processes, or affective style as I have referred to the entire domain (Davidson, 1992), form the core of what has traditionally been regarded as personality (e.g., Gray, 1982; Tellegen, 1985) as well as early childhood temperament (Goldsmith et al., 1987). In addition, affective style is also related to psychopathology. Virtually all forms of major psychopathology involve dysfunctions of emotion. Some theorists have argued that individual differences in the capacity to experience certain emotions may constitute a diathesis that alters an individual's vulnerability to particular types of psychopathology (e.g., Meehl, 1975).

It is hardly necessary to remind readers of the enormous number of ways in which individuals might differ in emotion-related activity. Psychologists have invented a myriad of schemes for parsing individual differences in emotion. One of the central points of this essay is that the manner in which individual differences are parsed should honor what is known of the underlying biology. Said another way, the underlying biology can be used as a guide to help establish the natural fracture points for specifying individual differences. Thus, a type of biological factor analysis can be performed in which associations among variables might be sought based on what is known of the common brain mechanisms that are implicated (see Luria, 1973, for examples).

Another issue that is well known but still deserves to be underscored is that since we are dealing with putative trait-like differences when we describe individual differences in emotion-related activity, it is essential that the measures we use to infer such differences are reliable and valid. Several different types of reliability are important to establish for a trait measure including test-retest and internal consistency. Biological measures that reflect emotion-related activity are no exception and should be subjected to the same psychometric criteria we require of our paper-and-pencil measures (see Tomarken et al., 1992, for an example).

The Multi-Componential Nature of Emotion: Implications for Individual Differences

Emotion is a construct that subsumes a heterogeneous group of processes. There are many ways in which emotion can be parsed. First, it is important to distinguish between the perception and production of emotion. The perception of emotional cues appears to be implemented in different neural circuitry from the production of emotional responses (see Davidson & Tomarken, 1989; Davidson, 1993, for reviews). Within each of these categories, further differentiation is in order. The perception of visual emotional cues is mediated by different brain mechanisms compared with the perception of auditory emotional cues (see Etcoff, 1989, for review). Even within the visual modality, it is likely that facial cues are differently mediated than nonfacial visual cues, since there is now considerable evidence implicating specialized neurons in the superior temporal sulcus that mediate the perception of faces (e.g., Rolls, 1992). On the production side, a variety of different schemes have been proposed to differentiate more finely among different components of emotional production. Several authors have proposed models of emotions that distinguish among verbal reports, behavior, and physiology (e.g., Davidson, 1978). Other investigators have drawn our attention to the highly differentiated nature of the expressive system, with particular emphasis on facial expressions of emotion (Ekman, 1993). Only certain types of expression are expected to show concordance with physiology and self-report, requiring the investigator to make rather subtle distinctions among expression types. The importance of recognizing the multi-componential nature of emotion for the study of individual differences is the likelihood that individuals may differ in certain emotion processes and not others.

Parsing Individuals on the Basis of Biology: An Alternative Strategy in the Study of Affective Style

One way to discover natural patterns of associations among variables related to affective style is to compare affect-related behavior and physiology in individuals who differ on a biological index that is putatively related to at least certain aspects of affective style. I will give one example of how biology can be used as a fulcrum to pry apart differences in affective style among individuals and illustrate aspects of the neural circuitry that implement such differences. In the final section of this essay, I will highlight the new questions raised by this corpus of data and address the issue of the underlying mechanisms that might mediate such individual differences.

Data on the effects of unilateral lesions on affective symptomatology (see Davidson, 1984; Davidson, 1992, for reviews) suggest that patients with left-sided frontal lesions are more likely to exhibit depressive symptoms compared with patients showing comparable lesions in the right hemisphere. These data raise the interesting possibility that individual differences in patterns of anterior activation asymmetry in neurologically intact individuals are associated with biases in affective responding. In several previous articles and essays (Davidson, 1993; Davidson & Tomarken, 1989) I have argued that individual differences in anterior activation asymmetry reflect an individual's vulnerability or susceptibility to respond with certain types of positive or negative affect, given the requisite elicitor. The left anterior region is hypothesized to be specialized for approach-related emotion, while right anterior zones are hypothesized to be specialized for withdrawal-related emotion. Individual differences in patterns of activation in these regions will therefore reflect the degree to which these systems are primed. Thus, for example, an individual with decreased activation in the left anterior region would be expected to have an underaroused approach system and so be particularly vulnerable to sadness and depression. An individual with increased activation in right anterior regions would be expected to have a primed withdrawal system and be particularly vulnerable to those emotions and forms of psychopathology that have a strong withdrawal component (e.g., fear, disgust, and anxiety disorders). An individual with increased activation in the left anterior region would be expected to have a primed approach system and therefore should likely be resilient in the face of stress and show a disposition toward positive affect. I will now briefly review the considerable corpus of data that supports this model. These data will then be used to ask questions about the mechanisms that underlie these individual differences.

Using scalp-recorded electrophysiological measures, we have measured the baseline brain electrical activity of large samples of subjects. These data are Fourier-transformed, and power in the alpha frequency band is extracted. A wealth of previous evidence indicates that alpha power is inversely related to activation (Shagass, 1972). By examining differences in the amount of alpha power from homologous electrode sites, we can make inferences about asymmetries in activation in different cortical regions. We have recently demonstrated that individual differences in prefrontal and anterior temporal activation asymmetry are reliable. In particular, we examined the test-retest stability over a period of approximately one month of these measures of activation asymmetry and found them to show moderate stability (*r*'s between .66 and .73). At each of the two recording sessions, we obtain measures from eight one-minute trials. The data from each of these trials are aggregated together to form a single asymmetry metric for each scalp region at each testing session. Each of these eight one-minute trials can be considered as individual items on a test and we can compute the internal consistency reliability (coefficient alpha). Although it is rare for statistical techniques of this kind to be applied to physiological data, we believe that it is essential if they are to be used as trait-like indices. We found that the internal consistency reliability of the measures was very high ($>.85$). These methodological studies were important in establishing that we could use the electrophysiological measures to reliably assess individual differences in baseline measures of anterior activation asymmetry.

In several studies, we assessed relations between the electrophysiological measures of anterior asymmetry and several constructs related to individual differences in emotion. We (Tomarken et al., 1992) found that subjects with more right-sided prefrontal and anterior temporal activation reported more intense negative and less intense positive dispositional mood than their more left-side activated counterparts. We (Wheeler, Davidson, & Tomarken, 1993) also found that subjects with greater right-sided anterior activation at baseline reported more intense negative affect in response to short film clips designed to elicit fear and disgust. These relations remained significant after baseline mood was partialled out in hierarchical regressions. In another study we (Kang et al., 1991) found that subjects with extreme right-frontal activation had less natural killer cell activity than their left-frontal counterparts and in very recent work, we (Davidson, Coe, Donzella, & Ershler, 1993) replicated this finding and extended it by showing that baseline measures of anterior asymmetry also predict reactivity of immune measures to stress. In particular, subjects with greater baseline right-sided activation showed a larger decline in natural killer cell activity in response to both a naturally occurring and an experimentally produced stressor. In other recent work we have examined the antecedents of these forms of affective style in infants and toddlers. First we (Davidson & Fox, 1989) showed that 10-month-old infants who cried in response to a one-minute episode of maternal separation showed greater right-sided frontal activation during a prior baseline period compared with those who showed no evidence during this period. Then we (Davidson, Finman, Straus, Rickman, & Kagan, 1993) demonstrated that toddlers selected as being extremely wary and reticent of approaching novel objects and people had significantly less left frontal activation during a prior baseline recording. These findings with infants and young toddlers suggest that individual differences in anterior asymmetries are present early in life and reflect temperamental qualities that can be reliably coded from behavioral observations.

The corpus of evidence that we have amassed over the past several years indicates that individual differences in anterior activation asymmetries are related to different features of affective style. We have found that subjects with greater right-sided anterior activation report more dispositional negative affect, show more intense negative emotion in response to film clips designed to elicit such emotion, and have decreased baseline natural killer cell activity compared with their left-activated counterparts. We have also found that depressed subjects show less left-sided anterior activation and have demonstrated that this pattern is present even in remitted depressives who are currently euthymic. The pattern of decreased left-sided anterior activation is also present among toddlers who show a temperamental style characterized by wariness to approach novel objects and people (see Davidson, 1992a, for reviews of this work). Parsing individuals on the basis of physiological measures of brain function thus reveals systematic differences in their dispositional mood and patterns of reactivity to emotional stimuli and emotionally challenging events. The data also suggest that approach-related positive and withdrawal-related negative affect are meaningful dimensions along which individuals may be classified.

Affective Style: Mechanistic Considerations

These findings raise many questions about the mechanisms that might underlie the individual differences we have considered. The most obvious include: (1) What are the psychological mechanisms that are associated with increased or decreased intensity of reactivity to positive and negative elicitors?; (2) What are the proximal physiological mechanisms that give rise to the electrical differences we record?; (3) What are the neurochemical mediators of the asymmetries we have identified?; (4) Why does the control of certain types of positive and negative affect appear to be lateralized in the manner described? I will comment on some promising new research directions that address each of these four questions.

Psychological Mechanisms

When some subjects report more intense emotion of a particular type in response to an eliciting event than others, the differences between them may lie in one or more of several psychological characteristics. The subject reporting more intense emotion might experience a larger amplitude response compared with a subject reporting less intense emotion of a particular type. The subjects might also differ in the duration of the emotion they experience. This mechanism reflects the rapidity with which a person recovers from an emotionally charged event. Some subjects might experience rapid recovery for certain types of emotion, while others might show a more prolonged response. There are other possible mechanisms in addition to amplitude and recovery function. Future research is required to explicitly address the psychological mechanisms that underlie gross individual differences in affective style. For a variety of reasons, I have proposed that individual differences in frontal activation may be related to the rapidity with which subjects recover from an emotionally provocative event (see Davidson, 1993, for a discussion). In recent studies on the neural circuitry that implements fear in rodents, LeDoux (1992) has suggested that the prefrontal region participates in the extinction of emotional responses and thus has implicated the prefrontal cortex in the regulation of the duration of emotional responding.

Physiological Mechanisms

We have begun to examine a number of possible underlying physiological mechanisms that might give rise to the scalp electrical asymmetries we measure. One possibility is that such activation differences emerge from structural differences in anterior cortical zones. To obtain initial data relevant to this question, we (Davidson, Doss et al., 1993) have performed MRI scans and quantified certain features of cortical anatomy in subjects selected to be extreme left or extreme right frontally activated. We computed areal measures of frontal and posterior cortical regions, asymmetry, and skull thickness. On none of the measures was there any difference that even approached significance. We are currently conducting a study using the FDG-PET procedure to assess regional glucose metabolism in subjects differing on electrophysiological indices of anterior asymmetry so that we can specify with more precision the cortical and possibly subcortical regions that contribute to the electrical asymmetries we have studied.

Neurochemical Mediators

Related to the question above is one concerned with the neurochemical mediators of the asymmetries we have observed. A number of investigators have reported asymmetries in various neurotransmitter systems (see Tucker & Williamson, 1984, for review). Asymmetries have been reported in concentration of certain transmitters, in receptor densities, and indirectly by examining the differential consequences of unilateral damage on levels of different transmitters (see Wittling, 1993, for review). Dispositional differences in transmitter asymmetry characteristics may be related to important features of affective style. For example, in new research, we (Davidson, Kalin, & Shelton, 1993) have found that the asymmetrical response in frontal cortex to an acute administration of diazepam in rhesus monkeys is related to their dispositional propensity to freeze in response to a human intruder. Those monkeys that showed more freezing also showed more activation in the left frontal region in response to diazepam. One mechanism that might underlie this difference is an asymmetrical concentration of benzodiazepine receptors in the left and right prefrontal region. The high freezers might have relatively fewer receptors in the right than left frontal region compared with the low freezers.

Other transmitters are likely to be involved with different forms of affect. Recently Depue and his colleagues (Depue et al., in press) have reported that there are marked individual differences in dopamine function. The prefrontal cortex is a major cortical site for dopamine neurotransmission (Williams & Goldman-Rakic, 1993). By administering the D2 receptor agonist bromocriptine, they can make inferences about the functional activity level of the dopamine system by examining the magnitude of inhibition of prolactin. Subjects in whom prolactin inhibition is greater presumably have more active dopamine systems. Depue et al. (in press) have reported a remarkably high correlation between the magnitude of prolactin inhibition by bromocriptine (presumably a measure of the functional activity of the dopamine system) and dispositional positive affect ($r = .75$). Tucker and Williamson (1984) in their review have suggested on the basis of various strands of evidence that dopamine is more left-lateralized, particularly in the frontal region. It will be of great interest in future research to use new PET-receptor imaging methods to examine the asymmetrical distribution of dopamine receptors and their relation to dispositional positive affect.

Why Lateralization?

It is instructive to ask why the anterior cortical zones should be lateralized in the processing of positive and negative affect. Although we clearly do not now possess the requisite evidence to propose a definitive answer to this question, we can offer several tentative suggestions. Most approach and withdrawal behavior is bilaterally expressed, though there may be tendencies for the unilateral expression of approach behavior through reaching early in ontogeny (see Davidson, 1992a, for discussion). If most of the output is bilaterally expressed, it must be synchronized on the two sides of the body. Kosslyn (1987) has described the computational advantages of having such output controlled by a single processor located in one hemisphere. This seems to be the way nature solved the problem of speech control, since the muscles required for articulation are in the midline (e.g., mouth, tongue, vocal apparatus, etc.), yet the control of speech is highly lateralized. Approach movements require more fine manual control than withdrawal movements. Approach movements tend to be slower than withdrawal movements and emerge in the context of positive affect and unilateral pointing. Approach-related positive affect became lateralized to the left hemisphere because of the "snowball effect" (Kosslyn, 1987). This mechanism has been hypothesized to underlie some of the cognitive lateralization effects that have been uncovered in the literature. The mechanism basically accounts for the lateralization of processes that may have become associated with the primary lateralized control system (in this case, fine manual behavior associated with approach). It holds that since the processor for the output is primarily unilateral, the instructions to this processor, while initially bilateral, become shifted because of the effects of feedback and exercise on strengthening the within-hemisphere connections. On this view, we should expect to find positive associations between positive affect and cognitive functions that are controlled by the left anterior region. In recent work, we (Hoptman, Coyle, & Davidson, 1993) examined relations between dispositional positive affect, verbal fluency, and baseline frontal activation and found high positive correlations among these three domains of functioning. Positive affect-extroversion has also been found to be significantly associated with measures of receptive and expressive language in toddlers (age 2 years) and the affect measures at age 2 have been found to significantly predict individual differences in these language measures at 7 years of age (Slomkowsi, Nelson, Dunn, & Plomin, 1992). It is also notable that the behavioral measure best differentiating between inhibited and uninhibited toddlers is spontaneous speech and the primary difference in brain function that we have found to differentiate between these children is left frontal activation, with the uninhibited subjects showing significantly more activation in this region (see Davidson, 1992a, for review).

The understanding of the right hemisphere's contribution to emotion is somewhat more complex. A system designed to facilitate withdrawal from noxious and aversive events must be rapid and capable of operating without extensive cortical processing. Shifts in autonomic function may also be more common in withdrawal behavior since the occurrence of such behavior is typically more sudden, metabolically demanding, and discrepant with the foreground processing than approach behavior. A variety of evidence suggests that both efferent and afferent connections between certain autonomic effectors and forebrain structures are more extensive for the right hemisphere (see Porges et al., 1993; Wittling, 1993, for reviews). Thus, the right hemisphere system that controls withdrawal is tightly coupled to the autonomic effectors that support this form of action. I suggest that the negative affect/withdrawal system may be more specialized to the temporal polor region that receives direct projections from the amygdala, whose outputs from the central nucleus have been directly implicated in the control of autonomic changes associated with negative affect (see LeDoux, 1992, for review). Whenever we have recorded brain electrical activity from the anterior temporal region, we have found that withdrawal-related negative affect produces reliable shifts toward right-sided activation in this region. We have also found that baseline anterior temporal region asymmetries are associated with dispositional negative affect (Tomarken et al., 1992) and in very recent work, we found that only anterior temporal and not frontal asymmetry predict decrements in immune function in response to negative events (Davidson, Coe, Donzella, & Ersher, 1993). The fact that we have also found effects in the prefrontal region related to withdrawal behavior and negative affect we believe is a function of the lack of spatial resolution in the scalp EEG. We are now using positron emission tomography and functional magnetic resonance imaging to obtain much more precise regional localization.

Summary and Conclusions

This essay provides an outline of a theory relating anterior cortical asymmetries to affective style. It underscores the value of parsing individual differences on the basis of known biological distinctions. Individual differences in prefrontal and anterior temporal activation asymmetry are stable over time and are related to a network of affect-related differences that establish the validity of this construct. Left prefrontal activation is associated with dispositional positive affect, greater positive reactivity to positive affective stimuli, and more effective natural killer cell activity. In toddlers it is associated with a sociable, outgoing temperamental style. Left prefrontal activation is also associated with a certain cognitive profile in both toddlers and adults, the core of which is more facile language function and, in adults, better verbal fluency. Right anterior temporal activation is associated with dispositional negative affect. The anterior temporal activation is hypothesized to reflect, in part, upstream influences from the amygdala. This system is viewed as capable of rapid action and recruitment of the requisite autonomic changes to support this action. The fact that individuals show stable levels of activation asymmetry in these cortical regions implies that there are dispositional differences in the level of tonic activation in these systems that underlies the constellation of individual differences we have described.

Personality Dimensions and Emotion Systems

JEFFREY A. GRAY

There is a vast literature on the measurement of human individual differences. It is now generally agreed that the statistical space encompassing all the traits so far described requires only a small number of independent dimensions. These cover the domains of both ability and personality or temperament (terms between which I do not distinguish). There are no known relationships of substantial magnitude or consistency between emotional reactivity and the ability domain, so we can ignore the general intelligence dimension and its subfactors. We may assume, however, that the personality domain reflects parameter values (Gray, 1968) that determine, for a particular individual, the operating characteristics of fundamental emotion systems (of the kind described in the answer to Question 6), alone and in interaction with one another. In the personality domain, current best estimates of the number of independent dimensions range from three (Eysenck & Eysenck, 1985) to about five (Costa & McCrae, 1992; Goldberg, 1990; Zuckerman, 1991). The Eysenckian estimate of three fits well with the postulate (see the answer to Question 6) that there are three fundamental emotion systems. This estimate is also consistent with Tellegen's (1985) conclusion that there are three independent dimensions of variation in mood, although work to date suggests that two of these account for considerably more variance than does the third. Thus, if we assume that emotion, mood, and personality are all manifestations of the same fundamental organization of the brain, the clearest basis for analysis at present would posit three related independent dimensions of variation in each case.

These arguments lead to the adoption, as a framework for the description of personality, Eysenck and Eysenck's (1985) three dimensions of extraversion-introversion (E), neuroticism (N), and psychoticism or psychopathy (P). It is important to note, however, that while the techniques of multivariate statistical analysis (particularly, factor analysis) on which these dimensions are based are able to determine the *number* of independent sources of variation in a given correlation matrix (obtained, e.g., from a battery of personality inventories), they cannot by themselves establish a nonarbitrary *location* of the factors used to describe these sources of variation. Thus it cannot be assumed that a particular dimensional description of personality derived in this way (e.g., the Eysenckian one adopted here) embodies a one-to-one correspondence between the dimensions employed and the fundamental emotion systems whose variation between individuals gives rise, *ex hypothesi*, to personality.

In conformity with these arguments, I have proposed (Gray, 1970) that individual differences in the reactivity of the BIS to its adequate stimuli (as defined by Figure 3 in the answer to Question 6) may underlie a dimension of personality ("trait anxiety") that, in terms of Eysenck's scheme, is approximately a 30-degree rotation of his N dimension in the two-dimensional space defined also by E; high trait anxiety is thus a mixture of high neuroticism and high introversion, with high neuroticism being the more important component (by a factor of approximately two) in the mix. Similarly, I have proposed (Gray, 1970) that individual differences in the reactivity of the BAS to its adequate stimuli (Figure 1 in the answer to Question 6) underlie a dimension of "impulsivity" that is a 30-degree rotation of Eysenck's E dimension; high impulsivity would thus be a mixture of high neuroticism and high extraversion, with high extraversion being the more important component. Tellegen (1985) and Eysenck and Eysenck (1985) prefer the only slightly different hypothesis that neuroticism directly reflects the reactivity of the BIS; and extraversion, that of the BAS. Given the emotions attributed to activation of these two systems (see my answer to Question 6), it can be predicted from these hypotheses that neurotic (the Tellegen-Eysenck version) or neurotic-introverted (Gray's version) individuals should experience more negative affect (especially anxiety and that type of depression–"neurotic"–that is closely related to anxiety; Gray, 1982a); and that extraverted or neurotic-extraverted individuals should experience more positive affect (happiness).

The available data are consistent with these predictions (Argyle & Lu, 1990; Costa & McCrae, 1980; Tellegen, 1985). It has not yet been possible, however, to distinguish between the Tellegen-Eysenck and Gray versions of the hypotheses (Gray, 1994). In the light of this difficulty, it might seem reasonable to choose the Tellegen-Eysenck version. This has the major virtues of simplicity and of consistency with the vast amount of factor-analytic data that has gone into the making of Eysenck's two dimensions of personality, N and E. However, a problem is posed by other data sets for the adoption of this view.

Eysenck's (1981) general theory of introversion-extraversion supposes that, under conditions of low arousal, introverts will show learning and performance that is superior to those of extraverts; and that, under conditions of high arousal, these relationships will be reversed. His model has no natural place for reward and punishment as such (though these are relevant variables in setting the level of arousal). Thus, the hypothesis that extraverts will show greater positive affect than introverts, even though Eysenck has adopted it (Eysenck & Eysenck, 1985, p. 141), sits rather separately from the rest of his theory. In Gray's (1970) approach, in contrast, the variables of reward and punishment (acting via the BAS and BIS, respectively, as outlined previously) are central concepts. Based on these concepts, the specific hypotheses (1) that trait anxiety reflects individual differences in the reactivity of the BIS, (2) that trait impulsivity reflects individual differences in the reactivity of the BAS, and (3) that trait anxiety and impulsivity are 30-degree rotations of neuroticism and introversion-extraversion, respectively, jointly predict that, other things being equal, introverts will learn and perform better than extraverts if punishment is used, whereas extraverts will do better than introverts with reward.

Consider now what predictions one might try to derive about the roles of reward and punishment from the Tellegen-Eysenck hypothesis concerning positive and negative affect. If we preserve the conceptual link (central to the present approach) between affect and reinforcement, it must follow from this hypothesis that extraverts relative to introverts will learn and perform better with reward (N having no influence); and that neurotic relative to stable individuals will learn and perform better with punishment (E having no influence). There is a major problem with this position: Existing data on the influence of reward and punishment on performance as a function of E converge on the conclusion that, irrespective of level of arousal, introverts are superior to extraverts if punishment is used, whereas extraverts are superior to introverts if reward is used (Boddy, Carver, & Rowley, 1986; Gray, 1981; Lahey et al., in press; Newman, 1987; Quay, 1988). This outcome is incompatible both with Eysenck's (1981; Eysenck & Eysenck, 1985) overall model and with the Tellegen-Eysenck hypothesis. For the former, it is an embarrassment (Gray, 1981) that extraverts do better than introverts with reward (unless the experimental conditions are highly arousing, which has not typically been the case in the relevant experiments); for the latter, it is an embarrassment that introverts and extraverts differ when punishment is used (since the effects of this variable should be influenced by the neuroticism dimension only).

These issues require much more empirical research before they are finally resolved. At present, however, it appears that there are two major dimensions of personality that reflect parameter values for the BIS and BAS, respectively; influence, therefore, sensitivity to stimuli associated with punishment or with reward, respectively; influence also the predisposition to experience anxiety/neurotic depression and happiness, respectively; and lie at 30-degree rotations of Eysenck's dimensions of N and E, respectively.

If these arguments are correct, there must in addition be a third dimension, corresponding roughly to Eysenck's P dimension in personality space, to Tellegen's constraint dimension in mood space, to the operating parameters of the FFS in emotion-system space, and to the predisposition to display fight or flight behavior (accompanied by rage/anger or terror/panic). At each of these levels, however, this dimension has been much less studied than the other two we have considered (for some suggestions, see Gray, 1983).

Individual Differences in Emotion

RICHARD LAZARUS

Undoubtedly, no two discrete emotional episodes are exactly alike, which I think can also be said for any psychological event. Although there are important features in common within episodes of anger, anxiety, guilt, shame, pride, love, and so forth, differences—often quite major—can always be found. For the scientist concerned with emotion, the epistemological choice—depending on one's purpose—is to decide whether to emphasize similarities or differences.

When we want to generalize—that is, to find universal mechanisms—we look at commonalities. When we want to make accurate descriptions of emotional phenomena, or to assess the causal variables underlying individual differences, we are apt to be sensitized to these differences. The similarities and differences in emotional episodes between individuals, and within individuals across occasions and over time, are the basic data of the effort to generalize about the common processes or particularize about the observed variation.

Attitudes of Scientists Toward Individual Differences

For the most part, psychologists and other social scientists have been ambivalent about individual differences. On the one hand, we presume that science is a search for general principles or universals, an outlook that is a product of the mechanistic tradition. Find the invariant process and presumably we will have a principle that applies in all contexts.

On the other hand, people differ greatly in their behavior and states of mind. This should come as no surprise. Astronomers know that the planets revolving around the earth are very different from each other in their orbits and physical charactistics, though they also follow the basic laws of physics. Even though we are all humans and follow the basic laws of physics and biochemistry, our individual bodies show enormous variation, as do our minds. Variation is just as common, salient, and important as universal mechanisms, and if our interest lies in practical intervention, it may be even more salient.

In my professional lifetime, general psychologists have usually treated individual differences as a nuisance, as errors of measurement, and, most unwisely, as deviations from natural laws that are best ignored or smoothed over. For example, they try to fit these variations to a regression line, which permits a mathematical generalization about what is being observed. Though personality psychology often seems most interested in uniform principles that apply to people in general, of all other branches of psychology it has a vested interest in stable individual differences and their origins, which presumably include the developmental history of an individual as well as that individual's inherited and adventitious constitutional makeup.

As was firmly recognized by Kurt Lewin (1931, 1935), if we keep our heads, there should be no inherent conflict between general laws and variations among individuals. Yet from a practical standpoint, we can never predict an individual event accurately from a general principle. One of Lewin's important contributions was to affirm that prediction requires that we know the variables operating in the psychological situation, which determine where the individual event fits within the universal law.

Lewin believed in the importance of studying individual cases to assess the variables operating in the psychological situation at a particular moment, including those pertaining to the environment and the personality (e.g., needs and ways of thinking). Lewin has also been quoted by Allport (1937, p. 324) as saying graphically, in a related vein, that "The same fire that hardens the egg softens the butter."

The ambivalence of psychology about individual differences arises from the narrow definition of science as having the task of finding general principles. But if we are to take individual differences seriously, the environmental and psychological context in which an emotion occurs must remain a major focus (see also Shweder, 1991, for an extended discussion of universals and variations). A useful theory of the emotions must provide for both kinds of knowledge—the general principles whereby emotions are aroused and regulated, and the environmental and personality variables that help us understand similarities and differences in individual episodes of emotion.

Two Perspectives on Individual Differences

Psychologists deal with individual differences in a number of ways, including celebrating or ignoring them. When attention is focused on differences—similarities, of course, constitute the opposite side of the same comparative coin—one of two perspectives or research designs is adopted, namely, between-subjects or within-subjects. In the first we are comparing the emotional response in two or more individuals; in the second we are comparing the emotional response of an individual with him or herself across occasions or as the emotion process unfolds and changes over time.

In the case of the between-subjects or *interindividual* perspective as I will refer to it, even when the same emotion, say, anger, is involved in two discrete episodes, some of the variation we observe derives from differences in the environmental situation provoking the anger. This is one reason why we have many terms for anger, each suggesting variants of the conditions of arousal and the quality of the emotional state itself, for example, defensive anger, righteous anger, disdainful anger or scorn, gloating anger, and so on.

There are two standard explanations—which as I argue later are incomplete—of the emotional variation found in the interindividual perspective. One explanation is that what has changed during the encounter, or what is different across occasions, is the provoking environmental situation.

The other explanation is that people vary in their response to the same provoking psychological situation because of variable individual goal hierarchies, generalized beliefs about self and world, and situational beliefs. All these affect the appraisal an individual makes of what is happening, which shapes the quality and intensity of the emotional response.

In the within-subject, or *intraindividual perspective* as I refer to it, we observe variations in the emotional response, say, anger, on different occasions. On one occasion, for example, it is righteous anger and on another it is hurt anger. Or we may observe that the person who is at first angry in a two-person encounter becomes conscious of and appalled by the injustice of his or her own angry outburst and the hurt response of the recipient of the anger. This change in appraisal changes the emotional state from the original anger to guilt or shame. In effect, we observe variation both in the kind of anger over time within the same individual and in the kind of emotion itself, which may shift from anger to guilt over time or occasions in accordance with the other person's response.

Here too, there are two standard but incomplete explanations for the intraindividual variation in emotion across occasions or over time. One is that the environmental situations provoking the emotion differ. For example, the righteous anger comes about because the attack was patently unjustified and did a grievous wrong, which provoked the righteousness of the anger; or, perhaps, the recipient of the attack secretly believed it was deserved, but doesn't want to admit it, which gives the righteousness a defensive quality. On the other hand, the hurt anger stemmed from a situation in which the provocation came from a loved one whose action toward a needy paramour lacked the expected sensitivity and consideration.

The intraindividual variation over time—that is, the change from anger to guilt—could also be explained by reference to differences in the environmental situation. In effect, what provoked the original anger is one set of social circumstances, and what provoked the guilt is another set; presumably the guilt reaction was the result, in part, of the injured response of the recipient, and the realization on the part of the perpetrator—fed by this injured response—that he or she had acted badly.

The other explanation, which could be argued just as easily, is that the intraindividual variation was caused by changes in the salience of goals or beliefs, which changed over the course of the emotion process. These personality changes, in turn, led to different appraisals of the significance of what was happening.

It is important to add that similarities between people in the emotions manifested across occasions can also be explained in the same ways—that is, attributed either to commonalities in the provoking environmental situations or in the operative personality variables. And, in a parallel fashion, environmental and personality differences are equally viable as explanations of variations in emotion within the same person over occasions and time. There is a symmetry in all these explanations of inter- and intraindividual similarities and differences. This symmetry has been diagrammed in Table 1.

If, for example, one asks which emotions tend to be correlated, the answer from the interindividual perspective is that people who report higher levels of happiness also report being more sociable and affectionate, have higher self-esteem, and are more responsive than others to the external world (see also Wessman & Ricks, 1966, for similar findings). In effect, with data derived from a between-subjects frame of reference, happiness is a trait having a number of personality correlates.

If, however, the research strategy is intraindividual, one finds that happiness is brought about by distinct events that lead to a sense of security and more freedom to be oneself and to express how one feels. In other words, within-subjects research designs provide data that reflect variations in the social conditions of an emotion, which influence appraials and the emotions that flow from them. Instead of revealing the trait side of emotions, intraindividual research strategies reveal emotions as reactions to particular social circumstances.

Failure to take into account the perspective from which data are derived can lead to real anomalies of understanding. For example, in an interindividual research strategy, compared with others people who often report feeling happy also report often feeling sad, suggesting that happiness and sadness go together as emotions. In other words, the two emotions are positively correlated across persons, which means that those who often experience one often experience the other too. However, in an intraindividual research strategy, when a person feels happy he or she is not likely to feel sad, suggesting that these emotions are not compatible, at least at the same moment or in the same social context. In effect, the two emotions are negatively correlated.

There is no necessary contradiction in the two types of data if we recognize that different psychological questions are asked in each perspective (see Broverman, 1962, and Marceil, 1977, for a more detailed analysis). Different answers to the question of how emotions are organized in the mind are obtained because the question asked in interindividual research designs is different from what is asked when the research design is intraindividual. Not to specify the frame of reference leaves the original question about how emotions are organized in the mind ambiguous. It is of the utmost importance to employ the perspective that is appropriate to the question we want to ask.

TABLE 1. Environment and Personality in the Inter- and Intraindividual Perspectives

Interindividual		Intraindividual	
Same emotion	Same environment Same personality	Same emotion	Same environment Same personality
Different emotion	Different environment Different personality	Different emotion	Different environment Different personality

The Processes Underlying Individual Differences in Emotion

My general comments about the inter- and intraindividual perspectives have not yet answered the question as it was phrased, which concerns the processes on which individuals differ in emotion-related activity. The answer, of course, depends on one's theory about the emotion process, which involves the differential arousal of one of a number of emotions and the regulation or expression of that emotion.

In my theory, the central process is *appraisal*. All the variables that contribute to an emotion operate through this process, on which relational meaning depends. If two individuals appraise the same situation differently, their emotional response will differ. And if they appraise different situations in the same way, their emotional response will be the same. Even *coping*, which is a fundamental ingredient of the emotion process in both emotion arousal and regulation, works by influencing and changing how the individual appraises the significance of what is happening and how it might be dealt with.

The main individual difference *variables* affecting appraisal are contained both in the environment in which people find themselves and in their personalities. Substantive *environmental variables* include demands, constraints, and resources (including social network and support variables), and adaptational outcomes. Formal environmental variables include the ambiguity of the environmental display, which potentiates a greater role in appraisal of personality variables, and the imminence of an outcome.

Personality variables include goal hierarchies and beliefs about self and world, which include the existential solutions to questions about the meaning of life that are favored by the individual, and the individual's sense of control over his or her fate (cf. optimism or pessimism), a variable that has been a favorite in stress-related research for some time.

This analysis implies a systems theory in which inter- and intraindividual variation in the appraisal process and the variables contributing to it will result in different emotion-related activity. Each variable contributes to the appraisal underlying the emotional response and its regulation by coping. As such, these appraisals contribute to inter- and intraindividual differences in the emotional response. In empirical research on the emotion process, to leave out any of these variables and the processes—especially appraisal—that they influence is to risk adding to the indeterminacy of the analysis.

Broad Dimensions of Temperament and Personality

MARY K. ROTHBART

In responding to this question, I will be discussing individual differences in emotion-related activity within the domain of temperament. We have defined temperament as constitutionally based individual differences in reactivity and self-regulation, expressed behaviorally in emotionality, activity level, and attention (Rothbart & Derryberry, 1981). Reactivity can be indexed via the intensive (threshold, intensity) and temporal (rise time, recovery time, latency) parameters of responsiveness of somatic, autonomic, endocrine, and reticular activating systems.

In theoretical terms, we have found it helpful to think about temperamental reactivity as organized according to major emotional-motivational systems, including fear, anger/frustration, positive affect and anticipation, and possibly affiliation (Rothbart, Derryberry, & Posner, 1994). Motivational patterns are built into each of these systems in addition to basic emotions. For each system, neural networks of attention also serve to regulate reactivity at a central level, and variability in dimensions of attentional control is of major interest in the study of temperament (Rothbart, 1991; Rothbart & Posner, 1985).

Emotional-motivational systems can be seen to carry out a very important kind of information processing within the individual nervous system, addressing the question: What is the significance of this event or situation to me? (LeDoux, 1989). This processing may be viewed in relation to the activity of neural circuits that support the analyses of location, time of occurrence, and identification of events, and some of these analyses may require considerable time to be completed. Emotional processing can be extremely rapid, receiving inputs from very early stages of perceptual processing. It may also result after extensive cognitive processing has occurred, or in response to the semantic labels attached to an event. The outputs of emotional analyses include changes in the individual's alertness, direction of attention, and somatic, autonomic, and endocrine processes (Derryberry & Rothbart, 1984). Individuals may differ in reactivity for each of these components of response, but results emerging from the psychological study of temperament and personality suggest that emotional-motivational systems are organized at a central level.

Dimensions reflecting basic emotional-motivational systems and attention have emerged from questionnaire studies involving parent reports of infant temperament (Rothbart & Mauro, 1990). Thomas, Chess, Birch, Hertzig, and Korn's (1963) nine dimensions of temperament, derived from content analysis of parent-reported infant behaviors, have formed the basis for much research to date. These include the dimensions of Intensity, Threshold, Approach/Withdrawal, Mood, Adaptability, Attention Span/Persistence, Distractibility, Rhythmicity, and Activity Level. However, problems have been found with this list. First, the constructs were not defined so as to be conceptually independent of each other. In some cases, parent report instruments designed to measure the dimensions thus employ items that could as easily be assigned to one temperamental dimension as another. Second, some constructs (e.g., Intensity and Threshold) suggest a homogeneity of reactions across stimulus and response modalities that laboratory studies have been unable to demonstrate (Strelau, 1983). Because Thomas et al. (1963) intended their dimensions to be used chiefly for clinical purposes, issues of discriminant validity and homogeneity of scales did not pose a problem for them, but for researchers seeking to develop psychometrically sound and theoretically useful measuring instruments, item-level factor analytic work was indicated.

In a review of item-level factor analytic studies of infant temperament, we have found a "shorter list" of temperament factors to have been extracted from items based on Thomas and Chess' (1977) original nine dimensions (Rothbart & Mauro, 1990). This list includes the dimensions of fear, general irritability (including frustration reactions), and positive affect, as well as attentional persistence, in addition to activity level and rhythmicity (Rothbart & Mauro, 1990). These dimensions show considerable similarity to dimensions identified by other researchers of temperament in children.

The temperamental dimension of fear corresponds to a degree with Garcia-Coll, Kagan, and Reznick's (1984) construct of behavioral inhibition, although in the latter model, behavioral inhibition constitutes one pole of a bipolar dimension, with uninhibited behavior constituting the other pole. The behavioral inhibition construct is in turn similar to Thomas and Chess' (1977) original temperamental dimension of Approach-Withdrawal, which includes positive affect and approach to novelty at one pole and distress and behavioral withdrawal at the other. These constructs illustrate clearly that in temperament theory, individual differences in emotionality are often explicitly linked to related behaviors and motivations, including approach, withdrawal, and inhibition.

I (Rothbart, 1991) and others (Gray, 1975; MacDonald, 1988), however, have argued that, rather than constituting a single dimension, approach and fear are separable dimensions that are mutually inhibitory under circumstances of environmental novelty and challenge. Such a model allows us to consider individuals who might be highly positively reactive under familiar circumstances, but who become inhibited or withdrawing (fearful) under conditions of novelty, i.e., individuals who are quite changeable across situations. The item-level factor analytic work on parent reports of infant temperament also suggests that positive affect/approach and fear are separable dimensions (Rothbart & Mauro, 1990).

In laboratory measures of temperament in infancy, we have observed infants' reactions to stimuli varying in novelty, intensity, and accessibility, and have found latency, duration, and intensity of emotional reactions to be positively intercorrelated, with consistency of individual reaction across stimuli designed to evoke fear, frustration, and smiling and laughter (Rothbart, Derryberry, & Hershey, in preparation). These observations allow us to make composite assessments of individual differences for fear, distress to limitations (anger/frustration), and positive affect in the laboratory. In a small longitudinal sample of infants, measures of emotionality in the laboratory have proved predictive of later mothers' reports about the children's emotionality (Rothbart, Ahadi, & Hershey, 1993; Rothbart et al., in preparation). We have found moderate stability from infancy to middle childhood (age 7 years) in children's fearfulness and reactions to frustration, as well as in their positive excitement about events (approach/anticipation), related to infant smiling and laughter. We feel these results are particularly persuasive about both the structure of temperamental individual differences and their stability over time, even when assessed by very different methods (laboratory observation in infancy and mother reports at age 7).

In recent scale-level factor analyses of the Children's Behavior Questionnaire, a parent-report measure of temperament in children 3 to 8 years old, we have consistently recovered three broad factors (Ahadi & Rothbart, 1994). One, labeled Surgency/Extraversion, is defined primarily by scales of Approach, High Intensity Pleasure, Activity Level, Impulsivity, and negative loadings of Shyness. A second factor, defined by scales of Discomfort, Fear, Anger/Frustration, and negative loadings of Soothability, corresponds to a broad factor of Negative Affectivity. A third dimension, defined by loadings for the scales of Inhibitory Control, Attentional Focusing, Low Intensity Pleasure, and Perceptual Sensitivity, is labeled Effortful Control. We have argued that the Effortful Control dimension reflects a level of organization not seen in early infancy that is related to the development of attentional systems (Rothbart et al., 1993; Rothbart & Ahadi, in press). Effortful Control is a particularly important dimension of temperamental variability because, while not an emotional construct, attentional processes serve regulatory functions over the emotions and their expression. Effortful Control is also important because it allows the individual to act in directions counter to those indicated by immediate cues of reward and punishment (Rothbart, 1991). The basic structure for childhood temperament in our measure has been replicated in the United States (e.g., Kochanska, DeVet, Goldman, Murray, & Putnam, 1993) and has emerged from analysis of data from 6 and 7 year olds in China (Ahadi, Rothbart, & Ye, 1993).

During the period when students of temperament in infancy and childhood have been identifying "shorter lists" of broad temperament dimensions, students of adult personality have increasingly been concluding that there are five (or three) major dimensions of individual differences in personality, with the former labeled the "Big Five" (Goldberg, 1980). Of these three or five factors, two appear to strongly involve emotionality, a third less strongly, and they seem interestingly related to dimensions of emotional variability found in infancy and childhood.

In Tellegen's (1985) factor analytic personality research, three orthogonal personality factors have been derived: Positive Emotionality, including feelings of pleasurable engagement, well-being, and social potency, Negative Emotionality, and Constraint. Adults' scores on measures of Positive Emotionality are positively correlated with their mood assessments of Positive Affectivity, i.e., their tendency to endorse mood descriptive adjective terms like enthusiastic, elated, excited, and active versus drowsy, dull, and sluggish (Tellegen, 1985; Watson & Tellegen, 1985). The Negative Emotionality trait includes feelings of negative engagement, stress, worry, and resentment, and is positively related to measures of Negative Affectivity in mood, i.e., the tendency to endorse items like distressed, fearful, hostile, and nervous versus calm, placid, and relaxed. A third orthogonal personality factor, called Constraint, includes characteristics of cautiousness, timidity, and restraint versus impulsivity and sensation-seeking. Although this latter factor at first inspection seems less related to emotionality than the first two, it includes aspects of behavioral inhibition identified in late infancy as timidity and behavioral restraint (Garcia-Coll et al., 1985), as well as the dimension of Effortful Control we have identified in childhood (Ahadi & Rothbart, in press; Rothbart & Ahadi, 1994).

Tellegen (1985) has noted similarities between these three factors and Eysenck's (1967, 1976) "Big Three" personality factors of Extraversion (corresponding to Positive Emotionality), Neuroticism (Negative Emotionality), and Psychoticism (Constraint), and between Positive Emotionality and Gray's (1975) Behavioral Activation System, and Negative Emotionality and Gray's Behavioral Inhibition System, although as I have previously suggested, behavioral inhibition may be more closely related to timidity and caution than to the negative affect identified in Tellegen's Negative Emotionality construct.

The "Big Five" broad personality factors have been put forward by numerous other factor-analytically oriented personality researchers, including McCrae and Costa (1987), Digman and Inouye (1986), Goldberg (1980), and John (1989). They have been extracted from both self-report and peer description data, and found in both adults and school-age children. The Big Five factors include Extraversion, Agreeableness, Conscientiousness, Neuroticism, and Openness, with Extraversion showing conceptual overlap with Positive Emotionality, Neuroticism with Negative Emotionality, and Conscientiousness with Constraint.

Given such commonalities in at least the labels used to describe individual differences in emotionality, it is intriguing to consider the possibility of developmental continuities on these dimensions. In our investigations of developmental stability of temperament, we have found fear assessed in the laboratory in infancy to predict later parent-reported fear, shyness, and (negatively) approach/anticipation at age 7, while positive affect (smiling and laughter) predicted later approach/anticipation, and frustration predicted later anger and aggression (Rothbart et al., in preparation). Research across much longer periods suggests substantial stability of shyness or behavioral inhibition (Rothbart, 1989a).

Nevertheless, caution in making direct mappings from individual differences in infants' emotionality to that of adults' is warranted. We may consider, for example, the factor of Negative Emotionality or Neuroticism. Negative Emotionality (and Neuroticism, as denoted by its label) in the adult contains strong connotations of negative social adjustment. Thus, Goldberg's (1980) self-descriptive adjectives for Neuroticism includes the terms envious, fretful, jealous, touchy, and insecure. Watson and Clark's (1984) Negative Affect (NA) mood scale includes feelings of nervousness, tension, worry, anger, scorn, revulsion, guilt, self-dissatisfaction, sense of rejection, and "to some extent" sadness. Although Watson and Clark stress the emotional aspects of these states, they also comment that high NA persons "by most definitions can be considered poorly adjusted" (p. 480).

By the content of these scales alone, it thus appears likely that cognitive structures concerning the self and life experiences of success and failure might strongly affect Negative Emotionality in the adult. Even though a low threshold for distress may predispose an individual to later mental suffering, negative social experience would be expected to be strongly influential in its development. Another caution in taking Negative Emotionality at face value in adult self-reports is recent research on repressive style, suggesting that some persons who are physiologically highly reactive to negative affect may report that they experience very little of it (Weinberger, Schwartz, & Davidson, 1979).

Developmental work will be needed to clarify these continuity and stability issues, but we may nevertheless tentatively identify at least three broad dimensions of individual differences in emotionality from both the temperament and personality literatures: positive affect (related to approach), negative affect, and fear (related to behavioral inhibition), in addition to individual differences in attention and activity. These dimensions are very broad, and they leave open the likelihood that a number of finer grained individual differences in emotionality will be usefully employed in our research (Rothbart, 1991). These might include individual differences in the temporal qualities of the emotions. In our research on 7-year-old children, we have found parent-reported soothability or falling reactivity in the children to be related to a number of parent-reported behavioral problems. Rising and falling characteristics of psychophysiological reactivity have also been related to individual differences in temperament, and may prove useful in future work (Rothbart, 1989b).

It is likely that we will ultimately identify individual differences in emotionality at both broad and more fine-grained levels, and that these differences will provide a powerful base for our work on the influence of socialization on the individual (see Rothbart & Ahadi, 1994; Rothbart et al., 1993). Current examples of such work are research by van den Boom (1989), who has related neonatal distress proneness and parental behavior to later attachment classification, and by Kochanska (1991), who has related toddler behavioral inhibition and parental socialization to the child's later susceptibility to guilt and conscience.

Returning now to the issue of the dimensions of individual differences in emotion-related activity, I have suggested that, within temperament, we focus on individual differences in the major emotional-motivational systems and components of these systems. Going beyond temperament, it is certainly likely that variability will exist in other emotions such as pride, shame or guilt. These more cognitively based emotions, however, go beyond the domain of temperament, although they may be influenced by it.

Afterword: How Do Individuals Differ in Emotion-Related Activity?

PAUL EKMAN
RICHARD J. DAVIDSON

Lazarus provides the only psychologically based answer to the question of individual differences in emotion. While Davidson, Gray, and Rothbart all approach the question from a more biological standpoint, there is not much overlap among them, and it is not easy to discern whether they would disagree with each other.

Lazarus offers a very interesting history of how psychologists have typically avoided individual differences and focused instead on general laws. His distinction between intraindividual differences, how a particular individual's emotional responses vary, and interindividual differences, variations across individuals in their emotional responses, is very useful. The other three contributors deal only with interindividual differences.

Both forms of individual differences for Lazarus are attributable to how appraisal operates, with changing environments (intraindividual) and personality characteristics (interindividual) encouraging one or another type of appraisal. More specifically, it is the differences between people in their goal hierarchies and beliefs about the self and the world that are posited to be responsible for interindividual differences in emotion. This would seem to imply the potential for easily accomplished change in interindividual differences in emotion, and in personality itself. The other contributors imply that individual differences are more fixed and less susceptible to change.

Rothbart deals only with temperament, constitutionally based individual differences in reactivity and self-regulation, which are expressed behaviorally in emotionality, activity level, and attention. She believes that these differences are organized according to the major emotional and motivational systems, and expects differences for fear, anger, positive affect, anticipation, and possibly attachment. As a developmental psychologist, she notes that individual differences in the various components of emotional reactivity (somatic, autonomic, and endocrine processes) although organized centrally may appear developmentally at different points. She notes that approach and fear are separate temperamental dimensions.

Approach and withdrawal are the key individual differences Davidson has studied, and he apparently believes the propensity or vulnerability to one or the other is a major way in which individuals differ in affective style. His central point, one Gray and Rothbart take for granted, but which Lazarus would protest, is that our approach to individual differences should "honor biology," taking account of the rapidly expanding knowledge of the brain. He usefully takes as an example individual differences in intensity of self-reported emotions, and raises the question as to whether this might be due more to differences in amplitude of an emotional response or to differences in recovery. Two individuals might both give more intense self-reports (of one or all emotions?) and yet that might be because one has greater amplitude and the other lesser recovery. More sensitive self-report techniques, informed by such ideas, perhaps could elucidate those potential differences in subjective experience. Lazarus does not attend to such specifics in individual differences, and, if he did, presumably would have to attribute them to differences in goals and beliefs.

Gray has a more narrow focus in his briefer contribution. He, along with Davidson, believes that individual differences in emotions, moods, and personality are all manifestations of the same differences in the fundamental organization of the brain. Most of his contribution deals with how Eyesenck's dimensions relate to his own work on the dimensions of personality that influence sensitivity to stimuli associated with reward or punishment, and influence the predisposition to experience anxiety/neurotic depression and happiness. There is general agreement between Gray and Davidson over the fundamental dimensions of individual differences in affective style. Davidson describes an approach system that is conceptually analogous to Gray's Behavioral Activation System. The withdrawal system in Davidson's theorizing is analogous to Gray's Behavioral Inhibition System. Davidson and Gray emphasize different anatomical substrates of these systems. Gray's work is based mostly on studies with rodents while Davidson's work is based mostly on human studies, so some of the differences in emphasis may reflect genuine species differences in the mediation of these different behavioral tendencies. It remains for future research to more systematically characterize the functional neuroanatomy of these systems in humans.

Question 11

What Develops in Emotional Development?

Two Aspects of Emotional Development: Expression and Elicitation

LINDA A. CAMRAS

Emotional Facial Expressions

The pioneering work by Ekman and others (Ekman & Friesen, 1971; Ekman, 1972; Izard, 1971) on the universal recognition of emotional facial expressions raises questions about the developmental origins of these expressions and their relation to emotion. Although various possibilities have been proposed (Ekman, 1979), the position advanced by Izard (1991; Izard & Malatesta, 1987) as one component of his Differential Emotions Theory (DET) has received considerable attention in recent years from developmental psychologists. According to this position, emotional expressions are innately tied to emotion-specific neural processes and subjective experiences. These are the core components of the discrete emotions. During the course of development, the discrete emotions emerge as structured wholes according to a maturational timetable. Thus, in infancy, when an emotion is experienced, its corresponding facial expression will be produced (at least during the first year of life when voluntary inhibition of expression is assumed not to occur). One practical consequence of this is that investigators would presumably be able to use facial expression as their sole index of infant emotions.

Empirical research on infant facial expression does not provide convincing evidence for DET's current theoretical position (see reviews in Camras, 1991,1992; Camras, Malatesta, & Izard, 1991; Oster, Hegley, & Nagel, 1992). Most important, there does not appear to be an innate concordance between infant emotions and their corresponding facial configurations as specified by differential emotion theorists (see Izard, Dougherty, & Hembree's, 1983, AFFEX coding system). For example, the facial configurations of "surprise" and "enjoyment" are regularly observed in situations in which the corresponding emotions are unlikely to be experienced (e.g., neonatal smiles during REM sleep; "surprise" configurations to familiar but exciting stimuli; Camras, 1992). In addition, some situations are generally acknowledged to elicit particular emotions in infants as indexed by their action responses (e.g., fear in response to stranger approach; surprise in response to apparent violations of object permanence), yet the corresponding facial configurations are rarely or never seen (e.g., Hiatt, Campos, & Emde, 1979). Lastly, the facial configurations described for the discrete negative affects of sadness, anger, and pain/discomfort are seen in such a wide range of situations that they appear more reasonably interpreted as expressions of qualitatively undifferentiated distress rather than discrete negative emotions (Camras, 1992).

These findings suggest that there is no innate concordance between discrete emotions and the facial configurations described by differential emotions theorists (Izard et al., 1983). Instead, these facial configurations seem to emerge as expressions of affective states related to—but not identical to—adult emotions such as anger, sadness, and surprise. During the course of development, these facial configurations eventually become associated with those emotions they are identified with in studies of expression recognition. In addition, developmental changes may occur in the fine-grained morphology of some expressions (e.g., eye-widening replacing eye-narrowing in the anger configuration described by Izard et al., 1983; see Oster, Hegley, & Nagel, 1992).

Because an innate concordance between facial expressions and their corresponding adult emotions has often been assumed by investigators of infant expressive behavior (Malatesta, Culver, Tesman, & Shepard, 1989; Sullivan & Lewis, 1989), little research has been conducted to investigate the development of this relationship. However, as a preliminary step to such an investigation, I have made a number of informal observations on the expressive development of my daughter Justine from infancy through early childhood. The examples presented here (see also Camras, 1991) focus on the development of relationships between Izard et al.'s (1983) AFFEX-specified "anger," "sadness," and "pain" facial configurations and other observable aspects of emotion such as eliciting situations and nonfacial (i.e., instrumental and vocal) behaviors.

During her first two months, Justine produced the "anger," "sadness," and "pain" configurations in a wide range of emotion-inducing situations (e.g., limb restraint, bath, sour vitamin, pacifier removal). While the three facial configurations were sometimes accompanied by different forms of body activity, observers in a systematic judgment study (Camras, Sullivan, & Michel, 1993) did not associate these body actions with qualitatively discrete emotions. Furthermore, Justine often cycled among these facial configurations within a single bout of crying. Thus, these configurations appeared to be associated with a qualitatively similar emotional response, herein called "distress," rather than the discrete negative affects of anger, sadness, and pain.

By age 2, however, Justine appeared to differentially produce the "anger" and "sadness" facial patterns in conjunction with other behaviors that might be judged anger-appropriate or sadness-appropriate by most adults. For example, the anger-related facial pattern would often be accompanied by loud crying and intense physical activity that seemed to be either instrumentally or expressively related to anger (e.g., hitting the agent of frustration, waving her arms but not actually striking at the frustrating agent). The sadness-related facial configuration was accompanied by more restrained sobbing and either the absence of body activity or even a dramatic display of behavioral inhibition (i.e., collapsing to the floor in "grief"). Furthermore, these patterns of response to some extent appeared to become differentially associated with anger-appropriate versus sadness-appropriate frustrating circumstances (e.g., circumstances in which a favorable change might or might not be effected).

Nevertheless, even at age 2, the anger configuration sometimes appeared in circumstances in which Justine appeared to be distressed rather than angry. For example, Justine sometimes produced this configuration while seeking comfort from her mother after accidentally hurting herself. Thus, the relationship between facial configuration and nonfacial indices of anger was not invariant. Similarly, even for adults, emotions may not always be accompanied by their corresponding stereotypic facial expression (Ekman, 1992). For example, in a recent study by Tomarken and Davidson (Davidson, 1992), phobic subjects were found to produce disgust expressions when confronted with their phobic stimuli although they reported experiencing both disgust and fear.

What type of theory can accommodate both developmental shifts in the relationship between facial expression and emotion and also the possible incomplete concordance of expression and emotion even in adulthood? One possibility may be proposed based on dynamical systems theory. Dynamical systems theory was developed to address certain limitations identified in hierarchical "top-down" models of behavior in which a central executive agent or "command program" was assumed to control the selection and temporal sequencing of behavioral elements (Bernstein, 1967; Fogel & Thelen, 1987; Kugler, Kelso, & Turvey, 1982; Thelen & Ulrich, 1991). Within the domain of motor action, such models are thought to overburden the controlling agent with a monumental number of computations to accommodate small variations in task demand and action context (e.g., position of the body when reaching is initiated; location and characteristics of reaching target). According to dynamical systems theory, the control of some elements of an action sequence may reside in contextual factors particular to the action situation and/or synergistic relationships among noncentral, lower order behavioral components. For example, if one is walking over slightly uneven ground, balance is maintained via synergistic compensations among lower-order muscle groups rather than continuous monitoring and adjustments by a central motor program. Thus, dynamical systems theory asserts that behavioral output is as much a product of specific task demands as it is of a central controlling agent.

Regarding development, there are several dynamical systems principles designed to explain shifts from one organized behavioral system to another (e.g., from walking to running) and these may also be usefully applied to developmental change (Fogel, Nwokah, Dedo, Messinger, Dickson, Matusov, & Holt, 1992; Fogel & Thelen, 1987). According to dynamical systems theory, a shift to a new behavioral system may take place when some component of the system reaches a "critical value." For example, in the domain of motor development, Thelen (1985) has provided persuasive evidence that the shift from crawling to walking occurs when the fat:muscle ratio in the infant's legs reaches a critical value rather than when a new "central program" matures. In addition, dynamical systems theorists assert that components of a system need not develop in synchrony. Thus, some elements (e.g., leg cycling) may develop earlier than others and may be present before they function as part of the target behavioral system (e.g., walking). When at some point in time, the final key component (termed the "control parameter") develops or reaches a critical value, the target system will be organized. Later further reorganizations of a system may take place as new components emerge or reach their critical values. A last important principle relevant to development is the notion that control parameters may differ across systems or may change with age. For example, while the fat:muscle ratio may serve as the control parameter for the development of walking, it may not serve the same function in the development of stair climbing or reaching.

Applied to the domain of expressive development, the dynamical systems perspective can readily account for ontogenetic shifts in the relationship between expression and emotion as described above for the anger and sadness configurations. According to this view, components of affect may initially develop in an independent fashion and only later become organized into the target emotions. Thus, "anger" and "sadness" facial expressions may develop earlier than other components of these affects (e.g., instrumental actions, emotion-specific cognitions). At some point in development, a key constituent factor will achieve a "critical value" and catalyze the organization of components into the target system. For example, for anger and sadness, one might speculate that this occurs when the infant becomes capable of the appropriate emotion-specific cognitive appraisals. At this point, the anger and sadness facial configurations might be recruited in anger and sadness emotion episodes because these emotions are more mature analogues of the high versus low distress intensities with which we associate the expressions in early infancy.

Dynamical systems theory can also accommodate the possibility that emotional facial expressions are not invariably produced as part of an emotion episode in either infancy or adulthood. That is, facial expressions would not be assumed to be direct "read-outs" of a central emotion program (Buck, 1991) but would be determined by specific contextual factors that may often—but not always—occur in stereotypic emotion situations. Thus, during the course of development, facial expressions would come to be recruited in those situations in which other emotion-appropriate responses are also produced (e.g., cognitive appraisals, instrumental actions). However, in some circumstances, observable facial expressions may not be generated unless particular contextual factors are introduced. In other situations, facial responses may not veridically reflect the emotion content of the episode. For example, recall that in the study by Tomarken and Davidson previously described, phobic subjects produced "disgust" rather than fear expressions. This may have occurred because such configurations involve narrowing or even closing the eyes and served as a defensive response functionally appropriate to the demands of the experimental situation. In dynamical systems terms, the subjects' behavior was dictated by the task as well as the emotion.

Although task demands have been acknowledged in previous conceptualizations of expressive behavior, such formulations have assumed a normative "top-down" process of expression production that may at times be subjected to interference in accord with social or personal display rules. In contrast, a dynamical systems perspective would not assume an "interference" model but would instead argue that central and contextual factors may be equally important in the initial construction of the expressive act.

Emotion Elicitation

Emotional development also includes changes in the emotional significance of some stimulus situations. These changes in stimulus appraisal (and/or noncognitive stimulus "appreciation"; Barrett & Campos, 1987) may result from developments in the domains of cognition, motor behavior, and social interaction. An instructive example of such development was found in a recent study by Camras, Oster, Campos, Miyake, and Bradshaw (1992) in which responses to nonpainful arm restraint by 5- and 12-month-old Japanese and American infants were examined. This study showed that older infants in both cultures became upset more quickly than younger infants did (although infants in both cultures and at both ages eventually produced similar facial and nonfacial signs of negative affect). The investigators interpreted this finding as indicating that infants' evaluation of arm restraint is not biologically "fixed," but tied to developmental status particularly in the domains of motor and cognitive development. Between 5 and 12 months of age, directed reaching and grasping proceed from being newly emergent to highly developed motor skills. Furthermore, major advances in intentional behavior and elaboration of goals take place (Bertenthal, Campos, & Barrett, 1984). Thus older infants are more likely than younger ones to have experienced and thus expect successful goal attainment via controlled arm and hand movements. Consequently, they may value control over their arm movements more than younger infants and more quickly come to evaluate the restraint as a significant impediment.

While the findings described above suggest that stimulus evaluation may change with development, they leave open the possibility that evaluation-emotion relationships may themselves be invariant (e.g., once the evaluation "significant impediment" is made, then rage or anger will be invariably elicited). However, as suggested earlier, it is possible that the emotion elicited may also change with development. For example, younger infants may respond to impediments with distress while toddlers and older children may respond with anger. That is, as development proceeds, emotional responses to impediments may change in form and be more clearly interpretable as indicating a discrete emotion.

Experience and Understanding of Emotions, Relationships, and Membership in a Particular Culture

JUDY DUNN

Ideas and arguments concerning *what* develops in emotional development have chiefly focused on the issue of when, as children grow through infancy and early childhood, different emotions are first seen, and on the question of how cognitive developmental changes are linked to such developments in emotional expression and response. My comments will be directed not at this question of the timing of the appearance of expressions of anger, fear, and surprise in infancy, but instead at how developments in children's emotional expression and experiences are linked to developments in their social relationships and their understanding of others. Four themes that recur in recent work on emotional development will be discussed; for each of these, a focus on children's emotions in the context of their close relationships raises new questions concerning the nature of emotional development and suggests a range of differing answers to the initial question posed.

The Circumstances That Elicit Particular Emotions Change as Children Grow Up

The first theme concerns developmental changes in the events that elicit emotions. The circumstances that lead a 10 month old to show anger, fright, amusement, or frustration include very different events from the sources that frighten, frustrate, or amuse a 4 year old or an adult. Clearly, as children grow up, and their goals, relationships, and understanding of other people change, so the eliciting circumstances for these emotions change too.

What does this imply for the emotions that individuals experience? Facial expressions may remain the same at the different ages—but it is by no means clear that the emotions experienced are the same, as the circumstances that elicit them change. It appears unlikely that what is experienced by an individual is the same when the events that precipitate the emotional expression are very different. In what sense is the amusement of an 8 month old tickled by his father the *same* emotion as the amusement of an 8 year old at a dirty joke? Is the fear of a baby picked up by an unfamiliar person the *same* as that of an adolescent waiting for her exam results? In considering this issue, Campos and his colleagues suggest that it is useful to think of each basic emotion as a "family," in which all members share features of feeling tone and (perhaps) relations between the organism's goals, and events, but in which there are also clear differences between different instances of the emotion—such as those linked to developmental differences in the circumstances that elicit the emotion over the lifespan (Campos, Barrett, Lamb, Goldsmith, & Stenberg, 1983).

Thus, even for the "core" emotions that we can trace from early infancy, and for which continuity in facial expression exists, there are important changes in the eliciting conditions, and I would argue that these changes in themselves imply important changes in the emotional experiences of the individual. The emotion someone experiences cannot be regarded as independent of the particular circumstances that give rise to it—and that means as independent of the understanding, goals, and relationships of the individual at that point in development. Since these eliciting circumstances change with development, this implies change too in the emotions experienced. So one answer to the question "What develops in emotional development?" must be the circumstances that elicit particular emotions, and consequently the *experience of these emotions*.

New Emotions Appear in the Second and Third Year of Life

A second theme in developmental studies of emotion concerns the appearance of complex new emotions as children grow from infancy to childhood. It is now widely acknowledged that during the course of their second and third years, young children begin to express emotions not seen in their earlier infancy: pride, shame, guilt, jealousy, and embarrassment. The expression of these emotions is clearly linked to a new appreciation of the standards of others, the expectation of approval or disapproval of others, or the interaction between others, and to the development of a sense of self and therefore of injury—potential or real—to the self. It is frequently assumed that the cognitive changes underlying the developments in social understanding, sense of self, and appreciation of social rules *lead* to the emergence of the new emotions. The new emotions are seen as developing as a result of the children's increasing cognitive maturity.

However, a focus on children's emotional behavior in real-life situations suggests that the interrelations between these developments are surely more complex. A number of lines of evidence from research on children's emotional behavior within their families indicate that situations in which young children are experiencing jealousy or envy not only reveal but may well foster children's most mature capabilities of argument and their ability to understand and anticipate others' actions (Dunn, 1988; Dunn & Slomkowski, 1992). And experiences of shame and embarrassment may in themselves contribute to children's self-consciousness, their reflection on their own abilities and performance, and those of others. The question

"What develops in emotional development?" becomes, importantly, "What develops *with*, or *as a result of* emotional development?" And the answer includes, I would argue, *understanding other people*, *understanding the social world*, *understanding one's self*.

Developments in the Regulations of Emotion

Among those interested in emotional development, a third theme, the topic of *regulation* of emotion, has received perhaps more attention than any other in recent years (see, e.g., Garber & Dodge, 1991). Two issues have been the chief focus of interest, the development of "impulse control"—the increasing control children exert over their frustration, anger, or distress during early childhood—and the clinical implications of individual differences in such emotional control. There are clearly major achievements in such emotional control during the preschool years, as children begin to argue rather that assault, to wait rather than wail, and to control their impatience or frustration. But to focus solely on the "damping down" of extremes of anger or distress would be gravely to misrepresent the striking developmental changes in children's emotional behavior and understanding during this period. If we think of affect regulation not solely as a private "homeostatic" mechanism, but as including children's increasing ability to influence not only their own emotions but those of others, and to use others to meet their own needs and influence their own emotional states, then it becomes clear that there are very broad changes in the second and third year of life in the nature of children's emotional regulation, and that these changes reflect profound changes in the nature of children's relationships.

For example, the growth of children's communication skills and of their understanding of others leads to a wide range of new powers of control over their own affective states. They become able to explain their own state and enlist aid or comfort when distressed; they are able to express their affection and ask for love. It is important to broaden the notion of emotional needs beyond the urgent situations of pain and extreme distress to include the need to feel good about oneself and to maintain a happy equilibrium, and here children's new communicative abilities mean that they are able to share positive experiences, draw attention to their successes, *tell* their parents that they are enjoying something—or simply that they *love* them—and start conversations about what they like. Most important, they have a new medium for sharing jokes—a core feature of close relationships. They also become able to exercise some manipulative power over their own future emotional states, as for instance in their new ability to evade or redirect parental disapproval or punishment. They can and do begin to practice deception about their own emotional states, in order to achieve their own desires or to evade unpleasant consequences.

Particularly striking are the developments in children's ability to understand and influence others' emotional states over this developmental period. There are notable changes in the elaboration and success with which children *comfort*, *tease*, and *joke* with others through their second, third, and fourth years; the significance of their joking and teasing behavior lies both in the evident pleasure they experience in sharing their positive affect with particular others and in manipulating the emotions of another, and in the understanding of others' emotions that this behavior reflects. The development of these features of emotion regulation are important not only because they demonstrate children's growing ability to control their own emotions, but because they reflect a new intimacy and power of expression that children have achieved in their close relationships. In their ability to influence the emotions of their parents and siblings these young children demonstrate the richness and elaboration of their relationships, a richness that highlights how narrow our conception of their attachment relationships has been—solely in terms of insecurity. In answer to the question of what develops with, or as a result of emotional development, we should include the development of *intimacy and power in close relationships*.

Language, Culture, and Emotional Development

A fourth theme concerns links between language and emotional development. The ability and propensity to talk about and reflect on emotions show remarkable developments in the preschool and early childhood years (Brown & Dunn, 1991; Dunn & Brown, 1991). Why is this important in emotional development? On the one hand it makes it possible for children to understand and (possibly) to distance themselves from emotional experiences, through discussion and reflection with others, and it enables them "to share their personal experience of the world with others, including 'being with' others in intimacy, isolation, loneliness, fear, awe, and love" (Stern, 1985, p. 182). On the other hand, it leads children to participate in the shared cultural concepts of emotion of their particular world, which can differ widely across cultures (Shweder & LeVine, 1984). To the question of what develops with emotional development, then, our answer should include not only *understanding of one's own and others' emotions*, but *membership in a particular culture*.

Intersystem Connections

CARROLL E. IZARD

Emotional development consists of the processes whereby the emotions system achieves an increasingly complex matrix of functional links with the other subsystems of the individual—the physiological/drive, perceptual, cognitive, and action systems. Conceived in this way, emotional development is facilitated and constrained by development within each of the organismic subsystems. For example, an individual cannot respond with contempt or shame until maturation and cognitive development have enabled the acquisition of a sense of self and self-other discrimination.

As defined here, emotional development is the cornerstone of personality development, the coordination of all the subsystems for the purpose of interpersonal and person-environment transactions. Development that leads to harmonious interactions of all the subsystems provides the basis for effective coping, creative behavior, and physiological and psychological well-being (cf. Seeman, 1989). Inappropriate or deficient connections among systems lead to personality disorder or psychopathology (Izard & Harris, in press).

Conceived as an integral part of individual or personality development, emotional development might be viewed primarily as a matter of achieving intersystem connections and communication lines. Indeed, much of the current body of research on emotional development concerns the development of relations between the cognitive and emotions systems. I think of this aspect of emotional development as the development of affective-cognitive structures and view these phenomena as the most common building blocks of mind, memory, and the traits of personality (Izard, 1971, 1992; Izard, Libero, Putnam, & Haynes, 1993).

The emotions system is defined as the matrix of relations that organizes and regulates the functioning of the several discrete emotions. The discrete emotions can operate separately, but, more commonly, they operate as members of an interrelated group or pattern (Blumberg & Izard, 1986; Izard, 1972). Although I agree with Tomkins (1962, 1991) that there are some innate relations among discrete emotions, conditioning and social learning and other types of experience are the source of many of the connections among emotions. The child who is regularly and harshly punished for expressing anger seems likely to develop a connection between anger and fear (of punishment). Hence, feelings of anger may become a learned activator of fear.

Development in Relation to a Particular Emotion

To describe the development of a discrete emotion, which may be viewed as a subsystem within the emotions system, it is necessary to consider each of its three components—neural-evaluative, expressive, experiential. In this context, the term component refers to functional units that are highly interrelated and that normally interact harmoniously. As used here, component does not mean that there is a categorical separation among entities. The three components have extensive interconnections, and each component can, and typically does, influence the others. Nevertheless, the concept of emotion components is useful, particularly in a discussion of development. The processes of development may differ among components.

Development and the Neural-Evaluative Component

The substrates of the neural-evaluative component consist of the structures and pathways involved in the process of evaluating the significance of internal and external stimuli. At the functional level, the neural-evaluative component is the process of emotion activation. The neural-evaluative process, or emotion activation, normally leads to the expressive and experiential components. Of course, the expressive and experiential components also have neural substrates, which may have some structures common to the neural-evaluative component and some that are different (see LeDoux, 1987).

Differential emotions theory (Izard, 1977; Izard & Malatesta, 1987) holds that the neural-evaluative component is functional for a few emotions at birth and for several others by the end of the first six or seven months of life. The differentiation and maturation of the substrates of the neural-evaluative component, as well as cognitive development and social learning, are involved in the emerging capacity to respond with emotions like contempt, shame, and guilt. The emergence of these emotions is coordinated with cognitive development because they are a function of self-consciousness, social comparison, and other higher order cognitive processes. Thus, these emotions derive from emotional development or the development of intersystem connections. That these emotions depend on cognitive development and the development of intersystems connections does not affect the hypothesis that they have innate determinants.

Development and Emotion Expressions

Noting that all components of an emotion have neural substrates serves as a reminder that all components, like the nervous system as a whole, continue to develop after birth. At the same time, evidence for the innateness and universality of the facial expressions of some discrete emotions (Ekman, Sorenson, & Friesen, 1969; Izard, 1971; Izard, 1980) suggests that the expressive component of these emotions is pre-adapted (Izard & Malatesta, 1987). Apparently, no postnatal development is required for these features of the emotions system to become functional. If we assume that these expressions are not random responses but consequents of the process of emotion activation, then the structures of the neural-evaluative component of these emotions must also be functional at birth. The question of whether there is an experiential component corresponding to these early-infancy expressions has been discussed but not settled (e.g., Izard & Malatesta, 1987; Lewis & Michalson, 1983).

Although some components of some emotions are functional at birth, this does not preclude developmental processes, even in the pre-adapted components. Expressions that are pre-adapted are more instinct-like in early infancy than they will appear in later years. Through maturation and learning, instinct-like expressions become controlled emotion signals that may be veridical or deceptive (Ekman & Friesen, 1982; Izard et al., 1987; Izard & Malatesta, 1987). Thus, development of the expressive component eventually enables the individual to regulate (exaggerate, attenuate) an expression and even to dissociate emotion expression and emotion experience (cf. Bonanno & Singer, 1990; Weinberger, 1990).

On the other side of the coin, there is little or no evidence as to how or whether development influences the morphology of the innate/universal expressions. There is no evidence that post-natal expressive behavior follows the widely applicable differentiation-integration principle of development. No one has shown for any expression that there is first a global, undifferentiated response that gradually becomes differentiated and then hierarchically integrated into a well-organized pattern.

There is evidence from an extensive longitudinal study that the expressions of certain emotions that are present at birth or that emerge within the first three months remain stable in early development (Izard, Fantauzzo, Castle, Haynes & Slomine, 1993). In this study, the facial behavior of 88 2.5- to 9-month-old infants was recorded in a variety of positive and mildly stressful situations. A total of 20,816 expressions were coded with objective, anatomically based coding systems. Full-faced, partial, and blended expressions of interest, joy, sadness, and anger accounted for 98 percent of all facial behavior. Full-face expressions of all four of these emotions were present by 2.5 months. Inspection of the frequencies of these discrete emotion expressions revealed no developmental trends between 2.5 and 9 months of age.

A subset of 53 infants in this study were observed in the same conditions at the same ages. The distribution of expressions for this subsample was essentially the same as that for the total group, but it also met the assumptions for formal analysis. A mixed model repeated measures MANOVA for each expression category revealed no significant effects for age.

The data of the Izard et al. (1993) study showed that for each of a limited set of expressions, the basic form or morphology of the movement configuration is present by 2.5 months and remains stable through the first nine months. The stability of these facial-movement configurations helps ensure the effectiveness of the social-communicative function of emotion expressions in the preverbal infant.

There is very little empirical data on the kind of development that occurs in the expressive component after early infancy. It is reasonable to assume that culture and idiosyncratic learning modify emotion expressions. Even if we accept this assumption, we still do not know how much the modifications apply to deliberate or voluntary expressions compared to spontaneous expressions. We also do not know the extent to which people modify the morphology of the expression compared to other techniques of expression regulation—reducing the expression to a single signal in one facial region, attenuating the intensity of the expression, substituting one expression for another, and so on. Undoubtedly culture, social learning, and individual-specific experiences produce some changes in expression morphology. Surely, experience helps determine the structure of expression blends, expressions that contain signals of more than one emotion. However, developmental changes in the morphology of a particular discrete emotion are probably constrained by whatever adaptive value has accrued to the social-communication function of veridical emotion expressions.

An important aspect of development in relation to emotion expressions is the development of individual differences in expressiveness. Biological differences in emotion thresholds, as well as social learning, contribute to differences in proneness to experience and express the various emotions. Research on mother-child relations and personality development has shown that mothers are characterized by individual differences in the extent to which they display their emotions around their children and that these individual patterns of expressiveness influence the social development (quality of attachment) of their children (Izard, Haynes, Chisholm, & Baak, 1991).

Development and Emotion Experience and Emotion-Cognition Relations

I define emotion experience primarily in terms of motivation. It is a particular *quality* of consciousness, primarily feeling or affective tone. It eludes precise description but several descriptors capture some of its aspects—motivating condition, feeling state, change or shift ("bias") in perception, cues for cognition, action readiness, action tendency. I view emotion experience (motivational / feeling state) as a direct product of the neural-evaluative or emotion activation process.

As defined here, emotion experience does not change with development. More specifically, the basic motivational/feeling state of an emotion is invariant (cf. Campos & Barrett, 1984; Emde, 1980). (What changes, as I discuss later, is the development of connections among emotions and cognition.) The present definition of emotion experience is consistent with the proposition that the neural component and the basic morphology of the expressive component of emotions are determined primarily by genetic processes and biological maturation. Having genetic determinants does not mean that they have to be in place and fully functional at birth (see Scarr & Kidd, 1983). It probably does mean that there is a timetable or schedule for their emergence, in most cases a schedule that is coordinated with developmental schedules in other systems. For example, the fear system does not emerge until the infant's sympathetic nervous system and the organs and systems it innervates are strong enough to withstand the effects of this potentially life-threatening emotion experience. As already noted, the infant cannot experience contempt, shame, or guilt until cognitive development has enabled the acquisition of a sense of self and self-other discrimination.

Emotion experience, except possibly that of contempt, shame, and guilt, does not *require* cognition at either the input or output side of emotion activation (see Izard on Question 5). Often cognition does instigate the emotion activation process, and in these cases cognition can be considered a distal cause of emotion experience. Even when cognition is a distal cause of emotion experience, it is neurochemical activity that generates the motivational/feeling state or conscious experience of emotion.

Because emotion experience shifts and focuses perception and is cue-producing in nature, it typically recruits cognitive processes. This brings us to a domain that does show enormous developmental changes—connections between emotions and cognition. As emotion experience shifts and focuses perception and engages the cognitive system, the stage is set for the development of emotion-cognition relations. As already noted, an emotion experience-cognition association or bond is called an affective-cognitive structure (Izard, 1977). This combination of motivational state and cognition is what some emotions theorists call emotion experience, and emotion experience defined in this way (what I call affective-cognitive structures) is certainly subject to developmental changes. Anything defined in terms of cognition will surely change with cognitive development. I can argue that emotion experience is invariant over the lifespan because I have defined it as a noncognitive motivational condition, generated directly by neurochemical processes.

I have speculated that the first mental structures are emotion experiences and that one of the first affective-cognitive structures is the associative bond of enjoyment and the image of the mother's face (Izard, 1978, 1993). The formation of this affective-cognitive structure begins at about three to five weeks of age, when the social smile emerges and the infant achieves the capacity to perceive the contours of the human face. This is before the infant can discriminate among faces and probably before the development of appraisal capacities have enabled the infant to anticipate mother's actions. At this age and until age four or five months, the infant smiles at friendly faces indiscriminately. The development of the bond between the feeling of joy and an image of the mother's face (a primal affective-cognitive structure) depends on the emergence of perceptual discrimination, recognition memory, and storage-retrieval capacities. With the advent of verbal representation and other higher order cognitive processes and months of social interactions, this initial affective-cognitive structure can become the nexus of a complex of affective-cognitive structures that constitute the mental representation of a secure attachment to the mother.

The infant's mental representation of the attachment figure and the attachment relationship is modified and elaborated through continued learning and experience. The result is a coherent and cohesive network of affective-cognitive structures that can be conceived as an interpersonal trait. Individual traits of personality emerge in similar fashion, through the development of bonds among particular emotions and particular sequences of cognition and action (Izard et al., 1993). The processes of linking emotions, cognition, and action patterns are influenced by both experience and genetic factors. Genetic makeup plays a significant role in determining emotion experience thresholds and proneness to experience certain emotions (cf. Kagan et al., 1988; Tangney, 1990), and these characteristics, in turn, are determinants of traits and dimensions of the developing personality.

Summary

Emotional development consists primarily of the development of links among emotions and cognition and the establishing of coherent and cohesive patterns of emotion, cognition, and action. A highly significant part of emotional development is the development of emotion regulation. Emotion experiences are the primary motivating and organizing conditions underlying the processes of emotional development. These processes are influenced by both genes and experience. Conceiving emotional development in this way makes it a large part of the development of personality.

Some features of the emotions system, the overall organization of the discrete emotions as a functional complex, are primarily a matter of biological development and the unfolding of genetic processes. Evidence suggests that this is true for the morphology of the expressions of the basic emotions. There is no evidence of postnatal developmental changes in the structure of the pattern of movements that signal an emotion or in the neuromuscular underpinnings of these patterned movements. There is evidence that the expressions of several emotions are present at birth or within a few weeks thereafter and that the form of these expressions remains constant over the first nine months of life.

I have defined emotion experience as the motivational condition generated directly by the neurochemical activity set in motion by the neural-evaluative or emotion activation process. Defined in this way, emotion experience does not require cognitive antecedents, constituents, or consequents. More important, for the present question, emotion experience as motivational condition is hypothesized to be invariant over the lifespan. The motivational state specific to joy or sadness or anger or fear remains constant. What develops in this domain is emotion-cognition relations, affective-cognitive structures, and patterns of emotion-cognition-action sequences. Emotion experience is seen as the organizing and motivating force in these processes, and these processes are viewed as central in emotional development and in the development of personality.

Meaning and Emotional Development

RICHARD LAZARUS

Not being a developmental psychologist, I am inclined to defer to those who have, for a long time, given attention to many of the questions I will address below, for example, Campos, Barrett, Lamb, Goldsmith, and Stenberg (1983), Emde (1984), Lewis and Michalson (1983), Sroufe (1979), and others who have centered attention on cognitive development and emotion in older children, such as Dunn (1988), Harris (1989), Stein and Trabasso (1990), and a growing number of others.

However, developmental issues regarding the emotions, particularly those concerning cognition, motivation, and coping, are so important for a well-rounded theory of emotion that I should nevertheless have some input on this question. I will limit myself to the programmatic statement of the variables whose development (Lazarus, 1991c) should be studied along with what I have written about emotion theory.

Although the developmental changes taking place in early childhood are profound, I take development to include also changes in personality and life settings in later life as well. With respect to the latter, the nature and variations in developmental change are not yet clear, and although I have contributed some ideas and information (e.g., Folkman, Lazarus, Pimley, & Novacek, 1987) about coping in aging, I will concentrate here on early development.

The emotion process is influenced by a number of basic variables, some of which serve as antecedents and some mediating processes. It is useful to regarded emotion as a special system of interdependent variables, each influencing various aspects of the emotion process; and each separate emotion, such as anger, anxiety, pride, and so forth, is generated and regulated by some of these variables. It is these variables, therefore, whose development is crucial to emotion theory, some of them undoubtedly being more central than others. In this brief essay, I focus on what I regard as the key antecedent and mediating variables in the generation of the emotions.

Antecedent Variables

Since emotion expresses a particular kind of relational meaning, namely, how the person-environment relationship bears on personal well-being, the person and the environment constitute the main sets of antecedent variables relevant to the emotions. The latter, obviously, are not directly influenced by development, and so can be ignored in this comment. However, it might be worth pointing out that they consist of environmental demands, constraints, and opportunities, as well as formal properties such as imminence and ambiguity, which also influence emotion.

Development is highly relevant, of course, to personality variables. What then are the central personality variables of the emotion process? I want to consider two, one being motivational, the other having to do with self or ego. I deal with motivation in the concept of an *individual goal hierarchy*, which defines the values and goals that are most and least important to the person. Important goals carry the implication of commitments, which is reflected in how much effort and persistence an individual is willing to expend to attain them even in the face of daunting obstacles. Remember, it is not just the presence of goal commitments that generates emotion, but an encounter with the environment must makes one or another of these goals salient in the transaction. The encounter provides information about the fate, actual or potential, of goal striving.

We know very little about the development of motivation, less even than we know about the development of the emotions—for example, which ones and at what age do they manifest themselves? We assume that physiological drives are universal, though perhaps not equally strong in different individuals (as in the sex drive). However, the point in life when particular social motives emerge and become organized hierarch--ically in a developing individual is an issue of considerable importance, not only for emotional development but for individual differences in general adaptation as well.

If, for example, goals to achieve or affiliate with others are not yet present at a particular age, these goals cannot be a causal antecedent of negative or positive emotions. Predicting the emotion process in a goal-relevant encounter with the environment as the infant develops depend, therefore, on what we know about the emergence and consolidation of these goals. Equally important, we need to rely also on their place in the goal hierarchy, that is, which ones are most and least important to the individual.

In speaking of a goal hierarchy, I believe we are also assuming some kind of emerging *self* or *ego-identity*, which, as Hilgard (1949) long ago observed, organizes goals in terms of their relative importance and regulates which one is to be acted on under given conditions. To the extent that emotions result from a judgment that something personally important is at stake, a developing child's mind must be capable of sensing that its commitments are engaged in an encounter before an emotion can take place. This kind of appraisal probably becomes possible very early, perhaps in the first few months. In addition, as Hilgard observed, there would be no defense mechanism without a self or ego-identity to defend.

Therefore, I am forced to conclude that there must be an elemental self or ego for emotion to occur, one that specifies and distinguishes one's own individual interests in the world from that of others. I say this though aware of suggestions from cultural anthropology and social constructivists that such a concept may vary in importance and kind—at least overtly and in language—in different cultures. And I am inclined to think, in accord with Stern (1985), that the developmental work of forming such a system, which is probably mandated biologically as a structure, though probably not in its contents, begins very early, perhaps within the first few months of postnatal life. At present, there is little agreement about how to think about and study the problem (see also Lewis, 1990; Lewis & Michalson, 1983).

In Lazarus (1991c) I distinguished among six types of ego-involvement, each of which is probably involved a different way in each of the emotions. These types include self- and social-esteem, moral values, ego-ideals, meanings and ideas, other persons and their well-being, and life goals. I am convinced that some emotions are brought about because particular ego-involvements are engaged in an encounter that contribute to the appraisal process.

For example, anger and pride draw on encounters relevant to self- and social esteem; guilt on internalized moral values; shame on internalized ego-ideals; anxiety on meanings and ideas that have existential significance; sadness, on the other hand, depends on any irrevocable loss regardless of the goal commitment involved, and so any type of goal that has been permanently lost is relevant for this emotion. However, I suspect that the goal commitments that have the greatest power to generate sadness, namely, those that are part of the self or ego, are capable of producing the most intense and prolongued emotions and moods.

Mediating Process Variables

The two key mediating process variables in my analysis are appraisal and coping, with coping subordinate to appraisal because, whether it changes the realities of the person-environment relationship or the way it is attended to or construed, its effects are mediated by changed relational meanings, in effect, by appraisal. This analysis ignores perception and attention, which undoubtedly play a role in the emotion process, probably by affecting appraisal and also being an aspect of coping. To have an emotion depends on noticing what is happening. However, I have not centered my concern on perception and attention, per se, as individual difference variables that could be relevant to the emotions.

The most important point to make about mediating process variables is that, to understand and predict the emotions of an individual requires that we also assess the knowledge, appraisal, and coping capabilities of a child at any given developmental stage. Lazarus and Smith (1988) have recently distinguished between knowledge and appraisal, which play different roles in the generation of an emotion. *Knowledge* has to do with what we believe (therefore, what we think we know) about how things work in the world. *Appraisal* is an evaluation of this knowledge and the inputs in an encounter about the significance of what is happening for personal well-being. I have argued (Lazarus, 1991c) that knowledge is a necessary but not sufficient condition of emotion but appraisal is both necessary and sufficient. There is also a growing body of observation about the development of *knowledge* and *appraisal*.

A child who is unable to recognize an external source of thwarting, sense that its self-esteem has been demeaned, or infer the basis for blame, cannot experience anger as it is appraised and experienced by an adult. Therefore, the crucial research task for appraisal theory is to learn what children at different developmental stages know about how things work in the world, and their capacity to evaluate the relational meanings important in the generation of an emotion.

Though there is also substantial overlap among them suggesting an emerging consensus, appraisal theorists (e.g., Frijda, 1986; Lazarus, 1991c; Roseman, 1984, 1991; Scherer, 1984; Smith & Ellsworth, 1985, 1987; Weiner, 1986) have emphasized somewhat different components and patterns of appraisal for different emotions. For example, most of them cite a motivational component as well as one signifying goal congruence or incongruence, which imply the environmental contingencies involved in harm and benefit. They also tend to agree on the importance of the direction of accountability and its role in blame, which seems widely appreciated as a factor in anger.

Though there has been some sporadic interest, there has been little observation about the development of the *coping process*. To the extent that coping is important in both emotion generation and regulation of the emotion process in general, it will be necessary to examine how children cope at different developmental stages. I think its importance is, indeed, very great.

Here is a rudimentary list of what might be called coping skills on which the emotional life depends, defined as developmental questions.

At what age can a child control environmental input by turning its head toward and away from threatening or rewarding objects and events? This is an early form of coping. Does its development correlate with later forms of coping? When and how does locomotion, and the appraisals it potentiates, make it possible for a child to approach or avoid encounters that have positive and negative significance? This might also be treated as a form of coping, which should be regarded as a developmental advance. At what point in development can a child manipulate the environment and its relationship with it verbally and symbolically rather than merely concretely and motorically—clearly a Piagetian and Wernerian issue on which there has been considerable research and theory? When does a child recognize that it can use emotion in manipulating others so that this capacity can be added to its coping repertoire? At what stage of life can a person first manipulate his or her construals of what is happening to regulate individual emotional reactions? For example, when can a developing child make excuses for someone who generated anger by distancing from distressing observations, by denying a threat? By what stage of life can a child realize that its own displays of happiness or other emotions may have important social consequences, making it useful to control them?

Similar questions can be asked with respect to all the powerful coping processes, both problem focused and emotion focused (e.g., denial, distancing, attention avoidance, and positive thinking, which adults learn to use—sometimes productively, sometimes counterproductively—throughout their lives). These very important questions have not, in the main, been much studied in developmental research, yet they profoundly influence the emotion process.

Summing Up

It seems to me that the task of understanding emotional development is best served by examining the acquisition, from infancy on, of the key individual difference variables that antecede the generation of emotions, and, even more important, the key mediating process variables that create relational meanings in short-term encounters and in the long-term existential issues of our lives.

The antecedents of greatest importance are *goal commitments* and *how they are organized* in the person, including types of ego-involvement, or variables of self, if one prefers that term. These personality variables, and their individual variations, are juxtaposed in an adaptational encounter with physical and social environmental variables, which have a major bearing on what people want or find aversive. These encounters and the transactions they produce, particularly interpersonal ones, generate the emotions.

Emotions occur because people understand at some level that they have a personal stake in the confrontation with the other person or physical environment, the outcome of which could involve either harm or benefit. *Appraisal*—based on what one knows about the world and defined as the way this knowledge is evaluated in the context of adaptational encounters—refers to the process whereby people and animals sense the significance of what is happening for their personal well-being. Each emotion is the result of an evaluation of the specific harm or benefit that has already taken place or will eventuate in an adaptational encounter. The process of appraisal results in what I call *relational meaning* by taking into account both the personal stakes and what is being confronted in the environment in that encounter.

This means that to understand emotional development requires that one also understand what a child at any age senses about the way things work—that is, its knowledge of emotion-relevant variables, as well as its capacity to make a complex set of appraisal decisions, that combine to produce the relational meaning. I believe this is the central task in the study of emotional development.

Finally, since *coping* alters relational meaning through its effects on the appraisal process, its development is also an indispensable task in developmental research on emotional development. Even babies, much less fully developed adults, are not totally passive, and at some point in their development they begin to shut out some aspects of their environment and attend to others, ultimately locomoting to and from threats and rewarding agents, and eventually manipulating the environment in very complicated verbal and symbolic ways. The possibilities of emotion generation, and emotion regulation, are greatly modified as children increase their repertoire of coping skills. Therefore, the study of emotional development must also include the study of how coping changes over the life course, and how the results of that coping influence the appraisal process.

Emotional Development Yields Lots of "Stuff" . . . Especially Mind "Stuff" That Emerges from Brain "Stuff"

JAAK PANKSEPP

Traditional answers to this question will focus on the increasingly sophisticated interactions a child has with its world. From a psychological perspective, I would say that the main thing that develops in emotional development is the linking of internal affective values to new life experiences. However, in addition to the epigentic processes related to each individual's personal emotional experiences leading to unique emotional habits and traits, there is also a spontaneous neurobiological unfolding of emotional and behavioral systems during childhood and adolescence (Hall & Oppenheim, 1987). Some neuroemotional processes are strongly influenced by prenatal experiences, for instance, the ability of early hormonal tides to control the brain substrates of gender identity (Crews, 1987; Kincl, 1990; Ziegler & Bercovitch, 1990). Modern neuroscience is showing that the brain is not as unchanging a computational space as is commonly assumed. Neurochemical systems develop and remold at both pre- and post-synaptic sites throughout the lifespan of organisms. Receptor fields proliferate and shrink during specific phases of ontogentic development (Insel, 1992), and they can show permanent changes in response to life events (Insel, Kinsley, Mann, & Bridges, 1990). Indeed, neurons in specific adult motivational systems can expand and shrink depending on the environmental challenges and the resulting hormonal tides an animal is exposed to (Schumacher, Coirini, Pfaff, & McEwen, 1990; Yang & Hatton, 1988). It is becoming increasingly clear that there is a dynamic interaction between environmental events and genetic events in the brain (e.g., Kwak, Young, Morano, Watson, & Akil, 1992; Young, Mezey, & Seigel, 1986). With such complexities, it is a risky business to suppose that the stages of emotional and moral development that we see in human children are simply due to the specific life experiences they have acquired. At the same time, it is foolhardy to push the biological view too far. Even with identical genetic backgrounds, there is a great deal of epigenetic diversity in the fine details of the nervous system. Only the general groundplans for brain connectivities are encoded within the genes, and probably quite indirectly at that (e.g., via expressions of various trophic factors). Neural growth is responsive to a large number of internal and external stochastic processes that lead to a diversity of detailed differences in every nook and cranny of the brain. But despite the infinite variety in the details, the overall plan of the mammalian brain has been highly conserved.

After birth, a great deal of neural unfolding remains to be completed in every species, and we can be reasonably confident that the maturation of specific neural systems does establish essential conditions for the unfolding of certain forms of emotionality. A few examples: (1) Social bonding (imprinting) processes are especially sensitive at certain times of life (Hess, 1973). (2) The separation distress system seems to exhibit increasing sensitivity during the initial phase of postnatal development, a long-plateau period, and a gradual decline during puberty (Scott, Stewart, & DeGhett, 1973). (3) Rough-and-tumble play exhibits a similar pattern (Panksepp, Siviy, & Normansell, 1984). (4) Rats exhibit strong tendencies for maternal behavior during early juvenile development, at times comparable to those when human children are especially infatuated by dolls and play-mothering (Brunelli & Hofer, 1990). (5) Parental tendencies are heralded by neurochemical changes, even genetic de-repression within the oxytocin system, which helps promote maternal intent (Jirikowski, Caldwell, Pilgrim, Stumpf, & Pedersen, 1989). (6) And of course, emotional aspects of sexuality mature at puberty under the sway of genetically controlled hormonal progressions, "developing" gender-specific impulses that were "exposed" as neurohormonal engrams during infancy (Kincl, 1990). Although many psychosocial specifics develop concurrently, depending on the unique life experiences of individuals, the natural unfolding of neurobiological processes underlying emotionality should not be minimized. Indeed, we need to consider how the experience of important life events feed back onto the structure of the systems. For instance, does an enriched environment invigorate the exploratory systems of the brain? Do repeated experiences of social loss in early childhood change the vigor and configuration of separation-distress systems of the brain? Answers to such compelling questions can now be achieved with certain long-lasting neuronal markers (such as fluoro-gold) that can be administered at specific times of psychoneurological development to see whether the morphological patterns in specific neuronal circuits are remodeled under the sway of specific environmental/emotional challenges. When we finally begin to do such experiments, we will truly be addressing the pervasive nature-nurture interactions that help mold the brain/mind throughout maturation.

Emotional Development: Changes in Reactivity and Self-Regulation

MARY K. ROTHBART

It would be very difficult to give a complete answer to this question, even in a list form. However, several interesting aspects of emotion and development can be touched on here. First, the age of onset of particular emotions appears to vary with development, as does the age of onset of particular components of emotional-motivational systems. Linked to these developments are the child's development of cognitive capacities. Self-regulatory influences on the emotions, including behavioral inhibition and the attentional systems, also develop. Throughout development, the social environment influences the emotions, facilitating, inhibiting, and directing their expression. Finally, developments in the emotional domain influence other important developmental processes and events. This discussion briefly considers each of these points.

First, we consider age of onset, or the time at which the emotion comes "on line" for the individual. Some emotions are expressed in the newborn, but the expression of other emotions is not observed until later in development. Thus distress is observed in the newborn infant (Izard, 1978a,b). Smiling is observed 2 to 12 hours after delivery, but vocal behavior resembling laughter is not seen until about 5 weeks of age (see Rothbart, 1973; Wolff, 1963). Anger/frustration reactions have been observed at 2 months of age (Lewis, Alessandri, & Sullivan, 1990), whereas inhibitory aspects of fear to novel stimuli are not usually demonstrated until 8 to 9 months of age (Schaffer, 1974).

The fear example points up a second way in which emotions develop. If emotions are viewed as part of organized emotional-motivational systems, as I have argued in response to Question 10, then some components of a system can be seen to develop at an earlier age than others. Recent findings suggest that distress proneness in 4-month-old infants, accompanied with behavioral activation, predicts later behavioral inhibition, a later developing component of the fear response (Kagan, Snidman, & Arcus, 1992). Behavioral approach and avoidance, components of positive and negative emotional-motivational systems respectively, also develop along with the greater motor capacities of the infant at 4 to 6 months.

The appearance of the emotions in the infant's repertoire is also linked to the development of cognitive capacities. For example, aspects of the orienting reaction are related to smiling to exogenous stimuli (Brock, Rothbart, & Derryberry, 1986), and memory changes between 7 and 9 months of age are related to anticipatory fear (Kagan, 1979; Sroufe, 1979). Emotions such as pride and shame depend on a concept of the self that is not achieved until toward the end of the second year. Lewis, Sullivan, Stanger, and Weiss (1989) have demonstrated relations between the development of self-concept and the appearance of the self-related emotions of embarrassment and pride. Advances in cognitive and language capacities are also requisite to the child's ability to identify and label emotions as experienced and expressed by the self and others (Bretherton & Beeghly, 1982), and moral emotions such as guilt may be dependent on children's understanding and internalization of rules.

The stimulus conditions sufficient to elicit the emotions also change with development, with new stimuli becoming adequate to elicit the emotions and others decreasing in adequacy over time. Consider smiling and laughter: both sensory events and novel stimuli are highly stimulating to the young infant after development of the orienting reaction by 2 to 3 months, and it is relatively easy to provide the "boosts" and "jags" (Berlyne, 1960, 1969) that elicit positive affect (Sroufe & Waters, 1976). Thus, repetitive banging of a spoon on a table may lead to repeated laughter in a 6 month old. Such simple events are much less likely to lead to pleasure in the older child and adult, who have habituated to much of the excitement elicited by environmental events. Older infants become increasingly reactive to more complex forms of novelty or incongruity (Sroufe & Waters, 1976), and more highly stimulating events, such as riding a roller coaster, may be sufficient to elicit smiling and laughter in the older person.

The experience of incongruity within a safe context, which can lead to both positive emotion and the experience of humor (Berlyne, 1960; Rothbart, 1973) will also be influenced by what the person knows, so that the individual's developing knowledge base allows for different kinds of pleasure depending on its breadth and depth. The context of safety itself will vary. For an infant close to a year of age, it may require the mother's presence (MacDonald & Silverman, 1978); in the older child, it may require that laughter be directed at someone other than the self; in the adult, it may require that a joke be told by a member of the ingroup to another ingroup member for pleasure to occur (LaFave, Mannell, & Guilmette, 1977). Stimuli effective in eliciting distress also change with development. The young infant may be overstimulated by stimulus intensities that do not affect the older child, and the older child may be distressed by social slights or threats to the perception of self-worth that have no impact on the infant (see discussion by Kagan, 1974; Rothbart, 1989c).

Cognitive development will also influence the effectiveness of stimuli in eliciting the emotions. In frustration reactions, the 2 month old shows anger/frustration to a failure of expectations; the 4 month old shows anger/frustration to both failure of expectations and the cessation of positive experiences (Lewis et al., 1990). Capacities for means-ends reasoning late in the first year provide a basis for irritability when the infant's achievement of means is blocked. Development of moral reasoning can lead to anger at others when moral principles are not followed, and to guilt when they are not followed by the self. Older children can rank order stimuli according to their value, including rankings of the self in relation to others, affecting emotions of pride and shame. Children become increasingly aware of failure and may be distressed by learning their relative standing in comparison with others (Ruble, Boggiano, Feldman, & Loebl, 1980). By adulthood, individuals will also use "downward comparisons" to enhance their feelings about themselves (Wills, 1981, 1990).

Psychological processes (such as attention) that serve to regulate the expression of emotion also develop. Thus, development of the infants' ability to disengage attention from visual stimuli that might become overstimulating is related to mother's reports of lower infant susceptibility to the negative affects at 4 months (Johnson, Posner, & Rothbart, 1991; Rothbart, Ziaie, & O'Boyle, 1992). Techniques for self-distraction from emotion will continue to be useful across development. Children's ability to effortfully control behavior, including expression of emotions, also follows a developmental course that begins in late infancy and likely continues throughout childhood. The development of language is another powerful regulator for the emotions (Kopp, 1992). The communication of the young child's state, which previously could only be conveyed through emotional expression can be conveyed in words when language is acquired. This communication is increasingly facilitated as the child becomes more proficient at language.

Development of components of one emotional reaction may also regulate the expression of another emotional reaction. For example, behavioral inhibition to novelty, part of the fear reaction developing late in the first year, is related not only to the inhibition of behavioral approach but also to inhibition of the expression of positive affect (Rothbart, 1988).

The developmental course of the expression of the emotions will be influenced by experience. Social learning theory emphasizes the ways in which individuals may be reinforced or punished for emotional displays. In older children, the expression of emotion is also directly socialized: Children come to recognize which emotions should be expressed at particular times, and are able to behaviorally regulate their expression of emotions (Saarni, 1979, 1982). It is likely that this ability is related to individual characteristics of high behavioral inhibition and effortful control (Rothbart, 1991).

The development of self-regulation influences the experience and expression of the emotions, but from the earliest days, emotion is regulated by others, and many of our emotions and cognitions about emotion will be developmentally shaped in a social context. It is interesting to note cultural variations that have been observed in the development of infants' attachment-related emotions with the mother. In Northern Europe, high-distress proneness in the newborn predicts later more "avoidant" attachment patterns, including low levels of expression of negative emotion (Grossman, Grossman, Spangler, Suess, & Unzner, 1985; van den Boom, 1989). In Japan, on the other hand, newborn high-distress proneness predicts more "ambivalent" patterns with relatively high expression of negative emotion (Miyake, Chen, & Campos, 1985; van Ijzendoorn & Kroonenberg, 1988). These patterns may be related to Northern European mothers' tendencies to avoid interaction with infants who become highly distressed, and Japanese mothers' tendencies to remain in contact with the child even when the child is distressed (van den Boom, 1988). In Northern Europe, children thus appear more likely to develop means for self-regulation and self-soothing that do not require the parent. In Japan, soothing is much more likely to require regulation by others.

It is likely that individual differences in the emotions will influence development within other domains. Mastery or effectance motivation is strongly tied to the child's experiences of reward and success, punishment and failure (Harter, 1978), and these experiences in turn are related to the individual's susceptibility to distress, the positive emotions, and the behavioral inhibition component of fear. For some more fearful and easily discouraged children, encouragement and providing graded positive experiences may be important in the development of mastery motivation and effectance; for others, it is necessary to keep positive approach tendencies under control.

Finally, we have suggested that individual differences in the rate of development of components of the emotions and self-regulatory capacities may greatly influence the nature of the child's experience (Rothbart, Ahadi, & Hershey, 1993; Rothbart & Derryberry, 1981). In particular, children whose behavior is highly controlled either by fear (behavioral inhibition) or attention (effortful control) may have less direct experience with objects and people during a period when children with later-developing controls are gaining much procedural knowledge in these domains. On the other hand, children with early controls will gain much in observational learning and adult approval for self-control. Adding a developmental view of the emotions, personality and socialization affords us a much richer and more complex view of each of these domains.

Afterword: What Develops in Emotional Development?

RICHARD J. DAVIDSON
PAUL EKMAN

All students of emotion agree that emotions change with development—that is, that there are certain age-related changes in various aspects of emotional reactivity. There is a diversity of views about what changes over the course of development, and why those changes occur, among the contributors who addressed this question. For anyone who has observed infants at different ages over the first several years of life, the differences in emotional behavior are striking. How to account for such changes and relate them to other systems that are undergoing parallel developmental transitions is the major challenge.

As Lazarus has noted, it is important to underscore at the outset that while the contributors have dealt with early development, age-related changes in emotional processing occur later in life as well. We know relatively little about such transitions and anticipate an increased emphasis on this developmental period in future research.

The development of emotion in early life critically depends on the maturation of the central nervous system, which, in humans in particular, is still undergoing major structural and functional changes postnatally. Panksepp speculates that specific developmental milestones in the ontogeny of emotion may be tied to the maturation of particular neural systems. The neural changes that occur with development provide the substrate for critical periods that enable certain milestones in emotional development to occur. For example, Panksepp cites social bonding and separation distress as two phenomena that depend on critical periods in neural development. Panksepp also makes the important point that the relation between biology and experience is bidirectional. Environmental events can alter the function and structure of the nervous system, thereby modifying the neural substrate of emotional circuits in the brain. Moreover, if such environmental events occur during particular critical periods, these changes may be very enduring and, in certain cases, permanent.

Several authors (Rothbart, Camras, Dunn, Lazarus) have noted that one of the most striking features of emotional development is that the stimulus conditions sufficient to elicit emotion change with development. What is amusing to a 1, 5, and 10 year old is very different. Instead of emphasizing stimulus conditions per se, Lazarus draws attention to developmental changes in the goals that are salient at different ages. These age-related changes in the salience of goal states will mediate which stimulus conditions are likely to provoke different emotions at different ages.

Dunn addresses the issue of whether the experience of two putatively identical emotions that occur at different ages in response to differing stimulus conditions are indeed the same. She suggests that as the circumstances associated with the elicitation of a particular emotion change, it is very likely that the experience of the emotion also changes. This can occur even though the facial expression remains the same. It would be important to determine what aspects of the physiology of emotion might also be constant and which aspects would vary when the same emotion occurs at different ages. A related point is whether when the same emotion is called forth by the same event (say, a joke that is found amusing by 3 year olds and 7 year olds), to what extent is the emotional experience the same or different?

Dunn's position is at variance with that proposed by Izard, who suggests that the core emotional experience associated with each discrete emotion does not change with development. Moreover, early in life, these core emotional experiences, he says, are closely tied to the appearance of discrete facial expressions of emotion. Izard contends that the morphology of emotional expressions remains relatively invariant once the particular configuration first emerges. For Izard, the major tasks of emotional development are the emergence of links between emotion and cognition, and the development of emotion regulation.

The issue of how the emergence of different facial signs of emotion is related to the underlying experience and processing of emotion is a central focus for Camras. She notes that early in development different facial expressions may be displayed in similar situations and a particular facial expression may co-occur with other behaviors that are both emotion-appropriate and emotion-inappropriate. Camras criticizes "top-down" theories that postulate particular facial "read-outs" of central states. Instead, she adopts a dynamical systems perspective that holds that the control of some elements of response are dictated by contextual factors.

Several commentators (Dunn, Rothbart) emphasize relations between emotional development and cognitive development. Clearly, the emergence of certain emotions critically depends on the realization of certain cognitive milestones. For example, Dunn notes that new emotions, such as pride, shame, guilt, jealousy, and embarrassment, appear in the second and third years of life. These emotions critically depend on the maturation of certain cognitive capabilities. Dunn also makes the very important point that the direction of causality between cognitive and emotional development goes both ways. The emergence of new emotions during the second and third years not only is the result of new cognitive capabilities, but also fosters more mature capabilities such as the capacity to argue, understand, and anticipate the actions of others.

Another major theme common to many authors is the issue of emotion regulation. Important developmental changes occur in the infant's capacity to regulate its emotions. Regulation itself is very complicated and includes a potentially extremely broad set of procedures. Rothbart notes that important links exist between the development of attention and the infant's maturing capacity to regulate emotion. Lazarus underscores the role of coping skills and suggests that there are important developmental changes in the nature and availability of such skills. Dunn takes a very broad view of regulation and emphasizes the child's growing ability to understand and influence others' emotional states. In their second, third, and fourth years there are notable changes in the degree to which children comfort, tease, and joke with others. These developments permit the child to more effectively share certain emotional experiences with others and to influence the emotions of their parents and siblings. According to Dunn, these developments are so important because they reflect a new intimacy that children have achieved in their close relationships.

Finally, several authors have commented on the role of culture in emotional development. Camras raises the possibility of cultural influences on expressivity as a function of mothers' communication styles and attitudes about the acceptability of certain expressive displays. Dunn links the emergence of language and the associated development of emotion talk as providing a crucial opportunity for the child to participate in the shared cultural concepts of emotion.

The diversity of views about emotional development underscores the complexity and importance of this topic. Changes in different components of emotional functioning are one of the most salient characteristics in all of development. Many factors influence emotional development, and it is clear from the commentators that developmental changes in emotion play a crucial role in guiding the individual along the trajectory toward adulthood.

Question 12

What Influences the Subjective Experience of Emotion?

I Feel, Therefore I Am—I Think

JAMES R. AVERILL

The terms "feeling" and "emotion" are often used interchangeably. For example, in most contexts, "I feel angry" means much the same as "I am angry." This fact has led some theorists to think that emotions are *really* feelings, or at least that feelings are essential features of emotions. Unfortunately, such an essentialist position regarding feelings does not help clarify the meaning of emotion. The reason is twofold.

First, "feeling" is one of the vaguest terms in the English language. I can feel the prick of a pin, the touch of velvet, the cold of a winter day, and the pounding of my heart after climbing six flights of stairs. Sometimes, I feel ill or nauseous. At other times I feel confused and disoriented. Once in a great while, I even feel knowledgeable or enlightened. Now and then, I also feel like going to a movie. And all too often, I feel like doing nothing. To say that emotions involve feelings is thus not very informative.

Second, feelings are neither necessary nor sufficient conditions for being in an emotional state. The person who is angry, jealous, envious, afraid, in love, and so forth, is sometimes the last and not the first to recognize that condition. Such would not be the case if feeling angry, say, was a necessary condition for being angry. Conversely, a person can feel angry without being angry, which would not be the case if feelings were sufficient conditions for being emotional.

This last state of affairs (e.g., feeling angry without being angry) may at first seem counterintuitive. An analogy might help to clarify the issue. "Feeling" an emotion can be compared with "hearing" voices. No matter how vivid and realistic a voice might seem, the experience will not be considered real (but rather hallucinatory) unless there is some adequate stimulus to account for its occurrence. Similarly, a person may "feel" a particular emotion, but unless the circumstances are adequate, the feeling will not be considered real. Hypomania illustrates the point. The person who is hypomanic may claim to be happy, but the happiness is dismissed as a mask for depression. Hypomania is not exceptional in this regard. Feelings of anger and other emotions can also be illusory, even hallucinatory (Averill, 1993).

But even if we grant that the concept of feeling is vague and that feelings are neither necessary nor sufficient conditions for emotional states, it is nevertheless true that subjective experience is among the more prototypic features of emotion. Any general framework for the analysis of emotion must give an account of emotional feelings.

The Doctrine of the Immaculate Perception

According to Freud, the feeling of anxiety serves as a signal to the individual (ego) that danger is present. Many more recent theorists of diverse persuasion have also viewed emotional feelings, not just anxiety, as a form of information. There is clearly something to this idea. I may feel angry, sad, or happy without fully realizing why, in which case the feeling itself may provide valuable information about my situation.

I believe, however, that it is easy to overinterpret the notion of feelings-as-information. During the last century, Nietzsche parodied what he called the "Doctrine of the Immaculate Perception," that is, the notion that we are the passive recipient of experiences implanted in us from without. It is the nature of doctrines, however, that they do not die easily, and the doctrine of the immaculate perception has proven no exception. During the 1950s a variety of researchers developed what they called the "new look" in perception. The point they tried to make was similar to Nietzsche's, but now supported by empirical evidence. Even simple perceptual experiences are active, motivated phenomena: Within limits, we see what we want to see, and we hear what we want to hear.

Consider again the case of a person who hears voices when no one is actually speaking. In extreme cases (e.g., paranoid hallucinations), the person may be assailed by the voices, which seem to come from without and are experienced as very real. Yet, the voices are the person's own doing, responses he or she makes but attributes to outside sources. As previously mentioned, emotional feelings, too, can be hallucinatory. That is not typically the case, but the dividing line between an hallucination and an ordinary (veridical) experience has less to do with the underlying mechanism as with the mode of activation. An ordinary perceptual experience is a response activated by an appropriate stimulus; an hallucination is a perceptual response activated by an inappropriate (often internal) stimulus.

I would suggest that emotional feelings are also responses the individual makes, responses that can be veridical or not, depending on the circumstances. This is not to deny the value of feelings as information. It is simply a recognition that concepts like experience versus behavior, stimulus versus response, and input versus output cannot do justice to underlying psychological reality. Feelings are part of the complex pattern of responses that constitute an emotional episode; they are what might be called self-informative responses.

Feelings Of, Feelings About, and Feeling Like

Earlier, I described a variety of uses of the term "feeling." For simplicity, these uses can be divided into three broad categories: "feelings of," "feelings about," and "feeling like." The first of these categories can be illustrated by the following thought experiment. Imagine that you are in a physician's office about to receive an inoculation against tetanus. As the nurse plunges the needle into your arm, he asks: Did you feel anything? You might respond by describing the momentary pain as the needle punctured the skin, the queasy feeling in your stomach, and so forth. This is what I mean by feelings *of* (e.g., a feeling of pain, of queasiness). Now imagine that you are at an art show and a friend asks: How do you feel about that picture? You might respond by giving an evaluation of the work—you think it is beautiful, provocative, disgusting, trite, or whatever. That is what I mean by feelings *about*.

Two types of emotion theories can be distinguished, corresponding roughly to the distinction between feelings of and feelings about. The well-known theory of William James is a good example of the former. According to James, emotions are basically feelings of bodily changes as they occur. Carl Jung provides an equally good illustration of the second view. According to Jung (1921), emotional feelings are essentially value judgments—feelings about. From a Jungian standpoint, if I am asked to describe my emotional feelings, I would not describe bodily sensations; instead, I would indicate how I evaluate the situation.

Most contemporary theories of emotion tend to combine feelings of and feelings about. Schachter's (1964) two-factor theory provides a good example. According to Schachter, emotional experience results when proprioceptive cues from bodily reactions (feelings of) are added to the appraisals (feelings about) the person makes of the situation.

A third type of theory corresponds roughly to the expression, "feeling like," as in "I feel like running." Instrumental responses (e.g. running) also make an important contribution to how we feel. Is escape possible? Should I fight to overcome a potential harm? Or is there nothing I can do? Depending on how these questions are answered, a person may feel fear, anger, or depression. Instrumental responses have been particularly emphasized by behaviorally oriented theorists (cf. self-perception theory—Laird & Bresler, 1992). It must be emphasized, however, that the instrumental response need not be actual; the mere possibility of a response is often enough to alter the nature of an emotional experience (cf. Lazarus's, 1991, notion of secondary appraisal, which focuses on an individual's cognitions, and Gibson's, 1979, concept of affordances, which focuses on information in the stimulus array).

In sum, bodily reactions, cognitive appraisals, and instrumental responses (actual or potential) may all contribute to emotional feelings. In my opinion, however, too much research and debate has been expended in an effort to demonstrate which of these (or subcategories of these, such as visceral arousal or expressive reactions) is the primary or *real* source of emotional feelings. It takes no fancy instruments or sophisticated laboratory studies to recognize that the relative importance may vary from one emotion to another (e.g., fear vs. hope), from one situation to another (e.g., anger experienced during a faculty meeting vs. anger experienced during a barroom brawl), and from one person to another (e.g., an emotionally labile extravert vs. a stolid introvert).

The debate over the true source of emotional feelings has tended to mask other, more important issues concerning the nature of emotional experience. An emotional feeling is not the mere sum of its parts (bodily sensations *plus* cognitive appraisals *plus* instrumental responses). As stated earlier, feelings are (self-informative) responses in their own right. I will now try to clarify the nature of that feeling/response.

Prereflexive Versus Reflexive Experience

Emotional feelings, it is sometimes said, are "prereflexive" (e.g., Sartre, 1948). This is a variation on the "doctrine of the immaculate perception" discussed earlier. However, if the arguments I have made thus far have any validity, then emotional feelings, like almost all other human experience, are "reflexive." The distinction between prereflexive and reflexive experience is admittedly rather vague and subject to varying interpretations. To a limited extent, it overlaps with the distinction between feelings *of* and feelings *about*, but the overlap is far from complete. Without getting into a detailed discussion, I will simply illustrate how I intend the distinction. Imagine the type of feelings a dog might have, or a whale. Infrahuman animals are aware of events in their environment, and they are aware of their own responses to those events. But with the possible exception of chimpanzees and gorillas (who demonstrate the rudiments of self-awareness), infrahuman animal are not aware of being aware; that is, they lack the cognitive capacity to reflect on the meaning of their own experiences.

In contrast to lower animals, human beings are not simply aware of, and responsive to, their immediate environment, they are aware of their own awareness, conscious of their own consciousness, so to speak. This "higher-order" awareness is what I mean by reflexive experience. And what makes reflexive experience possible? The capacity for symbolic thought. The most notable manifestation of that capacity is language. For example, feelings of anger are necessarily informed by the concept of anger—to the extent that they are feelings of anger and not just inarticulate experiences of frustration and displeasure. Language is not, however, the only way that concepts can be expressed. Art, music, and ritual are all symbolic activities by which concepts—particularly emotional concepts—find expression. But however manifest, if it were not for the capacity for symbolic thought, our emotional life would be little richer than that of a dog or a whale.

To further illustrate the distinction between reflexive and prereflexive experience, imagine two people listening to an orchestra. One is a critic assigned to review the performance; the other is a novice attending a concert for the first time. Do the critic and novice hear the same music? At the level of prereflexive experience, the answer might be a qualified Yes; but at the level of reflexive experience, the answer is No. The same sound waves impinge on the ears of both the critic and the novice, and both may find the experience enjoyable. However, when subsequently relating the experience to friends, or writing a review for assignment, they most likely would describe their experiences very differently. Their friends might even wonder whether the two had attended the same performance.

It might be objected that the critic and the novice "hear" the same music but that each in retrospect interprets the experience differently. However, reflexive experience need not be retrospective. People are quite capable of interpreting an experience as it occurs—indeed, in anticipation of its occurrence. In fact, I would argue that completely prereflexive (uninterpreted) experience is a myth, at least on the human level.

Dennett (1991) has presented a "Multiple Drafts" model of consciousness that may help to clarify this issue. According to Dennett's model, information entering the nervous system is being continuously "edited" before being passed along for further processing. At no point during the process can we say that editing is complete and the final product viewed (consciously experienced), as though it were projected on a screen in some "Cartesian theater" of the mind. One implication of this model is that the nature of conscious experience will vary depending on when (and where in the brain) we make a probe. If we probe early in the process, we may obtain responses indicative of particular discriminations (e.g., if we ask our music critic to press a button every time she hears a certain note), but the experience will lack coherence. If we probe late in the process (the next day, perhaps, as the critic writes her review), the result may be a rationally reconstructed report that lacks detail. When is the optimal time to make a probe? That, of course, depends on the purpose of the probe. At no point in time, however, is the experience revealed by the probe more *real* than at another time. "Most important, the Multiple Drafts model avoids the tempting mistake of supposing that there must be a single narrative (the 'final' or 'published' draft, you might say) that is canonical—that is the *actual* stream of consciousness of the subject" (Dennett, 1991, p. 113).

I will have more to say about the narrative structure of emotional feelings. But first, another distinction—and traditional source of confusion—needs clarification.

Subjective Versus Objective Experience

Emotional feelings are often described as subjective as opposed to objective. To the extent that subjective experience is regarded as simpler and less amenable to analysis (*De gustibus non est disputandum*), the distinction between subjective and objective tends to reinforce the distinction between prereflexive and reflexive experience. That, I believe, is a mistake.

The distinction between subjective and objective experience is based on the fact that all experience (animal or human, prereflexive or reflexive) has two poles—a subject pole and an object pole. For example, on a rainy day I see a rainbow on the horizon. The rainbow is the *object* of my experience; I am the *subject*, the one who sees. Other persons could presumably see the same rainbow, but not exactly the way I do. When the unique contributions of individual observers are subtracted, what remains is an "objective" description of the rainbow as, for example, we might find in a textbook on physical optics. When the emphasis is on the seer rather than the seen, as in an artist's rendition of the rainbow, the description is "subjective."

Feelings are subjective in the sense that they take into account the subject ("inner") pole of experience, and are not concerned exclusively with the external object in and of itself. This, incidentally, was one reason Wundt (1897) was led to distinguish feelings from sensations in his famous tripartite theory of feeling.

However, when speaking of the "subjective pole of experience," the term "experience" covers not only elementary feelings in the sense of Wundt, but also complex evaluations, as in the case of most emotional appraisals (cf. the earlier discussion of "feelings of" vs. "feelings about"). Moreover, the subjectivity of experience does not necessarily imply conscious awareness. At the most fundamental level, subjectivity refers to the *relation* of the subject to the object. Usually, that relation is manifest in consciousness, but this is not necessarily the case. Both subjective and objective judgments can, and on occasion do, proceed outside of awareness.

Biographical Versus Epistemological Subjectivity

The above sense of subjectivity (i.e., as taking into account the relation between subject and object) must be distinguished from another sense, namely, as a biased, irrational, even deluded form of judgment. Calhoun (1989) has called this latter sense *epistemological subjectivity*. It is illustrated by such statements as "You can't trust his judgment; he is too subjective." Emotions can be subjective in this sense; but so, too, can ostensibly rational arguments.

Calhoun (1989) contrasts epistemological subjectivity with *biographical subjectivity*. The latter is illustrated by such statements as "I find that picture disgusting" or "Your attitude makes me angry." Such statements do not necessarily imply a biased or irrational judgment. They do, however, imply that the instigating conditions are evaluated in relation to the subject's own interests and values (cf. feelings about). Emotions are subjective in this sense—they make events meaningful by placing them within the context of the individual's own history and goals.

Calhoun (1989) argues that biographical and not epistemological subjectivity distinguishes emotional from nonemotional states. Her argument is persuasive, but an important qualification must be noted. People are not simply free to choose their emotions on the basis of their personal history, interests, and values alone. What is most characteristic about emotions is not their biographical nature, but their *relational* nature, as discussed above. And it is society, more than biography, that determines the kind of subject-object relations that constitute the various emotions. In other words, biographical subjectivity (subject-object relations) can be epistemologically objective (verifiable across subjects).

The Temporal Dimension: Feelings as Narrative Accounts

To summarize thus far, feedback from bodily reactions, cognitive appraisals, and instrumental responses all may contribute to how a person feels when emotional. By themselves, however, they do not singly or in combination constitute an emotional experience. The latter is a higher order (reflexive) experience that takes into account the relation between the subject and object (subjectivity). To complete this sketch of emotional feelings, a temporal dimension must also be added. The subject-object relation implied by emotional concepts (and that informs emotional experience) is not static, but extends in time.

Emotions differ greatly in their temporal course. A sudden fright may last for only a few moments; but an episode of anger often lasts for hours or even days; of grief, for months or even years; and of love, perhaps for a lifetime. Needless to say, extended emotional episodes do not entail constant and uninterrupted sensory experiences, any more than they entail constant and uninterrupted bodily reactions or thoughts about the object. However, like readers of a text, we often fill in gaps in our immediate experience, based on the past and anticipated course of events. (In reading a text, for example, we typically do not notice typographical errors, such as misspelled words or missing letters; knowing what should be there, we "see" what isn't there.)

Consider how odd it would be for a person to say, "For ten seconds, I felt deep and genuine grief over the death of my son." Even if the person were to explain that the feeling recurred frequently over a period of months, we might still wonder about the sincerity of her grief. (At best, she would be like the music critic cited earlier who responded only to certain notes in a performance.) Or take the person who expresses feelings of love even though he knows that in the morning he will want nothing more to do with his "lover." What is odd in these examples is the lack of a temporal perspective, a coherent narrative that ties the elements together into a dynamic whole. Such a perspective is not ancillary to feelings of love or grief; it is what adds the warm glow and deep agony we associate with love and grief.

Emotional feelings are not like snapshots that capture only events of the moment. Instead, they resemble motion pictures that depict a story. In fact, as I have argued elsewhere with respect to anger (Averill, 1993), emotional feelings *are* stories we tell ourselves in order to guide and account for our own behavior (see Gergen & Gergen, 1988, and Sarbin, 1986, for related arguments). The only thing I would add, drawing on Dennett's (1991) "Multiple Drafts" model of conscious experience, is that the stories that help constitute our feelings are never complete, but are always open to "editorial revision."

To conclude, one final question remains: Who writes the scripts for our emotional stories (feelings)? Ultimately, of course, each person does, based on his or her own past experiences, present circumstances, and future aspirations. But an individual is not free to write just any story. When discussing Calhoun's (1989) notion of biographical subjectivity, I noted that it is society, more than personal biography, that determines the types of subject-object relations that help constitute the emotions. More specifically, the personal-biographical subjectivity discussed by Calhoun is a particularization of a social-historical subjectivity. In this sense, an emotional syndrome can be conceived abstractly as kind of social role that must be interpreted by the individual in order to be experienced; a person feels emotional just to the extent that he or she becomes engrossed in an emotional role, like a deep actor who experiences the part he or she is playing (Averill, 1980, 1991).

Why Emotions Vary in Intensity

GERALD L. CLORE

Why Emotions Involve Feelings

An important issue in the design of information-processing systems concerns how to schedule limited attentional and processing resources. Animate systems, whether living or robotic, appear more likely to succeed if ongoing processing can be interrupted when important situations arise (Simon, 1967). Understanding emotions involves not only figuring out how appraisals about the personal significance of situations are made, but also how the results of appraisals govern cognitive processing. A possible answer comes from considering the nonemotional processes involved in governing attentional processes.

In both higher and lower organisms, attentional and information-processing resources appear to be sense driven. External stimuli capture attention and processing resources through sensory organs devoted to visual, auditory, or other sensory stimulation. Bright lights and loud noises, for example, are effective ways of capturing someone's attention, a fact well known to both advertisers and small children. One of the functions of emotion seems to be to redirect cognitive processes, and it is interesting that emotion does this in the same way that an external stimulus does. The main difference is that, in the case of emotion, the sensory stimulation that captures attention is internally generated. This internal stimulation comes in the form of emotional feelings generated by affective appraisal processes, but they have the same attention-grabbing power as external stimuli. Just as in the case of externally stimulated sensory cues, the greater the intensity of these internally generated feelings, the more completely they command attention and redirect processing resources. For the system to work well, however, this intensity should reflect the urgency of the appraised situation, so that resources can be devoted to important matters. I will discuss recent work on this relationship—the relationship between the importance of situations and emotional intensity.

Emotional Intensity

The Cognitive Structure of Emotional Intensity

A curious thing about emotion research is that psychologists have paid relatively little attention to the fact that emotions vary in intensity of subjective experience. This is surprising in part because, both within and between people, variation in intensity is one of the most salient aspects of emotional experiences. An adequate account of emotion, therefore, would have to address the question of what determines intensity (Frijda, Ortony, Sonnemans, & Clore, 1992).

Our general view is that the intensity of emotions depends on a number of variables, all of which are present in the construal of the situation that gives rise to the emotion in the first place. Thus, to address the question of intensity, one needs a general conception of how emotion-inducing situations are appraised. Ortony, Clore, and Collins (Ortony et al., 1988) proposed that such appraisals are based on three kinds of cognitive structures—goals, standards, and attitudes. The variables that govern the intensity of emotion, according to this view, include the importance of the particular goals, standards, and attitudes that underlie a given emotional episode. Which of the many possible emotions occur depends on one's focus of attention. One can focus on the outcome of events as relevant to one's goals, the actions of agents as relevant to one's standards, or the attributes of objects as relevant to one's attitudes (or tastes). A distinctive affective reaction corresponds to each focus so that one can be pleased or displeased about events, approve or disapprove of actions, or like or dislike objects. The intensity of pleasure or displeasure depends on how desirable or undesirable an event is perceived to be, which in turn depends on the importance of relevant goals. The intensity of approval or disapproval depends on how praiseworthy or blameworthy an action is, which in turn depends on the importance one attaches to relevant standards. And the intensity of liking or disliking depends on how appealing or unappealing an object is, which depends on the importance of relevant attitudes. (Note that, since emotions are states, it is not dispositional liking and disliking that are being referred to but states of liking and disliking in the moment.)

Specific emotions are differentiations of these three affective reactions, and their intensity is similarly a function of the importance of the goals, standards, and attitudes on which they are based. The structure shown in the following figure is thus a hierarchical one in which emotions lower in the hierarchy are necessarily influenced by variables active at higher levels.

Also shown in the figure are local variables that affect particular groups of emotions that share the same eliciting conditions. For example, it indicates that the degree of *expectation deviation* should influence the intensity of emotions such as pride, shame, or anger, which are based on perceptions of the praiseworthiness or blameworthiness of actions. Thus, one might admire an old lady who dives into a river to save a drowning child more than a lifeguard who does so. The figure also indicates that the degree to which an outcome is seen as *deserved* should influence the intensity of emotions such as pity or resentment that are concerned with outcomes to others. The more one's colleague was seen as undeserving, for example, the more one might resent the colleague being awarded a large pay raise. The figure indicates that

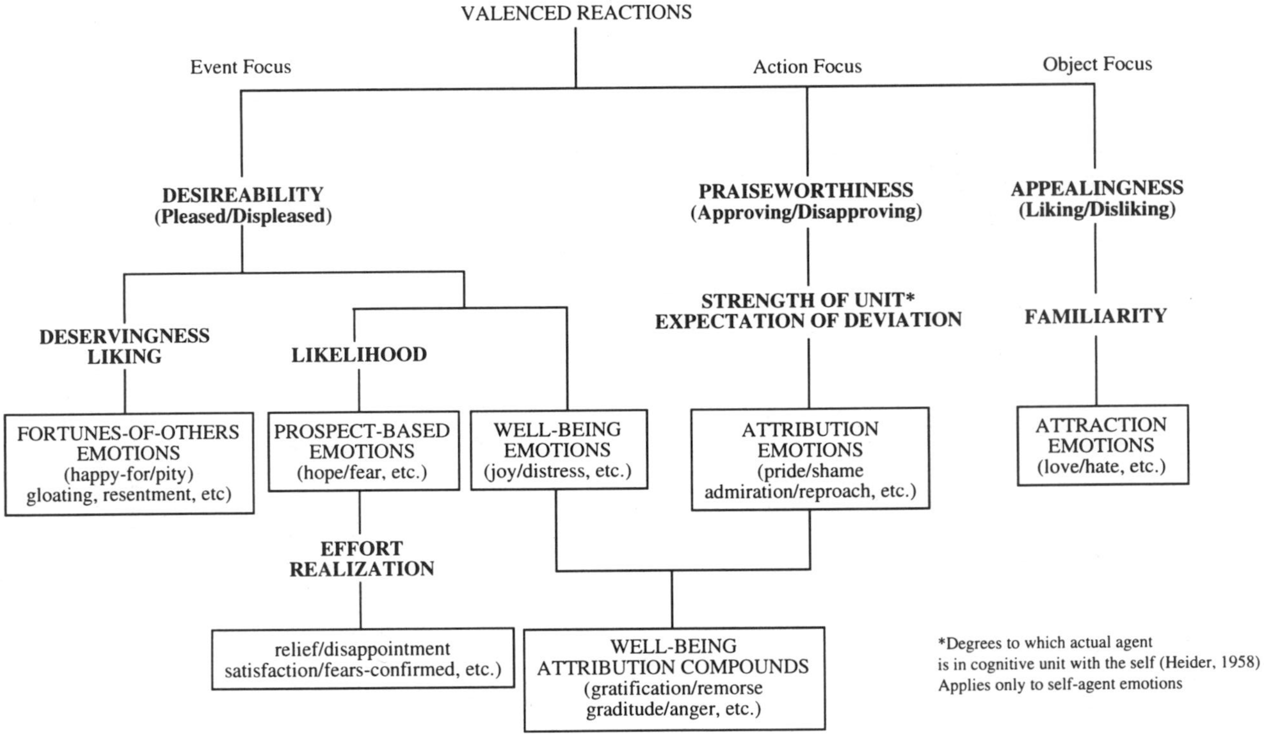

Global and local cognitive variables that govern the intensity of 22 emotion types according to Ortony, Clore, and Collins (1988).

the perceived *likelihood* of an outcome should influence such prospect-based emotions as fear. Thus, one is more fearful when a frightening prospect seems likely than when it seems unlikely. In addition, not pictured are global variables that influence the intensity of all emotions (e.g., *surprisingness, proximity, sense of reality*).

Basketball Study

One study designed to test predictions about the cognitive factors in emotions and emotional intensity was a study of sports fans (Clore, Ortony, Brand, & Levine, in preparation). Self-reports of emotion were obtained from nearly 100 college basketball fans during 20 basketball games. The fans answered questions and made predictions before, during, and after games seen both live and on television. The reports of their emotions were cluster analyzed separately for wins and losses. Consistent with the theory, three clusters of emotions emerged separately in both the win and the loss data sets. The loss data showed goal-based emotions (e.g., disappointment, depression), standard-based emotions (e.g., anger, embarrassment), and an attitude-based emotion (e.g., momentary disliking toward the coach). Similarly, the win data also showed some goal-based emotions (e.g., relief, being pleased), some standard-based emotions (e.g., pride, admiration), and an attitude-based emotion (momentary liking for the coach). In addition, the variables that predicted these qualitatively different experiences followed expectations from theory. Goal-based emotions were experienced when games were seen as important and the score was close, standard-based emotions were experienced when the teams played especially well or poorly, and attitude-based emotions depended on whether fans did or did not have strong positive attitudes toward the team.

The results for emotional intensity were also consistent with theory. The intensity of being embarrassed and other standard-based emotions that depend on approval or disapproval were made more intense by perceptions that the team had "not played well," had "not hustled," and did not have "a desire to win"—all factors concerned with standards of play. In contrast, disappointment and other event-based emotions were made more intense by perceptions that the game was an important one and that the outcome was unexpected—factors concerned with goals and outcomes. Thus, some emotions reflected disapproval of the team for not trying hard enough, while some others reflected a focus on the outcome of events relevant to an important goal.

Intensity and Goal Importance

In line with the general neglect of emotional intensity as a research topic, the hypothesis that the intensity of emotional experience should vary with the importance of relevant goals and concerns has also received little attention. But since this is a fundamental assumption of a cognitive view, it is a hypothesis worth testing. Does the intensity of emotional experience vary with the importance of underlying goals and concerns? On the negative side, one can readily think of situations that would seem to challenge the hypothesis. Sometimes, for example, people get quite upset over seemingly unimportant occurrences such as spilling a cup of coffee or misplacing something. Similarly, sports fans react strongly when their team loses, even though the fate of their team is probably peripheral to their real goals in life.

Indeed, in the basketball study, we asked fans about the importance of the teams' success in the context of their general life goals. In that context, how well the team did was generally not very important. However, since many of these same fans indicated that they reacted with great intensity at the game, the importance values of goals must be highly situated. Methodologically, that implies that one may need to specify the context when obtaining goal importance values. Theoretically, it implies that the goal importance hypothesis must be modified so that it concerns the *momentarily* perceived importance (or salience) of a goal.

Sporting events provide an especially good example of the situated nature of goal importance, and viewing sporting events in this way provides an interesting angle on their emotional function. A primary function of all entertainment, including spectator sports, film, theater, and so on, may be to allow one to escape from the unremitting burden of real-world goals and concerns (e.g., that taxes are unpaid, articles are unfinished, etc.). Seeing one's team win or lose can be intense because inside the stadium one focuses primarily on the game, and the goals that are activated are the limited set of goals relevant to the game. Such events, although intense, are relaxing because they allow one to take a vacation in an artificial world with a simplified goal structure, one in which the goals are fully attainable within the event.

The Concept of Emotional Intensity

In addition to the fact that goal importance values are situated, another obstacle to understanding when emotion will be intense concerns the concept of intensity itself. Frijda et al. (1992) propose that one needs to distinguish multiple aspects of emotional intensity. In particular, we argued that the *amplitude* of a reaction is distinct from its *duration*. One might very well get upset in the moment over spilled coffee or over a loss by one's favorite sports team, but such reactions may not last long. In contrast, important events, even when not reacted to extremely in the moment, may be dwelled on for some time. In other words, goal importance may influence the overall emotional impact of a situation through the duration of an emotional reaction, as well as (or instead of) through its momentary amplitude (Sonnemans, 1991). A study by Pfennig, Clore, and Ortony (1991, May; see also Ortony, 1990, August) shows that the more that events are relevant to one's goals, the greater the duration of the emotional reactions that result.

Thanksgiving Study

One obstacle to testing the goal importance hypothesis has been the difficulty of measuring goals. The basic strategy in the Thanksgiving study was to elicit from college students a sample of goals and desires regarding a fixed period of time, in this case the Thanksgiving vacation. This period has the advantage that it involves the potential for emotionally intense experiences as students try to integrate themselves back into their families for the vacation. As a way of getting them to think about the vacation period, subjects were asked to describe in some detail the kinds of things that were likely to happen over the break. With these probable events in mind, they also listed 15 goals and desires for the period using an elicitation procedure developed by Emmons (1986). Each goal was rated on various attributes, including the difficulty of the goal, the likelihood of achieving the goal, its importance, and so on.

During the Thanksgiving break, respondents recorded five emotional events each day. They described the events briefly and rated the intensity of their reaction and how long the feelings lasted. After the holidays, they rated the relevance of each goal to each emotional event. They also indicated how much they had thought about the event, how long the feelings lasted, and how strongly they still felt about it. The results suggest that goal importance is more likely to affect the duration than the amplitude of emotional reactions. The most powerful predictor of duration was the total goal relevance of an event (the number of goals involved and the degree to which each was relevant). Thus, the more an event is seen to affect specific goals, the more intensely one may react in the sense that it may influence emotional feelings and preoccupation over time. The results suggested that one might want to think of emotional intensity as a function of the total area under the curve (amplitude × duration) rather than merely of the amplitude of the reaction. It should be noted that recent research by Fredrickson and Kahneman (1993) shows that differences in the duration of an aversive event are given little weight in retrospective views of intensity, but their research concerned the duration of exposure to an aversive stimulus instead of the duration of an emotional reaction to the stimulus.

Cognitive Restructuring

A question of some interest is how the cognitive variables discussed above actually influence the intensity of subjective experience. There are doubtless many possible ways to approach such a question, but, at the cognitive level, the intensity of an experience (emotional or otherwise) may be a direct function of the amount of cognitive restructuring involved. To take a nonemotional example, consider one's reaction to an amazing vista. As one looks out at the vista, the intensity of the experience would presumably be tied to some implicit comparison of that view with something else, such as what one expected, the scene just beforehand, other vistas, and so on. It may be difficult to maintain the feeling of awe or amazement to the extent that one gets used to the scene and comes to have a clear mental model of it, so that the mere sight of the scene no longer restructures anything. When one vacations in the mountains, or in the midst of some other natural wonder, it can be distressing that one adapts to the surrounding beauty so quickly. Looking at photographs or thinking about the experience later can regenerate some of the intensity of the actual experience, even though stimulus vividness is much reduced. That is, the representational dynamism afforded by contrasts between the photographs and the new context may allow some new experience of amazement.

The applicability of the cognitive change hypothesis to the emotions we (Ortony et al., 1988) have classified as goal-based (left branch of the previous figure) is reasonably straightforward. Consider an intense emotional experience, such as grief over the death of a spouse. Assuming the marriage involved a close relationship of long standing, there might be few aspects of the grieving person's life that would not be changed or for which the mental representation would not be restructured. The experience might be intense to the extent that the person has to accommodate mentally to an endless number of violated assumptions about the other's presence. In general, the intensity of event-based emotions depends on the desirability of the event, which depends on the centrality of relevant goals, and hence on the amount that a change in the goal dislocates the rest of one's network of goals.

It is interesting to consider the experience of suspense from this perspective. What makes suspense an intense experience may be the fact that one alternately entertains first one outcome and then another, each with opposite implications. As one's cognitive model of the situation flip flops in this way, a lot of cognitive restructuring is experienced and the overall experience of intensity increases correspondingly. In a similar vein, discovering that one's spouse has been having an affair of long standing or reinterpreting established family relationships in the course of psychotherapy are peculiarly intense emotional experiences both in magnitude and duration, presumably because so much mental content becomes restructured.

The hypothesis also applies to the emotions we classify as standard-based emotions. The intensity of the shame one feels for one's shameful act, for example, (or the contempt for another person's contemptuous act) might depend on how much the appraisal changes one's view of oneself (or one's view of the other person). For example, one's conception of a priest who does some immoral act would presumably change more than one's conception of a criminal who does the same thing, and one's judgment of blameworthiness and the intensity of moral outrage should be correspondingly greater toward the priest. An application of the same principle can be seen in the heightened potential for embarrassment typical of adolescence. Without a firmly rooted sense of self, the self-image of the adolescent can change rapidly after committing an embarrassing act, an experience to which adults, with more firmly rooted senses of themselves, are less vulnerable.

The cognitive restructuring hypothesis is also relevant to the emotions classified by Ortony et al. (1988) based on reactions to objects on the basis of tastes or attitudes (the right branch of the previous figure). Consider the intensity of affective reactions to humor, music, or drama. The most satisfying examples of these genres are those in which later developments build on earlier ones. The audience is more intensely satisfied, for example, when the punch line to a joke clears up prior ambiguities, when the final movement of a symphony unifies previously distinct themes, and when the last act of a play resolves formerly unresolved problems. Humor is not so satisfying when the humorist fails to build a sufficiently well-developed cognitive structure to be transformed by the punch line. Racial, religious, and other stereotypes may be as prevalent as they are in humor, in part because they provide, without undue effort, ready-made expectations and cognitive structures with which the humorist can work (for a provocative theory of humor, see Wyer & Collins, 1992). In an analogous process, both symphonic and jazz performances are often built around simple melodic themes that stay firmly in memory to serve as the basis for variations. But rhythmic and melodic transformations are only satisfying when a representation of the untransformed theme is cognitively available to be restated and embellished. The amount of change in cognitive structure is not the same thing as the amount of raw stimulus change available to the senses. In a well-written drama, the introduction of one new fact can change completely one's cognitive construction of the events and people involved. But splicing scenes from a different drama into the middle of a film, for example, although it would constitute a large stimulus change, would not restructure one's representation of the ongoing drama, and hence would not intensify the emotions produced by it.

One attractive feature of this approach is that it handles well the curious contextual-embeddedness of emotions to which I alluded earlier. The fact that fans at a basketball game (or viewers of a dramatic film) find themselves responding with intense emotions, even though the outcome has no real bearing on their important goals, is to be expected from the cognitive reorganization hypothesis. All that is required for emotional intensity is the experience of cognitive reorganization. The potential for such restructuring exists whenever one is sufficiently invested to generate an elaborate model of the situation and to attend fully to it.

Overall magnitude of cognitive reorganization and change appears to offer one way of thinking about the machinery of emotional intensity, a way that is compatible with a cognitive approach emphasizing the appraisal of events, agency, and objects (Ortony et al., 1988). It is not clear whether intensity of feeling is the experience of cognitive reorganization per se or whether it is the experience of physiological arousal triggered by such change. But it seems not unreasonable to view such affective experiences as disappointment and such nonaffective experiences as amazement as experiences of dramatic cognitive restructuring, a process in which the magnitude of cognitive change is the intensity of disappointment or amazement.

Summary

This essay began with the assertion that attention in animate systems is usually driven by externally generated sensory cues, and that emotion commands attention and processing resources in a similar way through internally generated cues. A set of global and local cognitive variables were outlined that are believed to contribute to the intensity of specific emotions. Among the most general factors was the importance of the particular goal or concern on which an emotion is based. To deal with complications in this goal-importance hypothesis, we noted that the importance of goals is context dependent, and that the concept of emotional intensity may need to include the duration as well as the amplitude of an emotional reaction. Finally, the idea was proposed that the ultimate cognitive variable in emotional intensity is the extent to which cognitive restructuring takes place.

Emotional Experience Is an Output of, Not a Cause of, Emotional Processing

JOSEPH E. LEDOUX

Emotion has a bad reputation. It is viewed as somehow more subjective than other psychological processes and as a result is regarded as more difficult to study. However, can we really say that emotion is more subjective than memory, perception, and imagery, each of which has been studied in great detail and with great success by psychologists and cognitive scientists? But, you might reply, these are information-processing functions and they can be studied objectively; emotion is just experience. But this argument doesn't go very far either. To the extent that emotions are elicited by stimuli (including internal stimuli), emotions involve information processing. And just as we have made a great deal of progress in understanding how the brain processes objective stimulus features, such as color, without having much understanding of how these features are experienced as qualia (i.e., redness), so too can we study how emotion is processed in the absence of any understanding of how emotional qualia are experienced.

The point is that experience has too long stood in the way of a serious study of emotion. The problem of experience is a general problem for psychology, not a specific problem for emotion theory. The study of emotion can and should charge ahead on the question of how the brain processes emotional stimuli. Just as it is hoped that the experience of color will someday be understood by studies of color processing, emotional experiences ideally will be illuminated by studies of emotional processing. Emotional processing is the entry point to emotional experience.

What, then, is the nature of emotional experience? Is it any different from nonemotional conscious experience? Obviously, emotion "feels" different from nonemotion. However, it seems possible to me that while the content of the emotional experience is different from the content of nonemotional experience, the underlying mechanism may be the same. I believe that it is most parsimonious to assume that there is one mechanism of consciousness. Usually, this mechanism is busily filled with the trivial and mundane aspects of daily life. At the same time, it can be directed toward objects or ideas of interest. However, our control over consciousness is quickly lost if we encounter a threatening object. Activation of an emotion network, such as the fear network, by unconscious information processing directs our consciousness toward the most likely sources of the arousal. And once the emotional system takes hold of consciousness, it is difficult to direct awareness to less pressing matters or to future events, regardless of how pressing the future events are expected to be when they occur.

Thus, my suggestion is that emotional experience is mediated by the same mechanism that mediates other aspects of conscious experience. The difference between emotional experience and other kinds of experience lies not in the nature of the consciousness mechanism but in the systems that provide the inputs to the consciousness mechanism and the kinds of information that become represented as conscious content. In Question 8, I described some aspects of the unconscious processing mechanisms (evaluative mechanisms) that might be at the heart of the emotional processing system and thus would be the raw materials of emotional consciousness.

I would like to close with two implications of this view. First, if emotional and nonemotional experiences are mediated by a common experience mechanism, elucidation of the mechanism of emotional experience will help clarify the nature of conscious experience in general. Second, emotional experience is initially an output of emotional-processing systems, not an integral part of the system that activates and processes emotional information. However, once emotional experiences occur, they come to exert important influences on subsequent emotional processing. It is important to keep this dual role of emotional experience in mind. On the one hand, it is a consequence of emotional processing and, on the other, it becomes a cause of additional emotional phenomena. Because these two roles have not usually been recognized, emotional experience has been a confusing aspect of emotion. The challenges facing us in this area are to first understand how emotion is processed unconsciously, then to understand how unconscious emotional processing leads to emotional experiences, and finally to understand how emotional experiences, once present, affect the course of the emotional episode.

Evolution Constructed the Potential for Subjective Experience Within the Neurodynamics of the Mammalian Brain

JAAK PANKSEPP

In some unfathomed way, affective feelings arise from the neurodynamic activities in the brain's basic motivational and emotional systems. Our ignorance about these matters may continue for some time, for subjectivity and affectivity are the fuzzy dilemmas on whose horns neuroscience is reluctant to impale itself. However, the issue will have to be faced at some point, and it will have to be confronted in the animal brain research laboratory. Do animals have internal feelings or do they not? If they do, any model of the mammalian brain that does not account for them will be critically flawed. My assumption is that animals do have internal affective experiences, and for that reason I am willing to enter the hornet's nest of neurosubjectivity. I do this because I am convinced that no model of the brain will work unless central affective states that code intrinsic biological values are built into the system. Without them, there can be no appropriate guidance of behavior. In robots such values can be built in as specific perceptual templates ("sign-stimuli") that recognize objects to be sought and "cherished," but in higher animals a greater degree of generalization must be built into the system. In part, this may have been achieved by the evolution of affective states. In the context of trying to mechanistically understand the nature of subjectivity, it will be important to determine the neural basis of motivational feelings such as hunger, thirst, warmth, tiredness, and so on, and the affective nature of basic emotional feelings such as joy, anger, sadness, fear, and so on. Indeed, there seem to be as many distinct internally experienced affective states as there are basic motivational and emotional systems of the brain. Whether this is a perceptual illusion or a neurological fact needs to be determined. It is possible that many perceptually distinct feelings gain their affective intensity from a few shared mechanisms. Thus, feelings, whether motivational or emotional, have distinct cognitive and affective attributes, and they may be quite distinctly mediated in the brain.

The search for a hard scientific understanding of these affective experiences remains the single most troublesome question haunting the perimeter of the neuroscience revolution. Of course, mere psychological studies cannot yield much light on the nature of the underlying mechanisms. While psychology can describe the content and dynamics of consciousness, the brain sciences must seek to describe the precise mechanisms that permit this content. Perhaps advances in brain imaging will eventually allow us to visualize such processes in humans (Reiman, 1990; Zappulla et al., 1991), but the neurochemical and precise neurogeographic issues will be much more difficult to address without appropriate animal models. Major breakthroughs can be achieved when investigators of the animal brain come to terms with the neurodynamic nature of subjectivity. Of course, there will always be the philosophical and empirical conundrum: It is much easier to accept our own subjective awareness of feelings and emotions than to grant them to other people, and much harder yet to grant them to other species. Although we can never ultimately know whether other creatures have internally experienced feelings and self awareness, we must entertain a positive axiomatic answer to this question in order to plot any meaningful neuroscientific strategies. I think the circumstantial evidence is overwhelming that other animals do have internal feelings that are quite as strong as ours. Thus, I believe it a worthy task to continue struggling with the underlying brain issues. Although other species may not think and dwell on their internal states as much as humans, this lack of pondering probably reflects the low level of their linguistic-thought capacities, rather than any deficiency in their basic level of self-awareness. If awareness of oneself as an active organism does transpire in the deep recesses of the animal brain, we can be sure it will never be directly seen. It must be inferred. Perhaps we will have to emulate the particle physicists who had no options but to indirectly and theoretically probe the internal dynamics of atomic nuclei. Because of the centrality of the question for overall brain organization, I believe that the study of the subjective brain (*epistemics* as coined by Paul MacLean, 1990) remains the most important underdeveloped area of brain research. How, then, will we come to understand the neurobiological nature of subjective feeling states?

In considering this question, we have no option but to also fully consider the neuronal nature of "the self." Emotional feeling without some type of self-referencing seems impossible. I suspect that when we begin to fathom the nature of internal affective representations, we may be close to cracking the codes for some basic forms of self-consciousness that may be the root processes for all higher forms of self-awareness. In general, I suspect that we will make the most progress in understanding the basic nature of the primal forms of consciousness if we start by modifying Decartes' famous epithet: "I think, therefore I am" to "I feel, therefore I am," and then proceed to probe the neural nature of feelings.

If one is going to attribute subjective states to other animals, one must provide a reasonable evolutionary scenario as to why and how such internal feeling states could have emerged. An internally experienced state without a function is an improbable creature indeed. I suspect that some form of primitive self-awareness emerged in neural tissues as a most expeditious way for evolution to allow organisms to represent themselves as effective competitors in the world (Panksepp, 1990b), and I suspect that this process of "I-ness" first emerged within the confines of spontaneously active motor pattern generators of the brainstem. I also suspect emotional values are still anatomically linked and referenced to these intrinsic pattern generators.

Since our interactions with the world can be divided coarsely into sensory and motor processes, a reasonable starting point for any neural analysis of "I-ness" is to ask whether self-awareness mechanisms are more tightly linked to one or the other type of brain process. Perhaps they are evenly represented among sensory and motor functions, but everyday impressions generally tend to suggest that sensory processes are more important. But that may be a delusion reflecting how the primal motor representations of self are presently guided by multiple sensory inputs (especially those that can communicate intrinsic survival value). Thus, I would still entertain the idea that primitive self-awareness is more closely linked to motor pattern generators than to sensory processes in the brain. Indeed, such a scenario is suggested by single cell recordings that indicate that motor maps are neurogeographically more stable than sensory maps in primitive brain areas such as the superior colliculus. In that part of the brain sensory maps shift systematically in reference to the neurogeographically stable eye-movement maps (Sparks, 1988). In other words, the patterns of neuronal firing in the superior colliculi can be taken to indicate that self-related information processing exists in the ancient motor maps of the body rather than the sensory maps of the incoming world. It is also worth noting that this area of the brainstem is highly multimodal and, because of the massive convergence of many types of information, ideally suited to be a legislative area for ancient forms of self-awareness. Also, it is noteworthy that the central gray, situated just below the colliculi, is a key area through which emotional command circuits course, providing a ready avenue of communication between primitive forms of self-representation and affective processes.

Because of such data, I am also prone to believe that emotional feeling states, although capable of being triggered by sensory inputs, are more closely linked mechanistically with the motor pattern generator systems for emotive tendencies than to the sensory-perceptual analyzers that can activate the emotional command systems. For instance, emotional feelings may arise from an obligatory type of parallel neuronal processing that accompanies activity within the executive neural systems that synchronize and coordinate emotional outputs. Thus, the activity of circuits that coordinate crying may generate grief. Those that mediate fear and rage responses may elaborate the affective experiences of anxiety and anger. Of course, at present, these are little more than theoretical propositions that may help guide our fledgling empirical efforts in productive directions.

I would note that general neuronal principles that may apply for emotional affective states may not apply to motivational (i.e., body need) feeling states. For instance, aversive drive states (e.g., hunger, thirst, and cold) are probably linked to specific interoreceptive systems, while the external incentive stimuli relevant for these feelings (i.e., wetness, sweetness, and warmth) may be integrally linked to specific sensory inputs that intrinsically code biological values by generating positive or negative feeling states without any obligatory interactions with motor patterning systems. It should also be emphasized that the affective valence of incoming sensory information will be governed by the status of the pertinent homeostatic regulators, so that pleasure is amplified by stimuli that help re-establish regulatory constancies, and aversion is provoked by stimuli that tend to increase existing regulatory imbalances. The possibility that brain opioids are at the heart of such general affective read-out processes has been considered (Panksepp, 1981), but there are bound to be many other neurochemistries.

As all other brain processes, affective feelings are probably processed at several levels of the neuroaxis, and at the highest levels of the neuroaxis, basic emotional feelings may be experienced as sentiments and appetites. For instance, the more subtle feelings and cognitive strategies related to the basic emotional states may be elaborated in specific paleocortical zones—with fear and anger elaborated largely in the temporal lobes, anticipatory/expectancy/planning processes in median and orbitofrontal zones of frontal cortex and grief and separation distress in cingulate areas (Panksepp, 1985, 1989).

Although there appears to be no credible empirical resolution of these important issues on the horizon, I suspect that the evolution of the internal awareness of emotional and motivational states was a relatively efficient way for the nervous system to index the biological relevance of events. If a brain system was able to rapidly encode sensory inputs and motor processes with values, survival and reproduction were maximized in ever more competitive environments. In presently unknown ways, these values were apparently most efficiently represented as subjective experienced feeling states. Because of their apparent importance in evolution, I see no credible alternative to the proposition that all mammals probably experience essentially similar types of basic emotional and motivational feeling states. If this proposition is true, anthropmorphically guided animal brain research may be a way to begin to fathom how the underlying brain mechanisms operate in humans (Panksepp, 1982). Partially for this reason, I have advocated an approach to the study of the brain called "affective neuroscience" (Panksepp, 1990c, 1991, 1992). Of course, this is not to deny that on top of the basic emotional and motivational mechanisms all mammals share, extra layers of subtlety were surely added by the unique cerebral potentials of each species, but, without working out the more primitive mechanisms, those will probably prove to be even thornier issues than the ones posed here. In any event, even with the best animal brain research, abundant room will always remain for the scientific documentation of the grand subtlety and diversity of emotions experienced by humans, the final expressions of which are surely molded by unique educational and cultural experiences. In a multitude of ways, each human can also stylize and personalize the archetypical affective experiences that all mammals still share. But much of this will continue to lie in the realms of art and social engineering rather than science.

The Vicissitudes of Mood: A Schematic Model

DAVID WATSON
LEE ANNA CLARK

In our response to Question 2, we argued that the bulk of affective life is spent in mood states that do not clearly correspond to distinct emotions. Accordingly, in responding to the current question, we will examine the broader issue of what factors influence mood, as opposed to the subjective experience of emotion per se.

Even a cursory examination of the relevant literature indicates that mood can be affected by an incredible variety of forces. Therefore, we do not attempt to offer a comprehensive catalog of influences here. Instead, we present a general conceptual scheme that classifies the potentially important factors into four broad types: (1) *exogenous factors* (i.e., transient environmental factors), (2) *endogenous rhythms* (i.e., innate biological processes that are associated with a natural cyclicity in affective experience), (3) *traits and temperament* (i.e., characteristic mean level differences in the tendency to experience positive and negative mood states), and (4) *characteristic variability* (i.e., stable individual differences in the extremity of one's mood fluctuations). Joint consideration of these four broad types of influences offers a useful working model for understanding the vicissitudes of mood. We discuss each of these in turn, and then consider how they operate conjointly.

Exogenous Factors

By "exogenous factors" we mean short-term situational or environmental variables that produce significant fluctuations in mood. An enormous body of research has examined the influence of exogenous variables, so that we cannot offer anything resembling a comprehensive list of potentially important factors. Instead, we will focus on a few broad types that illustrate some important general principles.

First, we must review our conceptual model of affective experience (which is more fully articulated in our response to Question 2). In brief, mood experience can be classified most parsimoniously along two very general dimensions—Positive

Affect and Negative Affect—that reflect the extent to which a person is currently experiencing pleasurable (e.g., joyful, enthusiastic, energetic, confident, alert) and distressing (e.g., nervous, irritable, guilty, sad, upset) feelings, respectively. Moreover, these two broad dimensions are largely independent of one another; thus, for example, currently experiencing a significant amount of Negative Affect places no necessary restriction on the extent to which one is simultaneously experiencing pleasurable, positive feelings.

Given the distinctiveness and independence of these dimensions, it is not surprising that they tend to be influenced by different types of exogenous factors. Specifically, Negative Affect is elevated in response to stressful events and aversive stimuli. For instance, marked increases in Negative Affect have been observed in individuals who are undergoing surgery and dental treatments, anticipating a painful or invasive medical procedure, or viewing a gruesome or disgusting film (see Spielberger, Gorsuch, Lushene, Vagg, & Jacobs, 1983; Watson & Clark, 1984). Similarly, Negative Affect is elevated in situations involving evaluation or scrutiny by others, and in response to failure, criticism, and other negative feedback (Spielberger et al., 1983; Watson & Clark, 1984). Corroborating our earlier assertion, Positive Affect is less strongly and consistently influenced by stressful and aversive stimuli.

What factors consistently influence the experience of positive mood states? Most notably, a growing body of evidence indicates that Positive Affect is elevated when people are socializing (e.g., Clark & Watson, 1988; Watson, 1988a). However, some social activities are clearly more pleasurable than others, and some types of socializing are not associated with enhanced positive mood. For example, Clark and Watson (1988) found that physically active and epicurean activities (e.g., skiing, parties, eating and drinking with others) were associated with marked increases in Positive Affect, whereas sedentary and relatively formal social interactions (e.g., club meetings, lessons) were not. Nevertheless, the relation is remarkably broad and robust, and most types of social activity are associated with transient increases in positive mood.

Having said this, we must also note that the temporal/causal sequencing of this relation is rather complex. That is, some evidence clearly indicates that pleasurable social events lead to transient increases in Positive Affect (Clark & Watson, 1988; McIntyre, Watson, Clark, & Cross, 1991). However, other data suggest that elevated levels of Positive Affect lead to an enhanced desire for social activity and to actual increases in social behavior (e.g., Cunningham, 1988). It therefore appears that positive mood and social activity mutually influence one another.

Positive Affect is also elevated in situations involving strenuous exercise or other intense physical activity (Clark & Watson, 1988; Watson, 1988a). There is also some tendency for Negative Affect to decrease in these situations, but the effect is clearly greater for Positive Affect. More generally, it seems that Positive Affect is highly responsive to variations in activity level; simply put, it appears that it is easier to induce a state of high Positive Affect through *doing* than through *thinking*, whereas the reverse is true for Negative Affect.

Although different types of events have reliable and systematic effects on mood, we must emphasize that individuals show marked differences in their responses to these situations. Moreover, people do not simply respond passively to events occurring in their environment; rather, individuals are active agents whose appraisals (i.e., cognitive interpretations) of these situations are critically important in shaping their responses (Lazarus, 1966). Indeed, the significance of a situation cannot be understood fully without also considering the individual involved. For instance, a certain score on an examination might be construed as failure by one person, leading, in turn, to a transient episode of Negative Affect; the same score, however, might be viewed as evidence of success by another, leading to an entirely different affective response. Thus, the mood-eliciting properties of situations critically depend on the subjective appraisals of the individuals involved.

Finally, we should note that exogenous factors do not consist simply of discrete situations and events, but also include the changing physical features of the environment. Thus, mood is responsive to various aspects of the physical environment, including weather (e.g., temperature, humidity, atmospheric ionization, degree of sunshine), noise level, degree of crowding, ambient odors, and so on (e.g., Clark & Watson, 1988; Ehrlichman & Halpern, 1988). However, specific relations between these variables and Positive and Negative Affect have not yet been established.

Endogenous Rhythms

Endogenous processes also cause marked fluctuations in affect. By "endogenous rhythms," we are referring to internal biological processes that are associated with recurring cyclic patterns in mood. We will consider three internal rhythms here. First, Positive Affect shows a consistent diurnal pattern that reflects the influence of endogenous circadian rhythms (e.g., Clark, Watson, & Leeka, 1989; Thayer, 1978, 1989). Specifically, Positive Affect is relatively low on awakening, and remains low during the early morning. It rises until it peaks at some point during the middle of the day; it then falls throughout the evening until another low point is reached late at night. Other investigators (e.g., Thayer, 1978) have also found evidence of a "siesta effect"—a secondary trough in Positive Affect that occurs sometime during the mid- to late afternoon—but we have not observed this pattern in our own data. In contrast, Negative Affect does not exhibit a systematic diurnal rhythm (Clark et al., 1989).

Two additional points regarding this circadian rhythm in Positive Affect are noteworthy. First, the effect appears across different types of positive mood states. For example, in addition to examining general Positive Affect, Clark et al. (1989) assessed four specific positive moods: Excitement (excited, enthusiastic, inspired), Attentiveness (alert, attentive, interested), Pride (proud, determined), and Activity (active, strong). All four scales showed remarkably similar circadian patterns. Second, this diurnal pattern is also general across individuals: In the two studies reported by Clark et al. (1989), 78 percent of the subjects showed a mean increase in general Positive Affect between 9 A.M. and noon, and 85 percent showed a corresponding mean decrease between 9 P.M. and midnight. Thus, regardless of their preferred sleep-wake patterns, most individuals show the same basic circadian rhythm.

The biological processes that produce this diurnal cyclicity have not been clearly established. Some evidence links it to the so-called "strong oscillator" that regulates internal body temperature, REM sleep, and certain hormonal systems. However, other data suggest that these circadian mood fluctuations are at least partly due to the "weak oscillator" that controls the sleep-wake cycle and related functions. On the basis of these data, we have speculated that the observed rhythmicity in Positive Affect results from an interaction between these two oscillators (Clark et al., 1989).

Interestingly, Positive Affect—but not Negative Affect—also appears to follow a seasonal cycle. Specifically, Positive Affect levels tend to be highest in the spring, and then decline slightly in the summer and fall; they drop to their lowest point during the winter before reviving again the following spring (Bradburn, 1969; Smith, 1979). This phenomenon may represent a normal-range version of seasonal affective disorder, a bipolar illness that typically is characterized by a severe, atypical depression during the late fall and winter, followed by a manic episode during the spring or summer (Kasper & Rosenthal, 1989). This manic-depressive cycle is, of course, associated with enormous fluctuations in positive mood; in fact, Depue, Krauss, and Spoont (1987) have argued that bipolar disorder is caused by marked fluctuations in a biobehavioral "Behavioral Engagement" system that is strongly linked to the subjective experience of Positive Affect.

The evolutionary significance of these seasonal effects is not entirely clear, but most researchers agree that they are related to similar seasonal changes (e.g., in activity level, reproduction, and metabolic rate) that are observed in many animal species. In fact, Kasper and Rosenthal (1989) suggest that these seasonal effects can be viewed as a human equivalent of hibernation, and that the fall/winter depression originally developed as a highly efficient means of energy conservation (due to a decreased metabolic rate) during a time of scarce food supplies.

A third rhythmic effect concerns the menstrual cycle in women. Strong mood effects have been attributed to the various phases of this cycle, both in the popular media and in clinical lore. Therefore, it is surprising that the evidence has been inconsistent and somewhat inconclusive, although most studies have observed some increase in Negative Affect before and during menstruation (Thayer, 1989). Our own data suggest that menstrual mood effects are relatively modest in most women; moreover, the changes that we have observed have primarily been found on Positive Affect. Clearly, this is a topic that warrants more serious research attention.

Traits and Temperament

The factors we have considered thus far help to explain the marked mood fluctuations that each person experiences. In contrast, the final two categories clarify how individuals characteristically differ from one another. In this third category, we again consider the constructs of emotional traits and temperaments that we discussed previously in connection with Question 2. To recapitulate, emotional traits can be defined as the propensity to experience a corresponding mood. For example, the trait of Positive Affectivity represents one's characteristic tendency to experience positive mood states. Individuals high in Positive Affectivity have a high mean level of Positive Affect, and tend to experience frequent and intense episodes of positive mood; conversely, those lower on the trait have a generally lower mean level of

Positive Affect. Similarly, Negative Affectivity is a trait that represents one's characteristic predisposition to experience negative mood states. Each of these emotional traits is, in turn, a core component of a more general dimension of temperament: Negative Affectivity is a central, organizing feature of Neuroticism, whereas Positive Affectivity is a core component of Extraversion.

These trait/temperamental factors can be viewed as characteristic baselines that represent each person's typical or mean level of Positive and Negative Affect. Of course, each individual varies tremendously around his or her own baseline, in response to the exogenous and endogenous factors we have already considered. However, these fluctuations in no way negate the fact that baseline affective levels vary substantially from individual to individual.

What causes these marked individual differences in mean affective levels? As we discussed in response to Question 2, both Negative Affectivity/Neuroticism and Positive Affectivity/Extraversion have a strong genetic basis that has been hypothesized to reflect differential biological sensitivities to punishment and reward, respectively. In addition to this biological substrate, cognitive and attitudinal factors also play an important role, particularly in the case of Negative Affectivity/Neuroticism. For example, those who are high in Negative Affectivity/Neuroticism are more likely to view life situations as stressful and threatening, and as beyond their ability to cope; in contrast, those low on the dimension are more likely to view these same experiences as challenges that can be mastered successfully. In addition, high scorers are more likely to interpret ambiguous situations and stimuli negatively, and to see problems where others do not (Clark & Watson, 1991a; Watson & Clark, 1984). In other words, returning to our earlier discussion regarding life situations, this general dimension of Negative Affectivity/Neuroticism is associated with systematic individual differences in subjective appraisal.

Characteristic Variability

Emotional traits and temperaments reflect stable individual differences in *mean* affective levels. However, evidence indicates that individuals also show characteristic differences in mood *variability*. For example, Larsen, Diener, and their colleagues have conducted several studies examining the trait of Affect Intensity, which reflects the general intensity or magnitude of one's affective responses (for a review, see Larsen & Diener, 1987). Persons high in Affect Intensity respond more strongly to both positive and negative mood-eliciting stimuli; accordingly, they characteristically show more pronounced fluctuations—and hence greater variability—on both Positive and Negative Affect. Note that this further implies that positive mood variability is significantly related to negative mood variability. We have, in fact, found this to be the case in our own studies of daily mood.

In a related line of research, Depue et al. (1987) have argued that characteristic variability is an inherent feature of Behavioral Engagement (BE). As noted earlier, BE is a biobehavioral system that is strongly associated with the experience of Positive Affect. Depue et al. present evidence suggesting that individuals can be meaningfully classified not only in terms of their mean BE level, but also according to their characteristic degree of fluctuation around this central tendency. Moreover, Depue et al. view these two BE indices – mean level and characteristic variability – as relatively independent of one another. For example, those high in variability can have a high mean BE level, a relatively low average level, or else fall somewhere in between these extremes. Depue et al. further argue that most people exhibit fairly modest characteristic variations in their BE level; the notable exceptions, however, are individuals suffering from cyclothymia and bipolar disorder, who show enormous fluctuations on this dimension.

In our view, individual differences in characteristic variability are likely to be extremely important in understanding affective experience, and they surely warrant more serious research attention. However, we should also note that analyses of our own data suggest that positive mood variability is likely to prove more interesting than negative mood variability. This is because variability in Negative Affect is strongly correlated with mean level scores on Negative Affectivity/Neuroticism. For example, in three daily mood studies involving nearly 300 subjects, negative mood variability correlated from .60 to .80 with the overall mean level of Negative Affect. Accordingly, negative mood variability may yield little useful information beyond that already obtainable from existing trait and temperament measures. In contrast, positive mood variability is only weakly related to mean affective levels; in the same three daily mood studies, positive mood variability had correlations ranging from only -.12 to .37 with mean level scores on Positive and Negative Affect. Thus, assessing characteristic variability in Positive Affect is likely to yield important incremental information about affective experience.

Integration and Conclusion

Taken together, these four classes of factors yield a reasonable working model of affective experience. As we have noted, emotional traits and temperaments serve as a general baseline that determine one's overall level of Positive and Negative Affect. In contrast, the three remaining types are responsible for the marked mood fluctuations that each individual experiences; these three classes of factors therefore produce substantial variation around each person's baseline levels. On the one hand, exogenous factors produce marked, but highly irregular, fluctuations in mood that reflect a person's responses to changing environmental conditions; on the other hand, endogenous biological rhythms are responsible for the patterned cyclicity of affective experience, especially positive affective experience. Finally, these substantial mood fluctuations can themselves be viewed dispositionally; thus, factors such as Affect Intensity reflect general individual differences in the magnitude of one's affective responses to endogenous and exogenous influences.

Afterword: What Influences the Subjective Experience of Emotion?

PAUL EKMAN
RICHARD J. DAVIDSON

Clore and LeDoux, a cognitive psychologist and a neuroscientist, agree that emotional experience focuses our attention. They diverge from that point of agreement. LeDoux emphasizes unconscious information processing that activates an emotion network. Consciousness is directed toward the most likely source of the arousal. (It would be interesting to know the extent to which that direction toward the source is determined by phylogenetic as compared to ontogenetic factors.) Clore's discussion of how the intensity of emotional experience depends on goals, standards, and attitudes implies a process that more typically may be conscious. Clore also discusses the importance of both the intensity and duration of emotional experience, suggesting that duration is related to goals, and intensity to how much cognitive restructuring occurs.

Panksepp's position seems compatible with LeDoux, when he says that internal awareness of emotional and motivational states is a way for the nervous system to index the biological relevance of events. He suggests that emotional feeling states are linked more to motor pattern generator systems than to the sensory perceptual analyzers. Panksepp's claim that all mammals have the same emotional feelings and all mammals have self-awareness is in marked contrast to Averill. Although Panksepp allows for social and individual experience to stylize and personalize emotional experience, emotional experience is not a social invention, as it apparently is for Averill. Emotional feelings for Averill are stories we tell ourselves to guide our behavior and account for it. Unlike his contributions to other questions, Averill does not tell us whether there is any biological contribution to these feelings, but the implication is that there is not. Averill also argues that feelings are not a crucial issue in defining emotions, for we can have emotions without being aware of them, and feelings that are not emotions are common. However, he does acknowledge that subjective experience is "among the more prototypic features of emotion."

Watson and Clark primarily focus on moods, not emotions, although their discussion of exogenous influences on moods could have been written about emotions. Consistent with their position in their contributions to other questions, moods are reduced to positive and negative affect. They tell us that individuals differ not just in their typical mood and the strength of that mood, but also in how much variation in moods occurs. They do not address the question of how the subjective feelings of moods might differ from the subjective feelings that occur with emotions.

LeDoux makes a very important observation toward the beginning of his contribution when he notes that the problem of experience is not unique to the study of emotion. We also experience memories, percepts, images, and so on. The lack of a solution to the problem of experience and consciousness has not impeded research in these other areas, nor should it in the case of emotion. We can make great progress on the question of how the brain processes emotional stimuli and produces emotional responses without solving the consciousness question, just as we have made strides understanding color perception without cracking the qualia code.

Epilogue

Affective Science: A Research Agenda

PAUL EKMAN
RICHARD J. DAVIDSON

In the Afterwords following each chapter we highlighted agreements and disagreements about each of the twelve questions. Here we will first consider a few issues that cut across those questions, identifying what we believe to be common ground and providing our own perspective on three issues about which there is divergence. Then, we will take up each of the twelve questions and present some of our ideas about the research that would move the field forward.

While we attempted not to inject our own judgments in the Afterwords, this chapter by necessity has to reflect our own beliefs. The other contributors to this book would likely offer different judgments about what are the major disagreements among researchers worth commenting upon, and many would propose a different research agenda. Here we do not claim to provide the final word; there is no one best view or research agenda, precisely because there are too few data. There is a lot more argument in the responses to the twelve questions than data to argue about. Our goal is for the reader to finish this book thinking about what research on emotion needs to be done. If the reader disagrees with us about what research should be done, and that disagreement serves to stimulate thought about what research the reader wishes to pursue, we will have accomplished our objective.

We did circulate an earlier version of this chapter to five of the contributors, who represent a wide range of viewpoints. While we benefited from their criticisms and made changes in what we have written in response to their suggestions, none of them will agree with all of what we say in this chapter. At this juncture there are many paths for research to follow. The choice of which research path to take reflects judgments about what is (most) important, what is likely to pay off, and what kind of research a person finds most enjoyable to do. Ten years from now, we will better be able to see which paths have been most productive.

What Most Students of Emotion Agree About

We originally did not include the word "most" in the title of this section, but we found, to our surprise, that there is some dissent about some of the points we present in this section.[1] At the least, all scholars and investigators characterize emotion as involving multiple elements, and would endorse most of the elements and functions in the following list.

1. There is information processing and evaluation of events that provoke an emotion. There is divergence about just how to characterize those processes, and to what extent there might be universal features.
2. There are expressive and physiological changes that are to some extent distinctive for each emotion. There is divergence about: (a) whether there is a distinctive signal for every emotion, although nearly all agree that there is a distinctive signal for some emotions; (b) whether there are distinctive changes in autonomic nervous system activity and in central nervous system activity for each emotion; and (c) the extent to which there might be universals in signals or in some of the physiological changes that occur.
3. There is retrieval of relevant memories, expectations, and methods for coping with the emotion-provoking event.
4. Emotion involves a subjective experience, a feeling state, which may include awareness of some or all of these elements. For some theorists, this is the only essential element in emotion; for others, subjective experience is not essential. And some would argue that we may not always be aware of our emotional feelings when we are in the midst of an emotion.

Emotion is not a peripheral phenomenon but involves the organism totally. Emotional experience shapes and reflects individual personality development. Emotion serves a number of functions, although investigators differ in whether they agree with each of the functions listed below or how important they consider any one of these functions to be.

1. Emotions have motivational properties, to the extent to which people seek to maximize the experience of positive emotions and to minimize the experience of negative emotions.
2. Emotions organize behavioral and physiological patterns to deal with emotion-evoking events, interrupting less important ongoing activities. At high-intensity levels, emotions may disorganize behavior and planning.
3. Emotional signals inform others, which is crucial, not only in infancy but throughout life in social interactions.
4. One's emotional experience affects one's well-being and may have implications for one's physical health.

What Students of Emotion Disagree About

- Are emotions best conceptualized in terms of discrete states or dimensions?

Most of those who work from evolutionary viewpoint, examining emotional responses, have postulated a number of discrete emotions, such as anger, fear, disgust, and so forth. Most of those who emphasize cognition, studying the language of emotion or attributions about emotional states, have postulated a set of emotional continua or dimensions, such as pleasant–unpleasant, unaroused–aroused, approach–avoid, and so on. There are exceptions, of course; for example, Lazarus, a cognitive psychologist, postulates discrete emotions, and Davidson, a psychophysiologist, postulates approach--avoidance as a fundamental dimension in distinguishing among emotions.

We see no contradiction between a discrete and dimensional approach to emotion; these two formulations are useful for different purposes. No set of dimensions so far proposed adequately captures the known differences among discrete emotions. Yet many of the emotion dimensions can usefully describe variations in the experience of any particular discrete emotion. Some of the emotion dimensions can also distinguish among the discrete emotions.

An intensity dimension can distinguish variations in the strength of anger episodes, fear episodes, etc. Perhaps also some emotions have a more narrow range of intensity variations than others (e.g., there may be a greater range in the intensity of anger experiences than in the intensity of surprise experiences). A pleasant to unpleasant dimension can distinguish between groups of emotions: anger, fear, disgust, and sadness are unpleasant, while relief, contentment, amusement, and pride are pleasant. The pleasant–unpleasant dimension can describe differences within each group of emotions, although that is less certain. Is anger always more unpleasant than fear? The pleasant–unpleasant dimension should not, however, be used to distinguish different instances of the same emotion. While some fear experiences, for example, are more unpleasant than other fear experiences, those differences might better be captured by the intensity dimension rather than a pleasant–unpleasant dimension. An approach–avoid dimension can also be used to describe different instances of the same emotion (e.g., anger involving approach versus anger involving avoidance), as well as to distinguish among emotions (anger usually involves approach and disgust usually involves avoidance). An active--passive dimension can distinguish among different instances of the same discrete emotion, or among emotions (e.g., there is typically more activity in anger than in sadness).

- How Many Emotions Are There?

This is not a meaningful question to those who take a dimensional approach, and they cite disagreement among discrete emotion researchers about the number of emotions in support of their stance. Among discrete emotion researchers, the answer to the question of how many emotions there are depends on the type of evidence they consider.

There is consistent evidence for pan-cultural facial expressions for five emotions: anger, fear, sadness, enjoyment, and disgust (reviewed in Ekman, 1989; see also counter claim by Russell, 1994, and replies by Ekman, 1994, and Izard, 1994). There is still disagreement about whether there is a pan-cultural signal for surprise, contempt, and shame/guilt. Study of the emotion lexicon suggests roughly the same emotions (i.e., Shaver, Schwartz, Kirson, & O'Connor, 1987), although there is little cross-cultural data. Evidence exists for emotion-specific autonomic nervous system (ANS) activity in the case of anger, fear, disgust, and sadness (Ekman, 1992a; Levenson, 1992;

Levenson, Ekman, Heider, & Friesen, 1992). Although replicated within Western and in a non-Western culture, researchers are still arguing over the evidence (Ortony & Turner, 1990; Tassinary & Cacioppo, 1992; Zajonc & McIntosh, 1992). There is evidence for distinguishing positive from negative affect with EEG-based measures of regional brain activity (Davidson, 1992). There is no information so far about whether it is possible to distinguish among different negative emotions, such as anger, fear, disgust, and sadness, though sadness-based psychopathology (depression) can be distinguished from fear-based psychopathology (phobias) on EEG.

Part of the disagreement about the number of emotions can be resolved by considering emotions not as single unitary states but as families of related affective states (see Ekman, 1992b; Lazarus, 1991; Shaver et al., 1987). Each emotion family shares commonalities in their expression, physiological activity, and in the types of appraisal that call them forth. These shared characteristics within an emotion family should distinguish one emotion family from another. Later in this chapter we discuss research necessary to elucidate the concept of emotion families. Part of the disagreement about how many emotions there are comes also from a failure to distinguish among different affective phenomena (see Chapter 2).

- What is the gold standard for knowing that an emotion has occurred?

Is there a sine qua non for emotion? The answer at this time must be No. The investigator must use multiple methods to study emotion, including, whenever possible, measures of behavior, subjective experience, and physiology.

We believe that researchers should not rely exclusively on self-reports. Too much of what we know about emotion has come from questionnaires in which subjects who are not having an emotion try to remember or imagine what they would be thinking or feeling if they were having an emotion. How people account for their emotions provide important data, but we should not assume that accounts given when not experiencing an emotion are going to closely resemble accounts given during or immediately after an emotional episode, and an account may differ in interesting ways from other sources of information about what transpires during an emotional episode. Quite a separate potential problem is the near exclusive reliance on questionnaires or ratings scales rather than free responses to assess subjective experience.

Emotion talk during an interaction can provide continuous information about how emotion is experienced over time (see Marchitelli & Levenson, 1992). All too often, however, it is not emotion talk but reports on rating scales obtained after an emotional episode or series of episodes that are the primary source of information about subjective experience. Rosenberg and Ekman (1994) have shown that such retrospective self-reports are vulnerable to recency effects (see also Ptacek, Smith, Espe, & Raffety, 1994). The use of a rating dial during an emotion episode (Levenson, Sher, Grossman, Newman, & Newlin, 1980; Sher & Levenson, 1982) can provide on-line continuous information, but at the cost of limiting the number of emotions that can be considered and at the risk of interfering with the emotional experience. Rosenberg and Ekman (1994) and Levenson and Gottman (1983) and Gottman and Levenson (1985) have used different techniques for obtaining data on subjective experience by having subjects review a videotape of their interaction.

A Research Agenda

- Question 1: Are There Basic Emotions?

We will consider two areas of research: study of a culture that is reported not to have one of the emotions that others claim to be universal, and research to elucidate the concept of emotion families.

Research on "Absent" Emotions The position of social constructionists, such as Averill and Shweder, is bolstered by reports of cultures in which a particular emotion supposedly does not occur. For example, Signe Howell (personal communication, June 1985) said that anger is not present in the cultures she studied. If there truly is no trace of anger, no pattern of behavior when provoked, insulted, or frustrated, no evidence of anger displaced onto other targets, it would directly contradict the position of those who presume emotions to be universal. (See Ekman's, Panksepp's, and Scherer's replies to Question 1.)

The universalists can deal with reports from anthropology about "absent" emotions by presuming that the anthropologist must have missed subtle signs of the emotion, or that the emotion occurs but is not named, or that its manifestations were discouraged early in life. Such a view is buttressed by Levy's (1984) observations that while Tahitians do not either label or recognize sadness, sadness nevertheless was apparent in the behavior of Tahitians. Tahitians, Levy said, show sad expressions and behavior when experiencing a rejection by a loved one, but they interpret their behavior as sickness, not sadness, and do not relate it to the rejection. Unfortunately, there is no film or video record, or any other means, of substantiating Levy's claim.

To determine whether an emotion is truly absent in a culture would require that anthropologists and psychologists collaborate in careful examination of such a culture. Simply having more than one observer, in particular observers who differ in their position on universality, would be a vast improvement over the current state of knowledge which is based almost always on the observations of one person. Video recordings of naturally occurring and experimentally arranged interactions would be crucial to determine whether there is any hint of the absent emotion. Extensive and intensive interviewing to learn how the members of the culture construe social events which in other cultures commonly call forth the absent emotion should be conducted. Study of the early years of life could attempt to determine if socialization involves inhibiting the experience of the absent emotion. Elicitors known to call forth emotions at a very early age in Western cultures, such as the visual cliff for fear and arm restraint for anger, should be used.

The verified identification of cultural settings in which there is no trace of an emotion such as anger or fear, in adults, children, or infants, would require fundamental revisions in the position of many of the contributors to this book: Davidson, Dunn, Ekman, Frijda, Goldsmith, Izard, Kagan, Lazarus, LeDoux, Levenson, Panksepp, and Scherer. The failure to find such evidence should give pause to Averill, Clore, and Schweder. Regrettably, because of intercultural communication, direct and through mass media, the time left to do such research is nearly over.

Elucidating the Concept of Emotion Families The concept of emotion families (see Ekman's reply to Question 1) suggests that each emotion, such as anger, fear, disgust, and so forth, is composed of a group of related states that share certain features (appraisals, expressions, subjective feelings, physiology), and differ on those features from other emotions. Although this is an attractive metaphor, the concept of families is vague and not well based empirically. Ekman has used the metaphor of a theme and variations, which implies a central, core set of features. Rather than a theme and variations, perhaps families should be considered to be composed of siblings all of whom equally well represent that emotion, with no one sibling a better or more central representative of what distinguishes one family from another.

Research on each of the features mentioned here—appraisals, expressions, subjective feelings, and physiology—could help to resolve which metaphor is correct, and whether the concept of an emotion family has utility. Such research requires examination of multiple instances of at least two different emotions, such as anger or fear. Naturalistic observations of the different social occasions in which each emotion occurs would provide information about the commonalities in emotion antecedents. Videotape recordings would allow identification of expressions, speech, and other behaviors that are specific to one or the other emotion. Experimental inductions of each emotion would also be necessary to obtain additional data on the physiology, subjective experience, and information about how the person experiencing the emotion accounts for and explains why the emotion occurred.

Emotion researchers must utilize methodological developments from other areas of the biobehavioral sciences where this form of question has arisen. The issue here is whether different emotions are types or taxons, rather than varying on a dimensional continuum. A type or taxon is a categorical entity, even if it is associated with variations on continuous measures (e.g., heart rate). For example, we know that although the distribution of IQ scores in any large sample is normal, those at the low end include subjects who possess a taxon different from the remainder of the sample. Some of these individuals may have Down's syndrome, one consequence of which is to impair IQ. Thus, even though these subjects fall on the lower tail of a normal distribution, it would not be appropriate to consider all of these subjects as varying along the same dimension. In the same way, two emotions might differ in heart rate or some parameter of brain activity. Rather than assume that such variation is dimensional, we can ask whether the distribution of scores obtained during each of the two emotions is best captured by a taxonomic model or by a continuous, dimensional model.

In the last decade, statistical procedures have been developed to assess taxonicity (see Meehl, 1992, for a discussion). Taxonicity has been a key issue in psychopathology research where investigators have been interested in whether subjects who score at the extremes of a distribution on a certain trait are best regarded as a type or simply on the end of the continuum of a distribution. Where a large sample size is available with scores on a continuously distributed variable (e.g., heart rate) from two or more emotions, it is possible to use these statistical techniques to make inferences about the extent to which the data conform to a discrete (taxon) model or a dimensional one.

• Question 2: How are emotions distinguished from moods, temperament, and other related affective constructs?

Considering how central distinctions among the concepts of emotion, mood, and temperament have been, it is striking how little empirical research has actually been performed on these topics. Most of the commentators on this chapter proposed a relationship between mood and emotion, in which mood somehow alters the probability of emotion. Little is known about the mechanism for such putative effects.

How could we structure our research to answer this vexing question? The first choice is whether or not to preselect subjects on the basis of some mood disposition measure. Although that would seem to be the obvious decision, it is not certain whether people who score high on a mood predisposition measure are always in that mood, and if they are not in that mood during the laboratory session, then there is no way to observe the effects of the mood. The alternative is to bring subjects into the laboratory and assess their mood at that time, selecting only those who report experiencing a specific mood. Such screening is more cumbersome, requiring a larger number of subjects.

The second choice is what measure of mood to use. Should it be something such as the PANAS, which measures only a positive or negative mood, or should it be a measure of more specific negative or positive moods? The answer to this will depend on the question that the research is designed to answer.

The third issue is what tasks to provide that might be sensitive to mood effects. Consider the dynamics of emotional reactivity in response to standardized elicitors. We use the presentation of film clips, for example, to illustrate the various ways in which mood can affect emotional reactivity. Subjects who display high positive mood may experience positive affect earlier in the presentation of the visual stimulus. A second possibility is that such subjects might experience more intense positive emotion, with no differences in the timing of the response. A third possibility is that the positive mood subjects will exhibit a longer persistence of the positive emotion once it is elicited. These indices of rise time, intensity, and persistence can be examined using both behavioral and physiological measures sensitive to emotion. To know whether these relationships between mood and emotion were specific to the particular elicitors that were chosen, it would be important to replicate this basic procedure with other types of emotion elicitors.

Ekman has proposed that one important distinction between emotion and mood is that emotion has distinctive facial expressions, while mood does not. Although little empirical research is actually available to substantiate this claim, no one has yet to identify a facial expression that has been observed in a mood state that is not one of the emotional expressions. Although we think it not likely to be productive, a search for mood-specific facial expressions could be done by bringing subjects into the laboratory who differ in some dimension of mood and then videotape them unobtrusively; their facial behavior could be measured with the Facial Action Coding System (FACS) (Ekman & Friesen, 1978).

Ekman has proposed that mood might be reflected in tonic differences in the muscular activity of the face. This could be checked in similar studies in which EMG is used to measure facial activity in subjects who were known to be in one or another specific mood. This needs to be done separately from the search for visible facial movement, as described previously, since EMG is likely to inhibit at least some observable facial actions.

Davidson's proposal that mood may bias cognition while emotion may bias action is difficult to approach empirically. However, one testable prediction that follows from this proposal is that mood should result in more cognitive constraint than emotion. This pattern may arise simply as a function of the fact that mood persists while emotion is more phasic. Thus, if a subject is probed on information-processing measures after the induction of an emotion or mood, it may be that whatever emotion is being studied has already dissipated to some extent compared with the pre-task period. In contrast, mood, by at least some commentators' definitions, is likely to persist into the task period and thus influence the information-processing measures more than the emotion would. There are many ways in which these ideas might be tested. One strategy would be to manipulate mood and emotion separately and examine their effect on some information-processing measure. After each manipulation (i.e., one designed to affect primarily mood and one to affect emotion) subjects could then be tested on a task designed to assess automatic allocation of visual attention (using the visual probe, reaction-time technique; see Matthews 1990) to determine if the manipulation of mood results in a more pronounced change in visual attention than the manipulation of emotion. The basic prediction in this study is that the mood manipulation would bias visual attention toward positive stimuli more than the emotion manipulation, despite the fact that the reaction-time measure would occur in closer temporal proximity to the emotion elicitor than to the mood elicitor. One psychological mechanism that might account for this type of effect is that emotion more often than mood has an identifiable object. Since mood is less likely to be directed at a specific object, it may be available to bias general cognitive processing.

- Question 3: What is the function of emotions?

While virtually all theorists of emotion have offered commentaries on the functional significance of emotion, preciously little empirical research has actually been performed on this topic. In part, this is due to ambiguities about what is meant by the term *function*. Here we consider function in terms of what are the immediate changes or consequences that ensue when there is some evidence that an emotion is occurring.

Some of the relevant variables may be difficult to assess in a laboratory. For example, many commentators (see the responses to Question 3) have proposed that one function of emotion is to prime particular action tendencies. However, most laboratory situations place severe constraints on the types of action subjects are permitted to perform. It has therefore been very difficult to study this issue directly; investigators have, for the most part, opted for an easy way out by asking subjects to report on their action tendencies. Just how closely such measures are to actual action is unclear.

One type of research that is critically needed is more naturalistic studies of social interaction, particularly in infants and young children, where both emotion and action can be readily observed. Schoolyard play might be the canonical context for the conduct of such research. Observations in these settings would permit the examination of whether particular types of action reliably followed the display of certain emotions. The emotions could be inferred on the basis of facial and vocal behavior. If there are a small set of action sequelae for different emotions, then there should be frequent observable pairings of emotional expression, followed by particular types of action. If Clore's analysis is correct, then there should be considerable heterogeneity in the form of actions, but the goal of the action should remain relatively invariant within an emotion class. A coding system for goal orientation of action would have to be developed for this purpose. In studies of adult subjects who are seated in chairs in a laboratory, it is difficult to obtain any real action suitable for measurement.

There is some disagreement among commentators on the extent to which emotion influences cognition. This issue was also considered in the previous question on the relationship between emotion and mood, since one distinction that has been proposed is based on their differing functions with respect to action and cognition. Among the essays written in response to this question, there are two principal views with respect to how emotions influence cognition. One view holds that any such influence is on automatic cognitive operations, while another view suggests that emotions affect more extended appraisals. One of the critical problems in conducting research on this issue has been mentioned in the discussion of Question 2 – the difficulty of knowing whether the induced affective change is best conceptualized as an emotion or a mood. What is needed are experiments that induce emotions which are immediately followed by tests of both automatic and controlled processes that are matched on basic content and task difficulty. Any differential effects on one versus the other type of cognitive activity can then be assessed. It may well be that some emotions are more likely to affect one type of process, while other emotions may affect another type of process. While such studies have not yet been performed, there are suggestive data from studies of psychopathology where anxiety has been found to more likely affect automatic processes while depression is more likely to affect controlled processes (see, e.g., Mineka & Sutton, 1992). While anxiety and depression are neither emotions nor moods, the evidence does underscore the potential utility of conducting this type of research with normal affective processes.

A number of the commentators offered suggestions concerning the nature of emotional dysfunction. One prevalent theme mentioned by several writers is the idea that emotion expressed out of context, or prolonged beyond the usual duration, may be dysfunctional. These suggestions underscore the critical need for research on the temporal dynamics of emotional processing. We now have good tools to begin to characterize the time course of different response systems that reflect emotion. The duration of physiological and expressive changes in response to standardized emotion elicitors that are short in duration can be measured to obtain information on the persistence of the affective response following the eliciting stimulus. This type of study will provide new information on the duration of responses in different systems. It is likely that the time constant of affective change will differ across response systems, though the implications of this possibility have not been explicitly considered in discussions of the function of emotion.

Another type of dysfunction that may be the precursor to depression involves the failure to engage a positive event. At least some depression is characterized by a pervasive lack of interest and inability to experience pleasure. In this case, the dysfunction is not in the prolonged duration of negative affect, but rather the inability to engage the positive affect system. Both behavioral and physiological measures of positive affective response to appropriate incentives can be measured to assess this form of dysfunction.

- Question 4: How is evidence of universals in antecedents of emotion explained?

There is now considerable information from questionnaire studies about the common beliefs within and across cultures about the typical events that precede an emotion (c.f. Boucher & Brandt, 1981; Scherer, Walbott, & Summerfield, 1986). Although very important, we conceive of this information as accounts about emotion antecedents that may only partially represent what actually occurs if we were to examine emotional behavior in situ.

Information from questionnaire studies can provide one basis for specifying where and when we should expect to see specific emotions occur. Based on those findings, naturalistic observation and laboratory inductions could test how often these antecedents do actually evoke one or another emotion. In addition to obtaining observer ratings of emotional behavior, and video records which could later be measured, the people manifesting an emotion should be interviewed, to record their account of what they feel and why they feel it. By that means it would be possible to determine how an account of an antecedent event obtained soon after an emotional episode might differ from accounts about those antecedent events given by people who are not experiencing the emotion. Regardless of the degree of correspondence between these accounts, information about what people feel and what they believe brought about their feelings gathered immediately upon the observational evidence that an emotion is occurring will be invaluable to our understanding.

Diary studies offer another opportunity to learn about the antecedent events that commonly precede emotions. One problem that must be overcome is how to secure rich diary information without having the diary recordings become enormously intrusive. We also need to have studies in which there is both diary and observational data so we can learn about the type of emotional events that are typically not reported or are underrepresented in diaries.

Ekman proposed that often events antecendent to emotion are appraised automatically and therefore often the person is not conscious of the appraisal process. This possibility presents serious difficulties for self-report technology, since the very phenomenon of interest would be inaccessible to the measurement technology. The modern armamentarium of the cognitive scientist includes methods that can be used to make indirect, albeit rigorous inferences about such putative nonconscious cognitive processes. For example, if it is hypothesized that loss is a universal antecedent of sadness, pictures and words could be presented following a sadness induction, with the subjects asked to perform a lexical decision task (for the pictures, the task would be to specify whether a picture could be named by a word). Stimuli that included loss themes could be interspersed with other irrelevant stimuli. The basic prediction in this type of study is that reaction time would be faster to the loss themes following a sadness induction compared with the induction of another emotion.

• Question 5: What are the minimal cognitive prerequisites for emotion?

Let us distinguish the circumstances during which two types of appraisal processes occur. In one circumstance the latency is in milliseconds and the person may not be aware of what set off the emotion until after the emotion is in process. In the second circumstance, the latency is longer, and the person typically is aware of what it is that is setting off an emotion as it begins to gradually unfold. For Ekman (1977), the appraisal in the first circumstance is automatic; in the second, the appraisal is extended.

Although it is probably more of a continuum than a dichotomy, this distinction draws our attention to the fact that emotions can occur without extensive neocortical processing. When emotions occur automatically, the people experiencing the emotion cannot tell us about their appraisal process. They can only tell us how they account for their emotional behavior. Important as such accounts are, their import is to tell us how people describe the processes that occur during and after an emotion episode, not the processes that precede and lead to the emotion. It is only when the emotion is brought about through extended appraisal that we can learn about the cognitive processes by asking people about them.

The first empirical step, we believe, is to learn about the type of events that precede automatically activated emotions as compared to emotions that result from extended appraisal. The chief marker of an emotion resulting from automatic cognitive processes would be very short latency. What are the consistencies in emotions that occur from automatic appraisal? How varied are they? Do they resemble emotions that occur through extended appraisal?

Next, we need to begin to study the nature and characteristics of the automatic appraisal process itself. In the discussion of Question 4, we alluded to modern cognitive science procedures for making inferences about nonconscious processes. We believe that such procedures can be usefully applied to the question of automatic appraisals to determine which cognitive processes have been nonconsciously activated and to characterize their time course. Certain physiological techniques can also be used to make similar inferences (e.g., startle probe and event-related potential procedures).

• Question 6: Is there emotion-specific physiology?

Most of the commentators agree that whatever emotion-specific patterning is present is likely to be found in studies of central nervous activity. While some evidence of emotion-specific patterning in the autonomic nervous system (ANS) that has appeared in the past decade is promising, some of the commentators question the logic of expecting invariant autonomic patterns to mark particular emotions. These commentators maintain that because different instances of the same emotion may lead to different actions, ANS activity, which provides support for action, will not be emotion specific. The contrary view maintains that if specific actions have been adaptive in particular emotional contexts in the history of the species, it is likely that these preparations for action will have been preserved, and therefore emotion-specific ANS activity might be found. This is not simply a matter of debate, however, since there is now some evidence of emotion-specific ANS activity.

The most robust findings, however, have been obtained in response to the Directed Facial Action (DFA) task, where subjects are asked to voluntarily produce specific patterns of facial action. While there is some preliminary evidence (Levenson, Carstenson, Friesen & Ekman, 1991) that the same emotion-specific patterns are found with a very different task, this has yet to be demonstrated for each of the emotions they studied, and has yet to be replicated. Moreover, the DFA, as well as most other laboratory procedures, has been gathered in circumstances in which no action by the subjects is relevant for dealing with the emotions that are aroused.

The obvious next step to further clarify this matter is to examine autonomic patterning with subjects in which an emotion is aroused with several likely actions possible. This can be most easily done with an imagery task in which the same emotional experience is elicited with different action patterns. For example, subjects could be instructed to imagine that someone is trying to harm them and they are feeling afraid and they are trying to (a) flee, (b) hide, or (c) fend off the attacker (Lang [1979] did related work along these lines, but unfortunately included in his instructions some of the very changes in physiology—for example, increased heart rate—which are of interest.) We should note that an imagery task may not provide an adequate test, however, since the subject knows that no action can or will be taken. Nevertheless, it is a reasonable next step in pursuit of this issue.

Great progress has been made in studies of other animals where specific circuits are implicated in certain types of simple emotional learning. This work has clearly underscored the important contributions of the amygdala to emotional behavior. As Davidson has noted, however, there exist several case reports questioning the importance of the role of amygdala in human emotion. What is needed are studies in humans that use neuroimaging procedures with good spatial resolution, such as positron-emission tomography (PET) and functional magnetic resonance imaging (fMRI). These methods provide sufficient resolution to examine the functional activity in the amygdala. Using standardized probes to elicit emotion, including procedures virtually identical to those used in animal studies that have clearly implicated the amygdala, such as fear-potentiated startle (e.g., Davis, Hitchcock, Rosen, 1987) and classical conditioning (e.g., LeDoux, 1992), functional activity in the amygdala can be examined.

Of particular theoretical importance will be the study of different emotions that either belong to the same dimension or represent other dimensions. For example, among negative emotions, both fear and disgust are often associated with a strong withdrawal component, while anger and sadness are not. Certain forms of positive affect involve a strong approach component (e.g., anticipating receiving a desired appetitive stimulus), while other types of positive affect do not involve approach (e.g., the contentment that follows the receipt of a desired goal). It will be important to characterize the functional neuroanatomy of the circuits that track the approach–withdrawal dimensions and those that differentiate among emotions within a dimension.

Panksepp raises the important issue of possible neurochemical differences among emotions. This area has been virtually ignored in the human research literature (though see Depue, Luciana, Arbis, Collins & Leon, in press), although relevant animal data exist. Recent endocrine studies have discovered changes that occur over very short time spans (e.g., Carnes, Goodman, Lent, 1991). We can take the lead from the type of animal studies summarized by Panksepp and search for evidence of endocrine profiles that might distinguish between certain forms of positive and negative affect. However, studies using conventional sampling strategies have not found differences in HPA activity that differentiate between positive and negative affect, though this question is worth revisiting with more sophisticated sampling techniques.

Another strategy is to conduct studies that involve the administration of certain drugs that change mood or emotion in a laboratory context, while functional neuroanatomic and behavioral measures can be obtained. It would be informative to learn how changes in regional brain function induced by the drug administration are associated with changes in emotional state.

Ideally, studies can be conducted that include autonomic, central (via PET or fMRI), and endocrine measures simultaneously. Only in this way will the interrelation among these response systems be examined. As of this writing, there are virtually no studies in the literature that have looked at central and autonomic measures at the same time.

- Question 7: Can we control our emotions?

There are clearly many different ways in which people control their emotions. They range from avoiding potentially aversive stimuli, to inhibiting the expression of emotion, to using exogenous and endogenous distracters, as well as many other ways. It is also apparent that people engage in strategic maneuvers to increase the frequency and duration of positive affect. For future research on this topic to flourish, researchers will need to begin to specify the mechanism(s) by which control can be established.

It is probably most appropriate to choose a limited number of control strategies and characterize them in more mechanistic terms. For example, one form of control might be to mentally disengage from the emotion. This disengagement process might be similar to the disengage component of attention that has been characterized by Posner and colleagues in their PET studies of attention subcomponents. It may be that the capacity to disengage from an ongoing emotion critically depends on the prefrontal cortex. One characteristic of patients with frontal lobe damage is that they perseverate, though perseveration in emotional domains has not been systematically studied. Emotional perseveration may reflect a deficit in the capacity to disengage from an emotion, once it begins.

To investigate an individual's skill at terminating an emotion once it has been triggered, it would be informative to conduct a study that involved the presentation of a strong emotional stimulus that has been previously found to produce a change in emotion that persists following the offset of the stimulus (certain film clips have this characteristic). Immediately following the offset of the stimulus, subjects would be presented with one of two different cues. One cue would signify that subjects should attempt to terminate the ongoing emotional response, while the second cue would signify that the subject should do nothing. The advantage of presenting these cues after the termination of the eliciting stimulus is to prevent strategies from occurring that might result in alterations in how the emotional information is initially processed. While such strategic differences during encoding (i.e., alterations in appraisal) are another important form of emotion regulation, they may be different from the sorts of strategies people invoke to manage emotion once it occurs.

Another strategy that is critically needed in the study of emotional control is a developmental approach. As the chapter on development has underscored, one of the most salient changes that occurs with development is the capacity to control emotion. It would be informative to perform both naturalistic and experimental research longitudinally to examine the developmental changes in the capacity to control emotion. These developmental changes could be examined in relation to maturational changes in certain aspects of brain function.

If the prefrontal region is critical for certain forms of emotional control as some have suggested (e.g., Davidson, 1993), it would also be informative to conduct experimental studies on patients with frontal lobe damage to better characterize their deficit in emotional control. Perhaps such patients can take advantage of exogenous cues for emotional control, but fail when the control process depends entirely on endogenous processes.

Finally, once standard procedures are adopted to assess emotional control objectively, it is possible to examine individual differences in this skill. It would be informative to know if such individual differences are associated with systematic differences in patterns of regional brain function.

The most immediate need is for the development of objective paradigms to assess different aspects of emotional control using standardized emotional probes. Levenson and Gross have begun to do this in the context of their work on the inhibition of facial behavior during the presentation of emotional film clips. This approach needs to complemented with procedures that instruct subjects to begin the control strategy after they have received the emotional input to rule out basic differences in perceptual and attentional function during the presentation of the emotional stimulus. Once these assessment tools are developed, they can be applied in a variety of contexts to begin to address questions of mechanism.

• Questions 8 & 9: Can emotions be nonconscious? What is the relation between emotion and memory?

We have combined our comments on these two questions since they are so intimately tied together. To illustrate why these two questions should be addressed together, recall the clinical procedure that Korsakoff used in his interviews with amnesic patients. He would walk into each of his patient's rooms with his hand extended to shake theirs in greeting. Unbeknownst to the patient, Korsakoff would have a thumbtack between his fingers so that he would prick the patient as he shook their hand. When he would revisit the patient's room the next day or several days later, he would first ask the patient who he was. His amnesics were totally unaware of having any previous encounter with him. He would then offer his hand in greeting. His patients would refuse to shake his hand or would grimace when extending their hand toward him. In modern terminology, we would say that the patients had an affective implicit memory of the unpleasant handshake. However, because of their severe amnesia, they were incapable of explicitly encoding the identity of the doctor and so exhibited the peculiar dissociation between explicit and implicit recognition.

While clinical observations of this sort have been available for quite some time, little systematic research has been performed on this topic. It would be useful to study amnesics with both positive and negative affect elicitors to determine if implicit affective memory is equally robust for information of each valence.

We know very little about the differential characteristics of conscious versus nonconscious emotional memories. Paradigms have been developed that successfully show the acquisition of an unconscious affective memory. Using classical conditioning, Öhman has shown that backwardly masked faces can acquire signal value by pairing with an aversive stimulus, despite the fact that subjects are completely unaware of having seen those faces in the past. In the backward masking procedure, an emotional face is presented briefly and then followed immediately by a neutral face. The phenomenal experience of the subject in this case is that only a neutral face has been presented. If LeDoux is correct in his analysis of the neural substrates of these effects, we would expect that learning the association between the face and the aversive US would depend on the amygdala. If the stimuli were not masked and therefore visible, we would expect subjects to acquire both explicit and implicit information about the stimulus and therefore such learning should include the participation of both the amygdala as well as the hippocampus. These hypotheses could be tested in a study involving each of these conditions during which measures of regional cerebral blood flow are acquired with either PET or fMRI.

We also know little about the relative persistence of implicit affective information. A productive research design might be one that exposed one group of subjects to faces that are backwardly masked and conditioned to an aversive stimulus (producing an unconsciously conditioned emotional response), while another group is exposed to the identical faces in the absence of masking, but conditioned to the same aversive stimulus. A third group might be exposed to the same faces in the absence of any conditioning. Tests of recognition and liking of the faces could then be performed at 6-month intervals to determine if the implicit information persists as long or even longer than the explicit information.

The suggestions here all concern situations in which subjects might be unaware of the stimulus that produces the emotion. Another important form of unconscious affect arises when subjects are unaware of an emotional response they emit—that is, they cannot report on an emotional process that is occurring in themselves. Most individuals have had the experience of interacting with another person and observing subtle changes in the individual's facial expression of emotion of which the expressor appears to be unaware. Researchers who have viewed videotape of interpersonal interaction that is emotionally charged are consistently impressed with the high density of facial and other expressive behavior that occurs over time. In strict information-processing terms, it is unlikely that working memory has sufficient capacity to represent all of the behavior that occurs at any given point, since the density of the outflow is so high in these circumstances.

While such anecdotal observations are common, harnessing the phenomenon in a tractable laboratory paradigm has remained a difficult empirical challenge. One strategy that might be worth exploring is an interruption paradigm. Two individuals might be engaged in a dyadic interaction that is being monitored (via video) by expert facial coders. When a coder detects what appears to be a particular facial expression displayed by one participant, a signal is given to the target subject and she or he is asked to press one of seven buttons labeled with prototypic facial expressions of emotion. The subject is asked to press the button that most resembles the facial expression he was displaying in the period immediately preceding the signal. Signals can be presented during both expressive periods and control periods when the subject was displaying no visible facial action. Researchers can code the ongoing stream of facial behavior after the fact. The objective coding could then be compared with the subject's responses, and the frequency of unambiguous discrepancies between the objectively coded and subjectively experienced expressive periods could then be determined. There might well be individual differences in the extent to which subjects are aware of their expressive behavior (see, e.g., Weinberger, Schwartz, & Davidson, 1979). Of course, such an interruption strategy may prove unworkable or too costly if subjects, once interrupted, become preoccupied with the likelihood of being interrupted again.

We wish to note one other topic that relates to unconscious emotion and memory that has received almost no research attention—emotion in dreams (see Merritt, Stickgold, Pace-Schott, Williams, & Hobson, 1994, for a recent exception). The little work that has been performed indicates that dream content is often laden with emotion, and yet it is recalled relatively infrequently. We know almost nothing about the extent to which emotion in dreams is consistent within subjects and whether it is associated with patterns of waking emotion and mood. Are differences in post-sleep mood associated with variations in the emotional content of dreams from the preceding night? Can we use physiological measures (e.g., EEG measures of prefrontal asymmetry, as in Davidson, 1992; startle probe measures, as in Lang, Bradley, & Cuthbert, 1990) to obtain unobtrusive indices of at least the predominant valence of dream content? Such physiological measures can be obtained in the laboratory and then related to ratings of the emotional content of dreams elicited by reports following REM awakenings.

- Question 10: How do individuals differ in emotion-related activity?

This is a very active area of research, but it is an area of research that requires large sample sizes, and ideally longitudinal study. Individual differences in emotion should be manifest in the magnitude, latency, and recovery time to return to a baseline state. Research should determine if individual differences cut across or are specific to each of the emotional response systems (physiological, expressive, subjective). We also do not know if individual differences are emotion specific, specific to hedonic grouping (consistent among all negative or among all positive emotions), or are general across all emotions. Crucial, too, is the consistency in individual differences across the life span (see the following discussion under Question 11).

We do not know of research that has determined whether any of the individual differences we have outlined are more or less in evidence with weak, as compared to very intense, emotional provocations. The threshold for evoking any emotional response at all may itself be another aspect of emotion in which individuals differ. Still another interesting possibility is that the initial moments during an emotional reaction may show less variability across individuals than the subsequent moments as the emotion unfolds and develops.[2]

An individual differences strategy can offer a powerful test of hypotheses about the underlying physiological substrates of emotion. For example, if an investigator hypothesizes that physiological pattern X is specific to a particular discrete emotion or dimension of emotion, then individuals can be measured on physiological pattern X and studied to determine if they differ in the predicted way in their emotional reactivity. A concrete example of the utility of this strategy is the recent work of Davidson on individual differences in prefrontal asymmetry and their relation to emotional reactivity. In a series of studies Davidson and his colleagues (e.g., Tomarken, Davidson, & Henriques, 1990; Wheeler, Davidson, & Tomarken, 1993) have found that subjects with more right-sided prefrontal activation exhibit more intense negative responses to negative emotional stimuli.

- Question 11: What develops in emotional development?

Change in different components of emotion is one of the most salient features of human development across the lifespan. Research on this topic is also one of most demanding because of the problem of developing equivalent elicitors at different ages. For example, one of the questions that several commentators addressed concerned the issue of whether the core experience of an emotion remained invariant across development. To study this issue, researchers would need equivalent elicitors at different ages, for if differences were found in some parameter of emotional experience, a question would immediately arise as to whether the elicitors were really equivalent at the different ages. Different experiences might be produced by different elicitors.

Panksepp proposes that certain changes in affective development are associated with the maturation of specific central nervous system processes. This is a critical issue to investigate in both animal and human studies. However, it is necessary to go beyond mere descriptive correlations between patterns of central nervous system changes and developmental shifts in emotional processing. There are so many changes that occur in parallel in the central nervous system that establishing an association between a change in one component of neural structure or function and emotional development would be woefully inadequate. What is needed are studies that manipulate the brain in a specific way and then observe the effects of the manipulation on the hypothesized component of emotional development. For example, some investigators (e.g., Denenberg & Yutzey 1985; Fox & Davidson, 1984) have suggested that the regulation of negative affect (i.e., its voluntary inhibition) is mediated in part by interhemispheric inhibition of the right hemisphere by the left hemisphere via the corpus callosum. If this is true, individuals with lesions in the corpus callosum should show a specific deficit in this form of inhibition, though other aspects of emotional functioning should be relatively intact. This hypothesis can be examined in animal studies by performing an experimental callosotomy and then observing the animal over the course of development. If this were done in rhesus monkeys, we would expect to see in normal monkeys a period during which separation protest would peak and then be followed by a more attenuated response. If this diminution in separation protest that is observed with development is mediated in part by interhemispheric inhibitory pathways, lesions of the corpus callosum should disrupt the achievement of this particular developmental milestone. Human infants born with agenesis of the corpus callosum might profitably be followed to examine the same sorts of questions.

There exists considerable disagreement in the field concerning the significance of early facial expressions of emotion (compare Camras and Izard). One view holds that facial expressions of discrete emotions are invariant across the lifespan and provide an accurate read-out of emotional state. The other extreme posits that the same pattern of facial behavior may denote different states since contextual factors are important determinants of the facial configuration at each moment. We need better descriptive data on a larger sample of individuals. It would be informative to know how particular expressions are associated with both antecedent conditions and action sequelae at different ages. For example, we could choose one or two emotional expressions and chart the antecedents and consequences of the same expression at different ages longitudinally. This would provide a needed corpus of data that would be informative regarding the significance of facial expression at different ages.

Another issue in need of additional research attention is the relationship between affective and cognitive developmental milestones. Dunn has argued that the emergence of new emotions during the second and third years of life influences the development of new cognitive skills. It would be interesting to use an age-held-constant design in which children who did versus those who did not exhibit certain emotions (e.g., shame, embarrassment) were studied to determine their proficiency in certain cognitive skills, such as accuracy in anticipating the actions of others. This would be another way to establish the relationship between the acquisition of emotional and cognitive milestones.

- Question 12: What influences the subjective experience of emotion?

We advocate more use of procedures that allow subjects to respond freely to questions about their feelings. Although analysis of free responses is more cumbersome, there are a number of emotion lexicons that can be used to categorize free responses. Since there is no consensus about what set of emotion categories would be most useful, findings should include information not just by category, but must include the specific responses that were categorized. Once a free response is obtained, it may often be useful to ask subjects to give an intensity rating for the emotion they have named. We (Davidson, Ekman, Saron, Senulis, & Friesen, 1990; Ekman, Davidson, & Friesen, 1990; see also, Levenson, Ekman, & Friesen, 1990) use a procedure in which the subject is asked to rate the intensity of the emotion on a nine-point scale, anchored at one end with "No feeling of that emotion" and at the other end with "Most intense experience of that emotion they have ever had." It may also be useful to consider adjusting such intensity ratings on the basis of additional information in which subjects are asked to rate their own most intense experience of each emotion as compared to what they believe is the most intense experience of an emotion that anyone might ever have (see Ekman, in preparation).

Other procedures for calibrating subjects' ratings have also been developed. For example, some subjects use the upper end of the scale more than the lower end, while others show the reverse pattern. In other words, there are systematic biases that people display in their use of such rating scales. Wheeler, Davidson, and Tomarken (1993) have developed a regression-based procedure to remove the variance associated with global rating biases from simple Likert-type scales. They have demonstrated that when such procedures are used, the relation between self-reported emotion and physiology is improved.

It would also be useful to explore the utility of having subjects describe emotional experience in other than verbal terms. Colors, sounds, and other types of visual images could be explored, to determine if there is consensus. No one, for example, has pursued the findings of Clynes (1973) which suggested different patterns of motor activity occurred when subjects were asked to report on different emotions by touching a pressure transducer.

In addition to reports about emotions, it would be useful to also probe the memories and sensations of subjects. See the work of Levenson and Tsai (in preparation), Rime, Philippot, & Cisamolo (1990), and Scherer and Wallbott (1994) for studies of the sensations reported to occur with different emotions.

We need to know how subjects report their subjective experience of each emotion when they are in a baseline state, as compared to how the same subjects report their subjective state during or after an emotional episode. There are a number of techniques for obtaining reports of subjective experience during emotional episodes. Most commonly used is a self-report given immediately after an emotional episode. Even with a brief emotion induction, such as the viewing of a one-minute stimulus film, more than one emotion may occur. Recent evidence (Rosenberg & Ekman, 1994) shows that retrospective reports overrepresent the last emotion felt, not the earlier emotions. Retrospective reports, however, do allow more extensive questioning about the experience without contaminating the experience. Having subjects rate their emotions during an emotional episode deals with the problems of retrospective reports, but at the cost of diminishing the information that can be obtained. It is probably not feasible to have subjects rate more than the intensity of positive and negative emotion, or one or two specific emotions. And even then, the rating task itself may interfere with the emotional experience. Another procedure is to have subjects view the interaction in which their emotions occurred (Levenson & Gottman, 1983) or the film that evoked the emotion (Rosenberg & Ekman, 1994), providing information about the emotions they remember having felt initially. Gottman and Levenson (1985) have obtained continuous ratings using a joystick in the viewing task, but have only recorded emotions as positive or negative. Rosenberg and Ekman had their subjects stop the stimulus film whenever they remembered having felt an emotion; at that point, the subject provided a differentiated close-ended report of specific emotions.

With any of these techniques for reporting emotion, it would be important to determine which components of the emotion package (facial expressions, vocalizations, central and peripheral physiology) are most correlated with subjective experience. This may not be the same across emotions, across techniques for sampling emotions, across development, across individuals, or across cultures.

Conclusions

We adopted the phrase "affective science" because we believe emotions cannot be fully understood unless we also understand the other affective phenomena which border on emotion. We need to elucidate how emotions differ from moods, from preferences, from emotional traits, and emotional disorders. And understanding of each of these phenomena requires research that will to a large extent use the same methods.

We believe that programmatic research is required on each of the fundamental questions we have raised in this book if we are to see substantial progress. Methods are now available for instigating emotion in a number of different ways, and for measuring many different aspects of emotional experience. While questionnaires will undoubtedly always be part of the research enterprise in affective science, we hope to see less exclusive reliance upon them, and more use of observational methods and psychobiological assays. The examination of multiple emotions, each evoked more than one way, with comparisons to naturally occurring instances, at different points in the life span, are all needed. By definition, such work will require collaborations among investigators, from different subspecialties within psychology and to some extent also between psychologists and colleagues in other disciplines (e.g., linguistics, sociology, anthropology, neuroscience, psychiatry, zoology, among others).

Just as the study of cognition provided a unifying theme for psychology in the 1970s, we believe that emotion can serve a similar role in the 1990s. Emotion is relevant to many branches of psychology, including clinical, developmental, social, personality, comparative, and cognitive psychology as well as behavioral neuroscience. It has the potential to tie different areas together and to foster interdisciplinary bridges. In an era when the discipline of psychology is becoming increasingly fractionated, the prospect of a more integrated approach that takes into account different levels of analysis is appealing. Emotion is a topic that holds out such a promise.

There is a new generation of investigators just now or recently trained, and a lifetime of research to be done in affective science. Questions about the nature of emotion will be with us for a long time, but we hope there will be decisive data on some of the fundamental questions posed in this book within the next decade. Arguments about how best to interpret those data will probably remain with us for a long time.

Notes

1. This section is based on an earlier manuscript prepared by Paul Ekman with input from Richard Davidson, Robert Levenson, and Klaus Scherer.
2. Jack Block made this suggestion.

References

Abelson, R. P. (1983). Whatever became of consistency theory? *Personality and Social Psychology Bulletin, 9,* 37–54.

Adamec, R. E., (1991). Functional differences in temporal lobe sensory processing of threatening stimuli in the cat. *Physiology and Behavior, 49,* 455–464.

Adams, D. B. (1979). Brain mechanisms for offence, defense, and submission. *Behavioural and Brain Sciences, 2,* 201–241.

Aggleton, J. P. (1992). The functional effects of amygdala lesions in humans: A comparison with findings from monkeys. In J. P. Aggleton (Ed.), *The amygdala: Neurobiological aspects of emotion, memory, and mental dysfunction* (pp. 453–483). New York: Wiley-Liss.

Aggleton, J. P., & Mishkin, M. (1986). The amygdala: sensory gateway to the emotions. In R. Plutchik & H. Kellerman (Eds.), *Emotion: Theory, research and experience* (Vol. 3) (pp. 281–299). Orlando: Academic Press.

Ahadi, S. A., & Rothbart, M. K. (in press). Temperament, development and the Big Five. In G. Kohnstamm & C. Halverson (Eds.), *The developing structure of temperament and personality from infancy to adulthood.* Hillsdale, NJ: Lawrence Erlbaum.

Ahadi, S. A., Rothbart, M. K., & Ye, R. (1993). Child temperament in the U.S. and China: Similarities and differences, *European Journal of Personality*, 359–378.

Akiskal, H. S. (1990). Toward a clinical understanding of the relationship between anxiety and depressive disorders. In J. D. Maser & C. R. Cloninger (Eds.), *Comorbidity of anxiety and mood disorders* (pp. 597–607). Washington, DC: American Psychiatric Press.

Alheid, G. F., & Heimer, L. (1988). New perspectives in basal forebrain organization of special relevance for neuropsychiatric disorders: The striatopallidal, amygdaloid, and corticopetal components of substantia innominata. *Neuroscience, 27,* 1–39.

Allport, G. W. (1937). *Personality: A psychological interpretation*. New York: Holt, Rinehart & Winston.

Amaral, D. G., Price, J. L., Pitkänen, A., & Carmichael, S. T. (1992). Anatomical organization of the primate amygdaloid complex. In J. P. Aggleton (Ed.), *The amygdala: Neurobiological aspects of emotion, memory, and mental dysfunction* (pp. 1–66). New York: Wiley-Liss.

Amsel, A. (1958). The role of frustrative nonreward in noncontinuous reward situations. *Psychological Bulletin, 55,* 102–119.

Anderson, N. H. (1971). Integration theory and attitude change. *Psychological Review, 78,* 171–206.

Argyle, M., & Lu, L. (1990). The happiness of extraverts. *Personality and Individual Differences, 11,* 1011–1017.

Arnold, M. B. (1960). *Emotion and personality*. New York: Columbia University Press.

Averill, J. R. (1968). Grief: Its nature and significance. *Psychological Bulletin 70,* 721–748.

Averill, J. R. (1979). The functions of grief. In C. Izard (Ed.), *Emotions in personality and psychopathology* (pp. 339–368). New York: Plenum.

Averill, J. R. (1980). A constructivist view of emotion. In R. Plutchik & H. Kellerman (Eds.), *Theories of emotion* (pp. 305–340). New York: Academic Press.

Averill, J. R. (1982). *Anger and aggression: An essay on emotion*. New York: Springer-Verlag.

Averill, J. R. (1984). The acquisition of emotions during adulthood. In C. Z. Malatesta & C. E. Izard (Eds), *Emotion in adult development* (pp. 23–43). Beverly Hills, CA: Sage.

Averill, J. R. (1985). The social construction of emotion: With special reference to love. In K. Gergen & K. Davis (Eds.), *The social construction of the person* (pp. 89–109). New York: Springer-Verlag.

Averill, J. R. (1988). Disorders of emotion. *Journal of Social & Clinical Psychology, 8,* 247–268.

Averill, J. R. (1989). Stress as fact and artifact: An inquiry into the social origins and functions of some stress reactions. In C. D. Spielberger, I. G. Sarason, & J. Strelau (Eds.), *Stress and anxiety,* Vol. 12 (pp. 15–38). Washington, DC: Hemisphere.

Averill, J. R. (1990a). Inner feelings, works of the flesh, the beast within, diseases of the mind, driving force, and putting on a show: Six metaphors of emotion and their theoretical extensions. In D. E. Leary (Ed.), *Metaphors in the history ofpsychology* (pp. 104–132). New York: Cambridge University Press.

Averill, J. R. (1990b). Emotions as related to systems of behavior. In N. L. Stein, B. Leventhal, & T. Trabasso (Eds.), *Psychological and biological approaches to emotion* (pp. 385–404). Hillsdale, NJ: Lawrence Erlbaum.

Averill, J. R. (1991). Emotions as episodic dispositions, cognitive schemas, and transitory social roles: Steps toward an integrated theory of emotion. In D. Ozer, J. M. Healy, Jr., & A. J. Stewart (Eds.), *Perspectives in personality* (Vol. 3a, pp. 139–167). London: Jessica Kingsley.

Averill, J. R. (1993). Illusions of anger. In J. T. Tedeschi & R. B. Felson (Eds.), *Social interactionist approaches to aggression and violence*. Washington, DC: American Psychological Association.

Averill, J. R. (in press). Emotions as episodic dispositions, cognitive schemas, and transitory social roles: Steps toward an integrated theory of emotion. In A. J. Stewart, D. Ozer, & R. Hogan (Eds.), *Perspectives in personality.* Vol. 3. Greenwich, CT: JAI.

Averill, J. R., Catlin, G., & Chon, K. K. (1990). *Rules of hope*. New York: Springer-Verlag.

Averill, J. R., & Nunley, E. P. (1988). Grief as an emotion and as a disease. *Journal of Social Issues, 44,* 79–95.

Averill, J. R., & Nunley, E. P. (1992). *Voyages of the heart: Living an emotionally creative life*. New York: Free Press.

Averill, J. R., & Thomas-Knowles, C. (1991). Emotional creativity. In K. T. Strongman (Ed.), *International review of studies on emotion* (Vol. 1, pp. 269–299). London: Wiley.

Ax, A. F. (1953). The physiological differentiation between fear and anger in humans. *Psychosomatic Medicine, 15,* 433–442.

Baeyens, F., Eelen, P., & Van den Bergh, O. (1990). Contingency awareness in evaluative conditioning: A case for unaware affective-evaluative learning. *Cognition and Emotion, 4,* 3–18.

Bahrick, R. E., & Watson, J. S. (1985). Detection of intermodal proprioceptive-visual contingency as a potential basis of self-perception in infancy. *Developmental Psychology, 21,* 963–973.

Baile, C. A., McLaughlin, C. L., & Della-Ferra, M. A. (1986). Role of cholecystokinin and opioid peptides in control of food intake. *Physiological Review, 66,* 172–234.

Baldwin, H. A., Britton, K. T., & Koob, G. F. (1990). Behavioral effects of corticotropin-releasing factor. In D. Ganten & D. Pfaff (Eds.), *Current topics in neuroendocrinology,* Vol. 10, *Behavioral aspects of neuroendocrinology* (pp. 1–14). Berlin: Springer-Verlag.

Bandler, R. (1988). Brain mechanisms of aggression as revealed by electrical and chemical stimulation: A central role for the midbrain periaqueductal grey region. In A. N. Epstein & A. R. Morrison (Eds.), *Progress in Psychobiology and Physiological Psychology,* Vol. 13 (pp. 67–154), New York: Academic Press.

Bard, P., & Mountcastle, V. B. (1948). Some forebrain mechanisms involved in the expression of rage with special reference to suppression of angry behavior. *Research Publications of the Association for Research on nervous and mental Disease, 27,* 362–404.

Barlow, D. H. (1988). *Anxiety and its disorders: The nature and treatment of anxiety and panic.* New York: Guilford.

Baron, R. M., & Boudreau, L. A. (1987). An ecological perspective on integrating personality and social psychology, *Journal of Personality and Social Psychology, 53,* 1222–1228.

Barrett, K. C., & Campos, J. J. (1987). Perspectives on emotional development II: A functionalist approach to emotions. In J. D. Osofsky (Ed.), *Handbook of infant development* (2nd ed.) (pp. 555–578). New York: Wiley-Interscience.

Batson, C. D., Shaw, L. L., & Oleson, K. C. (1992). Differentiating affect, mood, and emotion: Toward functionally based conceptual distinctions. In M. S. Clark (Ed.), *Emotion* (pp. 294–326). Newbury Park, CA: Sage.

Beagley, W. K., & Holley, T. L. (1977). Hypothalamic stimulation facilitates contralateral visual control of a learned response. *Science, 196,* 321–322.

Beck, A. T. (1976). *Cognitive therapy and the emotional disorders.* New York: International Universities Press.

Beck, A. T. (1987). Cognitive models of depression. *Journal of Cognitive Psychotherapy, An International Quarterly, 1,* 5–37.

Bedford, E. (1962). Emotions. In V. C. Chappell (Ed.), *The philosophy of mind.* (pp. 110–126). Englewood Cliffs, NJ: Prentice-Hall.

Bellelli, G. (1991). Nostalgia. *Cahiers Internationales de Psychologie Sociale, 11,* 13–25.

Berger, T. W., & Thompson, R. F. (1978). Identification of pyramidal cells as the critical elements in hippocampal neuronal plasticity during learning. *Proceedings of the National Academy of Science, 75,* 1572–1576.

Berkinblit, M. B., Feldman, A. G., & Fukson, O. I. (1986). Adaptability of innate motor patterns and motor control mechanisms. *Behavioral and Brain Sciences, 9,* 585–638.

Berkowitz, L. (1989). Frustration-aggression hypothesis: Examination and reformulation. *Psychological Bulletin, 106,* 59–73.

Berkowitz, L. (1990). On the formation and regulation of anger and aggression. *American Psychologist, 45,* 494–503.

Berkowitz, L. (in press). Towards a general theory of anger and emotional aggression: Implications of the cognitive-neoassociationistic perspective for the analysis of anger and other emotions. In R. S. Wyer & T. K. Srull (Eds.), *Advances in social cognition* (Vol. 6): *Perspectives on anger and emotion.* Hillsdale, NJ: Lawrence Erlbaum.

Berlin, B., Breedlove, D., & Raven, P. (1968). Covert categories and folk taxonomies. *American Anthropologist, 70,* 290–299.

Berlyne, D. E. (1960). *Conflict, arousal and curiosity.* New York: McGraw-Hill.

Berlyne, D. E. (1969). Laughter, humor, and play. In G. Lindsey & E. Aronson (Eds.), *The handbook of social psychology,* Vol. 3. Reading, MA: Addison-Wesley.

Berlyne, D. E. (1971). *Aesthetics and psychobiology.* New York: Appleton-Century-Crofts.

Bernstein, N. (1967). *Coordination and regulation of movements.* New York: Pergamon.

Bertenthal, B., Campos, J., & Barrett, K. (1984). Self-produced locomotion: An organizer of emotional, cognitive and social development in infancy. In R. Emde & R. Harmon (Eds.), *Continuities and discontinuities in development* (pp. 175–210). New York: Plenum.

Bless, H., Bohner, G., Schwarz, N., & Strack, F. (1990). Mood and persuasion: A cognitive response analysis. *Personality and Social Psychology Bulletin, 16,* 331–345.

Bless, H., Hamilton, D. L., & Mackie, D. M. (1990). *Mood effects on the organization of person information.* Unpublished manuscript.

Blum, G. S. (1954). An experimental reunion of psychoanalytic theory with perceptual vigilance and defense. *Journal of Abnormal and Social Psychology, 49,* 94–98.

Blumberg, S. H., & Izard, C. E. (1986). Discriminating patterns of emotions in 10- and 11-year-old children's anxiety and depression. *Journal of Personality and Social Psychology, 51* (4), 852–857.

Boddy, J., Carver, A., & Rowley, K. (1986). Effect of positive and negative reinforcement on performance as a function of extraversion-intraversion: Some tests of Gray's theory. *Personality and Individual Differences, 7,* 81–88.

Bodenhausen, G. V. (1993). Emotions, arousal, and stereotypic judgments: A heuristic model of affect and stereotyping. In D. M. Mackie & D. L. Hamilton (Eds.), *Affect, cognition, and stereotyping: Interactive processes in group perception* (pp. 13–37). San Diego: Academic Press.

Bolles, R. C. (1970). Species-specific defense reactions. *Psychological Review, 77,* 3248.

Bolles, R. C. (1990). Where did everybody go? *Psychological Science, 1,* 107–113.

Bolles, R. C., & Fanselow, M. S. (1980). A perceptual-defensive model of fear and pain. *Behavioral and Brain Sciences 3,* 291–323.

Bonnano, G. A., & Singer, J. L. (1990). Repressive personality style: Theoretical and methodological implications for health and pathology. In J. L. Singer (Ed.), *Repression and dissociation* (pp. 435–470). Chicago: University of Chicago Press.

Bonnano, G. A., & Stilling, N. A. (1986). Preference, familiarity, and recognition after repeated brief exposure to random geometric shapes. *American Journal of Psychology, 99,* 403–415.

Bornstein, R. F. (1987). *Subliminal mere exposure effects and conscious cognition: A study of attitude changes in response to stimuli perceived without awareness.* Doctoral Dissertation. State University of New York at Buffalo.

Bornstein, R. F. (1989). Exposure and affect: Overview and meta-analysis of research, 1968–1987. *Psychological Bulletin, 106,* 265–289.

Bornstein, R. F., Leone, D. R., & Galley, D. J. (1987). The generalizability of subliminal mere exposure effects: Influence of stimuli perceived without awareness on social behavior. *Journal of Personality and Social Psychology, 53,* 1070–1079.

Boucher, J. D. (1983). Antecedents to emotions across cultures. In S. H. Irvine & J. W. Berry (Eds.), *Human assessment and culture factors* (pp. 407–420). New York: Plenum.

Boucher, J. D., & Brandt, M. E. (1981). Judgment of emotion: American and Malay antecedents. *Journal of Cross-Cultural Psychology, 12,* 272–283.

Bower, G. H. (1981). Mood and memory. *American Psychologist, 36,* 129–148.

Bower, G. H. (1990). Mood-congruity of social judgments. In J. Forgas (Ed.), *Emotion and social judgments.* Oxford: Pergamon.

Bower, G. H. (1992). How might emotions affect memory? In S. A. Christianson (Ed.), *Handbook of emotion and memory.* Hillsdale, NJ: Lawrence Erlbaum.

Bowlby, J. (1980). *Attachment and loss, Loss: Sadness and depression,* Vol. 3. New York: Basic Books.

Bradburn, N. M. (1969). *The structure of psychological well-being.* Chicago: Aldine.

Breger, L., Hunter, I., & Lane, R. W. (1971). *The effect of stress on dreams.* New York: International Universities Press.

Brentano, F. (1874). *Psychologie vom empirischen Standpunkt.* Leipzig: Duncker & Humboldt.

Breslau, N. (1985). Depressive symptoms, major depression, and generalized anxiety: A comparison of self-reports on CES-D and results from diagnostic interviews. *Psychiatry Research, 15,* 219–229.

Breslau, N., & Davis, G. C. (1985). DSM-III Generalized Anxiety Disorder: An empirical investigation of more stringent criteria. *Psychiatry Research, 14,* 231–238.

Bretherton, I., & Beeghly, M. (1982). Talking about internal states: The acquisition of an explicit theory of mind. *Developmental Psychology, 18,* 906–921.

Brewin, C. R. (1989). Cognitive change processes in psychotherapy. *Psychological Review, 96,* 379–394.

Bridges, R. S., Numan, M., Ronsheim, P. M., Mann, P. E., & Lupini, C. E. (1990). Central prolactin infusions stimulate maternal behavior in steroid-treated, nulliparous female rats. *Proceedings of the National Academy of Sciences, 87,* 8003–8007.

Briggs, J. L. (1970). *Never in anger: Portrait of an Eskimo family.* Cambridge, MA: Harvard University Press.

Briggs, J. L. (1978). The origins of non-violence: Inuit management of aggression. In A. Montagu (Ed.), *Learning non-aggression* (pp. 54–93). Oxford: Oxford University Press.

Broadhurst, P. L. (1975). The Maudsley reactive and nonreactive strains of rats: A survey. *Behavior Genetics, 5,* 299–319.

Brock, S. E., Rothbart, M. K., & Derryberry, D. (1986). Heart rate deceleration and smiling in 3-month-old infants. *Infant Behavior and Development, 9,* 403–414.

Brodal, A. (1982). *Neurological anatomy.* New York: Oxford University Press.

Brothers, L., Ring, B., & Kling, A. (1990). Response of neurons in the macaque amygdala to complex social stimuli. *Behavioral Brain Research, 41,* 199–213.

Broverman, D. M. (1962). Normative and ipsative measurement in psychology. *Psychological Review, 4,* 295–305.

Brown, G. W., Harris, T., & Copeland, J. R. (1977). Depression and loss. *British Journal of Psychiatry, 130,* 1–18.

Brown, J. R., & Dunn, J. (1991). "You can cry, Mum": The social and developmental implications of talk about internal states. *British Journal of Developmental Psychology, 9,* 237–256.

Brownstein, M., Arimura, A., Sato, H., Schally, A. V., & Kizer, J. S. (1975). The regional distribution of somatostatin in the rat brain. *Endocrinology, 96,* 1456–1461.

Brunelli, S. A., & Hofer, M. A. (1990). Parental behavior in juvenile rats: Environmental and biological determinants. In N. A. Krasnegor and R. S. Bridges (Eds.), *Mammalian parenting: Biochemical neurobiological and behavioral determinants,* (pp. 372–399). New York: Oxford University Press.

Buck, R. (1985). Prime theory: An integrated view of motivation and emotion. *Psychological Review, 92,* 389–413.

Buck, R. (1991). Motivation, emotion and cognition: A developmental-interactionist view. In K. Strongman (Ed.), *International review of studies on emotion,* Vol. 1 (pp. 101–142). Chichester: Wiley.

Buck, R. W. (1979). Individual differences in non-verbal sending accuracy and electrodermal responding: The externalizing-internalizing dimension. In R. Rosenthal (Ed.), *Skill in nonverbal communication* (pp. 140–170). Cambridge, MA: Oelgeschlager, Gunn & Hain.

Bunge, M. (1990). What kind of discipline is psychology: autonomous or dependent, humanistic or scientific, biological or sociological? *New Ideas in Psychology, 8,* 121–137.

Bush, L. K., Barr, C. L., McHugo, G. J., & Lanzetta, J. T. (1989). The effects of facial control and facial mimicry on subjective reactions to comedy routines. *Motivation and Emotion, 13,* 31–52.

Buss, A. H., & Plomin, R. (1984). *Temperament: Early developing personality traits.* Hillsdale, NJ: Lawrence Erlbaum.

Buunk, B., & Hupka, R. B. (1987). Cross-cultural differences in the elicitation of sexual jealousy. *The Journal of Sex Research, 23,* 12–22.

Cacioppo, J. T., Klein, D. J., Bernston, G. G., & Hatfield, E. (1993). The psychophysiology of emotion. In M. Lewis & J. Haviland (Eds.), *Handbook of emotions* (pp. 119–142). New York: Guilford.

Cacioppo, J. T., Petty, R. E., Losch, M. L., & Kim, H. S. (1986). Electromyographic activity over facial muscle regions can differentiate the valence and intensity of affective reactions. *Journal of Personality and Social Psychology, 50,* 260–268.

Cacioppo, J. T., Uchino, B. N., Crites, S. L., Snydersmith, M. A., Smith, G., Bernston, G. G., & Lang, P. J. (1992). Relationship between facial expressiveness and sympathetic activation in emotion: A critical review, with emphasis on modeling underlying mechanisms and individual differences. *Journal of Personality and Social Psychology, 62,* 110–128.

Cador, M., Robbins, T. W., & Everitt, B. J. (1989). Involvement of the amydala in stimulus-reward associations: Interaction with the ventral striatum. *Neuroscience, 30,* 77–86.

Calhoun, C. (1989). Subjectivity & emotion. *Philosophical Forum, 20,* 195–210.

Campos, J. J., & Barrett, K. C. (1984). Toward a new understanding of emotions and their development. In C. E. Izard, J. Kagan, & R. B. Zajonc (Eds.), *Emotions, cognition, and behavior* (pp. 229–263). New York: Cambridge University Press.

Campos, J. J., Barrett, K. C., Lamb, M. E., Goldsmith, H. H., & Stenberg, C. (1983). Socioemotional development. In P. H. Mussen (Ed.), *Handbook of Child Psychology,* Vol. 11 (pp. 783–915). New York: Wiley.

Campos, J. J., Campos, R. G., & Barrett, K. C. (1989). Emergent themes in the study of emotional development and emotion regulation. *Developmental Psychology, 25,* 394–402.

Camras, L. A. (1991). Conceptualizing early infant affect: View II and Reply. In K. Strongman (Ed.), *International review of studies on emotion* (pp. 16–28, 33–36). New York: Wiley.

Camras, L. A. (1992). Expressive development and basic emotions. *Cognition and Emotion, 6,* (3, 4), 269–284.

Camras, L. A., Holland, E. A., & Patterson, M. J. (1993). Facial expression. In M. Lewis & J. Haviland (Eds.), *Handbook of emotions* (pp. 199–208). New York: Guilford.

Camras, L. A., Malatesta, C., & Izard, C. (1991). The development of facial expressions in infancy. In R. Feldman & B. Rime (Eds.), *Fundamentals of nonverbal behavior* (pp. 73–105). Cambridge: Cambridge University Press.

Camras, L., Oster, H., Campos, J., Miyake, K., & Bradshaw, D. (1992). Japanese and American infants responses to arm restraint. *Developmental Psychology, 28*(4), 578–583.

Camras, L., Sullivan, J., & Michel, G. (1993). Do infants express discrete emotions? Adult judgements of facial, vocal, and body actions. *Journal of Nonverbal Behavior, 17,* 171–186.

Cannon, W. B. (1927). The James-Lange theory of emotions: A critical examination and an alternative theory. *American Journal of Psychology, 39,* 106–124.

Cannon, W. B. (1929). *Bodily changes in pain, hunger, fear and rage.* New York: Appleton.

Carnes, M., Goodman, B.M. & Lent, S.J. (1991). High resolution spectral analysis of plasma adrenocorticotropin reveals a multifactorial frequency structure. *Endocrinology, 128,* 902–910.

Carver, C. S., & Scheier, M. F. (1990). Origins and functions of positive and negative affect: a control-process view. *Psychological Review, 97,* 19–35.

Cassirer, E. (1908). *Substanzbegriff und Funktionsbegriff.* Leipzig: B. Cassirer.

Cattell, R. B. (1946). *Description and measurement of personality.* New York: World Book Co.

Cattell, R. B., & Scheier, I. H. (1961). *The meaning and measurement of neuroticism and anxiety.* New York: Ronald Press.

Christensen, A., & Heavey, C. L. (1990). Gender and social structure in the demand/withdraw pattern of marital conflict. *Journal of Personality and Social Psychology, 59,* 73–81.

Clark, H. H., & Clark, E. (1977). *Psychology of language.* New York: Harcourt Brace Jovanovich.

Clark, L. A. (1989). The anxiety and depressive disorders: Descriptive psychopathology and differential diagnosis. In P. C. Kendall & D. Watson (Eds.), *Anxiety and depression: Distinctive and overlapping features* (pp. 83–129). New York: Academic Press.

Clark, L. A., & Watson, D. (1988). Mood and the mundane: Relations between daily life events and self-reported mood. *Journal of Personality and Social Psychology, 54,* 296–308.

Clark, L. A., & Watson, D. (1991a). General affective dispositions in physical and psychological health. In C. R. Snyder & D. R. Forsyth (Eds.), *Handbook of social and clinical psychology* (pp. 221–245). New York: Pergamon.

Clark, L. A., & Watson, D. (1991b). Tripartite model of anxiety and depression: Psychometric considerations and taxonomic implications. *Journal of Abnormal Psychology, 100,* 316–336.

Clark, L. A., Watson, D., & Leeka, J. (1989). Diurnal variation in the positive affects. *Motivation and Emotion, 13,* 205–234.

Clark, M. S., & Isen, A. M. (1982). Toward understanding the relationship between feeling states and social behavior. In A. Hastorf & A. M. Isen (Eds.), *Cognitive social psychology.* New York: Elsevier.

Clore, G. L. (1992). Cognitive phenomenology: Feelings in the construction of judgment. In L. Martin & A. Tesser (Eds.), *The construction of social judgment* (pp. 133–164). Hillsdale, NJ: Lawrence Erlbaum.

Clore, G. L., & Ortony, A. (1984). Some issues for a cognitive theory of emotion. *Cahiers de Psychologie Cognitive, 4,* 53–57.

Clore, G. L., & Ortony, A. (1988). Semantic analyses of the affective lexicon. In V. Hamilton, G. Bower, & N. Frijda (Eds.), *Cognitive science perspectives on emotion and motivation* (pp. 367–398). Amsterdam: Martinus Nijhoff.

Clore, G. L., & Ortony, A. (1991). What more is there to emotion concepts than prototypes. *Journal of Personality and Social Psychology, 60,* 48–50.

Clore, G. L., Ortony, A., Brand, S., & Levine, S. (1992). *The joy of victory and the agony of defeat: Emotions and the sports fan.* Manuscript in preparation.

Clore, G. L., Ortony, A., & Foss, M. (1987). The psychological foundations of the affective lexicon. *Journal of Personality and Social Psychology, 53,* 751–766.

Clore, G. L., & Parrott, W. G. (1991). Moods and their vicissitudes: Thoughts and feelings as information. In J. Forgas (Ed.), *Emotion and social judgment* (pp. 107–123). Oxford: Pergamon.

Clore, G. L., & Parrott, W. G. (1994). Cognitive feelings and metacognitive judgments. *European Journal of Social Psychology, 24*, 101–115.

Clore, G. L., Parrott, W. G., Schwarz, N., & Wilkin, N. (1990). *Does emotional bias occur during encoding or judgment?* Unpublished manuscript.

Clore, G. L., Schwarz, N., & Conway, M. (1994). Emotion and information processing. In R. S. Wyer & T. K. Srull (Eds.), *Handbook of social cognition*, 2nd ed.) (pp. 323–417). Hillsdale, NJ: Lawrence Erlbaum.

Clynes, M. (1973). Sentics: Biocybernetics of emotion communication. *Annals of the New York Academy of Sciences, 220*, 55–131.

Colby, C. Z., Lanzetta, J. T., & Kleck, R. E. (1977). Effects of expression of pain on autonomic and pain tolerance responses to subject-controlled pain. *Psychophysiology, 14*, 537–540.

Cook, E., Hodes, R., & Lang, P. (1986). Preparedness and phobia: Effects of stimulus content on human visceral conditioning. *Journal of Abnormal Psychology, 95*, 195–207.

Corteen, R. S., & Wood, B. (1972). Autonomic responses to shock-associated words in unattended channel. *Journal of Experimental Psychology, 94*, 308–313.

Costa, P. T., & McCrae, R. R. (1980). Influence of extraversion and neuroticism on subjective well-being: Happy and unhappy people. *Journal of Personality and Social Psychology, 38*, 668–678.

Costa Jr., P. T., & McCrae, R. R. (1992). Four ways five factors are basic. *Personality and Individual Differences, 13*, 653–665.

Crepeau, L., & Panksepp, J. (1988). Dual olfactory system and cat smell-attenuated juvenile rat play. *Neuroscience Abstracts, 14*, 1104.

Crews, D. (Ed.) (1987). *Psychobiology of reproductive behavior: An evolutionary perspective.* Englewood Cliffs, NJ: Prentice-Hall.

Crook, J. H. (1980). *The evolution of human consciousness.* Oxford: Oxford University Press.

Csikszentmihalyi, M. (1975). *Beyond boredom and anxiety: The experience of play in work and games.* San Francisco, CA: Jossey-Bass.

Cunningham, M. R. (1988). Does happiness mean friendliness? Induced mood and heterosexual self-disclosure. *Personality and Social Psychology Bulletin, 14*, 283–297.

Cushman, P. (1991). Ideology obscured: Political uses of the self in Danial Stern's infant. *American Psychologist, 46*, 206–219.

Cutting, J. (1990). *The right cerebral hemisphere and psychiatric disorders.* New York: Oxford University Press.

D'Andrade, R. (1991). Some propositions about the relation of culture to human cognition. In J. Stigler, R. A. Shweder, & G. Herdt (Eds.), *Cultural psychology: Essays on comparative human development* (pp. 65–129). New York: Cambridge University Press.

Dantzer, R., Bluthe, R.-M., Koob, G. F., & Le Moal, M. (1987). Modulation of social memory in male rats by neurohypophyseal peptides. *Psychopharmacology, 91*, 363–368.

Darwin, C. (1872). *The expression of the emotions in man and animals.* London: Murray. (Reprinted, Chicago: University of Chicago Press, 1965.)

Davidson, R. J. (1978). Specificity and patterning in biobehavioral systems: Implications for the behavior change. *American Psychologist, 33*, 430–436.

Davidson, R. J. (1984). Affect, cognition and hemispheric specialization. In C. E. Izard, J. Kagan, & R. Zajonc (Eds.), *Emotion, cognition and behavior* (pp. 320–365). New York: Cambridge University Press.

Davidson, R. J. (1992a). A prolegomenon to the structure of emotion: Gleanings from neuropsychology. *Cognition and Emotion, 6*(3, 4), 245–268.

Davidson, R. J. (1992b). Anterior cerebral asymmetry and the nature of emotion. *Brain and Cognition, 6,* 245–268.

Davidson, R. J. (1992c). Emotion and affective style: Hemispheric substrates. *Psychological Science, 3,* 39–43.

Davidson, R. J. (1993). Parsing affective space: Perspectives from neuropsychology and psychophysiology. *Neuropsychology, 7,* 464–475.

Davidson, R. J., Coe, C., Donzella, B., & Ershler, W. (1993). Relations between cortical activation asymmetries and immune function during baseline and emotional challenge conditions. In preparation.

Davidson, R. J., Doss, R., & Tomarken, A. J. (1993). Relations between individual differences in electrophysiological asymmetry and MRI-derived measures of cortical morphometry. Unpublished data.

Davidson, R. J., Ekman, P., Saron, C., Senulis, J., & Friesen, W. V. (1990). Approach/withdrawal and cerebral asymmetry. *Journal of Personality and Social Psychology, 58,* 330–341.

Davidson, R. J., Rickman, M. O., Finman, R., Straus, A., Rickman, M. D., & Kagan, J. (1993). Behavioral inhibition and frontal brain function in children. In preparation.

Davidson, R. J. & Fox, N. A. (1989). Frontal brain asymmetry predicts infant's response to maternal separation. *Journal of Abnormal Psychology, 98,* 127–131.

Davidson, R. J., Kalin, N. H., & Shelton, S. E. (1993). Lateralized response to diazepam predicts tempermental style in rhesus monkeys. *Behavioral Neuroscience, 107,* 1106–1107.

Davidson, R. J., & Tomarken, A. J. (1989). Laterality and emotion: An electrophysiological approach. In F. Boller and J. Grafman (Eds.), *Handbook of Neuropsychology.* Amsterdam: Elsevier.

Davis, M. (1992). The role of the amygdala in conditioned fear. In J. P. Aggleton (Ed.), *The amygdala: Neurobiological aspects of emotion, memory, and mental dysfunction* (pp. 255–306). New York: Wiley-Liss.

Davis, M., Hitchcock, J. M., & Rosen, J. B. (1987). Anxiety and the amygdala: Pharmacological and anatomical analysis of the fear-potentiated startle paradigm. In G. H. Bower (Ed.), *The psychology of learning and motivation,* Vol 21 (pp. 263–305). San Diego: Academic Press.

Davison, G. C., & Neale, J. M. (1990). *Abnormal psychology* (5th ed.). New York: Wiley.

Dennett, D. C. (1991). *Consciousness explained.* Boston: Little, Brown.

Denenberg, V. H. & Yutzey, D. A. (1985). Hemispheric laterality, behavioral asymmetry and the effects of early experience in rats. In S. D. Glick (Ed.), *Cerebral lateralization in non-human species* (pp. 110–135). New York: Academic Press.

DeNoble, V. J., Hepler, D. J., & Barto, R. A. (1989). Cysteamine-induced depletion of somatostatin produces differential cognitive deficits in rats. *Brain Research, 482,* 42–28.

DeOlmos, J., Alheid, G., & Beltramino, C. (1985). Amygdala. In G. Paxinos (Ed.), *The rat nervous system* (pp. 223–334). Orlando: Academic Press.

Depue, R. A., & Iacono, W. G. (1989). Neurobehavioral aspects of affective disorders. *Annual Review of Psychology, 40,* 457–492.

Depue, R. A., Krauss, S. P., & Spoont, M. R. (1987). A two-dimensional threshold model of seasonal bipolar affective disorder. In D. Magnusson & A. Öhman (Eds.), *Psychopathology: An interactional perspective* (pp. 95–123). San Diego: Academic Press.

Depue, R. A., Luciana, M., Arbisi, P., Collins, P., & Leon, A. (in press). Dopamine and the structure of personality: Relation of agonist-induced dopamine activity to positive emotionality. *Journal of Personality and Social Psychology.*

Depue, R. A., & Spoont, M. R. (1987). Conceptualizing a serotonin trait. *Annals of the New York Academy of Sciences, 487,* 47–62.

Derryberry, D., & Rothbart, M. K. (1984). Emotion, attention, and temperament. In C. Izard, J. Kagan, & R. Zajonc (Eds.), *Emotion, cognition and behavior* (pp. 132-166). Cambridge: Cambridge University Press.

de Rivera, J. (1977). *A structural theory of the emotions.* New York: International Universities Press.

DeVries, G. J., Buijs, R. M., Van Leeuwen, F. W., Caffe, A. R., & Swaab, D. F. (1985). The vasopressinergic innervation of the brain in normal and castrated rats. *The Journal of Comparative Neurology, 233,* 236–254.

De Waal, F. (1982). *Chimpanzee politics.* London: Jonathan Cape.

DeWied, D., & van Ree, J. (1989). Neuropeptides: Animal behaviour and human psychopathology. *European Archives of Psychiatry and Neurological Sciences, 238,* 323–331.

Diener, E., & Emmons, R. A. (1984). The independence of positive and negative affect. *Journal of Personality and Social Psychology, 47,* 1105–1117.

Diener, E., & Iran-Nejad, A. (1986). The relationship in experience between various types of affect. *Journal of Personality and Social Psychology, 50,* 1031–1038.

Diener, E., & Larsen, R. J. (1984). Temporal stability and cross-situational consistency of affective, behavioral, and cognitive responses. *Journal of Personality and Social Psychology, 47,* 871–883.

Digman, J. M., & Inouye, J. (1986). Further specification of the five robust factors of personality. *Journal of Personality and Social Psychology, 50,* 116–123.

Doi, T. (1973). *The anatomy of dependency.* Tokyo: Kodansha International.

Downer, J. D. C. (1961). Changes in visual gnostic function and emotional behavior following unilateral temporal lobe damage in the "split-brain" monkey. *Nature, 191,* 50–51.

Drago, F. (1990). Behavioral effects of prolactin. In. D. Ganten & D. Pfaff (Eds.), *Current topics in neuroendocrinology, Vol. 10* (pp. 263–290). Berlin: Springer-Verlag.

Duffy, E. (1941). The conceptual categories of psychology: A suggestion for revision. *Psychological Review, 48,* 177–203.

Duffy, E. (1962). *Activation and behavior.* New York: Wiley.

Dumas, G. (1948). *La vie affective.* Paris: Presses Universitaires de France.

Dünker, J. (1979). Mimischer Affektausdruck und sprachliche Kodierung. Ph.D. Thesis. University of Zurich, Zurich, Switzerland.

Dunn, J. (1988). *The beginnings of social understanding.* Cambridge, MA: Harvard University Press.

Dunn, A. J., & Berridge, C. (1990). Physiological and behavioral responses to corticotropin-releasing factor administration: Is CRF a mediator of anxiety or stress responses? *Brain Research Reviews, 15,* 71–100.

Dunn, J., & Brown, J. R. (1991). Relationships, talk about feelings, and the development of affect regulation in early childhood. In J. Garber & K. Dodge (Eds.), *Affect regulation and dysregulation in childhood* (pp. 89–108). Cambridge: Cambridge University Press.

Dunn, J., & Slomkowski, C. (1992). Conflict and the development of social understanding. In C. U. Shantz & W. W. Hartup (Eds.), *Conflict and development* (pp. 70–92). Cambridge: Cambridge University Press.

Edwards, K. (1990). The interplay of affect and cognition in attitude formation and change. *Journal of Personality and Social Psychology, 59,* 202–216.

Ehrlichman, H., & Halpern, J. N. (1988). Affect and memory: Effects of pleasant and unpleasant odors on retrieval of happy and unhappy memories. *Journal of Personality and Social Psychology, 55,* 769–779.

Eibl-Eibesfeldt, I. (1972). Similarities and differences between cultures in expressive movements. In R. A. Hinde (Ed.), *Nonverbal communication* (pp. 20–33). Cambridge, MA: Cambridge University Press.

Eibel-Eibesfeldt, I. (1989). *Human ethology.* New York: Aldiné de Gruyter.

Eich, E. (1992). *Mood-state dependent memory: Resolving the conflicting data.* Paper presented at the convention of the Western Psychological Association, Portland, OR, April 1992.

Eichenbaum, H. (1992). The hippocampal system and declarative memory in animals. *Journal of Cognitive Neuroscience, 4*(3), 217–231.

Ekman, P. (1972). Universals and cultural differences in facial expressions of emotion. In J. Cole (Ed.), *Nebraska symposium on motivation, 1971* (pp. 207–283). Lincoln: University of Nebraska Press.

Ekman, P. (Ed.). (1973). *Darwin and facial expression.* New York: Academic Press.

Ekman, P. (1977). Biological and cultural contributions to body and facial movement. In J. Blacking (Ed.), A. S. A. Monograph 15, *The anthropology of the body* (pp. 39–84). London: Academic Press.

Ekman, P. (1979). About brows: Emotional and conversational signals. In J. Aschoff, M. von Cranach, K. Foppa, W. Lepenies, & D. Ploog, *Human ethology* (pp. 169–202). Cambridge: Cambridge University Press.

Ekman, P. (1984). Expression and the nature of emotion. In K. Scherer & P. Ekman (Eds.), *Approaches to emotion* (pp. 319–344). Hillsdale, NJ: Lawrence Erlbaum.

Ekman, P. (1992). An argument for basic emotions. *Cognition and Emotion, 6,* 169–200.

Ekman, P. (1992). Are there basic emotions? A reply to Ortony and Turner. *Psychological Review, 99,* 550–553.

Ekman, P. (1992). Facial expressions of emotion: New findings, new questions. *Psychological Science, 3*(1), 34–38.

Ekman, P. (1993). Facial expression and emotion. *American Psychologist, 48,* 384–392.

Ekman, P., & Davidson, R. J. (1993). Voluntary smiling changes regional brain activity. *Psychological Science, 4,* 342–345.

Ekman, P. (1994). Strong evidence for universals in facial expressions: A reply to Russell's mistaken critique. *Psychological Bulletin, 115,* 268–287.

Ekman, P. (in preparation). *Reports of the intensity of emotional experience.*

Ekman, P., Davidson, R. J., & Friesen, W. V. (1990). The Duchenne smile: Emotional expression and brain physiology II. *Journal of Personality and Social Psychology, 58,* 342–353.

Ekman, P., & Friesen, W. V. (1969). The repertoire of nonverbal behavior: Categories, origins, usage, and coding. *Semiotica, 1,* 49–98.

Ekman, P., & Friesen, W. (1971). Constants across cultures in the face and emotion. *Journal of Personality and Social Psychology, 17*(2), 124–129.

Ekman, P., & Friesen, W. V. (1975). *Unmasking the face.* Englewood Cliffs, NJ: Prentice-Hall.

Ekman, P., & Friesen, W. V. (1982). Felt, false, and miserable smiles. *Journal of Nonverbal Behavior, 6*(4), 238–252.

Ekman, P., & Friesen, W. V. (1986). A new pan cultural expression of emotion. *Motivation and Emotion, 10,* 159–168.

Ekman, P., Friesen, W. V., O'Sullivan, M., Chan, A., et al. (1987). Universals and cultural differences in the judgments of facial expressions of emotion. *Journal of Personality and Social Psychology, 53,* 712–717.

Ekman, P., Friesen, W. V., & Simons, R. C. (1985). Is the startle reaction an emotion? *Journal of Personality and Social Psychology, 49,* 1416–1426.

Ekman, P., Levenson, R. W., & Friesen, W. V. (1983). Autonomic nervous system activity distinguishes between emotions. *Science, 221,* 1208–1210.

Ekman, P., O'Sullivan, M., & Matsumoto, D. (in press). Confusions about contest in the judgment of facial expression: A reply to "Contempt and the relativity thesis." *Motivation and Emotion.*

Ekman, P., Sorenson, E. R., & Friesen, W. V. (1969). Pan-cultural elements in facial displays of emotions. *Science, 164*(3875), 86–88.

Elias, N. (1977). *The civilizing process.* New York: Urizen.

Ellsworth, P. C. (1991). Some implications of cognitive appraisal theories of emotion. In K. T. Strongman (Ed.) *International review of studies on emotion* (pp. 143–161). New York: Wiley.

Ellsworth, P. C. (in press). Sense, culture, and sensibility. In H. Markus & S. Kitayama, *Emotion and culture.* Washington DC: American Psychological Association.

Ellsworth, P. C., & Smith, C. A. (1988). From appraisal to emotion: Differences among unpleasant feelings. *Motivation and Emotion, 12,* 271–302.

Emde, R. (1980). Levels of meaning in infant development. In W. A. Collins (Ed.), *Minnesota symposium on child psychology,* Vol. 13 (pp. 1–37). Hillsdale, NJ: Lawrence Erlbaum.

Emde, R. N. (1984). Levels of meaning for infant emotions: A biosocial view. In K. R. Scherer & P. Ekman (Eds.), *Approaches to emotion* (pp. 77–107). Hillsdale, NJ: Lawrence Erlbaum.

Emmons, R. A. (1986). Personal strivings: An approach to personality and subjective well-being. *Journal of Personality and Social Psychology, 51,* 1058–1068.

Epstein, S. (1983). A research paradigm for the study of personality and emotions. In M. M. Page (Ed.), Personality: Current theory and research. *Nebraska Symposium on Motivation, 1982* (pp. 92–154). Lincoln: University of Nebraska Press.

Erdelyi, M. H. (1974). A new look at the New Look: Perceptual defense and vigilance. *Psychological Review, 81,* 1–25.

Etcoff, N. L. (1989). Asymmetries in recognition of emotion. In F. Boller and J. Grafman (Eds.), *Handbook of Neuropsychology,* Vol. 3 (pp. 363–382). Amsterdam: Elsevier.

Everitt, B. J., Morris, K. A., O'Brien, A., & Robbins, T. W. (1991). The basolateral amygdala-ventral striatal system and conditioned place reference: Further evidence of limbic-striatal interactions underlying reward-related processes. *Neuroscience, 42,* 1–18.

Eysenck, H. J. (1967). *The biological basis of personality.* Springfield, IL: Charles C Thomas.

Eysenck, H. J. (Ed.). (1976). *The measurement of personality.* Baltimore, MD: University Park Press.

Eysenck, H. J. (Ed.). (1981). *A model for personality.* New York: Springer-Verlag.

Eysenck, H. J., & Eysenck, M. W. (1985). *Personality and individual differences: A natural science approach.* New York: Plenum.

Farah, M. J. (1990). *Visual agnosia: Disorders of object recognition and what they tell us about normal vision.* Cambridge: MIT Press.

Fehm-Wolfsdorf, G., & Born, J. (1991). Behavioral effects of neurohypophyseal peptides in healthy volunteers: 10 years of research. *Peptides, 12,* 1399–1406.

Fehr, B., & Russell, J. A. (1984). Concept of emotion viewed from a prototype perspective. *Journal of Experimental Psychology: General Section, 113,* 464–486.

Field, T., & Walden, T. (1982). Perception and production of facial expression in infancy and early childhood. In H. Reese & L. Lipsitt (Eds.), *Advances in child development and behavior* (pp. 169–211). New York: Academic Press.

Fishbein, M., & Ajzen, I. (1975). *Belief, attitude, intention, and behavior.* Reading, MA: Addison-Wesley.

Fisher, L. A., & Brown, M. R. (1990). Corticotropin-releasing factor: Central regualtion of autonomic nervous and visceral function. In D. Ganten & D. Pfaff (Eds.), *Current topics in neuroendocrinology,* Vol. 10, *Behavioral aspects of neuroendocrinology* (pp. 15–32). Berlin: Springer-Verlag.

Fiske, S. T. (1982). Schema-triggered affect: Applications to social perception. In M. S. Clark & S. T. Fiske (Eds.), *Affect and cognition: the 17th Annual Carnegie Symposium on Cognition* (pp. 55–78). Hillsdale, NJ: Lawrence Erlbaum.

Flood, J. F., Garland, J. S., & Morley, J. E. (1990). Vasoactive intestinal peptide (VIP): An amnestic neuropeptide. *Peptides, 11:* 933–938.

Flood, J. F., & Morley, J. E. (1988). Effects of bombesin and gastrin-releasing peptide on memory processing *Brain Research, 460,* 208–210.

Fogel, A., Nwokah, E., Dedo, J., Messinger, D., Dickson, L., Matusov, E., & Holt, S. (1992). Social process theory of emotion: A dynamic systems approach. *Social Development, 1*(2), 122–142.

Fogel, A., & Thelen, E. (1987). The development of early expressive and communicative action. *Developmental Psychology, 23,* 747–761.

Folkman, S., & Lazarus, R. S. (1985). If it changes it must be a process: Study of emotion and coping during three stages of a college examination. *Journal of Personality and Social Psychology, 48,* 150–170.

Folkman, S., & Lazarus, R. S. (1990). Coping and emotion. In N. Stein, B. Leventhal, & T. Trabasso (Eds.), *Psychological and biological approaches to emotion* (pp. 313–332). Hillsdale, NJ: Lawrence Erlbaum. Modified and reprinted in L. J. Menges (Special Ed.). (1988). *Social Science in Medicine, 26,* 309–317.

Folkman, S., Lazarus, R. S., Pimley, S., & Novacek, J. (1987). Age differences in stress and coping processes. *Psychology and Aging, 2,* 171–184.

Forgas, J. P., & Bower, G. H. (1987). Mood effects on person perception judgments. *Journal of Personality and Social Psychology, 53,* 53–60.

Forgas, J. P., & Bower, G. (1988). Affect in social and personal judgments. In K. Fiedler & J. Forgas, (Eds.), *Affect, cognition, and social behavior* (pp. 183–208). Toronto: C. J. Hogrefe.

Forgas, J. P., Bower, G. H., & Krantz, S. E. (1984). The influence of mood on perceptions of social interactions. *Journal of Experimental Social Psychology, 20,* 497–513.

Forgas, J. P., & Moylan, S. (1991). Affective influences on stereotype judgments. *Cognition and Emotion, 5,* 379–397.

Forster, E. M. (1939). Not listening to music. In *Two cheers for democracy.* London: Edward Arnold.

Fowles, D. (1980). The three arousal model: Implications of Gray's two-factor learning theory for heart rate, electrodermal activity and psychopathy. *Psychophysiology, 17,* 87–104.

Fox, N. A. (1991). If it's not left, it's right. *American Psychologist, 46,* 863–872.

Fox, N. A. & Davidson, R. J. (1984). Hemispheric substrates of affect: A developmental model. In N. A. Fox & R. J. Davidson (Eds.), *The psychobiology of affective development* (pp. 353–381). Hillsdale, NJ: Lawrence Erlbaum.

Fox, N. A., & Davidson, R. J. (1986). Taste-elicited changes in facial signs of emotion and the asymmetry of brain electrical activity in human newborns. *Neuropsychologia, 24,* 417–422.

Fredrickson, B. L., & Kahneman, D. (1993). Duration neglect in retrospective evaluations of affective episodes. *Journal of Personality and Social Psychology, 65,* 45–55.

Fredrickson, B. L., & Levenson, R. W. (1992). *Positive emotions speed recovery from negative emotional arousal.* Manuscript submitted for publication.

Freud, S. (1894). The defence neuro-psychoses. In E. Jones (Ed.), *Sigmund Freud: Collected papers,* Vol. 1. New York: Basic Books, 1959.

Freud, S. (1915). Instincts and their vicissitudes. In E. Jones (Ed.), *Sigmund Freud: Collected papers,* Vol. 4 (pp. 60–83). New York: Basic Books, 1959.

Frijda, N. H. (1986). *The emotions.* Cambridge: Cambridge University Press.

Frijda, N. H. (1987). Emotion, cognitive structure, and action tendency. *Cognition and Emotion, 1,* 115–143.

Frijda, N. H. (1988). The laws of emotion. *American Psychologist, 43,* 349–358.

Frijda, N. H. (1993a). The place of appraisal in emotion. *Cognition and Emotion, 7,* 357–388.

Frijda, N. H. (1993b). Moods, emotion episodes, and emotions. In J. Haviland & M. Lewis (Eds.), *Handbook of emotions.* (pp. 381–403). New York: Guilford.

Frijda, N. H., Kuipers, P., & ter Schure, E. (1989). Relations among emotion, appraisal, and emotional action readiness. *Journal of Personality and Social Psychology, 57,* 212–228.

Frijda, N. H., Mesquita, B., Sonnemans, J., & Van Goozen, S. (1991). The duration of affective phenomena, or emotions, sentiments and passions. In K. Strongman (Ed.), *International review of emotion and motivation* (pp. 187–225). New York: Wiley.

Frijda, N., Ortony, A., Sonnemans, J. & Clore, G. (1992) The complexity of intensity: Issues concerning the structure of emotion intensity. In M. Clark (Ed.), *Review of personality and social psychology,* Vol. 11 (pp. 60–89), Newbury Park, CA: Sage.

Fulker, D. W. (1981). The genetic and environmental architecture of psychoticism, extraversion, and neuroticism. In H. J. Eysenck (Ed.), *A model for personality* (pp. 88–122). New York: Springer-Verlag.

Fuller, J. L., & Thompson, W. R. (1978). *Foundations of behavior genetics.* St. Louis: Mosby.

Funkenstein, D. H., King, S. H., & Drolette, M. (1954). The direction of anger during a laboratory stress-inducing situation. *Psychosomatic Medicine, 16,* 404–413.

Furness, J. B., Bornstein, J. C., Murphy, R., & Pompolo, S. (1992). Roles of peptides in transmission in the enteric nervous system. *Trends in Neurosciences, 15,* 66–71.

Gabriel, M., Slatwick, S. E., & Miller, J. D. (1976). Multiple unit activity of the rabbit medial geniculate nucleus in conditioning, extinction, and reversal. *Physiological Psychology, 4,* 124–134.

Gachev, G. (1987). Natsional'nye obrazy mira. *Voprosy literatury, 10,* 156–191.

Gallagher, D. J., & Clore, G. L. (1985, May). *Emotion and judgment: Effects of fear and anger on relevant and irrelevant cognitive tasks.* Paper presented at the Midwestern

Gallagher, M., & Holland, P. C. (1992). Understanding the function of the central nucleus: Is simple conditioning enough? In J. P. Aggleton (Ed.), *The amygdala: Neurobiological aspects of emotion, memory, and mental dysfunction* (pp. 307–321). New York: Wiley-Liss.

Ganten, D., & Pfaff, D. (Eds.) (1988). *Current topics in neuroendocrinology,* Vol. 8. *Neuroendocrinology of Mood.* Berlin: Springer-Verlag.

Garber, J., & Dodge, K. (1991). *The development of affect regulation and dysregulation.* Cambridge: Cambridge University Press.

Garcia-Coll, C. T., Kagan, J., & Reznick, J. S. (1984). Behavioral inhibition in young children. *Child Development, 55,* 1005–1019.

Gardiner, S. M., & Bennett, T. (1989). Brain neuropeptides: actions on central cardiovascular control mechanisms. *Brain Research Reviews, 14,* 79–116.

Gehm, T., & Scherer, K. R. (1988). Relating situation evaluation to emotion differentiation: Nonmetric analysis of cross-cultural questionnaire data. In K. R. Scherer (Ed.), *Facets of emotion: Recent research* (pp. 61–78). Hillsdale, NJ: Lawrence Erlbaum.

Gellhorn, E., & Loofburrow, G. N. (1963). *Emotion and emotional disorders.* New York: Haber Medical Division.

Gerber, E. (1986). Rage and obligation: Samoan emotion in conflict. In G. White & J. Kirkpatrick (Eds.), *Person and experience; Exploring Pacific ethnopsychologies*. Los Angeles: University of California Press.

Gergen, K. J., & Gergen, M. (1988). Narrative and the self as relationship. In L. Berkowitz (Ed.), *Advances in experimental social psychology,* Vol. 21 (pp. 17–56). New York: Academic Press.

Gibson, J. J. (1979). *An ecological approach to visual perception.* Boston: Houghton-Mifflin.

Giles, D. E., Rush, A. J., & Roffwarg, H. P. (1986). Sleep parameters in bipolar I, bipolar II, and unipolar depressions. *Biological Psychiatry, 21,* 473–482.

Glanzmann, P. (1985). Anxiety, stress and performance. In B. D. Kirkcaldy (Ed.), *Individual differences in movement.* Lancaster, England: MTP Press.

Gloor, P. (1960). Amygdala. In J. Field, H. W. Magoun, & V. E. Hall (Eds.), *Handbook of physiology: Neurophysiology,* Vol. II (pp. 1395–1420). Washington, DC: American Physiological Society.

Goddard, G. (1964). Functions of the amygdala. *Psychological Review, 62,* 89–109.

Goldberg, L. R. (1980, May). *Some ruminations about the structure of individual differences: Developing a common lexicon for the major characteristics of human personality.* Paper presented at the annual convention of the Western Psychological Association, Honolulu, Hawaii.

Goldberg, L. R. (1990). An alternative "description of personality": The Big-Five factor structure. *Journal of Personality and Social Psychology, 59,* 1216–1229.

Goldsmith, H. H. (1986). Heritability of temperament: Cautions and some empirical evidence. In G. A. Kohnstamm (Ed.), *Temperament discussed: Temperament and development in infancy and childhood* (pp. 83–96). Lisse, The Netherlands: Swets & Zeitlinger.

Goldsmith, H. H. (1989). Behavior-genetic approaches to temperament. In G. A. Kohnstamm, J. E. Bates, & M. K. Rothbart (Eds.), *Temperament in childhood* (pp. 111–132). Chichester: Wiley.

Goldsmith, H. H. (1993). Temperament: Variability in developing emotion systems. In M. Lewis & J. M. Haviland (Eds.), *Handbook of emotion* (pp. 353–364). New York: Guilford.

Goldsmith, H. H., Buss, A. H., Plomin, R., Rothbart, M. K., Thomas, A., Chess, S., Hinde, R. A., & McCall, R. B. (1987). Roundtable: What is temperament? Four approaches. *Child Development, 58,* 505–529.

Goldsmith, H. H., & Campos, J. J. (1982). Toward a theory of infant temperament. In R. N. Emde & R. J. Harmon (Eds.), *The development of attachment and affiliative systems.* New York: Plenum.

Goldsmith, H. H., & Campos, J. J. (1986). Fundamental issues in the study of early temperament: The Denver Twin Temperament Study. In M. E. Lamb, A. L. Brown, & B. Rogoff (Eds.), *Advances in developmental psychology, 4* (pp. 231–283). Hillsdale, NJ: Lawrence Erlbaum.

Gomperts, W. (1992). *The opkomst van de sociale phobie.* Amsterdam: Bert Bakker.

Gorman, J. M., Liebowitz, M. R., Fyer, A. J., & Stein, J. (1989). A neuroanatomical hypothesis for panic disorder. *American Journal of Psychiatry, 146,* 148–161.

Gottman, J. M. & Levenson, R. W. (1985). A valid procedure for obtaining self-report of affect in marital interaction. *Journal of Consulting and Clinical Psychology, 53,* 151–160.

Gottman, J. M., & Levenson, R. W. (1988). The social psychophysiology of marriage. In P. Noller & M. A. Fitzpatrick (Eds.), *Perspectives on marital interaction* (pp. 182–200). Clevedon, England: Multilingual Matters Ltd.

Gottman, J. M., & Levenson, R. W. (1993). *Male withdrawal from marital conflict.* Manuscript submitted for publication.

Graeff, F. G. (1987). The anti-aversive action of drugs. In T. Thompson, P. B. Dews, & J. Barrett, (Eds.), *Advances in Behavioural Pharmacology,* Vol 6. Hillsdale, NJ: Lawrence Erlbaum.

Graham, D. T. (1962). Some research on psychophysiologic specificity and its relation to psychosomatic disease. In R. Roessler & N. S. Greenfield (Eds.), *Physiological correlates of psychological disorder* (pp. 221–238). Madison: University of Wisconsin Press.

Gray, J. A. (1968). The Lister Lecture 1967. The physiological basis of personality. *Advancement of Science, 24,* 293–305.

Gray, J. A. (1970). The psychophysiological basis of introversion-extraversion. *Behavioural Research and Therapy, 8,* 249–266.

Gray, J. A. (1971). *The psychology of fear and stress.* London: Weidenfeld & Nicholson.

Gray, J. A. (1975). *Elements of a two-process theory of learning.* New York: Academic Press.

Gray, J. A. (1981). A critique of Eysenck's theory of personality. In H. J. Eysenck (Ed.), *A model for personality* (pp. 246–276). Berlin: Springer-Verlag.

Gray, J. A. (1982a). *The neuropsychology of anxiety: An enquiry into the functions of the septo-hippocampal system.* Oxford: Oxford University Press.

Gray, J. A. (1982b). Précis of *The neuropsychology of anxiety:* An enquiry into the function of the septo-hippocampal system. *Behavioural & Brain Sciences, 5,* 469–484.

Gray, J. A. (1983). Where shall we search for biologically based dimensions of personality? *Zeitschrift für Differentielle und Diagnostische Psychologie, 4,* 165–176.

Gray, J. A. (1985a). Anxiety and the brain: pigments aren't colour names. *Bulletin of the British Psychological Society, 38,* 299–300.

Gray, J. A. (1985b). Issues in the neuropsychological study of anxiety. In A. H. Tuma & J. D. Maser (Eds.), *Anxiety and the anxiety disorders* (pp. 5–26). Hillsdale, NJ: Lawrence Erlbaum.

Gray, J. A. (1987). *The psychology of fear and stress* (2nd ed.). Cambridge: Cambridge University Press.

Gray, J. A. (1990). Brain systems that mediate both emotions and cognitions. In J. A. Gray (Ed.), Special issue of *Cognition and Emotion, Psychobiological aspects of relationships between emotion and cognition* (pp. 269–288). Hillsdale, NJ: Lawrence Erlbaum.

Gray, J. A. (1991). Fear, panic and anxiety: What's in a name? *Psychological Inquiry, 2,* 77–78.

Gray, J. A. (1994). The neuropsychology of the emotions: Framework for a taxonomy of psychiatric disorders. In *Emotions: Essays on emotion theory* pp. 29–59. Hillsdale, NJ: Lawrence Erlbaum.

Gray, J. A. (in press). The neuropsychology of anxiety and schizophrenia. In M. S. Gazzaniga (Ed.), *The Cognitive Neurosciences.* Cambridge, MA: MIT Press.

Gray, J. A., Feldon, J., Rawlins, J. N. P., Hemsley, D. R., & Smith, A. D. (1991). The neuropsychology of schizophrenia. *Behavioral and Brain Sciences, 14,* 1–20.

Greenberg, L. S., & Safran, J. D. (1984). Integrating affect and cognition: A perspective on the process of therapeutic change. *Cognitive Therapy and Research, 8,* 559–578.

Gross, C. G. (1973). Interotemporal cortex and vision. In E. Stellar & J. M. Sprague (Eds.), *Progress in physiological psychology,* Vol. 5 (pp. 77–123). New York: Academic Press.

Gross, C. G. (1992). Representation of visual stimuli in inferior temporal cortex. *Philos. Trans. Royel Society of London [Biol.], 335,* 3–10.

Gross, J. J., & Levenson, R. W. (1993). Emotional suppression: Physiology, self report, and expressive behavior. *Journal of Personality and Social Psychology, 64,* 970–986.

Grossman, K., Grossman, K. E., Spangler, G., Suess; G., & Unzner, L. (1985). Maternal sensitivity and newborn orientation responses as related to quality of attachment in

Northern Germany. In I. Bretherton & E. Waters (Eds.), *Growing points of attachment theory and research. Monographs of the Society for Research in Child Development, 50*, 233–256.

Guignon, C. (1984). Moods in Heidegger's being and time. In C. Calhoun & R. C. Solomon (Eds.), *What is an emotion? Classical readings in philosophical psychology* (pp. 230–243). New York: Oxford University Press.

Hall, W. G., & Oppenheim, R. W. (1987). Developmental psychobiology: Prenatal, perinatal, and early postnatal aspects of behavioral development. *Annual Review of Psychology, 38*, 91–128.

Harré, R. (1986). An outline of the social constructionist viewpoint. In R. Harré (Ed.), *The social construction of emotions*. Oxford: Basil Blackwell.

Harris, P. L. (1989). *Children and emotion: The development of psychological understanding*. Oxford: Basil Blackwell.

Harrison, A. A. (1977). Mere exposure. In L. Berkowitz (Ed.), *Advances in experimental social psychology*, Vol. 10 (pp. 39–83). New York: Academic Press.

Harter, S. (1978). Effectance motivation reconsidered: Toward a developmental model. *Human Development, 21*, 34–64.

Healy, D., & Williams, J. M. G. (1988). Dysrhythmia, dysphoria, and depression: The interaction of learned helplessness and circadian dysrhythmia in the pathogenesis of depression. *Psychological Bulletin, 103*, 163–178.

Hebb, D. O. (1949). *The organization of behavior*. New York: Wiley.

Hebb, D. O. (1970). *Textbook of psychology*. New York: Saunders & Roe.

Heider, K. G. (1991). *Landscapes of emotion: Mapping three cultures of emotion in Indonesia*. New York: Cambridge University Press.

Henke, P. G. (1990). Limbic system modulation of stress ulcer development. *Annals of the New York Academy of Science, 597*, 201–206.

Henke, P. G. (1992). Stomach pathology and the amygdala. In J. P. Aggleton (Ed.), *The amygdala: Neurobiological aspects of emotion, memory, and mental dysfunction* (pp. 323–338). New York: Wiley-Liss.

Henry, J. P. (1986). Neuroendocrine patterns of emotional response. In R. Plutchik & H. Kellerman (Eds.), *Emotion: Theory, research and experience*, Vol. III. *Biological foundations of emotions* (pp. 37–60). New York: Academic Press.

Hess, E. H. (1973). *Imprinting: Early experience and the developmental psychobiology of attachment*. New York: Van Nostrand.

Hiatt, S., Campos, J., and Emde, R. (1979). Facial patterning and infant emotional expression: Happiness, surprise, and fear. *Child Development, 50*, 1020–1035.

Hilgard, E. R. (1949). Human motives and the concept of the self. *American Psychologist, 4*, 374–382.

Hinde, R. A. (1974). *Biological bases of human social behavior*. New York: McGraw-Hill.

Hinde, R. A. (1987). Comment. *Child Development, 58*, 505–529.

Hiroi, N., & White, N. M. (1991). The lateral nucleus of the amygdala mediates expression of the amphetamine-produced conditioned place preference. *Journal of Neuroscience, 11*(7), 2107–2116.

Hobson, J. A., Lydic, R., & Baghdoyan, H. E. (1986). Evolving concepts of sleep cycle generation: From brain centers to neuronal populations. *Behavioral and Brain Sciences, 9*, 371–448.

Hobson, J. A., & Steriade, M. (1986). Neuronal basis of behavioral state control. In V. B. Mountcastle (Ed.), *Handbook of physiology—The nervous system*, Vol. IV, section 1 (pp. 701–823). Bethesda: American Physiological Society.

Hochschild, A. R. (1979). Emotion work, feeling rules, and social structure. *American Journal of Sociology, 85,* 551–575.

Hofstede, G. (1984). *Culture's consequences: International differences in work-related values.* Beverly Hills, CA: Sage.

Holroyd, K. A., & Gorkin, L. (1983). Young adults at risk for hypertension: Effects of family history and anger management in determining responses to interpersonal conflict. *Journal of Psychosomatic Research, 27,* 131–138.

Holstedge, G., Kuypers, H. G. J. M., & Dekker, J. J. (1977). The organization of the bulbar fibre connections to the trigeminal, facial and hypoglossal motor nuclei. II. An autoradiographic tracing study in cat. *Brain, 100,* 265–286.

Holzman, W. S., & Bitterman, M. E. (1956). A factorial study of adjustment to stress. *Journal of Abnormal and Social Psychology, 52,* 179–185.

Hopkins, D. A., & Holstedge, G. (1978). Amygdala projections to the mesencephalon, pons and medulla oblongata in the cat. *Experimental Brain Research, 32,* 529–547.

Hoptman, M. J., Coyle, D. J., & Davidson, R. J. (1993). *Relations between EEG asymmetries and neuropsychological function, I: Anterior functions.* Paper presented at the Society for Psychophysiology Research, 1993.

Horowitz, M. J. (1976). *Stress response syndromes.* New York: Jason Aronson.

Horowitz, M. J. (1988). *Introduction to psychodynamics.* New York: Basic Books.

Horvath, F. E. (1959). Psychological stress: A review of definitions and experimental research. In L. von Bertalanffy & A. Rapaport (Eds.), *General systems,* Vol. V. Ann Arbor, MI: Society for General Systems Research.

House, A., Dennis, M., Warlow, C., Hawton, K., & Molyneux, A. (1990). Mood disorders after stroke and their relation to lesion location. *Brain, 113,* 1113–1129.

Hull, D. L. (1976). Are species really individuals? *Systematic Zoology, 25,* 174–191.

Hume, D. (1759). *A treatise on human nature: Vol. 2. Of the passions.* London: John Noon.

Hume, D. (1967). *A treatise of human nature.* L. A. Selby-Bigge (Ed.). Oxford: Clarendon Press. (Original work published 1739.)

Hunt, M. M. (1959). *The natural history of love.* New York: Knopf.

Hyde, J. S., & Sawyer, T. F. (1979). Correlated characters in selection for aggressiveness in female mice: II. Maternal aggressiveness. *Behavior Genetics, 9,* 571–577.

Insel, T. R. (1992). Oxytocin: A neuropeptide for affiliation—Evidence from behavioral, receptor autoradiographic and comparative studies. *Psychoneuroendocrinology,* 3–35.

Insel, T. R., Kinsley, C. H., Mann, P. E., & Bridges, R. S. (1990). Prenatal stress has long-term effects on brain opiate receptors. *Brain Research, 511,* 93–97.

Isen, A. M. (1970). Success, failure, attention and reaction to others: The warm glow of success. *Journal of Personality and Social Psychology, 15,* 294–301.

Isen, A. M. (1984). Toward understanding the role of affection cognition. In R. S. Wyer, Jr., & T. K. Srull (Eds.), *Handbook of social cognition,* Vol. 3. Hillsdale, NJ: Lawrence Erlbaum.

Isen, A. M. (1987). Positive affect, cognitive processes and social behavior. In L. Berkowitz (Ed.), *Advances in experimental social psychology,* Vol. 20 (pp. 203–253). New York: Academic Press.

Isen, A., & Means, B. (1983). The influence of positive affect on decision-making strategy. *Social Cognition, 2,* 18–31.

Isen, A. M., Shalker, T., Clark, M., & Karp, L. (1978). Affect, accessibility, of material in memory, and behavior: a cognitive loop? *Journal of Personality and Social Psychology, 36,* 1–12.

Izard, C. (1971). *The face of emotion.* New York: Appleton-Century-Crofts.

Izard, C. E. (1972). *Patterns of emotions: A new analysis of anxiety and depression.* New York: Academic Press.

Izard, C. E. (1977). *Human emotions.* New York: Plenum.

Izard, C. E. (1978a). On the development of emotions and emotion-cognition relationships in infancy. In J. M. Davidson, & R. J. Davidson (Eds.), *The psychobiology of consciousness.* New York: Plenum.

Izard, C. E. (1978b). On the ontogenesis of emotions and emotion-cognition relationships in infancy. In M. Lewis & L. A. Rosenblum (Eds.), *The development of affect* (pp. 389–413). New York: Plenum.

Izard, C. E. (1980). Cross-cultural perspectives on emotion and emotion communication. In H. Triandis & W. J. Lonner (Ed.), *Handbook of cross-cultural psychology,* Vol. 3. Boston: Allyn & Bacon.

Izard, C. E. (1991). *The psychology of emotions.* New York: Plenum.

Izard, C. (1992). Basic emotions, relations among emotions, and emotion-cognition relations. *Psychological Review, 99*(3), 561–565.

Izard, C. E. (1993). Four systems for emotion activation: Cognitive and noncognitive processes. *Psychological Review, 100*(1), 68–90.

Izard, C. (1994). Innate and universal facial expressions: Evidence from developmental and cross-cultural research. *Psychological Bulletin, 115,* 288–299.

Izard, C., Dougherty, L., & Hembree, E. (1983). *A system for identifying affect expressions by holistic judgments (AFFEX).* Newark: Instructional Resources Center, University of Delaware.

Izard, C. E., & Harris, P. (in press). Emotional development and developmental psychopathology. In D. Cicchetti & D. J. Cohen (Eds.), *Manual of developmental psychopathology.* New York: Wiley.

Izard, C. E., Haynes, O. M., Chisholm, G., & Baak, K. (1991). Emotional determinants of infant-mother attachment. *Child Development, 62*(5), 905–917.

Izard, C. E., Fantauzzo, C. A., Castle, J. M., Haynes, O., & Slomine, B. S. (1993). *The morphological stability and social validity of infants' facial expressions in the first nine months of life.* Submitted for publication.

Izard, C. E., Hembree, E. A., & Huebner, R. R. (1987). Infants' emotion expressions to acute pain: Developmental change and stability of individual differences. *Developmental Psychology, 23*(1), 105–113.

Izard, C. E., Libero, D. Z., Putnam, P., & Haynes, O. M. (1993). Stability of emotion experiences and their relations to traits of personality. *Journal of Personality and Social Psychology, 64,* 847–860.

Izard, C., & Malatesta, C. (1987). Perspectives on emotional development I: Differential emotions theory of early emotional development. In J. D. Osofsky (Ed.), *Handbook of infant development* (pp. 494–554). New York: Wiley.

Jackendoff, R. (1987). *Consciousness and the computational mind.* Cambridge: Bradford Books, MIT Press.

Jacoby, L. L., Kelley, C. M., Brown, J., Jasechko, J. (1989). Becoming famous overnight: Limits on the ability to avoid unconscious influences of the past. *Journal of Personality and Social Psychology, 56,* 326–338.

Jacobs, W. J. & Nadel, L. (1985). Stress-induced recovery of fear and phobias. *Psychological Review, 92,* 512–531.

Jacobs, W. J., Nadel, L., & Hayden, V. C. (1992). Anxiety disorders. In D. J. Stein & J. E. Young (Eds.), *Cognitive science and clinical disorders* (pp. 211–233). San Diego: Academic Press.

James, W. (1890/1950). *Principles of psychology.* New York: Dover.

James, W. (1884). What is emotion? *Mind, 9,* 188–205.

Jarrell, T. W., Gentile, C. G., Romanski, L. M., McCabe, P. M., & Schneiderman, N. (1987). Involvement of cortical and thalamic auditory regions in retention of differential bradycardia conditioning to acoustic conditioned stimulii in rabbits. *Brain Research, 412,* 285–294.

Jemmott, J. B., & Locke, S. E. (1984). Psychosocial factors, immunologic mediation, and human susceptibility to infectious diseases: How much do we know? *Psychological Bulletin, 95,* 78–108.

Jirkikowski, G. F., Caldwell, J. D., Pilgrim, C., Stumpf, W. E., & Pedersen, C. A. (1989). Changes in immunostaining for oxytocin in the forebrain of the female rat during late pregnancy, parturition and early lactation. *Cell and Tissue Research, 256,* 411–417.

Joels, M., & de Kloet, E. R. (1992). Control of neuronal excitability by corticosteroid hormones. *Trends in Neurosciences, 15,* 25–28.

John, O. P. (1989). Towards a taxonomy of personality descriptors. In D. M. Buss & N. Cantor (Eds.), *Personality psychology: Recent trends and emerging directions* (pp. 261–271). New York: Springer-Verlag.

Johnson, M. H., Posner, M. I., & Rothbart, M. K. (1991). Components of visual orienting in early infancy: Contingency learning, anticipatory looking and disengaging. *Journal of Cognitive Neuroscience, 3,* 335–344.

Johnson-Laird, P. N. (1988). *The computer and the mind: An introduction to cognitive science* (7 pp.). Cambridge: Harvard University Press.

Johnson-Laird, P. N., & Oatley, K. (1989). The language of emotions: An analysis of a semantic field. *Cognition and Emotion, 3,* 81–123.

Johnson-Laird, P. N., & Oatley, K. (1992). Basic emotions, rationality and folk theory. *Cognition and Emotion, 6,* 201–223.

Jones, E. G., & Powell, T. P. S. (1970). An anatomical study of converging sensory pathways within the cerebral cortex of the monkey. *Brain, 93,* 793–820.

Jones, H. E. (1935). The galvanic skin reflex as related to overt emotional expression. *American Journal of Psychology, 47,* 241–251.

Jones, H. E. (1950). The study of patterns of emotional expression. In M. Reymert (Ed.), *Feelings and emotions* (pp. 161–168). New York: McGraw-Hill.

Jones, H. E. (1960). The longitudinal method in the study of personality. In I. Iscoe & H. W. Stevenson (Eds.), *Personality development in children* (pp. 3–27). Chicago: University of Chicago Press.

Jouvet, M. (1972). The role of monoamines and acetylcholine-containing neurons in the regulation of the sleep-waking cycle. In *Ergebnisse der physiologice,* Vol. 64. *Neurophysiology and neurochemistry of sleep and wakefulness* (pp. 166–308). Berlin: Springer-Verlag.

Jung, C. G. (1960). Symbol formation. In H. Read, M. Fordham, & G. Adler (Eds.), *The collected works,* Vol. 8 (pp. 45–61). (Trans. from the German by R. F. C. Hull.) New York: Pantheon (copyright held by Bollinger Foundation, Inc.).

Jung, C. G. (1971). *Psychological types, Collected works,* Vol. 6. Princeton, NJ: Princeton University Press. (Original work published 1921.)

Kagan, J. (1974). Discrepancy, temperament and infant distress. In M. Lewis & L. A. Rosenblum (Eds.), *The origins of fear* (pp. 229–248). New York: Wiley.

Kagan, J. (1979). Structure and process in the human infant: The ontogeny of mental representation. In M. H. Bornstein & W. Kessen (Eds.), *Psychological development from infancy: Image to intention* (pp. 159–182). Hillsdale, NJ: Lawrence Erlbaum.

Kagan, J. (1991). A conceptual analysis of the affects. *Journal of the American Psychoanalytic Association, 39* (suppl), 109–129.

Kagan, J., Reznick, J. S., & Snidman, N. (1988). Biological bases of childhood shyness. *Science, 240,* 167–171.

Kagan, J., & Snidman, N. (1991a). Infant predictors of inhibited and uninhibited profiles. *Psychological Science, 2,* 40–44.

Kagan, J., & Snidman, N. (1991b). Temperamental factors in human development. *American Psychologist, 46,* 856–862.

Kagan, J., Snidman, N., & Arcus, D. M. (1992). Initial reactions to unfamiliarity. *Current Directions, 1,* 171–174.

Kalin, N. H., & Shelton, S. E. (1989). Defensive behaviors in infant rhesus monkeys: Environmental cues and neurochemical regulation. *Science, 243,* 1718–1721.

Kang, D. H., Davidson, R. J., Coe, C. L., Wheeler, R. W., Tomarken, A. J., & Ershler, W. B. (1991). Frontal brain asymmetry and immune function. *Behavioral Neuroscience, 105,* 860–869.

Kaplan, J. R., Pettersson, K., Manuck, S. B., & Olsson, G. (1991). Role of sympathoadrenal medullary activation in the initiation and progression of atherosclerosis. *Circulation, 84,* 23–32.

Kapp, B. S., Pascoe, J. P., & Bixler, M. A. (1984). The amygdala: A neuroanatomical systems approach to its contributions to aversive conditioning. In N. Buttlers & L. R. Squire (Eds.), *Neuropsychology of memory* (pp. 473–488). New York: Guilford.

Kapp, B. S., Whalen, P. J., Supple, W. F., & Pascoe, J. P. (1992). Amygdaloid contributions to conditioned arousal and sensory information processing. In J. P. Aggleton (Ed.), *The amygdala: Neurobiological aspects of emotion, memory, and mental dysfunction* (pp. 229–254). New York: Wiley-Liss.

Kapp, B. S., Wilson, A., Pascoe, J., Supple, W., & Whalen, P. J. (1990). A neuroanatomical systems analysis of conditioned bradycardia in the rabbbit. In M. Gabriel & J. Moore (Eds.), *Learning and computational neuroscience: Foundations of adaptive networks* (pp. 53–90). Cambridge: MIT Press.

Kasper, S., & Rosenthal, N. E. (1989). Anxiety and depression in seasonal affective disorders. In P. C. Kendall & D. Watson (Eds.), *Anxiety and depression: Distinctive and overlapping features* (pp. 341–375). San Diego: Academic Press.

Kaufman, I. C., & Rosenblum, L. A. (1967). The reaction of separation in infant monkeys: Anaclitic depression and conservation-withdrawal. *Psychosomatic Medicine,* 648–676.

Kenealy, P. (1988). Validation of a music mood induction procedure: Some preliminary findings. *Cognition and Emotion, 2,* 41–48.

Kihlstrom, J. F. (1987). The cognitive unconscious. *Science, 237,* 1445–1452.

Kihlstrom, J. F. (1990). The psychological unconscious. In L. Pervin (Ed.), *Handbook of personality: Theory and research* (pp. 445–464). New York: Guilford.

Kim, J. J., & Fanselow, M. S. (1992). Modality-specific retrograde amnesia of fear. *Science, 256,* 675–677.

Kincl, F. A. (1990), *Hormone toxicity in the newborn.* Berlin: Springer-Verlag.

Kitayama, S. (1991). Impairment of perception by positive and negative affect. *Cognition and Emotion, 5,* 255–274.

Klinger, E. (1975). The consequences of committment and disengagement from incentives. *Psychological Review, 82,* 1–25.

Kluver, H., & Bucy, P. C. (1937). "Psychic blindness" and other symptoms following bilateral temporal lobectomy in rhesus monkeys. *American Journal of Physiology, 119,* 352–353.

Kochanska, G. (1991). Socialization and temperament in the development of guilt and conscience. *Child Development, 62,* 1379–1392.

Kochanska, G., DeVet, K., Goldman, M., Murray, K., & Putnam, S. P. (1993). *Conscience development and temperament in young children.* Unpublished manuscript.

Koolhaas, J. M., van den Brin, T. H. C., Roozendaal, B., & Boorsma, F. (1990). Medial amygdala and aggressive behavior: Interaction between testosterone and vasopressin. *Aggressive Behavior, 16,* 223–229.

Kopp, C. B. (1989). Regulation of distress and negative emotions: A developmental view. *Developmental Psychology, 25,* 343–354.

Kopp, C. B. (1992). Emotional distress and control in young children. In. N. Eisenberg & R. A. Fabes (Eds.), *Emotion and its regulation in early development; New directions for child development, 55,* 41–56.

Kosslyn, S. M. (1987). Seeing and imagining in the cerebral hemispheres: A computational approach. *Psychological Review, 94,* 148–175.

Kosslyn, S. M., Davidson, R. J., Hobson, J. A., Horowitz, M. J., Hugdahl, K., Spiegel, D., & Rose, R. (1993). Cognitive neuroscience analyses of psychiatric phenomena: A user's guide. In preparation.

Kovecses, Z. (1989). *Emotion concepts.* New York: Springer-Verlag.

Krantz, D. S., & Manuck S. B. (1984). Acute psychophysiologic reactivity and risk of cardiovascular disease: A review and methodologic critique. *Psychological Bulletin, 3,* 435–464.

Krettek, J. E., & Price, J. L. (1978). Amygdaloid projections to subcortical structures within the basal forebrain and brainstem in the rat and cat. *Journal of Comparative Neurology, 178,* 225–254.

Kroon, R. M. (1988). *Aanleidingen en structuur van schuldgevoel.* Masters thesis, Psychology Department, Amsterdam University.

Kugler, P., Kelso, J., & Turvey, M. (1982). On the control and co-ordination of naturally developing systems. In J. Kelso & J. Clark (Eds.), *The development of movement control and co-ordination* (pp. 5–78). New York: Wiley.

Kunst-Wilson, W. R., & Zajonc, R. B. (1980). Affective discrimination of stimuli that cannot be recognized. *Science, 207,* 557–558.

Kwak, S. P., Young, E. A., Morano, I., Watson, S. J., & Akil, H. (1992). Diurnal corticotropin-releasing hormone mRNA variation in the hypothalamus exhibits a rhythm distinct from that of plasma corticosterone. *Neuroendocrinology, 55,* 74–83.

LaFave, L., Mannell, R., & Guilmette, A. M. (1977). An irony of irony: The left-handed insult in intragroup humour. In A. J. Chapman & H. C. Foot (Eds.), *It's a funny thing, humour* (pp. 283–285). London: Pergamon.

Lagerspetz, K. (1961). Genetic and social causes of aggressive behavior in mice. *Scandinavian Journal of Psychology, 2,* 167–173.

Lahey, B. B., McBurnett, K., Loeber, R., & Hart, E. L. (in press). Psychobiology of conduct disorder. In G. P. Sholevar (Ed.), *Conduct disorders in children and adolescents: Assessments and interventions.* Bethseda: American Psychiatric Press.

Laird, J. D. (1989). Mood affects memory because feelings are cognitions. *Journal of Social Behavior and Personality, 4,* 33–38.

Laird, J. D., & Bresler, C. (1992). The process of emotional experience: A self-perception theory. In M. S. Clark (Ed.), *Review of personality and social psychology,* Vol. 13 *Emotion* (pp. 213–234). Newbury Park, CA: Sage.

Lakoff, G. (1987). *Women, fire, and dangerous things.* Chicago: University of Chicago Press.

Lang, P. J. (1979). A bioinformational theory of emotional imagery. *Psychophysiology, 16,* 495–512.

Lang, P. J. (1988). What are the data of emotion? In V. Hamilton, G. Bower, & N. Frijda (Eds.), *Cognitive science perspectives on emotion and motivation* (pp. 173–194). Amsterdam: Martinus Nijhoff.

Lang, P. J., Bradley, M. M., & Cuthbert, B. N. (1990). Emotion, attention and the startle reflex. *Psychological Review, 97,* 377–398.

Lang, P. J., Greenwald, M. K., Bradley, M. M., & Hamm, A. O. (1993). Looking at pictures: Affective, facial, visceral and behavioral reactions. *Psychophysiology, 30,* 261–273.

Lange, C. (1887). *Ueber Gemuthsbewegungen.* Leipzig: Theodor Thomas.

Lanzetta, J. T., Cartwright-Smith, J., & Kleck, R. E. (1976). Effects of nonverbal dissimulation on emotional experience and autonomic arousal. *Journal of Personality and Social Psychology, 33,* 354–370.

Lanzetta, J. T., & Orr, S. P. (1986). Excitatory strength of expressive faces: Effects of happy and fear expressions and context on the extinction of a conditioned fear response. *Journal of Personality and Social Psychology, 50*(1), 190–194.

Laresen, R. J. & Ketelaar, T. (1991). Personality and susceptibility to positive and negative emotional states. *Journal of Personality and Social Psychology, 61,* 132–140.

Larimer, J. L. (1988). The command hypothesis: A new view using an old example. *Trends in Neurosciences, 11,* 506–510.

Larsen, R. J., & Diener, E. (1987). Affect intensity as an individual difference characteristic: A review. *Journal of Research in Personality, 21,* 1–39.

Larsen, R. J., & Ketelaar, T. (1991). Personality and susceptibility to positive and negative emotional states. *Journal of Personality and Social Psychology, 61,* 132–140.

Lashley, K. (1956). Cerebral organization and behavior. In H. Solomon, S. Cobb, & W. Penfield (Eds.), *The brain and human behavior* (pp. 1–18). Baltimore: Williams and Wilkins.

Lazarus, R. S. (1966). *Psychological stress and the coping process.* New York: McGraw-Hill.

Lazarus, R. S. (1981). The stress and coping paradigm. In C. Eisdorfer, D. Cohen, A. Kleinman, & P. Maxim (Eds.), *Models for clinical psychopathology* (pp. 177–214). New York: Spectrum.

Lazarus, R. S. (1982). Thoughts on the relation between emotion and cognition. *American Psychologist, 37,* 1019–1024.

Lazarus, R. S. (1984). On the primacy of cognition. *American Psychologist, 39*(2), 124–129.

Lazarus, R. S. (1991a). Cognition and motivation in emotion. *American Psychologist, 46,* 352–367.

Lazarus, R. S. (1991b). Progress on a cognitive-motivational-relational theory of emotion. *American Psychologist, 46,* 819–834.

Lazarus, R. S. (1991c). *Emotion and adaptation.* New York: Oxford University
Press.

Lazarus, R. S. (1993). From psychological stress to the emotions: A history of changing outlooks. *Annual Review of Psychology, 44,* pp. 1–21 (Palo Alto: Annual Reviews Inc.)

Lazarus, R. S., Deese, J., & Osler, S. F. (1952). The effects of psychological stress upon performance. *Psychological Bulletin, 49,* 293–317.

Lazarus, R. S., & Folkman, S. (1984). *Stress, appraisal, and coping.* New York: Springer-Verlag.

Lazarus, R. S., & Launier, R. (1978). Stress-related transactions between person and environment. In L. A. Pervin & M. Lewis (Eds.), *Perspectives in interactional psychology* (pp. 287–327). New York: Plenum.

Lazarus, R. S., & McCleary, R. A. (1951). Autonomic discrimination without awareness: A study of subception. *Psychological Review, 58,* 113–122.

Lazarus, R. S., & Smith, C. A. (1988). Knowledge and appraisal in the cognition-emotion relationship. *Cognition and Emotion, 2,* 281–300.

Leboyer, M., Bouvard, M. P., Launay, J.-M., Tabuteau, F., Waller, D., Dugas, M., Kerdelhue, B., Lensing, P., & Panksepp, J. (1992). Brief Report: A double-blind study of naltrexone in infantile autism. *Journal of Autism and Developmental Disorders, 22,* 311–321.

LeDoux, J. E. (1984). Cognition and emotion: Processing functions and brain systems. In M. S. Gazzaniga (Ed.), *Handbook of cognitive neuroscience* (pp. 357–368). New York: Plenum.

LeDoux, J. E. (1986). Sensory systems and emotion: A model of affective processing. *Integrative Psychiatry, 4,* 237–248.

LeDoux, J. E. (1987). Emotion. In F. Plum (Ed.), *Handbook of physiology. I: The nervous system.* Vol. V, Higher functions of the brain (pp. 419–460). Bethesda, MD: American Physiological Society.

LeDoux, J. E. (1989). Cognitive-emotional interactions in the brain. *Cognition and Emotion, 3,* 267–289.

LeDoux, J. E. (1990). Information flow from sensation to emotion: Plasticity in the neural computation of stimulus value. In M. Gabriel, & J. Moore (Eds.), *Learning and computational neuroscience: Foundations of adaptive networks* (pp. 3–52). Cambridge: MIT Press.

LeDoux, J. E. (1991). Emotion and the limbic system concept. *Concepts in Neuroscience, 2,* 169–199.

LeDoux, J. E. (1992a). Brain mechanisms of emotion and emotional learning. *Current Opinion in Neurobiology, 2,* 191–198.

LeDoux, J. E. (1992b). Emotion and the amygdala. In J. P. Aggleton (Ed.), *The amygdala: Neurobiological aspects of emotion, memory, and mental dysfunction* (pp. 339–351). New York: Wiley-Liss.

LeDoux, J. E. (1992c). Emotion as memory: anatomical systems underlying indelible neural traces. In S. Christianson (Ed.), *The handbook of emotion and memory: Research and theory* (pp. 269–288). Hillsdale, NJ: Erlbaum.

LeDoux, J. E., Iwata, J., Cicchetti, P., & Reis, D. J. (1988). Different projections of the central amygdaloid nculeus mediate autonomic and behavioral correlates of conditioned fear. *Journal of Neuroscience, 8,* 2517–2529.

LeDoux, J. E., Ruggiero, D. A., & Reis, D. J. (1985). Projections to the subcortical forebrain from anatomically defined regions of the medial geniculate body in the rat. *Journal of Comparative Neurology, 242,* 182–213.

LeDoux, J. E., Sakaguchi, A., & Reis, D. J. (1984). Subcortical efferent projections of the medial geniculate nucleus mediate emotional responses conditioned to acoustic stimuli. *Journal of Neuroscience, 4,* 683–698.

Lehrman, D. S. (1953). A critique of Konrad Lorenz's theory of instinctive behavior. *Quarterly Review of Biology, 28,* 337–363.

Lehrman, D. S. (1964). The reproductive behavior of ring doves. *Scientific American, 211,* 48–54.

Levenson, R. W. (1988). Emotion and the autonomic nervous system: A prospectus for research on autonomic specificity. In H. Wagner (Ed.), *Social psychophysiology and emotion: Theory and clinical applications* (pp. 17–42). London: Wiley.

Levenson, R. W. (1992). Autonomic nervous system differences among emotions. *Psychological Science, 3,* 23–27.

Levenson, R. W., Carstensen, L. L., Friesen, W. V. & Ekman, P. (1991). Emotion, physiology and expression in old age. *Psychology and Aging, 6,* 28–35.

Levenson, R. W., Ekman, P., & Friesen, W. V. (1990). Voluntary facial action generates emotion-specific autonomic nervous system activity. *Psychophysiology, 27,* 363–384.

Levenson, R. W., Ekman, P., Heider, K., & Friesen, W. V. (1992). Emotion and autonomic nervous system activity in the Minangkabau of West Sumatra. *Journal of Personality and Social Psychology, 62,* 972–988.

Levenson, R. W., & Gottman, J. M. (1983). Marital interaction: Physiological linkage and affective exchange. *Journal of Personality and Social Psychology, 45*, 587–597.

Levenson, R. W., & Gottman, J. M. (1985). Physiological and affective predictors of change in relationship satisfaction. *Journal of Personality and Social Psychology, 49*, 85–94.

Levenson, R. W., & Mades, L. L. (1980). *Physiological response, facial expression, and trait anxiety: Two methods for improving consistency.* Paper presented at the meeting of the Society for Psychophysiological Research.

Leventhal, H. (1984). A perceptual motor theory of emotion. In K. R. Scherer & P. Ekman (Eds.), *Approaches to emotion* (pp. 271–292). Hillsdale, NJ: Lawrence Erlbaum.

Levenson, R. W., Sher, K. J., Grossman, L. M., Newman, J., & Newlin, D. B. (1980). Alcohol and stress response dampening: Pharmacological effects, expectancy, and tension reduction. *Journal of Abnormal Psychology, 89*, 528–538.

Levenson, R. W., & Tsai, J. L. (in preparation). Experimental test of a model of ethno-cultural influences on emotion.

Leventhal, H., & Scherer, K. (1987). The relationship of emotion to cognition: A functional approach to a semantic controversy. *Cognition and Emotion, 1*, 3–28.

Levy, Robert I. (1973). *The Tahitians. Mind and experience in the Society Islands.* Chicago: University of Chicago Press.

Levy, R. I. (1978). Tahitian gentleness and redundant controls. In A. Montague (Ed.), *Learning non-aggression.* New York: Oxford University Press.

Levy, R. I. (1984a). The emotion in comparative perspective. In K. R. Scherer & P. Ekman (Eds.), *Approaches to emotion* (pp. 397–412). Hillsdale, NJ: Lawrence Erlbaum.

Levy, R. I. (1984b). Emotion, knowing and culture. In R. A. Shweder & R. A. LeVine (Eds.), *Culture theory: Essays on mind, self and emotion.* New York: Cambridge University Press.

Lewin, K. (1931). The conflict between Aristotelian and Galileian modes of thought in contemporary psychology. *Journal of Genetic Psychology, 5*, 141–177.

Lewin, K. (1935). On Aristotelian and Galilean science. In K. Lewin, *Towards a dynamic theory of personality* (pp. 16–23). New York: McGraw-Hill.

Lewis, M. (1990). The development of intentionality and the role of consciousness. *Psychological Inquiry, 1*, 231–283.

Lewis, M., Alessandri, S. M., & Sullivan, M. W. (1990). Violation of expectancy, loss of control, and anger expressions in young infants. *Developmental Psychology, 26*, 745–751.

Lewis, M., & Michalson, L. (1983). *Children's emotions and moods: Developmental theory and measurement.* New York: Plenum.

Lewis, M., Sullivan, M., Stanger, C., & Weiss, M. (1989). Self-development and self-conscious emotions. *Child Development, 60*, 146–156.

Lewis, V. L., & Williams, R. N. (1989). Mood-congruent vs. mood-state-dependent learning: Implications for a view of emotion. *Journal of Social Behavior and Personality, 4*, 157–171.

Leyhausen, P. (1967). Biologie von Ausdruck und Eindruck (Teil 1). *Psychologische Forschung, 31*, 113–176.

Lindsley, D. B. (1951). Emotions. In S. S. Stevens (Ed.), *Handbook of experimental psychology* (pp. 473–516). New York: Wiley.

Luria, A. R. (1973). *The working brain.* New York: Basic Books.

Lutz, C., & White, G. M. (1986). The anthropology of emotions. *Annual Review of Anthropology, 15*, 405–436.

Lyons, W. (1980). *Emotion.* Cambridge: Cambridge University Press.

McCall, R. B. (1986). Issues of stability and continuity in temperament research. In R. Plomin & J. Dunn (Eds.), *The study of temperament: Changes, continuities and challenges.* Hillsdale, NJ: Lawrence Erlbaum.

McClelland, J. L., & Rumelhart, D. E. (1986). *Parallel distributed processing: Explorations in the microstructures of cognition.* Cambridge, MA: MIT Press.

Maccoby, E. E., & Jacklin, C. S. (1974). *The psychology of sex-differences.* Stanford: Stanford University Press.

McCrae, R. R., & Costa, P. T., Jr. (1987). Validation of a five-factor model of personality across instruments and observers. *Journal of Personality and Social Psychology, 52,* 81–90.

MacDonald, K. B. (1988). *Social and personality development: An evolutionary synthesis.* New York: Plenum.

MacDonald, N. E., & Silverman, I. W. (1978). Smiling and laughter in infants as a function of level of arousal and cognitive evaluation. *Developmental Psychology, 14,* 235–241.

MacDougall, J. M., Dembroski, T. M., & Krantz, D. S. (1981). Effects of types of challenge on pressor and heart rate responses in Type A and B women. *Psychophysiology, 18,* 1–9.

McFarlane, A. C. (1986). The longitudinal course of posttraumatic morbidity: The range of outcomes and their predictors. *Journal of Nervous and Mental Disease, 176,* 30–39.

McIntyre, C. W., Watson, D., Clark, L. A., & Cross, S. A. (1991). The effect of induced social interaction on positive and negative affect. *Bulletin of the Psychonomic Society, 29,* 67–70.

Mackintosh, N. J. (1983). *Conditioning and associative learning.* New York: Oxford University Press.

MacLean, P. D. (1952). Some psychiatric implications of physiological studies on frontotemporal portion of limbic system (visceral brain). *Electroencephalogr. Clinical Neurophysiology, 4,* 407–418.

MacLean, P. D. (1990). *The triune brain in evolution: Role in paleocerebral functions.* New York: Plenum.

Malatesta, C. Z. (1990). The role of emotions in the development and organization of personality. In R. A. Thompson (Ed.), *Socioemotional development* (pp. 1–56). Lincoln: University of Nebraska Press.

Malatesta, C., Culver, C., Tesman, J., & Shepard, B. (1989). The development of emotion expression during the first two years of life. *Monographs of the Society for Research in Child Development, 54*(1–2), 1–136.

Mancia, B., & Zanchetti, A. (1981). Hypothalamic control of autonomic function. In P. J. Morgane & J. Panksepp (Eds.), *Handbook of the hypothalamus, Vol. 3, Pt. B, Behavioral studies of the hypothalamus* (pp. 47–202). New York: Marcel Dekker.

Mandler, G. (1975). *Mind and emotion.* New York: Wiley.

Mandler, G. (1982). The structure of value. In M. S. Clark & S. T. Fiske (Eds.), *Affect and cognition* (pp. 3–36). Hillsdale, NJ: Lawrence Erlbaum.

Mandler, G. (1984). *Mind and body: The psychology of emotion and stress.* New York: Norton.

Mandler, G., Nakamura, Y., & VanZandt, B. J. S. (1987). Nonspecific effects of exposure on stimuli that cannot be recognized. *Journal of Experimental Psychology: Learning Memory, and Cognition, 13,* 646–648.

Marceil, J. C. (1977). Implicit dimensions of ideography and nomothesis: A reformulation. *American Psychologist, 32,* 1046–1055.

Markus, H. R., & Kitayama, S. (1991). Culture and the self: Implications for cognition, emotion, and motivation. *Psychological Review, 98,* 224–253.

Marshall, G. D. & Zimbardo, P. G. (1979). Affective consequences of inadequately explained physiological arousal. *Journal of Personality and Social Psychology, 37,* 970–988.

Martin, L. L. (1986). Set/Reset: Use and disuse of concepts in impression formation. *Journal of Personality and Social Psychology, 51,* 493–504.

Martin, L. L., Seta, J. J., & Crelia, R. A. (1990). Assimilation and contrast as a function of people's willingness and ability to expend effort in forming an impression. *Journal of Personality and Social Psychology, 59,* 27–37.

Martin, L. L., Ward, D. W., Achee, J. W., & Wyer, R. S. (1993). Mood as input: People have to interpret the motivational implications of their moods. *Journal of Personality and Social Psychology, 64,* 317–326.

Maslach, C. (1979). Negative emotional biasing of unexplained arousal. *Journal of Personality and Social Psychology, 37,* 953–969.

Mason, J. W. (1975). Emotion as reflected in patterns of endocrine regulation. n. L. Levi (Ed.), *Emotions: Their parameters and measurement* (pp. 143–153). New York: Raven Press.

Masson, J. L., & Patwardhan, M. V. (1970). *Aesthetic rapture: The Rasadhyaya of the Natyasastra.* Poona, India: Deccan College Postgraduate and Research Institute.

Mathews, A. (1990). Why worry? The cognitive function of anxiety. *Behavior Research and Therapy, 28,* 455–468.

Matlin, M. W. (1971). Response competition, recognition, and affect. *Journal of Personality and Social Psychology, 19,* 295–300.

Mathews, A., May, J., Mogg, K., & Eysenck, M. (1990). Attentional bias in anxiety: Selective search or defective filtering? *Journal of Abnormal Psychology, 99,* 166–173.

Matsumoto, D., & Ekman, P. (1989). American-Japanese cultural differences in intensity ratings of facial expressions of emotion. *Motivation and Emotion, 13,* 143–157.

Mauro, R. (1988). Opponent process in human emotions? An experimental investigation of hedonic contrast and affective interaction. *Motivation and Emotion, 12,* 333–351.

Mauro, R., Sato, K., & Tucker, J. (1992) The role of appraisal in human emotions: A cross-cultural study. *Journal of Personality and Social Psychology, 62,* 301–317.

Maxson, S. C., Shrenker, P., & Vigue, L. C. (1983). Genetics, hormones, and aggression. In B. B. Svare (Ed.), *Hormones and aggressive behavior* (pp. 179–196). New York: Plenum.

Mayer, J. D., Salovey, P., Gomberg-Kaufman, S., & Blainey, K. (1991). A broader conception of mood experience. *Journal of Personality and Social Psychology, 60,* 100–111.

Meehl, P. E. (1975). Hedonic capacity: Some conjectures. *Bulletin of the Menninger Clinic, 39,* 295–307.

Meehl, P. E. (1992). factors and taxa, traits and types, differences of degree and differences in kind. *Journal of Personality, 60,* 117–174.

Mellerup, E. T., & Rafaelsen, O. J. (1979). Circadian rhythms in manic-melancholic disorders. In W. B. Essman & L. Valzelli (Eds.), *Current developments in psychopharmacology,* Vol. 5 (pp. 51–66).

Melton, R. J. (in press). Effects of induced mood on task performance. *Personality and Social Psychology Bulletin.*

Menon U., & Shweder, R. A. (1992). Kali's tongue: Cultural psychology and the power of "shame" in Orpissa, India. In H. Markus & S. Kitayama (Eds.), *Culture and the emotions.* Forthcoming APA publication.

Merbaum, M., & Hefez, A. (1976). Some personality characteristics of soldiers exposed to extreme war stress. *Journal of Consulting and Clinical Psychology, 44,* 1–6.

Merleau-Ponty, M. (1962). *Phenomenology of perception* (C. Smith, Trans.). London: Routledge & Kegan Paul.

Merritt, J. M., Stickgold, R., Pace-Schott, E., Williams, J., & Hobson, J. A. (1994). Emotion profiles in dreams of men and women. *Consciousness and Cognition, 3,* 46–60.

Mervis, C. B., & Rosch, E. (1981). Categorization of natural objects. *Annual Review of Psychology, 32,* 89–115.

Mesquita, B., & Frijda, N. H. (1992). Cultural variations in emotions: A review. *Psychological Bulletin, 112,* 179–204.

Mesulam, M. M., van Hoesen, G., Pandya, D. N., & Geschwind, N. (1977). Limbic and sensory connections of the inferior parietal lobule (area pg) in the rhesus monkey: A study with a new method for horseradish peroxidase histochemistry. *Brain Research, 136,* 393–414.

Michotte, A. E. (1950). The emotions as functional connections. In M. Reymert (Ed.), *Feelings and emotions* (pp. 114–126). New York, McGraw-Hill.

Miller, N. E. (1951). Learnable drives and rewards. In S. S. Stevens (Ed.), *Handbook of experimental psychology* (pp. 435–472). New York: Wiley.

Miller, N. E. (1978). The evidence for the antiatherogenicity of high-density lipoprotein cholesterol level. *Lipids, 13,* 914–919.

Mineka, S., Davidson, M., Cook, M., & Keir, R. (1984). Observational conditioning of snake fear in rhesus monkeys. *Journal of Abnormal Psychology, 93*(4), 355–372.

Mineka, S., & Sutton, S. K. (1992). Cognitive biases and the emotional disorders. *Psychological Science, 3,* 65–69.

Mishkin, M. (1965). Visual mechanisms beyond the striate cortex. In R. N. Russell (Ed.), *Frontiers in physiological psychology.* New York: Academic Press.

Miyake, K., Chen, S., & Campos, J. J. (1985). Infant temperament, mother's mode of interaction, and attachment in Japan: An interim report. In I. Bretherton & E. Waters (Eds.), *Growing points of attachment theory and research. Monographs of the Society for Research in Child Development, 50,* 276–297.

Moran, T. H., Schwartz, G. J., & Blass, E. M. (1983) Organized behavioral responses to lateral hypothalamic electrical stimulation in infant rats. *The Journal of Neuroscience, 3,* 10–19.

Moreau, J.-L., Cohen, E., & Lieblich, I. (1984). Ventral tegmental self-stimualtion, sensory reactivity and pain reduction in rats selected for high and low rats of lateral hypothalamic self-stimulation. *Physiology & Behavior, 33,* 825–830.

Moreland, R. L., & Zajonc, R. B. (1977). Is stimulus recognition a necessary condition for the occurrence of exposure effects? *Journal of Personality and Social Psychology, 35,* 191–199.

Moreland, R. L., & Zajonc, R. B. (1979). Exposure effects may not depend on stimulus recognition. *Journal of Personality and Social Psychology, 37,* 1085–1089.

Morgan, C., & Averill, J. R. (1992). True feelings, the self, and authenticity: A psychosocial perspective. In D. D. Franks & V. Gecas (Eds.), *Social perspectives on emotion,* Vol. 1 (pp. 95–124). Greenwich, CT: JAI.

Morley, J. E., & Blundell, J. E. (1988). The neurobiological basis of eating disorders: Some formulation. *Biological Psychiatry, 23,* 53–78.

Moore, B., Underwood, B., & Rosenhan, D. L. (1984). Emotion, self, and others. In C. Izard, J. Kagan, & R. Zajonc (Eds.), *Emotions, cognition and behavior* (pp. 464–483). Cambridge: Cambridge University Press.

Morris, W. N. (1989). *Mood: The frame of mind.* New York: Springer-Verlag.

Mowrer, O. H. (1947). On the dual nature of learning—A reinterpretation of "conditioning" and "problem-solving." *Harvard Educational Review, 17,* 102–148.

Mowrer, O. H. (1960). *Learning and behavior.* New York: Wiley.

Murphy, S. T., Monahan, J. L., & Zajonc, R. B. (under review). *The diffusion of nonconscious affect.*

Murphy, S. T., & Zajonc, R. B. (1987, August-September). *Affect and awareness: Comparisons of subliminal and supraliminal affective priming.* Paper presented at the 95th Annual Convention of the American Psychological Association, New York.

Murphy, S. T., & Zajonc, R. B. (1988, August). *Non-conscious influence of affective and cognitive processes.* Paper presented at the 96th APA Convention, Atlanta, Georgia.

Murphy, S. T., & Zajonc, R. B. (1993). Affect, cognition, and awareness: Affective priming with suboptimal and optimal stimulus. *Journal of Personality and Social Psychology, 64,* 723–739.

Murray, E. A. (1992). Medial temporal lobe structures contributing to recognition memory: The amygdaloid complex versus the rhinal cortex. In J. P. Aggleton (Ed.), *The amygdala: Neurobiological aspects of emotion, memory, and mental dysfunction* (pp. 453–470). New York: Wiley-Liss.

Myers, F. (1979). Emotions and the self: A theory of personhood and political order among the Pintupi Aborigines. *Ethos: Journal of the Society for Psychological Anthropology 7,* 343–370.

Naumann, E., Bartussek, D., Kaiser, W., & Gehm-Wolfsdorf, G. (1991). Vasopressin and cognitive processes: Two event-related potential studies. *Peptides, 12,* 1379–1384.

Negro-Vilar, A., & Conn, P. M. (Eds.) (1988). *Peptide hormones: Effects and mechanisms of action.* Boca Raton, FL: CRC Press.

Newman, J. D. (Ed.). (1988). *The physiological control of mammalian vocalizations.* New York: Plenum.

Newman, J. P. (1987). Reaction to punishment in extraverts and psychopaths: Implications for the impulsive behavior of disinhibited individuals. *Journal of Research in Personality, 21,* 464–480.

Niedenthal, P. M. (1987). *Unconscious affect in social cognition.* Ph.D. Thesis, University of Michigan.

Niedenthal, P. M. (1990). Implicit perception and affective information. *Journal of Experimental Social Psychology, 26,* 505–527.

Notarius, C. I., & Levenson, R. W. (1979). Expressive tendencies and physiological responses to stress. *Journal of Personality and Social Psychology, 37,* 1204–1210.

Oatley, K. (1992). *Best laid schemes: The psychology of emotions.* Cambridge: Cambridge University Press.

Oatley, K., & Jenkins, J. M. (1992). Human emotions: Function and dysfunction. *Annual Review of Psychology, 43,* 55–85.

Oatley, K., & Johnson-Laird, P. (1987). Towards a cognitive theory of emotion. *Cognition and Emotion, 1,* 51–58.

Obrist, P. A. (1981). *Cardiovascular psychophysiology.* New York: Plenum.

Ohman, A. (1986). Face the beast and fear the face: Animal and social fears as prototypes for evolutionary analyses of emotion. *Psychophysiology, 23,* 123–145.

Ohman, A., Dimberg, U., & Esteves, F. (1989). Preattentive activation of aversive emotions. In T. Archer & L.-G. Nilsson (Eds.), *Aversion, avoidance and anxiety* (pp. 169–193). Hillsdale, NJ: Lawrence Erlbaum.

Ono, T., & Nishijo, H. (1992). Neurophysiological basis of the Kluver-Bucy syndrome: Responses of monkey amygdaloid neurons to biologically significant objects. In J. P. Aggleton (Ed.), *The amygdala: Neurobiological aspects of emotion, memory, and mental dysfunction* (pp. 167–190). New York: Wiley-Liss.

Ormel, J., & Schaufeli, W. B. (1991). Stability and change in psychological distress and their relationship with self-esteem and locus of control: A dynamic equilibrium model. *Journal of Personality and Social Psychology, 60,* 288–299.

Ortony, A. (1990, August). *The cognition-emotion connection.* Paper presented at the Ninety-Eighth Annual Convention of the American Psychological Association, Boston, Massachusetts.

Ortony, A. (1991). Value and emotion. In G. Kessen, A. Ortony, & F. Craik (Eds.), *Memories, thoughts and emotions: Essays in memory of George Mandler* (pp. 317–353). Hillsdale, NJ: Lawrence Erlbaum.

Ortony, A., & Clore, G. L. (1989). Emotion, mood, and conscious awareness. *Cognition and Emotion, 3,* 125–137.

Ortony, A., Clore, G. L., & Collins, A. (1988). *The cognitive structure of emotions.* New York: Cambridge University Press.

Ortony, A., Clore, G. L., and Foss, M. S. (1987). The referential structure of the affective lexicon. *Cognitive Science, 11,* 341–364.

Ortony, A., & Turner, T. J. (1990). What's basic about basic emotions? *Psychological Review, 97,* 315–331.

Oster, H., Hegley, D., & Nagel, L. (1992). Adult judgments and fine-grained analysis of infant facial expressions. *Developmental Psychology, 28*(6), 1115–1131.

Osgood, C. E., Suci, G. J., & Tannenbaum, P. H. (1957). *The measurement of meaning.* Urbana: University of Illinois Press.

Panksepp, J. (1979). A neurochemical theory of autism. *Trends in Neurosciences, 2,* 174–177.

Panksepp, J. (1981). Brain opioids: A neurochemical substrate for narcotic and social dependence. In S. Cooper (Ed.), *Progress in theory in psychopharmacology* (pp. 149–175). London: Academic Press.

Panksepp, J. (1982). Toward a general psychobiological theory of emotions. *The Behavioral and Brain Sciences, 5,* 407–467.

Panksepp, J. (1985). Mood changes: In P. J. Vinken, G. W. Bruynm, & H. L. Klawans (Eds.), *Handbook of clinical neurology,* Vol. 1 *(45), Clinical neuropsychology* (pp. 271–285) Amsterdam: Elsevier.

Panksepp, J. (1986). The anatomy of emotions. In R. Plutchik and H. Kellerman (Eds.), *Emotion: Theory, research and experience,* Vol. III, *Biological foundations of emotions* (pp. 91–124). New York: Academic Press.

Panksepp, J. (1989a). Les circuits des emotions. *Science & Vie, 168,* 58–67.

Panksepp, J. (1989b). The neurobiology of emotions: Of animal brains and human feelings. In H. Wagner & T. Manstead (Eds.), *Handbook of social psychophysiology.* Chichester: Wiley.

Panksepp, J. (1990a). Psychology's search of identity: Can "mind" and behavior be understood without understanding the brain? *New Ideas in Psychology, 8,* 139–149.

Panksepp, J. (1990b). The psychoneurology of fear: Evolutionary perspectives and the role of animal models in understanding human anxiety. In R. Burrows (Ed.), *Handbook of anxiety, Vol. 3* (pp.3–58). Amsterdam: Elsevier.

Panksepp, J. (1990c). A role for affective neuroscience in understanding stress: The case of separation distress circuitry. In S. Puglisi-Allegra & A. Oliverio (Eds.), *Psychobiology of stress* (pp. 41–57). Dordrecht, the Netherlands: Kluwer Academic Publishers.

Panksepp, J. (1990d). Gray zones at the emotion/cognition interface. In J. A. Gray (Ed.), Special issue of *Cognition and Emotion, Psychobiological Aspects of Relationships Between Emotion and Cognition* (pp. 289–302). Hillsdale, NJ: Lawrence Erlbaum.

Panksepp, J. (1991). Affective neuroscience: A conceptual framework for the neurobiological study of emotions. In K. Strongman (Ed.), *International reviews of studies in emotions, Vol. 1* (pp. 59–99). Chichester: Wiley.

Panksepp, J. (1992). A critical role for "affective neuroscience" in resolving what is basic about basic emotions: Response to Ortony and Turner. *Psychological Review, 99,* 554–560.

Panksepp, J. (1993). Neurochemical control of moods and emotions: Amino acids to neuropeptides. In M. Lewis & J. Haviland (Eds.), *The handbook of emotions* (pp. 87–107). New York: Gulford.

Panksepp, J., & Abbott, B. (1990). Modulation of separation distress by a-MSH. *Peptides, 11,* 647–653.

Panksepp, J., & Lensing, P. (1991). Nalterxone treatment of autims: A synopsis of an open-trial with four children. *Journal of Autism and Developmental Disorders, 21,* 135–141.

Panksepp, J., Normansell, L., Herman, B., Bishop, P., & Crepeau, L. (1988). Neural and neurochemical control of the separation distress call. In J. D. Newman (Ed.), *The physiological control of mammalian vocalizations* (pp. 263–299). New York: Plenum.

Panksepp, J., Sacks, D. S., Crepeau, L. J., & Abbott, B. B. (1991). The psycho- and neurobiology of fear systems in the brain. In M. R. Denny (Ed.), *Aversive events and behavior* (pp. 7–59). Hillsdale, NJ: Lawrence Erlbaum.

Panksepp, J., Siviy, S., & Normansell, L. (1984). The psychobiology of play: Theoretical and methodological perspectives. *Neuroscience and Biobehavioral Reviews, 8,* 465–492.

Panksepp, J., Siviy, S. M., & Normansell, L. A. (1985). Brain opioids and social emotions. In M. Reite and T. Fields. (Eds.), *The psychobiology of attachment and separation* (pp. 3–49). New York: Academic Press.

Papousek, H., & Papousek, M. (1974). Mirror-image and self-recognition in young human infants: A new method of experimental analysis. *Developmental Psychobiology, 7,* 149–157.

Parrott, W. G. (1988). The role of cognition in emotional experience. In W. J. Baker, L. P. Mos, H. V. Rappard, & H. J. Stam (Eds.), *Recent trends in theoretical psychology* (pp. 327–337). New York: Springer-Verlag.

Parrott, W. G., & Sabini, J. (1990). Mood and memory under natural conditions: Evidence for mood incongruent recall. *Journal of Personality and Social Psychology, 59,* 321–336.

Pavot, W., Diener, E., & Fujita, F. (1990). Extraversion and happiness. *Personality and Individual Differences, 12,* 1299–1306.

Pedersen, C. A., Caldwell, J. D., Jirikowski, G., & Insel, T. R. (Eds.) (1992). Oxytocin in maternal, sexual and social behaviors. *Annals of the New York Academy of Sciences* New York: Academy of Sciences.

Penick, S., & Solomon, P. R. (1991). Hippocampus, context, and conditioning. *Behavioral Neuroscience, 105,* 611–617.

Pennebaker, J. W. (1991). *Opening up: The healing power of confiding in others.* New York: William Morrow.

Pennebaker, J., & Beall, S. K. (1986). Confronting a traumatic event: Toward an understanding of inhibition and disease. *Journal of Abnormal Psychology, 95,* 274–281.

Pennebaker, J., Hughes, C. F., & O'Heeron, R. C. (1987). The psychology of confession: Linking inhibitory and psychosomatic processes. *Journal of Personality and Social Psychology, 52,* 781–793.

Pennebaker, J., Kiecolt-Glaser, J. K., & Glaser, R. (1988a). Disclosure of traumas and immune function: Health implications for psychotherapy. *Journal of Consulting and Clinical Psychology, 56,* 239–245.

Pennebaker, J., Kiecolt-Glaser, J. K., & Glaser, R. (1988b). Confronting traumatic experience and immunocompetence: A reply to Neale, Cox, Valdimarsdottir, and Stone. *Journal of Consulting and Clinical Psychology, 56,* 638–639.

Perkins, M. (1966). Emotion and feeling. *Philosophical Review, 75,* 139–160.

Pervin, L. A. (1986). Ideographic and nomothetic aspects of affect. In L. Van Langenhove, J. M. De Waele, & R. Harre (Eds.), *Individual persons and their actions: Essays in honor of J. P. De Waele.* Brussels: Free University of Brussels.

Pfaffman, C. (1960). The pleasures of sensation. *Psychological Review, 67,* 253–268.

Pfennig, J. L., Clore, G. L., & Ortony, A. (1991, May). *Predicting emotional intensity: the role of goal importance.* Paper presented at the Midwestern Psychological Association, Chicago.

Phillips, R. G., & LeDoux, J. E. (1992). Differential contribution of amygdala and hippocampus to cued and contextual fear conditioning. *Behavioral Neuroscience, 106,* 274–285.

Phillips, R. G., & LeDoux, J. E. (1992). Overlapping and divergent Projections of CA1 and the Ventral Subiculum to the Amygdala. *Society of Neuroscience Abstracts, 18,* 518.

Piderit, T. (1867). *Mimik und Physiognomik.* Detmoldt: Meyer.

Pitkänen, A., & Amaral, D. G. (1991). Demonstration of projections from the lateral nucleus to the basal nucleus of the amygdala: A PHA-L study in the monkey. *Experimental Brain Research, 83,* 465–470.

Plomin, R., & Bergeman, C. S. (1991). The nature of nurture: genetic influence on "environmental" measures. *Behavioral and Brain Sciences, 14,* 373–428.

Plutchik, P. (1980). *Emotion: A psychobioevolutionary synthesis.* New York: Harper & Row.

Polanyi, M. (1966). *The tacit dimension.* Garden City, NY: Doubleday.

Pollard, C. A., Pollard, H. J., & Corn, K. J. (1989). Panic onset and major events in the lives of agoraphobics: A test of contiguity. *Journal of Abnormal Psychology, 98,* 318–321.

Porges, S. W., Doussard, J. A., & Maiti, A. K. (in press). Vagal tone and the physiological regulation of emotion. In N. A. Fox (Ed.), *Emotion regulation: Behavioral and biological considerations.* Monograph of the Society for Research in Child Development.

Posner, M. I., & Rothbart, M. K. (1992). Attentional mechanisms and conscious experience. In A. D. Milner & M. D. Ruggs (Eds.), *The neurophysiology of consciousness* (pp. 91–111). San Diego: Academic Press.

Post, S., & Mai, J. K. (1980). Contribution to the amygdaloid projection field in the rat: A quantitative autoradiographic study. *J. Hirnforsch, 21,* 199–225.

Pribram, K. H., & McGuiness, D. (1975). Arousal, activation, and effort in the control of attention. *Psychological Review, 82,* 116–149.

Price, J. L., & Amaral, D. G. (1981). An autoradiographic study of the projections of the central nucleus of the monkey amygdala. *Journal of Neuroscience, 1,* 1242–1259.

Ptacek, J. T., Smith, R. E., Espe, K., Raffety, B. (1994). Limited correspondence between daily coping reports and retrospective coping recall. *Psychological Assessment, 6,* 41–49.

Puglisi-Allegra, S., & Oliverio, A. (Eds.) (1990). *Psychobiology of stress.* Dordrecht, Germany: Kluwer Academic Publishers.

Quay, H. C. (1988). The behavioral reward and inhibition system in childhood behavior disorders. In L. M. Bloomingdale (Ed.), *Attention deficit disorder,* Vol. 3 (pp. 176–186). New York: Pergamon.

Randall, W. C., & Priola, D. V. (1965). In W. C. Randall (Ed.), *Nervous control of the heart* (pp. 214–244). Baltimore: Williams and Wilkens.

Reiman, E. M. (1990). Positron emission tomography in the study of panic disorder and anticipatory anxiety. In G. D. Burrows, M. Roth, & R. Noyes Jr. (Eds.), *Handbook of anxiety,* Vol. 3, *The neurobiology of anxiety* (pp. 289–305). Amsterdam: Elsevier.

Reisenzein, R., & Hofmann, T. (1990). An investigation of dimensions of cognitive appraisal in emotion using the repertory grid technique. *Motivation and Emotion, 14,* 1–26.

Reisenzein, R., & Schönpflug, W. (1992). Stumpf's cognitive-evaluative theory of emotion. *American Psychologist, 47,* 34–45.

Rescorla, R. A. (1988). Behavioral studies of Pavlovian conditioning. *Annual Review of Neuroscience, 11,* 329–352.

Rholes, W. S., Riskind, J. H., & Lane, J. W. (1987). Emotional states and memory biases: Effects of cognitive priming and mood. *Journal of Personality and Social Psychology, 52,* 91–99.

Ricci-Bitti, P. O. (1989). The universality of facial expression of emotion. In W. Schönpflug (Ed.), *Bericht über den 36. Kongress der Deutschen Gesellschaft für Psychologie* (pp. 332–343). Göttingen: Hogrefe.

Rime, B., Philippot, P., & Cisamolo, D. (1990). Social schemata of peripheral changes in emotion. *Journal of Personality and Social Psychology, 59,* 38–49.

Roberts, W. W., & Berquist, E. (1968). Attack elicited by hypothalamic stimulation in cats raised in social isolation. *Journal of Comparative and Physiological Psychology, 66,* 590–596.

Roberts, R. J., & Weerts, T. C. (1982). Cardiovascular responding during anger and fear imagery. *Psychological Reports, 50,* 219–230.

Roberts, W. W. (1980). ^{14}C deoxyglucose mapping of first-order projections activated by stimulation of lateral hypothalamic sites eliciting gnawing, eating, and drinking in rats. *Journal of Comparative Neurology, 194,* 617–638.

Robertson, H. A., Martin, I. L., & Candy, J. M. (1978). Differences in benzodiazepine receptor binding in Maudsley reactive and Maudsley non-reactive rats. *European Journal of Pharmacology, 50,* 455–457.

Robinson, R. G., & Downhill, J. E. (in press). Lateralization of psychopathology in response to focal brain injury. In R. J. Davidson & K. Hugdahl (Eds.), *Brain asymmetry.* Cambridge, MA: MIT Press.

Rolls, E. T. (1990). A theory of emotion, and its application to understanding the neural basis of emotion. In J. A. Gray (Ed.), *Psychobiological aspects of relationships between emotion and cognition* (pp. 161–190) (Special issue of *Cognition and Emotion*). Hillsdale, NJ: Lawrence Erlbaum.

Rolls, E. T. (1990). Theoretical and neurophysiological analysis of the functions of the primate hippocampus in memory. In *Cold Spring Harbor symposia on quantitative biology* (pp. 995–1006). Cold Spring Harbor Laboratory Press.

Rolls, E. T. (1992). Neurophysiological mechanisms underlying face processing within and beyond the temporal cortical visual areas. In V. Bruce, A. Cowey, A. W. Ellis, & D. I. Perrett (Eds.), *Processing the facial image* (pp. 11–21). Oxford: Oxford University Press.

Rolls, E. T. (1992). Neurophysiology and functions of the primate amygdala. In J. P. Aggleton (Ed.), *The amygdala: Neurobiological aspects of emotion, memory, and mental dysfunction* (pp. 143–165). New York: Wiley-Liss.

Rosaldo, M. Z. (1980). *Knowledge and passion: Ilongot notions of self and social life.* Cambridge: Cambridge University Press.

Roseman, I. J. (1984). Cognitive determinants of emotion: A structural theory. In P. Shaver (Ed.), *Review of personality and social psychology,* Vol. 5, *Emotions, relationships, and health* (pp. 11–36). Beverly Hills, CA: Sage.

Roseman, I. J. (1991). Appraisal determinants of discrete emotions. *Cognition and Emotion, 5,* 161–200.

Roseman, I. J., Spindel, M. S., & Jose, P. E. (1990). Appraisals of emotion-eliciting events: Testing a theory of discrete emotions. *Journal of Personality and Social Psychology, 59,* 899–915.

Rosenberg, E. L., & Ekman, P. (in press). Coherence between expressive and experimental systems in emotion. *Cognition and Emotion.*

Rothbart, M. K. (1973). Laughter in young children. *Psychological Bulletin, 80,* 247–256.

Rothbart, M. K. (1988). Temperament and the development of inhibited approach. *Child Development, 59,* 1241–1250.

Rothbart, M. K. (1989a). Behavioral approach and inhibition. In S. Reznick (Ed.), *Perspectives on behavioral inhibition* (pp. 139–157). Chicago: University of Chicago Press.

Rothbart, M. K. (1989b). Biological processes of temperament. In G. Kohnstamm, J. Bates, & M. K. Rothbart, (Eds.), *Temperament in childhood* (pp. 77–110). Chichester: Wiley.

Rothbart, M. K. (1989c). Temperament and development. In G. Kohnstamm, J. Bates, & M. K. Rothbart (Eds.), *Temperament in childhood* (pp. 187–248). Chichester: Wiley.

Rothbart, M. K. (1991). Temperament: A developmental framework. In A. Angleitner & J. Strelau (Eds.), *Explorations in temperament: International perspectives on theory and measurement* (pp. 61–74). New York: Plenum.

Rothbart, M. K., & Ahadi, S. A. (1994). Temperament and the development of personality. *Journal of Abnormal Psychology, 103*, 55–60.

Rothbart, M. K., Ahadi, S. A., & Hershey, K. L. (1993). Temperament and social behavior in childhood. *Merrill-Palmer Quarterly, 40*, 21–39.

Rothbart, M. K., & Derryberry, D. (1981). Development of individual differences in temperament. In M. E. Lamb & A. L. Brown (Eds.), *Advances in developmental psychology*, Vol. 1 (pp. 37–86). Hillsdale, NJ: Lawrence Erlbaum.

Rothbart, M. K., Derryberry, D., & Hershey, K. (in preparation). *Stability of temperament in childhood: Laboratory infant assessment to parent report at seven years.* Manuscript, University of Oregon, Eugene, Oregon.

Rothbart, M. K., Derryberry, D., & Posner, M. I. (1994). A psychobiological approach to the development of temperament. In J. E. Bates & T. D. Wachs (Eds.), *Temperament: Individual differences at the interface of biology and behavior* (pp. 83–116). Washington, DC: American Psychological Association.

Rothbart, M. K., & Mauro, J. A. (1990). Questionnaire measures of infant temperament. In J. W. Fagen & J. Colombo (Eds.), *Individual differences in infancy: Reliability, stability and prediction* (pp. 411–429). Hillsdale, NJ: Lawrence Erlbaum.

Rothbart, M. K., & Posner, M. (1985). Temperament and the development of self-regulation. In L. C. Hartlage & C. F. Telzrow (Eds.), *The neuropsychology of individual differences: A developmental perspective* (pp. 93–123). New York: Plenum.

Rothbart, M. K., Ziaie, H., & O'Boyle, C. G. (1992). Self-regulation and emotion in infancy. In N. Eisenberg & R. A. Fabes (Eds.), *Emotion and its regulation in early development; New directions for child development, 55*, 7–24.

Rothbaum, F., Weisz, J. R., & Snyder, S. S. (1982). Changing the world and changing the self: A two-process model of perceived control. *Journal of Personality and Social Psychology, 42*, 5–37.

Rozin, P., & Fallon, A. E. (1987). A perspective on disgust. *Psychological Review, 94*(1), 23–41.

Rubinow, D. R. (1986). Cerebrospinal fluid somatostatin and psychiatric illness. *Biological Psychiatry, 32*, 342–365.

Ruble, D. N., Boggiano, A. K., Feldman, N. S., & Loebl, J. H. (1980). Developmental analysis of the role of social comparison in self-evaluation. *Developmental Psychology, 16*, 105–115.

Russchen, F. T., Amaral, D. G., & Price, J. L. (1985). The afferent connections of the substantia innominata in the monkey, *Macaca fascicularis. Journal of Comparative Neurology, 242*, 1–27.

Russell, J. A. (1983). Pancultural aspects of the human conceptual organization of emotions. *Journal of Personality and Social Psychology, 45*, 1281–1288.

Russell, J. A. (1991a). Culture and the categorization of emotions. *Psychological Bulletin, 110*, 426–450.

Russel, J. A. (1994). Is ther universal recognition of emotion from facial expression? A review of cross-cultural studies. *Psychological Bulletin, 115*, 102–141.

Russell, J. A. (1991b). In defense of a prototype approach to emotion concepts. *Journal of Personality and Social Psychology, 60,* 37–47.

Russell, J. A., & Mehrabian, A. (1977). Evidence for a three-factor theory of emotions. *Journal of Research in Personality, 11,* 273–294.

Ryle, G. (1949). *The concept of mind.* London: Hutchinson.

Ryugo, D. K., & Weinberger, N. M. (1978). Differential plasticity of morphologically distinct neuron populations in the medial geniculate body of the cat during classical conditioning. *Behavioral Biology, 22,* 275–301.

Saarni, C. (1979). Children's understanding of display rules for expressive behavior. *Developmental Psychology, 15,* 424–429.

Saarni, C. (1982). Social and affective functions of nonverbal behavior: Developmental concerns. In R. Feldman (Ed.), *Development of nonverbal behavior.* New York: Springer-Verlag.

Sagi, A., & Hoffman, M. L. (1976). Empathic distress in the newborn. *Developmental Psychology, 12*(2), 175–176.

Said, S. I., & Mutt, V. (Eds.) (1988) *Vasoactive intestinal peptide and related peptides. Annals of the New York Academy of Sciences,* 527.

Saper, C. B., Loewy, A. D., Swanson, L. W., & Cowan, W. M. (1976). Direct hypothalamic-autonomic connections. *Brain Research, 117,* 305–312.

Sarason, I. G. (1960). Empirical findings and theoretical problems in the use of anxiety scales. *Psychological Bulletin, 57,* 403–415.

Sarbin, T. R. (1986). Emotion and act: Roles and rhetoric. In R. Harré (Ed.), *The social construction of emotions* (pp. 83–97). Oxford: Basil Blackwell.

Sartre, J. P. (1948). *The emotions: Outline of a theory.* B. Frechtman (Trans.). New York: Philosophical Library.

Sastre, P. J., & Jouvet, M. (1979). Le comportement onirique du chat. *Physiology & Behavior, 22,* 979–989.

Scarr, S., & Kidd, K. K. (1983). Developmental behavior genetics. In M. M. Haith & J. C. Campos (Eds.), *Handbook of child psychology* (pp. 345–433). New York: Wiley.

Schacter, D. L. (1987). Implicit memory: History and current status. *Journal of Experimental Psychology: Learning, Memory and Cognition, 13,* 501–518.

Schachter, S. (1964). The interaction of cognitive and physiological determinants of emotional states. In L. Berkowitz (Ed.), *Advances in experimental social psychology,* Vol. 1 (pp. 49–80). New York: Academic Press.

Schachter, S. (1975). Cognition and centralist-peripheralist controversies in motivation and emotion. In M. S. Gazzaniga & C. B. Blakemore (Eds.), *Handbook of psychobiology* (pp. 529–564). New York: Academic Press.

Schachter, S., & Singer, J. E. (1962). Cognitive, social, and physiological determinants of emotional state. *Psychological Review, 69,* 379–399.

Schaffer, H. R. (1974). Cognitive components of the infant's response to strangeness. In M. Lewis & L. A. Rosenblum (Eds.), *The origins of fear* (pp. 11–24). New York: Wiley.

Scheler, M. (1923). *Wesen und Formen der Sympathie.* Frankfurt: Schulte-Buhmke.

Scherer, K. R. (1984a). Emotion as a multicomponent process: A model and some cross-cultural data. In P. Shaver (Ed.), *Review of personality and social psychology,* Vol. 5 (pp. 37–63). Beverly Hills, CA: Sage.

Scherer, K. R. (1984b). On the nature and function of emotion: A component process approach. In K. R. Scherer & P. Ekman (Eds.), *Approaches to emotion* (pp. 293–318). Hillsdale, NJ: Lawrence Erlbaum.

Scherer, K. R. (1985). Emotions can be rational. *Social Science Information, 24,* 331–335.

Scherer, K. R. (1986). Vocal affect expression: A review and a model for future research. *Psychological Bulletin, 99,* 143–165.

Scherer, K. R. (1988a). Criteria for emotion-antecedent appraisal: A review. In V. Hamilton, G. H. Bower, & N. H. Frijda (Eds.), *Cognitive perspectives on emotion and motivation* (pp. 89–126). Dordrecht: Kluver Academic Publishers.

Scherer, K. R. (1988b). *Facets of emotion: Recent research.* Hillsdale, NJ: Lawrence Erlbaum.

Scherer, K. R. (1992). What does facial expression express? In K. Strongman (Ed.), *International Review of Studies on Emotion.* Vol. 2 (pp. 139–165). Chichester: Wiley.

Scherer, K. R. (1993a). Neuroscience projections to current debates in emotion psychology. *Cognition and Emotion, 7,* 1–41.

Scherer, K. R. (1993b). Studying the emotion-antecedent appraisal process: An expert system approach. *Cognition and Emotion, 3/4,* 325–355.

Scherer, K. R. (submitted). Cross-cultural differences in emotion-antecedent appraisal. Manuscript submitted for publication. University of Geneva.

Scherer, K., & P. Ekman (Eds.) (1984). *Approaches to emotion.* Hillsdale, NJ: Lawrence Erlbaum.

Scherer, K. R., & Walbott, H. G. (1986). How universal and specific is emotional experience? Evidence from 27 countries on five continents. *Social Science Information, 25,* 1–14.

Scherer, K. R., & Wallbott, H. G. (1994). Evidence for universality and cultural variation of differential emotion response patterning. *Journal of Personality and Social Psychology, 66,* 310–328.

Scherer, K. R., Wallbott, H. G., Matsumoto, D., & Kudoh, T. (1988). Emotional experience in cultural context: A comparison between Europe, Japan, and the USA. In K. R. Scherer (Ed.), *Facets of emotion: Recent research* (pp. 5–30). Hillsdale, NJ: Lawrence Erlbaum.

Scherer, K. R., Wallbott, H. G., & Summerfield, A. B. (Eds.). (1986). *Experiencing emotion: A crosscultural study.* Cambridge: Cambridge University Press.

Schmajuk, N. A., & Gray, J. A. (in prep). Latent inhibition: a neural network approach.

Schnurr, P. P. (1989). Endogenous factors associated with mood. In W. N. Morris, *Mood: The frame of mind* (pp. 35–70). New York: Springer-Verlag.

Schumacher, M., Coirini, H., Pfaff, D. W., & McEwen, B. S. (1990). Behavioral effects of progesterone associated with rapid modulation of oxytocin receptors. *Science, 250,* 691–694.

Schwarz, N. (1990). Happy but mindless? Mood effects on problem solving and persuasion. In R. M. Sorrentino & E. T. Higgins (Eds.), *Handbook of motivation and cognition,* Vol. 2 (pp. 527–561). New York: Guilford.

Schwarz, N., Bless, B., & Bohner, G. (1991). Mood and persuasion: Affective states influence the processing of persuasive communications. In M. Zanna (Ed.), *Advances in experimental social psychology,* Vol. 24 (pp. 161–199). San Diego: Academic Press.

Schwarz, N., & Clore, G. L. (1983). Mood, misattribution, and judgments of well-being: Informative and directive functions of affective states. *Journal of Personality and Social Psychology, 45,* 513–523.

Schwarz, N., & Clore, G. L. (1988). How do I feel about it? The informative function of mood. In K. Fiedler & J. Forgas (Eds.), *Affect, cognition, and social behavior* (pp. 44–62). Toronto: C. J. Hogrefe.

Schwarz, N., Robbins, M., & Clore, G. L. (1985, May). *Explaining the effects of mood on social judgment.* Paper presented at the Midwestern Psychological Association, Chicago.

Schwartz, G. E., Weinberger, D. A., & Singer, J. A. (1981). Cardiovascular differentiation of happiness, sadness, anger and fear following imagery and exercise. *Psychosomatic Medicine, 43,* 343–364.

Scott, J. P., Stewart, J. M., & DeGhett, V. J. (1973). Separation in infant dogs. In E. C. Senay & J. P. Scott (Eds.), *Separation and depression: Clinical and research aspects* (pp. 3–32). Washington, DC: American Association for the Advancement of Science, Publication 94.

Seamon, J. J., Brody, N. & Kauff, D. M. (1983a). Affective discrimination of stimuli that are not recognized: Effects of shadowing, masking, and cerebral laterality. *Journal of Experimental Psychology: Learning, Memory, and Cognition, 9*, 544–555.

Seamon, J. J., Brody, N., & Kauff, D. M. (1983b). Affective discrimination of stimuli that are not recognized: II. Effect of delay between study and test. *Bulletin of Psychonomic Society, 21*, 187–189.

Seeman, J. (1989). Toward a model of positive health. *American Psychologist, 44*, 1099–1109.

Seligman, M. (1971). Phobias and preparedness. *Behaviour Therapy, 2*, 307–320.

Seligman, M. E. P. (1970). On the generality of the laws of learning. *Psychological Review, 77*, 406–418.

Seligman, M. E. P., & Hager, J. E. (1972). *Biological boundaries of learning*. New York: Appleton-Century-Crofts.

Shagass, C. (1972). Electrical activity of the brain. In N. S. Greenfield & R. A. Sternbach (Eds.), *Handbook of psychophysiology* (pp. 263–328). New York: Holt, Rinehart & Winston.

Shand, A. F. (1920). *The foundations of character: A study of the emotions and sentiments*. London: Macmillan.

Shapiro, L. E., & Insel, T. R. (1990). Oxytocin receptor distribution reflects species-typical patterns of social behavior. *Neuroscience Abstracts, 26*, Abstract #186.6.

Shaver, P., Schwartz, J., Kirson, D., & O'Connor, C. (1987). Emotion knowledge: Further exploration of a prototype approach. *Journal of Personality and Social Psychology, 52*, 1061–1086.

Shepard, R. N. (1984). Ecological constraints on internal representation: Resonant kinematics of perceiving, imagining, thinking, and dreaming. *Psychological Review, 91*, 417–447.

Sher, K. J. & Levenson, R. W. (1982). Risk for alcoholism and individual differences in the stress-response-dampening effect of alcohol. *Journal of Abnormal Psychology, 91*, 350-367.

Shevrin, H. (1990). Subliminal perception and repression. In J. L. Singer (Ed.), *Repression and dissociation: Implications for personality theory, psychopathology, and health*. Chicago: University of Chicago Press.

Shweder, R. A. (1991a). Rethinking culture and personality theory. In R. A. Shweder (Ed.), *Thinking through cultures: Expeditions in cultural psychology* (pp. 269–312). Cambridge, MA: Harvard University Press.

Shweder, R. A. (1991b). On pseudo-empiricism, pseudo-deductionism and common-sense. *Psychological Inquiry, 2*, 366–371.

Shweder, R. A. (1992). The cultural psychology of the emotions. In M. Lewis & J. Haviland (Eds.), *Handbook of emotions*. New York: Guilford.

Shweder, R. A. (1993). Everything you ever wanted to know about cognitive appraisal theory without being conscious of it. *Psychological Inquiry, 4*, 322–326.

Shweder, R. A., & LeVine, R. A. (1984). *Culture theory*. Cambridge: Cambridge University Press.

Shweder R. A., Much, N. C., Mahapatra, M., & Park, L. (in press). The "Big Three" of morality (autonomy, community, divinity) and the "big three" explanations of suffering. In A. Brandt, P. Rozin, & S. Katz (Eds.), *Morality and health*. Palo Alto, CA: Stanford University Press.

Shweder, R. A., & Sullivan, M. (1993). Cultural psychology: Who needs it? *Annual Review of Psychology, 44*, 497–523.

Siegel, A., & Brutus, M. (1990). Neural substrates of aggression and rage in the cat. In A. N. Epstein & A. R. Morrison (Eds.), *Progress in psychobiology and physiological psychology, Vol. 14* (pp. 135–234). New York: Academic Press.

Silberman, E. K., & Weingartner, H., (1986). Hemispheric lateralization of functions related to emotion. *Brain and Cognition, 5,* 322–353.

Simon, H. A. (1967). Motivational and emotional controls of cognition. *Psychological Review, 74,* 29–39.

Sinclair, R. C., & Mark, M. M. (1992). The influence of mood state on judgment and action: Effects on persuasion, categorization, social justice, person perception, and judgmental accuracy. In A. Tesser & L. L. Martin (Eds.), *The construction of social judgments.* Hillsdale, NJ: Lawrence Erlbaum.

Singer, J. A. (1990). Affective responses to autobiographical memories and their relationship to long-term goals. *Journal of Personality, 58,* 535–563.

Sinha, R., Lovallo, W. R., & Parsons, O. A. (1992). Cardiovascular differentiation of emotions. *Psychosomatic Medicine, 54,* 422–435.

Sinnott, W. (1966). *The bridge of life: From matter to spirit.* New York: Simon and Schuster.

Slomkowski, C. L., Nelson, K., Dunn, J., & Plomin, R. (1992). Temperament and language: Relations from toddlerhood to middle childhood. *Developmental Psychology, 28,* 1090–1095.

Smedslund, J. (1991). The Pseudo-empirical in psychology and the case for psychologic. *Psychological Inquiry, 2,* 325–338.

Smith, C. A. (1989). Dimensions of appraisal and physiological response in emotion. *Journal of Personality and Social Psychology, 56,* 339–353.

Smith, C. A., & Ellsworth, P. C. (1985). Patterns of cognitive appraisal in emotion. *Journal of Personality and Social Psychology, 48,* 813–838.

Smith, C. A., & Ellsworth, P. C. (1987). Patterns of appraisal and emotion related to taking an exam. *Journal of Personality and Social Psychology, 52,* 475–488.

Smith, O. A., Astley, C. A., Devito, J. L., Stein, J. M., & Walsh, R. E. (1980). Functional analysis of hypothalamic control of the cardiovascular responses accompanying emotional behavior. *Fed. Proceedings, 39*(8), 2487–2494.

Smith, O. A., & DeVito, J. L. (1984). Central neural integration for the control of autonomic responses associated with emotions. *Annual Review of Neuroscience, 7,* 43–65.

Smith, T. W. (1979). Happiness: Time trends, seasonal variations, intersurvey differences, and other mysteries. *Social Psychology Quarterly, 42,* 18–30.

Snidman, N., & Kagan, J. Heart rate reactivity and behavior. Unpublished manuscript.

Sokal, R. R., & Sneath, P. H. A. (1963). *Principles of numerical taxonomy.* San Francisco: Freeman.

Sokolov, E. N. (1963). *Perception and the conditioned reflex.* Oxford: Pergamon.

Solomon, R. L. (1980). The opponent-process theory of acquired motivation: The costs of pleasure and the benefits of pain. *American Psychologist, 35,* 691–712.

Sonnemans, J. (1991). *Structure and determinants of emotional intensity.* Doctoral dissertation. University of Amsterdam.

Sparks, D. (1988). Neural cartography: Sensory and motor maps in the superior colliculus. *Brain Behavior and Evolution, 31,* 49–56.

Spielberger, C. D. (1975). Anxiety: State-trait-process. In C. D. Spielberger & I. Sarason (Eds.), *Stress and anxiety,* Vol. 1 (pp. 115–143). New York: Wiley.

Spielberger, C. D., Gorsuch, R. L., Lushene, R., Vagg, P. R., & Jacobs, G. A. (1983). *Manual for the State-Trait Anxiety Inventory.* Palo Alto, CA: Consulting Psychologists Press.

Spielberger, C. D., Johnson, E. H., Russell, S. F., Crane, R. J., Jacobs, G. A., & Worden, T. J. (1985). The experience and expression of anger: Construction and validation of an anger expression scale. In M. A. Chesney & R. H. Rosenman (Eds.), *Anger and hostility in cardiovascular and behavioral disorders.* (pp. 5–30). New York: Hemisphere/McGraw-Hill.

Sroufe, L. A. (1979). Socioemotional development. In J. D. Osofsky (Ed.), *Handbook of infant development.* New York: Wiley.

Sroufe, L., & Waters, E. (1976). The ontogenesis of smiling and laughter: A perspective on the organization of development in infancy. *Psychological Review, 83,* 173–189.

Squire, L. R. (1987). Memory: Neural organization and behavior. In F. Plum (Ed.), *Handbook of physiology,* Section 1: *The nervous system,* Vol. V, *Higher functions of the brain* (pp. 295–371). Bethseda: American Physiological Society.

Squire, L. R. (1992). Memory and the hippocampus: A synthesis from findings with rats, monkeys, and humans. *Psychological Review, 99,* 195–231.

Stefanacci, L., Farb, C. R., Pitkänen, A., Go, G., LeDoux, J. E., & Amaral, D. G. (1992). Projections from the lateral nucleus to the basal nucleus of the amygdala: A light and electron microscopic PHA-L study in the rat. *Journal Comparative Neurology, 323,* 2–17.

Stein, N., & Levine, L. L. (1989). Thinking about feelings: The development and organization of emotional knowledge. In R. E. Snow & M. Farr (Eds.), *Aptitude, learning, and instructions: Cognition, conation, and affect,* Vol. 3 (pp. 165–198). Hillsdale, NJ: Lawrence Erlbaum.

Stein, N. L., & Trabasso, T. (1990). Children's understanding of changing emotional states. In C. Saarni & P. L. Harris (Eds.), *Children's understanding of emotion* (pp. 50–77). New York: Cambridge University Press.

Stein, N. L., & Trabasso, T. (1992). The organisation of emotional experience: Creating links among emotion, thinking, language and intentional action. *Cognition and Emotion 6,* 225–244.

Steiner, J. E. (1979). Human facial expressions in response to taste and smell stimulation. *Advances in Child Development and Behavior, 12,* 257–295.

Stemmler, G. (1989). The autonomic differentiation of emotions revisited: Convergent and discriminant validation. *Psychophysiology, 26,* 617–632.

Stenberg, C. R., & Campos, J. J. (1990). The development of anger expressions in infancy. In N. Stein, B. Leventhal, & T. Trabasso (Eds.), *Psychological and biological approaches to emotion* (pp. 247–282). Hillsdale, NJ: Lawrence Erlbaum.

Steptoe, A. (1981). *Psychological factors in cardiovascular disease.* New York: Academic Press.

Steriade, M., Gloor, P., Llinas, R. R., Lose da Silva, F. H., & Mesulam, M.-M. (1990). Basic mechanisms of cerebral rhythmic activities. *Electroencephalography and Clinical Neurophysiology, 76,* 481–508.

Steriade, M., & Llinas, R. (1988). The functional states of the thalamus and the associated neuronal interplay. *Physiological Reviews, 68,* 649–742.

Stern, D. N. (1985). *The interpersonal world of the infant: A view from psychoanalysis and developmental psychology.* New York: Basic Books.

Stern, W. (1938). *General psychology from the personalistic perspective,* (H. D. Spoerl, Trans.). New York: Macmillan.

Stewart, J., de Wit, H., & Eikelboom, R. (1984). Role of unconditioned and conditioned drug effects in the self-administration of opiates and stimulants. *Psychological Review, 91,* 251–268.

Storm, C., & Storm, T. (1987). A taxonomic study of the vocabulary of emotions. *Journal of Personality and Social Psychology, 53,* 805–816.

Strack, F., Martin, L. L., & Stepper, S. (1988). Inhibiting and facilitating conditions of the human smile: unobtrusive test of the facial feedback hypothesis. *Journal of Personality and Social Psychology, 54,* 768–777.

Strack, F., Schwarz, N., Bless, H., Kubler, A., & Wanke, M. (1990). *Remember the priming episode. Episodic cues may determine assimilation vs. contrast effects.* (Manuscript submitted for review.)

Strelau, J. (1983). *Temperament personality activity.* New York: Academic Press.

Strelau, J. (1987). Emotion as a key concept in temperament research. *Journal of Research in Personality, 21,* 510–528.

Stumpf, C. (1899). Uber den Begriff der Gemühtsbewegung. [On the concept of emotion]. *Zeitschrift für Psychologie und Physiologie der Sinnesorgane, 21,* 47–99.

Sullivan, M., & Lewis, M. (1989). Emotion and cognition in infancy: Facial expressions during contingency learning. *International Journal of Behavioral Development, 12*(2), 221–237.

Sundstrom, E., Archer, T., Melander, T., & Hokfelt, T. (1988). Galanin impairs acquisition but not retrieval of spatial memory in rats studied in the Morris swim maze. *Neuroscience Letters, 88,* 332–335.

Suomi, S., & Harlow, H. (1976). The facts and functions of fear. In M. Zuckerman & C. D. Spielberger (Eds.), *Emotions and anxiety* (pp. 3–34). Hillsdale, NJ: Lawrence Erlbaum.

Swanson, L. W. (1983). The hippocampus and the concept of the limbic system. In W. Seifert (Ed.), *Neurobiology of the hippocampus* (pp. 3–19). London: Academic Press.

Swanson, L. W., Sawachenko, P. E., Rivier, J., & Vale, W. (1983). Organization of ovine corticotropin-releasing factor immunoreactive cells and fivers in the rat brain: An immunohistochemical study. *Neuroendocrinology, 36,* 165–186.

Swerdlow, N. R., & Koob, G. F. (1987). Dopamine, schizophrenia, mania and depression: Toward a unified hypothesis of cortico-striato-palildo–thalamic function. *Behavioral and Brain Sciences, 10,* 197–245.

Tajfel, H. (1982). *Social identity and intergroup relations.* Cambridge: Cambridge University Press.

Takeuchi, Y., Mclean, J. H., & Hopkins, D. A. (1982). Reciprocal connections between the amygdala and parabrachial nuclei: Ultrastructural demonstration by degeneration and axonal transport of horseradish peroxidase in the cat. *Brain Research, 239,* 538–588.

Tangney, J. P. (1990). Assessing individual differences in proneness to shame and guilt: Development of the self-conscious affect and attribution inventory. *Journal of Personality and Social Psychology, 59,* 102–111.

Tassinary, L. G., & Cacioppo, J. T. (1992). Unobservable facial actions and emotion. *Psychological Science, 3,* 28–33.

Teasdale, J. D., & Fogarty, S. J. (1979). Differential effects of induced mood on retrieval of pleasant and unpleasant events from episodic memory. *Journal of Abnormal Psychology, 88,* 248–257.

Tellegen, A. (1985). Structures of mood and personality and their relevance to assessing anxiety, with an emphasis on self-report. In A. H. Tuma & J. D. Maser (Eds.), *Anxiety and the anxiety disorders* (pp. 681–706). Hillsdale, NJ: Lawrence Erlbaum.

Tellegen, A., Lykken, D. T., Bouchard, T. J., Jr., Wilcox, K. J., Segal, N. L., & Rich, S. (1988). Personality similarity in twins reared apart and together. *Journal of Personality and Social Psychology, 54,* 1031–1039.

Thayer, R. E. (1978). Toward a psychological theory of multidimensional activation (arousal). *Motivation and Emotion, 2,* 1–34.

Thayer, R. E. (1989). *The biopsychology of mood and arousal.* New York: Oxford University Press.

Thelen, E. (1985). Developmental origins of motor coordination: Leg movements in human infants. *Developmental Psychobiology, 18*(1), 1–22.

Thelen, E., & Ulrich, B. (1991). Hidden skills. *Monographs of the Society for Research in Child Development,* Serial No. 223, *56*(1), 1–98.

Thines, G., Costall, A., & Butterworth, G. (Eds.) (1991). *Michotte's experimental phenomenology of perception.* Hillsdale, NJ: Lawrence Erlbaum.

Thomas, A., & Chess, S. (1977). *Temperament and development.* New York: Brunner/Mazel.

Thomas, A., Chess, S., Birch, H. G., Hertzig, M. E., & Korn, S. (1963). *Behavioral individuality in early childhood.* New York: New York University Press.

Thomas, E. (1988). Forebrain mechanisms in the relief of fear: The role of the lateral septum. *Psychobiology, 16,* 36–44.

Toates, F. M. (1988). Motivation and emotion from a biological perspective. In V. Hamilton, G. Bower, & N. Frijda (Eds.), *Cognitive science perspectives on emotion and motivation* (pp. 3–36). Amsterdam: Martinus Nijhoff.

Tobias, B. A., Kihlstrom, J. F., & Schacter, D. L. (1992). Emotion and implicit memory. In S.-A. Christianson (Ed.), *The handbook of emotion and memory: Research and theory* (pp. 67–92). Hillsdale, NJ: Lawrence Erlbaum.

Tomarken, A. J., Davidson, R. J., & Henriques, J. B. (1990). Resting frontal brain asymmetry predicts affective responses to films. *Journal of Personality and Social Psychology, 59,* 791–801.

Tomarken, A. J., Davidson, R. J., Wheeler, R. E., & Doss, R. C. (1992). Individual differences in anterior brain asymmetry and fundamental dimensions of emotion. *Journal of Personality and Social Psychology, 62,* 676–687.

Tomarken, A. J., Davidson, R. J., Wheeler, R. W., & Kinney, L. (1992). Psychometric properties of resting anterior EEG asymmetry: Temporal stability and internal consistency. *Psychophysiology, 29,* 576–592.

Tomarken, A. J., Mineka, S., & Cook, M. (1989). Fear relevant selective associations and covariation bias. *Journal of Abnormal Psychology, 98,* 381–394.

Tooby, J., & Cosmides, L. (1990). The past explains the present: Emotional adaptations and the structure of ancestral environment. *Ethology and Sociobiology, 11,* 375–424.

Tomkins, S. S. (1962). *Affect, imagery, consciousness,* Vol. I. *The positive affects.* New York: Springer-Verlag.

Tomkins, S. S. (1963). *Affect, imagery, consciousness,* Vol. II. *The negative affects.* New York: Springer-Verlag.

Tomkins, S. S. (1984). Affect theory. In K. R. Scherer & P. Ekman (Eds.), *Approaches to emotion* (pp. 163–196). Hillsdale, NJ: Lawrence Erlbaum.

Tomkins, S. S. (1991). *Affect, imagery, consciousness,* Vol. III. New York: Springer-Verlag.

Tranel, D., & Hyman, B. T. (1990). Neuropsychological correlates of bilateral amygdala damage. *Archives of Neurology, 47,* 349–355.

Trevarthen, C. (1979). Communication and cooperation in early infancy. A description of primary intersubjectivity. In M. Bullowa (Ed.), *Before speech: The beginnings of human communication.* London: Cambridge University Press.

Tucker, D. M., & Williamson, P. A. (1984). Asymmetric neural control systems in human self-regulation. *Psychological Review, 91,* 185–215.

Turner, B. H., Mishkin, M., & Knapp, M. (1980). Organization of the amygdalopetal Projections from modality-specific cortical association areas in the monkey. *Journal of Comparative Neurology, 191,* 515–543.

Turner, T. J., & Ortony, A. (1992). Basic emotions: Can conflicting criteria converge? *Psychological Review, 99,* 566–571.

Ungerleider, L. G., & Mishkin, M. (1982). Two cortical visual systems. In D. J. Ingle, M. A. Goodale, & R. J. W. Mansfield (Eds.), *Analysis of visual behavior* (pp. 549–586). Cambridge: MIT Press.

van den Boom, D. (1988). *Neonatal irritability and the development of attachment: Observation and intervention.* Doctoral dissertation, University of Leiden, The Netherlands.

van den Boom, D. (1989). Neonatal irritability and the development of attachment. In G. Kohnstamm, J. Bates, & M. K. Rothbart (Eds.), *Temperament in childhood.* Chichester: Wiley.

Vanderhaeghen, J.-J. & Crawley, J. N. (Eds.) (1985). Neuronal choleocystokinin, *Annals of the New York Academy of Sciences, 448.*

Van der Kolk, B. (1987). *Psychological trauma.* Washington, DC: American Psychiatric Press.

Van Essen, D. C. (1985). Functional organization of primate visual cortex. In A. Peters & E. G. Jones (Eds.), *Cerebral cortex* (pp. 259–328). New York: Plenum.

Van Goozen, S., & Frijda, N. H. (1992). Emotion words used in six European countries. *European Journal of Social Psychology, 22,* 89–95.

van Ijzendoorn, M. H., & Kroonenberg, P. M. (1988). Cross-cultural patterns of attachment: A meta-analysis of the strange situation. *Child Development, 59,* 147–156.

Varela, F. J., Thompson, R., & Rosch, E. (1991). *The embodied mind.* Cambridge, MA: The MIT Press.

Wallbott, H. G., & Scherer, K. R. (1986). How universal and specific is emotional experience? Evidence from 27 countries on five continents. *Social Science Information, 25,* 763–795.

Wallbott, H. G., & Scherer, K. R. (in press). Cultural differences in experiencing shame and guilt. In K. Fischer & J. Tangney (Eds.), *The self-conscious emotions.* New York: Guilford.

Watson, D. (1988a). Intraindividual and interindividual analyses of Positive and Negative Affect: Their relation to health complaints, perceived stress, and daily activities. *Journal of Personality and Social Psychology, 54,* 1020–1030.

Watson, D. (1988b). The vicissitudes of mood measurement: Effects of varying descriptors, time frames, and response formats on measures of Positive and Negative Affect. *Journal of Personality and Social Psychology, 55,* 128–141.

Watson, D., & Clark, L. A. (1984). Negative Affectivity: The disposition to experience aversive emotional states. *Psychological Bulletin, 96,* 465–490.

Watson, D., & Clark, L. A. (1991). Self- versus peer-ratings of specific emotional traits: Evidence of convergent and discriminant validity. *Journal of Personality and Social Psychology, 60,* 927–940.

Watson, D., & Clark, L. A. (1992a). Affects separable and inseparable: On the hierarchical arrangement of the negative affects. *Journal of Personality and Social Psychology, 62,* 489–505.

Watson, D., & Clark, L. A. (1992b). On traits and temperament: General and specific factors of emotional experience and their relation to the five-factor model. *Journal of Personality, 60,* 441–476.

Watson, D., & Clark, L. A. (in press). Extraversion and its positive emotional core. In R. Hogan, J. A. Johnson, & S. R. Briggs, *Handbook of personality psychology.* San Diego, CA: Academic Press.

Watson, D., Clark, L. A., & Tellegen, A. (1988). Development and validation of brief measures of positive and negative affect: The PANAS scales. *Journal of Personality and Social Psychology, 54,* 1063–1070.

Watson, D., & Pennebaker, J. W. (1989). Health complaints, stress, and distress: Exploring the central role of Negative Affectivity. *Psychological Review, 96,* 234–254.

Watson, D., & Slack, A. K. (1993). General factors of affective temperament and their relation to job satisfaction over time. *Organizational Behavior and Human Decision Processes, 54,* 181–202.

Watson, D., & Tellegen, A. (1985). Toward a consensual structure of mood. *Psychological Bulletin, 98,* 219–235.

Weber, M. (1947). *Theory of social and economic organization.* London: William Hodge.

Wegner, D. M. (1989). *White bears and other unwanted thoughts.* New York: Viking Press.

Wehr, T. A., Jacobsen, F. M., Sack, D. A., Arendt, J., Tamarkin, L., & Rosenthal, N. E. (1986). Phototherapy of seasonal affective disorder. *Archives of General Psychiatry, 43,* 870–875.

Weinberger, D. A. (1990). The construct validity of the repressive coping style. In J. L. Singer (Ed.), *Repression and dissociation* (pp. 337–386). Chicago: University of Chicago Press.

Weinberger, D. A., Schwartz, G. E., & Davidson, R. J. (1979). Low-anxious, high-anxious, and repressive coping styles: Psychometric patterns and behavioral and physiological responses to stress. *Journal of Abnormal Psychology, 88,* 369–380.

Weinberger, N., Ashe, J., Metherate, R., McKenna, T., Diamond, D., Bakin, J., Lennartz, R., & Cassady, J. (1990). Neural adaptive information processing: A preliminary model of receptive-field plasticity in auditory cortex during Pavlovian conditioning. In M. Gabriel & J. Moore (Eds.), *Learning and computational neuroscience: Foundations of adaptive networks* (pp. 91–138). Cambridge: MIT Press.

Weiner, B. (1985). An attributional theory of achievement motivation and emotion. *Psychological Review, 92,* 548–573.

Weiner, B. (1986). *An attributional theory of motivation and emotion.* New York: Springer-Verlag.

Weingartner, H., Kaye, W., Gold, P., Smalleberg, S., Peterson, R., Gillin, J. C., & Ebert, M. (1981). Vasopressin treatment of cognitive dysfunction in progressive dementia. *Life Sciences, 29,* 2721–2726.

Weiskrantz, L. (1956). Behavioral changes associated with ablation of the amygdaloid complex in monkeys. *Journal of Comparative Physiology and Psychology, 49,* 381–391.

Wessman, A. E., & Ricks, D. F. (1966). *Mood and personality.* New York: Holt, Rinehart.

Wheeler, R. E., Davidson, R. J., & Tomarken, A. J. (1993). Frontal brain asymmetry and emotional reactivity: A biological substrate of affective style. *Psychophysiology, 30,* 82–89.

Whitlock, D. G., & Nauta, W. J. H. (1956). Subcortical projections from the temporal neocortex in Macaca mulatta. *Journal of Comparative Neurology, 106,* 183–212.

Whitman, R., & Alexander, J. (1968). On gloating. *International Journal of Psycho-analysis, 49,* 732–738.

Whorf, B. L. (1956). Science and linguistics. In J. B. Carroll (Eds.), *Language, thought, and reality: Selected writings of Benjamin Lee Whorf* (pp. 207–219). Cambridge, MA: MIT Press.

Whybrow, P. C., Bauer, M. S. (1988). Effects of peripheral thyroid hormones on the central nervous systems: Relevance to disorders of mood. In D. Ganten & D. Pfaff (Eds.), *Current topics in neuroendocrinology,* Vol. 8. *Neuroendocrinology of mood* (pp. 309–327). Berlin: Springer-Verlag.

Wierzbicka, A. (1985). *Lexicography and conceptual analysis.* Ann Arbor, MI: Karoma Publishers.

Wierzbicka, A. (Ed.) (1990). Special Issue on the Semantics of the Emotions. *Australian Journal of Linguistics, 10,* (2).

Wierzbicka, A. (n.d.). Talk about emotions: semantics, culture and cognition. Unpublished manuscript, Department of Linguistics, Australian National University.

Will, B. E. (1977). Neurochemical correlates of individual differences in animal learning capacity. *Behavioral Biology, 19,* 143–171.

Williams, S. M., & Goldman-Rakic, P. S. (1993). Characterization of the dopaminergic innervation of the primate frontal cortex using a dopamine-specific antibody. *Cerebral Cortex, 3,* 199–222.

Wills, T. A. (1981). Downward comparison principles in social psychology. *Psychological Bulletin, 90,* 245–271.

Wills, T. A. (1990). Similarity and self-esteem in downward comparison. In J. Suls & T. A. Wills (Eds.), *Social comparison: Contemporary theory and research* (pp. 51–78). Hillsdale, NJ: Lawrence Erlbaum.

Wittgenstein, L. (1953). *Philosophical investigations.* Oxford: Basil Blackwell.

Wittling, W. (in press). Brain asymmetry in the control of autonomic-physiological activity. In R. J. Davidson & K. Hugdahl (Eds.), *Brain asymmetry.* Cambridge, MA: MIT Press.

Wolff, P. H. (1963). Observations on the early development of smiling. In B. M. Foss (Ed.), *Determinants of infant behavior,* Vol. 2. New York: Wiley.

Woods, S. C., & Porte, J. D. (1983). The role of insulin as a satiety factor in the central nervous system. In A. J. Szabo (Ed.), *CNS regulation of carbohydrate metabolism: Advance in metabolic disorders,* Vol. 10. New York: Academic Press.

Wundt, W. (1897). *Outlines of psychology* (C. H. Judd, Trans.). New York: Gustav E. Stechert.

Wyer, R. S., & Collins, J. E. (1992). The theory of humor elicitation. *Psychological Review, 99,* 663–688.

Wyer, R. S., & Srull, T. K. (Eds.). (1984). *Handbook of social cognition* (Vol. 1). Hillsdale, NJ: Lawrence Erlbaum.

Wynn, P. C., Hauger, R. L., Holmes, M. C., Millan, M. A., Catt, K. J., & Aguilera, G. (1984). Brain and pituitary receptors for corticotropin releasing factor: Localization and differential regulation after adrenalectomy. *Peptides, 5,* 1077–1084.

Wynne, L., & Solomon, R. L. (1955). Traumatic avoidance learning: Acquisition and extinction in dogs deprived of normal peripheral autonomic function. *Genetic. Psychology Monographs 52,* 241–284.

Yang, Q. Z., & Hatton, G. I. (1988). Direct evidence for electrical coupling among rat supraoptic nucleus neurons. *Brain Research, 463,* 47–56.

Young, W. S. III, Mezey, E., & Seigel, R. E. (1986). Quantitative in situ hybridization reveals increased levels of corticotropin-releasing factor mRNA after adrenalectomy in rats. *Neuroscience Letters, 70,* 198–203.

Zajonc, R. B. (1968). The attitudinal effects of mere exposure. *Journal of Personality and Social Psychology,* Monogr. 9 (2, part 2).

Zajonc, R. B. (1980). Feeling and thinking: Preferences need no inferences. *American Psychologist, 35,* 151–175.

Zajonc, R. B. (1984). On primacy of affect. In K. R. Scherer & P. Ekman (Eds.), *Approaches to emotion* (pp. 259–270). Hillsdale, NJ: Lawrence Erlbaum.

Zajonc, R. B. (1985). Emotion and facial efference: A theory reclaimed. *Science, 228,* 15–21.

Zajonc, R. B., & McIntosh, D. N. (1992). Emotions research: Some promising questions and some questionable promises. *Psychological Science, 3,* 70–74.

Zajonc, R. B., Murphy, S. T., & Inglehart, M. (1989). Feeling and facial efference: Implications of the vascular theory of emotions. *Psychological Review, 96,* 395–416.

Zappulla, R. A., LeFever, F. F., Jaeger, J., & Bilder, R. (1991). Windows on the brain: Neuropsychology's technological frontiers. *Annals of the New York Academy of Sciences, 620.*

Ziegler, T. E., & Bercovitch, F. B. (Eds.) (1990). *Socioendocrinology of primate reproduction, Monographs in Primatology,* Vol. 13. New York: Wiley-Liss.

Zipf, G. K. (1949). *Human behavior and the principle of least effort.* Cambridge, MA: MIT Press.

Zola-Morgan, S., Squire, L. R., Alvarez-Royo, P., & Clower, R. P. (1991). Independence of memory functions and emotional behavior: Separate contributions of the hippocampal formation and the amygdala. *Hippocampus, 1*(2), 207–220.

Zuckerman, M. (1979). *Sensation seeking.* Hillsdale, NJ: Lawrence Erlbaum.

Zuckerman, M. (1984). Sensation-seeking: A comparative approach to a human trait. *The Behavioral and Brain Sciences, 7,* 413–471.

Zuckerman, M. (1991). *Psychobiology of personality.* Cambridge: Cambridge University Press.

Zuckerman, M., Klorman, R., Larrance, D. T., & Spiegel, N. H. (1981). Facial, autonomic, and subjective components of emotion: The facial feedback hypothesis versus the externalizer-internalizer distinction. *Journal of Personality and Social Psychology, 41,* 929–944.

Index